# THE ROUTLEDGE COMPANION TO LITERATURE AND ECONOMICS

The study of literature and economics is by no means a new one, but since the financial crash of 2008, the field has grown considerably with a broad range of both fiction and criticism. *The Routledge Companion to Literature and Economics* is the first authoritative guide tying together the seemingly disparate areas of literature and economics.

Drawing together 38 critics, the *Companion* offers both an introduction and a springboard to this sometimes complex but highly relevant field. With sections on "Critical Traditions," "Histories," "Principles," and "Contemporary Culture," this book looks at examples from Medieval and Renaissance literature through to poetry of the Great Depression and novels depicting the 2008 financial crisis. Covering topics from Austen to austerity, Marxism to modernism, the collated essays offer indispensable analysis of the relationship between literary studies and the economy.

Representing a wide spectrum of approaches, this book introduces the basics of economics, whilst engaging with essential theory and debate. As the reality of economic hardship and disparity is widely acknowledged and spreads across disciplines, this *Companion* offers students and scholars a chance to enter this crucially important interdisciplinary area.

**Matt Seybold** is an Assistant Professor of American Literature and Mark Twain Studies at the University of Alabama, USA. He publishes on American literature and economics.

**Michelle Chihara** is an Assistant Professor of English at Whittier College, USA, as well as Editor of the Economics and Finance section of the *Los Angeles Review of Books*. She publishes both fiction and nonfiction, with emphasis on economics, finance, and contemporary culture.

ROUTLEDGE COMPANIONS TO LITERATURE SERIES

Also available in this series:

**THE ROUTLEDGE COMPANION TO LITERATURE AND RELIGION**
*Edited by Mark Knight*

**THE ROUTLEDGE COMPANION TO INTER-AMERICAN STUDIES**
*Edited by Wilfried Raussert*

**THE ROUTLEDGE COMPANION TO THE ENVIRONMENTAL HUMANITIES**
*Edited by Ursula K. Heise, Jon Christensen and Michelle Niemann*

**THE ROUTLEDGE COMPANION TO INTERNATIONAL CHILDREN'S LITERATURE**
*Edited by John Stephens, with Celia Abicalil Belmiro, Alice Curry, Li Lifang and Yasmine S. Motawy*

**THE ROUTLEDGE COMPANION TO PICTUREBOOKS**
*Edited by Bettina Kümmerling-Meibauer*

**THE ROUTLEDGE COMPANION TO WORLD LITERATURE AND WORLD HISTORY**
*Edited by May Hawas*

**THE ROUTLEDGE COMPANION TO PAKISTANI ANGLOPHONE WRITING**
*Edited by Aroosa Kanwal and Saiyma Aslam*

**THE ROUTLEDGE COMPANION TO LITERATURE AND ECONOMICS**
*Edited by Michelle Chihara and Matt Seybold*

For more information on this series, please visit: www.routledge.com/literature/series/RC4444

# THE ROUTLEDGE COMPANION TO LITERATURE AND ECONOMICS

*Edited by Matt Seybold and Michelle Chihara*

Routledge
Taylor & Francis Group
LONDON AND NEW YORK

First published 2019 by Routledge

2 Park Square, Milton Park, Abingdon, Oxon OX14 4RN
605 Third Avenue, New York, NY 10017

*Routledge is an imprint of the Taylor & Francis Group, an informa business*

First issued in paperback 2021



*British Library Cataloguing-in-Publication Data*
A catalogue record for this book is available from the British Library

*Library of Congress Cataloging-in-Publication Data*
Names: Seybold, Matt, editor. | Chihara, Michelle, editor.
Title: The Routledge companion to literature and economics / edited by Matt Seybold and Michelle Chihara.
Description: Abingdon, Oxon : New York, NY; Routledge, 2019. | Includes index.
Identifiers: LCCN 2018022717 | ISBN 9781138190870 (hardback : alk. paper) |
ISBN 9781317278115 (web pdf) | ISBN 9781317278108 (epub) |
ISBN 9781317278092 (mobikindle)
Subjects: LCSH: Economics and literature. | Economics in literature.
Classification: LCC PN51.R734 2019 | DDC 809/.933553—dc23
LC record available at https://lccn.loc.gov/2018022717

ISBN: 978-1-138-19087-0 (hbk)
ISBN: 978-1-03-217856-1 (pbk)
DOI: 10.4324/9781315640808

Typeset in Bembo
by codeMantra

# CONTENTS

# CONTRIBUTORS

**Lauren Bailey** is a Ph.D. candidate in English at the City University of New York, Graduate Center. Her dissertation explores the crossover among the gothic, inheritance plot, and global economy of Victorian Britain by examining the disruptive force of foreign objects in nineteenth-century British literature. She has completed institutes and fellowships in Writing & Thinking at Bard College, Archival Research at the New-York Historical Society, and History of Political Economy at Duke University, and has received research awards and grants from her institution, the British Association for Victorian Studies, Rocky Mountain Modern Language Association, and the History of Economics Society.

**Jennifer J. Baker** is an Associate Professor of English at New York University, where she specializes in eighteenth- and nineteenth-century American literature and culture. She is the author of *Securing the Commonwealth: Debt, Speculation, and Writing in the Making of Early America* (Johns Hopkins, 2005) and the co-editor of a special issue of *Early American Literature* on "Economics and Early American Literature." She is currently at work on a book on American Romanticism and the life sciences.

**Mary McAleer Balkun** is a Professor of English at Seton Hall University. Her research interests include material culture and body studies in early America, and the American gothic and grotesque. She is the author of *The American Counterfeit: Authenticity and Identity in American Literature and Culture* (U. of Alabama, 2006), co-editor with Susan C. Imbarrato of *Women of the Early Americas and the Formation of Empire* (Palgrave, 2016), and associate editor of *The Greenwood Encyclopedia of American Poets and Poetry: From the Colonial Era to the Present* (2015) and *The Greenwood Encyclopedia of American Poets and Poetry* (2005). She is currently at work on *New World Upside Down*, a study of the early American grotesque.

**David Buxton** is a Professor at Université de Paris Nanterre, France, and the author of numerous books and articles on literature, cinema, television, and psychoanalysis.

**Christopher Chen** is an Assistant Professor of Literature at the University of California at Santa Cruz, and a 2016–17 Institute for Humanities Research Fellow. Chen has published articles, poetry, interviews, and reviews in *boundary 2, South Atlantic Quarterly, The Los Angeles*

*Review of Books, Crayon*, and *1913: A Journal of Forms*. He is completing a book-length comparative study of contemporary African American and Asian American experimental poetry. His research focuses on twentieth- and twenty-first-century U.S. poetry and poetics, the history and prehistory of American capitalism, and contemporary theories of comparative racialization.

**Michelle Chihara** is an Assistant Professor of English at Whittier College and Editor of the Economics & Finance section of *The Los Angeles Review of Books*. Her academic research analyzes contemporary American cultural production in the thick economic and historic context of the most recent financial panic. The working title of her current project is *Behave: The Cultural Turn to Behavioral Economics in 2006–2016*. Her research, prose and fiction, can be found in *Postmodern Culture, Studies in American Fiction, Mother Jones, The Santa Monica Review, The Los Angeles Review of Books,* and *n+1,* among others.

**Eleanor Courtemanche** is an Associate Professor of English at the University of Illinois at Urbana-Champaign, where she teaches British Victorian literature, and is the author of *The "Invisible Hand" and British Fiction, 1818–60: Adam Smith, Political Economy, and the Genre of Realism* (Palgrave, 2011). She has written articles on Dickens and Hayek, Karl Marx and Heinrich Heine, and on Victorian utopias and the TV show *Porlandia*. She is currently writing a book entitled *Fragile Capitalism*.

**Paul Crosthwaite** is a Senior Lecturer in English Literature at the University of Edinburgh. His publications include *Trauma, Postmodernism, and the Aftermath of World War II* (Palgrave, 2009); articles in *Angelaki*, *Cultural Critique*, *Cultural Politics*, *New Formations*, *Public Culture*, *The Review of Contemporary Fiction*, and *Textual Practice*; and, as editor, *Criticism, Crisis, and Contemporary Narrative: Textual Horizons in an Age of Global Risk* (Routledge, 2011) and *Show Me the Money: The Image of Finance, 1700 to the Present* (Manchester, 2014). He is currently completing a monograph on the market logics of contemporary fiction.

**Lana L. Dalley** is a Professor of English at California State University, Fullerton, where she teaches nineteenth-century British literature. She's published numerous articles on women's writing and political economy and is the co-editor of *Economic Women: Essays on Desire and Dispossession in Nineteenth-Century British Culture* (Ohio State, 2014).

**Laura Finch** is currently at the University of Michigan as a member of the Society of Fellows and an Assistant Professor in the Department of English Language and Literature. After this fellowship, she will be joining MIT as a member of the English Department. She received her PhD in 2016 from the University of Pennsylvania in the program in Comparative Literature and Literary Theory. She is currently completing her book manuscript entitled *Intimate Economies: Financial Citizenship and Literary Form in the Contemporary Novel* and is starting work on her second project *Girlish: Empire, Capital, and Impossible Subjects*.

**Andrew Galloway** is a Professor of English at Cornell University, and teaches medieval literature. His books include *Medieval Literature and Culture* (2006), *The Cambridge Companion to Medieval English Culture* (2011), and *The Cambridge Companion to Piers Plowman* (2014), co-edited with Andrew Cole. He has published over eighty essays and chapters, primarily on late-medieval literature and historical writing in their contexts and was awarded Cornell's Provost's Award for Distinguished Scholarship in 2009. His current projects concern the economic meanings of the transformations of "the lyric" from the late Middle Ages to the Renaissance (for *What Kind of a Thing is the Medieval English Lyric?*), Chaucer's parallels to and differences from Adam Smith (for *Money, Commerce, and Economics in Late Medieval English Literature*), and the relationship among land-law, the satire, and authorship in the fourteenth-century poem *Piers Plowman* (for *Studies in the Age of Chaucer*).

**Richard Godden** is a Professor of English at University of California, Irvine. He writes on the relation between economic structure and narrative form, with particular attention to the ways in which under-thought or unthinkable aspects of any regime of accumulation register linguistically as contested semantic content, which sedimented materials condition what stories can and cannot be told. His account of the narrative poetics of the financial turn (working title, "Paper Graveyards") will conclude a four-volume study of the poetics of a fordist century. The preceding volumes are *Fictions of Capital* (Cambridge, 1990), *Fictions of Labor* (Cambridge, 1997), and *William Faulkner: An Economy of Complex Words* (Princeton, 2007).

**Christian P. Haines** is an Assistant Professor of English at Dartmouth College. He has published in journals including *Angelaki*, *boundary 2*, and *Genre*, and co-edited a special issue of *Cultural Critique*, "What Comes After the Subject?" (Spring 2017). He is finishing up a book on contemporary and nineteenth-century U.S. literature, entitled *A Desire Called America: Biopolitics, Utopia, and the Literary Commons*.

**Kimberly Hall** is an Assistant Professor of English and Digital Media Studies at Wofford College. Her work on social media has been published in *Television & New Media*, *Women & Performance*, and *A modern*. She is currently working on a book manuscript about the historical development of observational media projects.

**Howard Horwitz** is a Professor of English at the University of Utah and the author of *By the Law of Nature* (1991) as well as dozens of articles, primarily on the intersections of political economy and literary culture from colonial America to the present. Publications can be found in *American Literary History*, *ELH*, *boundary 2*, and *Configurations*, among other places.

**Brian Hurley** is an Assistant Professor of Japanese Literature, Film, & Culture at Syracuse University. His research has appeared in *The Journal of Japanese Studies*, *Representations*, and the Japanese-language journal of literary criticism *Bungaku*. He is currently working on a book manuscript that examines the confluence of literature and thought in modern Japan.

**Joseph Jonghyun Jeon** is a Professor of English at University of California, Irvine. He is the author of *Vicious Circuits: Korea's IMF Cinema and the End of the American Century* (Stanford, forthcoming) and *Racial Things, Racial Forms: Objecthood in Avant-Garde Asian American Poetry* (Iowa, 2012). He is currently working on a project about Asian/Latin American cultural production in the context of the U.S.-centered, global free-trade regime that governed global trade from the 1980s through the present.

**Alissa G. Karl** is an Associate Professor of English at the State University of New York, Brockport. Her research investigates the intersection of economics and literary and cultural forms in the twentieth and twenty-first centuries. She is the author of *Modernism and the*

*Marketplace: Literary Culture and Consumer Capitalism in Rhys, Woolf, Stein and Nella Larsen* (Routledge, 2009) and the co-editor of the collection *Neoliberalism and the Novel* (Routledge, 2016). Currently, she is finishing a monograph titled *Novels, Machines and the Twentieth-Century Economic Imaginary,* and undertaking new work on the novel and the precariat in the economic present.

**Peter Knight** is a Professor of American Studies at the University of Manchester. He is the author of *Conspiracy Culture: From Kennedy to The X Files* (Routledge, 2000), *The Kennedy Assassination* (Edinburgh, 2007), and *Reading the Market: The Genre of Financial Capitalism in Gilded Age America* (Johns Hopkins, 2016). He was the co-curator with Paul Crosthwaite and Nicky Marsh of the exhibition and book *Show Me the Money: The Image of Finance, 1700 to the Present* (Manchester, 2014) and is the co-editor of the Palgrave Series in Literature, Culture and Economics.

**Andrew Kopec** is an Assistant Professor of English at Purdue University, Fort Wayne. His work on literature and economics has appeared in journals such as *PMLA*, *ELH*, *Early American Literature*, and *The Eighteenth Century: Theory and Interpretation*, as well as in edited volumes. A recipient of fellowships and grants from the Library Company of Philadelphia and the Purdue Research Fund, he is currently writing his first book, *The Pace of Panic: American Romanticism and the Business Cycle.*

**Timothy (Tim) Kreiner** is a Lecturer in the Department of English at Yale University. His writing on poetry and politics has appeared in or is forthcoming from *Contemporary Literature, Los Angeles Review of Books, Lana Turner,* and *Viewpoint.* He is completing a book of literary history, *The Long Downturn and its Discontents: Poetry, Culture Wars, and the New Left*, about the ins and outs of poetry, social movements, and political economy.

**Andrew Lawson** is a Reader in English at Leeds Beckett University. His most recent publications are *Downwardly Mobile: The Changing Fortunes of American Realism* (Oxford University Press, 2014) and an edited collection, *Class and the Making of American Literature: Created Unequal* (Routledge, 2014). He is currently working on a study of the entrepreneur in early America.

**Mark Garrett Longaker** is an Associate Professor in the departments of Rhetoric and Writing, English, and Communication Studies at the University of Texas at Austin. He is the author of *Rhetoric and the Republic: Politics, Civic Discourse, and Education in Early America* (U. of Alabama, 2007), *Rhetorical Style and Bourgeois Virtue: Capitalism and Civil Society in the British Enlightenment* (Penn State, 2015), and, with Jeffrey Walker, *Rhetorical Analysis: A Brief Guide for Writers* (Pearson, 2010). His recent scholarly work investigates the intersection of rhetorical theory and the liberal political tradition with special attention to the writings of John Locke.

**Nicky Marsh** is a Professor of English at the University of Southampton. Her recent articles include "The Cosmopolitan Coin: What Modernists Make of Money" in *Modernism/Modernity.* She is currently completing a monograph called *The Empire Without Credit: Money and Meaning in America.*

**Regina Martin** is an Associate Professor of English at Denison University, where she specializes in British literature, 1870–present, examining intersections between literature of that period and economic theory, history, and institutions. She has published articles in *PMLA*, *Criticism*, and *Twentieth-Century Literature* among other journals. She is currently working on a book manuscript entitled *Finance Capital and British Modernism, 1870–1940.*

**Annie McClanahan** is an Assistant Professor of English at the University of California, Irvine. Her first book, *Dead Pledges: Debt, Crisis, and 21st Century Culture* (Stanford, 2016), won the 2017 ASAP Book Prize. Her work has appeared in *Representations, theory & event, boundary2, Journal of Cultural Economy, Journal of American Studies, South Atlantic Quarterly,* and elsewhere. She currently holds a Mellon Foundation New Directions Fellowship through which she is studying microeconomics toward a book tentatively titled *A Cultural History of the Microeconomic Century.*

**Robbie Moore** is a Lecturer in the English Program at the University of Tasmania. He is a recipient of the *Henry James Review*'s Leon Edel Prize, and has an ongoing research interest in literature and cities. He is currently completing a book on the hotel in modernist culture.

**Christopher Newfield** is a Professor of Literature and American studies at the University of California, Santa Barbara. Much of his research is in Critical University Studies, which links his enduring concern with humanities teaching to the study of how higher education continues to be reshaped by industry and other economic forces. His most recent books on this subject are *The Great Mistake* (2016), *Unmasking the Public University* (2008), and *Ivy and Industry* (2003). He writes about higher education policy for the *Huffington Post, Insides Higher Ed,* and the *Chronicle of Higher Education,* as well as his own blog, *Remaking the University.*

**Sharada Balachandran Orihuela** is an Assistant Professor of English and Comparative Literature at the University of Maryland, College Park. She specializes in nineteenth-, twentieth-, and twenty-first-century hemispheric American literature. Her first book, *Fugitives, Smugglers, and Thieves: Piracy and Personhood in American Literature*, is forthcoming from the University of North Carolina Press. Her articles have appeared in *Arizona Quarterly, J19: The Journal of Nineteenth-Century Americanists,* and *Environmental Communication.*

**Stephen M. Park** is an Assistant Professor at Loyola University Maryland, where he teaches in the English Department and in the Latin American and Latino Studies Program. His first book is *The Pan American Imagination: Contested Visions of the Hemisphere in Twentieth Century Literature* (U. of Virginia, 2014). His work continues to focus on Hemispheric approaches to American Literature, and his current book project is entitled *Economic Fictions: NAFTA, North American Literature, and the Logic of Free Trade.*

**Matt Seybold** is an Assistant Professor of American Literature & Mark Twain Studies at Elmira College, where he also edits MarkTwainStudies.org, the official website of the Center for Mark Twain Studies. His research focuses on the intersection of economics, mass media, and literary culture in the United States. Recent publications can be found in *American Studies, T. S. Eliot Studies Annual, Henry James Review, Reception, Mark Twain Annual, Western Humanities Review, Aeon Magazine,* and the *Los Angeles Review of Books.* The working title of his current project is *The Rhyme of Crisis: A General Theory of Economy and Media.*

**Alison Shonkwiler** is an Associate Professor of English at Rhode Island College and the author of *The Financial Imaginary: Economic Mystification and the Limits of Realist Fiction*

(Minnesota, 2017). She co-edited, with Leigh Claire La Berge, *Reading Capitalist Realism* (Iowa, 2014) and teaches twentieth- and twenty-first-century American literature. She is currently at work on a project on contemporary cultures of work.

**Michael Szalay** is the Chair of the English Department at the University of California, Irvine. He is the author of *New Deal Modernism: American Literature and the Invention of the Welfare State* (Duke, 2000) and *Hip Figures: A Literary History of the Democratic Party* (Stanford, 2012). He is now finishing a book on the origins and rise of prestige television.

**Imre Szeman** is a University Research Professor of Communication Arts at the University of Waterloo, where he teaches cultural studies and environmental communication. His recent book-length projects include *Energy Humanities: An Anthology* (Johns Hopkins, 2017), *Fueling Culture: 101 Words for Energy and Environment* (Fordham, 2017), and *Petrocultures: Oil, Politics, Culture* (McGill-Queen's, 2017). He is completing work on *Energy Cultures* (co-edited with Jeff Diamanti) and *On Petrocultures: Globalization, Culture, Energy – Selected Essays, 2001–17.*

**Michael Tratner** is the Mary E. Garrett Alumnae Professor of English at Bryn Mawr College, specializing in Modernism and Film Studies. His last book was entitled *Crowd Scenes: Movies and Mass Politics* (Fordham, 2008) and he is currently working on a history of love and money in literature, tracing relationships between economic theories and sexuality from the mercantilism of *Romeo and Juliet* to the neoliberal cyborg economics of the movie *Avatar.*

**Kyle Wanberg** is a Clinical Assistant Professor in Global Liberal Studies at New York University. His research areas include anticolonial literature and theory, literary representations of finance, and translation studies, and he has published work in several books and journals including *The European Journal of English Studies, Comparative Literature Studies, Canadian Review of Comparative Literature,* and *Journal of Literary Theory and Comparative Literature.* His first single-author book, *The Pit of Babel,* is forthcoming.

**Henry B. Wonham** is a Professor of English at the University of Oregon. He is the author of *Mark Twain and the Art of the Tall Tale* (Oxford, 1993) and *Playing the Races: Ethnic Caricature in American Literary Realism* (Oxford, 2004), and with Lawrence Howe co-edited the collection of essays entitled *Mark Twain and Money: Language, Capital, and Culture* (U. of Alabama, 2017).

**Alden Sajor Marte-Wood** is a Ph.D. candidate in English at the University of California, Irvine, where he works on Asian American and Southeast Asian Anglophone literature. His work has been published in *Post Script: Essays in Film and the Humanities* and he has writing in the forthcoming *Bloomsbury Handbook to Literary and Cultural Theory.* His dissertation situates Filipino/American cultural production within transpacific capitalist networks of flexible accumulation.

# 1
# INTRODUCTION

*Michelle Chihara and Matt Seybold*

William Wordsworth considered Adam Smith a literary critic, though a bad one. "For both Smith and Wordsworth," Thomas Ford says, "literary criticism and political economy remained inextricably interwoven" (Ford 2013: 576). John Stuart Mill, whose *Principles of Political Economy* (1848) was "the most-read tract on economics since Adam Smith's *Wealth of Nations*" (Nasar 2011: 32), asserted that "the primary and perennial sources of all social evil are ignorance and want of culture." He prescribed "preaching and popular writing…national galleries, theatres, and public games" to the masses who, he hoped, via such encounters might acquire the rationality upon which classical economic models of human behavior depended. To maximize the social utility of such media, it was to be delivered and curated by "the more instructed and cultivated" (Mill 2006: 213–14), like Mill himself, who published criticism on Samuel Coleridge, Alfred Tennyson, and other poets.

Karl Marx similarly shows "a passionate interest in literature" (Prawer 1976: 399). Like Mill, he searched for "what linked intellectual and artistic pursuits to a nation's economy" (3), coming to believe "that a fundamental alteration of modes of exchange and production will be necessary to allow everyone the chance to develop artistic and appreciative faculties which are stunted and starved in a capitalist society" (400). Marx's writings sustained the covalence between literary criticism and political economy through much of the twentieth century, codified by a line of self-consciously Marxist critics. But while Marxist literary criticism or cultural Marxism thrived, the belletrism of Smith, Mill, and other classical (and even neoclassical) political economists was among the casualties of the marginal revolution of the late nineteenth century, and particularly the Keynesian synthesis of the mid-twentieth century, as economists increasingly severed themselves from their disciplinary roots in philosophy, rhetoric, and politics, seeking to style themselves as scientists inspired by mathematics, physics, and engineering.

John Maynard Keynes, though he was as dismissive of Marx as he was of such delusional scientism, was among the last canonical economists to share Marx's "passionate interest." Like Marx, he frequently proclaimed his own literary amateurism, preferring to characterize himself as a patron of the arts and an admiring friend of literary modernists. But Keynes's rigorous attention to narrative structure, linguistic precision, metaphor, and other elements of style, as well as the breadth of his published work, reveals this as a false modesty. Even more than his commentary on novels, plays, and poems, Keynes's shared intellectual genealogy with contemporary literary theory and cultural studies is evidenced by his sensitivity to the direct and indirect effects of mass media on what he called the "animal spirits" of the populace. The psychological effects of popular culture (which Keynes still viewed as predominantly textual) were translated rapidly into financial markets by readers who were also consumers and investors, and thereafter into politics and policy-making, which were increasingly sensitive to economic conditions. Keynes argued that in nations unified by organized finance and mass media, the two infrastructures developed a mutual dependence which ensured that, as Gertrude Stein put it, "Money is what words are. / Words are what money is." (165)

This aspect of Keynes's *General Theory* (1936) was not easily translated into the quantitative methods that dominated after his death, and thus both the psychoanalytic and media theory aspects of Keynes's *oeuvre* were largely ignored by economists of the Keynesian synthesis and the neoliberal hegemony which followed. Starting in 1985, Deirdre McCloskey began a slow process of resuscitating her profession's attentiveness to the expression and proliferation of their arguments, the flawed assumption and representational limitations of their preferred methods, and the unassailable human unreliability which undercut economic positivism. The emergence of her "rhetorical economics" (later "humanomics") paralleled that of New Economic Criticism, a subfield of literary criticism which is a recognizable predecessor to the brands of scholarship contained in and considered by this volume.

The mutual imbrication of literary and economic knowledge is much more fully explored in the following pages. "Classical Economics" by Eleanor Courtemanche, "Neoclassical Economics" by Regina Martin, "Keynes and Keynesianism" by Matt Seybold, "Modernism and Macroeconomics" by Michael Tratner, "Neoliberalism" by Alissa Karl, and "Rhetorical Economics" by Mark Longaker specifically expand upon elements of the above overview. We offer this synopsis at the outset to establish, as we begin to examine the complex and counterintuitive relationship between the two disciplines which give this companion its title, that they have not always been, and perhaps need not be, adversaries or anathema, though they frequently are treated as such by economists and literary scholars alike. As Elizabeth Hewitt puts it, in her "Vexed Story of Economic Criticism" (2009), "Of all the interdisciplinary couplings, perhaps the marriage between literary studies and economics has been the most tempestuous—the most likely to alternate between devotion and repudiation" (618). Superficially, it would seem that literary studies have, since 2008, cycled into a period of repudiating economics, but the nature of this era's repudiation is, we argue, distinct, as it is not so much an alternative to devotion as the synthesis of shared roots. This collection begins with an essay by Christopher Newfield which looks out at a global neoliberal capitalism in decline and asks: Does economics need us (*us* being SASH, the qualitative Social Sciences, Arts, and Humanities)? Newfield answers with a resounding yes, placing literary knowledge of the economy at the center of an answer to neoliberal economization (see also Brown 2015). "We need to see the humanities as what they are about to become," he writes, "central disciplines for a planet that must for the first time either devote itself to sustainable development or die."

According to Mark Osteen and Martha Woodmansee, editors of *The New Economic Criticism* (1999), economic criticism last fell out of favor during the mid-twentieth century, while "the profession was dominated by the allegedly apolitical procedures of New Criticism" (13). During this period, as English and Economics departments each indulged their own brand of navel-gazing formalism, their repudiation of each other was characterized by apathy, not animosity. Not so in 2018. Contemporary econo-literary criticism is, paradoxically, energetically engaged with the history of economic thought and methods of economic analysis *and* openly hostile toward economics' prevailing disciplinary hegemony and its perceived program of institutional and cultural imperialism. In this introduction, we—that is, it should probably be noted, two professors credentialed by and employed in English departments—examine the "tempestuous marriage" with particular attention to (1) the most persistent tradition of repudiation: Marxist Literary Criticism, (2) the most recent, receding period of devotion: New Economic Criticism, and (3) how (and why) contemporary econo-literary criticism breaks the cycle by absorbing its extremes.

We began imagining this collection at the 2015 ACLA Annual Meeting in Seattle. Routledge Senior Editor, Polly Dodson, noticed, shrewdly, an uptick in panels, papers, and plenaries explicitly engaging finance and economics. The title of the seminar we organized in 2015—"Literary Finance: Why Now?"—conspicuously echoed the question she was asking herself, and thus we found ourselves preparing a proposal for the *Routledge Literary Companion* series. This volume retains several topics and contributors from that ACLA seminar (see Christian P. Haines's "Financialization" and Alden Wood's "Consumption," for instance). But it would be disingenuous to suggest that it concretely answers the question of *why* a sizable community of scholars trained in literary and cultural studies have chosen to spend the last decade (or longer) fastidiously reading political economy, economic history, business journalism, Wall St. memoirs, microeconomics textbooks, and many other tediously "unliterary" genres which make up what Leigh Claire La Berge calls "financial print culture" (La Berge 2014). The reasons why scholars engage economics and finance so deeply are various and sometimes divergent. What this volume demonstrates, however, is that these scholars approach economic texts and contexts with rigorous attention to the disciplinary vocabulary, methodological assumptions, and intellectual history of economics.

But, by spending so many hours engaging with what might be compellingly be characterized as capitalist apologia, mustn't we also ask: Are we complicit, just as economists are, in rationalizing and normalizing an unsound and exploitative ideology? Acquiescence to capitalism is elicited by social pressure, propaganda, and force, at least as much as it is by logic, persuasion, and disinterested analysis, as orthodox economic mythology claims. This is not to say that the production of an objectively defensible brand of capitalism is unimaginable, but merely that the existing Anglo-American brand shames all those who attempt to defend it on its merits.

The critics in this volume represent a wide spectrum of approaches, methodologically and politically. While the more explicitly Marxist blush at their proximity to the word *economics*, as opposed to the more overtly combative *capitalism*, we suspect that all would want to avoid complicity with the structures that have historically aligned academic economists with the corridors of power, from Chile to Washington, D.C. But beyond orthodoxies, simply by putting the terms *literature* and *economics* into conversation, we raise questions about the nature of the critique being performed. In *Critique and Postcritique* (2017), Elizabeth Anker and Rita Felski delineate the contemporary debates about the role and function of the humanities writ large. They note that many scholars feel that critique, in general, or literary critique, in particular, has "become just another familiar pedagogical tool and research method in the neoliberal university," "[s]afely housed in the Routledge anthology and the freshman composition class." This critique of critique calls "contemporary forms of reading and reasoning" to account "for being insufficiently radical or oppositional" (Anker & Felski 2017: 13).

Within Marxist literary debates, charges of being "insufficiently radical or oppositional" are common. And literature, as represented by a *Routledge Companion* or a university course, is frequently part of structures that perpetuate social distinction. Literature, as a specialized form of knowledge, has roots in both religious institutions and a belletristic bourgeoisie. But questions about critique's complicity in the neoliberal university must be contextualized in the larger debates about the role of the academy in society and in its own self-analysis. The fact that critique within the academy has failed to spark the revolution hardly seems a penetrating insight, particularly in light of Newfield's research on the corporatization of the university, most recently in *The Great Mistake* (2016). In the essay that follows, he sees "opposition emerg[ing] in activity rather than systematic argument." We see econo-literary criticism as part of this activity that instantiates its opposition, and in doing so stands up for literature, for the liberal arts, and for the value of inter- and intradisciplinary dialogues within a university understood as a public good and not a neoliberal institution. If this articulation of value is itself insufficiently radical or potentially bourgeois, we are sure colleagues, including those who have contributed to this volume, will let us know.

Internecine Marxist debates have, at least since the early twentieth century, always been marked by vituperative invective. The "method wars" within the academy are no exception. Sometimes, these debates are turf wars in disguise. But at other times, as with the debates around critique itself, disagreement over methods can expand the overall territory of scholarship. Since Georg Lukács broke with the group of expatriate Left intellectuals known as the Frankfurt School over their allegiance to Soviet Russia, Marxist aesthetic theorists have articulated widely varying methods. Neoclassical economists have tended to dismiss what is effectively a caricature of Marx's labor theory of value, or his account of base and superstructure. On this, the canon of Marxist aesthetic theorists might agree. That might be the extent of their consensus. Max Horkheimer, Theodore Adorno, Raymond Williams, and Walter Benjamin all articulated their own versions of cultural Marxism with their own idiosyncratic definitions of ideology, culture, and society. This lineage is present in this volume. Louis Althusser's influence is clear in Alden Wood's use of interpellation and, via Pierre Macherey, in David Buxton's account of serialized culture in the age of finance.

The critic who is conspicuous in his (relative) absence from the expansive territory delineated in these pages is Fredric Jameson. This may be because in method wars, as in the Marxist wars, everyone is trying to get beyond a Jamesonian anxiety of influence. In *Capitalist Realism* (2009), Mark Fisher echoed Jameson (and Slavoj Zizek) by claiming that it is easier to imagine the end of the world rather than the end of capitalism. (Fisher was working on a contribution to this volume before his untimely death. We hope his legacy is nevertheless evident in these pages.) In *Reading Capitalist Realism* (2014), Alison Shonkwiler and Leigh Claire La Berge expanded on the concept of capitalist realism "to provide a language and terminology for what comes *after* a Jamesonian critique at its most totalizing, suffocating and yet unassailably correct" (La Berge & Shonkwiler 2014: 2). The terms of the Jamesonian critique have not become any less pressing. As recently as 2014, Shonkwiler and La Berge observed that "capitalism has intensified its claim on its established terrain and further foreclosed upon imaginable alternatives" and wrote that "capitalist realism presumes that things have gotten worse" (3). And that was before the dramatic rise of right-wing populism which is both mobilized by and contributes to staggering inequalities of wealth and concentrations of power.

Jameson has been criticized as expressing the failures of the postmodernism that he criticized. Anker and Felski describe him as a "lightning rod for recent debates" because of his "unapologetic embrace of allegorical and homological modes of reading" (6). A wide spectrum of critics in postcolonial criticism—Aijaz Ahmad, most famously—pushed back against his writing on national allegory for his flattening of Third World literature (see Ahmad 1986, 1992). Jameson acknowledged, in a 1989 issue of *New Left Review*, that people seemed to think that because he had "'become' a postmodernist" he "must have ceased to be a Marxist in any meaningful (or in other words stereotypical) sense" (31). And yet, Jameson's symptomatic readings remain relevant. Recent books by Geoff Mann and Wendy Brown testify that it has gotten no easier in the past decade to imagine the end of capitalism, even though, as Matt has written elsewhere, "since 2008 finance has been an emperor with no clothes…the fictiveness of finance capital now stands so ludicrously exposed that even those who benefit from its sustained pretenses seem shocked that their imaginary wealth continues to reproduce itself." The work of Jameson still casts a long guiding shadow over literary criticism, Marxist theory, and this volume.

The brush that tars both the critic and her topic is commonly wielded at literary critics who write about finance and economics. The argument is that in their commitment to its seductive formal complexity, they reproduce the ideology of the objects of their critique. The cult of formal difficulty in literature ports easily, in other words, to a seductive new economy of signs in finance. And the conventional objection to Jameson's homological method is leveled at many of his contemporaries, who were relatively briefly identified as New Economic Critics, including Marc Shell, Walter Benn Michaels, Jean-Joseph Goux, and Kurt Heinzelman. In 1999, Osteen and Woodmansee argued that "their work … laid the foundation for virtually all the literary economic criticism that has followed" (14). By "expos[ing] and analyz[ing] this historical and philosophical parallels—usually termed homologies—between economic and linguistic systems," New Economic Criticism "retains the singular advantage of enabling one to study social forms 'from the inside,' and thereby to discover how certain essentials in human social behavior transcend historical and cultural differences" (14–15). The homology between economics and literature—or, as both Shell and Stein would likely prefer, between money and words—was "the major assumption upon which economic criticism has been built" (15). While it is true that "Shell's work … opened seemingly infinite avenues for future work" (16), work like that discussed and performed in this volume, the homological method also, too often, dead-ended in what Nicky Marsh calls "somewhat tautological assumptions" (Marsh 2017: 486) and readings that were more suggestive than substantive.

In 1991, when Osteen and Woodmansee coined *New Economic Criticism* to name a Midwest MLA panel, the most recent of what they would later identify as the field's core texts were Jameson's *Postmodernism* (1991) and Howard Horwitz's *By The Law of Nature* (1991). Horwitz, as a scholar who both contributed to *The New Economic Criticism* and anticipated many of its limitations (and who has been a visible organizer and mentor figure for econo-literary scholars emerging during the global financial crisis), personifies, along with Michael Tratner, the undeniable link between Osteen and Woodmansee's volume and our own. His chapter on "Social Want" interpolates three figures—Marx, McCloskey, and Keynes—who appear consistently throughout both volumes, but are nowhere else made so directly conversant with one another. Osteen and Woodmansee recognized Horwitz as "the first of the new breed" who, with a "nuanced methodology" built around isomorphism, "avoids the traps of homology hunting" (21). Horwitz's work satisfies McCloskey's demand that literary scholars "consider first the economy of the producer/author, including his or her local division of labor, class, etc." (12). But though Horwitz demonstrates in *By The Law of Nature* deep immersion in the distinct economic texts and contexts of the nineteenth-century United States—its trusts, its tariffs, its locofocoism, and its penny paper political economy—it is not because he views the economics of Marxists, Keynesians, or Monetarists as anachronistic. McCloskey's own corpus, especially her recent Bourgeois Trilogy (2006–16), testifies that compelling economic theories often emerge when economists reach beyond conventions of temporality and territory. Keynes's famous warning that "we assume the present is a much more serviceable guide to the future than a candid examination of past experience would show it to have been hitherto" (Keynes 1973b: 114) offers, unintentionally, a rationale for projecting economic theories backward upon the archive which, consciously or unconsciously, informs their conception, instead of the horizons of their publication.

As Eleanor Courtemanche puts it in her chapter (which also offers an insightful analysis of New Economic Criticism), economic criticism thrives when "historically-inflected critics tease … apart various strands of classical and neoclassical economic theory that had previously been left to economics departments." This volume reflects that both historicist and isomorphic methods flourish in the twenty-first century. In the "Histories" part of the volume, readers will find essays pitched to the conventional periodizations of English graduate programs. The authors of these chapters survey the economic history of the eras in question and identify influential works of political economy associated with their specialization, while also modeling how to interpret poems, plays, fiction, and creative nonfiction in light of connections to the world beyond the text. The "Principles" section features essays on a series of essential economic concepts. While the contributors to this section do, whenever possible, locate the historical origins of the principles they interrogate, they also treat them as objects of chronic critique and often as potentially (and sometimes misleadingly) homologous with critical methods, rhetorical techniques, and literary genres.

In the spirit of their efforts, we should note that *principle* is a loaded word in economics, as classical and neoclassical economists frequently signaled their aspirations to canonization by giving their *magnum opuses* the title *Principles of Political Economy*, in the tradition of Mill, Thomas Robert Malthus, David Ricardo, and Alfred Marshall. There is, as such, an incongruence between what students in literary studies associate with *principles*, and what economists associate with the term. In "Literary Principles as Against Theory" (1985), Christopher Ricks argues that *principles* are "modest and practicable" (321) applications "rooted" to their "given situation" (323). Principles, according to Ricks, "admit contradictions" (323) and "permit … counter-principles" (325), while "a theory, because its reputability is constituted of elaborated concatenation, cannot accommodate a counter-theory" (325) and is "hostile to contradictions" (323). Theories do not contain, as T. S. Eliot puts it, "a recognition, implicit in the expression of every experience, of other kinds of experience that are possible" (325). By Ricks's definition (and Eliot's), the *Principles* published by the likes of Ricardo and Marshall are unmistakably works of theory. They make strong claims to comprehensiveness and universality. Keynes signaled his self-conscious break from this tradition by ironically titling his crowning achievement *The General Theory*, even though it is primarily a series of highly circumstantial principles, loosely framed by a theory that economics cannot aspire to anything more than that, because economic circumstances are "not homogenous through time." Insofar as it is a theory, the *General Theory* is a theory that aims to end economic theory by exposing it as intrinsically irrational. The fact that Keynes, via his title, supplemented his explicit economic critique of Ricardo with an implicit linguistic critique demonstrates why McCloskey believes that contemporary economic rhetoric is debased by comparison, to a degree which compromises its conceptual utility, and emphasizes the vitality of the skills language and literature scholars bring to economic texts.

Osteen and Woodmansee's *New Economic Criticism* collection remains highly relevant, as evidenced by how often it is referred to in the chapters which follow, but that ubiquity is also attributable to its paucity of successors. Few ensuing attempts have been made to sustain New Economic Criticism as a coherent and collaborative community of scholars. There has been, especially in the past decade, a steady stream of critical works that *could* be called New Economic Criticism, but they rarely are. Osteen and Woodmansee admitted that they named *New Economic Criticism* in an attempt to draw upon the vogue of New Historicism. They succeeded in being fashionable. New Economic Criticism has largely disappeared from the academic lexicon. It was, perhaps, a matter of poor branding, as it was misleading to call economic criticism "new," even in 1999, since the field had been flourishing, by Osteen and Woodmansee's own admission, for at least two decades, beginning with the publication of Shell's *The Economy of Literature* (1978) and Heinzelman's *The Economics of Imagination* (1980). It was never entirely clear how New Economic Criticism distinguished itself from "old" economic criticism by Lukács, Williams, Rehard Flory, and William Charvat, nor why it tried.

New Economic Criticism was not a wholesale rejection of Marxist Literary Criticism, but New Economic Critics did tend to treat Marx as part of a historical continuum of economic thought, not an invalidation of it—as a purveyor of useful principles, not a grand exclusionary theory. Osteen and Woodmansee identify Jameson's *Postmodernism* and Benn Michaels's *The Gold Standard and the Logic of Naturalism* (1987)—both indebted to Cultural Marxism—as core texts in the emerging field. But they were also persuaded by McCloskey that literary critics had a "blind spot" because their "knowledge of economics begins and ends with Karl Marx" (12). McCloskey, a rare economist committed to revolutionizing her discipline from within, was arguably the central figure in New Economic Criticism, and her influence is still felt in this volume. But several literary scholars, notably Horwitz and Stanley Fish, thought that McCloskey was "caught between antifoundationalist impulses and a deep loyalty to University of Chicago-style economic orthodoxy" (23). McCloskey's work is belatedly making an impact on economics itself, a generally encouraging sign, but the accommodations she has made to her Chicago School peers, becoming an icon of civil libertarianism, suggest that Horwitz's assessment in his *New Economic Criticism* essay was precocious. Econo-literary critics have, as McCloskey hoped, expanded the range of their engagement with the history of economic thought. Simultaneously, many Marxists have been broadening their perspectives in an effort to update the Marxian critique, developed during industrialization, for an epoch of deindustrialization (and least in the Global North) and, especially, financialization.

The interdisciplinary collaborations that seemed so promising in 1990s failed to materialize in the following decade, which is one explanation for the decline of New Economic Criticism. Large numbers of economists and economic historians wrote books claiming that they had predicted the global financial crisis, notably Robert Shiller's *The Subprime Solution* (2008), Nouriel Roubini's *Crisis Economics* (2010), and Thomas Piketty's *Capital In The Twenty First Century* (2013). But while all of these economists begin with the urgency of the need for a new understanding, they have not, as a discipline, been able to get beyond what economic historian Philip Mirowski calls their inability to question the "legitimacy of neoclassical microeconomics" (Mirowski 2013: 283). Mirowski, whose *Against Mechanism* (1988), *More Heat Than Light* (1989), and *Never Let A Serious Crisis Go To Waste* (2013) bring fatal flaws in the neoclassical orthodoxy to light from within a deep knowledge of the field, is a rare exception. But, under a new banner and with minimal involvement from economists themselves, collaborations like those Osteen and Woodmansee anticipated have coalesced since 2008 in a series of working groups, institutions, and interdisciplinary collections, frequently united under a loose rubric like Cultural Economy or Critical Finance Studies.

Critical Finance Studies scholars have been building on work that does not take the neoclassical microeconomic models as given, even as they seek new understandings of economics. Groups like the Critical Finance Group at Warwick University or the Critical Labor and Finance Studies research cluster at the University of Arizona bring together scholars across disciplines. Some of these scholars come from literature and cultural studies backgrounds but now seem more political economists, while some come from other disciplines but have turned to literary terms of analysis; all have made crucial contributions to the qualitative knowledge necessary today. Many contributors to this volume are part of such groups. The UCI Center for Culture & Capital lists a number of scholars in this volume as members, and has provided both intellectual and material support for the work.

There are also a number of books by literature scholars which have a substantial impact upon this collection, but whose authors are not represented within it. These include Anna Kornbluh's *Realizing Capital* (2014), Sarah Brouillette's *Literature and Creative Economy* (2014), Leigh Claire La Berge's *Scandals and Abstractions* (2015), Supritha Rajan's *A Tale of Two Capitalisms* (2015), Bruce Robbins's *The Beneficiary* (2017), and Aimee Bahng's *Migrant Futures* (2018).

The reader may notice that the scholars and collectives listed earlier tend to use the term *finance* and not *economics*. Deindustrialization coincided with the rapid growth of the finance, insurance, and real estate sectors in the Global North during the final decades of the twentieth century, which is also the period in which "finance" came to mean "the economic." As La Berge writes in her analysis of the 1980s, "finance came to stand in metonymically for 'the economy' in the sense that the representation of the financial sector of economic activity is the closest thing we have to the representation of an economic totality" (4). Our use of *economics* gestures toward economic histories that predate the metonymy of finance. It is not a concession to finance's centrality, nor to the ahistoric "economization" associated with neoliberalism (see Brown 2015). As Timothy Mitchell details in *Carbon Demoracy* (2011), a history of democracies and oil, the emergence and rise of "the economy" as a governing abstraction was man-made, along with fossil fuel-based capitalist democratic states. Given the power this abstraction now expresses, it is a social construct worth deconstructing.

For at least as long as it has been legitimized by integration into Western governance and academia, the discipline of economics has taken capitalism as given, and has tolerated, even exacerbated, the protection of affluence and excess at the expense of institutional violence and the creation of poverty by the willfully inefficient distribution of resources. Economists are routinely called upon to rationalize limitations of access to education, healthcare, and legal protection which disproportionately disadvantage minorities and enable harmful upward redistributions of wealth. Over the past year, democratically elected administrations in both the US and the UK have enacted policies of trade and taxation explicitly justified by outdated and widely discredited economic theories. The famous maxim from the conclusion of Keynes's *General Theory*, that "madmen in authority, who hear voices in the air, are distilling their frenzy from some academic scribbler of a few year back," rendering us all "slaves of some defunct economist" (383) have never rung more true. Orthodox economists are disproportionately responsible for the perpetuation of profoundly anti-intellectual and antidemocratic rhetorics. They face severe "incentives problems," to borrow their own euphemism. To accept and acknowledge that most of the economic theories and models which are taught to undergraduates and MBAs reflect nothing more than their creators' yearning for mathematical elegance and the academic prestige incumbent therein is to risk the exalted positions onto which economists cling, not only as disproportionately well-compensated members of the professoriate, but as influential (and also well-compensated) consultants to government and private industry. Economists have put the stamp of (pseudo-)science on austerity measures, executive compensation packages, deregulation that facilitates fraud and exploitation, and other forms of subsidized graft. So far as they are concerned, the proceeds do trickle down. Economists who, like McCloskey and Mirowski, expose the fatuous expertise of many of their peers face predictably severe professional sanction. As such, economists's capacity for self-reform is limited and progress away from conventions is exceedingly slow, even when they have been soundly debunked.

The rising prominence of behavioral economists like Shiller and Richard Thaler, who won the Nobel Prize in 2013 and 2017, might inspire hope that economists may yet rise to defeat their professional "zombies" from within (see Quiggin 2010). But, as Michelle discusses in her chapter, the behavioral method, like Keynesianism before it, runs the risk of "synthesizing" an entirely new set of risks and perverse incentives into an even more seductive account of the democratic subject, within the rising tyranny of metrics. Many behaviorists have turned their attention to social issues and seem to promise an awareness of capitalism's intrinsic inequality, but ultimately they deliver their more accurate predictive instruments into the service of a quietist "optimization" of the regime that creates injustice.

But though behavioral economics may be compromised, its origin story, told and retold in popular books by Thaler, Nassim Taleb, and Michael Lewis, is evidence that economics can be improved by interdisciplinary collaborations which need not actually involve economists. Important works on economic history and theory are being written by evolutionary biologists like David Sloan Wilson, geographers like David Harvey and Geoff Mann, political scientists like Wendy Brown, and psychologists like Daniel Kahneman and Amos Tversky, who broke the ground upon which Shiller and Thaler's research now stands. In this volume, Richard Godden locates within the structure of finance capital a formal imperative, a historically specific impulse to allegory in the moment of the turn to finance. Paradigm shifts come from those within the academy who know the disciplines that need shifting well. While it might be hard to imagine Godden's groundbreaking work in *William Faulkner: An Economy of Complex Words* (2007) being recognized with a Nobel Memorial Prize in Economics, it probably seemed equally outrageous to imagine Kahneman, who won in 2002, as a laureate in the decade after he and Tversky published *Judgment Under Uncertainty* (1982). Interdisciplinary critiques of economics can and should be used to strengthen the society built around them.

In the Anker and Felski volume, the editors see themselves working in the spirit of "testing out new possibilities and alternatives" (2) rather than coming to an epistemological consensus. Working under the assumption that each critic in this volume may be operating under a slightly different take on "literature" and "economics," we, too, leave open questions of epistemology, in the spirit of defending the space to contain the larger debates. We hope this capacious space will both stabilize the need for knowledge of literature and destabilize other forms of knowing. Donna Haraway argues then in current debates about the social construction of knowledge that there are "*four* very tempting positions." These temptations include (1) a total rejection of epistemological realism, (2) "the analysis of power through Marxist, feminist and anticolonial frameworks," (3) "the perspective of scientists themselves," and (4) the "master temptation," "to look always through the lenses ground on the stones of the complex histories of gender and race in the constructions of modern science around the globe" (Anker & Felski 2017: 61) According to Heather Love, the "dynamism" of Haraway's work is lost when critics miss her ambivalence. All of these temptations are also critical resources for Haraway. Love writes that she draws on them *and* uses them by "mining the tensions between them as well as their moments of intersection or complementarity" (61).

Increasingly since 2016, mainstream commentators have reductively appropriated Benn Michael's argument that attention to "identity politics" comes at the expense of attention to "class" (see Benn Michaels 2006). Ideally, the dynamic space opened up by considering that literature *and* economics together is one that avoids all such reductive totalizing. Ideally, by avoiding a totalizing theory of literature and economics, we can mine the tensions among the critics represented here, staging ambivalence around the four temptations, using them all as a resource and yet avoiding being seduced. In her chapter, Annie McClanahan draws on the work of Marxist feminists like Silvia Federici to analyze the reproductive metaphors that govern political economy's accounts of secular stagnation. With careful attention to definitions of "race" and the structural processes within capitalism that produce racial difference, Christopher Chen and Timothy Kreiner, in their chapter on American poetry and Audre Lorde, draw on the tradition of black Marxism and Cedric Robinson and Frantz Fanon. Meanwhile, Michael Szalay, in his chapter on the AOL Time Warner merger, draws on Marx and geographer Edward W. Soja to explain how these companies "promised a space in which over-accumulated capital would not die, but would instead remain dynamic and continue to expand" such that "global media would become more important than government...by becoming the form of appearance of global capital in expansion." Szalay is one of five scholars who, in the final section of the volume, herald a brand of econo-literary criticism that, without entirely abandoning the methods of Marxist Literary Criticism and New Economic Criticism traced here, must be described as even "newer." These scholars take concerns with serialization, genre, medium, and regimes of production to create literary knowledge of the economy around aggressively contemporary objects—podcasts, prestige television, and hip-hop musicals—which must be considered native to late capitalism.

Dawn McCance notes that since Michel Foucault, we have known that power is not "superstructural" or a top-down affair, but that "cultural representations both produce power and render it fragile—and are intelligible only in this double sense" (McCance 2000: 1). Foucault gave a powerful account of discourse's complicit relationship to power. He predicted many aspects of neoliberalism's rise (see Foucault 2008). However, Foucault also troublingly seemed to endorse some of the very aspects of free-market orthodoxy about which he was so prescient (see Zamora & Behrent 2016). We do not imagine that literature can or should represent an entirely autonomous field from power or from the capitalist social relations under which it is produced. We do believe in the importance of literary knowledge in the face of the political and social matrix that creates us and that today threatens to destroy us.

As recently as last year, Matt wrote, in a review essay for the Economics & Finance section of *The Los Angeles Review of Books* which Michelle edits:

> We find ourselves looking at nearly two centuries during which economics has wasted larger proportions of our money, talent, and attention with each passing generation. One is tempted...to wonder whether the 'Queen of the Social Sciences' is a dry cellar, a cactus land, a paralyzed force, a headpiece filled with straw. What part of the record of economics should persuade us economists aren't altogether expendable? *What are the roots that clutch, what branches grow, out of this stony rubbish?*

Serious engagement with economics does not imply acceptance of its legitimacy, but economics needs scholars from outside its compromised walls. Something Brook Thomas wrote in response to our proposal in 2015 has stuck with us: "Economics plays too important a role in society for its study to be confined to economics departments." The scholars represented here, their forms of knowledge and engagement, might be able to carry water to the waste land of contemporary economics. Charles Dickens habitually satirized specific works of political economy, not out of disrespect for the discipline, but rather to protect, as he put it, "the real useful truths of political economy" from "those who see figures and averages, and nothing else" (Henderson 2000: 142). Nearly a century later, Keynes echoed Dickens when he wrote,

> Economics is a science of thinking in terms of models joined to the art of choosing models which are relevant to the contemporary world...to convert a model into a quantitative formula is to destroy its usefulness as an instrument of thought.
>
> *(Keynes 1973b: 296, 300)*

The reason "good economists are scarce," Keynes posited, was that while neither the art nor the science of economics "require a highly specialized intellectual technique," the mind which possesses both "appears to be a very rare one" (297).

## References

Ahmad, Aijaz. (1992) *In Theory: Classes, Nations, Literatures*, New York: Verso.
Ahmad, Aijaz. (1987) "Jameson's Rhetoric of Otherness and the 'National Allegory'," *Social Text* 17: 3–25.
Anker, Elizabeth S. and Felski, Rita. (2017) *Critique and Postcritique*, Durham, NC: Duke University Press.
Benn Michaels, Walter. (2006) *The Trouble with Diversity*, New York: Metropolitan.
Benn Michaels, Walter. (1987) *The Gold Standard and the Logic of Naturalism: American Literature at the Turn of the Century*, Berkeley: University of California Press.
Brown, Wendy. (2015) *Undoing the Demos: Neoliberalism's Stealth Revolution*, Brooklyn, NY: Zone Books.
Fisher, Mark. (2009) *Capitalist Realism: Is There No Alternative?* New York: Zero Books.
Ford, Thomas H. (2013) "The Romantic Political Economy of Reading: Or, Why Wordsworth Thought Adam Smith was the Worst Critic Ever," *ELH* 80.2: 575–95.
Foucault, Michel. (2008) *The Birth of Biopolitics*, New York: Palgrave Macmillan.
Godden, Richard. (2007) *William Faulkner: An Economy of Complex Words*, Princeton, NJ: Princeton University Press.
Goux, Jean-Joseph. (1994) *The Coiners of Language*, Norman: University of Oklahmoma Press.
Heinzelman, Kurt. (1980) *The Economics of Imagination*, Amherst: University of Massachusetts Press.
Henderson, James P. (2000) "'Political Economy Is a Mere Skeleton Unless...': What Can Social Economists Learn from Charles Dickens?" *Review of Social Economy* 58.2: 141–51.
Hewitt, Elizabeth. (2009) "The Vexed Story of Economic Criticism," *American Literary History* 21.3: 618–31.
Horwitz, Howard. (1991) *By the Law of Nature: Form and Value in Nineteenth-Century America*, New York: Oxford University Press.
Jameson, Frederic. (1991) *Postmodernism, or, the Cultural Logic of Late Capitalism*, Durham, NC: Duke University Press.
Jameson, Frederic. (1989) "Marxism and Postmodernism," *New Left Review* 176: 31–45.
Keynes, John Maynard. (1973a) *The Collected Writings of John Maynard Keynes, Vol. XII: The General Theory of Employment, Interest, and Money*, London: Macmillan St. Martin's.
Keynes, John Maynard. (1973b) *The Collected Writings of John Maynard Keynes, Vol. XIV: The General Theory & After, Part II: Defense & Development*, London: Macmillan St. Martin's.
La Berge, Leigh Claire. (2014) *Scandals and Abstractions: Financial Fiction of the Long 1980s*, Oxford: Oxford University Press.
La Berge, Leigh Claire and Shonkwiler, Alison. (2014) *Reading Capitalist Realism*, Iowa City: University of Iowa Press.
Marsh, Nicky. (2017) "The Cosmopolitan Coin: What Modernists Make of Money," *Modernism/modernity* 24.3: 485–505.
Marshall, Alfred. (1890) *Principles of Economics*, London: Macmillan.
McCance, Dawn. (2000) "Introduction," *Mosaic* 33.3: v–viii.
McCloskey, Deirdre N. (1985) *The Rhetoric of Economics*, Madison: University of Wisconsin Press.
Mann, Geoff. (2017) *In The Long Run We Are All Dead: Keynesianism, Political Economy, and Revolution*, New York: Verso.

Mill, John Stuart. (2006) *Collected Works of John Stuart Mill, Vol. 4: Essays on Economics and Society, 1824–1845*, Indianapolis, IN: Liberty Fund.
Mirowski, Philip. (2013) *Never Let a Serious Crisis Go to Waste*, New York: Verso.
Mitchell, Timothy. (2011) *Carbon Democracy: Political Power in the Age of Oil*, New York: Verso.
Nasar, Sylvia. (2011) *Grand Pursuit: The Story of Economic Genius*, New York: Simon & Schuster.
Newfield, Christopher. (2016) *The Great Mistake: How We Wrecked Public Universities an How We Can Fix Them*, Baltimore, MD: Johns Hopkins University Press.
Osteen, Mark and Woodmansee, Martha. (1999) *The New Economic Criticism: Studies at the Intersection of Literature and Economics*, London: Routledge.
Prawer, S. S. (1976) *Karl Marx and World Literature*, Oxford: Clarendon Press.
Quiggin, John. (2010) *Zombie Economics: How Dead Ideas Still Walk among Us*, Princeton, NJ: Princeton University Press.
Ricardo, David. (1817) *On the Principles of Political Economy and Taxation*, London: John Murray.
Ricks, Christopher. (1996) *Essays in Appreciation*, Oxford: Oxford University Press.
Seybold, Matt. (2017a) "The End of Economics," *Los Angeles Review of Books* (July 3). www.lareviewofbooks.org/article/the-end-of-economics/.
Seybold, Matt. (2017b) "Ain't Nothing like the Real Thing? Maybe," *boundary 2 online* (November 22). www.boundary2.org/2017/11/matt-seybold-aint-nothing-like-the-real-thing-maybe/.
Shell, Marc. (1978) *The Economic of Literature*, Baltimore, MD: Johns Hopkins University Press.
Stein, Gertrude. (1936) *The Geographical History of America*, New York: Random House.
Tversky, Amos and Kahneman, Daniel. (1982) *Judgment under Uncertainty: Heuristics and Biases*, Cambridge: Cambridge University Press.
Zamora, Daniel and Behrendt, Michael C. (2016) *Foucault and Neoliberalism*, Hoboken, NJ: Wiley.

# PART I

# Critical traditions

# 2
# WHAT IS LITERARY KNOWLEDGE OF ECONOMY?

*Christopher Newfield*

This chapter argues that literary criticism has resources and perspectives that oppose key premises of Western capitalism. I won't argue that literary criticism offers a general critique Western capitalism, both because the former is clearly not a unified body of views and because opposition emerges in activity rather than systematic argument. I don't engage in theoretical elaboration here. I'm interested in showing only that these practices and perspectives are right under our noses—and that they should be under the noses of economists and policymakers as well.

## Homo non-oeconomicus

The general question, what is literary knowledge, is as old as literature itself. Commentary as far back as Plato holds that knowledge isn't the right word when referring to literature. Many have claimed that literature subtracts or destroys knowledge, forcing other disciplines or "faculties" to shoulder the burden of adding to it. More recently, critics such as Amanda Anderson, Simon During, Rita Felski, and Helen Small have offered careful arguments for the kind of knowledge produced by literature and its critics. This work offers a range of excellent briefs for literary knowledge across a broad terrain. But why does economics belong on this broad literary terrain?

There are at least two reasons why it should—and why literary scholars should keep developing the literary contribution to economic thought. The first is that economic policy needs new ideas. It has paddled itself up a creek from which the discipline of economics seems unable to help it escape. The works of political economists like Giovanni Arrighi, Mark Blyth, James Galbraith, David Harvey, Greta Krippner, Thomas Piketty, Bernard Stiegler, Wolfgang Streeck, and Yanis Varoufakis suggest that Western economies have entered an impasse of creditor-dominated low growth that will continue to increase inequality and political conflict. Some innovation economics—such as the work of Robert Gordon—claims that the main wave of technological innovation is behind us and productivity growth will not return to mid-twentieth-century levels for decades, if ever. Meanwhile, attempts to rekindle growth in the old mold of the Industrial Revolution—more technology driven by ever-greater use of energy—will now produce unacceptable increases in environmental damage. Economics needs the imagination, theories, and materials of literary and cultural study (LCS) to find sustainable paths forward.

Second, there are the stakes for literary study itself. Literary study lacks the kind of research infrastructure assumed by the natural and even the social sciences. LCS does not have the funding to do the purchasing and operating of equipment, data collection, regular travel, archiving, visualization, and dissemination that ground empirical research in science and technology fields. This relative poverty does not detract from the conceptual, historical, and analytical richness of humanities disciplines. And yet, the lack of infrastructure limits the creation and circulation of findings in the forms that public knowledge currently recognizes as valid. In the next twenty years, LCS could become a set of service disciplines that will be expected to focus on teaching the important crafts of reading and writing as a kind of general *pre*-major. Doctoral programs would continue to shrink, and advanced courses would be replaced by general overviews that can be standardized across different campuses and platforms. In this context, we need to explicate, now more than ever, the meaning of literary knowledge.

My experience is that most nonliterary people assume that literature and criticism produce no actual knowledge about the world outside the text. They doubt that "literary knowledge" is a thing. For example, not long ago, a literature grad student in my department got a fellowship to take courses across campus that shared an Environmental Studies doctoral emphasis. He told me that during the last week in a sociology grad seminar on climate change, the group was to discuss T.C. Boyle's novel *San Miguel*, which is built around some environmental dilemmas. One of the first questions, from a sociology grad student, was, "What were we supposed to learn from this novel?" "Nothing," the professor replied, to general chuckling. The lit grad raised his hand to state a few claims about environmentalism that Boyle had made. Before he could speak, the professor continued, "fiction doesn't say anything about the world as such, but it's the end of the quarter and I thought you needed a break." Not to overread an anecdote, but we are up against widespread skepticism about literature as knowledge, and it is perhaps at its most intense among our also insecure neighbors in the qualitative social sciences.

In general, knowledge has standing by being recognized as knowledge by *other people's* disciplines: epistemological standing isn't self-conferred. Literature offers knowledge if sociologists and chemists think it does, not just if literature professors do. The disciplines operate with rigorous ownership structures. The economy is owned by economics and by related specialties found in business schools. How does it register that Jennifer Egan wrote an excellent novel, called *A Visit from the Goon Squad* (2010), about the psychosocial effects of the late capitalist music industry? It is a study of neoliberalism's *homo oeconomicus*. But even with its 2011 Pulitzer Prize, Egan's book lacks public status as a description of *Capitalism in the 21st Century*, in contrast to the economist Thomas Piketty's book by that title. If we can't say what literary knowledge is and what it contributes to cross-disciplinary investigations, how can we have literary knowledge of economy?

There's a long tradition of thinking that literature is on the side of whatever is not reason, but the situation seems to have gone from bad to worse. Kant, at the end of the eighteenth century, could spread humanistic inquiry across the "lower faculties" while giving these a unique guardian role of protecting knowledge from state interference. But C.P. Snow, in the 1950s, went on to segregate literature and the humanities into the lesser of "two cultures" and labeled it an obstruction to the superior culture of science. We live with a hardened version of this divide today: the STEM disciplines are prized as the saviors of the knowledge economy by political and business leaders that include many humanities graduates, like Barack Obama. The other disciplines, which I label SASH (Social Sciences, Arts, and Humanities) are often classed as luxuries, nice for those who can afford them. In Britain, the Cameron government has written the superfluity of non-STEM fields into statute by eliminating their government funding: they are now supported entirely by fees, whose cap the Tories tripled to £9,000. Making matters worse, we now have quantitative methodologies crossing through the iron curtain that used to separate them from the qualitative: cognitive scientists such as Michal Kosinski claim that big data allow them to describe and explain human behavior in ways that writers cannot (Kosinski et al. 2013). Other disciplines, while patrolling their ownership structures, no longer recognize those of the arts and letters that claim to be privileged observers of the history and meaning of human life. Steven Pinker, a prominent cognitive scientist, recently wrote a very long book on the evolution of human nature and society for which his lack of *historical* expertise clearly posed no obstacle. He has also published a book about how academics should write. You don't need to be a writing professor to be an expert on writing, or a historian to discuss historical development, but the same is not true of organic chemistry or cognitive psychology.

And yet, if I have not depressed you too much, you may be remembering the other side of story, which is the mass popularity of story itself. Global production of narrative grows without limit; it now circulates better than ever and in every imaginable form. The humanities are one of the most popular activities on the planet—the hearing and telling of stories of every kind. Science, politics, economics, all of today's "higher faculties," trail behind in the sweepstakes of daily circulation. Undergraduate students are aware of this, and continue to take courses that teach them both how to analyze texts and how to make them—even when they are not majoring in the departments that house them. Lousy funding has not prevented the arts and humanities from serving as the heart of "maker culture"—a diffuse cultural tendency that links arts and technology in collaborative forms of learning-by-doing. And yet, the popularity of practices like creative nonfiction does not rest on the belief that they make knowledge in any classic sense.

Can we retell a story about contemporary thought in which the humanities are not marginal but central—and central because of the knowledge they make? I'd like to see if I can convince any of you that literary knowledge of economy is one answer to neoliberal *economization*, which reduces value to private market goods and subjectivity to the preparation to compete to maximize these (Brown 2015). Literary knowledge of economy not only points toward sustainable economics, but also expresses a kind of self, a *homo non economicus*, that is good in itself and also essential to the next economy.

## The humanities as subjective empiricism

A central function of human life is this narrative function—unending acts of private and social self-representation that are consistently self-reflexive. In *The Value of the Humanities* (2013), Small argues that humanities disciplines should resist the traditional "gadfly role" descended from Socrates, in which humanities critics act, in Small's phrase, as "isolated agitants" *rather than* pursuing "critical inquiry that is a 'social practice'" (Small 2014: 139). She says, in other words, that we should reject the dualisms of reason/emotion and public/private in which the humanities are mostly about private affect, and see the exploration of interiority as continuous with publicly recognizable critical inquiry.

Literature is good at not just linking private and public works, but at describing their continuous coproduction. Small has as good a summary as I have read of the characteristic modes in which the humanities pursue these public–private thought–affect inquiries. The humanities can be contingently identified, she writes, by

> Their tendency to value qualitative above quantitative reasoning; their distrust of proceduralism; their greater faith in interpretative than in positivistic thinking; their orientation as much toward historical analysis as toward synchronic structural analysis; and their attention to the role of the perceiver in ascertaining even the most philosophically secure of knowledge claims; (relatedly) their interest in the specificity of the individual response (its content and its style) over and above the generalized or collective response, and their concern with what can be known or understood even though it is incapable of empirical verification.
>
> *(Small 2014)*

This nicely identifies seven core elements of humanities knowledge. It is qualitative, non-proceduralist, interpretative, historical, standpoint-dependent, individual, and, most perplexing and yet powerful, unverifiable-yet-real. In today's knowledge world, these are powerful modes that have an important but underestimated role.

All this is good for unapologetically centering on the unpredictable unfolding of minute-by-minute individual existence—conditioned by the forces of history, but not *determined* by them. Small's conclusion is that humanities scholars must not follow the "guardianship model of democracy," in which liberal arts elites steer the populace in accordance with their higher learning. We might best, Small concludes, "be content to be unimportant: just careful, or scholarly, or fanciful, or pleasurable but not particularly consequential" (150).

I agree that humanities academics must find a normal place in an ecosystem of variable knowledge contributions. I'd also emphasize that the humanities fields—and here literature and its criticism—generate practical knowledge obtained through distinctive modes—non-procedural, interpretative, unverifiable-yet-real, and the rest.

What always strikes me about literary texts is a simple thing: the density of their empirical detail. They are more *precise* than are sociology texts on the same topics. One can imagine an article on "Intergenerational Bimodalities and Transchronological Ideations During Academic Family Holidays: A Bloomsbury Group Case Study." And then, one can read the opening of Virginia Woolf's *To the Lighthouse* for something different:

> "Yes, of course, if it's fine tomorrow," said Mrs. Ramsay. "But you'll have to be up with the lark," she added.
>
> To her son these words conveyed an extraordinary joy, as if it were settled, the expedition were bound to take place, and the wonder to which he had looked forward, for years and years it seemed, was, after a night's darkness and a day's sail, within touch. Since he belonged, even at the age of six, to that great clan which cannot keep this feeling separate from that, but must let future prospects, with their joys and sorrows, cloud what is actually at hand, since to such people even in earliest childhood any turn in the wheel of sensation has the power to crystallise and transfix the moment upon which its gloom or radiance rests, James Ramsay, sitting on the floor cutting out pictures from the illustrated catalogue of the Army and Navy stores, endowed the picture of a refrigerator, as his mother spoke, with heavenly bliss. It was fringed with joy. The wheelbarrow, the lawnmower, the sound of poplar trees, leaves whitening before rain, rooks cawing, brooms knocking, dresses rustling—all these were so coloured and distinguished in his mind that he had already his private code, his secret language, though he appeared the image of stark and

> uncompromising severity, with his high forehead and his fierce blue eyes, impeccably candid and pure, frowning slightly at the sight of human frailty, so that his mother, watching him guide his scissors neatly round the refrigerator, imagined him all red and ermine on the Bench or directing a stern and momentous enterprise in some crisis of public affairs.
>
> "But," said his father, stopping in front of the drawing-room window, "it won't be fine."
>
> Had there been an axe handy, a poker, or any weapon that would have gashed a hole in his father's breast and killed him, there and then, James would have seized it. Such were the extremes of emotion that Mr Ramsay excited in his children's breasts by his mere presence; standing, as now, lean as a knife, narrow as the blade of one, grinning sarcastically, not only with the pleasure of disillusioning his son and casting ridicule upon his wife, who was ten thousand times better in every way than he was (James thought), but also with some secret conceit at his own accuracy of judgement. What he said was true. It was always true. He was incapable of untruth; never tampered with a fact; never altered a disagreeable word to suit the pleasure or convenience of any mortal being, least of all of his own children, who, sprung from his loins, should be aware from childhood that life is difficult; facts uncompromising; and the passage to that fabled land where our brightest hopes are extinguished, our frail barks founder in darkness (here Mr Ramsay would straighten his back and narrow his little blue eyes upon the horizon), one that needs, above all, courage, truth, and the power to endure.
>
> "But it may be fine—I expect it will be fine," said Mrs Ramsay...

Standard empirical evidence consists of three statements—*if* it's fine tomorrow; it *won't* be fine; but it *may* be fine. And then, Woolf, the literary artist, adds in all the invisible and unverifiable data that get at the actually existing hidden world. Conflict, intensity, deviance from rules, and norms are hallmarks of the psychic world as it actually is. My only point here is that the qualities of humanities knowledge that Helen Small outlines emerge from the textual *data*. Literary craft in all genres is an empirical craft, eliciting the half-seen and the unseen from the psychological lives of the multitude, one person at a time. A master like Woolf can do this at the keystroke level. These are literary data, psychic and interpsychic detail, "half-created half-perceived," no less empirical for being imagined, and reconstructed by the author on the basis of thousands of experiential data points.

Literary knowledge is a subjective empiricism resting on data whose existence depends on the author's narrative. Fredric Jameson has been getting at something similar:

> Reading then involves what Wittenberg (following Kant's example) will ingeniously and pertinently call 'the fabula a priori'. Even when reading those patently false narratives called novels, we still believe in something, namely the fabula; and this holds, as he demonstrates, for the so-called experimental or modernist novel fully as much as for the allegedly traditional kind. But in that case, there is at least one term we can get rid of for good, and that is the word 'fiction': fiction is a fiction, if you prefer, and in a world where everything is narrative, we can eliminate it. 'Fiction' was the now discarded theory that the fabula could be either true or false; whereas, if you want to put it that way, the fabula is always true.
>
> *(Jameson 2015)*

Neither Jameson, nor I mean to solve epistemological issues with this formulation, but to be explicit about something obvious: we should recognize literature for its wealth of unique data about humanity's inner life, represented by individuals often but not always in interaction with other people, social systems, and things.

## Knowledge of economy

So can we proceed serenely on to ask about literary knowledge of *economy*? Subjectivity needs us (and democracy can really use us too). Does economics need us as well?

A first step in literary economy is to investigate the *mode of production* of *literature*. I've discussed this at length elsewhere (Newfield 2008, 2016), and it is beyond my scope here, so I'll retreat to what is familiar research ground for me: What is the mode of production of academic knowledge about literature? What is the mode of production of literary criticism?

This would seem to be the terrain of Marxist literary criticism. Jameson continues to preside over this subdiscipline and shape its destiny. But in terms of specific commentary on literary economics, Jameson's work is something of an approach and avoid. For example, toward the end of a review of Slavoj Zizek's book, *The Parallex View*, Jameson writes the following:

> [Zizek] believes (as I do) that Marxism is an economic rather than a political doctrine, which must tirelessly insist on the primacy of the economic system and on capitalism itself as the ultimate horizon of the political situation (as well as of all the other ones – social, cultural, psychic and so forth). Yet it was always a fundamental mistake to think that Marxism was a 'philosophy' which aimed at substituting the 'ultimately determining instance' of the economic for that of the political. Karl Korsch taught us eighty years ago that for Marxism the economic and the political are two distinct and incommensurable codes which say the same thing in radically different languages.
>
> *(Jameson 2006)*

Jameson defers the economy as a horizon, where it has a paradoxical combination of three features. It is determinate. It is not determinate (of the political or, by extension of the socio-cultural, because the economic is *incommensurable* with these). And the economic is disembodied, rather than embodied in institutions and practices that have immediate causal power.

There is a problem here, but it is *not* the paradoxical complexity. Paradoxical complexity is an essential contribution of literary knowledge. It allows readers to understand that opposites collide and yet coexist, and influence situations together. It depicts our *actual* world. The sheer difficulty of literature is linked to its efforts to avoid the error of linear causality and single sources. The reduction of psychological or social situations to single, determinate causes is one of the most destructive habitual limits of human cognition. It pervades policy arenas. Jameson has called paradoxical complexity "structural causality," which includes multiple and indirect causes, and which requires "cognitive mapping." Lying behind these is dialectical thinking: the simple thesis is always wrong, but necessary, and its negation by an antithesis will, in turn, need to be negated until some kind of synthesis is achieved, which will resemble the original thesis while being different. The exasperating difficulty of these processes—the opacity of the necessary terms like "negation of the negation"—is the heart of its validity.

We have just bumped into a second feature of literary knowledge, which is the retention of internally contradictory forms of *structural* causality *rather* than the reduction of forces to linear causality as is common in other disciplines. All social and cultural phenomena emerge from multiple sources that exist in a state of dynamic interaction at all times. Reducing effects to a single cause—Houston's housing is relatively affordable because it has no property zoning—always creates confusion and generally bad policy. To wax melodramatic, either humanity acquires the habit of the regularized mass utilization of structural causality, or we will never understand anything in time to fix it. Literary knowledge helps people through *all* the entanglements. (I realize that Jameson has been rejected in some quarters by being turned into Exhibit A of deterministic "symptomatic reading." But I think the value of grasping the structural causality of phenomena, including those in literary texts, is so important as to be worth the risk.) Literary knowledge of economy will analyze and express the economy's internal contradictions and incommensurabilities without reducing them to linear or material causalities.

## The post-neoliberal subject in literature

But we also need to move past the disembodied status of the economy in Jamesonian Marxist literary criticism. This would be the place to reference and analyze the last decade of research in the domain of literature and economics. This work constitutes a mini-renaissance brought to us by a diverse host of scholars that includes Paul A. Cantor, Stephen Cox, Richard Dienst, Miranda Joseph, Anna Kornbluh, Colleen Lye, Randy Martin, Annie McClanahan, Christopher Nealon, and many others. One theme has been the difference that financialization makes, and a second has been the damage done to individual agency by finance capitalism and the neoliberal policy frameworks that enable it. The literary tradition does not speak with one voice, and I'm going to read a novel that treats the neoliberal consolidation as both destructive and unsuccessful.

I offer a quick rehearsal of features of LCS that I see as particularly important to literary knowledge of economy. First, critical theory long ago rejected the traditional base-superstructure model of the relation between economics and culture that saw economics determining culture and subjectivity in a fairly linear way. Second, theory also established that an entity like "neoliberal subjectivity" is an unstable construction that must be continuously made and remade. Third, many forms of literature, particularly the Western novel that includes ample tracts of free indirect discourse, offer what I think of as literature's equivalent of big data about psychology, which I have just called "subjective empiricism," in which an individual's consciousness is detailed on the basis of the author's almost unlimited number of experiences, conscious and unconscious. Fourth, literature and its criticism are particularly good at representing structural causality, which includes multiple, contradictory, and *indirect* causes. Literary knowledge helps people through *all* the entanglements, and so to explain to someone the economics of our weak recovery—or the Syrian Civil War—you find yourself, pretty soon, speaking some kind of novel.

Finally, literary knowledge of economy will analyze and express the economy's internal contradictions. It unveils internally contradictory forms of structural causality, in preference to the reconciliation of forces which may occur in other disciplines. It will unveil incommensurabilities—for example, the incommensurability between the economic demand that one adapts one's human capital to the economy and the subjective process of forming that human capital itself. In other words, a liberal arts student may consciously seek to develop her creative capabilities to better fit with the knowledge economy, and yet have an intellectual life that does not fit this, except when coerced through direct economic pressure.

A prime exploration of economic incommensurability is a novel about neoliberalism in the music industry, Jennifer Egan's *A Visit from the Good Squad* (2011). It returns us to the Western version of the crisis of creativity in the contemporary economy. Egan's novel analyzes the experience of writers, musicians, and their professional colleagues before and after neoliberalism's entrenchment in the 1980s.

The hallmark of the music industry in this work is the failure of anyone in authority to nurture any musician, ever. There is no university-style cultivation of talent in view. Most of the main characters grow up together in San Francisco in the 1980s, after the social movement basis of the music scene has disappeared. The "real musician" in the group spends most of his adult life as a low-income outsider. The big success story from the group, named Bennie, is an agent and executive, in a state of deep confusion mixed with self-loathing, and in any case not "creative" at all.

Bennie's brother-in-law, Jules, is a serious journalist who gets shunted into celebrity coverage as newspapers get disrupted by Internet-based new media. One day, he is forced to take a nineteen-year-old rising star named Kitty Jackson to a fancy lunch to interview her for a puff piece. After a completely empty interview, he decides to get her out of the restaurant for a walk in Central Park, one block away, in what he calls "an attempt to salvage this assignment and, in a larger sense, my once-promising, now-dwindling literary reputation." Jules' effort to rescue some noncommercial artistry somehow leads to an impulsive sexual assault on Kitty Jackson, which also fails. Jules is arrested, tried, convicted, and imprisoned. His career and identity are both destroyed.

At one point in prison, Jules describes his sexualized homicidal rage against a young woman whom he could or should have read as something of a fellow victim of neoliberalism: The celebrity order is neoliberalism in action, requiring the maximization of the self's human capital for the industry's process of translating artistry into a quantified return on investment. But Egan goes out of her way, in a couple of violent passages, to describe the extremity of Jules' inability to fit with the economic imperative of his job. His identity is essentially annihilated in the presence of a celebrity like Kitty Jackson, in which he becomes "indistinguishable… from every other non-Kitty Jackson"—a pure nonentity (Egan 2011: 127). Jules has killed his neoliberal self. Egan, the author, seems to be saying that the artist can escape neoliberalism only by committing a crime that ensures he will never be allowed to function as an artist again.

Obviously, this is a stupid solution. But *Goon Squad* is full of stupid solutions—this attempted rape and a recorded death through self-induced illness, as well as homelessness, kleptomania, and serial betrayal. They all signal determined (though misguided and ineffective) attempts to evade neoliberal subjectivity. Egan would seem to agree with Wendy Brown, Aihwa Ong, Lionel Wee, and others on the basic parameters of neoliberal subjectivity. She then focuses on the incommensurability between the system's demands and a livable self. The effect of the novel, judging from my experience of having taught it many times to undergraduates, is to assure the reader that first, neoliberalism is an imposed identity and, second—not a huge surprise to them—when your identity has something to do with creative aspiration, neoliberalism will get you to sabotage if not destroy yourself.

And yet at this point in the history of capitalism and critical theory, incommensurability may strike most of us as an inadequate strategy. It points out that creativity and human capital are not the same, and are for most people mutually exclusive, without providing grounds for an alternative. *Goon Squad* does offer few characters creating their own *homo* non-*oeconomicus*. For example, Sasha, agent-mogul Bennie's former executive secretary, stages a successful escape to a largely self-made world as an artist and mother in the California desert. Scotty, the "authentic" musician, having played in obscurity his whole life, finally gets an audience for his outsider music and is at least temporarily celebrated for his genius. But none of these solutions are particularly satisfying, and none will work outside of individual contexts.

Whether intentionally or not, Jennifer Egan has written a novel about creativity without criticism. It is about creativity in a neoliberalized culture industry, which means that the traditional demand for continuous competition—assessed by revenues—is accompanied by a newer demand for continuous self-development without industry support. But *Goon Squad*'s characters never discuss the business structure or neoliberal rules of the music industry. None of the characters has an analysis. The partial exception is Jules, and his critique is driven by the need to explain the sexual assault that ensured his self-destruction. The novel avoids putting psychological, artistic, and economic issues together. Because it does *not* introduce what I would call literary knowledge of economy, the novel offers two spheres in blocked juxtaposition: a culture industry focused on milking (not cultivating) individual talent, and the individual miseries of the self-cultivators who are at odds with the economy even if they survive pretty well. The aporia is neither resolved nor analyzed.

And yet, it's a wonderful novel. When I ask myself why I think this, I realize that the reason is Egan's literary knowledge of economy that does *not* exist in the mode of criticism. She represents a wide range of ways in which neoliberalism prompts efforts to create homo *non*-oeconomicus (see Cohen 1993: 1–17). The characters' acts have several common features as they flop around like fish that have been landed by the great neoliberal fisherman:

A They are engaged in lifetime *Bildung*. (We have a profane illumination in such a book of "Bildung for all.")

B They perform Bildung as a counter to the negation of politics—the internally contradictory and apparently dysfunctional self is a source of the negation of the negation of politics.

C They attempt a local shift in their immediate social *ethos* via a full range non-foundational "interpretative gestures" (Yves Citton). They think of the character of the immediate society that they want, and use critique, intervention, interruption (including bad ones like Jules' assault), and reconstruction in shifting combinations that literature captures better than just about anything else.

Literary knowledge of economy has a fourth feature which I've just illustrated with Egan: detailed descriptions of actually existing *homo non-oeconomicus*, beleaguered and negational, but pervasive and emerging. It is my conviction that these four features put literary knowledge—in principle—at the cutting edge of building an emerging economic order.

## The economy needs us

To give a sense of why I think this, I'll end with a short account of this emerging economy.

We have at least two available ways of thinking about neoliberal capitalism. The first is neoliberalism's deterministic horizon of capitalist economy creating the conformist entrepreneurial neoliberal subject. The other is a homo non-oeconomicus structured around agency and structural incommensurabilities.

The first way of thinking sees capitalism as the fully neoliberal innovation economy. It can be traced to Joseph A. Schumpeter and the legion of descendants who created neoclassical innovation economics. It has enjoyed popularizers like Thomas Friedman in books like *The Lexus and the Olive Tree* (1999) and *The World is Flat* (2005). It also has Marxist critics who accept the basic premises.

This model operates with three interrelated assumptions: (1) capitalism replaces human labor with technology, and succeeds by being technology-intensive (and energy-intensive);

(2) capitalism always absorbs autonomous labor into managerial systems (bourgeois knowledge labor as well as traditional industrial labor); (3) because of 1 and 2, capitalism may expand without limit. We have an iron triangle of petroleum-tech-management-growth and its modified *homo oeconomicus*.

The second perspective holds that while this system may have worked well at one time, it no longer does. As one writer puts it, Western economic dynamism arose from

> the vitalism of the Baroque era and the expressionism of the Romantic period. In view of the explosion in poetry, music, and art in the 'creative' sector of the economy, it should not surprise us that imagination exploded in the rest of the economy too.

But, he continues, vested interests have replaced "indigenous innovation" that came from the grass roots. Educational systems are contracting, and "Schools are doing less to expose the young to the great books of adventure and personal development." The author of these words is a neoclassical economist and 2006 Nobel Laureate, Edmund S. Phelps. For Phelps and the other economists who recognize an innovation crisis in the West, the neoliberal system is no longer sustaining itself internally, and is already in decline.

The sense that neoliberal capitalism is neither stable nor inevitable was developed in the work of world-systems theorist Giovanni Arrighi, particularly in his last book, *Adam Smith in Beijing* (2007). Arrighi synthesized research on East Asian economic history to claim that all along there have been alternative pathways of economic development over the past several centuries. Focusing on the East Asian pathway, Arrighi noted that it never did follow Schumpeter's neoliberal principle of replacing human labor with technology but retained complex labor on a mass scale. While the Western pathway consisted of the famous Industrial Revolution, East Asia had an *industrious revolution*. Referring to his main intellectual source, Kaoru Sugihara, Arrighi writes that he "does not question the competitive advantages of the wage-labor-based, large-scale production typical of the European path" propelled by military dominance (Arrighi 2007: 72), but suggests that the situation has now changed.

The European or Western pathway cannot expand indefinitely because it has its own limits, and this has now become obvious environmentally through unprecedented levels of toxic pollution and climate crisis. The West's limits derive from its strengths. Schumpeterian technological innovation involves the loss of human skill and know-how (and justifies huge concentrations of capital), and managerialism entails the loss of self-management skills and powers of social collaboration. The East Asian pathway had its own weaknesses, but retained major strengths, Arrighi writes,

> Most notably, [it offered the] preservation of a labor force capable of performing multiple tasks well; of responding flexibly to variations in the natural and social environment of production; and of anticipating, preventing, and solving problems relating to the management of production...it is also typical of recent theories of so-called flexible production.
>
> *(Arrighi 2007: 72–3)*

Of course, the current Chinese economy contains deeply coercive, dictatorial, and exploitative elements. But it is also true that this one party state has supported the highest levels of sophisticated manufacturing capability in the world—as good in some sectors as Germany's, and often better than those of the United States. iPhones are not only cheaper to assemble in China: California workers no longer have the hybrid skills at scale to make them at all.

I don't want to whitewash an industrious economy, which is as miserable, exploitative, and unjust as anything devised by the West's industrial economies. And yet, some mainstream economic sociology is now bearing out Arrighi's view of East Asian labor capabilities (see Breznitz & Murphree 2011). What it suggests is a set of new rules.

The pathway *ahead* will *limit* the replacement of skilled labor by technology in new partnerships between them. New interpretative practices will allow sustainable societies that don't need the crutch of growth.

It will require often inefficient and parasitic management to be replaced by genuine self-management.

It will be more labor-intensive and less energy-intensive. There will be no latitude for endless expansion and its unsustainable side effects.

LCS should generally side with the second given its methodological habitus. Literature and critical theory, speaking very broadly, posit that *economy* determines *subjectivity* only across a gap of incommensurability. This apparent paradox has the effect of constituting psychic possibilities *and* seeing the psyche (and its cultural effects) as incommensurable with these apparently determinant forces. In grasping this double condition, theorists like Judith Butler have long argued that power is both pervasive and unable to replicate itself perfectly. Another particularly influential formulation of this phenomenon—to repeat a determinate economic horizon that operates indeterminately across incommensurable points—was the concept which I mentioned earlier, the profane illumination, which refers to an understanding that is discontinuous with history conceived of as causally determinant time. The profane illumination recovers or reflects or creates (there are useful difficulties here) moments of rupture within history, moments of revolutionary possibility that Benjamin called *jetztzeit*, when the flow of history is interrupted. Such a pause or break must be observed and also created by actors, artists, political revolutionaries, novelists, and literary and cultural analysts.

What all this means is this: not only is a non-neoliberal self clearly registered and highly articulated in literature, but this self has an underappreciated *economic* destiny as well. This is the fifth aspect of literary knowledge. Through subjective empiricism, paradoxical reason, self-reflexivity about modes of production, and the noneconomic self, LCS develops the kind of knower, the kind of actor, suited to the post-neoliberal, post-managerial economies to come.

I realize that this is cryptic. I hope it is also telegraphic. The next economic transformation will reverse at least in part "industrial" teleology by replacing technology with complex and elaborated interpretative practices.

So with all this in mind, here's how I think we should tell the story of literary knowledge. It has appeared marginal, recessive, and even retrograde throughout the period of the Industrial Revolution. Its home fields of literature and criticism have produced types of dissent that had little reach outside the disciplines of literature and languages. In relation to STEM, literature and criticism have been locked in as "lower faculties," denied their Kantian role as interpreters of the conditions of truth. And yet, we have preserved essential creative capabilities, in Martha Nussbaum's sense. These include empiricism of interiority, interpretation across incommensurabilities, self-formation or Bildung for everyone, and care for the character of society tied more closely to human wants.

The very least that the field of LCS should do is explore the possibility that this combination of capabilities will form the central features of the pathway of post-capitalism that is now struggling into being. We need to ignore the cues coming from most academic leaders, who are now more than ever devoted to serving a Western techno-economic pathway that is in decline. We need to see the humanities as what they are about to become, central disciplines for a planet that must for the first time either devote itself to sustainable development or die.

Voting for the first of these, humanities scholars must recognize that the economy needs us, the planet needs us, we need us, and we need us to take much stronger stands. What would it mean to think and act as though literature were in power?

## References

Arrighi, Giovanni. (2007). *Adam Smith in Beijing: Lineages of the 21st Century*, New York: Verso Books.

Breznitz, Dan & Murphree, Michael. (2011). *Run of the Red Queen: Government, Innovation, Globalization, & Economic Growth in China,* New Haven, CT: Yale University Press.

Brown, Wendy. (2015). *Undoing the Demos: Neoliberalism's Stealth Revolution*, New York: Zone Books.

Cohen, Margaret. (1993). *Profane Illumination: Walter Benjamin & The Paris of Surrealist Revolution*, Berkeley: University of California Press.

Jameson, Frederic. (2006). "First Impressions," (review of *The Parallax View*), *London Review of Books* 28 (17). www.lrb.co.uk/v28/n17/fredric-jameson/first-impressions.

Jameson, Frederic. (2015). "In Hyperspace," *London Review of Books* 37 (17). www.lrb.co.uk/v37/n17/fredric-jameson/in-hyperspace.

Kosinski, Michal, Stillwell, David, & Graepel, Thore. (2013). "Private Traits and Attributes Are Predictable from Digital Records of Human Behavior," *Proceedings of the National Academy of Sciences* 110 (15), 5802–5.

Newfield, Christopher. (2008). *Unmaking the Public University: The Forty-Year Assault on the Middle Class*, Cambridge, MA: Harvard University Press.

Newfield, Christopher. (2016). *The Great Mistake: How We Wrecked Public Universities and How We Can Fix Them*, Baltimore, MD: Johns Hopkins University Press.

Phelps, Edmund S. (2015). "What Is Wrong with the West's Economies?," *The New York Review of Books*, 13 August 13. www.nybooks.com/articles/archives/2015/aug/13/what-wrong-wests-economies/.

Small, Helen. (2014). "The Public Value of the Humanities," unpublished conference paper, Oxford University.

# 3

# THE POLITICS OF FORM AND POETICS OF IDENTITY IN POSTWAR AMERICAN POETRY

*Christopher Chen and Timothy Kreiner*

Postwar US poetry is haunted by the question of how elaborations of antiracist and feminist poetics came to be severed both from one another and from the critique of political economy in the wake of the "New Left" (Van Gosse 2008). These developments in US poetry have been driven by broader theoretical debates over the relationship between capitalism and so-called "identity politics" (Jenkins 2014) as they have unfolded across a sweeping cross-disciplinary "cultural turn" (Chaney 2002). In the postwar era, the retreat to *kulturkritik* by Western Marxists (Anderson 1979), along with the relatively recent equation of racial justice with what Canadian political philosopher Charles Taylor has called a politics of cultural recognition (Taylor 1994), combined to make culture a suture point between what many critics see as discrepant political discourses. Typically, this turn to culture in social theory has been defined through the consignment of Marx's systematic critique of the basic categories and premises of political economy to the ash heap of totalizing historical grand narratives. Accounting for how contemporary US poets represent the complex relationship between racial identity and capitalism, therefore, forces us to confront an ideological terrain structured by an entrenched opposition between culture and political economy. Since 1970 or so, that opposition has given rise to what we call the antinomies of postwar poetics, wherein distinct aesthetic programs are associated with seemingly incommensurable political projects keyed to discrete social subjects. Turning toward both black feminist and contemporary Marxist feminist social reproduction theory, in our argument, helps dissolve those antinomies. The resultant view opens onto a more incisive reckoning of how contemporary poetry registers the co-constitutive character of race, gender, and class as politically contested social locations in postwar US poetry.

## The rise of the Poetry Wars and the fall of the new left

The Poetry Wars of the 1970s–1990s, in which an avowedly anticapitalist poetic avant-garde defined itself in opposition to what it took to be a formulaic mainstream verse culture, were deeply informed by the rise and fall of the New Left. From the heady days when the "movement of movements" was on everyone's lips to the implosion of the New Left flagship Students for a Democratic Society amid fractious debates concerning race, gender, and imperialism, things quickly fell apart. We follow Van Gosse (2008), therefore, in using the term "New Left" in the more capacious sense of referring to the many and variegated new social movements of the 1960s and 1970s that was typical at the time, rather than the narrower sense that confined it to the student and antiwar movements in much subsequent scholarship. Two historical narratives dominate existing accounts of the period. For some, increasing militancy and the splintering of the core activist group, the Students for a Democratic Society (SDS), into antagonistic political demands organized around specific social identities betrayed the halcyon days of the Port Huron Statement. Todd Gitlin and Kirkpatrick Sale epitomize this view of left fragmentation. Sale's monumental study of SDS inaugurated the narrative of historical decline centered on student and antiwar movements. Gitlin's work (1987, 1995) influentially turned that historiographical trend to polemical ends. For others, however, the acrimony owes less to the betrayal of uniformly liberal values by days of rage or organizationally distinct concerns with racial and gender identity than missed connections and roads not taken for a variety of reasons including, above all, counterinsurgent state violence (see Dawson 2013). Where all critics agree, however, is that by the end of the 1970s the Women's, Black, Gay, Chicano, Puerto Rican, and Asian American Liberation Movements were in acrimonious retreat along with the student, antiwar, and rank-and-file rebellions that, together, comprised the New Left. In their wake, they left a host of unresolved theoretical questions and political antagonisms. Such divisions are registered in the disciplinary separations that continue to organize more recent accounts of a New Left not defined by the centrality of student and antiwar movements (see Gosse 2005: 211–19).

As liberation movements faded from the streets, American poetry provided a cultural proxy for their concerns in politically charged theoretical debates. Collectively known as the Poetry Wars, those debates were set in motion by the emergence of Language Writing as an explicitly anticapitalist project over the course of the 1970s. As readers familiar with the ins and outs of postwar poetic controversies will recall, in its early days that project was routinely articulated in opposition to the "expressive" first-person lyrics dominant at the dawn of the MFA program era headlined by the Iowa Writers Workshop. Fierce coterie debates were waged in little magazines, at poetry readings, and at local talk series (Kim 2000). Language Writers repeatedly critiqued so-called workshop poems in the vein of Robert Lowell's *Life Studies* and William Stafford's "Traveling Through the Dark" on the grounds that such cloying lyrics gave voice to bourgeois forms of subjectivity in the service of capital. These coterie debates were subsequently taken up by academic literary critics (Perloff 1984; McGann 1987; Middleton 1990). Language Writing, we were told repeatedly, sabotages the service of capital by poetry.

How, precisely, Language Writing did so was worried at length beginning in the mid-1970s. In polemics such as the *Politics of the Referent* symposium edited by Steve McCaffery (1977), Ron Silliman's "Disappearance of the Word and Appearance of the World" (1977), and Barrett Watten's "The Politics of Poetry: Surrealism and *L=A=N=G=U=A=G=E*" (1984), prominent Language Writers argued that experimental formalisms sabotage the smooth reproduction of class belonging greased by lyric modes. Often, those polemics depend upon functional analogies between linguistic and economic production. The force of such analogies varied. Some argued that poetic experiments disrupt the production of linguistic reference in ways akin to the downing of tools in the workplace (McCaffery 1977; Ross 1988; Hartley 1989). Others argued that poetic experiments raise class consciousness outside the workplace by making readers coproducers of textual meaning (Andrews 1977; Silliman 1987b; Bernstein 1992; Hejinian 2000). Neither literary road to overcoming capitalist social relations was particularly well-defined. Yet by the time those coterie debates entered the academy, questions concerning the class politics of literary form constituted "a surrogate social struggle" (xxii), as Silliman influentially put it in his introduction to the Language Writing anthology *In the American Tree* (1986). The debates surrounding that claim grew hotly contested and theoretically gnarled; they quickly eclipsed the rather more heterogeneous body of work from which the claim was abstracted. Today, therefore, Language Writing is best remembered for advancing the familiar "politics of form" according to which experimental formalisms are anticapitalist and expressive poetry is not.

That politics of form similarly eclipsed concerns with the critique of political economy. Virtually all observers take for granted the oddly cultural character of the Marxism on offer during the Poetry Wars. As George Hartley's definitive *Textual Politics and the Language Poets* (1989) makes clear, the peculiarly linguistic Western Marxism favored by Language Writers was an unruly mélange of Althusser, the Frankfurt School, and Gramsci unceremoniously mixed with structuralist linguistics and its post-structural variants. Those are names with which to conjure; we aim to conjure little with them. For our purposes, it is enough to note what all these intellectual currents share in the eyes of Perry Anderson. Anderson (1979) long ago remarked that the bureaucratic petrification of Marx's critique of political economy in the wake of the Second International helped push Adorno, Althusser, Benjamin, Gramsci, and Lukacs toward a variously shared *kulturkritik*. "The progressive relinquishment of economic or political structures as the central concerns of theory was accompanied by a basic shift in the whole centre of gravity of European Marxism towards philosophy" (49) with a particular attunement to culture. We need not share Anderson's prognosis that what was to be done was to rejoin the separated spheres of Marxian theory and the historical workers' movement, therefore, in order to note what was already clear in 1976. The turn toward cultural forms as a "surrogate social struggle" was, in the first instance, a turn away from what was widely perceived as a rigid and formulaic economism.

It was also a turn away from anticapitalist currents within the New Left. The peculiarly linguistic Western Marxism favored by champions of Language Writing as an anticapitalist project had little overlap with the global Maoism that animated the New Communist Movement, for instance. The organizations which comprised that movement were variously structured along racial and nationalist lines that were also internally riven by questions concerning gender, sexuality, and imperialism. The New Communist Movement was, at best, a microcosm of the antagonisms that shaped the New Left. Yet in Max Elbaum's definitive account (2002), what held the New Communist Movement together was a forthright and widely shared commitment to national liberation movements abroad and antiracist struggles at home as the leading edge of class struggle in the postwar world. Peasants, the unemployed, and Frantz Fanon's *lumpenproletariat* had more currency in the New Communist Movement than the historically white, male, industrial working class of traditional Marxism.

One finds little trace of those historical developments in the anticapitalist poetics of Language Writing. Indeed, the politics of form associated with Language Writing traffics in generic notions of class struggle between a bourgeoisie and working class that may have been lifted from the pages of nineteenth-century factory inspectors. Analogical relationships between cultural forms and social classes left both the composition of those classes and the forms of antagonism between them curiously undetermined just as the agents and sites of class struggle were being radically transformed in the postwar world. At the same time, the most prominent Marxist champions of functional analogies between linguistic and economic production in the Language Writing cohort were white men. Not surprisingly, therefore, in the annals of postwar poetic history, Language Writing is routinely aligned with a generic working-class subject traditionally composed of white male wage laborers.

## The politics of form and the poetics of identity

By the mid-1980s, the principal referents for social struggle in living memory were the Liberation Movements that formed the leading edge of the New Left in the 1970s. In ways that have proven as durable as they are false, the poetry associated with leading figures of those movements—including Amiri Baraka, Lorde, Adrienne Rich, Janice Mirikitani, and Rudolfo Gonzales—was widely understood as the unmediated expression of the "content" of various racial, gender, and sexual identities. Viewed as dependent upon literary conventions associated with the workshop poems of the era's literary mainstream, the poetry associated with New Left liberation movements thus existed in a politically ambiguous and frequently vexed relationship to the anticapitalist, avant-garde poetics of Language Writing. These taxonomic distinctions translated New Left organizational debates into a language of fundamentally distinct formal strategies, aesthetic programs, and poetic lineages.

This was especially true for the most ardently Marxist champions of Language Writing. Two years after the publication of *In the American Tree*, Silliman gave that opposition signal clarity in the anti-Maoist pages of the *Socialist Review*. In "Poetry and the Politics of the Subject" (1988), Silliman extends his earlier claim that the field of poetry constitutes a surrogate social struggle to argue that distinct poetic forms constitute discrete social struggles for different social subjects. Because different groups of people confront different political problems at the same time, Silliman reasoned, "many white heterosexuals" are "apt to call into question, if not actually explode, such conventions as narrative, persona, and even reference." Meanwhile, those groups who have not yet been "the subject of history," including "women, people of color, sexual minorities, [and] the entire spectrum of the 'marginal'" are apt to "appear much move conventional" because they "have a manifest political need to have their stories told" (63).

That view has proven remarkably durable. From the vantage of contemporary avant-gardes and their critical champions, the hegemony of lyric continues to presume a model of language as essentially referential, and the poem as a mimetic expression of the experiences of coherent, singular-speaking subjects. This remains the case even as both Flarf and Conceptual Poetry, to name two influential examples of what could be called twenty-first-century poetic avant-gardes, notably eschew the overtly anticapitalist politics of form associated with Language Writing (Dworkin and Goldsmith 2011; Gardner et al. 2017). At the same time, both retain the political charge associated with formalist experiments opposed to self-expression, autobiographical testimony, and ideals of experiential authenticity historically encoded in lyric conventions. Recent avant-garde experiments with nonnormative syntax have thus come to define poetic experimentation primarily in terms of the disruption of the empirical givenness of identity naturalized by the lyric "I" (Goldsmith 2011; Perloff 2012). According to influential proponents of this view, the denaturalization of the coherence of this lyric-speaking subject underwrites the politics of formal innovation—a politics that continues to be understood as fundamentally antithetical to a contemporary poetics of identity premised upon the representational visibility of marginalized racial subjects for example.

This politically charged division of literary labors naturalized an interpretive framework in which women, people of color, and queer poets embody what could be called a poetics of recognition organized around ideals of self-expression. White heterosexual men, on the other hand, have nothing to lose but their subject positions holding them prisoner in the house of class belonging. Since 1970 or so, this view of opposed poetic modes yoked to discrete social identities has structured contemporary poetic debates in which class, race, and gender are understood as analytically separable categories because of their persistent assignment to either expressive and experimental aesthetic programs. Keyed to different forms of aesthetic judgment, these programs, we would argue, remain bound to ongoing unresolved debates both over political strategy and over the complex historical relationship between capitalism and social identity. The antinomies of postwar poetics, in short, continue to structure interpretive approaches to poetic works that seem to straddle or bridge the divide between this influential genre distinction.

Within the broad ambit of the critique Silliman crystallized, for example, race remains a crucial boundary marker between identity and formal experimentation in which social identity and the lyric "I" are understood as essentially homologous kinds of expressive subjects. As critics such as Anthony Reed have begun to point out, a poetics of identity so defined drastically narrows interpretive approaches to contemporary black experimental poetry, for example, by establishing a "hermeneutic circle of lyricized and racialized reading" (Reed 2014: 97). For Reed, such rigid interpretive protocols, premised upon a highly contested conception of the category of the lyric (Jackson 2005), preemptively reduce poems within racially marked literary traditions to "expressions and experiences of a singular intending consciousness that is in turn metonymic for race" (98). More often than not, the specificity of class location falls outside the hermeneutic circle of such reading practices.

In recent decades, these critical premises have been repeatedly challenged by scholars such as Reed. Beginning with a series of anthologies attuned to formally innovative writing by women, the ongoing equation of feminist concerns with confessional verse has come to seem as historically false as it is theoretically anachronistic (O'Sullivan 1996; Sloan 1998; Rankine and Spahr 2002; Frost and Hogue 2006; Rankine and Sewell 2012). A like series of anthologies attuned to experimental writing by poets of color has similarly put paid the equally inaccurate and outdated equation of antiracist concerns with expressive poetics (Lew 1995; Nielsen and Ramey 2006; Giménez Smith and Chávez 2014; Nielsen and Ramey 2015). In the past two decades, a wealth of scholarship variously complicating the vexed relationships between postwar poetics and feminist or antiracist politics has also emerged. Thus, the rigid, politically charged division of literary labors in the wake of the New Left that partly owes to the emergence of Language Writing and what we have called the poetics of recognition has begun to loosen. This makes possible richer and more complex models of the relationship between social identity and poetic experiment. In addition to Reed, scholars such as Elizabeth Frost, Phillip Brian Harper, Dorothy Wang, Joseph Jeon, Lynn Keller, Linda Kinnahan, Nathaniel Mackey, Fred Moten, Aldon Lynn Nielsen, Evie Shockley, Juliana Spahr, Anne Vickery, and Timothy Yu have begun to pursue those lines of inquiry in terms of race and gender.

## "Coal": market relations and the material location of identity

Actually existing forms of postwar poetry and politics that were unapologetically feminist, antiracist, *and* anticapitalist remain less well remarked however. Consider, for instance, the foundational 1977 "A Black Feminist Statement" penned by the Boston and Cambridge-based Combahee River Collective (CRC)—a group of black women who in 1974 broke from what group members considered the more economically and sexually conservative politics of the National Black Feminist Organization. Today, this Statement is best remembered for its powerful articulation of the specific struggles black women face. The Statement's insistence that "This focusing upon our own oppression is embodied in the concept of identity politics" remains, in the eyes of many scholars, the locus classicus of an "identity politics" typically thought to be incompatible with a critique of political economy. Yet, the CRC Statement is unequivocal that while traditional Marxism has neglected concerns with race and gender, the notion of identity the Statement describes is a specifically racialized and gendered class position within a capitalist social order:

> We realize that the liberation of all oppressed peoples necessitates the destruction of the political-economic systems of capitalism and imperialism as well as patriarchy... We are not convinced, however, that a socialist revolution that is not also a feminist and antiracist revolution will guarantee our liberation. We have arrived at the necessity for developing an understanding of class relationships that takes into account the specific class position of Black women who are generally marginal in the labor force, while at this particular time some of us are temporarily viewed as doubly desirable tokens at white-collar and professional levels. We need to articulate the real class situation of persons who are not merely raceless, sexless workers, but for whom racial and sexual oppression are significant determinants in their working/economic lives. Although we are in essential agreement with Marx's theory as it applied to the very specific economic relationships he analyzed, we know that his analysis must be extended further in order for us to understand our specific economic situation as black women.
>
> *(Combahee 1979: 360)*

The peculiar definition of "identity politics" the CRC Statement offers is neither separatist nor unaware of class differentiation among black women. Rather, the Statement provides a broadly materialist account of the position of black women in society. That position is not only a relative class position within the labor force. In the eyes of the Statement, the position of black women is also fundamentally subordinated by a patriarchal black nationalist politics and by a hegemonic second wave feminism largely grounded in the experiences and political demands of middle-class white women within the New Left. This liminal position led the CRC and many subsequent black feminists to understand identity categories as referring to internally divided populations, and to conceive of their own political work as thus by definition coalitional.

The consequences of those divisions are especially visible in the writings of Harlem-born author Audre Lorde, who was a frequent participant in retreats organized by CRC members (Harris 2001). One of Lorde's most well-known poems, "Coal," presents an especially suggestive model for thinking through what E. San Juan Jr has called the "race/class problematic" (2003) and the interplay among race, class, and gender in the CRC's conception of "identity politics." Close reading the poem challenges poetic taxonomies that can otherwise obscure how racial and gender identities are deeply inscribed within capitalist social relations. Lorde's writing would seem to obviously fall on the side of a lyric expressivity aligned with a project of reclaiming rather than rejecting a poetics of identity—a reading that retraces the hermeneutic circle Reed describes wherein racial identity and the lyric "I" are understood as formally equivalent kinds of speaking subjects. And yet across Lorde's entire body of writing, the author repeatedly stages a powerful queer feminist critique of the problem of categorical identities understood as describing static objects rather than dynamic social relations. At the same time, Lorde's work draws attention to the analytic distortions and separations that categorical thinking inevitably introduces into attempts to understand social inequality.

Initially appearing in the author's first book of poems *The First Cities* (1968), "Coal" was subsequently republished, with small but significant revisions, in the author's 1976 collection of the same name. The poem is structured by an elaborate geological metaphor in which the earth is a figure for the multilayered, intersubjective structure of racial identity, and where the earth's depths conceal subterranean social forces that produce racially unequal claims on a diaphanous lyric "I." This "I" is assigned a relative economic value and positioned within atomized market relations through combined processes of racial, gender, and class formation that the poem dramatizes in terms of the transformation of coal into diamond.

The poem begins by isolating a single word, "I," on its own line in a move that invokes lyric conventions only to immediately question how this racially unmarked, purportedly universal pronoun might conceal the social location of speakers who claim it:

> I
> is the total black, being spoken
> from the earth's inside.
> *(Lorde 1997: 163)*

Forcing a racially unmarked lyric subject to confront its own conditions of possibility, the poem presents this lyric "I" as a kind of empty signifier initially shorn of predicates. This "I" does not speak. Instead, it is ultimately revealed to be "the total black, being spoken/From the earth's inside" by social forces beyond the immediate control of the speaker.

As a reference to both racial identity and coal, the "total black" doesn't imagine the racial delimitation of the "I" as a limiting particularity on the way to an unmarked universality. Instead, the racial specification of that "I" is precisely what allows it to address the conditions of its own emergence. This "I" is neither a kind of subjectless postmodern textuality that speaks nor inert material circumstances that mechanistically determine expression. What "is spoken" is revealed in the second stanza to be a fraught, ongoing conversation between subjects.

The poem's repeated references to "many kinds of open" imply that the "I" is not transparent and equally available to all. Openness seems to signal a shared condition of mutual dependence revealed by the relational, intersubjective character of language itself. A socially disembedded, departicularized "I" is likened to a diamond—an object that among other things suggests a traditional discourse of aesthetic value indexed to the artifactual, formally intricate, and highly wrought character of poetic utterance. The abstract emptiness of that "I," Lorde seems to insist, is a dead form that can only be brought to life, or pried "open," by the performative particularity of how a speaker might sound and how that performance might be "coloured/By who pays what for speaking":

> There are many kinds of open.
> How a diamond comes into a knot of flame
> How a sound comes into a word, coloured
> By who pays what for speaking.
> *(Lorde 1997: 163)*

Extending the geological metaphor by reconnecting the diamond to the process of its formation from coal, the poem plunges into a space "beneath" reified social forms where identities are made. It is a space where language functions as a simultaneously economic and erotic currency that can determine the relative worth of social identities through "who pays what for speaking." Here, economic exchange is also racially differentiating and governs how speech is "coloured." The pun implies that the social position of who speaks fundamentally alters the reception of what is spoken and so significantly enlarges or narrows the terrain of the expressible.

In particularizing this lyric "I," the poem seems to embody an identity-based expressive poetics while at the same time fundamentally defamiliarizing what is being "expressed." The poem does not conceive of identity as simply a particular attribute of individuals or groups. In insisting on the "total" nature of blackness here, the poem traces a vision of a collective social body mapped from a racially specific location in social space.

Broadly speaking, there are two possible allegorical interpretations of the "earth's inside" that the poem references. The first closely resembles the poetics of identity by affirming a positive association between racial identity and lyric expression. On this view, this underground space is the primordial source of black motherhood and a black feminist identity rooted in what Lorde elsewhere calls a "woman's place of power within each of us" (Lorde 1984: 37) which is "neither white nor surface; it is dark, it is ancient, and it is deep" (37). Likening poetry to a "quality of light by which we scrutinize our lives," (37) Lorde argues that the exploratory, unpredictable character of poetic language allows it to link experiences—"nameless and formless, about to be birthed, but already felt" (37)—to conceptual thought and ultimately to concerted political action. In poetry collections like *The Black Unicorn* (1978), these deep sources of identity are explicitly represented in terms of Afrocentric spirituality as well as Dahomean and Yoruban mythologies.

The second possible reading of this subterranean realm imagines blackness as a hierarchical social relation imposed upon individuals who are subject to a kind of systematic economic devaluation among other social constraints. On this view, identities are economically conditioned, compelled, and altered through the making and breaking of intersubjective attachments that establish the conditions of possibility for both intimate relationships and assembling political coalitions. This coalitional, transindividual space orients identity toward a social whole that is fundamentally distinct from a vision of the whole implied by the abstract universality of a sovereign, racially unmarked lyric "I." From this vantage, we might say that while the title marks the specific racial location of that "I," the poem lays bare the subterranean violence that makes that individual, racialized subject also an object of systemic forces beyond the boundaries of individual experience.

In light of those two views, the poem's references to the economic positioning of identity open onto forms of situated agency and what Lorde calls "places of possibility" that are precisely *not* defined through a political subject whose putative universality is defined primarily through its social unlocatability. At the same time, the second stanza imagines racial divisions as a form of enforced privation, market atomization, and social closure that drastically narrows the expressive capacity of the speaker.

Indeed, the poem implies that the possibility of communication is crucially shaped by economic exploitation governing the calculation of individual profit and loss. Market relations seem to function as a kind of distorted mirror image or underside of Lorde's expansive sense of the promise of erotic association and "the power which comes from sharing deeply any pursuit with another person" (Lorde 1984: 56). The reappearance of the language of economic exchange reveals how words map both the social bonds and the boundaries structured by a ubiquitous market logic:

> Then there are words like stapled wagers
> In a perforated book—buy and sign and tear apart—
> And come whatever wills all chances
> The stub remains
> An ill-pulled tooth with a ragged edge.

While "Some words are open," others remain incommunicable, seemingly trapped inside of the speaker's body—"breeding like adders" or breaking off like "An ill-pulled tooth" and lost. The visceral, embodied loss experienced by the speaker after their failed gamble configures the racial body as isolated and silenced—a kind of prison of social possibility. The stanza's focus on how far speech might travel beyond the body suggests that emancipatory political possibilities exist between subjects rather than simply within them as "whatever wills all chances" and its speculative investments. At the same time, the parallelism of similes in this stanza draws attention to how communicative action must continually confront the problem of establishing a grammar of likeness across essentially unlike social phenomena otherwise only bound together through market forces. The problem of likening the unlike here seems to mirror the operations of market forces that determine the relative value of speakers according to a single economic measure. While the poem presents language as governed by the grammar of atomized market relations determining "who pays what for speaking," the "wager" of language used here nevertheless seeks to connect and dereify rather than simply turn away from these forms of alienated sociality.

As the geological metaphor is extended to place the speaker on the other side of the earth in the final stanza, the poem repeats almost verbatim the rhetoric of the first with minor but meaningful syntactical variations. For the first time in the poem, the "I" is not spoken but speaks in order to make another social "wager":

> Love is a word another kind of open—
> As a diamond comes into a knot of flame
> I am black because I come from the earth's inside
> Take my word for jewel in your open light.

Language successfully and laboriously drawn up from the depths of the earth is here compared to a "jewel." In the symbolic economy of the poem, diamonds are not simply minerals but a commodity invested with a specific form of value through the rules governing human exchange. Similarly, the meaning and value of blackness is in the poem renegotiated at a moment of encounter whose outcome is unclear.

The final stanza completes a journey of understanding where "the total black" shifts from an ascriptive to an affirmative identity whose worth can be asserted despite the risk of its potential devaluation. That journey traverses both the material constraints of identity and the political necessity of crossing identitarian divides. The lyric "I," we might say, is where those two views meet in a "knot of flame" that binds together political concerns typically divided by the categories of race, gender, and class.

## Conclusion: the social reproduction of race, gender, and class

The issues raised by Lorde's brief poem take us to the heart of contentious contemporary debates about the race/class problematic in the wake of the "Poetry Wars," while illuminating how Lorde's socialism might inform her black feminist political commitments. The drama "Coal" stages between an ostensibly lyric "I" and the "total black" that determines "who pays what for speaking" explodes the antinomies of postwar poetics by offering one suggestive model of how readers might imagine an integral account of racial, gender, and class formation.

We might read this symbolic space in the poem, where coal and diamond are transformations of the same metaphorical social substance, in the context of what contemporary Marxist feminists have called a "hidden abode" of social reproduction. For social reproduction theorists, a "split between 'productive' waged work and unwaged 'reproductive' labour," as Nancy Fraser has argued, "has underpinned modern capitalist forms of women's subordination" (Fraser 62). As Angela Davis (2001) and Evelyn Nakano Glenn (1992) have pointed out, however, historically black women have been confined within segregated postbellum labor markets where many have been compelled to perform both waged domestic labor within white households and unwaged domestic labor for their own families.

The poem thus might be productively placed in conversation with a social reproduction problematic that gathers white supremacy, patriarchy, and capital together into a single analytic frame. Situating Lorde's black feminism within a social reproduction framework also allows a better account of the particulars of the poem where lived experience is significantly shaped by a logic of capital that is often simply naturalized, unnamed, or reduced to measures of income and wealth. The "open light" by which one can discern the skeletal architecture of a differentiated, market-mediated social whole reflects the difficulty that the speaker faces in assembling partial intersubjective relations into a single coherent "voice," or what critic Anna Carastathis (2016) has called a "coalition of one" (182). The poem's natal imagery indicates a metaphorical transformation, however fleeting, of a ubiquitous social atomization organized through market transactions. The iterative character of these market relations seems, at moments, to suggest a collective capacity for the self-renewal of social bonds consistently thwarted by entrenched racial divisions that are not overcome but instead exacerbated by the economically enforced molecularization of social activity.

By the same token, the poem's thematic concern with both economic processes and submerged violence sheds light on the pervasive but anachronistic exclusion of women and people of color from conceptions of the working class in postwar poetics. Against the grain of discourses of generic class belonging, Lorde's "Coal" recalls the postwar transformation of social classes that passed virtually unremarked in the contentious climate of the "Poetry Wars."

Indeed, today the traditional working-class literary critics have come to associate with some early Language Writers' anticapitalist polemics is largely a thing of the past in the eyes of economic and labor historians. At the same time, increasing scholarly attention paid to comparatively less well-known Marxist accounts of race elaborated by thinkers from Harry Haywood and Claudia Jones to Harry Chang and James Boggs lays bare the anachronism at the heart of such accounts. While employment in manufacturing did not peak until 1979 in absolute terms, the share of the total labor force employed in manufacturing entered permanent decline after 1966 (U.S. Bureau of Labor Statistics 2017a, 2017b). At the same time, women began to enter the formal labor force en masse during the 1960s. Many found employment in the low-wage but expanding service sector that absorbed the shares of the labor force manufacturers relinquished (Blackwelder 1997). Those trends increased sharply after 1970. Women's share of the labor force has hovered around 50% since 1990, while women have outnumbered men in the service sector since 1984 (Wood 2014). Manufacturers, meanwhile, continued shedding labor. Predictably, nonwhite workers bore the brunt of those job losses. Unemployment among black workers reached its postwar high in 1983, and has remained at least double that of white workers since 1970 (U.S. Bureau of Labor Statistics 2011). Meanwhile, as a growing body of research documents, the surplus of nonwhite workers excluded from the wage relation continues to be absorbed by a brutally racialized system of mass incarceration (Wacquant 2002; Gilmore 2007). There is no historical referent, in short, for theoretical conceptions of a working class that is not also profoundly gendered and racialized in the postwar US.

Lorde's poem traces the broad outlines of a unitary model of social domination and economic exploitation which Marxist feminists began to describe in the 1970s (Vogel 1987). The first iterations of that model emerged from so-called "dual system debates" rooted in value theoretical efforts to square class and gender (Sargent 1986). Those efforts were closely associated with the Wages for Housework campaign during the Women's Liberation Movement (Federici 1984). More recent iterations have addressed the sometimes race-blind character of those earlier models (Gimenez 2001; Ferguson 2008). Simply put, social reproduction theory extends Marx's critique of political economy beyond the factory walls. It does so while retaining the logical force of Marx's categories. It also does so while attending to aspects of social life organized by the law of value without necessarily contributing to either the mass or rate of profit. Rather than viewing race, gender, and class as discrete axes charting differential locations within a taxonomic grid, social reproduction theory defines race and gender as constitutive elements of capital accumulation (Ferguson 2016). The result is an emerging critique of political economy that encompasses forms of subordination both within and beyond the wage nexus (Viewpoint 2015). This emerging critical political economy thus moves beyond not only the opposition between gender and class, but also beyond the race/class distinction that continues to plague contemporary theorizing about the relationship between social identity and capitalism.

We want to conclude by arguing that reimagining what lies "beneath" categorical thinking in "Coal" reattaches social identity to political economy, while also mounting a powerful challenge to conceiving of class subjects in deracialized and degendered terms. This analysis requires readers to abandon an older base-superstructure model of the economic determination of essentially epiphenomenal racial identities in favor of an understanding of economic positioning as a kind of enabling constraint of identity formation, describing forms of political agency that are "open" but nevertheless racially situated in the poem. As Raymond Williams reminds us, "In practice [economic] determination is never only the setting of limits; it is also the exertion of pressures":

> As it happens this is also a sense of "determine" in English: to determine or be determined to do something is an act of will and purpose. In a whole social process, these positive determinations, which may be experienced individually but which are always social acts, indeed often specific social formations, have very complex relations with the negative determinations that are experienced as limits.
>
> *(Williams 87)*

Lorde's "Coal" offers a vision of coalitional practice that does not assume an immaterial, socially disembedded universalism as the ground or precondition of collective action that aims to transform these social conditions. The speaker of the poem seems to discover their freedom precisely through determination and not in spite of it.

The hermeneutic circle drawn by the antinomies of postwar poetics is particularly ill-suited to account for how the poem treats the meaning and dynamic structure of racial identity as neither fixed nor ontologically pregiven, and social class as immanently raced and gendered. At the same time, and despite its stylistic adherence to lyric conventions, the poem poses a significant challenge to both assigning an intrinsic and unchanging political valence to formal strategies, and to understanding racial identity as a politically unmediated object of recognition. On the contrary, "Coal" traces how a single intending consciousness seems to split or fracture into multiple registers of experience that illuminate unfamiliar and sometimes frightening aspects of the self. Discordant voices that seem to speak through the subject only later coalesce into a single call for recognition, but it is a demand to recognize the very intersubjective conditions of possibility that undergird any seemingly unitary identity. For the speaker, and for the contemporary social conditions the speaker addresses, there is no "I" without the "total black," and vice versa.

Lorde's "Coal" shifts between affirmative and ascriptive views of identity to underscore that the recognition of difference is the starting point rather than ultimate horizon for the poet's coalitional vision. Consequently, the poem's investigation of the changing conditions that come to define the complex meaning of identity as both situated and "open" suggests historically unrealized political possibilities typically foreclosed by the antinomies of postwar poetics. In place of formal distinctions shorn of their social referents, the "earth's inside" that binds race, gender, and class together in the poem maps fault lines that continue to drive contemporary poetic and political debates.

## References

Anderson, Perry. (1979) *Considerations on Western Marxism*. London: Verso.
Blackwelder, Julia Kirk. (1997) *Now Hiring: The Feminization of Work in the United States, 1900–1995*. College Station: Texas A&M University Press.
Carastathis, Anna. (2016) *Intersectionality: Origins, Contestations, Horizons*. Lincoln: University of Nebraska Press.
Chaney, David C. (1994) *The Cultural Turn: Scene-Setting Essays on Contemporary Cultural History*. London: Routledge.
Combahee River Collective. (1979) "A Black Feminist Statement." In *Capitalist Patriarchy and the Case for Socialist Feminism*, edited by Zillah R. Eisenstein, 362–72. New York: Monthly Review Press.
Davis, Angela Y. (1983) *Women, Race & Class*. New York: Vintage Books.
Dawson, Michael C. (2013) *Blacks in and out of the Left*. Cambridge, MA: Harvard University Press.
Dworkin, Craig Douglas, and Kenneth Goldsmith. (2011) *Against Expression: An Anthology of Conceptual Writing*. Evanston, IL: Northwestern University Press.
Elbaum, Max. (2002) *Revolution in the Air: Sixties Radicals Turn to Lenin, Mao and Che*. London: Verso.
Federici, Silvia. (1984) "Putting Feminism Back on Its Feet." *Social Text*, 9/10: 338–46.
Ferguson, Susan. (2016) "Intersectionality and Social-Reproduction Feminisms: Toward an Integrative Ontology." *Historical Materialism* 24 (2): 38–60.
Ferguson, Susan. (2008) "Canadian Contributions to Social Reproduction Feminism, Race and Embodied Labor." *Race, Gender & Class* 15 (1/2): 42–57.
Fraser, Nancy. (2014) "Behind Marx's Hidden Abode." *New Left Review* 86: 55–72.
Frost, Elisabeth A., and Cynthia Hogue. (2006) *Innovative Women Poets: An Anthology of Contemporary Poetry and Interviews*. Iowa City: University of Iowa Press.
Gardner, Drew, Nada Gordon, Sharon Mesmer, K. Silem Mohammad, and Gary Sullivan, eds. (2017) *Flarf: An Anthology of Flarf*. Washington, DC: Edge Books.
Gilmore, Ruth Wilson. (2007) *Golden Gulag: Prisons, Surplus, Crisis, and Opposition in Globalizing California*. Berkeley: University of California Press.
Gimenez, Martha E. (2001) "Marxism, and Class, Gender, and Race: Rethinking the Trilogy." *Race, Gender & Class* 8 (2): 23–33.
Giménez Smith, Carmen, and John M. Chávez. (2014) *Angels of the Americlypse: An Anthology of New Latin@ Writing*. Denver, CO: Counterpath.
Gitlin, Todd. (1995) *The Twilight of Common Dreams: Why America Is Wracked by Culture Wars*. New York: Metropolitan Books.
Gitlin, Todd. (1987) *The Sixties: Years of Hope, Days of Rage*. Toronto, ON: Bantam Books.
Glenn, Evelyn Nakano. (1992) "From Servitude to Service Work: Historical Continuities in the Racial Division of Paid Reproductive Labor." *Signs* 18 (1): 1–43.
Goldsmith, Kenneth. (2011) *Uncreative Writing: Managing Language in the Digital Age*. New York: Columbia University Press.
Gosse, Van. (2008) "A Movement of Movements: The Definition and Periodization of the New Left." In *A Companion to Post-1945 America*, edited by Jean-Christophe Agnew and Roy Rosenzweig, 277–302. Malden, MA: Blackwell Publishers.
Gosse, Van. (2005) *Rethinking the New Left: An Interpretive History*. New York: Palgrave.
Harris, Duchess. (2001) "From the Kennedy Commission to the Combahee Collective: Black Feminist Organizing, 1960–1980." In *Sisters in the Struggle: African American Women in the Civil Rights-Black Power Movement*, edited by Bettye Collier-Thomas and V. P. Franklin, 280–305. New York: New York University Press.
Hartley, George. (1989) *Textual Politics and the Language Poets*. Bloomington: Indiana University Press.

Jackson, Virginia Walker. (2013) *Dickinson's Misery: A Theory of Lyric Reading*. Princeton, NJ: Princeton University Press.
Jenkins, Richard. (2014) *Social Identity*. New York: Routledge.
Kim, Eleana. (2000) "Language Poetry: Dissident Practices and the Makings of a Movement." *Readme*. Retrieved from http://home.jps.net/~nada/language1.htm.
Lew, Walter K. (1995) *Premonitions: The Kaya Anthology of New Asian North American Poetry*. New York: Kaya Productions.
Lolordo, Nicholas. (2004) "Identity Poetics? Or, the Norton Anthology of Modern and Contemporary Poetry." *Postmodern Culture* 15 (1). Retrieved from http://pmc.iath.virginia.edu/issue.904/15.1lolordo.html.
Lorde, Audre. (2000) *The Collected Poems of Audre Lorde*. New York: Norton.
Lorde, Audre. (1984) *Sister Outsider: Essays and Speeches*. Berkeley, CA: Crossing Press.
McCaffery, Steve. (1977a) "The Death of the Subject: The Implications of Counter-Communication in Recent Language-Centered Writing." *Open Letter*, 7.
McCaffery, Steve. (1977b) "Politics of the Referent." *Open Letter*, 7: 60–99.
McGann, Jerome. (1987) "Contemporary Poetry, Alternate Routes." *Critical Inquiry* 13 (3): 624–47.
Middleton, Peter. (1990) "Language Poetry and Linguistic Activism." *Social Text*, 25/26: 242–53.
Nielsen, Aldon Lynn, and Lauri Ramey. (2015) *What I Say: Innovative Poetry by Black Writers in America*. Tuscaloosa: The University of Alabama Press.
Nielsen, Aldon Lynn, and Lauri Ramey. (2006) *Every Goodbye Ain't Gone: An Anthology of Innovative Poetry by African Americans*. Tuscaloosa: University of Alabama Press.
O'Sullivan, Maggie. (1996) *Out of Everywhere: Linguistically Innovative Poetry*. London: Reality Street Editions.
Perloff, Marjorie. (2012) "Poetry on the Brink: Reinventing the Lyric." *Boston Review*. June. Retrieved from http://bostonreview.net/forum/poetry-brink.
Perloff, Marjorie. (1984) "The Word as Such: L=A=N=G=U=A=G=E Poetry in the Eighties." *American Poetry Review* 13 (3): 15–22.
Rankine, Claudia, and Lisa Sewell. (2012) *Eleven More American Women Poets in the 21st Century: Poetics across North America*. Middletown, CT: Wesleyan University Press.
Rankine, Claudia, and Juliana Spahr. (2002) *American Women Poets in the 21st Century: Where Lyric Meets Language*. Middletown, CT: Wesleyan University Press.
Reed, Anthony. (2014) *Freedom Time: The Poetics and Politics of Black Experimental Writing*. Baltimore, MD: Johns Hopkins University Press.
Ross, Andrew. (1988) "The New Sentence and the Commodity Form: Recent American Writing." In *Marxism and the Interpretation of Culture*, edited by Cary Nelson and Lawrence Grossberg, 361–80. Urbana: University of Illinois Press.
Sale, Kirkpatrick. (1973) *SDS*. New York: Random House.
San Juan Jr., E. (2003) "Marxism and the Race/Class Problematic: A Re-Articulation." *Cultural Logic* 6 (13). Retrieved from http://clogic.eserver.org/2003/sanjuan.html.
Sargent, Lydia. (1986) *The Unhappy Marriage of Marxism and Feminism: A Debate of Class and Patriarchy*. London: Pluto Press.
Silliman, Ron. (1988) "Poetry and the Politics of the Subject." *Socialist Review*, 18: 62–8.
Silliman, Ron. (1987) "Disappearance of the Word, Appearance of the World." In *The New Sentence*, 7–18. New York: Roof.
Silliman, Ron. (1986) *In the American Tree*. Orono, ME: National Poetry Foundation.
Sloan, Mary Margaret. (1998) *Moving Borders: Three Decades of Innovative Writing by Women*. Jersey City, NJ: Talisman House, Publishers.
Taylor, Charles. (1994) *Multiculturalism: Examining the Politics of Recognition*. Princeton, NJ: Princeton University Press.
U.S. Bureau of Labor Statistics. (2017a) "All Employees: Manufacturing [MANEMP]." Retrieved from *FRED, Federal Reserve Bank of St. Louis*, https://fred.stlouisfed.org/series/MANEMP, August 24 2017.
U.S. Bureau of Labor Statistic. (2017b) "All Employees: Total Nonfarm Payrolls [PAYEMS]." Retrieved from *FRED, Federal Reserve Bank of St. Louis*, https://fred.stlouisfed.org/series/PAYEMS, August 24 2017.
U.S. Bureau of Labor Statistics. (2011) "Unemployment Rates by Race and Ethnicity, 2010." *The Economics Daily*, October. Retrieved from www.bls.gov/opub/ted/2011/ted_20111005.htm.

Viewpoint. (2015) "Social Reproduction." Special Issue, *Viewpoint Magazine* 5.
Vogel, Lise. (2013) *Marxism and the Oppression of Women: Toward a Unitary Theory.* Chicago, IL: Haymarket Books.
Wacquant, Loic. (2002) "From Slavery to Mass Incarceration." *New Left Review* 13: 41–60.
Watten, Barrett. (1984) "The Politics of Poetry: Surrealism and L=A=N=G=U=A=G=E." In *Total Syntax*, 31–64. Poetics of the New. Carbondale: Southern Illinois University Press.
Williams, Raymond. (1978) *Marxism and Literature.* Oxford: Oxford University Press.
Wood, Catherine A. (2014) "The Rise in Women's Share of Nonfarm Employment during the 2007–2009 Recession: A Historical Perspective." Bureau of Labor Statistics, United States Department of Labor. *Monthly Labor Review.* Retrieved from www.bls.gov/opub/mlr/2014/article/the-rise-in-women-share-of-nonfarm-employment.htm.

# 4
# RHETORICAL ECONOMICS

*Mark Garrett Longaker*

"The chief way that a rhetorical economics would differ from the present economics, to repeat, is that it would face the arguments." (McCloskey 1994: 387) Since one voice dominates the conversation about "rhetorical economics," this essay must begin and end with Deirdre McCloskey. McCloskey tells the story of sophistic rhetoric's valiant struggle against "architectural modernism"—not the literary movement favoring James Joyce, nor the historical period featuring the lost generation, but the epistemological disposition worshipping "Science with a big S": "mechanical rules" and an allergy to "ambiguity" (1994: xii). At times, McCloskey (1996) compares modernism to Platonism, a faith in truth and certainty. Against Platonism, she pits sophism, the considerate attention to "real arguments for the real problems of the day." As positivist science is the modernist's weapon, rhetoric—the awareness that "persuasion is all we humans have"—is the sophist's shield (1996: 232–3).

Every epic struggle needs a star-crossed romance and an evil villain. As modernist iron clanged against sophistic armor, rhetoric and economics, though fated for one other, were separated. Nefarious positivism won, claiming a new kingdom, "American economics," as its spoils (1998a: 144). The positivist priests brought with them the Methodologists, petty bureaucrats who censure all arguments failing to perform the hollow rituals of verification and falsifiability. Cramming all human knowledge into the procrustean beds of measurable observation and mathematical precision, modernism's despots threw rhetoric into exile.

Yet, even as the positivist overlords and their Methodologist underlings ruled the discipline of economics under a gray sky of prediction and objectivity, colorful blossoms emerged. Economists practiced rhetoric because they knew that "what distinguishes good from bad in learned discourse is not the adoption of a particular methodology, but the earnest and intelligent attempt to contribute to a conversation" (McCloskey 1998a: 144). Though their union was forbidden, rhetoric and economics quietly courted. All that remains, said McCloskey, is for economists to acknowledge this affair, to "give up their quaint modernism and open themselves officially to a wider range of discourse." She assured that this union would not crack their disciplinary foundations. Economists would "not need to abandon data or mathematical precision" for these are rhetoric's children. McCloskey suggested that economists "merely agree to examine their language in action and converse more politely with others in the conversations of humanity" (1998: 167). Exile the positivists, admit that economics loves rhetoric, and watch a thousand flowers bloom!

McCloskey's story, like most mythology, neglects history. To begin with, the positivists did not wither and die once the blinding light of rhetoric shined forth. They changed strategy. They regrouped. To this day, more than thirty years after she published her first essay on the fecund marriage between rhetoric and economics, we still find the old modernist presuppositions lurking about the halls of American economics departments. And, the marriage between rhetoric and economics was not so fated. It may have been orchestrated by McCloskey's persuasive prose. Furthermore, the wedded disciplines of rhetoric and economics did not find a stable home in the social sciences. Instead, the pair was better received by the humanities. Villains were neither executed nor exiled. Warring kingdoms did not find peace. Love did not emerge. It was arranged (albeit happily). Nonetheless, this is a happy story. As I will explain toward the end of this essay, rhetoric and economics remains a joyous and fruitful couple. The children of this union may yet bring the humanities and the social sciences together. Before I get to the happy ending, however, I should detail the particulars of McCloskey's argument and the responses it produced. As I will demonstrate in the paragraphs to come, McCloskey had a clever idea that inspired scholarly conversations. For these contemporary conversations alone, her "rhetorical economics" deserves to be called a scholarly tradition.

McCloskey's engrossing memoir, *Crossing* (1999), testifies to what a brave and adventuresome person she is. In the 1980s, she was already a tenured Chicago School economist when she began hanging around with rhetoric scholars such as Wayne Booth and wondering what would become of economics if its practitioners lost faith in their modernist commitments. In the later decades of the twentieth century, the natural and the social sciences were filled with arguments about truth and method. This conversation reached its nadir (or its apotheosis, depending on your perspective) in 1996 when *Social Text* published an article by physicist Alan Sokal, who argued that gravity is a social construct. Sokal later revealed that he was an old-school positivist who had pranked the social constructionists. Gravity was real, and postmodernists were chagrined. At the beginning of these rancorous disagreements, in 1983, McCloskey published her first essay on the rhetoric of economics; she expanded the argument into a book published in 1985 and revised it for a second edition in 1998. This book, *The Rhetoric of Economics*, along with *If You're So Smart: The Narrative of Economic Expertise* (1990) and *Knowledge and Persuasion in Economics* (1994) remain her definitive trilogy about rhetorical economics, McCloskey's effort to replace modernism with rhetoric.

While this essay's brevity will obviate any thorough summary, it will allow a quick glance at McCloskey's three principal claims: her methodological, her analytical, and her ethical theses. Later in the essay, I will discuss the scholarly conversations in response to these theses as well as McCloskey's most recent efforts toward a humanist economics. Those interested in a more careful play-by-play reconstruction of the scholarly conversation should consult Edward M. Clift's excellent essay (2009) on "The Rhetoric of Economics" and chapter 8, "Rhetoric, Mathematics, and the Nature of Neoclassical Economic Theory," in Philip Mirowski's *Against Mechanism* (1988a: 137–60). Clift, a rhetorician, and Mirowski, an economist, explore McCloskey's nuanced position while explaining its relevance to two unique disciplines. My essay, in contrast, explores the main questions and the research potential in this tradition of econo-literary criticism.

## The methodological, analytical, and ethical theses

As suggested in the paragraphs earlier, McCloskey (1998a) wanted famed economists such as Paul Samuelson, Gary Becker, and her mentor Milton Friedman to give up their positivism and to abandon their predictions. She was careful to point out that mathematical modeling, statistics, and empirical testing should remain (139), though she warned against the assumption that these methods could answer all questions or could lead to certain predictions. McCloskey aimed to replace positivism with a "grown-up economics" that modestly but appropriately aims "to know history, not to change it" (1990: 109). Her methodological thesis, therefore, had two important corollaries. First, the tried-and-true scientific methods of economic inquiry should be supplemented by humanistic methods: mathematics alongside hermeneutics. Second, lacking absolute certainty, economics should not presume the soothsayer's clarity. Grown-up economics is a methodologically eclectic and historically interpretive science.

In *The Rhetoric of Economics*, she praised quantification. Statistics can demonstrate the size of something (such as the level of market integration). But statistical arguments cannot answer questions about the importance of the difference: "How large is large?" While she praised mathematical precision in economic argumentation, she questioned the presumption that "once you have reduced a question to numbers, you have taken it out of human hands" (1998a: 100). In *If You're So Smart* (1990), McCloskey noted that any effort at prediction is both doomed to failure and driven by what she called "magical thinking"—the desire to control the future (1990: 98). This argument is especially interesting because it takes aim at Milton Friedman's belief that "economics as a positivist science is a body of tentatively accepted generalizations about economic phenomena that can be used to predict the consequences of changes in circumstances" (1953: 39). McCloskey qualified Friedman's thesis without abandoning his program. She said economics is a humanist science that can explain the consequences of changes in circumstances.

McCloskey's methodological thesis is the bedrock for her other two arguments. But before moving onto the other two theses, a caveat: McCloskey's rhetorical approach to economic methodology does not mean that "anything goes." "The alternative to blindered methodologies of modernism is not a mob warring against itself but a body of enlightened thinkers engaging in earnest conversation in which they know what rhetorics they use" (1998a: 175). Without a sainted Methodologist blessing the proper forms of investigation, economists will be aware of all the arguments and will judge for themselves. Their critical awareness and discernment will require training in the methods of rhetorical analysis.

McCloskey offers the "rhetorical tetrad" as a heuristic for applying "rhetoric…to economic science": Fact, Story, Logic, and Metaphor (1998a: 19). In the *Rhetoric of Economics*, she (1998a) published rhetorical analyses that notice facts, logic, and style in economic arguments. She discussed, for instance, analogy, metaphor, synecdoche, and irony in David Ricardo's arguments about distribution, Gary Becker's arguments about "human capital," and Robert Solow's work on income (35–49). She explained that John Muth's "positivist style" assured readers of his scientific credentials, making him a trustworthy and persuasive speaker (1998a: 61–3). And she looked at Robert Folger's use of numerous argumentative strategies, such as *paramologia*, *reductio ad absurdum*, and *argumentum a fortiori* (1998a: 80–3). In *If You're So Smart*, she rhetorically analyzed "stories," which include a wide variety of argumentative devices, from mathematical models (which McCloskey calls "stylized facts" [1990: 23]) to common narratives about the British economy. Like readers of literature, economists read aesthetically. They look for the "right ending" to their scientific narratives: an unintended consequence or a market equilibrium (1990: 29–30). Accepting McCloskey's analytical thesis, economists will understand how they argue and why they disagree.

Rhetorical analysis will have another unintended—ethical—consequence: It "can perhaps make economists more modest, tolerant, and self-aware" (1998a: 186). They will boast "less pretended omniscience and more real wisdom" (1990: 162). Following from her analytical arguments, the first part of McCloskey's ethical thesis begs for rhetorical humility. Forecasting follows from positivist "forming and testing hypotheses" (Friedman 1953: 42). Scientific hypotheses and rhetorical fortune-telling inevitably lead to pride (that goeth before the fall). The "American" question is therefore the title of her book: *If You're So Smart*, why ain't you rich? The second part of her ethical argument pleads for ethical speech. Borrowing a term from German philosopher Jürgen Habermas, McCloskey (1998a) suggested that economists replace Methodology with their practiced habits of good conversation: "Don't lie; pay attention; don't sneer; cooperate; don't shout; let other people talk; be open-minded; explain yourself when asked; don't resort to violence or conspiracy in aid of your ideas" (160). Arguments that fail to adhere to these standards should not be taken seriously.

With McCloskey's three theses in mind, the next segment of this essay will discuss the broader conversation about rhetorical economics, emphasizing trends and suggesting possibilities: What kinds of inquiry does/did rhetorical economics make available?

## The conversations about methodology, analysis, and disciplinarity

Most of the immediate response to McCloskey's work focused on the methodological thesis, ignoring her analyses altogether. Alexander Rosenberg (1988), one of her sternest methodological critics, voiced agreement with the analytical chapters (175). Even Austrian economists, who should be sympathetic to a humanistic–rhetorical approach, snarkily harrumphed at the methodological thesis (McCloskey 1994: 314–24). For example, Hans Hermann Hoppe (1989) accused McCloskey of "nihilism" and "ethical relativism" (179), while defending Ludwig Von Mises's call to rationalism. Others said nastier things (Rothbard 1989). The methodological thesis occupied a special section of *Economics and Philosophy* (1988), including a response from McCloskey and responses to her response. In the late 1980s, the conversation was no different, and the disagreements no more reconcilable than they would be six years later when McCloskey published a book-length refutation (*Knowledge and Persuasion in Economics* [1994]) of the methodologists who refuted her. For all the ink spilled, the methodological conversation was nearly over before it began. Positivists and die-hard empiricists dug in their heels. McCloskey defended her position. Even when scholars looked for common or new ground, they found the same battlefields. Since the late 1990s, very little has been said about methodology. The more productive and engaging conversation is about analysis.

In the early days, McCloskey's analytical arguments commanded substantive response (Lanham 1993: 168–70; Aune 2001: 174–8). More recently, they inspire a passing reference (Longaker 2006; Goodnight & Green 2010; Hanan et al. 2014; Colombini 2015). Nevertheless, analytical influence persists, contributing, though diffusely, to a range of arguments. Some analyses lead to historical conclusions (Bazerman 1993; Henderson 1993): How have economists argued and why? Some lead to disciplinary conclusions (Clower 1988; Mirowski 1988; Henderson & Dudley-Evans 1990; Swales 1993; McCloskey 1994: 111–78): How did the argumentative forms of economic discourse shape the discipline's formation? And some lead to pedagogical conclusions (Hewings 1990; Mason 1990): How does the rhetoric of economics inaugurate new students into—or alienate them from—the field? The budding scholar does not even have to use McCloskey's favored tools of rhetorical analysis (Dudley-Evans & Henderson: 1990; Backhouse et al. 1993). Genre theory (Swales 1993), Bakhtinian literary theory (Brown 1993), deconstruction (Mehta 1993), discourse analysis (Bloor & Pindi 1990), linguistics (Dudley-Evans 1993), affect theory (Chaput 2014), and hermeneutics (Gerard 1993) have all proven useful.

While there is a flourishing and varied tradition (and much remaining potential) in the analysis of economic discourse, many of the presuppositions that McCloskey aimed to set aside have survived even among those who ostensibly follow her lead. For instance, rhetorical analysis is still regularly described as a method of weeding out misleading arguments (Solow 1988; Avsar 2011). McCloskey's (1994) broad definition of rhetoric as "all means of unforced agreement" did not take seed where rhetoric's pejorative definition had deep roots (287). In many cases, the conversation about analysis led to more analyses, failing even to challenge tried-and-true assumptions, such as the notion that rhetoric merely represents the economy (Bichieri 1988; Goodwin 1988). On the other hand, some scholars have marshaled their analyses to support radical claims about language, disciplinary foundations, and politics. Some analyses conclude that rhetoric constitutes and shapes economic developments (Goodnight & Green 2010; Hanan 2014; Hanan et al. 2014). Some analysts have argued that the very foundations of the discipline must be rethought (Mirowski 1988), even though McCloskey and others have argued that the rhetorical analysis of economics bears no necessary political or disciplinary implications (Fish 1988). Daring to gainsay their grand dame, some analyses suggest that the political leanings of economic discourse should be overturned (Stettler 1995; Quinn 1996).

While the conversation about analysis has strayed from McCloskey's views, the conversation about disciplinarity sits close to her (1994) original purpose (127–63) and her most recent endeavors. The disciplinary conversation is both inwardly facing (toward economics) and outwardly facing (toward the economy). Her partner-in-rhetoric Arjo Klamer (1984) gazes inward, seeing the discipline of economics not as a science but rather as a conversation in which economists "not only construct models and conduct empirical tests" but "also argue on what a good model should look like" (238). In one especially vibrant analogy, Klamer (1987) described economists as a "tribe," complete with rituals and religions. His favored metaphor—the "conversation or, better, a bunch of conversations"—allows Klamer (2007) to analyze disciplinary culture, including networking, conferences, and rhetoric (xiv, 37–50, 91–125). Like Klamer, other scholars inwardly investigate the discipline of economics as a conversation (Waller and Robertson: 1990).

The outwardly focused scholarly conversation about disciplinarity features fewer voices but greater potential. Recent historical studies, for instance, investigate language's role in the formation of economic disciplines and in the early formation of "modern" epistemology (Poovey 1998). Writing in the last decades of the twentieth century, McCloskey rarely analyzed anything before World War II. Recent historical work suggests that the rhetorical constitution of the economic conversation began before the American Revolution. Equally interesting is McCloskey's twenty-first-century scholarly program, which she calls "humanomics." McCloskey now presents the economy (not the scholarly discipline but the production and distribution of scarce resources) as a conversation. Once gazing inwardly at disciplinary convention, now she gazes outward at industrial innovation. No matter where she looks, she finds rhetoric.

## The conversation about humanomics

Rhetorical economics belongs in the "traditions" section of this collection for two reasons. First, for three decades, scholars have used rhetoric to rethink their methodological presumptions, their disciplinary formation, and their discursive constitution. Second, McCloskey's humanomics revives a much older and nowadays "neglected link between the economy and culture," a conversation that began with Adam Smith, a tradition featuring the mathematician's models as well as "the anthropologist's and the aesthete's sense." This tradition is about "bourgeois virtue" (1998b: 300). McCloskey's early work on bourgeois virtue suggests that she is extending the disciplinary thesis (1994: 348). But the scope of her inquiry has changed dramatically. Her argument about bourgeois virtue applies to all humanity. McCloskey believes that capitalism—understood as a conversation—has ethically improved its participants as well as its bystanders while materially enriching its participants and even its critics.

In the first volume of her bourgeois-virtue trilogy, McCloskey defines all seven of the classical and Christian virtues as "bourgeois virtues": faith, hope, charity, justice, temperance, fortitude, and prudence. Against those who see the capitalist as a calculating utilitarian ("Max U," a man seeking maximum utility), McCloskey states, "bourgeois life has not in practice...excluded the other virtues. In fact, it has nourished them" (2006: 8). Playing with the economist's stylistic affection for variables represented in mathematical formulae, McCloskey declares, not by P(rudence) alone does capitalism prosper, nor does capitalism preach prudence only. Another variable—S(ociety)—must be added to the equation (2006: 424–5). Her chapters on the bourgeois virtue of love are particularly illustrative, for charity is often attributed to the devout priest or the committed friend, but never to the calculating stock trader. McCloskey, however, argues that the bourgeoisie has its own version of this Christian virtue—"altruistic hedonism." Though not "disinterested, particular, identifying" or "constraining," bourgeois love is good (2006: 114). In the acts of consumption and production, the bourgeoisie expresses and realizes their love for one another and for all humanity. They do not act strictly out of "self-interest," for "a loveless economy would not work" (2006: 123). Rather, the bourgeoisie pursues profit and consumes goods because they feel love in their hearts, and they believe that the honest pursuit of industry and pleasure is the best way to ameliorate society. Resulting is a desire "to be virtuous in business as elsewhere" (2006: 129). Therefore, altruistic hedonism is linked to the other virtues because it leads to the exercise of "temperance, humility, prudence, justice, solidarity, [and] faith" (2006: 112).

In her second volume, McCloskey causally attributes Western society's economic growth to new ideas. In *The Bourgeois Virtues* (2006), McCloskey defines the virtues. In *Bourgeois Dignity* (2010), she isolates the variables. While arguing like a moral philosopher, she emphasizes economics. While arguing like an economist, she emphasizes rhetoric. Borrowing her method from John Stuart Mill, McCloskey decides to: "take out what you can measure, and what's left is the impact of what you can't" (2010: 33). After accounting for the small effects of education, primitive accumulation, transportation, geography, natural resources, and a host of other factors, McCloskey concludes that "what's left standing is—let us pray—the not-directly-measurable innovation released by the rhetorical change" (2010: 37), *liberty* and *dignity* first valorized by seventeenth-century Dutch and eighteenth-century English (2010: 394). "Liberty to hope was a good idea and...a faithful economic life should give dignity and even honor to ordinary people" (2010: 26). Liberty and dignity made way for "the Bourgeois Deal: 'Let me get very rich by buying innovations low and selling them high (and please do refrain from stealing from me, or interfering), and I will make *you* pretty rich too'" (2010: 70). The bourgeois idea, a rhetorical variable, enabled innovation, an economic effect.

In her third volume, *Bourgeois Equality* (2016), McCloskey explores the rhetorical shift leading to modernity. And this most recent volume brings McCloskey back to rhetorical economics but with a wider scope. McCloskey analyzes a range of literary and historical sources, including but not limited to: Jane Austen's novels, Adam Smith's moral and legal writings, Benjamin Franklin's autobiographical musings, and English plays from the

Elizabethan to the Augustan eras. In all these sources, she sees evidence of the great valorization, that rhetorical shift toward liberty and dignity. The upshot of McCloskey's argument is that economists should look beyond strictly material factors, such as infrastructure, investment, laws, and regulations when accounting for growth and particularly when discussing modernity. Borrowing a term from the leftist political theorist Karl Polanyi while inventing her own, McCloskey writes, "all actual bourgeois people have nontrading relations in their lives, and the trading itself is *embedded*. Analysis of the embedded consequences is the scientific program of *humanomics*" (2016: 557 italics inserted).

McCloskey's humanomics anticipates a new scholarly era and respects a long-standing tradition. This conversation about humanomics need not exclusively involve economists. No economist myself, I (2015) have offered a modest contribution to the conversation about humanomics, arguing that many British Enlightenment thinkers wanted to sustain capitalism by practicing bourgeois virtue through the appreciation and the teaching of rhetorical skill. I confess a certain agnosticism regarding McCloskey's causal argument. I am not convinced that a particular method of teaching rhetorical style led to bourgeois virtue or to capitalism's success. But I accept McCloskey's historical and her definitional claims. Like McCloskey, many have seen themselves as a virtuous bourgeoisie, and they have also imagined the economy as a conversation. Through rhetoric, McCloskey and her predecessors have tried to sustain the social institutions surrounding, supporting, and interacting with what she calls "trade-tested innovation." The conversation about humanomics is a centuries-old tradition forgotten by economists and political theorists who—as McCloskey explains—focus too narrowly on what can be empirically quantified or mathematically analyzed. Rhetorical theorists, literary analysts, intellectual historians, and the like should chronicle, analyze, critique, and most importantly explain this tradition. May a thousand flowers bloom!

## References


Aune, J. (2001) *Selling the Free Market: The Rhetoric of Economic Correctness*, London: Guilford.

Avsar, R. (2011) "Mainstream Economic Rhetoric, Ideology and Institutions," *Journal of Economic Issues* 137–57.

Backhouse, R., T. Dudley-Evans, & W. Henderson (1993) "Exploring the Language and Rhetoric of Economics," in W. Henderson, T. Dudley-Evans, & R. Backhouse eds. *Economics and Language*, New York: Routledge. 1–20.

Bazerman, C. (1993) "Money Talks: The Rhetorical Project of the *Wealth of Nations*," in W. Henderson, T. Dudley-Evans, & R. Backhouse eds. *Economics and Language*, New York: Routledge. 173–99.

Bicchieri, C. (1988) "Should a Scientist Abstain from Metaphor?" in A. Klamer, D. McCloskey, & R. Solow eds. *The Consequences of Economic Rhetoric*, Cambridge: Cambridge University Press. 100–15.

Bloor, T. & M. Pindi (1990) "Schematic Structure in Economic Forecasts," in T. Dudley-Evans & W. Henderson eds. *The Language of Economics: The Analysis of Economics Discourse*, Hong Kong: Modern Language Publications and the British Council. 55–66.

Brown, V. (1993) "Decanonizing Discourses: Textual Analysis and the History of Economic Thought," in W. Henderson, T. Dudley-Evans, & R. Backhouse eds. *Economics and Language*, New York: Routledge. 64–84.

Chaput, C. (2014) "The Rhetorical Situation and the Battle for Public Sentiment: How Friedman Overtook Galbraith at the Dawn of Neoliberalism," in J. Hanan & M. Hayward eds. *Communication and the Economy: History, Value, Agency*, New York: Peter Lang. 187–208.

Clift, E. (2008) "The Rhetoric of Economics," in A. Lunsford, R. Eberly, & K. Wilson eds. *The Sage Handbook of Rhetorical Studies*, Los Angeles, CA: Sage, 197–215.

Clower, R. "The Ideas of Economists," in A. Klamer, D. McCloskey, & R. Solow eds. *The Consequences of Economic Rhetoric*, Cambridge: Cambridge University Press. 85–99.

Colombini, C. (2015) "Speaking Confidence: Bubble Denial as Market Authoritative Rhetorical Decorum," *Rhetoric Society Quarterly* 45: 117–37.

Dudley-Evans, T. (1993) "The Debate over Milton Friedman's Theoretical Framework: An Applied Linguist's View," in W. Henderson, T. Dudley-Evans, & R. Backhouse eds. *Economics and Language*, New York: Routledge. 132–52.

Dudley-Evans, T. & W. Henderson (1990) "The Organization of Article Introductions: Evidence of Change in Economics Writing," in T. Dudley-Evans & W. Henderson eds. *The Language of Economics: The Analysis of Economics Discourse*, Hong Kong: Modern Language Publications and the British Council. 67–78.

Fish, S. (1988) "Comments from Outside Economics," in A. Klamer, D. McCloskey, & R. Solow eds. *The Consequences of Economic Rhetoric*, Cambridge: Cambridge University Press. 21–30.

Friedman, M. (1953) "The Methodology of Positive Economics," in *Essays in Positive Economics*, Chicago, IL: University of Chicago Press. 3–43.

Gerard, B. (1993) "The Significance of Interpretation in Economics," in W. Henderson, T. Dudley-Evans, & R. Backhouse eds. *Economics and Language*, New York: Routledge. 51–63.

Goodnight, T. & S. Green (2010) "Rhetoric, Risk, and Markets: The Dot-Com Bubble," *Quarterly Journal of Speech*: 115–40.

Goodwin, C. (1988) "The Heterogeneity of the Economists' Discourse: Philosopher, Priest, and Hired Gun," in A. Klamer, D. McCloskey, & R. Solow eds. *The Consequences of Economic Rhetoric*, Cambridge: Cambridge University Press. 207–20.

Hanan, J. (2014) "From Economic Rhetoric to Economic Imaginaries: A Critical Geneology of Economic Rhetoric in U.S. Communication Studies," in J. Hanan & M. Hayward eds. *Communication and the Economy: History, Value, Agency*, New York: Peter Lang. 67–94.

Hanan, J. I. Ghosh, & K. Brooks (2014) "Banking on the Present: The Ontological Rhetoric of Neo-Classical Economics and Its Relation to the 2008 Financial Crisis," *Quarterly Journal of Speech* 100: 139–62.

Henderson, W. (1993) "The Problem of Edgeworth's Style," in W. Henderson, T. Dudley-Evans, & R. Backhouse eds. *Economics and Language*, New York: Routledge. 200–22.

Hoppe, H. (1989) "In Defense of Extreme Rationalism: Thoughts on Donald McCloskey's *The Rhetoric of Economics*," *Review of Austrian Economics* 3: 179–214.

Henderson, W. & T. Dudley-Evans (1990) "Introduction: The Analysis of Economics Discourse," in T. Dudley-Evans & W. Henderson eds. *The Language of Economics: The Analysis of Economics Discourse*, Hong Kong: Modern Language Publications and the British Council. 2–15.

Hewings, A. (1990) "Aspects of the Language of Economics Textbooks," in T. Dudley-Evans & W. Henderson eds. *The Language of Economics: The Analysis of Economics Discourse*, Hong Kong: Modern Language Publications and the British Council. 28–42.

Klamer, A. (2007) *Speaking of Economics: How to Get in the Conversation*, New York: Routledge.

Klamer, A. (1987) "As If Economists and Their Subject Were Rational," in J. Nelson, A. Megill, & D. McCloskey eds. *The Rhetoric of the Human Sciences: Language and Argument in Scholarship and Public Affairs*, Madison: University of Wisconsin Press. 163–83.

Klamer, A. (1983) *Conversations with Economists: New Classical Economists and Opponents Speak out on the Current Controversy in Macroeconomics*, Totowa, NJ: Rowman & Allanheld.

Lanham, R. (1993) *The Electronic Word: Democracy, Technology, and the Arts*, Chicago, IL: University of Chicago Press.

Longaker, M. (2015) *Rhetorical Style and Bourgeois Virtue: Capitalism and Civil Society in the British Enlightenment*, State College: The Pennsylvania State University Press.

Longaker, M. (2006) "John Locke's Monetary Argument: An Analysis with Methodological and Historical Implications," *Rhetoric Society Quarterly* 41: 125–44.

Mäki, U. (1993) "Two Philosophies of the Rhetoric of Economics," in W. Henderson, T. Dudley-Evans, & R. Backhouse eds. *Economics and Language*, New York: Routledge. 23–50.

Mäki, U. (1988) "How to Combine Rhetoric and Realism in the Methodology of Economics," *Economics and Philosophy* 4: 89–109.

Mason, M. (1990) "Analysis of a Passage from an Economics Textbook," in T. Dudley-Evans & W. Henderson eds. *The Language of Economics: The Analysis of Economics Discourse*, Hong Kong: Modern Language Publications and the British Council. 16–28.

McCloskey, D. (2016) *Bourgeois Equality: How Ideas, Not Capital or Institutions, Enriched the World*, Chicago, IL: University of Chicago Press.

McCloskey, D. (2010) *Bourgeois Dignity: Why Economics Can't Explain the Modern World*, Chicago, IL: University of Chicago Press.

McCloskey, D. (2006) *The Bourgeois Virtues: Ethics for an Age of Commerce*, Chicago, IL: University of Chicago Press.
McCloskey, D. (1998a) *The Rhetoric of Economics*, 2nd ed., Madison: University of Wisconsin Press.
McCloskey, D. (1998b) "Bourgeois Virtue and the History of *P* and *S*," *Journal of Economic History* 58: 297–317.
McCloskey, D. (1996) "Keynes Was a Sophist, and a Good Thing, Too," *Eastern Economic Journal* 22: 231–4.
McCloskey, D. (1994) *Knowledge and Persuasion in Economics*, Cambridge: Cambridge University Press.
McCloskey, D. (1990) *If You're So Smart: The Narrative of Economic Expertise*, Chicago, IL: University of Chicago Press.
Mehta, J. (1993) "Meaning in the Context of Bargaining Games: Narratives in Opposition," in W. Henderson, T. Dudley-Evans, & R. Backhouse eds. *Economics and Language*, New York: Routledge. 85–99.
Mirowski, P. (1988a) *Against Mechanism: Protecting Economics from Science*, Totowa, NJ: Rowman and Littlefield.
Mirowski, P. (1988b) "Shall I Compare Thee to a Minkowski-Ricardo-Leontief-Metzler Matrix of the Mosak-Hicks Type? Or, Rhetoric, Mathematics, and the Nature of Neoclassical Economic Theory," in A. Klamer, D. McCloskey, & R. Solow eds. *The Consequences of Economic Rhetoric*, Cambridge: Cambridge University Press. 117–45.
Peter, F. (2001) "Rhetoric vs. Realism in Economic Methodology: A Critical Assessment of Recent Contributions," *Cambridge Journal of Economics* 25: 571–89.
Poovey, M. (1998) *A History of Modern Fact: Problems of Knowledge in the Sciences of Wealth and Society*, Chicago, IL: University of Chicago Press.
Quinn, K. (1996) "A Rhetorical Conception of Practical Rationality," *Journal of Economic Issues* 30: 1127–42.
Rosenberg, A. (1988) "Rhetoric Is Not Important Enough for Economists to Bother about," *Economics and Philosophy* 4: 173–5.
Rothbard, M. (1989) "The Hermeneutical Invasion of Philosophy and Economics," *Review of Austrian Economics* 3: 45–59.
Solow, R. (1988) "Comments from Inside Economics," in A. Klamer, D. McCloskey, & R. Solow eds. *The Consequences of Economic Rhetoric*, Cambridge: Cambridge University Press. 31–7.
Stettler, M. (1995) "The Rhetoric of McCloskey's Rhetoric of Economics," *Cambridge Journal of Economics* (1995): 391–403.
Swales, J. (1993) "The Paradox of Value: Six Treatments in Search of a Reader," in W. Henderson, T. Dudley-Evans, & R. Backhouse eds. *Economics and Language*, New York: Routledge. 223–39.
Waller, W. & L. Robertson (1990) "Why Johnny (Ph.D., Economics) Can't Read: A Rhetorical Analysis of Thorstein Veblen and a Response to Donald McCloskey's *Rhetoric of Economics*," *Journal of Economic Issues* 4: 1027–44.

# 5

# LABOR WITHOUT VALUE, LANGUAGE AT A PRICE

## Toward a narrative poetics for the financial turn

*Richard Godden*

Marx defines language as "practical consciousness" made from "agitated air."[1] His description links cognition to its medium within the realm of practice (or the "practical"), where, for Marx, practicalities always, and in the last instance, derive from labor practice. What then, besides breath, agitates the air, as language, consciousness, and labor subsume one another? Stated reductively, and in terms of mysterious simplicity, Marx's labor theory of value posits labor under capital as the sole source of value, and value production as the motor of capital accumulation. It follows, following Marx, that a labor theory of language reflects and refracts the practices of value production, which practices are packed with agitations. Before attempting to demystify the key terms, "labor" and "value," I needs must situate language more generally among social practices. Here, the work of V.N. Volosinov will prove crucial.

For Volosinov, "the organizing center of any utterance, of any experience, is not within but outside—in the social milieu surrounding any being."[2] He adds that, "consequently, the whole route between inner experience ("the expressible") and outward objectification (the utterance) lies entirely across social territory."[3] Consciousness accordingly lives outside itself ("I" being immanent within "we"), doing so by way of words always and already occupied by prior usage, which uses reflect earlier contexts of use, and their users' relation to those contexts. Language, so understood, is inherently dialogic—semantic matter made from sedimented polyphony. Cited in an appendix to *Marxism and the Philosophy of Language*, Bakhtin might have been glossing Volosinov:

> The word is not a tangible object, but an always shifting, always changing, means of social communication. Its dynamism consists in its movement from speaker to speaker, from one context to another. Through it all, the word does not forget its path of transfer and cannot completely free itself from those concrete contexts into which it has entered.[4]

But why claim that words, unable to forget their paths, remain concretely cluttered? Because, as a form of practice, thrown forward with more or less vehemence toward reference, the word (whether from mouth, page, or screen) works on the world, which portion of the world (or referent), made to matter as linguistic matter, waits on further words to take it up, deploying its work as part of their semantic sediment.

Given that contexts linger within the verbal event, and persist as material residues after the event, in the form of its practiced intent, that event must be conditioned, under capital, by those relations that condition all relations—the social relations of value production. Accordingly, the event, at once linguistic and social, must be conditioned by its necessary relations to "labor," "value"...and a table. I introduce the table as the swiftest means through which to address the nature of the conjunction of labor and value within the commodity, or that through which capital appears to reproduce itself as a value.

In the first chapter of *Capital*, a table according to Marx famously dances:[5] made, by a carpenter for his own use, the table stays wooden and still. Taken by the carpenter to market, priced for sale and assuming, therefore, the form of a commodity—that is, "set in relation to all other commodities"[6]—the table dances, performing, I would suggest, a two-step whose steps are at odds with one another. Marx's dancing table, "evolv[ing] a wooden brain" out of which spins a body that "transcends sensuousness,"[7] is a monster fashioned from the incompatibility of "use" and "exchange," each a "value," each antagonistic to the other, yet required to exist under "price" as a "non-identical unity."[8] Agitated by the "unstable duality" of its "double body,"[9] the table dances, but what is the exact nature of its agitation? Perhaps it dances, in weightless delight, at its affinity through price with all other marketed items. Or, perhaps and also, the dance of affinity derives from the table's relation, as congealed labor power, to those other priced expressions of labor? "Use value" and "exchange value," each requiring the other under capital, sit ill in any object, person, or word which comes to market.

Let us suppose that the carpenter works not for himself, but for a company; accordingly, his labor, like the table, commands a price. In order that woodwork may be made comparable to office work or kitchen work, his labor must be abstracted, or measured for the notional quantity of its content, a quantity that can then be priced. By which means, labor power becomes abstract labor, which, in turn, becomes abstract labor time, yielding—through the dream of equivalency—a priceable entity, congealed in the commodity, be it a table, a document, or a side order of salad.[10] You can sit at the table, read the menu, taste the salad, but you cannot touch, read, taste the relations that bought eye to item, item to table, table to restaurant. These relations-in-things transcend the sensuousness that they substantiate, and as such might be considered "real abstract[ions],"[11] invisible yet making the substance of the meal possible, under capital. One should add that the meal costs. The restauranteur, as a capitalist, takes his profit from labor, understood to be the sole source of that value, doing so, more particularly from a distinction between the labor necessary to the reproduction of that labor (paid as a wage) and the labor surplus to the requirement of labor's reproduction: the "surplus labor" becomes the capitalist's "surplus value" (taken as profit).[12] Which is to say, concrete appearances perhaps to the contrary, for the capitalist, labor does not exist to make tables or meals, but to make value or profits—which profit, spent or reinvested, assumes and casts off the forms of labor, commodity, and money, even as it structures those entities through which it passes (labor, commodity, and money) in its drive to self-valorization, or its own increase.

To return briefly to the table, its preparation, and what it carries (in my example): if the table itself, the salad, the cook and waiter's work, and the figures on the bill are in fact phenomenal forms of invisible relations, their materiality needs must be recast as material compounded from opacity, distortion, dislocation, and secretion—an assemblage that amounts to a real that is really unreal. Given that capitalist relations of production, resting on the value of labor power, produce things radically foreign to that which forms them (the totality of their real relations and conditions), those things, the phenomenal world under capital, whose "manifestation[s] are equally forms of concealment,"[13] should strike us as "hieroglyph[s] which [have] to be deciphered."[14] That they do not, speaks in large part to our language. Put aphoristically, if, after Marx, language is best understood as "practical consciousness," does that mean that we are all practically unconscious as to the invisibilities that historically determine us, and if so, why?

To recognize that within the systematization of the global market, under neoliberal imperatives, few aspects of living escape "price"—and that consequently, "social synthesis [will]... be found within the exchange relation"[15]—is to lodge individual subjectivity (in intent, purpose, and practice) within the determinate social form of that relation, within, that is, the all-pervading and pervasively "real abstraction" of equivalency. Sohn-Rethel, addressing modern subjectivity, argues that intellection occurs behind the back of consciousness, or via "unconscious social practice" having to do with "the non-mental practice of commodity exchange, and the mediation of the money form."[16] He seeks thereby to "locate a material and historical basis for formal modes of thinking and practice."[17] I take "unconscious" or "non-mental" practices to refer to the cumulative abstractions inherent in capitalist money and the social relations latent in our use of it, where,

> abstraction belongs to the interrelationship of the exchanging agents and not to the agents themselves. For it is not individuals who cause the social synthesis but their actions. And their actions do it in such a way that, at the moment it happens, the actors know nothing of it.[18]

Put reductively, in the market (and under late capital we are all "in the market"), we are know-nothings, because our conscious practice knows little or nothing of what it does. Nonetheless, what we do, while it remains abstracted from us (or "unconscious" to us), forms the basis of our thought (consciousness). Furthermore, to add Marx to Sohn-Rethel, since we think in words, our language, as "practical consciousness," in and through its practice subjects us to opacity. Ergo, epistemologically, market structures that we do not know produce the forms of what we know, through market practices on our behalf, thereby conditioning the medium in which we do not know it. Cognitively and linguistically, we are subject to invisibilities. Such invisibilities, nonetheless, make themselves more or less visible: these emergencies might be called "contradictions."

In what follows, I seek to explore the linguistic dimensions of contradiction. Take the "identity of opposites," or systems of equivalents through which capital grows: equivalencies, called by Jacques Rancière, "impossible equations," structure all aspects of capitalist relations—labor, commodity, and price. Effectively, value emerges from a condensation of = signs. As already argued, diverse labor power can go to market only because rendered equivalent by a process of abstraction which nominally extracts that which they share, "abstract labor time."[19] By such means, the work of the carpenter, the cook, the student, and the CEO—though qualitatively different—became quantitatively one, and therefore comparable through price (the wage). But labor differences continue to agitate the market's indifference, since labor time—whether in the form of disputes over the length of the working day or board room bonuses—remains the site of social antagonism, itself reflective of the "myster[y] ... of the equivalent form,"[20] that permitted the magnitude of value to be measured through labor time, in order that an inequitable distribution of the former might maximize capital accumulation.

The postulated equality of disparate labors is replicated, though at a different level of abstraction, within that which labor produces, the commodity. As established, the table that dances unites incompatibilities of use and exchange within the notion of price. Its troubled body, congealing from person to thing, and subject to further transubstantiation—at least from the viewpoint of exchange—from thing to price, stands still to be sold due to being petrified by its price tag. As Sohn-Rethel puts it, "the business of exchange enforces abstraction … from the material activities of man … since objects of exchange are assumed to remain immutable for the duration of the transaction."[21] Whether in shop windows or on screens, goods may not be used. "Use" here has a double sense: first, usage, whether in production or distribution, is forgotten; second, the price unpaid precludes use until purchase. Yet since the good remains at once concrete (congealed labor that will not sell unless useful) and abstract (care of the obliterations affected by price[22])—screen or shop window notwithstanding—it like labor before it, retains a double nature, proving therefore contradictory and liable to agitations. Would-be purchasers just might, for whatever reason, recall the circumstances of the desired commodity's manufacture, and, holding the good in question neither cheap nor good at that price, refrain from purchase.

Price as the third prevalent form through which the value presents itself (labor, commodity, and money), like the structural elements, labor and commodity whose imperatives as part of capital it brings to realization, condenses and displaces the antitheses and antagonisms latent in the process of which it is the apogée. However, those processes remain hidden in the material forms that hold them: where the hidden differs from the lost, in that what is lost most typically stays lost, while the hidden waits to come from hiding.[23] The pressure of the antagonisms secreted within and by the hidden motions of value produces what Marx describes as moving contradictions,[24] doing so because many of the apparent unities internal to value production retain their unity only through "external antitheses."[25] Witness the passage of diverse labor powers into the singularity of abstract labor; or of use value into exchange value; or of persons into things having the form of commodity only through the reification of those persons. Doubled bodies are troubled bodies, containing "the possibility of crises" in their inclination to divide along the lines of their constitutive and "immanent contradictions."[26]

Seeking a figure for contradiction, Marx settled on ellipsis, of which he notes:

> It is a contradiction to depict one body as constantly falling towards another and at the same time as constantly flying away from it. The ellipse is a form of motion within which the contradiction is both realized and resolved.[27]

The ellipse marks a broken place: to confront a break is to confront an instance of a broken system, initially linguistic but also conceptual in the degree to which the sentence proposes to mean. To think through the ellipsis, rather than simply to read across its semantic hesitation, may be to recognize that the referents (persons, actions, and things), drawn syntactically into relation by the sentence, are themselves liable to the interruption enacted by the ellipse. As such, in Marx's terms, they become the bodies falling toward and away from one another, submitted by motion to a "semantic impertinence" that gives rise to a particular form of conceptual need in the reader. At the risk of making too much of an aside about a piece of punctuation, I would suggest that since syntax causes us to "see relationally," broken syntax, insofar as it intensifies relational seeing, promotes the insight that semantic materials are themselves made from relations that they are not, indeed from relations that, under capital, they may well exclude, repel, and occlude.[28] So read, ellipses, through signal contradiction and hesitation, may promote insight into the presence of certain types of contradiction.

An instance, whose familiarity may allow me a degree of shorthand even as it seeks to dispel abstraction: In F. Scott Fitzgerald's *The Great Gatsby* (1925), Gatsby and the narrator Nick Carraway consider Daisy Buchanan's voice:

> 'She's got an indiscreet voice,' I remarked. 'It's full of——' I hesitated.
> 'Her voice is full of money,' he said suddenly.
> That was it. I'd never understood before. It was full of money —— that was the inexhaustible charm that rose and fell in it, the jingle of it, the cymbals' song of it .... High in a white palace the king's daughter, the golden girl ....[29]

Dash and ellipsis so punctuate the passage that pause takes semantic form as pun, a figure whose speech situation grants it time for acoustic division. "Jingle," "cymbal," "golden," allow Carraway to recast, through hesitation, Gatsby's abrupt "money." Each pun prompts a semantic shift: "jingle" moves from sonic notation to loose change, while "golden" as the mineral form of the promise redeemable from notes (financial and musical) is devalued as a "symbol," both by its heard proximity to "jingle" and by Nick's procrastinating and ultimately evasive decoration of Gatsby's insight. So absolute is the damage done by the principle of ellipsis that even the speakers' proper names come apart. "Gat," the syllable shared by Gatz and Gatsby, in German means "hole," and in Dutch "hole, gap, break": Carraway will assure us that his has been a story of the Middle West,[30] a region settled initially by Germans, and in the later nineteenth century by Dutch farmers. But if Gatsby's remark, "Her voice is full of money," may be read as typical of his now named capacity to interrupt expectation, Carraway, also apt to his name, exhibits the knack of witnessing the holes, only in order to obscure them. "Carraway" joins "Daisy" and "Myrtle" in its derivation from horticultural dictionaries: the seeds of the caraway are traditionally thought to "ease the pains of colic" and have long been used in confectionary, cookery, and perfumery to enable digestion and evacuate noxious gases.[31] Lyric afflatus attends Carraway's style of speech. Sufficiently to trace the ellipse, as it conditions the rhythms of Carraway's prose more generally, would I believe be to recover the class antagonisms that divide his voice, lodging them in that last instance among the tangled and layered contradictions immanent in the abrupt generalization of the commodity form during the first decades of twentieth century—a period during which, "more and more of the activities of living [came] to be strained through the bars of the dollar sign."[32]

I offer the above as both a reading and an articulation of theory: the ellipses in Carraway's voice, while historically specific, also figure the doubled brokenness immanent (theoretically) in the commodity form. To pursue the principle of ellipsis is, as Herbert Marcuse notes of contradiction itself, "not to displace the actual identity of the thing"—be that thing money, voice, proper name or text, "but [to] produce this identity in the form of a process in which the potentiality of things unfold."[33] Volosinov offers a linguistic route to thing and person experienced as "potential" and "process," or to what Marx identifies as the moving contradictions, immanent as "forms of concealment" (labor, commodity, and price)[34] within Capital's realization of value. Plainly, contradiction, understood through ellipsis, amounts to an "undeveloped experience," resulting in an "ephemeral and haphazard" sense that what is, is also what is not[35]—a troubled feeling that has yet to become an idea. Volosinov identifies such intimations within language as "ideological scraps": emphasizing that they are difficult to detect, he casts them as, "miscarriages of social orientation, novels without heroes, performances without audiences."[36] Yet, it remains important to recognize that even occurrences, "at the very edge of semantic availability,"[37] remain "wholly a product of social interaction" forming from "a constant struggle of accents,"[38] even where those accents are realized through inflection, hesitation, and whisper. To dwell on the "theoretical" aspect of ellipsis as an exposure of semantic edges and abutments risks reducing Marx's insistence on language as "practical consciousness" which occurs in the throats of its users, and not merely in the minds of its theorists.

The struggle for Volosinov remains inextricable from an expanding economic base: "[n] ew aspects of existence ... once they make contact with the human word and human emotion"[39] do not coexist peacefully within prior semantic formulations. Rather, in re-evaluative disputes, words—ever "two-sided act[s]"[40]—are "torn apart by .... living contradictions."[41] At which point, the ellipsis within the contradiction may be recast as "a generative [semantic] process," occurring between structurally driven antagonistic accents, whereby meaning is traceably modified to the degree that, "nothing ... could be said to be absolutely fixed."[42] I would stress that "unfixing" here partakes of no laudatory vitalism:[43] instead, semantic volatility emerges from specifiable contradictions, which contradictions "clash in historical time," and accordingly seize and are the "seizures of unique historical instants."[44]

"1971" might stand as one such instant of historical seizure, although, like all such instants, it trails antecedents and projects consequences. In 1971, in the midst of what Robert Brenner characterizes as "the long downturn ... [and] descent into crisis" of U.S. manufacture (1965–73), the Nixon administration ended the Bretton Woods agreement that had linked the value of the dollar to a golden equivalent.[45] By closing the "gold window" and floating the U.S. dollar, Nixon was able to devalue its worth against other global currencies in a sequence of depreciations, thereby nominally aiding U.S. manufacturing competitiveness, while pursuing "an ultra-expansionist monetary policy."[46] But given the stagnancy of American manufacture, and the downward pressure on commodity prices attendant on increased international competition (from Germany and Japan), the freshened flows of dollar liquidity (credit) did not tend toward production. Caught in "the enigma of capital," whereby yesterday's profit or loan must be tomorrow's investment, much of the newly created money supply fled offshore.[47] U.S. transnational corporations, aided by their banking arrangements, invested heavily in foreign exchange trading, or joined "the irregulated recycling of petrodollars into practically unlimited loans for Third (and Second) World countries."[48] In the latter form, dollar-denominated global liquidity, as money at a price, yielded rent on money lent, or money made from money.

> As a result of these mutually reinforcing developments, by the mid 1970s the volume of purely monetary transactions carried out in offshore money markets exceeded the value of world trade many times over. From then on the financial expansion became unstoppable.[49]

If money obliterates its sources, money made from money, or in "purely monetary transactions," must compound that occlusion. During the 1970s, freed from gold as limit, the U.S. dollar, deployed by the state in almost "unlimited quantities"[50] to counter industrial decline, took the prevalent form of credit money; that is to say, money released from constraint either by a metallic measure, or by the requirement that its worth be pre-validated. Alain Lipietz draws a distinction between real and credit monies, the former representing "finished labor," the latter "value in process" or value as "anticipated realization."[51] Credit money can play the part of real money only for so long, before an absence of delivery on anticipation—or as deployed in a U.S. manufacturing base incapable of producing competitive goods at an average rate of profit—it loses credibility. At which point, it goes elsewhere (offshore into finance), or confronts its own status as a written symbol, neither good as gold, nor adequate measure of labor satisfactorily undertaken. Both options, occurring together, go some way to explain the serious monetary upheavals of the 1970s: six years of dollar devaluations (1972–78), a decade of accelerating inflation, and a consequent "major crisis of confidence in the U.S. dollar as a viable world money"[52]—all despite an overabundance of liquid capital at a loss for sufficient rates of return.

If social synthesis under capital should necessarily be located within the exchange relation, and that relation, in an historically specific seizure (1971–79), promotes a certain incredulity as to its index of value, might not that measure (exchange relation) seem simultaneously all important, and yet of no lasting importance? At such times, times of acute monetary uncertainty, the equating effect (or system of impossible equivalencies from within whose combined abstractions capital's value forms), may count more only to count less. Either way, counting will prove both prevalent and subject to doubt, creating a particular form of semantic volatility. Arjun Appadurai, writing in the wake of the global meltdown (2009), proposes that:

> In the course of the last century (but especially since 1970 or so), the machinery for measuring, modeling, managing, predicting, commoditizing, and exploiting risk has become the central diacritic of modern capitalism. Financial markets lead and shape other markets, financial capital vastly outstrips manufacturing or industrial capital, financial policymakers dominate global economic policy, and major economic crises are produced and prolonged by the runaway growth of risk instruments, markets and creative legal and accounting devices.[53]

Appadurai takes risks and the derivative—an instrument for the monetization of risk that allows "a small set of actors to take risks on risks," to the greater profit of a few[54]—as the object of his study. Derivative deals did indeed constitute the primary market and motor for the U.S. economy between 2000 and the Crunch.[55] I seek, however, to locate the "calculative habitus" underlying a "cultural disposition" orientated to price,[56] and through price to number, in an earlier phase of financialization—during the 1970s—when credit money first began to overwhelm the system with surplus, causing nonfinancial corporations to fly from a stagnating productive sector into the sphere of circulation, where profit in the "quasi world of money" might be made from what Costas Lapavitsas calls, "moneyness."[57]

What briefly is the quality of "moneyness" under such conditions and in such a moment? For Sohn-Rethel, the exchange abstraction (an abstraction already described as resulting from a series of compounded equivalencies, each essential, each impossible) dispenses with the empirical realities of time and space, "admit[ing] only of quantitative differentiation."[58] Accordingly, number registers quantity as it subsumes quality: or, as Sohn-Rethel puts it:

> the comparatives of 'more' and 'less' used in a deal of exchange do not imply a quantitative comparison between say, tons of coal and reams of paper, or of acres of land and yards of linen. The interrelational equation posited by an act of exchange leaves all dimensional measurements behind and establishes a sphere of non-dimensional quantity. This is the pure or abstract quality of cardinal numbers with nothing to define it but the relation of greater than (>) or smaller than (<) or equal to (=) some other quantity as such.[59]

As coal, paper, land, and linen, arguably liable to trail the record of their making, give way to tradeable exchange rates and equity prices, so "a physicality of the abstract,"[60] concretized through number, further displaces place, person, thing, or at least appears to do so. As finance pervades, expanding the work of abstraction, its impersonal, indifferent, and quantificatory measures, flowing through persons as lived but unthinkable or under-thought practices, subject language (as "practical consciousness") to the form of those practices whose primary imperative, in times of finance, needs must be price made from price. From money made from money, under the sign of price prime (or price$^2$), take language made from language, under the sign of number. At a loss for a reference or, better, given the supposed retreat of those contradictions generative of semantic density (the material of reference), language begins hypertrophically to refer only to itself. Such accounting, at the level of theory, gives rise to the post-structuralist turn, which slips signifier under signifier to the atrophy of the referent.[61]

Walter Abish, an author emphatically of the post-structuralist moment, apt to his moment and its incipient habit of calculation, transforms reading into counting by having the narrator of "In So Many Words" (1975) literally count the words that are "so many," in a manner that admits primarily of "quantitative differentiation." His story starts "60," a number that changes to "93" at the close of the first section—an explicable increase as soon as one realizes that the first italicized section anticipates the second: its words, ordered alphabetically, preempt the words of the second section, minus 33. Contraction occurs because recurrent terms (like "the" [16], "that" [4], "also" [2]) are represented only once. Given that the story consists of 160 sections (or 80 paired units), each prefaced by a number (its word count), counting accompanies reading at all points; indeed, characters within the story count and incline to number:

> 48
>
> American an and as bedroom bliss counting distance divides eight 8 extension 5 flat floor 4 grip had her horizontal in is joy line lips mean-time of I pacing prairie pride 7 she 6 soon steps take that the then thin 3 toward turns 2 was will window.
>
> 71
>
> In the meantime she was pacing the floor. The flat thin horizontal line that divides her thin lips is an extension of the distant horizon line in the prairie. She is counting, 1, 2, 3, 4, 5, 6, 7, 8, as she takes eight steps toward the bedroom ... soon her hands will grip the American joy, the American bliss, the American pride.[62]

She who counts to "8," though once silently, paces the floor of an eighth-floor apartment: her pattern (first 8 sounded, second 8 silent) exactly reverses the structural count of her story, where the reader's articulation of the first italicized instance of the 80 units (each sans syntax) presumably and rapidly falls silent. Note that "8" laid sideways amounts to the infinity sign, a re-angling prompted by "the flat thin line,"—a lineation that depends on "division" (by 2) and extends an inestimable distance. Distance, in this instance, proves less temporal and spatial than numerical, since it tacitly begs the question, "How many recurrent 8-counts can a single ellipse (3 dots) take, even when cut short by 'soon'?" She who paces anonymously does so in anticipation of a parting of her lips to admit in sequence three male members at the story's close. The narrator, not one of the three, though a prior partner, himself turns numerical in the next twinned unit:

> 83
>
> This is an introduction to the first person. I am sitting on the third barstool from the left.
>
> *(p. 82)*

The initial sentence, partially repeated four times during the story, in that it immediately follows "83," prompts the digitalization of "first," which, in turn, transfigures the first person pronoun ("I am"), and renders the barstool one of an arithmetical series, to which the narrator's account of the bartender's hands adds another ("Crack, crack, crack the sound of American working class knuckles [p. 83]). Figuring attends the narrator's subsequent account of the woman's gifts, given to a sequence of lovers: having been among their number, he "made a tidy bundle":

> 46
>
> I'm not complaining. I have a competent broker. Keep it up, he advised me. It was the American password. Keep it up. I'll try, I said gamely, although I preferred fucking George. I'll try, and bought 24,000 shares of Commonwealth Oil at an unusual low, 2¼.
> *(p. 84)*

A high number (24,000) at a low price (2¼) not only renders the count financial, but grants that which is "kept up" an economic profile: in the context of "password," coded for computer use by the two previous titles in the collection—"Read-Only Memory" (a storage file) and "Access" (a click, typically following a partially or fully numerical code)—that which rises, or indeed falls, responds to market graphics. Since the narrator twice characterizes "America's paranoia" as "fear of the limp prick" (p. 81), and the woman's "grip" as "accustomed to taking possession of perfection" (p. 80), we may assume that her triple grip on the national, "joy ... bliss ... pride" (p. 82), "one then two then three" (p. 97) at the story's conclusion, grasps high ("perfect") rather than low ("imperfect") numbers.

Innuendo functions oddly here. Typically, as clarified by D.A. Miller, the promiscuously prolific connotations of innuendo "excite the desire for proof" in denotative form—a glimpse of the "fluorescent literality" of the sexual scene, sustainedly conjured but finally undelivered by the connotative register.[63] Since Abish punctuates "In So Many Words" with "wangs," "fucks," "pricks," and "mouths," what remains to be seen? If innuendo (pervasive in the story) yields a doubled sign—which both is and is not that to which it refers—the consequent split referents divide, here, to occlude not members, but eroticized numbers. Accordingly, aggregates of abstract units emerge as the dirty secret invited by the reading experience, which aggregates are further monetized by the collection's title (*In the Future Perfect*). Credit monies operate in the future perfect, underpinning the volatile liquidity of the 1970s with a statistical certainty that surplus value *will* be realized. Liquidity's ample issuance, in a time of high finance, forces "prediction into being,"[64] realizing being itself as a "pseudo-concreteness,"[65] sedimented from anticipation. Actuality, infused with "moneyness," requires retroactive valorization if it is to add up to the perfection latent in its anticipated price. My reading of "In So Many Words" rests on a network of quasi-cabalistic allegorical recuperations extending from an initial bid that casts number as price prime, and lodges the "calculative habitus" of price prime within linguistic practice. As a coda, and borrowing from Walter Benjamin's *The Origin of German Tragic Drama* (1925), I shall ghost a bare case for the claim that an impulse to allegory exists as a formal imperative immanent in the structure of finance capital.

Benjamin deals with literary responses to the Thirty Years War, and arguably, by extension to the Weimar.[66] Those on whom he comments confront a fallen world marked "impermanent" by historical catastrophe. For Benjamin, allegory renders the ruins runic:

> In allegory the observer is confronted with the *facies hippocratica* of history, as a petrified primordial landscape. Everything about history that, from the very beginning, has been untimely, sorrowful, unsuccessful, is expressed in a face – or rather in a death's head....

> This is the heart of the allegorical way of seeing, of the baroque, secular explanation of history as the Passion of the world. The greater the significance, the greater the subjection to death, because death digs most deeply the jagged line of demarcation between physical nature and significance.[67]

Where reality is hollowed out by death, and any sense of intrinsic meaning has been evacuated, the allegorist abridges loss by the arbitrary introduction of emblematic significances. For "ruin" read "rune."[68] From the "remnant" take "voluptuous... significance."[69] On the fragment write "captions."[70] Benjamin's allegorists mourn the dead things that cause them grief, but do so with disrespect, since "[a]ny person, any object, any relationship can [to them] mean absolutely anything else."[71]

Dates are difficult, but certainly at some point between 1923 and 1926, Benjamin wrote of "the man in the street," that "money... brings him into perceived contact with things."[72] Arguably, such contact may founder for a variety of reasons: for the great Lutheran dramatists of the baroque, or so Benjamin argues, Luther's conviction that good works did not add up to Grace, "deprived human actions... of all value." Works and their objects, accordingly, yielded "for those who looked deep[est].... Something new... an empty world."[73] Suppose, for persons on the street in the Weimar, and for their theorist ("who looked deeper"), money, rather than Lutheran faith, forms the perceptual bridge between persons and things: might not "an empty world," arising from a very different source, prompt a linked aesthetic reaction? Benjamin suggests as much via his work on Baudelaire. In *The Arcades Project*, Benjamin notes that Baudelaire "ascribes the experience of allegory to... the experience of the commodity,"[74] specifying that, for Baudelaire, "allegory corresponds perfectly to the commodity fetish,"[75] which fetish, for Benjamin, involves "the assimilation of living to dead matter."[76] The comments, though addressed to Baudelaire (and in a further instance, to Flaubert), owe much to Marx for whom the commodity fetish turns famously on "the definite social relations between men... assuming the fantastic form of a relation between things."[77] From person to thing, with each element leaving some pieces of itself in its opposed term, thereby creating, "*material* relations between *persons* and ***social*** relations between ***things***."[78] Benjamin identifies the violence inherent in the transposition, noting, care of Baudelaire, "[s]adism and fetishism intertwine in those imaginations that seek to annex all organic life to the sphere of the inorganic."[79] To "seek" may not be to "achieve": Marx's term "fantastic" bespeaks a trick, one attended by "metaphysical subtleties," "theological niceties," "strange[ness]," and "enigma."[80] Confronted with the mid-nineteenth-century Parisian market as an *apparently* "inorganic sphere," littered with *seemingly* "dead matter," Benjamin's Baudelaire, for whom "[e]verything ... becomes allegory,"[81] "broods," and "rummages," trying on meaning as commodities try on prices, there being, "no traceable mediation between the two," where "the two" refers to a lack of mediation between "meaning and image," as between "merchandise and price tag." Consequently, for Benjamin's allegorist, "the modes of meaning fluctuate almost as rapidly as the price of commodities." Casting "price" as the "meaning" or "soul" of the commodity, and therefore as the focus both of the allegorist's "broodings," and of his desires as they attach to the fetish,[82] Benjamin gnomically insists, "[a]n inferno rages in the soul of the commodity, for all the seeming tranquility lent it by the price." He adds, as though to catch the quality of the "tranquil inferno," that "[i]n the final analysis, the image of petrified unrest called up by allegory is a[n] historical image."[83] Given that "allegory corresponds perfectly to the commodity fetish," one might identify "petrified unrest" as an affect shared both by Baudelaire's allegory and by Marx's fetish. In fact, that which exists in a state of "petrified unrest" is neither "dead" nor "inorganic": restlessness implies the residual presence of a body within the body of the fetish (as perhaps in the allegorical text), ready to burst out and enflame, annulling the form of its host.

Writing to Benjamin in 1940, about his work on the Baroque, Adorno locates the source of unrest: addressing "reification" (a term largely avoided by Marx, but nonetheless related to the transubstantiation of person and thing), he argues that reification is always attended by forgetting: "objects become thing-like, the moment they are retained for us without the continued presence of their other aspects: when something of them has been forgotten."[84] Since price, the acme of the fetish form, "obliterates" and renders "invisible" the "specific attributes" and "real elements" of the reproduction that it represents,[85] price fetishism might be said to promote amnesia over production, and more particularly over work (or better, abstract labor time) as value's source within capitalist accumulation. To forget so much is to empty the world of value.

Whereas the seventeenth-century baroque dramatist, for Benjamin, encounters a world "subject to death," and so absent of significance, Benjamin's Baudelaire, wandering through "Paris, the capital of the nineteenth century," encounters something equally new and empty, though emptied and mortified by different forces—the work of price, which work remains, for him, incomplete. Witness Benjamin's sense that in Baudelaire's poetry, "the image of the woman and the image of death intermingle in a third: that of Paris": by implication, just as the prostitute remains a death's head *and* a working woman, so the city, imbricated in her body, bifurcates—at once "death-fraught idyll" (or price) and "social… substrate" (or labor power congealed into "topographical formation").[86] In Marx's terms, the occlusion of labor by price remains incomplete, yielding, therefore, a doubled body, though the tension inherent in such duplicity may *appear* to lessen in time of capital flight into finance, for which flight Marx provides a prescient shorthand via his account of "fictitious capital."

As rent on money lent (or money made from money), "fictitious capital" effectively doubles the erasures inherent in the monetary form. "Pregnant" with itself, or "self-reproducing and self-expanding,"[87] and so without passage through production or consumption, finance capital amounts to the fetish-squared. Under the sign of "Price-Compounded," and endogamous in the degree to which it contains nothing but itself, "fictitious capital"—in Benjamin's terms—empties the world, preparing not merely "a paper graveyard," apt to allegorical purpose,[88] but proposing price itself as the ur-allegorical sign. The measure of price's allegorical productivity is the degree to which it renders production truly (though only and ever, apparently) invisible. "Fictitious capital" yields a world of appearances for which labor has no value beyond irritant (in its migratory, unemployable, or riotous forms), and price alone makes matter matter, thereby transforming linguistic matter (or semantics) after its own image into the arbitrary and allegorical sign. Of course, viewed from the perspective of labor's structural centrality to value, neither language nor price *can* be arbitrary, since both signifier and monetary terms are products of social relations in process. As a result, their materialities, however occluded, remain motivated: far from arbitrary, each residually indexes those relations that it assumes if only to cast off. Stated aphoristically, labor abides, though during the seizure of a financialized instant, it abides at great distance—in the expanding realm of non-understanding as it emerges from market acts to snag our thoughts and words: perhaps so far behind the back of consciousness that the possibility of reference seemingly recedes, acceding to the arbitrary signs of allegoresis. So read, allegory, in times of high finance, amounts to "an historical image" and index of the degree to which the real abstractions of price prime prove for a time pervasive.

## Notes

1 Karl Marx and Fredrick Engels, *The German Ideology*, ed. C.J. Arthur (London: Lawrence & Wishart, 1982), p. 51.
2 V. N. Volosinov, *Marxism and the Philosophy of Language*, trans., Ladislaz Matejka and I. R. Titnuk (New York: Seminar Press, 1973), p. 93.
3 *Ibid.*, p. 90.
4 M. M. Bakhtin, quoted by I. R. Titnuk, "Appendix II: The Formal Method and the Sociological Method (M.M. Baxtin, P. N. Medvedev, and V. N. Volosinov) in Russian Theory and Study of Literature," *Marxism and the Philosophy of Language*, p. 199.
5 Karl Marx, *Capital,* Vol. 1, trans., Ben Fowkes (London: Penguin, 1976), pp. 163–4.
6 *Ibid.*, p. 163.
7 *Idem.*
8 Moishe Postone, *Time, Labor and Social Domination* (Cambridge: Cambridge University Press, 2003), p. 139.
9 *Idem.*
10 For "abstract labor" and "abstract labor time," see Marx, *Capital,* Vol. 1, pp. 127–30.
11 The phrase is taken from Alfred Sohn Rethel, *Intellectual and Manual Labor: A Critique of Epistemology* (MacMillan: London, 1978), p. 20. See also Louis Althusser, "Cremonini, Painter of the Abstract," collected in his *Lenin and Philosophy and Other Essays,* trans., Ben Brewster (London: Monthly Review Press, 1971), p. 231. See also Alberto Toscano, "Materialism without Matter; Abstraction, Absence and Social Form," *Textual Practice,* Vol. 28, No. 7 (2014), pp. 1221–40, and, "The Open Secret of Real Abstraction," *Rethinking Marxism,* Vol. 20, No. 2 (2008), pp. 273–87. Toscano pursues the sources and implications of Etienne Balibar's observation, "Marx's Materialism Has Nothing to Do with Reference to Matter," *The Philosophy of Marx*, trans., Chris Turner (London: Verso, 2014), p. 23.
12 For the passage from "surplus labor" to "surplus value," see Marx, *Capital,* Vol. 1, Chapter 9, "The Role of Surplus Value," pp. 320–39.
13 Jacques Rancière, "The Concept and the Critique of Political Economy: From the *1844 Manuscripts* to *Capital*," collected in *Reading Capital: The Complete Edition*, Louis Althusser, Etienne Balibar, Pierre Macherey and Jacques Rancière, trans., Ben Brewster and David Fernback (London: Verso, 2015), p. 121.
14 *Ibid*, p. 112. Rancière's hieroglyphics gloss those of Marx,

> by equating their different products to each other as exchange values, they equate their different kinds of labor as human labor. They do this without being aware of it. Value, therefore, does not have its description branded on its forehead: it rather transforms every product of labor into a social hieroglyphic.
>
> Capital, *Vol. I, pp. 166–7*

15 Sohn-Rethel, *Intellectual and Manual Labor,* p. 41.
16 See Toscano's account of Rethel, "Materialism without Matter," pp. 1227.
17 Sohn-Rethel, *Intellectual and Manual Labor,* p. 33.
18 *Ibid.*, p. 45.
19 For "abstract labor time," see Marx, *Capital,* Vol. 1, pp. 140–63.
20 *Ibid.*, p. 149.
21 Sohn Rethel, *Intellectual and Manual Labor,* p. 48. See also, p. 25.
22 Marx argues that money renders invisible the specific attributes of that from which it may be thought to rise. See *Capital,* Vol. 1, p. 205.
23 See Malcolm Bull, *Seeing Things Hidden: Apocalypse, Vision and Totality* (London: Verso, 2000), p. 293.
24 Marx, *Capital,* Vol. 1, p. 209. David Harvey catches the centrality of motion to value when he writes of *Capital* as offering, "a broader and broader understanding of the [antagonistic] internal relations that keep capital in a perpetual state of contradictory unity and therefore, in perpetual motion." *A Companion to Marx's* Capital (London: Verso, 2010), p. 26.
25 Marx, *Capital,* Vol. 1, p. 209.
26 *Idem.*
27 Marx, *Capital,* Vol. 1, p. 198. True cognates, 'ellipse" and "ellipsis" both derive from the Greek, "to come short." In the case of the geometrical figure ("ellipse"), a plane bisecting a cone "comes short" of the angle of the cone, forming an ellipse along the edge of the intersection. "Ellipsis,"

similarly names a verbal incompletion. As late as the nineteenth century, the two words were sometimes used interchangeably. In presenting his formulae for the circuit of money capital ("M—C…P…C$^{1}$—M$^{1}$") Marx uses "dots [to] indicate that the circulation process is interrupted" (*Capital,* Vol. 2 [London: Penguin, 1991], p. 109). I am thankful to Joshua Clover, Devan Bailey and Andrea Henderson for their advice re: the ellipse/ellipsis distinction.

28 I take the phrases "semantic impertinence" and "seeing relationally" from Paul Ricoeur, "The Metaphorical Process as Cognition, Imagination and Feeling," *Critical Inquiry*, Vol. 5 (Autumn, 1978), pp. 145, 148. To read Ricoeur's concern for meaning, "depicted under the feature of the ellipsis" (p. 151) through Marx, might be to cast price as a primary agent of ellipse. In *Grundrisse,* Marx describes money as, "a highly energetic solvent." (Penguin, London, 1993), p. 507.

29 F. Scott Fitzgerald, *The Great Gatsby* (New York: Scribners, 2004), p. 120. Punctuation as in the original.

30 *Idem.*, p. 176.

31 *Culpepper's Compleat Herbal* (London: W. Forulsham, 1653).

32 Robert and Helen Lynd, *Middletown* (London: New York: Harcourt & Brace, 1929), pp. 80–1.

33 Herbert Marcuse, *Reason and Revolution: Hegel and the Rise of Social Theory* (London: Routledge, 1973), p. 124.

34 Rancière, *Reading Capital, the Complete Edition*, p. 107.

35 Volosinov, *Marxism and the Philosophy of Language,* p. 92.

36 *Idem.*

37 Raymond Williams, *Marxism and Literature* (Oxford: Oxford University Press, 1977), p. 134. For Williams' response to Volosinov, and his account of the semantic valencies of "social experiences in solution," see particularly Chapter 3, "Language" (pp. 21–44), and Chapter 9, "Structures of Feeling" (pp. 128–35).

38 Volosinov, *Marxism and the Philosophy of Language*, p. 93.

39 *Ibid.,* p.106.

40 *Ibid.,* p. 86.

41 *Ibid.,* p. 106.

42 *Idem.*

43 Volosinov's concern to derive semantics from antagonistic accents might usefully be contrasted with Gilles Deleuze and Felix Guattari's account of the "tensor" or "atypical expression," as typical of linguistic variation:

> the tensor … causes language to tend towards the limit of its elements, forms or notions, towards a near side or beyond of language … [in a] kind of transitivization of the phrase, causing the last term to react on the preceding term, back through the entire chain.
>
> *Deluze and Guattari,*
> A Thousand Plateaus, *trans., Brian Massumi*
> *(London: Bloomsbury, 2014 [originally 1988]), p. 116*

44 Frederic Jameson, *Valences of the Dialectic* (Verso: London, 2009), p. 120.

45 Robert Brenner, *The Economics of Global Turbulence, New Left Review*, No. 229 (May/June, 1998), p. 95.

46 Robert Brenner, *The Boom and the Bubble: The U.S. in the World Economy* (Verso: London, 2002), p. 27. Brenner refers to the ending of pegged exchange rates as a "turning point" and "pivotal shift."

47 David Harvey, *The Enigma of Capital and the Crises of Capitalism* (Profile Books: London, 2010). Harvey defines the "enigma" as a capital suplus absorption problem.

> In the absence of any limits or barriers, the need to reinvest in order to remain a capitalist propels capital to expand at a compound rate. This then creates a perpetual need to find new fields of activity to absorb the reinvested capital.
>
> *(p. 45)*

48 Giovanni Arrighi, *The Long Twentieth Century* (Verso: London, 2002), p. 299. Arrighi cites the following estimates: foreign exchange trading (1979) $17.5 trillion; total value of world trade (1979) $1.5 trillion. Or, and also in 1979, yearly transactions in the London Eurodollar market (temporary parking place for much of U.S. capital, seeking something financial to do) exceeded the value of world trade by a factor of 6. By 1986, that factor stood at 25 (p. 299).

49 *Idem.*

50 Ricardo Parboni, quoted by Arrighi, *The Long Twentieth Century*, p. 308.
51 Alain Lipietz, *The Enchanted Realm: Inflation, Credit and the World Crisis*, trans., Ian Patterson (London: Verso 1985), pp. 84–92.
52 Arrighi, *The Long Twentieth Century*, p. 317.
53 Arjun Appadurai, *Banking on Words* (Chicago, IL: University of Chicago Press, 2016), p. 44.
54 *Ibid.*, p. 125.
55 See Gérard Duménil and Dominique Lévy, *The Crisis of Neoliberalism* (London: Harvard University Press, 2011), pp. 110–12.
56 Appadurai, *Banking on Words*, p. 135.
57 Costas Lapavitsas, *Profiting without Producing: How Finance Exploits Us All* (London: Verso, 2013), pp. 16, 55.
58 Sohn-Rethel, *Intellectual and Manual Labor*, p. 57.
59 *Ibid.*, p. 47
60 *Ibid.*, p. 57.
61 See Joshua Clover, "Value / Theory / Crisis," *PMLA*, Vol. 27, No. 1 (January, 2012), p. 112. Foundational post-structuralist works were either written or gained traction during the 1970s: Derrida's *Of Grammatology* originally published in 1967, was first translated in 1976. Baudrillard wrote the essays collected in *For a Critique of the Political Economy of the Sign* during the late 1960s and early 1970s. Deleuze and Guattari's, *Anti-Oedipus: Capitalism and Schizophrenia* appeared first in 1972, followed two years later by Lyotard's *Libidinal Economy*.
62 Walter Abish, *In the Future Perfect* (London: Faber, 1984), p. 82. Originally published, 1975. With reference to Abish, subsequent pagination will refer to this edition, and will be included in the body of the essay.
63 D. A. Miller, "Anal Rope," *Representations*, Vol. 32 (Fall, 1990), p. 123.
64 Lauren Berlant, *Cruel Optimism* (Durham, NC: Duke University Press, 2011), p. 70.
65 Lipietz, *The Enchanted World*, p. 62.
66 See Eugene Lunn, *Marxism and Modernism* (London: Verso, 1982), pp. 184–7.
67 Walter Benjamin, *The Origin of German Tragic Drama*, trans., John Osborne (London: New Left Books, 1977), p. 166.
68 *Ibid.*, pp. 177, 176.
69 *Ibid.*, p. 184.
70 *Ibid.*, p. 185.
71 *Ibid.*, p. 175.
72 Benjamin, "These Surfaces for Rent," collected in his, *The Work of Art in the Age of Its Technological Reproducibility* (Cambridge, MA: Belknap Press, 2008), p. 173.
73 Benjamin, *The Origin of German Tragic Drama*, pp. 138–9.
74 Walter Benjamin, *The Arcades Project*, trans., Howard Eiland and Kevin McLaughlin (Cambridge, MA: Harvard U. P., 1999), [J66, 2], p. 346.
75 *Ibid.*, [J 79a, 4], p. 368.
76 *Ibid.*, [J 71, 3], p. 354.
77 Marx, *Capital*, Vol. 1, p. 165.
78 *Ibid.*, p. 166. Emphasis mine.
79 Benjamin, *The Arcades Project*, [J 71, 3], p. 354.
80 Marx, *Capital*, Vol. 1, pp. 164, 165.
81 Benjamin, "Paris, Capital of the Nineteenth Century: Exposé (of 1939)," collected in *The Arcades Project*, p. 21. As an epigraph to the section, "Baudelaire, or the Streets of Paris," Benjamin quotes from "Le Cynge" (Baudelaire), "Everything for me becomes allegory."
82 All references to the allegorist as "brooding" on the relation between meaning and price are taken from *The Arcades Project*, [J 80, 2; J 80a, 1], pp. 368–9.
83 *Ibid.*, [J 78a, 2], p. 366.
84 Theodore Adorno and Walter Benjamin, *The Complete Correspondence, 1928–1940*, trans., Nicholas Walter (London: Polity Press, 1999), p. 321.
85 Karl Marx, *Capital*, Vol. 3 (London: Lawrence and Wishart, 1984), p. 393.
86 Walter Benjamin, "Paris the Capital of the Nineteenth Century," in his, *The Work of Art in the Age of its Technological Reproducibility*, p. 105.
87 Marx, *Capital*, Vol. 3, pp. 393, 394.
88 Johann Christian Hallmann, quoted by Benjamin, *The Origin of German Tragic Drama*, p. 231, note.

# PART II

# Histories

# 6
# PREMODERN ECONOMICS
## Ideas, literature, and contexts

*Andrew Galloway*

Before the printing press, before professional theaters (featuring secular drama and professional actors attended by paying audiences), before living writers were identified as "authors" or "poets" (both of which terms were reserved in the Middle Ages to ancient or at least dead writers)—before the development of a fully monetary economy and expansive global consumerism, whose foundations become unmistakable by the sixteenth century, we find a world where both "economics" and "literature" occupied roles that will seem strange to us. From the sixteenth century on, treatises on "economics" in French, Dutch, and English were written and printed for general audiences, culminating in 1776 with Adam Smiths' monumental *Wealth of Nations* (see Monroe 1923; Courtemanche 2011). Before that, however, discussions of material economics were folded into writings on Christian ethics and moral theology, usually in Latin, by and for academics and other clerics (for medieval academic faculty were always clerics, though not necessarily priests, monks, or friars). The most explicit medieval discussions of material exchanges appeared amid considerations of fraud, faith, and justice, where medieval academics investigated, sometimes in detail, the ethics of worldly exchanges, but implicitly as part of the vast and dangerous *saeculum* of transient worldly treasure and sinful human appetites, all contrasted with the infinite treasury of heaven. Medieval literature often supplied even more trenchant and many-sided perspectives on the principles of economies and society, sometimes in as closely focused ethical arguments as those by the academics. At the core of both kinds of presentations were fascinations with piety and deadly sin, mingled with maintenance of an increasingly complex social hierarchy.

This might seem unpromising material for modern inquiry into economics *or* literature. But it provides a good opportunity to rethink concepts and categories we take for granted—and might force us to imagine a wider framework than modern Literature or Economics or History departments and specializations usually encourage. Certainly, the medieval domains of both academic and poetic production press us to ponder how ethics might still be crucial to economic theory and practice. What price was truly just, at any given moment or transaction, and how would merchants or civic or clerical authorities know? Was pricing even in sinful transactions, like prostitution, governed by principles of justice? What kind and amount of need, what begging, was legitimate? When was poverty great enough to free someone from legal persecution for theft of provisions? What interest could be charged on loans of money—if any? What profit was legitimate, and how might the intention rather than the material outcome factor into that?

All these topics, which encompass a long tradition of reconsideration of economics and society after western culture restarted intellectual and literate traditions following the cascading fall of Rome and its empire in the early fourth century, began with the monks, friars, and other "secular" male clerics (celibate or not) who filled the medieval universities between the twelfth and the sixteenth centuries (see Baldwin 1970; Langholm 1992, 1998). But academic commentaries and debates were not the only vectors of such discussions. Throughout the Middle Ages, poetry, both in a long and rich tradition of Latin—restarting much earlier than the invention of universities in the twelfth century and flourishing through all the centuries of western medieval culture—and in all the "vernacular" languages (that is, the ancestors of all modern languages of England and Europe), also addressed what we call economics. Often, to be sure, like the academic commentaries, discussions of economics in medieval literature presented abuses in the earthly economy as horrifying but interesting depths of sin, including the dark sides of a money economy of credit and debit that we take for granted. Consider charging interest on a loan, which even now can be called "usury" if the interest is high enough. Although moneylending for profit was common from the twelfth century on when trade, towns, and currency exchanges grew in significance, there is a long tradition both in literature and medieval economic theory behind Dante's location of usurers in the deepest part of the seventh circle of hell, among fraud and injustice, in his *Divine Comedy* (finished 1320). Dante's guide through hell, Virgil, reminds the narrator that man, after expulsion from the Garden of Eden, must earn his bread by the sweat of his brow. "If you remember Genesis at the beginning, it behooves man to gain his bread and to prosper. But because the usurer takes another way, he contemns Nature in herself and in her follower, for he puts his hope elsewhere" (*Inf.* 11.106–11). When Dante, the Pilgrim, sees the usurers, they are sitting in pain on burning sand amid leaping flames, while "from the neck of each hung a pouch, which had a certain color and a certain device, and thereon each seems to feast his eyes": the emblems of the noble families from which they came, emblazoned on the moneybags they would hold at the public tables where they plied their trade (*Inf.* 17.52–7).

For the academic moralists too, usury was metaphysically fraudulent, and intrinsically unjust. Usurers offer money as if it were an object temporarily leased then returned in its original physical reality, like a horse, which would justify some payment for the use; but in fact giving money in a loan used it up, like a bottle of wine, which ought to be repaid with another bottle of wine of exactly the same value. Making a living from the loan of something used up by demanding more than what was loaned was theft, not honorable labor—and not even really labor at all, since the time of the loan determined the interest charged, during which the moneylender shed not a drop of sweat for his profit, as in Dante's biblical condemnation. As the Dominican theologian Thomas Aquinas argued in the 1260s, usury makes double use of the same money: both "sinking it in exchange" of a loan (giving coins to the borrower, which transfers all the use of those coins to the borrower), and also, illicitly, requiring a further payment for that perfectly just and equal exchange, attaching illicit strings (see Aquinas's *Summa Theologiae*, quaestio 78). To many medieval commentators on usury, a *mutuum* ("loan") means, as the pieces of that word show, that "meum" (mine) becomes "tuum" (yours), period. This widespread (but false) etymology shows that the medieval world was slow to conceive of the materially inert object of money triggering widening market consequences on its own. Just as there was no intrinsic assumption of a "state," enforcing and containing all transactions and taxes of land and other "immoveable" property (although the more personal idea of "lordship," then that of the king and king's law, supplied a version of that framework), so the idea that a "market" would operate through its own force or "invisible hand," uncontrolled by human or divine morality, was repellant, like allowing sexuality to run rampant. Indeed, allowing money to "work" day and night with a loan "begetting" interest through holidays and work days alike violated both Christian laws and nature's laws of procreation and reproduction. For Aquinas, drawing on Aristotle, usury was an incestuous "breeding of money" from "barren metal" in which "the offspring resembles the parent" (see *Politics*: book 1, chapter 10). Thus, Dante's guide, Virgil, asserts of the usurers that "the smallest ring seals with its mark both Sodom and Cahors," the latter city a well-known century of usury, the former the archetypal, biblical city of sodomy. The desire for such lawlessly productive and debilitating wealth was itself unnatural, as seen in the hungry gazes of Dante's usurers at the bags with their trademark emblems of Dante's Florentine Christian usurers.

Dante touring that circle of hell does not need to mention Jews, already damned by their religion (and increasing persecuted as a monetary economic expanded, as in being ordered to wear yellow stars of David by the Fourth Lateran Council of 1215). Besides, Jews were allowed to lend money to Christians by both Christian and Jewish laws—conveniently for Christian culture. Loans were essential from the highest political levels down to small-scale manufacturers, used as often in the countryside as in the cities. By the fourteenth century, however, English borrowers often had to rely on Christian moneylenders, since the Jews were driven out of England in 1290 in Edward I's economically ill-conceived "purification" of his nation (possibly from a religious vow when he feared death by fever) (Mundill 1998). In the late fourteenth century, one Christian London merchant became a major supplier of loans to everyone from women silk-weavers to members of the royal family to poets like Chaucer and Gower (see Galloway 2011). Chaucer's Merchant, it is thought partly modeled on that very individual, is satirically portrayed as preoccupied "with his bargaines and with his chevisaunce," the latter a term for "usury" (282).

As these crosscurrents suggest, intellectual and literary history is many-sided, its positions—driven by broadly identifiable social locations and traditions but also less predictable values and insights—dialectical. Not all medieval writers were so unsympathetic to the complexities of earthly economics. The late thirteenth-century treatise "on contracts" by the maverick Italian Franciscan Peter of John Olivi (died 1298, before Dante had even started his *Divine Comedy*) opens with its first challenge to any moral governance of the universal propensity for profit: is it licit to sell something for more than it is worth, or to buy it for less than it is worth? It seems that it is: because otherwise "almost the entire community of those selling and buying would be sinning against justice, because nearly everyone wants to sell high and buy low" (*fere tota communitas vendencium et emencium contra iusticiam peccaret, quia fere omnes volunt care vendere et pro vili emere*) (95). This seems the weary capitulation of a late thirteenth-century moralist surrounded by a robust commercial world (Peter died in Narbonne). But Peter goes on to refute it at a stroke: no one wants to have fraud committed on himself, so, by the golden rule, no one should commit fraud on another by market timing. Peter is clear that the slightest fraudulent intention makes any contract "internally" usurious, regardless of the "external" form of the contract (132–4). Yet Peter's ways of thinking, if not his settled thoughts, were ahead of his time in a number of ways. He was precocious in considering valid the idea of opportunity cost, for example, or risk (measuring with an exacting eye the balance between "uncertain" gain or loss from opportunity or risk, and the "certain" fees demanded by the lender) among reasons why, as "some say," it might well be legitimate for someone lending money to charge more than its initial cost (228–31; see also Langholm 1992: 346–73). He is also the first western writer to present the idea of "capital" as distinct from money, defining "a certain 'seminal reason' of profitability which we commonly call 'capital'" (*quamdam racionem seminalem lucri quam communiter* capitale *vocamus*).

Here is the beginning of a notion of "the market" as a presence, a spectral force unto itself. But it has deep roots. Peter's phrase resourcefully draws on a curious term from the early medieval theologian St. Augustine (c. 400), whose "seminal reasons" are the nubs of the future forms of every living thing that God created when he created the world, insuring life's future varieties as well as those made at the instant of creation (see Gilson 1960: 206–8; Langholm 1992: 371–2). Although Peter in the 1290s is discussing simply the power of anything one has been loaned or wholly owns to be used for productivity—an idea found in many medieval scholastic discussions of property, lands, and money—his use of Augustine's "seminal reasons" to define "capital" without any one human agency and lacking any moral condemnation of capital's productive power as such is uncannily modern, if not quite as specified as Adam Smith's idea of a given entrepreneur's "circulating capital which furnishes the materials and wages of labour, and puts industry into motion" (Smith II 1976: 309).

Taken piecemeal, however, many of Peter's ideas are not so different from the long tradition of scholastic economics. Consider Peter's initial challenge that "nearly everyone wants to sell high and buy low" (see Langholm 1992: 198–248; Torrell 2005). This is taken straight from Aquinas, who also refutes it (IIa IIae q77 a1). Aquinas, in turn, quoted the line, "fere omnes volunt care vendere et pro vili emere," (almost everyone wants to sell high and buy low) from Augustine, writing shortly after the sack of Rome and the disintegration of the Roman Empire (Augustine 1991: 346). Such a motto is neither poetry nor economic theory; yet through the hands of Augustine, Aquinas, and Peter of John Olivi, this "protocapitalist" idea is a palpable threat to any moral economy, certainly to the emphatically moralizing economics of the Middle Ages. What can treatments of it disclose about medieval responses to the impulses of self-interest, concerning which Adam Smith is so memorably succinct—"it is not from the benevolence of the butcher, the brewer, or the baker, that we expect our dinner, but from their regard to their own interest" (Smith I 1976: 18)?

Augustine's motto concerning economic self-interest, which winds through the entire medieval period, prompts three questions. First, how did medieval intellectuals respond to that notion? Second, how did poets—less constrained by professional Christian obligations—regard the notion, and indeed any economic practices? Finally, how did the entire Middle Ages make the "Great Transition" from precapitalist economics to the capitalism of modernity, where we accept the motto as an obvious universal principle, indeed an ethic we might feel ashamed to ignore in the web of our social interactions—unless, as the Marxist medieval historian Lawrin Armstrong suggests, we may find in medieval notions of a "moral economy" some resistance to our "increasingly 'insane forms' of fictitious capital to subsidize unlimited consumption and growth" (29)?

## Capitalism's joke: the triumph of buy low, sell high

When Augustine introduces the motto that Peter of John Olivi and Aquinas later gravely consider, he does so in a wry anecdote straight from the late imperial Rome of bread and circuses. In his *On the Trinity* (c. AD 415), in order to show that humanity has a deep desire to recognize its own "unanimity within the same living and reason-using nature," Augustine tells a story about a comedian (*mimus*) who promised his audience that at his next show, he would announce what they all wanted:

> So on the appointed day a greater crowd than usual came along full of great expectations, and as the silence and suspense grew he said, so the story goes, "You all want to buy cheap and sell dear." In this saying of a frivolous comedian all found their own self-awareness expressed, and in their admiration for his telling them so unexpectedly a truth that was as plain to all of them as their own noses, they warmly applauded him. Now why should his promise to tell them what they all wanted have aroused such great expectations, if not because a man is normally in the dark about the wishes of other men?
>
> *(Augustine 1991: 346)*

The example is one of Augustine's many entertaining uses of everyday experience and anecdote to make a philosophical and theological point. Augustine eventually gets to the problem of universal desires expressed in faith, but the *mimus*'s joke leads him into a brief and, for Augustine, rare but very influential excursus on economic theory. As he knew from basic dialectical training, every condition can be defined by its opposite. So Augustine immediately follows this story with cases that might contradict the comedian's principle. An heir of a large estate, he proposes, might recklessly sell his patrimony cheaply, but pay top price to satisfy his vices. In a more pious spirit, someone might offer a higher price than what is asked as an act of spontaneous economic justice. Here, Augustine introduced the term the "just price," a notion that was to have a long tradition in medieval thought:

> I myself know a man who was offered a codex for sale, and when he realized that the seller was ignorant of its real value was therefore asking for much too little, he gave him the just price [*iustum pretium*] which was far more than he expected.

This brief moment offers one basis for the entire late medieval discussion of the "just price" and the ideal of a moral economy (see Langholm 1992: 225–37). As Langholm shows, there are bases for this notion in the passages from Aristotle's *Nicomachean Ethics* (e.g. book 9, chapter 1) on which the medieval writers he discusses were commenting. Augustine is hardly ever concerned with the mechanisms of worldly economics, but the fact that he locates the discussion here in remarks on "justice" suggests that he has encountered the problems of economic fraud, justice, negotiation, and social benefit directly or indirectly from Aristotle (which Augustine would know in Greek; Aristotle was not entirely translated into Latin until the 1260s, just before Aquinas used his ideas). In the *Nicomachean Ethics* (book 5, chapter 5), Aristotle discussed money, prices, and usury under "justice," which, like all virtues in Aristotle, involves a balance or equity. Since trade between craftsmen making different kinds of things is necessary, money was invented as a common measure to equalize the "proportion" of value of one to another (or perhaps equalize the social importance of one *craftsman* to another: commentators continue to debate Aristotle's precise meaning here) (see Langholm 1992: 181–95). As usual, however, the Christian Augustine's contribution was not to the study of rational economic choices, as the Greek Aristotle's generally was, but to the more emotional and psychological wells beneath rational calculation—that is, the state of the soul—that might cause a wider variety of economic behavior.

Augustine's remarks on economics are very brief, but few later medieval theologians would be so inventive. This is apparent even in the long history of medieval scholastics seeing to neutralize the "raw market" principles enshrined in the sixth-century Roman "body of civil law" (*Corpus Iuris Civilis*) and Digest compiled under Emperor Justinian, used for public law on the Continent throughout the Middle Ages. There, the *Corpus Iuris* repeatedly implies that commodities can be sold for whatever someone is willing to pay for them. In 1276, Henry of Ghent deliberated whether buying something cheaper and immediately selling it at a higher price is a sin. It is, he concluded, since the *Corpus Iuris* means "can *by law*" when it says "can be sold for whatever someone will pay for it." The Latin *potest* ("can") really mean *debet* ("ought to") (see Langholm 1982). Many other moral constraints were generated by medieval intellectual culture to tame whatever market conditions might take shape around the human propensity to buy low, sell high, which medieval culture saw more as the basis of fraud and violence than Hayekian "freedom" (for Hayek's version of freedom, see Chapter 14). A man dying of thirst might pay a fortune for a sip of water, but that does not make it ethical to charge a fortune for water to him (Olivi 2012: 110–11). Determining a "just price" meant determining all costs that went into something, with a small amount of necessary profit to sustain producers and their families.

But what was "necessary," and who determined it? This opened further questions about distinguishing real need from gratuitous or excessive desire, and here more creative thought is visible (see Tierney 1959; Galloway 2009). The problem of poverty occupied a major position in the theorizing of later medieval academics, in part because of the "new" religious order of the Franciscans with their vows of poverty and, initially, lives of actual urban begging (replaced by opulent arrangements by the late Middle Ages that made them a constant target of satire for hypocrisy), but in part because the growth of urban culture no less than periodic famine produced a new class of urban poor. All this put pressure on the ability of laws, academics, and poets to define both the principle of self-interest and the principle of protection of those in need—at least in "true" need, defining which was itself a problem with which literature often grappled as subtly as academic commentary.

## Medieval literary as economics

As the example from Dante shows, late medieval literature was certainly informed by scholastic traditions. But what about literature before the scholastic period of the thirteenth and fourteenth centuries? Poetry in the Old English period (before 1066) was not usually touched by Augustine's writings on the Trinity, much less any ancient pre-Christian writings like Aristotle's. How does a principle of economic self-interest or economic market freedom appear there, before the great age of literary satire and scholastic debate?

The only "secular" epic surviving in full from Anglo-Saxon England, *Beowulf*, is rich with economic inquiries and perspectives, but the recurrent principle is not that of the academic ideas of balance and justice, but instead a kind of proportionate retribution of an honor code. This did not need Aristotle. Scyld Shefing is introduced to show from the outset how to impose power on surrounding tribes, elite families, or even nations (*mægþ*) by terror and demand for tribute, a capacity available to Scyld because of his "glory-value" (*weorðmynda*), and resulting in what appears to be a minor empire based on conquest and tribute:

weorð-myndum þah,
oðþæt him æghwylc þara ymbsittendra
ofer hron-rade hyran scolde,

> gomban gyldan.                Þæt wæs god cyning! (lns. 8–11, my translation)
> [he prospered in glory-value, until every one of those peoples located around him beyond the whale-road (sea) had to obey him, give him tribute. He was a good king!]

The meaning of gold is never obvious, as discussions this early—perhaps four centuries after the collapse of the Roman Empire itself, and before the commercial "take off" of the eleventh century—make clear. In *Beowulf*, reward or money is the most meaningful not for trade but for personal honor and political peace. Scyld's "economy of tribute" seems to anticipate the view of the historian Christine Desan that money was originally created not as an abstract vehicle for a supposedly innate human need for exchange of goods, but from despotic political structures in which money began as tokens of tax that then were used in secondary markets anchored by the central lord's power to collect taxes. Only when this political circumstance was later forgotten, Desan argues, in the seventeenth and eighteenth centuries, did money seem to serve as the invisible measurement of value, and the notion of a "market" was born (see Desan 2014).

Money as such, "gyld," rarely figures in *Beowulf*; the dragon's hoard is the main other instance, framing the poem with two instances of aggressive and impersonal assertions of personal "value" (*weorð*). Between those is a succession of more discrete but more widely meaningful transactions, from rings of retainers to the ancient inherited armor with an established lineage, instanced in the sword that Hrothgar shows Beowulf, inscribed with "old runes" and the tale of feud. Exchange in *Beowulf* always includes exchanges of favors and advice, often in geopolitically consequential ways. Arriving at the house of the Danish king, Beowulf is adroitly reminded by the Danish king Hrothgar that Hrothgar harbored Beowulf's father, Ecgtheow, when the latter was in flight: "your father struck up a mighty feud… I settled the feud by payment [*feo*]" (lines 457–70). Even as Beowulf is announced, Hrothgar begins to frame their interaction as a debt exchanged: "Why, I knew him when he was only a boy;… the seafarers [*sæ-liþende*; "merchants"?] who used to carry / gifts of coins, our thanks to the Geats / said he had war-fame" (lines 372–80). In this sense, the "economy" includes gifts and counter-gifts, social and material debits and credits recalled as precisely as money would later be (see Davies and Fouracre 2010). Grendel's mother, Beowulf's second antagonist, acts in precise retaliation for the killing of her son. Here is equity, but in a far more complex economy than commerce could allow.

*Beowulf*'s period is often called a "dark" age, but it is so mostly to us; its own principles and measures were evidently precise and long-remembered. Even into the seventh century, when Christianity had arrived from Rome inspiring monasteries along the eastern edge of Britain from Canterbury to Northumbria, the hoard found at Sutton Hoo in East Anglia includes only a small and seemingly random set of coins: amid the sword-haft and glorious helmet aboard the boat left at Sutton Hoo were forty-two gold objects that mingled thirty-seven Merovingian imitations of Justinian's Byzantine "tremisses" (in thinner gold than the originals) with three unstruck blanks plus two small ingots. Philip Grierson ingeniously suggests that, since the longboat that carried these elegant military and ceremonial objects had benches for forty rowers, the coins and blanks were payments for rowers, a penny a rower, reserving the two ingots for the steersman (see Grierson 1970). But no living person would be on that ship. Instead, the ship was made to be given over to the "power of the flood" ("on flodes æht" 42), launched into the ocean at the death of the ruler it carried or commemorated, like the empty funeral ship launched in *Beowulf* carrying the body of Scyld Scefing no one knows where (lines 26–52). Ghostly rowers would need their penny to make the crossing.

The twelfth-century rise of academic inquiry and of the universities, fostered by the massive influence of the newly recovered texts by Aristotle, cohered with other major economic changes (noted both above and more fully below) to create a far more precisely and separately articulated realm of "economics" than is visible in *Beowulf* or other early medieval literatures. By the later Middle Ages, laws controlling prices and venues were widespread. Civic authorities policed vendors for market timing, as when they withheld their products during market day until other sources were exhausted and they could charge more—a practice for which many a dealer spent time in the stocks in fourteenth- and fifteenth-century England (see Britnell 1996a). In late medieval English literature too, mercantile self-interest is carefully observed, though satirized in the frames of Covetousness or Avarice (see Yunck 1963; Little 1971; Ladd 2010). We may think of Chaucer's Wife of Bath, who declares with some bitterness in regard to her aged body—the only commodity she still has—"Al is for to selle"; or Chaucer's Pardoner, who makes his profession out of his hypocritical sermon that avarice is the root of all evil (see Kernan 1974). Chaucer is capable, however, of suggesting a cohesive if often self-deluded political and social economy. The *Canterbury Tales* (c. 1386–99) is filled with clashes between high-minded but sometimes naïve lords, and mathematically shrewd and cynical entrepreneurs, and "professional" religious figures (monks, friars, and prioresses) may be in either mode, in a movement that can be seen to teeter toward the vision of Adam Smith (see Galloway 2018). Among Chaucer's satires, for example, the *Summoner's Tale* describes a cynically avaricious friar seeking to gain a major donation from a layman. When this "donation" turns out to be flatulence, as imponderable as any "spiritual" commodity like prayer or spiritual authority, a lord and his cunning squire debate how to divide the donation of a fart in precise (Aristotelian) equality to all the members of the friar's priory. Aristotle's "distributive justice" is here stretched to absurdity when an effort at measuring "value" is applied to an unmeasurable and unsalable resource (time, honor, spiritual authority, prayers, for which windy flatulence is a stand-in).

Chaucer's elitist London peer and associate, John Gower, usually avoids direct attention to commerce (apart from the sins of merchants in his French *Mirour de l'Omme*, "Mirror of Mankind"), but Gower constantly implies principles of commerce in dialectic with noble gift exchange throughout his tales collected in the English *Confessio amantis* ("Confession of a Lover"), as in several tales featuring circulating and mysteriously valuable chests (see Ladd 2010; Galloway 2014). Both Chaucer and Gower were regular customers of a London moneylending (Christian) merchant, whose connections similarly bridged noble, artisanal, and literary London, and whose "mercantile literacy" of accounting can be traced not only in his own surviving account book but also in their poetry and many of the literary works of the region (see Galloway 2011).

The survey of such concerns in the "age of Chaucer" can, of course, be expanded much further. Most significant for economic considerations and debates, however, is the endlessly revised poem *Piers Plowman*, with its highly learned but seemingly vagrant and impoverished narrator. This work is more openly a testimonial of its time of writing, from the late 1360s into the 1380s, that is, not long after the Black Death with its many disruptions of the labor pool, thus wages and laws attempting to constrain those changes, and during a time of pan-European currency shortages (enhancing attention to credit), increased vagrancy and debates about poverty such as the problem of defining the "deserving poor," all topics frequently if irresolutely taken up in the poem (see Middleton 1997; Scott 2004). The poem's initial debate between Meed (Reward, or Money) and Conscience frames the idea of naked desire for reward into different kinds of reward, along an axis both earthly and heavenly, and with different degrees of timing and quantifiability, "measurable" and "measureless." Earthly reward should be "measurable," Langland's Conscience argues, though Meed simply argues that everyone wants reward. For Conscience, this treats earthly rewards as if they were the kinds we get in heaven, unmeasurable, a violation of Aristotle's ideal of carefully (but elusively) balanced justice. For Meed, acknowledging this universal self-interest allows any community to sustain harmony and its shared goodwill (see Galloway 2006).

Although *Piers Plowman*, an epic of salvation and salvation history, is nearly as ambitious as Dante's *Comedia* or Milton's *Paradise Lost*, its willingness to sacrifice "high poetic" form and style in favor of investigating the ethics of various economies can make it seem sometimes "confused and monotonous... hardly a poem" (Lewis 1936: 161). But that view (from the period of High Modernism) depends on an idea of what a poem ought *not* to contain. A sense of how intellectually as well as poetically unique *Piers Plowman* is can be gleaned from the narrator's encounter near the end of the poem with the allegorical personification of Need. Here, Need lets the vagrant narrator in on a secret—or offers a last temptation. You can get away with anything without fear if you really need it. As the legal adage runs, "need has no law" (*necessitas non habet legem*). Thus, Need asks the narrator,

> Coudestow noght excuse the... [*could you not excuse yourself*]
> That thow nome [*took*] na moore than need thee taught,
> And need ne hath no law ne nevere shal falle in dette? ...
> And he cache in that caas [*If he takes something in that instance*] and come therto by sleighte, [*trickery*]
> He synneth noght, soothliche, [*he doesn't sin, truly*] that so wynneth his foode. ...
> So Nede, at gret nede, may nymen [*take*] as for his owene,
> Withouten conseil of Conscience or Cardynale Vertues.
>
> *20.6–7, 10, 14–15*

Where Dante would offer sheer condemnation of acknowledged abuses, Langland explores tricky economic ethical puzzles. Need's taunts offer official doctrine, but turn those on their head by expressing such doctrine self-servingly, since a personification of Need must necessarily speak for himself. Considering need impersonally, as a social condition requiring careful tending in an age before any "poor laws," defined some of the strongest contributions the Middle Ages made toward a "moral economy." But as soon as need is defined as a subjective condition, it instantly shifts the focus to self-interest, from *want* to *I want* (see Langholm 1992: 185–6; Galloway 2009). Langland's literary form of personification explores this problem. Poignant as many of Langland's reflections on the destitute often are (see especially those in the late "C" text, C.9.70–203), to speak of need on one's own behalf is precisely the relativist condition of consumerism and self-interest of modern economics and society. In Langland's unresolved confrontation with this paradox may lie one of the key pivots of the entire Middle Ages: teetering (in a different way than Chaucer) between collectively and impersonally defined idea of an economy of need—a perspective dismissed by Adam Smith four centuries later—and an economy explicitly focused on production, demand, and profit that Smith propounded, in which the presence of ethics, need, and the path to penance, compassion, and salvation (or impiety, violence, and hell) all vanish in the glare of both commercialization and self-interest.

## The "great transition"

But what really changed, and why? Having begun by examining the image of self-interest as a challenge or joke in medieval intellectual culture, and then following that through literary examples of narrative elaboration and ideological unraveling, it is logical to end by considering how the principle of self-interest became an entire economic system—if it did. To understand where we have been and where we now are, medievalists and everyone should try to understand how western culture navigated the "great transition" from precapitalist medieval economies to full-bore capitalism of wage labor, reinvestment of capital into the modes of production, a fundamentally monetary market, and prices and wages set by that market, all driven by the universal imperative to buy low, sell high (see Britnell 1996b; Dyer 2005; Campbell 2016). How did a Roman mime's joke become Smithian gospel, and modern reality?

One voice will be familiar by general repute at least. For Karl Marx in *Capital* (c. 1867), "feudal production" was "characterized by division of the soil amongst the greatest possible number of sub-feudatories" governing whom "the might of the feudal lord, like that of the sovereign, depended not on the length of his rent-roll, but on the number of his subjects, and the latter depended on the number of peasant proprietors" (Marx I 1990: 878). We recall the kind of dialectical satire between lords and entrepreneurs that Chaucer offers. Historians are nowadays sometimes reluctant to use "feudalism" to describe medieval society's structure of "service" and "loyalty," so varied are the arrangements in landholding, and so vague the modern and medieval range of uses of the relevant terms (see Reynolds 1994; Hudson 1997). Yet as early as Bede's Letter to Bishop Egbert (c. 734 AD), Bede mentions that the problem of sinful monasteries being given land means that such land will not be available to the knights who would otherwise be granted such lands in order to fight for the king; worse are those who pretend they will establish monasteries and through that guise purchase royal edits for hereditary land ownership—the category known as "bookland" in Anglo-Saxon England, which here seems to stand opposed to land-for-military-service (see Davies and Fouracre 2010: 89–115).

However how accurate Bede is, something like the ideal of land for service in a hierarchical sequence from laborers on up to the king continued to the thirteenth century, when it became more legally specified, in commentaries on civil law, such as the thirteenth-century Italian legal scholar Hostiensis's treatise *De feudis* found in his massive commentary on the *Digest* of Justinian (Reynolds 1994: 236). How far this contingent "holding" of land really defined ownership as contingent on service (and some intangible "feudal loyalty") is unclear. In the thirteenth century, peasants begin to be documented engaging in an active market in land, and by the fourteenth century, hereditary leases allowed them to buy and sell it more or less openly—a practice Langland in *Piers Plowman* still found reprehensible enough to present as a simile of a Christian's betrayal of loyalty to his basic faith (Dyer 2005: 46–51). But increasing numbers of gentry landowners found complex, if sometimes contentious legal maneuvers to transfer and bequeath feudal land (whose possession could not be directly transferred in a will until the sixteenth century) in what amounts to a widespread market (see Bellamy 1989). Changes are broadly visible at the bottom as well as the top of society: in c. 1300, roughly half the laborers were serfs; by c. 1600, only a small number had the legal identity of serfs, that is, those who owed various "customary" obligations of labor or, increasingly, rent, and were subject to various legal and financial burdens in their lives and on the lands to which they were supposed to remain attached, though also protected by "custom" from some of the market variations in rent to which "free-holders" were more subject.

Contracts for knightly service were similarly specified increasingly in contracts for life or other limited ways, whereby lords' retinues ballooned into private armies (with badges for "affinities") but involved wages and terms rather than vaguer and longer commitments. But this stage of "bastard feudalism" may be evidence of lordly households growing larger rather than traditional knightly retainers becoming more contractual and commodified supporters (see Bean 1989).

For Marx, "feudal production" fell apart by its own weight; the numbers of small peasant properties built up a "primitive accumulation" of wealth, but since such productivity was utterly dominated by feudal lords, it was not deployed as "capital" dedicated to the production of other surplus wealth until the former feudal lords in the fifteenth and sixteenth centuries sought to control directly the lands that the peasants had previously managed, usurping the "common lands" (the areas used by all for grazing and plowing in a rotation determined not by individual peasant landholding but by collective village agreement) and putting those out for lease, further driving the peasantry into the role of wage laborers. This is cogent, and is broadly followed by a number of modern Marxists, but it differs from other explanations for this period's historical change, such as those focused on rising commercialism, or on wider confluences of biological and climatic catastrophes.

The commercialist view was initially enunciated by Adam Smith a half-century before Marx. For Smith (c. 1776), the medieval lords—whom Smith shrewdly notes lived before official "feudal law" but whose power was enhanced by such later legal clarification—had long been the sole lord and patron of their local laborers, retainers, and artisans, in a system by which the lord gave back to them the whole of their sustenance and his surplus wealth in pursuit of his powers and the trappings of prestige of his lordship. Their lives, incomes, properties, and legal rights all depended, Smith remarked tartly, almost solely on his pleasure. Expanding networks of trade and manufacturing in the later Middle Ages brought out the structural problem in this: tradesmen and artisans became beholden not to one lord but to "a hundred or a thousand different customers," by which they were increasingly more "independent" in lives and outlook even while that solitary lord continued to dedicate his entire surplus to gaining the increasingly luxurious and expensive products that, thanks to that expanding market and manufacturing network, such laborers and artisans were now able to produce (Smith III 1976: 438). Such individuals were motivated not by prestige or fear but by the ethic of busy practicality or "industry," a condition of world-historical importance for Smith, even though its carriers acted "merely from a view to their own interest, and in pursuit of their own pedlar principle of turning a penny wherever a penny was to be got" (Smith III 1976: 440). For historians elaborating this view, cities became the nodes of change, "non-feudal islands in the feudal seas," as the great twentieth-century medieval non-Marxist economic historian Michael Postan states, in which charters of urban privileges were crucial, since that allowed householders in medieval towns to be personally free and to hold their land by "burgage tenure," a "fully-free title which approached very closely the concept of full untrammeled ownership represented by the Roman *proprietas*" (239–40). But as Marxists might (and do) object, the steeply hierarchical structures of cities can also be seen to emulate precisely the structure of oppression by lords over laborers, in this case craftsmen and artisans, of the rest of the feudal world, as Rodney Hilton argues (Hilton 1992). Stressing the darker Marxist view is Robert Brenner, while stressing more positive elements from a similar intellectual perspective is Dyer (Aston and Philpin 1987: 10–63; Dyer 2005).

Motives and feelings, of freedoms or constraints, are elusive historical targets, and Smith and Marx are as vulnerable as some of their modern followers to the criticism that they overemphasize either the "pedlar principle" or class conflict (see Aston and Philpin 1987). Less centered on attitudes or outlooks was the approach of Smith's contemporary, Thomas Malthus (c. 1798), who founded the principle of population pressures on resources as the engine of change. For modern scholars using Malthusianism in some measure (including Postan), the "feudal" order gave way when the expansions of food and population in the thirteenth century finally collapsed as the available lands and agricultural technology (whose innovation was never encouraged in a system in which the laborers were entirely and directly under the power of landlords) reached its limit. Along with climate change from the Little Ice Age (see Campbell 2005), this set the stage for the decimations of the population in the Great Famine of 1315–18, followed by the Black Death in 1348–9, a disease continuing in waves for decades until roughly half the laboring population had died—itself a situation that, arguably, unleashed more mobility, wage demands, and, in turn, new laws, followed by the Rising of 1381, a massive popular revolt that, though crushed, left a culture prone to weaken traditional social roles. New opportunities for agrarian and civic industries emerged with these demographic and attitudinal changes, freeing the laboring classes further from immediate personal lordship, but putting them more deeply into a web of royal bureaucracy and the structures of an administrative state. Indeed, another principle of cultural change is literacy, documentary bureaucracy, and finally the printing press (introduced in England in 1475), often touted as a major "agent of change" in creating modernity (see Eisenstein 1979; Clanchy 2012).

As John Hatcher and Mark Bailey argue, self-consciousness about how any "models" are deployed or combined to explain particular aspects of these massively complex changes is the key (Hatcher and Bailey 2001). The "great transition" remains too large to be either simply a march toward greater social alienation or an inspiring instance of human creative responses to severe climatic, biological, economic, philosophical, religious, and political shocks, much less the "discovery" of individuality that Renaissance scholars from the nineteenth century on have persistently proposed belongs to the world after 1500 (see the more subtle reassessment by Biow 2015). It is pertinent to end by questioning even the question. Periodization is too blunt a line to understand any of these strands or aspects of culture fully. Women's social and economic constraints, for instance, persisted across this period. The historical significance of this is often by negation. As Judith Bennett shows in her writing about the transition of late medieval ale-brewing and ale-selling from women to men across the "medieval-Renaissance" divide (c. 1300–1600), whenever professions begin to prosper, women tend to disappear from them (Bennett 1996). A similar phenomenon is visible in the transition of the role of midwives in childbirth to (male) physicians in the fifteenth and sixteenth centuries (see Blumenfeld-Kosinski 1991). It is challenging to characterize as a whole any period that leaves so many people behind, however fundamentally, it changed the circumstances of others. As Joan Kelly-Gadol asks, "did women have a Renaissance?" If "feudalism" ended in legal terms in the seventeenth century, many of its features of stateless domination and exploitation can reemerge in a post-national economy of global corporations. History does not start or end at one line, nor is "progress" an adequate term for describing continuities and disruptions of ideas, literature, and life.

## References

Alighieri, Dante. (1977) *The Divine Comedy*, Charles S. Singleton (trans.), Princeton, NJ: Princeton University Press.

Aquinas, Thomas. *Summa theologiae*, the Secunda secundae (Second Part of the Second Part) (IIa IIae). The original text is available at the online Corpus Thomisticum.

Aristotle. (1995) *The Complete Works of Aristotle: The Revised Oxford Translation*, 2 vols, Princeton, NJ: Princeton University Press.
Armstrong, Lawrin. (2016) *The Idea of A Moral Economy: Gerard of Siena on Usury, Restitution, and Prescription*, Toronto, ON: University of Toronto Press.
Aston, T. H. and Philpin, C. H. E. (1987) *The Brenner Debate: Agrarian Class Structure and Economic Development in Pre-industrial Europe*, Cambridge: Cambridge University Press.
Augustine, St. (1991) *The Trinity (De Trinitate)*, Edmund Hill (trans.), New York: New City Press.
Baldwin, John. (1970) *Masters, Princes and Merchants: The Social Views of Peter the Chanter and His Circle*, Princeton, NJ: Princeton University Press.
Bean, J. M. W. (1989) *From Lord to Patron: Lordship in Late Medieval England*, Manchester: Manchester University Press.
Bellamy, John G. (1989) *Bastard Feudalism and the Law*, Portland, OR: Areopagitica Press.
Bennett, Judith M. (1996) *Ale, Beer, and Brewsters in England: Women's Work in a Changing World, 1300–1600*, Oxford: Oxford University Press.
Biow, Douglas. (2015) *On the Importance of Being an Individual in Renaissance Italy: Men, Their Professions, and Their Beards*, Philadelphia: University of Pennsylvania Press.
Blumenfeld-Kosinski, Renate. (1991) *Not of Woman Born: Representations of Caesarean Birth in Medieval and Renaissance Culture*, Ithaca, NY: Cornell University Press.
Britnell, R. H. (1996a) *The Commercialisation of English Society, 1000–1500*, Manchester: Manchester University Press.
Britnell, R. H. (1966b) "Price-Setting in English Borough Markets, 1349–1500," *Canadian Journal of History* 31: 1–15.
Campbell, Bruce M. S. (2005) *The Great Transition: Climate, Disease and Society in the Late-Medieval World*, Cambridge: Cambridge University Press.
Chaucer, Geoffrey. (2005) *The Canterbury Tales*, Jill Mann (ed.), London: Penguin Books.
Clanchy, M. T. (2012) *From Memory to Written Record: England 1066–1307, Third Edition*, Oxford: Wiley-Blackwell.
Courtemanche, Eleanor. (2011) *The 'Invisible Hand' and British Fiction, 1818–1860*, London: Palgrave.
Davies, Wendy and Fouracre, Paul. (2010) *The Languages of Gift in the Early Middle Ages*, Cambridge: Cambridge University Press.
Desan, Christine. (2014) *Making Money: Coin, Currency, and the Coming of Capitalism*, Oxford: Oxford University Press.
Dyer, Christopher. (2005) *An Age of Transition? Economy and Society in England in the Later Middle Ages*, Oxford: Oxford University Press.
Eisenstein, Elizabeth. (1979) *The Printing Press as an Agent of Change*, Cambridge: Cambridge University Press.
Galloway, Andrew. (2018) "Crossing the Threshold: Geoffrey Chaucer, Adam Smith, and the Liminal Transactionalism of the Later Middle Ages," in Craig E. Bertolet and Robert Epstein (eds.), *Money, Commerce, and Economics in Late Medieval English Literature*, New York: Palgrave MacMillan.
Galloway, Andrew. (2014) "Gower's Kiste," in R. F. Yeager and Ana Sáez Hidalgo (eds.), *John Gower in England and Iberia: Manuscripts, Influences, Reception*, Suffolk: Boydell and Brewer.
Galloway, Andrew. (2011) "The Account Book and the Treasure: Gilbert Maghfeld's Textual Economy and the Poetics of Mercantile Accounting in Ricardian Literature," *Studies in the Age of Chaucer* 33: 65–124.
Galloway, Andrew. (2009) "The Economy of Need in Late Medieval English Literature," *Viator* 40 (2009): 309–31.
Galloway, Andrew. (2006) *The Penn Commentary on "Piers Plowman": C Prologue-Passus 4; B Prologue-Passus 4; A Prologue-Passus 4*, Philadelphia: University of Pennsylvania Press.
Gilson, Etienne. (1960) *The Christian Philosophy of St. Augustine*, New York: Random House.
Grierson, Philip. (1970) "The Purpose of the Sutton Hoo Coins," *Antiquity* 44: 14–18.
Hatcher, John and Bailey, Mark. (2001) *Modelling the Middle Ages: The History and Theory of England's Economic Development*, Oxford: Oxford University Press.
Hilton, R. H. (1992) *English and French Towns in Feudal Society: A Comparative Study*, Cambridge: Cambridge University Press.
Hudson, John. (1997) *Land, Law, and Lordship in Anglo-Norman England*, Oxford: Clarendon Press.
Kelly-Gadol, Joan. (1986) "Did Women Have a Renaissance?" rept. in *Women, History, and Theory: The Essays of Joan Kelly*, Chicago, IL: University of Chicago Press.

Kernan, Anne. (1974) "The Archwife and the Eunuch," *ELH* 41: 1–25.
Ladd, Roger A. (2010) *Antimercantilism in Late Medieval English Literature*, New York: Palgrave Macmillan.
Langholm, Odd. (1998) *The Legacy of Scholasticism in Economic Thought: Antecedents of Choice and Power*, Cambridge: Cambridge University Press.
Langholm, Odd. (1992) *Economics in the Medieval Schools: Wealth, Exchange, Value, Money and Usury According to the Paris Theological Tradition, 1200–1350*, Leiden: Brill.
Langholm, Odd. (1982) "Economic Freedom in Scholastic Thought," *History of Political Economy* 14: 260–83.
Langland, William. (2003) *Piers Plowman: A New Annotated Edition of the C-Text*, Derek Pearsall (ed.), Exeter: University of Exeter Press.
Lewis, C. S. (1936) *The Allegory of Love: A Study in Medieval Tradition*, London: Oxford University Press.
Little, Lester. (1971) "Pride Goes before Avarice: Social Change and the Vices in Latin Christendom," *American Historical Review* 76: 16–49.
Marx, Karl. (1990) *Capital: A Critique of Political Economy*, Ben Fowkes (trans.), London: Penguin.
Middleton, Anne. (1997) "Acts of Vagrancy: The C Version 'Autobiography' and the Statute of 1388," in Steven Justice and Kathryn Kerby-Fulton (eds.), *Written Work: Langland, Labor, and Authorship*, Philadelphia: University of Pennsylvania Press.
Monroe, Arthur. (1923) *Monetary Theory before Adam Smith*, Cambridge, MA: Harvard University Press.
Mundill, Robin R. (1998) *England's Jewish Solution. Experiment and Expulsion, 1262–1290*, Cambridge: Cambridge University Press.
Olivi, Pierre de Jean. (2012) *Traité des contrats*, Sylvain Piron (ed.), Paris: Les belles lettres.
Postan, M. M. (1972) *The Medieval Economy and Society: An Economic History of Britain in the Middle Ages*, London: Penguin.
Reynolds, Susan. (1994) *Fiefs and Vassals: The Medieval Evidence Reinterpreted*, Oxford: Oxford University Press.
Scott, Anne M. (2004) *Piers Plowman and the Poor*, Dublin: Four Courts Press.
Smith, Adam. (1976) *An Inquiry into the Nature and Causes of the Wealth of Nations*, Edwin Cannan (ed.), Chicago, IL: University of Chicago Press.
Tierney, Brian. (1959) *Medieval Poor Law: A Sketch of Canonical Theory and Its Application in England*, Berkeley: University of California Press.
Torrell, Jean-Pierre. (2005) *Aquinas's Summa: Background, Structure, and Reception*, Benedict M. Guevin (trans.), Washington, DC: Catholic University of America.
Yunck, John A. (1963) *The Lineage of Lady Meed: The Development of Medieval Venality Satire*, South Bend, IN: University of Notre Dame Press.

# 7

# JOHN SMITH AND THE VIRUS OF TRADE

*Andrew Lawson*

On a day in August, 1608, a pamphlet appeared at a bookseller's stand in St. Paul's churchyard, London, *A True Relation of Such Occurrences and Accidents of Note as Hath Happened in Virginia* by Captain John Smith. Smith's report was among the first examples of what would become a flood of pamphlets, ballads, plays, and fiction promoting English colonization by "narrat[ing] the heroic actions of early voyagers" (Kulikoff 2000: 42). But it is also a document that defines a new economic role for the upwardly mobile individual as an adventurer and trader in the service of the mercantilist state. Although *A True Relation* is sometimes little more than *res gestae*, a formless record of desultory facts, there is a strong narrating presence at its core, drawing the world in and shaping it around itself, as well as a definite view of that world as being primarily concerned with truck and barter, a complexly layered series of exchanges.

The basic fact of economic life for the English adventurers into Virginia was scarcity. Unable to supply their own needs, they depended on Algonquian-speaking natives belonging to the Powhatan chiefdom for food. In November, 1607, after his appointment to the position of Cape Merchant, the Company official in charge of the colony's store, Smith led a trading mission downriver, which he describes as follows:

> I was sent to the mouth of the river, to Kecoughtan, an Indian Town, to trade for Corn, and try the river for Fish, but our fishing we could not effect by reason of the stormy weather. The Indians thinking us near famished, with careless kindness offered us little pieces of bread and small handfuls of beans or wheat, for a hatchet or a piece of copper: In the like manner I entertained their kindness, and in like scorn offered them like commodities, but the Children, or any that showed extraordinary kindness, I liberally contented with free gift, such trifles as well contented them; finding this cold comfort, I anchored before the Town, and the next day returned to trade, But God (the absolute disposer of all hearts) altered their conceits, for now they were no less desirous of our commodities then we of their Corn: under colour to fetch fresh water, I sent a man to discover the Towne, their Corn, and force, to try their intent, in that they desired me up to their houses: which well understanding with four shot [armed men] I visited them. With fish, oysters, bread and deer, they kindly traded with me and my men, being no less in doubt of my intent, than I of theirs, for well I might with twenty men have

> freighted a Ship with Corn.... With sixteen bushels of Corn I returned towards our Fort: by the way encountered with two Canoes of Indians, who came aboard me, being the inhabitants of Waraskoyack, a kingdom on the south side of the river... with these I traded, who having but their hunting provision requested me to return to their Towne, where I should load my boat with corn, and with near thirty bushels I returned to the fort, the very name whereof gave great comfort to our despairing company.
>
> *(Smith* I *1986: 35–6)*

Twelve first-person pronouns linked predominately to active verbs: I was sent, I entertained and offered; I contented; I anchored; I sent; I visited; I doubted not; I might have freighted; I returned; I traded; I could have loaded a boat; I returned, the sequence culminating in the report of another successful expedition when "I unladed seven hogsheads into our store" (41). There are also three mentions of "trade," as well as references to "commodities" and "trifles," the marketable item referred to most frequently being "corn" (six mentions). In its diction, *A True Relation* reflects a cultural moment in which Britons were, in Jean-Christophe Agnew's words, "feeling their way around a *problematic* of exchange." They were "putting forward a coherent and repeated pattern of problems or questions about the nature of social identity, intentionality, accountability, transparency, and reciprocity in commodity transactions—the who, what, when, where, and why of exchange" (Agnew 1986: 9). More specifically, Smith writes in a period when, as described by Alan Everitt, "new methods of private bargaining were gradually breaking down the protective barriers of the customary marketing system" (Everitt 1967: 563).

The salient economic facts of life in the sixteenth century were soaring prices and falling wages. While the day wage of an agrarian laborer in 1609 had more than doubled since 1500, the cost of a basket of foodstuffs and consumables had more than quadrupled (Goldstone 1984: 1123). Price inflation meant that, by the late sixteenth century, there were increasing opportunities for profit in market exchange. The revolution in prices, in R. H. Tawney's words, "injected a virus of hitherto unsuspected potency, at once a stimulant to feverish enterprise and an acid dissolving all customary relationships" (Tawney 1969: 142). The virus of trade had "nourished itself like an alien body within the pores of feudal society" (Dobb 1946: 37).

Men and women worked the countryside as itinerant traders—petty chapmen, badgers, hawkers, hucksters, and peddlers—bringing dry goods, foodstuffs, and "unconsidered trifles" to out of the way places. Commercial farmers forestalled or evaded regulated local markets by dealing with middlemen—factors, jobbers, and brokers—or by selling directly to merchants in ports and market towns at prices set not by town officials but by the interaction of supply and demand, the "free-floating price and profit system" (Appleby 1978: 25). Face-to-face bargains were conducted via elaborate rituals in which prospective dealers made a series of lengthy "speeches" and "communications" before the bonds obligatory were sealed with solemn oaths and vows, in a language that was "repetitive and antique" and not always well understood (Everitt 1967: 561). In these exchanges of words, gestures, and paper, sincere expressions of being in earnest blended indeterminately with the "glozing terms" of masquerade and deceit. In one bargaining encounter described by Everitt, a Canterbury maltster named Thomas Fetherstone purchased barley from John Videon of Patrixbourne, drawing from him "many good bargains of corn, by which he was a great gainer," simply by calling him "cousin," and using "manifold and great protestations of love" (Everitt 1967: 558). Private trading was, in Fernand Braudel's words, "a revolution which went beyond the economy into social behaviour" (Braudel 1982: 47). The "criterion of exchangeability" had been removed from the "ritual confines of the marketplace" and embedded "in the midst of everyday life," in a "new and boundless silent trade" (Agnew 1986: 50).

On the face of it, the situation at the first contact between Indians and Englishmen in the Chesapeake was one that ideally facilitated the "reciprocal traffic, exchange, or movement of material goods through peaceful human agency" (Renfrew 1969: 152). Corn, or maize, was the most widely planted staple in the Chesapeake and the most important source of wealth, cultivated in special fields and offered as tribute to the paramount chief, Powhatan (Quitt 1995: 247). Algonquian leaders also distributed prestige goods—crystals, minerals, copper, shells, and ritual artifacts—invested with ancestral, divine, or primordial powers. Lacking natural sources of copper within his own territory, Powhatan relied on exchange with neighboring people, and was particularly irked by his dependence on the hostile Monacans (Mallios and Emmett 2004). The English had brought with them plentiful supplies of copper in the form of scrap metal from domestic manufacturing, and needed the corn growing everywhere in Powhatan fields (Hudgins 2005). But exchanges between Englishmen and Indians were structured by cultural differences.

Algonquian society was, in large part, a "gift economy," in which the exchange of goods was motivated by generosity and obligation. Gifts were not personal property, but were imbued with the soul or spirit of the giver; as such, they were more like a loan than a sale, and moved between individuals of equal rank, making them "permanently allied and perpetually independent" (Mallios 2006: 28). Since non-reciprocation violated the social bond created by gift exchange, it was seen as an aggressive act, tantamount to a declaration of war. Social life in the English colony functioned according to the norms of a "commodity economy" in which exchange was motivated by the desire for "immediate acquisition of material wealth" (Mallios 2006: 29). The goods exchanged were private property, "inert, inactive, soulless," their value assessed by the "cold reasoning of the merchant, the banker, the capitalist" (29). The only significant social relationship was "the economic one between equated exchange values" (29). Violations of economic exchange were theft, the unlawful possession of another individual's property, or inundation, the oversupply of a good in the market, leading to price falls and a falling off of trade.

The gift and commodity economies should not be seen as a binary system, as separate poles insulated from each other. Elements of commodity exchange already existed in Powhatan culture, and the rank-based English society contained its own forms of obligation. In the early contact period, there was considerable overlap between, and flexibility within, the two economies, whose dynamic interaction produced unstable and intricate mutations of cultural and economic practices. Smith's role was to attempt to police the blurred borders between exchange systems, and to manage disturbances or derangements in the market structure of equivalences. In *A True Relation*, Smith attempts "to portray the exchange of goods as a voluntary agreement between two parties" (McCarthy 1990: 46–7). But the fundamental problem was that the English consumed corn at a rate that exceeded the Indians' need for copper (Mallios 2006: 86). The English quickly inundated Powhatan society with trade goods, "so glutt[ing] the Savages with their commodities as they became not regarded" (Smith *I* 1986: 211). This meant that Powhatan, with a plentiful surplus and full knowledge of the colonists' greater need, could "set the terms of exchange" (McCarthy 1990: 47).

In their first face-to-face encounter, Powhatan promised to give Smith "Corn [and] Venison" in return for "Hatchets and Copper," as well as two large canons and a grindstone (Smith *I* 1986: 57). He would not "disturb" the settlers, but they would have to move nearer to his seat of power at Werowocomoco, where Smith would be his werowance or subordinate chief (57). As Powhatan's captive, Smith was in no position to bargain, so he simply "promised to perform" (57). While waiting for Smith to perform his promises, Powhatan kept the colonists alive, sending food supplies every other day. Smith acted as the colony's "market clerk," setting the price of food items in hatchets and copper (215). In *A True Relation*, Smith exults at his status among the Indians, who called him by his name and "deferred" to his "discretion" (61, 63). But Smith's economic role was being challenged by the rival logic of gift exchange, in which "greatness and authority" were obtained by "bounty, and liberality" (215). The fleet admiral, Sir Christopher Newport, sent Powhatan "great presents," while his crews conducted their own private trade with the Indians, having been granted "liberty to truck or trade at their pleasures" by the London Company (215). The result was a second inundation of copper and a corresponding inflation in the price of corn. The divergent tactics pursued by Smith and Newport undermined the English position in the tense negotiations with Powhatan that followed.

Powhatan's opening gambit was to refuse to trade for corn. The paramount chief was alarmed at the expansion of Anglo-Indian trade that had followed the arrival of the first supply of goods to the Jamestown colony, and by the challenge to his authority represented by lesser Algonquians conducting private trade with Newport's crews. Adopting a proud bearing that showed he "scorn[ed] to trade as his subjects did," Powhatan told Newport that it was "not agreeable" with his "greatnes[s]" to "trade for trifles" in a "peddling manner" (217). He insisted on seeing all of Newport's trade goods, selecting what he liked, and setting the goods' value. The element of compunction, with the assertion of the paramount chief's political authority, made the exchange look more like enforced tribute than gift offering. Powhatan was, in effect, tearing up the agreement that Smith would act as market clerk, and stepping into the role of exchange-rate arbiter himself. Newport responded by obeying the principle of asymmetrical exchange embedded in the gift economy. In an attempt to "out brave this Savage in ostentation of his greatness, and so to bewitch him with his bounty," he agreed to Powhatan's request, telling him that he could have what he liked (217). Committed to the commodity economy, Smith refused Powhatan's "offer" and asked "to see what he would give" for one "piece" first, so as to establish a going rate (71). Seeming to "despise" the cautious, calculating "nature of a Merchant," Powhatan suggested that if the colonists gave "freely," he would "requite" them "liberally" (71). Newport played along, offering twelve large copper cooking pots, only to be given the amount of corn that Smith had previously obtained for one small pot. Powhatan pressed home his advantage, insisting on trading for hatchets "at his own rate" (71). The English ended up receiving four bushels for their goods, when they had expected twenty hogsheads (217).

Outraged by what he saw as Newport's poor bargaining, Smith "glanced in the eyes of Powhatan many trifles," until the paramount chief "fixed his humour upon a few blew beads" (Smith *II* 1986: 156). A trope of English-colonizing discourse was that the Indians were "poor" people who lacked "skill and judgement in the knowledge and use of our things," leading them to "esteem our trifles before things of greater value" (Harriot 1955: 371). Seeing that Powhatan "importunately desired" the beads, Smith improvised a sales pitch, describing them as "being composed of a most rare substance of the colour of the skies, and not to be worn but by the greatest kings in the world" (Smith *II* 1986: 156). Powhatan, "half-mad to be the owner of such strange Jewells," offered half a bushel of corn (Smith *I* 1986: 71). The next day, Smith offered more beads, and secured two more bushels.

It's at this point of apparent success—the securing of corn supplies for trifles—that trade relations begin to break down. The colonists had violated the gift economy by refusing to relocate or to honor the other terms of Smith's first exchanges with Powhatan. They had violated the norms of both gift and economic exchanges by inundating the native world with trade goods, driving down their value and producing a glut of copper and trifles. When Newport prepared to leave for England with a cargo of "phantastical gold," Powhatan presented him with a farewell gift of twenty turkeys in return for twenty swords (220). The Powhatan emperor now insisted on a strict notion of equal exchange: one of what you desire of mine for every one of what I desire from you. As Martin Quitt points out, "[n]othing could have signalled more clearly Powhatan's understanding that exchange with the English had to be moved from unbalanced gift giving to balanced barter" (Quitt 1995: 250). Barter is typically seen by economists as a "primitive" form of exchange involving haggling or "negative reciprocity." But Caroline Humphrey suggests that we see barter as an "open-ended, potentially innovative, negotiable, transaction," in which "need not only answers need but can also create a new demand" (Humphrey 1985: 50). Powhatan was pursuing these open-ended possibilities, beginning with copper or beads, but discovering tools and weapons as exchangeable goods, while the English insisted monotonously on primitive trade in order to satisfy basic subsistence needs. Powhatan had abandoned gift-exchange norms in another, highly significant sense. With the market for copper glutted, he was no longer interested in trifles but in highly utilitarian objects (Richter 2007: 51–2). The turkeys-for-swords deal was a stunning display of the paramount chief's negotiating prowess. The problem for the English was now twofold: restoring a high exchange rate for copper and coping with Powhatan's flexibility and innovation.

The English attempted to shift the terms of exchange from the economic to the political, devising a strategy of assimilation modeled on the "surrender and regrant" policy pursued in Ireland (Canny 1976: 32–4). Newport presided over a bizarre ceremony in which Powhatan was "crowned" and acknowledged as an English chieftain, so long as he kneeled to the sovereign power of the English king. Powhatan refused to kneel, and in return for gifts of copper, a basin, a pitcher, and a bed gave only a pair of his old shoes and a cloak. Smith made it clear that he disapproved of the "strange Coronation" (Smith *II* 1986: 181). In a letter to the London Company, he pointed out that the sudden switch to a policy of gift-giving and symbolic rather than economic exchange threatened "the confusion of us all" (189). In every exchange, there was an inherent instability, a tendency of the terms of trade to alter almost imperceptibly, to shift or mutate in time and place. But an even more serious problem was that the Company's monopoly was being undermined as a result of "leakage by unauthorized entrepreneurs" (Games 2009: 129).

The situation in Virginia was designed to be one of the focused exchanges: formalized, restricted to relatively few contacts, and initiated by "high-ranking individuals" (Stewart 1989: 66). But the Virginia Company was acutely aware of the danger of broad-based exchanges proliferating in "a series of web-like or chain-like personalized relationships" (65–6). It was particularly anxious about the presence of visiting seafarers, warning the colony's leaders to "take Care that your Mariners that Go for wages Do not mar your trade" (Barbour 1969: 53). The Company was confronting what is now known as the principal-agent problem, in which "rational agents pursue their own private interests, most often free riding off of collective resources provided by principals"—like the East India Company captains who conducted their own private exchanges on official trading voyages (Erikson and Bearman 2006: 203). The focused exchange of elite men trading under government-granted monopolies was giving way to a new ethos of "free trade."

English traders, artisans, shopkeepers, and craftsmen held long-standing grievances at the granting of monopoly charters to private corporations, which they argued was a form of "engrossing" otherwise prohibited by statute. Corporations were permitted the "sole buying and selling" of a commodity to be "brought into few hands," when this ought to be "free and common to all the Citizens" of the commonwealth (Tawney and Power 1924: 266). In 1604, Sir Edwin Sandys told the House of Commons that since "all free subjects" were entitled to inherit land, they should also be entitled to "the free exercise of their industry, in those trades whereto they apply themselves," including the overseas trade (qtd. in Tawney 1969: 183; Rabb 1998: 95). Mariners were early adopters of the emerging free trade ethic. Private trade by mariners shipping goods on their own account was permitted by Northern European maritime law in lieu of wages, a form of "vernacular capitalism" known as portage (Pope 1995: 39). Newport's crews triggered a third inundation of European trade goods by holding night markets on board the *Mary and Margaret*, trading directly with the Indians.

Within six weeks, only twenty of the two or three hundred "hatchets, chisels, mattocks, and pickaxes" that came on the second supply remained (Smith *I* 1986: 240). The sailors also traded butter, cheese, beef, pork, aqua vitae, beer, biscuit, and oatmeal for furs. According to William Strachey, the mariners demanded payment in bills of exchange from colonists at a markup of "four or five for one" for pilfered goods (Strachey 1973: 71–2). All that the London Company could do was to condemn the "covetousness" of persons driven by the desire for "private lucre" and "sordid gain" (Virginia Company 1987: 256). Exchange, Marx writes, "bursts its local bounds," breaking through all "individual and local" limitations (Marx 1982: 183). The commodity is "a born leveller and cynic," always ready "to exchange not only soul, but body, with each and every other commodity" (179). The London Company's attempts to impose social control foundered the moment the mariners and colonists realized that everything was "saleable and purchasable," and that circulation was "the great social retort into which everything is thrown" (229).

Powhatan grasped the centrality of the criterion of exchangeability, but as paramount chief he was able to avoid contamination by the virus of trade. His last offer to Smith was "40 bushels" for "40 swords" (Smith *I* 1986: 245). When Smith asked how he had become so "forgetful" and ungenerous, Powhatan laughed, telling him that he "could eat his corn, but not his copper" (246). Powhatan had become "the consummate trader," denigrating the other party's goods while "boost[ing] the worth of his own" (Quitt 1995: 254). Smith resorted to glozing terms, assuring him that he had acted in good faith, "believing your promises to supply my wants," seeking to "satisfy your desire, and to testify my love" (Smith *I* 1986: 246). Powhatan's response was to shift to the terms of a gift economy in which Newport had always been more adept than Smith, giving "what I desired, ever taking what I offered him" (248). His other bargaining tactic was to insist on the political over the economic, telling Smith that the English had come not for trade but "to invade my people, and possess my Country" (246). Smith ended by telling Powhatan that it was "not our custom to sell our curtesy as a vendible commodity," implying that Powhatan's expressions of love were made only for the goods they might obtain (249). But this was precisely the English custom in the myriad individual bargains, the higgle-haggling and hard bargaining that constituted the "reticulate pattern" of inland trade (Agnew 1986: 48). The porous boundaries of exchange in this pattern meant that Smith's regulatory authority had drained away.

*A True Relation* is a key document from a vital moment in the transition from a traditional society based on status to a market society based on "rational self-interest and voluntary contractual obligation" (Wayne 1982: 104). From the perspective of commerce, we are in essence "the agents of our own obligations," responsible only to "items given and received in exchange" in "a mutual concurrence of free and independent wills" (Sacks 2001: 43, 42). The true relation is a purely economic one, in which "persons exist for one another merely as representatives and hence owners, of commodities" (Marx 1982: 178–9). It is "as the bearers of these economic relations that they come into contact with each other" (179). In this relationship of "reciprocal isolation and foreignness" (182), Smith represents copper, Powhatan corn. Both are recognizably human only insofar as they exhibit a willingness to make promises, to contract and exchange. Smith could neither exercise nor answer to a higher authority: cut loose by Powhatan, he was forced to "shift" for himself (Smith *I* 1986: 249). In doing so, he bequeathed a legacy to future colonists and Americans: the lonely, embattled, anarchic world of free market men.

## References

Agnew, J.-C. (1986) *Worlds Apart: The Market and the Theater in Anglo-American Thought, 1550–1750*, Cambridge: Cambridge University Press.

Appleby, J. (1978) *Economic Thought and Ideology in Seventeenth-Century England*, Princeton, NJ: Princeton University Press.

Barbour, P. L. (ed.) (1969) *The Jamestown Voyages under the First Charter, 1606–1609, Vol. 1, London: Cambridge University Press.*

Braudel, F. (1982) *Civilization and Capitalism: 15th–18th Century, Vol. 2: The Wheels of Commerce*, trans. Siân Reynolds, London: Collins.

Canny, N. P. (1976) *The Elizabethan Conquest of Ireland: A Pattern Established, 1565–76*, Hassocks: Harvester Press, 1976.

Dobb, M. (1946) *Studies in the Development of Capitalism*, London: Routledge & Kegan Paul.

Erikson, E. and Bearman, P. (2006) "Malfeasance and the Foundations for Global Trade: The Structure of English Trade in the East Indies, 1601–1833," *American Journal of Sociology* 112.1: 195–230.

Everitt, A. (1967) "The Marketing of Agricultural Produce," in *The Agrarian History of England and Wales, Vol. 4: 1500–1640*, Joan Thirsk (ed.), Cambridge: Cambridge University Press.

Games, A. (2009) *The Web of Empire: English Cosmopolitans in an Age of Expansion, 1650–1660*, New York: Oxford University Press.

Goldstone, J. A. (1984) "Urbanization and Inflation: Lessons from the English Price Revolution of the Sixteenth and Seventeenth Centuries," *American Journal of Sociology* 89.5: 1122–60.

Harriot, T. (1955) "A Brief and True Report of the New Found Land of Virginia (1590)," in *The Roanoke Voyages, 1584–1590, Vol. 1*, David Beers Quinn (ed.), London: Hakluyt Society.

Hudgins, C. C. (2005) "Articles of Exchange or Ingredients of New World Metallurgy? An Examination of the Industrial Origins and Metallurgical Functions of Scrap Copper at Early Jamestown (c. 1607–17)," *Early American Studies* 3.1: 32–64.

Humphrey, C. (1985) "Barter and Economic Disintegration," *Man* 20.1: 48–72.

Kulikoff, A. (2000) *From British Peasants to Colonial Farmers*, Chapel Hill: University of North Carolina Press.

McCarthy, F. (1990) "The Influence of 'Legal Habit' on English-Indian Relations in Jamestown, 1606–1612," *Continuity and Change* 5.1: 39–64.

Mallios, S. (2006) *The Deadly Politics of Giving: Exchange and Violence at Ajacan, Roanoke, and Jamestown*, Tuscaloosa: University of Alabama Press.

Mallios, S. and Emmett, S. (2004) "Demand, Supply, and Elasticity in the Copper Trade at Early Jamestown," *Journal of the Jamestown Rediscovery Center* 2. Web. Accessed 11 May 2015.

Marx, K. (1982) *Capital: A Critique of Political Economy, Vol. 1*, trans. Ben Fowkes, London: Penguin Books.

Pope, P. E. (1995) "The Practice of Portage in the Early Modern North Atlantic: Introduction to an Issue in Maritime Historical Anthropology," *Journal of the Canadian Historical Association* 6.1: 19–41.

Quitt, M. (1995) "Trade and Acculturation at Jamestown, 1607–1609: The Limits of Understanding," *William and Mary Quarterly* 52.2: 227–58.

Rabb, T. K. (1998) *Jacobean Gentleman: Sir Edwin Sandys, 1561–1629*, Princeton, NJ: Princeton University Press.

Renfrew, C. (1969) "Trade and Culture Process in European Prehistory," *Current Anthropology* 10: 151–69.

Richter, D. K. (2007) "Tsenacommacah and the Atlantic World," in *The Atlantic World and Virginia, 1550–1624*, Peter C. Mancall (ed.), Chapel Hill: University of North Carolina Press.

Sacks, D. H. (2001) "The Promise and the Contract in Early Modern England: Slade's Case in Perspective," in *Rhetoric and Law in Early Modern Europe*, Victoria Kahn and Lorna Hutson (eds.), New Haven, CT: Yale University Press.
Smith, J. (1986) *The Complete Works of Captain John Smith*, 3 vols, Philip L. Barbour (ed.), Chapel Hill: University of North Carolina Press.
Stewart, R. M. (1989) "Trade and Exchange in Middle Atlantic Region Prehistory," *Archaeology of Eastern North America* 17: 47–58.
Strachey, W. (1973) "A True Reportory," in *A Voyage to Virginia in 1609*, Lewis B. Wright (ed.), Charlottesville: University Press of Virginia.
Tawney, R. H. (1969) *Religion and the Rise of Capitalism: A Historical Study*, Harmondsworth: Penguin.
Tawney, R. H. and E. Power (eds.) (1924) *Tudor Economic Documents, Vol. 3*, London: Longmans, Green & Co.
Virginia Company. (1978) "A True Declaration of the Estate of the Colony in Virginia (November 1610)," in *New American World: A Documentary History of North America to 1612, Vol. 5*, D. B. Quinn (ed.), London: Macmillan.
Wayne, D. (1982) "Drama and Society in the Age of Jonson: An Alternative View," *Renaissance Drama* 13: 102–29.

# 8
# GOTHIC ECONOMIES
## Capitalism and vampirism

*Lauren Bailey*

John Polidori's "The Vampyre" (1819) presents us with one of the first vampires in British fiction. In this tale, readers face a supernatural villain that is as economic as it is monstrous. Lord Ruthven represents not only a member of the wealthy elite who preys upon those in lower socioeconomic positions, but also what becomes of unregulated self-interest in an economic system that promotes consumption for consumption's sake.

Straddling Enlightenment empiricism and Romantic aesthetics, Gothic fiction of the late eighteenth- and early nineteenth-century engages with both ancient folklore and budding theories of political economy as a way of understanding the cultural discourse contemporary to its time. Given that the Gothic is "a broken historical descent, a cultural heritage grown balefully strange," and a romance of "dislocated origin" (Duncan 1992: 23), this genre tends to work with history and timelines differently than others. Though Gothic fiction harkens back to the past, it does so as a way of grappling with current politico-economic conditions, living out society's fears of the unknown to their fullest and most horrifying potential.

Adam Smith's *Wealth of Nations* (1776) attempts to describe its own phenomena—economics. Smith sets out to gather information about the intricacies of societies, looking at how a society gathers its wealth, from where, and to what effect. The pretense of this project is observational science: that Smith produces an objective study of labor, trade, markets, and economic systems in the wake of the shift from mercantilism to capitalism. However, *Wealth of Nations* is in every way inflected by not just Smith's own moral philosophy, but with the late eighteenth-century drive toward empiricism and science. In what may seem like a curious section, Smith engages with contemporary physicians' theories on the preservation of a "healthful state of the human body" despite "very faulty regimen[s]," referring to diet and exercise. Likewise, Smith makes the argument that the "political body" functions much in the same way in that the "the wisdom of nature has ...remed[ied] many of the effects of the folly and injustice of man." Smith continues this analogy of bodies to the subject of reproduction, arguing in great detail that artificers, manufacturers, and merchants are neither "barren [nor] unproductive" (Smith 1976a: 673–4). Smith means here to suggest that the body of society functions through the cooperation of its several different moving parts. There is no intentionality here, only sheer function at the design of biology. Smith imagines both human body and global economy as adaptive systems. Though generally able to readjust and function without much direct intervention, there are still benefits to better diet and consequences to malnutrition—or to return to economic discourse, there is still a need for moderate regulation.

*Wealth of Nations* makes famous the metaphor of the "invisible hand," which in the nineteenth century becomes synonymous with laissez-faire economics. As many recent New Economic critics have pointed out, it is often misapplied to situations in which the state of the nation, economy, or being in general is left to destiny, fate, or God—and presumably to a positive end (see Courtemanche 2011). So then, any actions and all associated consequences, positive or negative, will somehow work themselves out to the benefit of all. However, this is not what Smith implies. Smith does not state that consequences will only ever be positive nor does he suggest that there is a beneficent presence which consciously drives all economic actions into happy outcomes. The explanation he offers is meant to illustrate the lack of relationality of self-interest to public interest, dismantling presumptions of cause/effect. More simply put, it is nearly impossible to trace the effect of an individual's action on a macroeconomic scale. Whether or not someone intends a particular effect when acting out a certain course of action, it has no bearing on what will actually happen. Smith writes:

> He generally, indeed, neither intends to promote the public interest, nor knows how much he is promoting it… by directing that industry in such a manner as its produce may be of the greatest value, he intends only his own gain, and he is in this, as in many other cases, led by an invisible hand to promote an end which was no part of his intention. Nor is it always the worse for the society that it was no part of it. By pursuing his own interest he frequently promotes that of the society more effectually than when he really intends to promote it. I have never known much good done by those who affected to trade for the public good.
>
> *(Smith 1976a: 456)*

Smith's text reads that in the interest of increasing society's annual revenue insofar as it affects the individual's capital, yes, individuals "direct [their] industry [so] that its produce may be of the greatest value." Yet, the individual does not act with direct intention to benefit the revenue of society. This idea of an invisible hand, then, refers to the unintentional, out-of-scale outcome of one's actions on a societal level, however incremental or incidental the individual's action may have been.

This experimental politico-economic theory comes two and a half decades after *The Theory of Moral Sentiments* (1759) in which Smith explores constructions of sympathy (see Greiner 2012). Smith understands there to be certain compulsory sentiments tethered to human nature and the experience of them as equal parts physical and intellectual, additionally molded by situation and upbringing. The sympathetic component of the human state, and its desire to exchange positions and sentiments with others, is crucial to his understandings of political economy. Indeed, the ongoing efforts of humans to understand one another are necessary to a well-functioning society. He argues that "…to feel much for others and little for ourselves, that to restrain our selfish, and to indulge our benevolent affections, constitutes the perfection of human nature" (Smith 1976b: 25). Smith's philosophies of political economy attempt to bridge together "two rival ways of representing complex social systems" just as fiction attempts to grapple with "networked effects, fantasies of infinite social interconnectedness, and unintended consequences" (Courtemanche 2011: 3).

This need for cultural and interpersonal connectedness within Smith's economic analysis is surely impacted by eighteenth-century social anxieties surrounding Britons' rapid increase and diversification of trade, development of several new, large-scale industries, expansion of global markets, and growth of empire (see Sussman 2000). The British body itself changed quite drastically in both composition and appearance throughout the 1700s. The social ramifications of these types of economic changes are notably widespread. By the end of the eighteenth century, Britain had found itself at the center of several international markets. The pursuit of free trade brought with it unparalleled access to new goods, many of which could be imported for far less than it would cost to produce them domestically. From a Smithian standpoint, "[i]f a foreign country can supply us with a commodity cheaper than we ourselves can make it, better buy it of them" (Smith 1976a: 457), so long as it is done in moderation, avoiding inflation of other markets and any detriment to supporting domestic industries. However, with "too many worldly goods" and a "dazzling array of products" comes "social mobility, arousing fears about the malleability of human personality and its trappings" (Festa 2009: 68). The desire for increased imperialism and capitalist exchange brings with it the risks of exposure and consumption of the outside and Other. What was once inaccessible, safely closed off and in the distance, is now circulating onto domestic land. The fears following the economic shifts of the market manage to seep into Polidori's Gothic narrative via Lord Ruthven's relentless, consumptive self-interest.

Gothic fiction often focuses on the inevitability of consequences, and "The Vampyre" makes it clear that unmitigated self-interest is horrific. Lord Ruthven effects sheer terror in those around him as they are trapped by their circumstances of supreme vulnerability and forced into victimhood. While the absence of sympathy makes Lord Ruthven the ideal villain, the fact that he has much in common with a successful capitalist makes him all the more threatening.

Lord Ruthven lacks sympathy and exists only as a parasitic form. He produces nothing and offers little-to-no reciprocation for the labor and life force he receives from others. Worse yet, his consumption corrupts those around him—"...his character was dreadfully vicious, for that the possession of irresistible powers of seduction, rendered his licentious habits more dangerous to society" (Polidori 2014: 91). Since the ability to consume increases with one's socioeconomic status, Lord Ruthven is a more dangerous consumer, or at the least, one with wider access and more damaging effect.

Although Smith acknowledges in *Wealth of Nations* that consumption can be "hurtful to society" if the expense of consumption comes "without increasing production, or establishing any permanent fund for supporting that expense" (294), he also claims that "consumption is the sole end and purpose of all production; and the interest of the producer ought to be attended to only so far as it may be necessary for promoting that of the consumer" (660). Thus, in a society that values consumerism above all, Lord Ruthven has free reign to use and discard others to whatever degree of callousness and vulgarity he prefers.

Initially, he fools young protagonist Aubrey and members of high social circles alike into believing that he has a "hatred of vice" (Polidori 2014: 89). They believe him to be of exceptionally high moral fiber. In fact, Aubrey is unable to envision a person who could be wholly self-interested in the first case: "the very impossibility of forming an idea of the character of a man entirely absorbed in himself... he soon formed this object into the hero of a romance" (90). Aubrey is swept away by Romanticism, having "cultivated more his imagination than his judgment" (90), more concerned with the sublime austerity of his surroundings than minding the cunning behavior and extortionist schemes of his companion.

Aubrey's naïveté in this instance is shared by all those around him as Lord Ruthven's crimes go undiscovered for lengthy periods of time. Believed to be quite charitable, Lord Ruthven offers substantial economic relief to many of those who approach him. He is "profuse in his liberality;—the idle, the vagabond, and the beggar, received from his hand more than enough to relieve their immediate wants" (90). Puzzlingly, Lord Ruthven refuses those who appear to be in the most need, though. In fact, he declines to aid those who are known to be quite virtuous, having fallen onto tough times from "misfortunes attendant even upon virtue," and rejects them "with hardly suppressed sneers" (91). Instead, he prefers to bequeath small fortunes to "the profligate… to allow him to wallow in his lust… to sink him still deeper in his iniquity" (91).

Lord Ruthven revels in the further demise of social deviants. This should not be confused with any ill-informed attempt at justice—he acts out of no concern for the community. Rather, he seeks profit for himself at the suffering of others: "…all those upon whom it was bestowed, inevitably found that there was a curse upon it, for they were all either led to the scaffold, or sunk to the lowest and the most abject misery" (91). Once low enough, he is able to strike without fear of repercussion. As a true testament to his capitalist villainy, Lord Ruthven not only derives great pleasure from watching others' descent into economic and therefore social disgrace, but feeds on them once they have fallen low enough that others disregard them. As a predator with its prey, "when he encountered the rash youthful novice, or the luckless father of a numerous family; then his very wish seemed fortune's law… his eyes sparkled with more fire than that of the cat whilst dallying with the half-dead mouse" (91). He increases his supply of goods at the expense of others, promoting consumption to the point of depletion, and stripping his victims of their resources beyond the extent of repair. He deliberately situates himself in positions of socioeconomic power in order to orchestrate the fall of others: "In every town, he left the formerly affluent youth, torn from the circle he adorned… many a father sat frantic, amidst… hungry children, without a single farthing… to satisfy their present craving" (91).

As much as his victims suffer economic losses, Lord Ruthven deliberately squanders his gains—simply because he can. He takes "no money from the gambling table; but immediately los[es], to the ruiner of many" (91), making his exit from the setting as abruptly as he had entered. As soon as his "affairs [are] embarrassed" (90), Lord Ruthven takes his leave of the scene, draining entire social networks of their financial resources.

As Lord Ruthven moves about different cities and countries, he leaves not only a trail of debt and destitution, but of missing women, who when finally found are nothing but drained corpses. In this fictional text as well as in nineteenth-century England itself, women are seen as particularly susceptible to the manipulation of capitalist ventures. As the marketplace expands, so too does the fear that women would fall victim to its whims, be it from the foreignness of its goods and men or the power of its economic force. As numerous young women with connections to Lord Ruthven end up missing or otherwise ruined after having been found no longer chaste, Aubrey realizes that

> his contempt for the adulteress had not originated in hatred of her character; but that he had required, to enhance his gratification, that his victim, the partner of his guilt, should be hurled from the pinnacle of unsullied virtue, down to the lowest abyss of infamy and degradation.
>
> *(92)*

Lord Ruthven is drawn to these women not for the appeal of vice but for their virtue—the status of ideal English womanhood. He delights in the idea that he might "throw fear into those breasts where thoughtlessness reigned" and is "as often among those females who form the boast of their sex from their domestic virtues, as among those who sully it by their vices" (89).

Well aware of his society's valuation of female virginity, Lord Ruthven deliberately manipulates women into the exchange of their sexual chastity for his attention. His pleasure is in driving down value, and in the case of the marriage market, the virtue of a young, marriageable woman is an invaluable commodity. With no interest in marriage and no sympathy for the women he coaxes into compromising situations, nor the families that he destroys along the way, he consumes so that others may not. With limited economic opportunities outside the home, marriage is the only possibility of economic stability for the vast majority of women. At the mercy of others in positions of more power, young women such as Ianthe, Aubrey's love interest, are found in a system that prioritizes the needs of vampires above their own. Ianthe warns Aubrey of a "living vampyre" who "feeds upon the life of a lovely female to prolong his existence for the ensuing months" (93), but Aubrey fails to either draw the connection to Lord Ruthven or fully grasp the brutal severity of his affectionless transactions. By the time that Aubrey confronts Lord Ruthven about his interest in using women simply for sport, knowing that his seduction will

> most likely end in the ruin of an innocent, though thoughtless girl...Lord Ruthven answered that his intentions were such as he supposed all would have upon such an occasion; and upon being pressed whether he intended to marry her, merely laughed.
>
> *(92)*

Lord Ruthven is thoroughly disinterested in the pain or humiliation that he causes others. This blatant disregard for the humanity of the women he seduces before ultimately draining of their vitality evokes feelings of horror while also drawing attention to the cruelty of one-sided economic exchanges. Lord Ruthven controls the terms of these exchanges with women entirely. He can take as much from them as he desires and give nothing in return.

After corrupting and murdering Ianthe, he moves onto gaining the attentions of Aubrey's sister. Using the social currency of his status, Lord Ruthven invests his time and energy in Miss Aubrey, who is defenseless against him:

> Who could resist his power? His tongue had dangers and toils to recount—could speak of himself as of an individual having no sympathy with any being on the crowded earth, save with her to whom he addressed himself;—could tell how, since he knew her, his existence, had begun to seem worthy of preservation, if it were merely that he might listen to her soothing accents;—in fine, he knew so well how to use the serpent's art, or such was the will of fate, that he gained her affections.
>
> *(100)*

His status as a confident, self-interested capitalist is highly advantageous. His small investment of dishonest communication enables him the management of their relationship, and her reputation, in full. He sits in the position of control, capable of withdrawing his support as readily as he supplied it. Worse, with the added power of having spoiled her credit, he can now cost Miss Aubrey her own social standing at his whim, as he reminds Aubrey, "...if not my bride today, your sister is dishonoured. Women are frail!" (101).

Aubrey cannot appeal to Lord Ruthven's sense of self-interest. There is nothing that he can offer the vampire that he could not just take on his own. Against a villain with the ability to take anything and as much as he desires, Aubrey can gain nothing from the advantages of Lord Ruthven. As Smith explains,

> It is not from the benevolence of the butcher, the brewer, or the baker, that we expect our dinner, but from their regard to their own interest. We address ourselves, not to their humanity but to their self-love, and never talk to them of our own necessities but of their advantages.
>
> *(Smith 1976a: 26–7)*

Without the power to act on his own behalf, and with no assistance, no charity, Aubrey is left without recourse. He dies devoid of his will and sense of self just as his sister's body is found, collapsed and drained of its blood.

The vampire in this tale acts as a manifestation of anxieties about unchecked self-interest and indulgence in a new economic system. The assumption that women are in special need of protection and regulation only heightens the Gothic effect of this story with its masculinized economic threat. Lord Ruthven's violent misadventures of material and metaphorical consumption play well upon looming fears of capitalism as something as gruesome as it is individualist. By showcasing what society suffers through its failure to protect the most vulnerable, "The Vampyre" epitomizes the dire consequences of an ineffectual regulatory system.

## References

Çelikkol, Ayse. (2011) *Romances of Free Trade: British Literature, Laissez-Faire, and the Global Nineteenth Century*, Oxford: Oxford University Press.

Courtemanche, Eleanor. (2011) *The 'Invisible Hand' and British Fiction, 1818–1860*, London: Palgrave Macmillan.

Duncan, Ian. (1992) *Modern Romance and Transformations of the Novel: The Gothic, Scott, Dickens*, Cambridge: Cambridge University Press.

Festa, Lynn. (2009) *Sentimental Figures of Empire in Eighteenth-Century Britain and France*, Baltimore, MD: Johns Hopkins University Press.

Greiner, Rae. (2012) *Sympathetic Realism in Nineteenth-Century British Fiction*, Baltimore, MD: Johns Hopkins University Press.

Polidori, John. (2014) "The Vampyre," in Corinna Wagner (ed.), *Gothic Evolutions: Poetry, Tales, Context, Theory*, Peterborough: Broadview Press.

Smith, Adam. (1976a) *An Inquiry into the Nature and Causes of the Wealth of Nations*, Oxford: Oxford University Press.

Smith, Adam. (1976b) *The Theory of Moral Sentiments*, Oxford: Oxford University Press.

Sussman, Charlotte. (2000) *Consuming Anxieties: Consumer Protest, Gender & British Slavery, 1713–1833*, Palo Alto, CA: Stanford University Press.

# 9
# THE PRINT REVOLUTION AND PAPER MONEY

*Mary McAleer Balkun*

From the earliest days of the nation's settlement, and despite scarce resources and few avenues for distribution, colonial Americans had access to printed material. The first printing press was brought to Cambridge, Massachusetts, from England in 1638 by Stephen Day, a former locksmith. The initial issue from the press was *The Freeman's Oath* (1639), followed the same year by an *Almanack* by William Pierce, a mariner. Then, in 1640, Day published the first book in English in America, *The Whole Booke of Psalmes* (the *Bay Psalm Book*). In 1685, William Bradford founded a press in Philadelphia, publishing "Kalendarium Pennsilvaniense" (for which he and the author, Samuel Atkins, were reprimanded, initiating a series of run-ins with the Pennsylvania government). In 1693, Bradford went to New York to establish a press there, and was ultimately printer of the first paper currency in that colony in 1709. But it is Benjamin Franklin who remains the best known of the colonial printers, primarily because of his *Autobiography*, where he details his time as an apprentice for his brother, James, publisher of the *New England Courant*, as well as his later efforts to establish his own business. Opening his shop in 1728, Franklin not only published the *Pennsylvania Gazette* and the iconic *Poor Richard's Almanack* but he was also one of the most successful printers of paper currency in the colonies, as well as a staunch advocate of paper money as opposed to specie. Finally, Franklin was a forerunner in the publication of English novels, producing three editions of Samuel Richardson's *Pamela* (1740), although novels were never an important part of his business. In the history of American printing, Franklin is a pivotal figure for many reasons, not least of which because in his person print culture, paper currency, and fiction intersect—a triad that would steadily gain in importance after the American Revolution and increase exponentially in the nineteenth century.

While printed matter was available from the mid-seventeenth century onward, albeit in limited form, the growth of print culture was relatively slow in the colonies. In *Letters of the Republic*, Michael Warner observes that by the mid-eighteenth century, "newspapers were being published regularly in the major towns," while "Pamphlets and broadsides were a familiar and normal feature of politics" (61). It was not until later in the century, however, that the print explosion resulted in the proliferation of newspapers and books. Describing the latter part of the century as "the heyday of the small newspaper," Warner observes that "more newspapers were founded in the 1790s than had been started in the entire century preceding" (125). However, as Cathy Davidson notes in *Revolution and the Word*, her seminal study of the American novel, printing in the early years of the Republic, was still hampered by certain material facts: supplies had to be imported from England, and in fact most books were also imported. She observes that

> only a limited number of books (chapbooks, almanacs, Bibles, and a few other steady sellers) were readily available to the populace at large. Although the Revolution had officially ended that world, almost half a century would elapse before American publishing would be consolidated into large dynastic houses and cheap books would become big business.
>
> *(74)*

In addition, distribution was difficult, a situation that would not be improved until new methods of transporting books were introduced, including better roadways and the railroad (Davidson 2004: 74).

There was also a direct correlation between class status and access to print culture, a connection that inevitably impacted the way printed matter was understood. In *The Republic in Print*, Trish Loughran asserts that despite the increased availability of printed matter by 1800, "most Americans lived beyond the reach of any printed matter that was not produced by their own local printer or privately sent to them through personal connections" (33), and print matter was still a luxury rather than a necessity (34). In addition, despite what authors might have preferred, "print played a smaller role in daily life than we might imagine" (33). The print revolution first impacted the "growing urban middle class whose literacy and hunger for printed commodities has been well documented" (34). As many others have indicated, print culture also resulted in such phenomena as the growing interest in personal privacy, which was itself related to the "emphasis on individual rights and freedoms that print helped develop" (Rubinstein 1994). More significantly, according to Geoffrey Rubinstein:

> Print injected Western culture with the principles of standardization, verifiability and communication that comes from one source and is disseminated to many geographically dispersed receivers. As illustrated by dramatic reform in religious thought and scientific inquiry, print innovations helped bring about sharp challenges to institutional control. Print facilitated a focus on fixed, verifiable truth.

On the other hand, print also led to questions about the very nature of reality and truth. This is most evident in debates about the novel, the genre that owes its existence, as we know it today, to print culture. But it also arises in connection with paper currency, the history of which is inextricably aligned with the history of printing in America.

In "Jedidiah Morse and the Transformation of Print Culture in New England, 1784–1826," Leon Jackson considers "printedness" and its impact on the new Republic, pointing out that printedness often centered on questions of "the location and nature of authority within printed texts" (3). While Jackson is referring primarily to controversies over "libel law, legislation on copyright, arguments over anonymity, calls for professionalization of authorship, and the proliferation of the popular press" (3), questions about the authority of the text had long been raised in connection with another form of printed matter: paper money. Warner's analysis of print culture in part rests on his premise that print is "constructed on the basis of its metonymic embodiment in printed artifacts" (61), and that this relationship also exists for printed currency. He argues not only that "It was not accidental that the public debates of print discourse took shape in relation to the emergent forms of currency and commerce" but that from the outset "Printers sold their products as goods and advertised other goods. They also printed the experimental new paper currencies of the eighteenth century, as well as increasingly detailed trade reports" (62). The result was an "economy of discourse" that is "the decisive feature of print capitalism" (63). In positing a form of exchange in which an abstract public is only made real through print, Warner's study raises fundamental questions about the very nature of money as both representational and as an object of exchange, and this is at the heart of the debates over paper as opposed to other forms of currency, such as in the paper versus specie debates.

Georg Simmel in *The Philosophy of Money* advances the theory that "money in terms of its pure concept…is nothing but the pure form of exchangeability. It embodies that element or function of things, by virtue of which they are economic" (138). From a poststructuralist perspective, because the material form of money has no direct relationship to its inherent value,

> money, like language, is a symbol that can never fully close the gap between representation and reality. This analogy leads to others: crediting a piece of money, for example, requires a suspension of disbelief not unlike what a reader brings to imaginative literature.
>
> *(Baker and Wertheimer 2006: 398)*

This is reminiscent of Roland Barthes' observation that the inscription on money—whether paper or metal—is one indication that money, either as index or sign, is "always subject to a writing" (40). Thus, debates over the relationship between the form of money and its perceived value, especially in a print culture, inevitably come back to the authority and truth value of the text on the page.

The questions and concerns associated with paper money have a long history in America, beginning with the first issue of print currency in 1690, which occurred in response to demands for payment from soldiers from New England and New York who had fought an unsuccessful campaign against Canada. Alan Watson points out,

> Although economic historians of the past generation have contended that the colonials possessed sufficient circulating media, including coins, and that complaints of inadequacy arose only when the colonials were unable to pay their debts or when they were seeking exemptions from restrictions on the emission of currency, such observations have generally been based on studies of the northern and middle provinces, or they have been derived from questionable extrapolations of disparate data.
>
> *(189)*

The 1690 issue marks the start of what Farley Grubb describes as the first of "two distinct epochs of paper money" (3) in the nation. It also introduces the primary and continuing reason for printing paper currency: shortages in the amount of specie available to colonial leadership to pay debts a colony had accrued (see Rothbard 2002). According to Grubb,

> paper money became useful as a circulating medium of exchange for facilitating private trade within the colony/state issuing it. By legal statute and precedent, people could always use their paper money to pay the taxes and mortgage payments owed to the government that had issued that specific paper money, which, in turn, gave that money a local 'currency'.
>
> *(3)*

However, as Adolphus Mordecai Hart explains (in the oldest history of American paper currency), the fluctuating value of the paper currency proved a problem from the start. Soon after it was distributed, the 1690 issue proved to be worth as just one-third of its value, possibly as the result of so-called "leather money" from Ireland that had made its way to the colonies and increased suspicion about paper currency (5). The instability of paper currency, however, did not prevent colonial governments from continuing to produce it, even in the face of English objections (see Watson 2002: 184), and to produce it in such quantities that it ultimately became worth even less than the paper on which it was printed. Massachusetts provides one example. Louis Jordan describes a situation where one could trade 6s of paper for a Spanish silver dollar in 1690 and by 1737 it required "22s6d in paper money to equal a Spanish dollar."

Exacerbating the problem, each colony produced its own currency, so that, as Grubb notes, "There could be as many different paper monies as there were separate colonies and states" (3). The colonies ultimately moved beyond producing paper currency in order to address emergency expenditures, and starting in the 1720s, there was a general movement "toward paper money, with a view to making it a permanent fixture within their colonies," with Pennsylvania leading the way and proving to be "the most successful colony in this movement" (3). According to Grubb, "It is the birth of this permanent peacetime paper money supply that Franklin will affect" (3). The escalating challenge of worthless paper currency ultimately resulted in the decision in 1749 by the Massachusetts House of Representatives, following an agreement in which England reimbursed the colony in specie for its help during the Louisbourg campaign of King George's War, to redeem all paper currency and thereby attempt to return the colony to a "hard currency" (Tarnoff 2011: 20). Ben Taroff explains that the ensuing debates pitted rich against poor, merchants against farmers, and lenders against debtors (20). The controversy resulted from two opposing philosophical attitudes about "value":

> Hard-money supporters... saw value as being fixed and intrinsic. They believed that money only had value in proportion to its metallic content, and that silver and gold alone provided the bedrock upon which the edifice of a secure economy could be constructed. Paper's proponents, on the other hand, thought of money in more utilitarian terms" and "if money was a standard of exchange agreed upon by a group of individuals...then a scrap of paper could serve the purpose just as well as a silver coin.
>
> *(22)*

These were not new arguments, nor were they limited to the events of 1749. John Dixon traces an array of responses to paper money: from John Colman, a Boston businessman, who "asked in 1720, 'What intrinsick value is there in Silver and Gold?'" to the Reverend John Wise, who "declared gold and silver 'empty Cyphers, in the Affairs of Mankind,'" to the clergyman Thomas Paine, who "aligned paper money with the 'Popish Doctrine of Transubstantiation,'" and, finally, to "one Cornelius Agrippa," who "rejected paper bills as 'a false Weight, and a false Ballance, which are an Abomination unto the lord'" (81). Sinful, deceitful, and even immoral, paper money "was a kind of illusionists's trick with potentially catastrophic consequences, an intrinsically deceitful medium that bred bad behavior" (Tarnoff 2011: 24).

These attitudes and concomitant fears are also evident in the paper money debates of the late eighteenth and early nineteenth centuries, when the expansion of printing meant that even greater numbers of bills could be produced more easily. The debates were fueled for years to come by the decision of the Continental Congress to finance the Revolutionary War effort by printing "Continental dollars," which it did in such increasing numbers that "by the spring of 1781, the Continentals were virtually worthless, exchanging on the market at 168 paper dollars to one dollar in specie." Murray Rothbard notes that "the collapse of the Continental currency gave rise to the phrase, 'not worth a Continental.'" In addition,

> several states issued their own paper money, and each depreciated at varying rates. Virginia and the Carolinas led the inflationary move, and by the end of the war, state issues added a total of 210 million depreciated dollars to the nation's currency.
>
> *(Rothbard 2002: 59–60)*

In fact, there was a direct correlation between the failed Continental and the new rules about printing and circulation of currency that were built into the Constitution. Kevin McLaughlin argues that the failed Continental dollar revealed a fear about paper money that would "not only drive monetary debate and policy in the nineteenth century, it also led to a sense of shame at the nation's paper origins" (46). The incident also led to Shay's Rebellion, a series of violent uprisings in 1786 and 1787 by farmers unable to pay their debts and facing the loss of their property.

Both the decision of the Massachusetts House of Representatives and that of the Continental Congress exemplify the basic fears about paper money that are outlined by Charles Gide in *Political Economy* (1883). In his analysis of Gide's theories in *The Coiners of Language*, Jean-Joseph Goux notes that, for Gide,

> the value of paper money is *precarious*, for it depends entirely on the legislator's will and can be annihilated by the very law that created it. If the Law demonetizes paper money, the bearer of notes is left with nothing but useless scraps of paper: the loss of legal value is the loss of all value,

a situation which does not apply to metallic money, according to Gide, because it has a "natural" or "intrinsic value…underpinning its legal value" (127). If, as Gide maintains, the only value in paper money is that conferred by law (128), then the next phase in paper currency seems most logical, since what Grubb describes as the second epoch begins with the ratification of the Constitution, which specifically denied to both the state and national legislatures the power to issue "bills of credit." This resulted in "the ascendance of a government-chartered and -regulated, but privately run, bank-based system of issuing paper money, an epoch we are still in today" (3).

Unfortunately, this restriction applied only to paper currency issued by the federal government. According to Stephen Mihm, banks were still able to issue notes that were essentially

> surrogates of money, slips of paper that could, in theory, be converted to real money (specie) when presented at the counter of the issuing bank. Within a few years of the ratification of the Constitution, a growing number of states had chartered banks and other corporations that could issue their own money.

As a result, the banks and corporations that issued notes increased from just a few in the 1790s, to approximately 250 by 1815, to 330 by 1830, to 901 by 1840, until, "By 1860, some 1,562 banks, or 'rag manufactories,' as one critic called them, churned out a dizzying stream of colorful bits of paper" (Mihm 2004). The effect, according to Mihm, was profound:

> With every bank commissioning money of its own design (and in denominations, sizes, and colors of its choosing) more than ten thousand *different* kinds of notes bobbed up and down in the streams of commerce by the late 1850s, continually changing hands and baffling the uninitiated.

However, not everyone at the turn of the century was opposed to banks as generators of paper currency. In one essay from the period, "The Utility of Country Banks Considered," the author maintains that banks increase the amount of available specie, as well as increasing "commerce and productivity" (Thompson 1996: 81). In addition, a bank's currency could be trusted to the extent that people had confidence in the firm that produced it; in that case, according to the anonymous author, "its promissory notes [would] have the same currency as gold and silver money" (81). The utilitarian perspective on money is most closely associated with a figure who was involved in the currency debates from his earliest days, and who was still weighing in on the matter near the end of his life: Benjamin Franklin.

As Grubb observes in "Ben Franklin and Birth of Paper Money":

> No other American was involved over as long a period of time with so many different facets of colonial paper money as was Benjamin Franklin… [He] arrived in Philadelphia the year paper money was first issued by Pennsylvania (1723), and he soon became a keen observer of and commentator on colonial money. He wrote pamphlets, treatises, and letters about paper money. He designed and printed paper money for various colonies. He entertained ideas about and proposed alternative monetary systems. As an assemblyman for the colony of Pennsylvania, he was involved in the debates during the 1740s and 1750s over the management of that colony's paper money. As a lobbyist for various colonies to the British court, he dealt with conflicts over colonial paper money that arose between Britain and her colonies in the 1760s and 1770s. Finally, at the end of his life as one of the preeminent Founding Fathers at the 1787 Constitutional Convention, he participated in constitutionally ending the first epoch and so helped usher in the second epoch of paper money in America.
>
> *(3–4)*

On more than one occasion, Franklin wrote in favor of a paper currency (although some critics note that his support also had its extrinsic rewards, since he was eventually given the contract to print Pennsylvania's money, and later printed money for Delaware and New Jersey). His first such effort was a pamphlet entitled "The Nature and Necessity of a Paper Currency," published anonymously in 1729, in which he makes the innovative argument "that money in circulation derived its value from the sum of all such transactions—all things made and all the services people exchange" (Levenson 2016: 31). In other words, money represents labor and its value inheres from that. In the latter part of the century, Franklin supported the system of bank-issued paper currency and even claimed to have purchased shares in the Bank of North America (Grubb 2006: 8).

Yet, Franklin's most important role in the saga of American currency may have been his successful efforts to combat counterfeiting, the single greatest threat to the validity and stability of money. While printers had resorted to a variety of methods to thwart counterfeiters, such as using "special typefaces and type ornaments, sometimes cut by hand, in the hopes that counterfeiters would find it too expensive to reproduce the banknotes" (Lynch 2007), nothing seemed to work consistently. And while the more experienced might be able to identify and avoid counterfeit currency, Jack Lynch observes that "the merchants who had to deal with them were baffled," and he cites David R. Johnson, who maintains that

> 'Rural colonists were not very familiar with paper money because their daily lives did not revolve around commercial transactions; furthermore, they had a deep prejudice against it because they did not regard it as 'real' money.' Because merchants lacked familiarity with authentic paper money, they could be fooled by some surprisingly amateurish counterfeits.

Franklin's solution—a process which was kept secret in his lifetime and not recovered until the 1960s–was based on the work of the master engraver, Joseph Breitnall, who invented a process for producing engravings of leaves. Franklin made a plaster cast of the leaf, and then used a copper plate press to add the image to the paper. Because the leaf cast was so intricate, the process was kept secret. Franklin's method was quite successful.

It is ironic that Franklin, known for his creation of a series of personae, identified the central requirement for a paper currency, aptly summarized by Tarnoff: people have to believe in it. In "Legal and Illegal Moneymaking: Colonial American Counterfeiters and the Novelization of Eighteenth-Century Crime Literature," Todd Barosky makes some important observations about the relationship between counterfeit paper money and fiction, specifically crime fiction of the mid-eighteenth century. These are equally relevant to American print culture in the late eighteenth and early nineteenth centuries, especially in light of the rise of the novel. Barosky contends that counterfeit money not only "complicates new forms of monetary symbolization, but it does so by contesting the capacity for symbolization itself, and thus seems not merely to change but actually to deny 'the meaning of meaning.'" He continues:

> The act of counterfeiting, insofar as it is successful, therefore functions as a critique of legitimized forms of monetary symbolization while also providing a model for theorizing the truth content of literary representations within a novelistic discourse characterized by the absence of durable frameworks of authority.
>
> *(536)*

Wendy Bellion discusses, in *Citizen Spectator*, how interest in—and fears about—imitation in this period extended not just to personal behavior but also to "signatures, letters, paper money, even paintings," which could be imitated for purposes of "fraud and deceit" (173). Anxieties about fiction are very much related to anxieties about the nature of truth and authority in relation to currency, and these concerns about money are actually addressed in works of fiction in this period.

The idea of reading as a transaction between text and reader, similar to transactions involving money, is a staple of econo-literary criticism, and much of this stems from the work of Jean-Joseph Goux and his "vision of homology between monetary and literary signification" (Hites 2016: 435). According to Goux:

> nineteenth-century literary realism drew on the convertibility of language to reality just as the monetary realism of the convertible note rested on a foundation of gold, both depending on neutral referential relations between signifier and signified, paper and gold, text and value, narrative and life.
>
> *(Hites 2016: 435)*

For example, Jennifer Jordan Baker points to Hugh Henry Brackenridge's *Modern Chivalry* (1792) as one example of a text that reflects contemporary fears about the insubstantiality of paper money, a novel where "people make promises they cannot keep and turn words into wind" (2). She also points back to Larzer Ziff's *Writing the New Nation*, where he argues that

> One signature of early American literature... was the fear that personal 'immanence' could be replaced entirely by textual 'representation,' thus creating a society in which people interact less with other individuals than with textual representations of those individuals in letters, pamphlets, newspaper pieces, and books.
>
> *(Baker 2008: 2; Ziff 1991: 17, 58)*

Baker adds that "Ziff aptly attributes this fear to a new concept of personal wealth based on abstract forms of wealth, such as paper money, stocks, mortgages, and loans" (2). A similar relationship in a contemporary monetary situation—in this case the panic of 1837, which pitted the "paper money men" against the "gold bugs"—is reflected in Edgar Allan Poe's story, "The Gold Bug" (1843). However, McLaughlin notes that Poe was not the first to engage the paper money debate in his fiction. In *Sot-Weed Redivivus* (1730), Ebeneezer Cooke enjoins the colony to "abandon its use of the besotting currency of 'Indian Weed'...in favor of 'Paper made of Rags'" (47).

This intersection of currency and fiction is even more overt in Charles Brockden Brown's fiction, especially *Arthur Mervyn* (1799), where "a contested $20,000 bank note is discovered sewn into a literary manuscript" (Baker 2008: 121). Baker also points to J. Hector St. Jean de Crèvecoeur's *Letters From An American Farmer* (1782), and the wife's concerns about "paper culture" in its various forms, whether Farmer James' literary aspirations or paper credit (159–60). In "Paper Money Gets Personal," Baker examines the eighteenth-century practice of having money serve as an actual character in a variety of literary genres: speeches, poems, essays, and tales. Finally, Marc Shell cites the common use of the metaphor of "ghostliness" by poets and economists of the period to describe paper money (6). As he explains, both paper money and artistic productions depend on the "willing suspension of belief," a fact that disturbed writers such as Melville, who was especially troubled by the "fear that all literature was, like money... a merely passable 'naught'—a mere cipher" (7). Shell adds,

> Credit, or belief, involves the very ground of aesthetic experience, and the same medium that seems to confer belief in fiduciary money (bank notes) and in scriptural money (created by the process of bookkeeping) also seems to confer it in literature.
>
> *(7)*

Ultimately, the print revolution brought to the foreground and even intensified fears and biases that had long existed in American politics, economics, and culture, especially in regards to paper money. The dollar became the repository for all questions about authenticity, authority, truth, reliability, individuality, and even independence. A common paper currency was the final signal that a rough assemblage of thirteen individual colonies was now a single unit, determining its own future, and writing its own story. The paper dollar was one of the many surfaces upon which that narrative would now be written.

## References

Baker, Jennifer J. (2008) *Securing the Commonwealth: Debt, Speculation, and Writing in the Making of Early America*, Baltimore, MD: Johns Hopkins University Press.

Baker, Jennifer J. (2006) "Paper Money Gets Personal: Reading Credit and Character in Early America," *Common Place* 6.3. Web. www.common-place-archives.org/vol-06/no-03/baker/.

Baker, Jennifer J. and Eric Wertheimer. (2006) "Introduction," *Early American Literature* 41.3: 397–403.

Barosky, Todd. (2012) "Legal and Illegal Moneymaking: Colonial American Counterfeiters and the Novelization of Eighteenth-Century Crime Literature," *Early American Literature* 47: 531–60.

Barthes, Roland. (1974) *S/Z: An Essay*, Richard Miller (trans.), New York: Hill and Wang.

Bellion, Wendy. (2011) *Citizen Spectator: Art, Illusion, and Visual Perception in Early National America*, Chapel Hill: University of North Carolina Press.

Davidson, Cathy N. (2004) *Revolution and the Word: The Rise of the Novel in America*, New York: Oxford University Press.

Dixon, John. (2010) "Between Script and Specie: Cadwallader Colden's Printing Method and the Production of Permanent, Correct Knowledge," *Early American Studies* 8.1: 75–93.

Goux, Jean-Joseph. (1994) *The Coiners of Language*, Norman: University of Oklahoma Press.

Grubb, Farley. (2006) "Benjamin Franklin and the Birth of a Paper Money Economy," Philadelphia, PA: Federal Reserve Bank of Philadelphia. Lecture. www.philadelphiafed.org/-/media/publications/economic-education/ben-franklin-and-paper-money-economy.pdf.

Hart, Adolphus Mordecai. (1851) *History of the Issues of Paper-Money in the American Colonies: Anterior to the Revolution*, St. Louis, MO: Union Print.

Hatfield, Stuart. (2007) "British Counterfeiting During the American Revolution," *Journal of the American Revolution*. https://allthingsliberty.com/2015/10/faking-it-british-counterfeiting-during-the-american-revolution/.

Hites, Sándor. (2016) "On Monetary and Literary Fictions," *Neohelicon* 43.2: 427–43.

Jackson, Leon. (1999) "Jedidiah Morse and the Transformation of Print Culture in New England, 1784–1826," *Early American Literature* 34.1: 2–31.

Jordan, Louis. "'Colonial Currency' and 'Introduction to Early Massachusetts Currency.'" www.coins.nd.edu/ColCurrency/CurrencyText/MA-1690-1750.html.

Levenson, Thomas. (2010) "Benjamin Franklin's Greatest Invention," *American History* 45.4: 26–33.

Loughran, Trish. (2007) *The Republic in Print: Print Culture in the Age of U.S. Nation Building, 1770–1870*, New York: Columbia University Press.

Lynch, Jack. (2007) "The Golden Age of Counterfeiting: Cashing in on Colonial Currency," *Colonial Williamsburg: The Journal of Colonial Williamsburg Foundation* 29.3: 20–4. www.history.org/Foundation/journal/Summer07/counterfeit.cfm.

McAuley, Louis Kirk. (2013) *Print Technology in Scotland and America, 1740–1800*, Lewisburg, PA: Bucknell University Press.

McLaughlin, Kevin. (1999) "Just Fooling: Paper, Money, Poe," *Differences: A Journal of Feminist Cultural Studies* 11.1: 38–67.

Mihm, Stephen. (2004) "Accept No Imitations: The Campaign against Counterfeits, Past and Present," *Common-Place* 4.4. www.common-place-archives.org/vol-04/no-04/mihm/.

Rothbard, Murray. (2002) *A History of Money and Banking in the United States*, Auburn, AL: Ludwig Von Mises Institute.

Rubinstein, Geoffrey. (1994) "Printing: History and Development," *Karmark*. http://karmak.org/archive/2002/08/history_of_print.html.

Shell, Marc. (1993) *Money, Language, and Thought: Literary and Philosophic Economies from the Medieval to the Modern Era*, Baltimore, MD: Johns Hopkins University Press.

Tarnoff, Ben. (2011) *Moneymakers: The Wicked Lives and Surprising Adventures of Three Notorious Counterfeiters*, New York: Penguin.

Thompson, James. (1996) *Models of Value: Eighteenth-Century Political Economy and the Novel*, Durham, NC: Duke University Press.

Warner, Michael. (1990) *Letters of the Republic: Publication and the Public Sphere in Eighteenth-Century America*, Cambridge, MA: Harvard University Press.

Watson, Alan D. (2002) "Counterfeiting in Colonial North Carolina: A Reassessment," *North Carolina Historical Review* 79.2: 182–97.

Ziff, Larzer. (1991) *Writing in the New Nation: Prose, Print, and Politics in the Early United States*, New Haven, CT: Yale University Press.

# 10
# THE ECONOMICS OF AMERICAN LITERARY REALISM

*Henry B. Wonham*

This essay seeks to offer preliminary reflections on an unwieldy but important question: did the late nineteenth- and early twentieth-century writers associated with the development of literary realism in America espouse a particular understanding of the economic circumstances in which they lived? Two of those writers, Mark Twain and Charles Dudley Warner, hinted at a deep homology between the era's literary and economic themes when they entitled their 1871 novel (and the period in which it is set) *The Gilded Age*, a phrase with unmistakable economic resonance. But did the diverse set of writers generally aligned with the aesthetic disposition of realism—William Dean Howells, Rebecca Harding Davis, Sarah Orne Jewett, Henry James, Mary Wilkins Freeman, Hamlin Garland, Charles W. Chesnutt, Theodore Dreiser, Sui Sin Far, Frank Norris, Stephen Crane, Zitkala-Ša, Edith Wharton, Abraham Cahan, Jack London, Upton Sinclair, and many others—did this group of writers share an overriding interpretation of the economic conditions that inspired Twain and Warner to give the period its notorious moniker?

Critics sometimes identify certain writers on this list as "naturalists," a term borrowed from the nineteenth-century French movement whose leading literary voice was Emile Zola. According to this distinction in terminology, Howells, Twain, Davis, Jewett, James, and some others might be considered predominately "realists," while Dreiser, Norris, Crane, and Garland would qualify as "naturalists" by virtue of their Zolaesque interest in "dispassionate or 'scientific' depictions of the more lurid aspects of everyday urban and industrial life, with a special focus on lower-class criminality, sexuality, and alcoholism" (Barrish 2011: 115). Like all classificatory terms in literary studies, especially imported terms, "Naturalism" raises complications in the American context, not least because very few of the writers typically grouped under this conceptual umbrella (with the exception of Norris) accepted the association. In this essay, I have followed Philip Barrish's wise example from *The Cambridge Introduction to American Literary Realism* by using the term sparingly, less as a way of distinguishing between individual writers or works than as a means of identifying thematic concerns shared by some of the writers which I include under the larger umbrella of American literary realism.

I have deliberately made my list of notable realists so long in order to suggest the inherent difficulty of establishing anything like consensus on even the most general questions of economic policy and principle. Mark Twain and Ida Tarbell, the muckraking journalist, may have shared a certain instinct for the disclosure of sham and corruption—and hence a certain claim to status among writers of something loosely defined as realism—but one of them was entirely welcome within the private executive offices of the Standard Oil Trust, while the other launched a literary crusade against the very same company (see Messent 2009). To pretend that realism as an aesthetic program was more invested in dismantling than in defending the power of corporations—to name just one of the period's pressing economic concerns—is to make light of fundamental differences of temperament and opinion. That said, it is worth considering whether American realists espoused an identifiable economic outlook in response to the period's tumultuous financial history. My provisional answer to the question is that they did.

Before considering the way writers responded to economic issues and events during the period associated with the rise of realism and naturalism (from roughly 1865 to 1910), it is important to identify the issues and events in question. This unsystematic overview owes much to Stuart Bruchey's *Enterprise* (1990) and Walter Licht's *Industrializing America* (1995). Economic historians point to several prevailing themes, the most important of which might be the cycle of rapid economic expansion and intermittent panic that characterized the period (see Bruner and Carr 2007). The American economy grew at a significant rate after the Civil War, as railroads, mines, manufacturing, agriculture, and heavy industry pushed westward, and yet postwar economic expansion was interrupted repeatedly by sudden panics in investor confidence, which often resulted in wide-scale contraction. One such shock occurred in 1869, when panic among Wall Street investors resulted in a 20% decline in the value of U.S. securities and a 50% drop in the price of wheat. After a brief recovery, the Panic of 1873 led to one of the deepest recessions in American history, during which 89 of the nation's 364 railroads failed and national unemployment reached 14%. The most devastating panic of the period occurred in 1893, when President Grover Cleveland was compelled to ask for J. P. Morgan's help in restoring the gold reserves of the U.S. Treasury, an exigency that underscored the unprecedented power of private banks and their close ties to the federal government.

Morgan's intervention proved successful, but his enormous profit from the bailout inspired broad resentment and helped fuel a populist movement that challenged both the political legitimacy of the gold standard and the morality of the capitalist system of finance more generally. Whether or not specific writers followed William Jennings Bryan and the populist wing of the Democratic Party in advocating the free coinage of silver—another hot-button issue of the day—they operated in an environment of dramatic economic volatility and increasingly broad distrust of large banks and corporations.

Another significant economic development of the period—one that no serious writer could fail to notice—was the rise of the labor movement. The nation's first important union, the Knights of Labor, was formed in 1869 on a platform opposed to both socialism and anarchism, and within fifteen years, it included 100,000 members. Other unions, like the American Federation of Labor, extended the fight for higher wages and better working conditions as part of an emerging consensus among working-class Americans that *laissez-faire* economics required systemic pushback from laborers, farmers, small business owners, and consumers. The writers of American realism and naturalism embraced the interests of laborers with widely varying degrees of enthusiasm—one might contrast the enthusiasm of Henry James and Edith Wharton, on the one hand, with that of Rebecca Harding Davis and Upton Sinclair on the other—but it is important to situate all of their aesthetic efforts within the context of pervasive labor unrest and the emerging phenomenon of organized labor in America.

One could go on *ad infinitum* listing developments that may have inspired literary reaction to the contemporary state of economic affairs. A short list of such developments would have to include the emergence of business conglomerates—corporate "trusts"—that sought to distort market values by establishing legal monopolies over key industries, as well as the federal government's initial efforts to challenge corporate consolidation through such legislation as the 1887 Interstate Commerce Act (regulating railroads) and the 1890 Sherman Anti-Trust Act (regulating the formation of trusts). The literary history of American realism is inseparably tangled up in these contending arguments over the compatibility or incompatibility of *laissez-faire* capitalism and public welfare. Other items that belong on a short list of significant economic developments during the period might include (but certainly should not be limited to): the expanding influence of Wall Street and the role of speculation in American economic affairs; and the emergence of serious theories of dissent in the work of such thinkers as Thorstein Veblen (the scourge of "conspicuous consumption"), Henry George (the prophet of the single-tax movement), and Washington Gladden (a champion of the Social Gospel).

It would be futile to venture a sweeping claim about the way writers of the period responded to this smorgasbord of large and small economic ideas, issues, and developments. Wherever consensus seems most likely to be found, as on the expanding influence of Wall Street speculation (presumably a development anathema to realist sensibilities, as suggested by Charles Dudley Warner's scathing 1889 Wall Street novel, *A Little Journey in the World*), the example of a prominent outlier disrupts agreement. Thus, as if on cue, Hank Morgan, the narrator of Twain's *A Connecticut Yankee in King Arthur's Court* (also published in 1889), creates the world's first stock market in sixth-century Camelot, an innovation that Hank (perhaps speaking for Mark Twain) understands as consistent with the introduction of modern technology, morality, and hygiene into the benighted romantic world of King Arthur's Court. The authors of American realism, it seems, including the collaborators who coined the era's gilded epithet, Warner and Twain, refuse to line up on the major economic issues of the day.

While consensus on specific questions may have been as elusive among writers as it was among economists of the period, in fact it seems plausible to argue that American realism *did* develop as a marginally coherent response to identifiable economic circumstances. Among recent critics, Andrew Lawson has argued most compellingly for such an understanding of realism's origins, which he discerns in "an antebellum cultural formation which privileges the local, the concrete, and the particular in response to the destabilizing and dematerializing effects of the market" (15). By "the market," Lawson means the abstract money economy, as distinguished from the object-centered domestic economy practiced in precapitalist households, where "use" prevailed over "profit" and "exchange" as the guiding logic behind the production and consumption of goods. The destabilizing effects of the transition from a domestic to a capitalist marketplace were most acutely felt by writers who experienced "at least some degree of downward social mobility," and so realism for Lawson is an "aesthetics of scarcity," practiced in response to a bewilderingly abstract new economic order (17). He dates the declining social status of the first realists to the Panic of 1837, a moment of widespread economic collapse, "in which 'reality' itself [was] put under a new kind of stress, and people [were] forced to ask new questions of it" (2). For the writers and readers who experienced the economic collapse of 1837, the questioning of reality produced "the demand for a new, mimetic literature, a literature that represents the solid world of fact as a counterweight to the misty and the undefined" (2).

Lawson's emphasis on 1837 as a watershed moment in the history of American literature is a unique and provocative move. Critics interested in the intersection of literature and economics generally link the emergence of a realist impulse in American fiction to the period of industrial expansion and corporate consolidation following the Civil War. In tracing the mimetic urge to a much earlier moment—one of fiscal contraction rather than expansion, and one felt most acutely by economically vulnerable women, in particular—Lawson disrupts numerous critical orthodoxies: instead of placing William Dean Howells, Henry James, and Hamlin Garland at the forefront of realist innovation, this argument features writers such as Rose Terry Cooke, Rebecca Harding Davis, Anna Warner, Sara Parton (Fanny Fern), and Eliza Buckminster Lee, all of whom serve as examples of "distressed gentry-class women" who pioneered the realist movement by projecting "a sense of precariousness and its concomitant need for the epistemological assurances of a mimetic fiction" (9). As the century progressed, the sense of economic precariousness spread, according to Lawson, becoming an aspect of middle-class experience more generally and "finding [its] fullest expression, after the Civil War, in the fiction of William Dean Howells, Henry James, and Hamlin Garland" (9). At this point, American realism becomes fully conscious of its "historic mission," which is to counterbalance "the conditions of weightlessness, unreality, and precariousness created by the transition to capitalism and the rise of the market economy" (17).

Lawson's argument offers a bracingly fresh understanding of realism's economic backstory, but his sense that the movement's major figures were philosophically opposed to market capitalism actually echoes a traditional theme in criticism. That theme has often played out in assessments of the fiction of William Dean Howells, the most outspoken defender of realism among the period's major critics, as well as one of the mode's most prolific and creative practitioners. Howells did not approve of the shady financial operations of large corporations and of Wall Street speculators, according to the traditional view, and his campaign for realism in American letters was thus in part an attempt to restore the fading image of an older American commercial life, one in which real goods were exchanged between real people on a basis of "simple, natural, and honest" commerce (Howells 1959: 12). *The Rise of Silas Lapham* (1885), the centerpiece of Howells's *oeuvre*, is the novel most frequently marshaled in support of this account of realism's backward-looking economic fixation, for it is the story of a simple Vermont farm boy's ascent of the social and economic ladder, culminating in his dramatic fall from fortune (which is also ironically his "rise" in ethical terms). Silas, the novel suggests, ultimately achieves moral redemption when he escapes the vicissitudes of the modern market economy, including the insidious stock market, where he dabbled like an opium-eater during the period of his prosperity.

Howells's stern treatment of Silas's economic aspirations created a lasting impression on literary critics, who have generally agreed with Edwin Cady that the novel is "a modern realistic version of a morality play," in which stock speculation is the name of sin (v). Another critic, Wayne Westbrook, has called *The Rise of Silas Lapham* "the *locus classicus* Wall Street novel," explaining that Silas emerges "from the shadows of misfortune, repentant, freed from the bondage of the money lust, cleansed of the taint of financial corruption, and morally transformed" (60). For these critics, Silas's story of redemption from the sinful taint of economic affairs provides a pattern for understanding realism's larger engagement with finance and industry. Late nineteenth-century economic conditions, characterized by abstractness, egoism, and dishonesty, in this view, enter the Howellsian realist novel so that they can be purged. Not all realists, to be sure, shared Howells's instinct for purgation; younger writers such as Frank Norris (*The Octopus* [1901]) and Theodore Dreiser (*The Financier* [1912]) took steady aim at business villains in their fiction, and the directness of their treatment of seedy economic subjects largely denotes the thin, sometimes obscure, line that separates the terms "realism" and "naturalism" in critical discourse. In either case, whether they cleansed their fiction of the taint of economics, like Howells, or dwelt at length upon its sordid operations, like Norris, literary realism and naturalism originate, as Lawson would explain, in opposition to "the destabilizing and dematerializing effects of the market" (15).

Some of the most influential critics working at the intersection of literature and economics have described American realism in precisely these terms. Walter Benn Michaels, whose *The Gold Standard and the Logic of Naturalism* (1987) remains after thirty years one of the most provocative approaches to that intersection, believes that American literary realism stands inherently at odds with the era's emerging culture of high finance. For Michaels, "the goal of realism," as an aesthetic disposition with overlapping social, political, and economic agendas, is to "minimize excess," including the vastly excessive returns of unearned income enjoyed by realism's categorically disreputable tycoons (41). As for so many other critics of American realism, *The Rise of Silas Lapham* is Michaels's representative text in the realist mode, and in that novel he discerns Howells's "fundamentally agrarian, anticapitalist vision of the world." Describing a plot resolution that epitomizes realism's enmity for speculation, he notes that the quiet "domestic economy" to which Silas returns at the end of the novel stands in "precarious opposition to the excesses of capitalism," especially as expressed in the novel's rendering of "the greedy and heartless stock market" (41). Michaels's book has had a commanding influence in literary studies, and more recent critics, such as Neil Brown, continue to expand on the basic premise that, in Brown's words, "the ethics and aesthetics of realism" run "counter to an emergent, unrestrained market capitalism and its moral vacuity" (4).

Realism may originate as a therapeutic reaction to the experience of economic uncertainty, as Lawson has persuasively explained, but the suggestion that Howells and his fellow realists were "anticapitalist" or "fundamentally agrarian" overstates the case. In fact, some recent critics, such as Nathaniel Cadle, have turned this argument on its head by linking American realism to Progressive efforts to extend U.S. influence—and the influence of U.S. financial institutions—across the globe. As a result of taking over the "Editor's Study" at *Harper's Monthly* in 1886, according to Cadle, Howells became immersed in the fiction of foreign authors, "which in turn led him to rethink the work of American literary realism within a much broader context" (77). Cadle situates Howells's turn toward global literature within "a widespread effort, across political and ethnic lines, to empower the United States through embracing and exploiting emerging modes of transnational circulation" (8). Accordingly, Howells's fiction of the late 1880s and afterward—like that of Henry James, Mark Twain, and other realists—exhibits a shift in focus from "primarily moral conflicts experienced by individual characters" toward "a more overt engagement with the broader social implications of unequal political representation and economic access" (18).

In this view, the defining feature of American realism is not its "anticapitalist vision of the world" but its promotion of *local color* as the portent and medium of a global tendency toward Americanization in the arts. Howells, more than any other writer of the period, worked tirelessly to position American realism at the center of this new global aesthetic paradigm, arguing that American local colorists were "part of the world movement in fiction toward greater naturalness and lifelikeness" (qtd. in Cadle 2014: 59). In a review of Mary Wilkins Freeman, he observed that "a new method was necessary in dealing with the new conditions, and the new method is world-wide, because the whole world is more or less-Americanized" (59). As Cadle explains, Howells believed that "American local color provided a model that foreign authors could employ to represent their own cultures," and his promotion of this aesthetic platform in the work of Armando Palacio Valdés, José Rizal, and many others thus reflected the widening reach of America's global influence in cultural affairs (62).

This emphasis on realism's role in what Howells considered the inevitable and desirable Americanization of the arts has the surprising effect of linking the campaign for realism to a much broader Progressive agenda, one neatly summarized by Woodrow Wilson in 1915: "We shall some day have to assist in reconstructing the processes of peace [because] we are more and more by force of circumstances the mediating Nation of the world in respect to its finance" (1). American neutrality was necessary, Wilson argued—paradoxically—because the U.S. was poised to adopt a new role in world affairs, that of a global mediator capable of overseeing "worldwide financial transactions" and "international disputes" (3). Realism, for Cadle, is the literary manifestation of this transnational turn in American thinking about "the increasingly global currents of U.S. society and culture" (4). Far from a rejection of capitalism and the vicissitudes of the modern market economy, this view understands realism as the expression of a Progressive hope that American culture, led by its fiscal currency and its financial institutions, might spread across the world, preparing the conditions for something wishfully described in Progressive discourse as "world-salvation" (29).

Of course, the Progressive agenda entailed more than a vision of America as the global mediator of "worldwide financial transactions." On the domestic front, that agenda also called for enhanced federal authority over economic institutions and processes, and here again an important affinity is discernable between the realist and the Progressive visions of America's global future. Lawson may be right that realism originates in "precarious" response to the nineteenth-century recurrent financial panics, and Silas Lapham's voluntary retreat to the farm in Vermont undeniably supports such a view of the genre as a defeated reaction to economic adversity. But Howells's next landmark novel, *A Hazard of New Fortunes* (1890), depicts American capitalism as a work in progress, one in which the state has the potential to act as an engine of social, political, and economic reforms. Echoing critics Thomas Peyser and Russ Castronovo, both of whom convincingly situate American realism within the ferment of international discourses of utopian reform, Cadle reads *A Hazard of New Fortunes* as an extended argument for "a planned economy that, not unlike the one proposed by Edward Bellamy in *Looking Backward* (1888), would resolve [what Howells in the novel calls] 'this economic chance-world in which we live'" (Peyser 1998; Castronovo 2007; Cadle 2014: 72). Both Howells and his mouthpiece in *Hazard*, Basil March, seek some assurance that "honest work shared by all" will bring "honest food shared by all," an assurance only the state can offer, as Basil realizes when he visits the immigrant processing facility at Castle Garden and then worries:

> In fact, it was after the simple strangers left the government care that March feared their woes might begin; and he would have liked the government to follow each of them to his home, wherever he meant to fix it within our borders. He made note of the looks of the licensed runners and touters waiting for the immigrants outside the government premises.
>
> *(272)*

In voicing March's humane wish to extend government protection of immigrants to the private sphere, Howells makes his novel an explicit instrument of Progressive reform.

My point in suggesting affinities between Howellsian realism and Progressive reform is not to insist that Lawson, Michaels, and other critics are wrong for describing realism as "fundamentally agrarian" and "anticapitalist." In some of its moods—perhaps exemplified by Twain's *Adventures of Huckleberry Finn* (1885) or Jewett's *The Country of the Pointed Firs* (1896)—realism may imagine for itself a precapitalist haven from economic abstraction and financial worry. That said, the major fiction of the realist movement in America seems to me far more significantly invested in the regulation and reform of capitalist institutions than in their sublimation or eradication. This is another way of saying that the real culprit in a seminal novel like *A Hazard of New Fortunes* is not capitalism, or the market economy, or Wall Street, but chance itself. Howells is not sure if the federal government possesses the moral fortitude or the wisdom to institute a regime of social justice within the "economic chance-world" in which we live, but if collective oversight can ensure that "honest work" brings "honest food," then he is willing to work toward that end within the existing system of economic relations. While exceptional cases abound, *this* is the general disposition of American realism toward the economic circumstances of the period. At some level, the spirit of reform—rather than that of rejection—informs the representation of economic and social institutions in works by all of the major figures I named at the outset of this essay: Howells, Rebecca Harding Davis, Sarah Orne Jewett, Henry James, Mark Twain, Charles Dudley Warner, Mary Wilkins Freeman, Hamlin Garland, Charles W. Chesnutt, Theodore Dreiser, Sui Sin Far, Frank Norris, Stephen Crane, Zitkala-Ša, Edith Wharton, Abraham Cahan, Jack London, and Upton Sinclair.

The same might even be said about the career of poor Silas Lapham, the poster child for American realism's purported antipathy for high finance. As we have seen, literary critics tend to applaud Silas's retreat to the farm in Vermont as a renunciation of business, but it is easy to forget that instead of retiring at the end of the novel, Silas actually becomes a more cautious and patient businessman. Having once made money so fast that he didn't have time to spend it, he recognizes after his financial collapse that the growth of his paint manufacturing operation "must be for a long time on a small scale compared with his former business," and, as a consequence of this recognition, the "bragging note" of his earlier success "was rarely sounded" (354). Far from abandoning business, he continues to push the Persis Brand, his highest quality paint, and when a West Virginia company buys up his remaining assets in a friendly consolidation, Silas becomes a part owner with "an interest in the vaster enterprise of the younger men" (361). He no longer trades stocks like an impulsive gambler but instead looks forward to the day when his company shares will get "to paying dividends again" (364). Silas may have given up stock trading as a game of chance, in other words, but he certainly has not rejected either capitalism or high finance. Rather, he has become a long-term investor, and the contentment he enjoys at the end of the novel should be understood less as a celebration of agrarian domesticity than as a consequence of his shift to a more rational, conservative investment strategy. While it is tempting to imagine that Silas emerges from his ordeal "cleansed of the taint of financial corruption, and morally transformed," as Westbrook has suggested, in fact it would be more accurate to regard him as a reformed and improved capitalist (60).

It is not a coincidence that as Silas becomes a better, more patient investor, his purview also shifts notably toward the international context, as when he looks out over Boston's Back Bay after his business failure and draws an aesthetic comparison that would have been unthinkable to him during his earlier life as a harried, thoroughly provincial man of business. Having been forced out of the fast lane by his financial reverses, he can now pause at his window and appreciate that "the hills, the naked trees, the spires and roofs had a black outline, as if they were objects in a painting of the French school" (311). Such uncharacteristic sensitivity and cosmopolitan awareness have come to Silas as byproducts of his pared-down financial identity, which has enabled what Cadle might call a transnational turn in his thinking about "the increasingly global currents of U.S. society and culture" (4). Perhaps it would be accurate to describe Silas at this point in the novel as something like a businessman-realist, or a realist in business affairs, which is to say—following Cadle—that his provincial eyes have been opened to the global marketplace. No longer the bragging, nouveau-riche rustic who played the stock market like a game of cards, he has become a long-term investor focused on global, rather than provincial values, a shift in perspective that allows him to appreciate for the first time the difference between fine workmanship and "obstreperous pretentiousness" in design (310). Tellingly, as he ruminates on this previously unnoticed distinction, Silas tries to remember "what Italian city it was" that inspired his architect's tasteful approach to brickwork (310). Aesthetic values associated with the global marketplace (and with literary realism's global currency) assert themselves here as correctives to Gilded Age provinciality and excess.

I have relied on Silas Lapham's career as a metonym for American realism's fraught engagement with the economic circumstances of the period, and in doing so I have portrayed Silas less as an anticapitalist than as a realist in business affairs. But what is a realist in business affairs? One way to answer the question would be to think about the way Progressive economists of the late nineteenth and early twentieth centuries challenged the neoclassical paradigm they had inherited from their precursors. In John Gambs's eloquent summary, the Standard theory of the great eighteenth-century economists modeled itself on the mechanistic sciences and sought to identify laws of economic activity comparable in scope and validity to the laws of gravity. "Standard theory," according to Gambs,

> explores economic life by first assuming the existence of a perfectly functioning economic universe governed by pure competition.... The universe is the basic plan, blueprint, diagram.... In it there are no monopolies... government intervention is negligible.... [T]here are no great wars, no great depressions, no great booms, no reconstruction after a great war.
>
> *(45)*

Within this perfectly unmolested universe of neoclassical economic theory, men and women pursue their selfish interests, seeking out markets where they can buy cheap and sell dear, and their efforts—as if guided by "an invisible hand"—result in a "beneficent and harmonious pattern" that promotes "the general interests of society" (Gambs 1952: 117). Gambs is quoting Adam Smith's famous phrase, which first appeared in *The Theory of Moral Sentiments* (1759):

> The rich... are led by an invisible hand to make nearly the same distribution of the necessaries of life, which would have been made, had the earth been divided into equal portions among all its inhabitants, and thus without intending it, without knowing it, advance the interest of the society.
>
> *(184)*

According to Gambs, the dissenting voices of the late nineteenth century tended to point out that "spinning fine theories in a world of abstraction" is one thing, while addressing "immediate problems" on a "down-to-earth realistic level" is quite another (107). These Progressive dissenters, such as the American economist David Ames Wells, insisted that the study of social, political, and economic conditions—the very conditions that were bracketed by Standard theory—was essential to economic analysis. They anticipate the approach of John Maynard Keynes, as outlined elsewhere in this volume. An event like the devastating Panic of 1873, Wells wrote, could only be intelligently discussed in light of "a clear and full recognition of... the causes and extent of the industrial and social changes and accompanying disturbances which have especially characterized the last fifteen or twenty years of the world's history" (1). This was a proclamation of realism in economic discourse. Neoclassical theory based its conclusions on an ideal that was, in Gambs's words, "as much unlike the reality to be explained as chess is unlike… atomic warfare." To the most ardent economic realists, "the whole business [of Standard theory]" was "reminiscent of the subtleties of medieval scholasticism" (Gambs 1952: 108).

Perhaps it is capricious to draw fuzzy analogies between literary aesthetics and economic analysis, but it is striking to notice how closely the campaign for realism in American fiction echoed Progressive dissent from neoclassical economic theory. In a famous passage from *Criticism and Fiction* (1891), Howells's manifesto in defense of realism, he gives a tongue-in-cheek speaking part to an imaginary character who is filled with the "spirit of pedantry." This character addresses a young scientist and would-be writer:

> I see that you are looking at a grasshopper there which you have found in the grass, and I suppose you intend to describe it. Now don't waste your time and sin against culture in that way. I've got a grasshopper here, which has been evolved at considerable pains and expense out of the grasshopper in general; in fact, it's a type. It's made up of wire and card- board, very prettily painted in a conventional tint, and it's perfectly indestructible. It isn't very much like a real grasshopper, but it's a great deal nicer, and it's served to represent the notion of a grasshopper ever since man emerged from barbarism. You may say that it's artificial. Well, it is artificial; but then it's ideal too; and what you want to do is to cultivate the ideal. You'll find the books full of my kind of grasshopper, and scarcely a trace of yours in any of them.
>
> *(13)*

Novelists and economists generally speak different languages, but I would submit that David Ames Wells and William Dean Howells were intellectual cousins, contemporary realists who considered the dominant theoretical paradigm in their respective spheres of discourse too much "unlike the reality to be explained." American realists, whether they spoke the language of economics of that of fiction, promoted a method of looking at complex problems, rather than a theoretically consistent interpretation of the economic system as a whole, such as one finds in either Adam Smith or Karl Marx. That is to say, American realists specialized, as Howells put it, in "the business of observing, recording, and comparing" (27). One cannot do better than this, I think, as a statement of realism's outlook on economic events of the period during which the mode flourished in American literary culture. Perhaps it would not be too frivolous to conclude that the writers and economists loosely aligned with Howells's commitment to observation, record-keeping, and comparison were, like Silas Lapham himself, realists in business affairs.

## References

Barrish, Phillip J. (2011) *The Cambridge Introduction to American Literary Realism*, Cambridge: Cambridge University Press.

Brown, Neil. (2005) "Pivots, Reversals, and Things in the Aesthetic Economy of Howells's *The Rise of Silas Lapham*," *Connotations* 15: 1–16.

Bruchey, Stuart. (1990) *Enterprise: Dynamic Economy of a Free People*, Cambridge, MA: Harvard University Press.

Bruner, Robert F. and Sean D. Carr. (2007) *The Panic of 1907: Lessons Learned from the Market's Perfect Storm*, Hoboken, NJ: Wiley.

Cadle, Nathaniel. (2014) *The Mediating Nation: Late American Realism, Globalization, and the Progressive State*, Chapel Hill: University of North Carolina Press.
Cady, Edwin. (1957) "Introduction" to *The Rise of Silas Lapham*, Cambridge, MA: Houghton Mifflin.
Castronovo, Russ. (2007) *Beautiful Democracy: Aesthetics and Anarchy in a Global Era*, Chicago, IL: University of Chicago Press.
Gambs, John S. (1952) *Man, Money, and Goods*, New York: Columbia University Press.
George, Henry. (1879) *Poverty and Plenty*, Garden City, NY: Doubleday.
Gladden, Washington. (1884) "Christianity and Wealth," *The Century* (October): 904–11.
Howells, William Dean. (1990) *A Hazard of New Fortunes*, New York: Oxford University Press.
Howells, William Dean. (1983) *The Rise of Silas Lapham*, New York: Penguin Books.
Howells, William Dean. (1959) *Criticism and Fiction, and Other Essays*, New York: New York University Press.
Lawson, Andrew. (2012) *Downwardly Mobile: The Changing Fortunes of American Realism*, New York: Oxford University Press.
Licht, Walter. (1995) *Industrializing America: The Nineteenth Century*, Baltimore, MD: Johns Hopkins University Press.
Messent, Peter. (2009) *Mark Twain and Male Friendship: The Twichell, Howells, & Rogers Friendships*, New York: Oxford University Press.
Michaels, Walter Benn. (1987) *The Gold Standard and the Logic of Naturalism*, Berkeley: University of California Press.
Peyser, Thomas. (1998) *Utopia and Cosmopolis: Globalization in the Era of American Literary Realism*, Durham, NC: Duke University Press.
Smith, Adam. (1976) *The Theory of Moral Sentiments*, New York: Oxford University Press.
Tarbell, Ida. (1904) *The History of the Standard Oil Company*, New York: McClure, Phillips.
Twain, Mark. (1889) *A Connecticut Yankee in King Arthur's Court*, New York: Charles Webster.
Veblen, Thorstein. (1994) *The Theory of the Leisure Class*, New York: Penguin.
Warner, Charles Dudley. (1889) *A Little Journey in the World*, New York: Harper & Brothers.
Warner, Charles Dudley and Mark Twain. (1873) *The Gilded Age: A Tale of To-day*, Hartford, CT: American Publishing Company.
Wells, David Ames. (1889) *Recent Economic Changes, and Their Effect on the Production and Distribution of Wealth and the Well-Being of Society*, New York: D. Appleton & Co.
Westbrook, Wayne W. (1980) *Wall Street in the American Novel*, New York: New York University Press.

# 11

# WOMEN'S WRITING AND THE MAINSTREAMING OF POLITICAL ECONOMY

*Lana L. Dalley*

> "Young ladies don't understand political economy, you know," said Mr. Brooke, smiling toward Mr. Casaubon, "I remember when we were all reading Adam Smith. *There* is a book, now. I took in all the new ideas at one time—human perfectibility, now. But some say, history moves in circles; and that may be very well argued; I have argued it myself."
>
> *(Eliot 1871–2: 17)*

It doesn't take the *Middlemarch* (1871) reader long to realize that Dorothea Brooke's uncle rarely knows what he's talking about; in this passage, as elsewhere, Mr. Brooke's confident proclamations about women's ignorance are undermined by his own lack of understanding. Although he praises Smith's *Wealth of Nations* (although, tellingly, not by name), his verbal fumbling makes readers question if he has, in fact, even read the book. It also leads readers to imagine that, on the one hand, young ladies very well might understand political economy and on the other, men very well might not. *Middlemarch* begins in 1831, just before the passage of the Reform Bill, nearly forty years before the time of its publication (1871–2). At both historical points (1831 and 1871), Adam Smith would have been a household name even if, like Mr. Brooke, the average citizen would have been hard-pressed to say something very substantial about his economic theories. In this way, "Adam Smith" became a kind of metonym for political economy and an intellectual currency for men like Mr. Brooke (see Eleanor Courtemanche's "Classical Economics"). Economics was increasingly preoccupying the nineteenth-century imagination and, yet, given women's struggle to viably participate in the economic system, it's easy to imagine—as Mr. Brooke does in *Middlemarch*—that women didn't think about economics like their male counterparts did. By tracking women's engagement with political economy in the nineteenth century, this essay will contribute to a growing body of research that shows women not only understood political economy, but that their writing helped secure its place in the Victorian cultural imagination (see Dalley and Rappaport 2014).

After the publication of *Wealth of Nations* in 1776, political economy came to be thought of as "the economy of empires," a more specific incarnation of its predecessor, *oeconomy*, which treated both the household economics and the economics of the state. Many scholars have pointed to this transition as seminal in the making of the modern liberal state, the formalization of the separate spheres ideology, and the consequent distancing of women from economic thought and practice (see Clark 1995; Davidoff and Hall 1987; Vickery 1993). While writers like Thomas Carlyle and John Ruskin put women on a domestic pedestal in their critiques of capitalism (a position predicated on their nonparticipation in waged labor), political economists like Adam Smith, Thomas Malthus, and John Stuart Mill had very little to say about how and where women fit into their economic worlds (see Carlyle 1843; Ruskin 1865). Indeed, there is a conspicuous absence of women in early political economy. And yet, clearly, women had a stake in economics—both the economics of empire and the economics of the home—and this essay will show how women writers made that stake evident and, in the process, helped mainstream political economy in the nineteenth century. Women's contributions were often collaborative—dependent on formal and informal networks of writers and thinkers—and took many forms including fictional exploration, textbook and essay writing, university work, and committee participation. And yet, despite their many contributions to political economy, the nineteenth-century "science" is still widely thought of as the domain of men, both in terms of its subject matter and its practitioners.

In the early 1830s, Harriet Martineau approached publisher Charles Fox with an unlikely idea, something, she argued, that had never been tried: she wanted to write a series of fictional tales illustrating the principles of political economy. Martineau's twenty-five tale series was published monthly for two years (1832–4) and aimed to educate the public about the key principles of political economy; the series was a commercial and critical success. While Martineau's plan was, indeed, original, she was not the first writer to forge economic and fictional discourses, nor was she the first woman to contribute meaningfully to political economy. In 1816, Jane Marcet published *Conversations on Political Economy*, which featured didactic conversations between the fictional characters Mrs. B and Caroline. Marcet wrote her *Conversations* to explicitly educate readers on the principles of political economy, while other early nineteenth-century writers, like Jane Austen and Maria Edgeworth, were more indirectly engaging with economic theory in their fiction. Edgeworth was lifelong friends with the political economist David Ricardo, and his collected letters show an ongoing dialogue between the two about questions of stock, foreign trade and exports, Irish politics, and provision for the poor. Edgeworth often went to Ricardo with pressing economic questions, and his influence can be seen in her treatment of land management, wealth, and financial dependence in novels like *Castle Rackrent* (1800), *The Absentee* (1812), *Patronage* (1814), *Ormond* (1817), and *Helen* (1834) (see Easton 2003; Picken 2016). During the same period, Austen was responding to contemporary economic debates in her domestic novels as she repeatedly wrestled with questions of inheritance, the tenuous financial position of women, and the subjective nature of value and its consequent volatility. Austen's personal records are notoriously sparse, so it's hard to determine with certainty what political economy, if any, she read; however, scholars have compellingly argued that Austen read Adam Smith (certainly *Theory of Moral Sentiments*, and likely *Wealth of Nations*) and that his thinking left an imprint on her fiction (see Chamberlain 2014; Elsie 2011; Poovey 2008). Although her novels are often remembered for their witty treatment of mercenary marriages and family politics, Austen was also writing about the emergent credit economy, the slave trade and imperial economics, and money. When thinking about the history of women's engagement with political economy, Austen and Edgeworth's fictional engagement with political economy can be read as indispensable precursors to the works of Marcet and, especially, Martineau. The idea that literary and economic discourses were not only compatible, but perhaps also had shared ground, was part of the development of economic theory and crucial to its more widespread dissemination; in the nineteenth century, moreover, imaginative literature would be one of the key ways that women influenced popular ideas about economics.

By the early nineteenth century, political economy occupied firm ground in nineteenth-century intellectual culture, but Martineau considered political economy's principles to be too abstract and difficult for the common reader to comprehend. Access to economic theory, Martineau thought, was like membership in an exclusive club and she wanted to make it more accessible to the general public. Marcet's *Conversations* was Martineau's own introduction to political economy and she came to Adam Smith only after reading Marcet, an example that, in itself, illustrates the powerful reach of women's writing about political economy. Martineau organized her stories around four key economic principles—Production, Distribution, Exchange, and Consumption—and "embod[ied] each leading principle in a character: and the mutual operation of these embodied principles supplied the action of the story" (Martineau 1877: 147). A series of fictional tales, she argued, would give readers "the science in a familiar, practical form. [Political economists] give us its history; they give us its philosophy; but we want its picture" (Martineau 1832: xi). Martineau's inkling that a series like *Illustrations* was "craved by the popular mind" seemed to be confirmed by its impressive sales. According to Elaine Freedgood, "[b]y 1843, the monthly sales had reached 10,000, several times that of many of Dickens's novels, which at 2,000 or 3,000 a month were considered highly successful" (213). Indeed, *Illustrations* was the key source of economic knowledge for many early nineteenth-century readers, prompting one reviewer to declare "[a]t this moment, no person is doing more good in England than this lady: perhaps no other female ever occupied the same proud position of a national instructress, on the topics of the country's most essential interests" (Anonymous 1832: 639). Even when reviewers praised *Illustrations*, though, their praise was heavily gendered, and in a way that came to characterize the critical response to women's writing about economics; women could participate in economics via domestic economies and fictional discourse but, in 1832 at least, the "science" of political economy remained the domain of men.

Martineau's role as national instructress was extended when she was commissioned to write a second series of tales, *Poor Laws and Paupers Illustrated* (1833–4). And yet, despite her widespread success, many critics were quick to point out that Martineau was a fiction writer, not an economist. For example, in a review of *Illustrations*, Edward Bulwer-Lytton wrote,

> She has taken the facts of Political Economy, woven a series of tales, of great and familiar interest, illustrative of the broader and more useful of its doctrines. It is as a writer of fiction, however that we only regard her.... As a political economist... we do not consider Miss Martineau entitled to high estimation.
>
> *(quoted in Logan 2004: 428)*

The distinction, of course, was inflected by gender; while it was acceptable for women to write *about* political economy, it remained difficult to think of them *as* political economists.

And, yet, Martineau seems to have thought of herself as an economist, writing in her *Autobiography* that, by fifteen, she was "becoming a political economist without knowing it" (55). The distinction between women as economists and women writing about economics persisted throughout the nineteenth century and is an important part of the history of women's writing and the mainstreaming of political economy. Many women who were actively writing about and engaging in economic discourse simultaneously refused to call themselves economists, or to even claim any formal knowledge of the subject. For most of the century, women writers were more likely to be thought of as popularizers of economic theory, rather than economists contributing to the discipline. For example, in the preface to the industrial novel *Mary Barton* (1848), Elizabeth Gaskell writes, "I know nothing of Political Economy, or the theories of trade. I have tried to write truthfully; and if my accounts agree or clash with any system, the agreement or disagreement is unintentional" (4). Gaskell aligns her writing with feminine sympathetic observation (the "truth" of what she's observed in Manchester), rather than economic theory perceived as part of masculine intellectual culture.

In truth, Gaskell did know something about political economy. Jane Marcet was a family friend and by the 1820s, Gaskell had read both her *Conversations on Chemistry* (1805) and her *Conversations on Political Economy* (Uglow 1999: 61). Gaskell was also familiar with Martineau's *Illustrations* and likely based several aspects of *Mary Barton* on "A Manchester Strike." It was one of only a few industrial tales by women written prior to *Mary Barton* and the setting, action, and characters in Gaskell's novel are reminiscent of those in Martineau's story. Like many other Victorian women, Gaskell also garnered knowledge about political economy from within her own family. Her father, William Stevenson, wrote a series on political economy in *Blackwood's Edinburgh Magazine* in 1824. And, most tellingly, in a letter to her daughter, Marianne, written in April 1851, Gaskell writes,

> Before you fully make up your mind [on the subject of a Protectionist Ministry], read a paper in the Quarterly on the subject of Free Trade, (written by Mr. George Taylor) in (I think) the year 1839; and then when you come home I will read with you Mr. Cobden's speeches. But first I think we should read together Adam Smith on the Wealth of Nations. Not confining ourselves as we read to the limited meaning which he affixes to the word "wealth."
>
> *(qtd. in Chapple and Pollard 1966: 148)*

Gaskell's willingness to challenge Smith's definition of wealth, and her apparent command of the material, suggests a confident understanding of political economy and makes readers question her claim of ignorance in *Mary Barton*. When tracing the history of women's engagement with political economy, this example is important because it illustrates the complexity of women's position within the growing corpus of economic writing. Like Gaskell, many Victorian women writers were writing about economics and engaging with economic theory, but their contributions remain obscured by the writers' dissembling and our own assumptions about gender and genre.

As the period progressed and the women's rights movement gained steam, many writers began to utilize the liberal vocabulary of classical theory to argue for women's economic self-dependence; at the same time, they held on to ideas about sexual difference that rendered the economic work of women necessarily distinct from that of men. This reconfiguring of economic theory found its way into the imaginative writing of Charlotte Bronte, Elizabeth Barrett Browning, George Eliot, Sarah Grand, and Olive Schreiner, to name just a few, demonstrating the far reach of economic thinking and the porous nature of generic boundaries in the period. Texts like *Shirley* (1849), *Aurora Leigh* (1856), *Adam Bede* (1859), *Middlemarch*, *The Heavenly Twins* (1893), and *Story of an African Farm* (1883) all engage, to greater and lesser degrees, the theories of political economy when crafting their fictional worlds. Aurora Leigh's burgeoning independence, for example, is predicated on liberal economic thinking and Hetty Sorrel commits infanticide for decidedly Malthusian reasons (see Dalley 2006, 2008). Similar to Martineau's earlier work, these fictional engagements asked readers to consider how economic thinking played out in real-life settings and this writing remains an important part of the cultural conversation about economics and the mainstreaming of political economy in the nineteenth century.

Alongside political economy's emergence in imaginative literature, economic theory was also finding its way into other proto-feminist writing at mid-century, specifically that of Barbara Leigh Smith Bodichon, Bessie Parkes, and other members of the Langham Place Group. During her time as a student at Bedford College in the early 1850s, Smith Bodichon (at the time, Barbara Leigh Smith) read and responded to Mill's *Principles*. A generous yearly income from her father allowed Smith Bodichon to travel extensively and, at the age of 22 (in 1849) to enroll "at the newly formed Ladies' College in Bedford Square where she studied law, political economy, and art" before beginning her feminist work with the Langham Place Group in 1854 (Lacey 2001: 21). It was at Bedford Square that Smith Bodichon read and responded to Mill, and her reaction to Mill's economic treatise is quite noteworthy (see Hernstein 1985; Hirsch 1998). In her notes on the text, she critiques his treatment of women, specifically citing the following subjects as missing from the *Principles*: "the Construct of Marriage is one; the Laws concerning Women is another, and there are many more" (qtd. in Lacey 2001: 3–4) She laments that one as influential as Mill does not critique "the injustice of their [men's] laws to women and the absurdity of the present Laws of Marriage and Divorce" because "there never was a tyranny so deeply felt yet borne so silently" (3–4). Smith Bodichon's early reading of Mill reveals some of the ways in which his economic writing fails to adequately incorporate gender within its interpretive framework. And yet, despite these shortcomings, Smith Bodichon and her contemporaries still relied heavily upon Mill's economic logic.

For Mill (and other classical theorists), individuality was tied to the right to possess private property. By extension, then, individuality was also anchored to an individual's right to earn wages, with which *he* can then purchase property. It is precisely this aspect of liberal economic theory that most served mid-Victorian feminist arguments about women's self-dependence. By utilizing the vocabulary of political economists like Mill, proto-feminist writers affixed their arguments for women's rights to possess property and earn wages to an ethics of individuality that very much marked the nineteenth century. They actively generated a feminist economic theory predicated on notions of self-dependence and usefulness and conceptualized in the language of classical political economy. They also, simultaneously, helped to mainstream political economy, and expand the scope of the discipline to include women, opening the door for the emergence of female economists in the final decades of the period; so, even though early political economists do not explicitly account for women in their work, their theories provided a framework for later inclusions of women.

Sexual difference, for example, was often characterized as just another facet of the division of labor. Most Victorian women's rights activists upheld the notion that women's character is decidedly moral and domestic, which enabled them to offer something new (and necessary) to the marketplace without threatening the work of men. In this way, they render domestic values as compatible with, rather than at odds with, economic values. This theoretical shift allows them to utilize the frameworks within classical theory, while simultaneously elucidating the shortcomings of those frameworks when accounting for women. For example, Smith Bodichon makes a compellingly modern argument for the proper recognition of women's domestic work in "Woman and Work" (1857):

> Women who act as housekeepers, nurses, and instructors of their children, often do as much for the support of the household as their husbands; and it is very unfair for men to

> speak of supporting a wife and children when such is the case. When a woman gives up a profitable employment to be governess to her own family, she earns her right to live. We war against idleness, whether of man or woman, and every one is idle who is not making the best use of the faculties nature has given them.
>
> *(qtd. in Lacey 2001: 41)*

Within this framework, women's domestic work is the key to the material progress of the individual male and, by extension, the material progress of the nation. This feminist revision of liberal economic theory—where the value of domestic labor is equal to the economic support provided by the male head of household—is built upon a sexual division of labor conceptualized along traditional ideological lines.

This point is illustrated most unequivocally in Parkes's "What Can Educated Women Do? (II)" (1860). Parkes, a close friend of Smith Bodichon and daughter of Mill's close friend Joseph Parkes, was a member of the Langham Place Group and editor of their journal, *The English Woman's Journal*, from 1858 to 1867. *The English Woman's Journal* was home to several essays about political economy written by women. In "What Can Educated Women Do?" Parkes addresses what she perceives as the shortcomings of political economy from a feminist perspective:

> From the first days in which political economy rose from the region of empirics into those of science a covert war has been waged as to how far it expressed the whole truth in regard to social well-being. The great laws which it defines stand up like rocks amidst the wild waves of theory and compel them to retire, yet natures in whom love and reverence predominate insist on supplementing their shortcomings by a higher principle. Nowhere is this more evident than in the writings of John Stuart Mill himself: indeed he occasionally retreats upon the moral intuitions of the human heart in a way that exposes him to censure from those who are willing to push intellectual conclusions to their farthest limits.... And so I believe that the opening of new paths to educated women will be a very great economical benefit, I see plainly that we have great moral interests also at stake which require to be jealously guarded, that we may not look to the political economy of the question only, but must take anxious care to build up the new theory in connection with the old reverence for all that makes a woman estimable: in gaining somewhat we must not lose more.
>
> *(qtd. in Lacey 2001: 171–2)*

Parkes's desire to combine political economy with the "old reverence of all that makes a woman estimable" signals her hesitancy to simply characterize women in the same terms as the Economic Man who figures in political economy. The language of separate spheres saturates the passage, and yet so does the language of women's economic liberation; this duality was characteristic of women's economic writing in the period. While perhaps such positions are difficult for a modern reader to reconcile, for many nineteenth-century feminists, sexual difference was a fundamental condition of women's economic liberation.

In the final decades of the period, many feminists anchored their ideas about women's rights to free market ideology, suggesting that women's full economic participation was the critical next stage of national economic development. In her essay "The Future of the Englishwoman" (1878), for example, Millicent Garrett Fawcett reads the feminist movement for equal education as a "phase of the free trade argument" (352), a declaration that underscores the belief held among many Victorian feminists that women's emancipation was dependent on the tenets of liberal economic theory. Just a few years earlier, Fawcett had taken a cue from Martineau and published her own fictional primer on economics, *Tales in Political Economy* (1874). In the preface to *Tales*, Garrett Fawcett writes:

> It is hoped that these little tales may be of some use to those who are trying to teach Political Economy. I cannot let them go to press without a word of apology to Miss Martineau for my plagiarism of the idea, which she made so popular thirty years ago, of hiding the powder, Political Economy, in the raspberry jam of the story.

She would go on to lecture in political economy at Queens College, London, and, in the 1890s, to be a member of the British Economic Association. In 1871, Fawcett co-founded Newnham College, Cambridge, with her husband, the economist Henry Fawcett, and in 1875, Mary Paley became the first female economics lecturer at the College. Like Fawcett, Paley frequently collaborated with her husband, Alfred Marshall, and the two would eventually coauthor a seminal textbook on political economy, *The Economics of Industry* (1879).

Clara Collet is perhaps the most well-known late-Victorian female economist. Collet's first introduction to political economy was as a student at University College, London. She subsequently became a member of the Royal Economic Society (the Society was founded in 1890 and Collet was one of only six women present at the inaugural meeting) and Assistant Commissioner on Labour to investigate aspects of women's work. In "The Economic Position of Educated Working Women" (1890), Collet writes, "One effect on the economic position of educated working women of such an extension of employment would be to enable them to measure their value" (21). Collet is more concerned with increased opportunities for women to work outside the home than with their unpaid domestic labor; she relies upon the lexicon of political economy to argue for middle-class women's participation in waged labor, highlighting her knowledge of liberal economic theory and demonstrating the extent to which individual value, within a capitalist society, increasingly came to be determined by one's ability to earn money. In most late Victorian feminist writing, a woman's right to earn money for her labor is an important step toward her becoming a rational and useful member of society.

And yet, at the same time as some thinkers were anchoring women's emancipation to liberal economics and the free market, another group were looking at the economics of gender from a different perspective, arguing that women's freedom was, in fact, contingent upon increased economic regulation. Beatrix Potter Webb and the Fabian Society critiqued the individualist premises of women's rights activists and argued that the unregulated market hurt women workers most acutely. Throughout her career, Webb worked to strengthen and extend workers protections, especially the Factory Acts, which she accused the "able and devoted ladies who have usually led the cause of women's enfranchisement" (1) of causing to be rejected. She, along with Sidney Webb, George Bernard Shaw, and Graham Wallace, founded the London School of Economics in 1895 and she and Sidney Webb founded the *New Statesman* journal in 1913.

"The ladies seem determined to make the science of Political Economy their own," declared a reviewer of *Illustrations* in August 1832,

> After all, we believe that there is something in the female mind which peculiarly fits it for elucidating, in a familiar manner, the intricacies of political economy. The economy of empires is only the economy of families and neighbourhoods on a larger scale.
>
> *(qtd. in Logan 2004: xx)*

The notion that women were particularly suited to write about political economy because of their role as domestic managers was one taken up by many of the writers discussed in this essay. It would be a mistake, though, to assume that these writers were only—or even primarily—concerned with the economics of the home; they had as much to say about empires as they did about their own neighborhoods. Women were instrumental in furthering the conversation about political economy and, in many cases, their work was more accessible and more widely distributed than that of the male economists they were engaging with.

And yet, the story of women's involvement with political economy is not an easy one to write; as this essay has shown, their involvement took many different forms in the nineteenth century, including journal articles and didactic tales, poetry and novels, the writing of textbooks, and the holding of University lectureships. The "plot" of the story is not linear or predictable; women's contributions are sometimes highly visible and other times they remain buried in the archives; they range from formal economic theory to informal engagements with the subject. By the end of the nineteenth century, though, women like Beatrix Potter, Clara Collet, Mary Paley, and Millicent Garrett Fawcett were making formal contributions to political economy—no longer regarded as merely "instructresses" or popularizers but as economists, demonstrating the extent to which women did, indeed, make the science of Political Economy their own.

## References

Anonymous. (1832) "Miss Martineau's Little Novels," *The Spectator* 210 (July 7): 639.

Carlyle, Thomas. (1843) *Past and Present*, London: Chapman and Hall.

Chamberlain, Shannon. (2014) 'The Economics of Jane Austen,' *The Atlantic* (August 3). www.theatlantic.com/business/archive/2014/08/the-economics-of-jane-austen/375486/.

Chapple, J. A. V. & Pollard, Arthur. (eds.) (1966) *The Letters of Mrs. Gaskell*, Manchester: Manchester University Press.

Clark, Anna. (1995) *The Struggle for the Breeches: Gender and the Making of the British Working Class*, Berkeley: University of California Press.

Collet, Clara. (1902) *Educated Working Women: Essays on the Economic Position of Women in the Middle Classes*, London: P.S. King & Son.

Copeland, Edward. (1995) *Women Writing about Money: Women's Fiction in England, 1790–1820*, Cambridge: Cambridge University Press.

Dalley, Lana. (2008) 'The Economics of "a bit o' victual," or Malthus and Mothers in *Adam Bede*,' *Victorian Literature and Culture* 36.2: 549–67.

Dalley, Lana. (2006) 'The Least "Angelical" Poem in the Language: Political Economy, Gender, and the Heritage of *Aurora Leigh*,' *Victorian Poetry* 44.4: 525–42.

Dalley, Lana & Rappoport, Jill. (eds.) (2014) *Economic Women: Essays on Desire and Dispossession in 19th-Century British Culture*, Columbus: Ohio State University Press.

Davidoff, Leonore & Hall, Catherine. (1987) *Family Fortunes: Men and Women of the English Middle Class, 1780–1850*, London: Routledge.

Easton, Fraser. (2003) "Cosmopolitical Literature: Exchangeable Value and National Development in Adam Smith and Maria Edgeworth," *Studies in Romanticism* 42.1: 99–125.

Eliot, George. (1994) *Middlemarch: A Study of Provincial Life*, New York: Penguin.

Fawcett, Millicent G. (1878) 'The Future of the Englishwoman,' *Nineteenth Century* 4: 347–57.

Ferber, Marianne A. & Nelson, Julie A. (1993) *Beyond Economic Man: Feminist Theory and Economics*, Chicago, IL: University of Chicago Press.

Freedgood, Elaine. (2000) *Victorian Writing about Risk: Imagining a Safe England in a Dangerous World*, Cambridge: Cambridge University Press.

Gallagher, Catherine. (2008) *The Body Economic: Life, Death, and Sensation in Political Economy and the Victorian Novel*, Princeton, NJ: Princeton University Press.

Gaskell, Elizabeth. (1848) *Mary Barton*, London: Chapman & Hall.

Greiner, Rae. (2012) *Sympathetic Realism in Nineteenth Century British Fiction*, Baltimore, MD: John Hopkins University Press.
Groenewegen, Peter. (1994) *Feminism and Political Economy in Victorian England*, Cheltenham: Edward Elger.
Henry, Nancy & Schmitt, Cannon. (2008) *Victorian Investments: New Perspectives on Finance and Culture*, Bloomington: Indiana University Press.
Herstein, Sheila R. (1985) *A Mid-Victorian Feminist, Barbara Leigh Smith Bodichon*, New Haven, CT: Yale University Press.
Hirsch, Pam. (1998) *Barbara Leigh Smith Bodichon, 1827–1891: Feminist, Artist, and Rebel*, London: Chatto and Windus.
Klaver, Claudia C. (2003) *A/moral Economics: Classical Political Economy and Cultural Authority in Nineteenth-Century England*, Columbus: Ohio State University Press.
Kuiper, Edith & Sap, Jolande. (1995) *Out of the Margin: Feminist Perspectives on Economics*, London: Routledge.
Lacey, Candida A. (2001) *Barbara Leigh Smith Bodichon and the Langham Place Group*, London: Routledge.
Laurence, Anne, Maltby, Josephine & Rutterford, Janette. (2008) *Women and Their Money, 1700–1950: Essays on Women and Finance*, London: Routledge.
Logan, Deborah. (2002) *The Hour and the Woman: Harriet Martineau's 'Somewhat Remarkable' Life*, DeKalb: Northern Illinois University Press.
Marshall, Alfred & Mary, Paley. (1879) *The Economics of Industry*, London: Macmillan & Co.
Marcet, Jane H. (1816) *Conversation on Political Economy*, London: Longman, Rees.
Martineau, Harriet. (1877) *Autobiography*, Boston, MA: James Osgood & Co.
Martineau, Harriet. (1832) *Illustrations of Political Economy, I to V*, London: Charles Fox.
Michie, Elsie. (2011) *The Vulgar Question of Money: Heiresses, Materialism, and the Novel of Manners from Jane Austen to Henry James*, Baltimore, MD: John Hopkins University Press.
Osteen, Mark and Woodmansee, Martha. (1999) *The New Economic Criticism: Studies at the Intersection of Literature and Economics*, London: Routledge.
Picken, Cassidy. (2016) "Maria Edgeworth's Poetics of Rent," *ELH* 83.1: 181–209.
Polkinghorn, Bette & Thomson, Dorthy L. (1998) *Adam Smith's Daughters: Eight Prominent Women Economists from the Eighteenth Century to the Present. Cheltenham: Edward Elger.*
Poovey, Mary. (2008) *Genres of the Credit Economy: Mediating Value in Eighteenth- and Nineteenth-Century Britain*, Chicago, IL: University of Chicago Press.
Pujol, Michele A. (1992) *Feminism and Anti-Feminism in Early Economic Thought*, Cheltenham: Edward Elger.
Ruskin, John. (1865) *Sesame and Lillies*, New York: Wiley.
Webb, Beatrice. (1896) *Women and the Factory Acts*, London: Fabian Society.
Uglow, Jane. (1999) *Elizabeth Gaskell: A Habit of Stories*, London: Faber and Faber.
Vickery, Amanda. (1993) "Golden Age to Separate Spheres?" *The Historical Journal* 36.2: 383–414.

# 12

# MODERNISM AND MACROECONOMICS

*Michael Tratner*

The word "macroeconomics" first appeared in print in 1945, a bit too late to be considered one of the sources of Modernist literary innovations. Furthermore, it alludes to such things as "aggregate demand" and "gross domestic product," concepts that seem far removed from T.S. Eliot's fragmented images or Virginia Woolf's streams of consciousness. However, this new branch of economics derives from the writings of John Maynard Keynes, who was an active member of the Bloomsbury intellectual group, often conversing with Eliot and Woolf, as Piero Mini has documented. Woolf even wrote an essay about economics, *Three Guineas* (1938), that bears some similarities to Keynes's theory, though it seems implausible to assert any direct influence. And an economic theorist who influenced Keynes—C.H. Douglas—is cited many times by two Modernist Poets, Ezra Pound and William Carlos Williams. The relationship between macroeconomics and Modernist literature is then not a result of direct influence but rather due to common reactions to socioeconomic developments in the early twentieth century.

The event most identified with macroeconomics and Keynes's theory is the Great Depression. A number of critics have traced the influence of Depression-era economic policies on the Modernism of the 1930s, most strikingly Michael Szalay, who coined the term "New Deal Modernism" in his detailed account of the way numerous writers reacted to Roosevelt's economic policies (see Szalay 2000). But New Deal policies—social security, welfare, and deficit spending—were not just reactions to the Depression; they were also efforts to fend off economic and political developments that the Depression threatened to extend worldwide: namely, the Communist Revolution of 1917 and the Fascist regimes that emerged in Italy in 1922 and later in Germany. Those new political systems sought to counter the same fundamental problem that macroeconomics sought to solve: massive economic suffering. The Depression seemed to reveal an impossible contradiction within Capitalism: it was creating great wealth and great poverty at the same time. What Communism and Fascism promised was the inclusion of the impoverished masses in the overall wealth. Individuals who joined these movements gained, as Hitler put it, the "magic influence" of a vast united nation: the feeling that "the power of thousands are accumulated in every individual" (479). In response to that appeal, Capitalism developed its own "magic influence" that also allowed individuals to feel that they could draw on the accumulated power of thousands, and the method used in Capitalist countries is at the core of macroeconomics: the provision by the government of funds to counter oppressive effects of the overall economic structure. Keynes's macroeconomic policies allow the individual to borrow power from thousands of other persons via the mechanism of government spending. And the money the government infuses into the society even goes beyond what the government actually has to offer: Keynes proposes using "deficit spending," giving away more than the government has collected in taxes, as a way of getting money to circulate in ways not shaped by the current economic system. Keynes's macroeconomics seeks to produce its own magic influence in creating a sense that there is more money available to everyone than is perhaps even really there.

Communism and Fascism sought overt changes in the structures of industries and businesses, though in very different ways. Keynes instead focused on a flaw in the way money circulates: too much is stuck in savings, so people do not have enough money to purchase what has been produced. And Keynes felt that this problem was partly a result of beliefs ingrained in people by the development of Capitalism. In an essay in 1931, he wrote, "the essential characteristic of capitalism" is "the dependence upon an intense appeal to the money-making and money-loving instincts of individuals as the main motive of the economic machine" (Keynes 2010: 293). In another essay, he says those money-loving instincts had made "the duty of saving nine-tenths of virtue," producing an "unstable psychological condition" that is "not natural" (20–1).

Previous economic theories had presented the individual as a rational agent, but a crucial part of Keynes's *General Theory of Employment, Interest and Money* (1936) derives from his belief that

> Most, probably, of our decisions to do something positive, the full consequences of which will be drawn out over many days to come, can only be taken as the result of animal spirits – a spontaneous urge to action rather than inaction, and not as the outcome of a weighted average of quantitative benefits multiplied by quantitative probabilities.
> *(161–2)*

"Animal spirits" is an unusual term to describe the basis of most decisions, and Keynes uses the term to describe an unusual vision of human irrationality. After Freud, the common understanding of irrationality is as the result of innate animal drives that would lead people to acts that would disrupt and destroy conventional society. Instead, Keynes sees irrationality and even "instincts" as the way people have been trained in order to fit into society. Hence, he believes that irrationality can be changed, but he fears the possible results:

> I think with dread of the readjustments of the habits and instincts of the ordinary man, bred into him for countless generations, which he may be asked to discard… To the use the language of today, must we not expect a general 'nervous breakdown'?
> *(Keynes 2010: 327)*

Keynes's vision of the need for what might be a terrifying change in deep unconscious feelings provides the strongest connection between his macroeconomic theories and modernism. Much of modernism is an effort to find new ways to think and feel, an effort to disrupt and change the ways people visualize or represent the world, and thereby change unconscious habits and conceptions.

Furthermore, several modernists directly identify economics as a crucial part of that effort to change people. The writer who shows the connection among economics, unconscious feelings, and modernism most vividly is Ezra Pound, who is usually treated as a fascist. But

Pound's *Cantos* present a strange version of Fascism which is much closer to macroeconomics: he equates Fascism to an economic theory known as "Social Credit," though Mussolini and Hitler, so far as I know, never made that equation. Social Credit is the creation of C.H. Douglas, an early twentieth-century economic theorist who argues that the social order has been distorted because the government and banks and certain rich people have restricted access to money by restricting credit, creating a blockage that doesn't allow most people to be able to buy things they want. As Pound puts it in Canto XXXVIII,

> there is and must be therefore a clog
> and the power to purchase can never
> (under the present system) catch up
> with prices at large.
>
> *(Pound 1986: 189)*

Pound also parallels Keynes in recommending government spending as the solution: citing Douglas, Pound writes in *The Cantos*, "any government worth a damn can pay dividends... instead of collectin' taxes" (231). Pound suggests then that the government can simply distribute credit to everyone to buy things and thereby release people from the blockages in the current social order. Pound argues that fascist governments are doing this, saying, "Douglas proposed to bring up the TOTAL purchasing power of the whole people by a per capita issue of tickets...Mussolini and Hitler wasted very little time PROPOSING. They started and DO distribute BOTH tickets and actual goods" (Pound 1973: 294). When the people have "TOTAL purchasing power," they are free of social restrictions, and society becomes a paradise.

Being free of social restrictions is to be in some sense entirely yourself as an individual—your deepest desires can be realized. Pound is quite explicit in indicating the connection between what is deep inside individuals and the overall economic system by saying that what is generally regarded as the most private part of private life—sexuality—is in fact shaped by the system of credit. In his most famous Canto, number XLV, he calls the bad system of credit he sees around him in the U.S. and Britain "usury," (or in Latin, "usura") and says that "Usura slayeth the child in the womb/ It stayeth the young man's courting/ It hath brought palsey to bed, lyeth/ between the young bride and her bridegroom" (230). Usury also wrecks art: "with usura... no picture is made to endure nor to live with... with usura the line grows thick." Pound's notion that economics has altered sexuality might seem strange, but was similarly suggested by many writers, as I have traced in *Deficits and Desires: Economics and Sexuality in Twentieth-Century Literature*.

Pound presents usury as making the modern world a hell on earth, in which there is no pleasure to be found because "the perverts... have set money-lust/ Before the pleasures of the senses" (61). Keynes similarly says Capitalism instills in people "the love of money as a possession—as distinguished from the love of money as a means to the enjoyments and realities of life" and such love of money is "a somewhat disgusting morbidity, one of those semi-criminal, semi-pathological propensities which one hands over with a shudder to the specialists in mental disease" (Keynes 2010: 329). For both Keynes and Pound, human psychology has been deeply distorted by the economic system.

Pound thinks that artists and poets have a role in countering the effects of usury, though not as great a role as the government. He believes that some artists can maintain contact with the natural world inside their bodies and thereby find something to counter the effects of the socioeconomic system. Most people, though, essentially have their consciousness entirely controlled by the surrounding social environment: "Their minds are, that is, circumvolved about them like soap-bubbles reflecting sundry patches of the macro-cosmos"

(Pound 2005: 92). Alec Marsh notes that the term "bubble" suggests "the traditional image of financial speculation, where hollow artificial values are allowed to expand until they burst," (112) which creates a sense that the "macro-cosmos" is at its core a result of macroeconomics. In contrast to those whose minds are full of artificial values, Pound argues that

> with certain others their conscious is 'germinal.' Their thoughts are in them as the thought of the tree is in the seed, or in the grass...And these minds are the more poetic, and they affect mind about them and transmute it.
>
> *(Pound 2005: 92)*

While the germinal poetic mind may be embedded in nature, its function is to transmute the "macro-cosmos" and perhaps break through the bubbles in which so many minds float. Poetry—a cultural product—alters the overall social order. Douglas makes a parallel statement about the source of economic value: "The factor transcending all others in importance in the modern world is the cultural inheritance by the aid of which wealth in practically unlimited quantity can be produced by a small and diminishing amount of human labour" (188–9). If we apply Douglas's theory to art, then we can say that the value of a poem derives more from the cultural inheritance—from its connection to the vast macro-cosmos of thought—than from individual labor. Pound follows that theory: his *Cantos* are built by drawing on an extensive list of cultural references—writings from early America, from Renaissance Italy, from many eras of Chinese history, from multiple languages, from politics, economics, and political treatises, as well as numerous literary works. We never see any individual in *The Cantos* with clarity. Pound does glorify certain great men—Confucius, Malatesta, Mussolini, and Jefferson—but it is for their role in shaping the overall social order. Those men and their words and acts appear only in fragments, and those fragments blend into fragments of other persons and other ages. Almost all modernist works have such a structure, being full of citations and references not only to the world around the artist but to historical events and cultures far removed, and we could say that this amounts to a "macroeconomic" method of producing value.

William Carlos Williams joined Pound in advocating Douglas's Social Credit, but did not at all agree with Pound that Douglas's vision was embodied in fascism; rather, Williams believed that Douglas's theory could work in the U.S. so that government-provided credit could free up the economic system without turning to fascism. Williams also finds Douglas's own writings to be a form of poetry. In an essay on Pound's *Cantos*, Williams writes,

> And so, when a light breaks and penetrates the blinding chaos in which we are sweltering – a name such as that of Douglas in England – it is poetry and Pound hails it not from a spirit of partisanship but as it is, a light from heaven.
>
> *(William 1954: 169)*

Williams is almost quoting Pound in reaching that conclusion, because in Canto XXXVIII, after the explanation of Douglas's theory which I cited earlier:

> there is and must be a clog
> and the power to purchase can never
> (under the present system) catch up with
> prices at large.

Pound immediately writes,

And the light became so bright and so blindin'
in this layer of paradise
that the mind of man was bewildered.
*(190)*

When Williams says that Douglas's theory is poetry, it is not of course because of its style or form, but because for Williams poetry is a breakthrough in both experience and expression—it is, in Pound's terms, a "germinal" act disrupting the "macro-cosmos." In *Spring and All*, Williams writes, "So most of my life has been lived in hell—a hell of repression lit by flashes of inspiration, when a poem such as this or that would appear" (Williams 1986: 203). Williams connects the hell of repression to economic issues by saying that it was particularly due to "the futility of acquisitive understanding" (202). And like Pound, he sees in the "repression" that he struggled against both sexual and economic issues, saying that the U.S. is mired in a conflict he calls "Love versus usury, the living hell-stink of today" (Williams 1954: 168).

Pound and Williams thus both conclude that there is a deep structure in society which has kept people repressed, kept them from being themselves, and that structure is economic at its core. Williams' early poems contain vivid images of the repression due to economic suffering. For example, in XVII, a poem beginning "The pure products of America/ go crazy," he presents a series of images of distorted personalities of impoverished persons because Americans have "no peasant traditions to give them / character" (217). A desolate young woman ends up "expressing with broken/ brain the truth about us" (218). But within this vision of people destroyed by money and lust, Williams finds

It is only in isolate flecks that
something
is given off

No one
to witness
and adjust, no one to drive the car.
*(219)*

Those isolate flecks are images of poetic inspiration, but there is no way to make use of those flecks, because there is no one to turn them into something that adjusts the system and changes the way that things are "driven."

Later, Williams writes a long poem, *Paterson* (1946), which makes as explicit as Pound does the belief that credit is the key to undoing repression in all its forms, particularly sexual. He presents the system of producing money as a perverse sexual act:

While in the tall
buildings (sliding up and down) is where
the money's made
        up and down
. . .
                predatory minds, un
affected
        UNINCONVENIENCED
                        unsexed, up
and down (without wing motion) This is how
the money's made    .    using such plugs
*(Williams 1963: 165)*

The "blockage" that Douglas, Pound, and Keynes theorize as distorting the circulation of money becomes here the entire system, plugging up desires and unsexing people. Williams, like Pound, focuses on banks as the key element in this distorted economic system. Williams says that the U.S. is suffering from

> the cancer, usury. Let credit
> out . out from between the bars
> before the bank windows.
> *(Williams 1963: 183)*

In the poem, he includes a momentary vision of the paradise that could be created if credit was unleashed, saying that the:

> Difference between squalor of spreading slums
> and splendor of renaissance cities
> Credit makes solid
> is related directly to the effort,
> work: value created and received,
> "the radiant gist" against all that
> scants our lives.
> *(185)*

People feeling their lives being scanted have wanted to dissolve into the accumulated power of thousands, all during the twentieth century: in the 1920s and 1930s, they sought that magic in communist and fascist movements, but those movements ultimately failed while Keynesian macroeconomics and some Modernist writers have continued to renew that dream.

Louis Zukofsky also turns to a macroeconomic solution to the horrors of the modern world in *A-8*, but he starts from a very different place than Pound, Williams, or Keynes. He quotes Marx and Lenin and highlights the suffering of laborers, who exist in a "death-like sleep / Bathed in the fire of labor" producing the "rage of an age" (61–2). He goes beyond Marx, though, in noting the rise of corporations, and fears that workers will turn to centralized authority—to dictatorship—to counter corporate power :

> The corporations have no souls.
> corporate life and corporate power
> ...
> It tends always to development.
> Always to consolidation...
> Even threatens the central government
> ...
> The people ... seek protection against it...
> Look for such protection, significantly enough,
> Not to their ... legislature,
> But to the single autocratic feature
> ... of government,
> The veto by... Executive... this...
> Something more imperial than republican.
> *(77)*

When Zukofsky tries to imagine a counter to the rise of an imperial—or fascist—government, he does not simply turn to the possibility of a Communist revolution as his quotes from Marx might suggest; rather, what he says sounds much more like the prescriptions of Douglas and Keynes:

> It is not by the consolidation
> Or concentration of powers (corporate bodies)
> But by their distribution,
> That good government is effected.
>
> *(90)*

Zukofsky presents a macroeconomic solution: that the government can counter the consolidation and concentration hurting the masses by creating a new distribution of powers and in particular of money.

Not all modernist writers end up suggesting macroeconomic policies as Pound, Williams, and Zukofsky do. Gertrude Stein resolutely opposes the very idea of the government distributing money or trying to adjust the economic system, but by examining how she includes such opposition in her art, we can nonetheless gain a sense of some ways that modernist techniques are tied to a macroeconomic vision. Stein asks, in a work entitled *The Geographical History of America* (1936), "Is Franklin Roosevelt trying to get rid of money… by destroying it?" (189). Luke Carson provides an explanation of what Stein may mean: "To destroy money, as Stein thought Roosevelt was trying to do, is to destroy the social bonds constituted by… debt, bonds created in… exchange" (71). For Stein, the exchange of money represents a kind of shared debt: the need to buy from each other means those in a community end up feeling indebted to each other. Money creates the very meaning of human interactions, and that meaning is lost when money derives from the abstract center of the government. As Stein puts it, "Perhaps Franklin Roosevelt wants to get rid of money by making it a thing having no meaning" (194). This relation of money to meaning leads to a remarkable conclusion:

> Money is what words are.
> Words are what money is.
>
> *(165)*

With that equation, Stein implies that when Roosevelt is destroying money, he is also destroying words, which also create meaning by being exchanged in communities. Stein's art seeks to restore words and meaning, but she cannot just write in a local or communal way: she has to turn to a presentation of a vast system and a long history to counter the effects of the new system, and hence she writes *The Geographical History of America.* This is a complex, modernist text, mixing comments on Washington, Napoleon, and Roosevelt with small scenes of people identified by first names that almost seem to float unmoored throughout history, all swirling in theories of human nature and the human mind. The text shows that Stein cannot simply ignore the macroeconomic view and present visions of the social bonds she wishes existed: rather, she has to create a vision of the macroeconomic system, in order to break it.

Even modernist works that appeared before the Great Depression were driven to present such a "macro" view of the world. *The Waste Land* (1922) is almost completely a vision of spaces, geographies, and buildings which largely interfere with or destroy individual thought and feeling. While the poem is often taken as representing the loss of myths and religion, Michael Levenson has argued rather that the poem derives its vision of devastation from an early essay by Keynes: "More than Jessie Weston, more than *The Golden Bough*, *The Economic*

*Consequences of the Peace* [by John Maynard Keynes] anticipates the ghostly modality of *The Waste Land*, the spectral insight into the fictions of modernity" (4). The poem has no solution to the mass devastation it shows, though it does hint at a Keynesian notion in the last section, declaring that "we have existed" only when we have realized that our lives are not to be measured by what is "to be found in our obituaries… Or under seals broken by the lean solicitor" (420). Instead of measuring us by what we have saved up, the poem says that we exist only in "a moment's surrender / Which an age of prudence can never retract"—in other words, when we break free of Victorian prudence and restraint and surrender or give away what Victorians would save up. But this suggestion of a break with what Keynes called the psychologically unnatural belief in saving remains only a very small moment in the poem.

The effort to break with the nineteenth-century attitudes and social structures is more extensively explored in modernist novels, particularly Virginia Woolf's. Her essay *Three Guineas* provides a way to understand her novels as aiming at the Keynesian goal of using economics to change the irrational, unconscious parts of the human psyche. The essay aims at ending war, but she stridently refuses to join any anti-war movement, or indeed any movement for any cause. What she proposes instead as a way to help end war is to change the way money is distributed: the title refers to three guineas that she gives to three organizations, without any requirements or descriptions of what should happen with that money. It is the sheer change of the distribution of money that she proposes which could possibly change unconscious attitudes sufficiently to end war.

Woolf's essay presents as the cause of war the way men are trained. First, she focuses on the fact the considerable money is spent educating men, making them feel dominant over the women in their lives, and causing them to join in the dance of society: "Here we go round the mulberry tree, the mulberry tree, the mulberry tree. Give it all to me, give it all to me, all to me. Three hundred millions spent upon war" (59). Then, she argues that men are further distorted by the professions they enter:

> And so competitive do they become that they will not share their work with others though they have more than they can do themselves. What then remains of a human being who has lost sight, and sound, and sense of proportion? Only a cripple in a cave. That of course is a figure, and fanciful; but that it has some connection with figures that are statistical and not fanciful—with the three hundred millions spent upon arms—seems possible.
>
> *(72)*

Woolf joins Keynes and Pound in saying that love of money destroys sensual experience, but she draws a further conclusion that it leads to violence.

Woolf's solution is to give "one guinea" to women's colleges and "one guinea" to an organization devoted to helping women enter the professions. She says that she is giving the money with no strings, no directions on how to use it. It is only the redistribution of money across society—a macroeconomic change—that she hopes would ultimately end war.

Woolf analyzes further that the economy devoted to male dominance leads to an unconscious structure in men, which she calls an "infantile fixation" (127). But unlike Freudian theories of "infantile fixations," she believes that this one can be changed: "must we not, and do we not, change this unalterable nature?" (140). The entire essay is devoted to saying that the redistribution of money can alter even "infantile fixations" of men. The effect on women she imagines as equally drastic: "It was the lady who could not earn money; therefore the lady must be killed" (133). Woolf herself was that lady, but found ways to make money—by running Hogarth Press—and so she has killed the "lady" she was. She writes as a person who has been reconstructed by a change in economics, just what she hopes her redistribution of money could accomplish for everyone.

The third guinea Woolf gives to an antiwar organization, but she refuses to join the organization or sign its petitions. She argues that only if she remains independent of all social groups can she escape the pressures that lead to war. Her independence is of course based on her having enough money to stand alone, which if extended to everyone could be an image of the elimination of all macroeconomic effects.

Woolf's novels can be seen as tracing the changes she advocates in *Three Guineas*. Consider Woolf's most personal novel, *To the Lighthouse* (1927). Though the novel is often seen as a version of her own childhood family in the form of the fictional Ramsays, what the novel traces is not just the interactions within that family but also the way that family sits in the surrounding socioeconomic world, and in particular the effect of that family upon an artist not in it: Lily Briscoe, whose ability to create a painting is inhibited by the family structure. Mrs. Ramsay holds the family together and presses for marriages, and while she leads a dinner party, Lily hears underneath it all "women can't write, women can't paint" (130).

Mrs. Ramsay herself has an impossible dream of ceasing "to be a private woman... and become what... she greatly admired, an investigator, elucidating the social problem" (18)—a woman earning her living. But, as Woolf argued in *Three Guineas*, the lady who cannot earn money must be killed, and so it requires the death of Mrs. Ramsay to alter the environment of the house enough to allow Lily to create her painting. Mrs. Ramsay's death is coincident with World War I, and during that period the family is replaced by working-class women whose presence was essentially invisible before the war. The working classes reconstruct the house, and so when Lily and the Ramsay family return, they are in a new environment. Instead of a dinner party overseen by Mrs. Ramsay, the family is now gathered into a boat skippered by a working-class youth. Lily no longer feels caught within that patriarchal world; she finds herself in a new kind of space, an open field, looking at the Ramsays in the boat and at the reconstructed house with no one in it. She and the Ramsay family are in different socioeconomic containers, and from her outside position, she can imagine a revised structure of gender roles. She turns Mrs. Ramsay and a child into an abstract triangle and concludes that "she would move the tree to the middle, and need never marry anybody" (262). She becomes a woman defined by her work as an artist, just what Woolf advocated as an answer to the war that interrupted the novel. She and Woolf can then finally say the last line in the novel, "I have had my vision" (287).

In Woolf's novels, as in much Modernist poetry, a sense of horror haunts the pleasant upper-class world, emerging from a surrounding socioeconomic system warping everyone's consciousness. Writers struggle to disrupt the words and images streaming through their minds, and many call for changes in the economic system to undo some of the deep distortions. Modernism is aligned with macroeconomics in the effort to change the "macrocosmos" that surrounds and fills the minds of everyone.

## References

Carson, Luke. (1999) *Consumption and Depression in Louis Zukofsky, Gertrude Stein, and Ezra Pound.* New York: St. Martin's.

Douglas, Clifford Hugh. (1933) *Social Credit.* New York: Norton.

Eliot, Thomas Stearns. (1971) *The Complete Poems and Plays, 1909–1950.* New York: Harcourt, Brace.

Hitler, Adolph. (1971) *Mein Kampf,* Ralph Mannheim (trans.). Boston, MA: Houghton Mifflin Company.

Keynes, John Maynard. (2010) *Essays in Persuasion*. Houndsmill, Basingstoke, and Hampshire: Palgrave Macmillan.
Keynes, John Maynard. (1936) *The General Theory of Employment, Interest and Money*. London: Macmillan.
Levenson, Michael. (1999) "Does the Waste Land Have a Politics?" *Modernism/Modernity* 6.3: 1–13.
Mini, Piero V. (1991) *Keynes, Bloomsbury and the General Theory*. New York: St. Martin's.
Nickels, Joel. (2012) *The Poetry of the Possible: Spontaneity, Modernism and the Multitude*. Minneapolis: University of Minnesota Press.
Pound, Ezra. (2005) *The Spirit of Romance*. New York: New Directions.
Pound, Ezra. (1986) *The Cantos of Ezra Pound*. New York: New Directions.
Pound, Ezra. (1973) *Selected Prose, 1909–1965*. New York: New Directions.
Stein, Gertrude. (1973) *The Geographical History of America*. New York: Vintage.
Szalay, Michael. (2000) *New Deal Modernism: American Literature and the Invention of the Welfare State*, Durham, NC: Duke University Press.
Tratner, Michael. (2001) *Deficits and Desires: Economics and Sexuality in Twentieth-Century Literature*. Palo Alto, CA: Stanford University Press.
Marsh, Alec. (1998) *Money and Modernity: Pound, Williams and the Spirit of Jefferson*. Tuscaloosa: University of Alabama Press.
Williams, William Carlos. (1986) *The Collected Poems of William Carlos Williams, 1909–1939*. New York: New Directions.
Williams, William Carlos. (1963) *Paterson*. New York: New Directions.
Williams, William Carlos. (1954) *Selected Essays of William Carlos Williams*. New York: Random House.
Woolf, Virginia. (1966) *Three Guineas*. New York: Harcourt Brace Jovanovich.
Woolf, Virginia. (1955) *To the Lighthouse*. New York: Harcourt Brace Jovanovich.
Zukofsky, Louis. (2011) *"A"*. New York: New Directions.

# 13
# AMERICAN MODERNISM AND THE CRASH OF 1929

*Paul Crosthwaite*

When Baz Luhrmann's *The Great Gatsby* opened in 2013, the critic Charles Moore spoke for many in observing that the film demonstrated one of the laws of adaptation: 'that the one thing worse than infidelity to the book is fidelity to it.' Luhrmann's film 'meticulously presents and builds everything that Fitzgerald describes, using computer generation as a substitute for imagination,' Moore continued; 'it is a would-be faithful film, and a terribly, terribly bad one.' By the same token, I'd argue, it's precisely where the film departs most sharply from the letter of F. Scott Fitzgerald's 1925 novel that it is truest to its spirit. Luhrmann and his co-writer Craig Pearce maintain the retrospective narrative frame provided by the story's participant-observer, Nick Carraway, but push it forward in time by some five years, to December 1929, when, as the film opens, we find Nick in a sanitarium, washed up, trying to dry out, and looking back on 'the summer of 1922' when 'the tempo of [New York] approached hysteria,' 'Wall Street boomed,' and 'the parties were bigger; the shows were broader; the buildings were higher; [and] the morals were looser.'

One reason why this shift is fitting, even as it takes a blatant liberty with the source text, is that locating the narrative present (the moment in which Nick is telling – more specifically, writing – the story) over seven years hence seems so much more in keeping with the novel's narratorial tone of wistfulness, irrevocability, and hard-come-by experience than its own ostensible narrative distance of, at most, two years, and perhaps a mere twelve months (see Fitzgerald 1991: 180, n.5.27; Fitzgerald's inconsistency on this point may itself be telling). A sense that Nick's narrative voice somehow emanates from a moment much later than the one in which it is expressly situated (later, therefore, than the novel's own date of publication) is reinforced when he describes a memento from his spell in New York: a timetable in whose 'empty spaces' he 'wrote down [...] the names of those who came to Gatsby's house that summer' (49). The time-table's relatively recent provenance – it is headed 'This schedule in effect July 5th, 1922' – is curiously at odds with its description: it is 'an old time-table now, disintegrating at its folds,' we're told, whose 'grey names' are just barely legible (49). No doubt Nick has had occasion to handle this document frequently as he has mulled over the events of that fateful summer, but the antique condition insistently assigned to it suggests a document many years, even decades, old, rather than one whose age might be more readily expressed in terms of months.

By placing its down-on-his-luck narrator at the very end of the 'Gatsby decade,' then, the most recent film adaption accords with the original's seemingly remote retrospective vantage point, from which a voice of experience ruefully contemplates the exuberance and optimism of a prolonged adolescence. Yet, Luhrmann and Pearce's relocation of Nick's framing narration to December 1929 also, of course, reflects a further intuition that many readers of the novel have felt: namely that, as Luhrmann puts it, 'in *Gatsby*, Fitzgerald … more or less predicts the Wall Street crash' of October of that year (Verghis 2013). The film, then, affords Nick the opportunity to look back on the disaster that, in the original, he (and his author) can only approximately prefigure. One of the most striking aspects of Fitzgerald's crafting of his novel, however, is the way in which he builds such a state of retrospection in the wake of disaster into his narrative's own structure. The disintegrating timetable in Nick's possession, for example, is remarkable not only for its prematurely (indeed, nigh-on preternaturally) aged condition, but also because of the baleful fates that, in the intervening period between its inscription and Nick's narration, turn out to have befallen so many of the party guests (or their relatives) whose names are recorded on it: fates ranging from sudden and mysterious hair whitening to divorce to imprisonment to drowning, suicide, and spousal murder (Fitzgerald 1991: 49–50). Nick's interpolated timetable is thus a text that, at some ill-defined but implicitly remote moment in the future, will unavoidably be read as presaging the unfortunate careers of the people it inventories. By juxtaposing the casualness of Nick's original act of inscription with the oracular quality it assumes in retrospect, Fitzgerald signals his own contrasting self-consciousness about the likelihood that his text will itself come to be read as having anticipated events transpiring only after (perhaps long after) its composition. The fact that this future orientation has a financial inflection is evident here from the presence on Nick's list of a Wall Street speculator – one James B. 'Rot-gut' Ferret – who 'came [to Gatsby's parties] to gamble,' and, when 'cleaned out,' had to rely on his stock 'fluctuat[ing] profitably next day' (50).

Such moments, then, help us to take the measure of the truth in the rarely tested truism that *The Great Gatsby* – like other novels of the period, as we'll see – forecasts the Great Crash, or at least *a* great crash. Proleptic writing of this kind invites – indeed, demands – proleptic reading – reading attuned to the ways in which a text may take as its referents not merely past or present events, but projected future ones. In this chapter, I try to give an indication of what a rigorous version of this reading practice – a kind of future-anterior historicism – might look like. Part of such a critical method, as I suggested a moment ago, must consist of an attempt to reconstruct not only how literary texts limn the shapes of things yet to come, but also how they anticipate precisely their own liability to be read in the shadow of them. My argument is that anticipatory impulses of this kind form parts of a wider modernist preoccupation with speculation, futurity, prophecy, and crisis in the early twentieth century, and that the particular economic conditions of the United States in the 1920s were peculiarly conducive to such proleptic imaginings. In the 1930s, moreover, modernist authors, I argue, strove both to understand how the preceding decade now seemed always to have been clouded by the financial disaster that brought it to a close, and how that crisis might itself portend still greater crises to come.

Financial crisis was a familiar fact of economic life in the United States in the late nineteenth and early twentieth centuries. The nation was wracked by major financial 'panics' – and accompanying slumps under in wider economic conditions – in 1869, 1873, 1893, 1907, 1914 (with the onset of the Great War), and 1920–21 (in the jarring adjustment to peacetime). Dotted among these upheavals of truly national (indeed often international) magnitude were numerous more localized banking and stock market panics, whose effects were largely confined to New York or other regions with significant financial institutions. 1922, however, saw the Dow Jones Industrial Average of leading US stocks recover strongly from the postwar depression and embark on an upward trajectory that would continue, with only infrequent and short-lived interruptions, throughout what one commentator, the editor and historian Frederick Lewis Allen, later called 'the seven fat years' (1922–28) (Allen 1935: 222). The ascent was rapid – measured by the Dow Jones, the average of industrial stocks rose 36% between 1921 and 1924 – and eventually reached astonishing heights: what would turn out to be the peak of the bull market on 3rd September 1929, when the Dow closed at 381.17 points, represented a 400% gain on the 1921 high (Klein 2001: 134, 194, 96).

The weeklong series of events that came to be memorialized as the Great Crash began toward the close of trading on Wednesday, 23rd October, when, following weeks of price declines amid signs of slowing in key sectors of the economy, the New York Stock Exchange was rocked by a sudden sell-off. The next day – 'Black Thursday' – a cascade of selling began from the opening bell and the market plummeted. There was a partial rally at the end of the week, but Black Monday and Black Tuesday – October 28th and 29th – were to follow, when the Dow fell 13% and then a further 12%. Prices continued to decline, albeit with less dramatic daily drops, until mid-November, when the Dow closed below 200 points. It would eventually bottom out at 41.22 points in mid-1932, in the depths of the Great Depression, having sustained a staggering 89% loss from its peak, and would not reach that peak again for well over twenty years (Traflet 2013: 14).

Looking back in the immediate aftermath of the crash, the journalist Garet Garrett ruefully contemplated the 'New Era' ethos that had been much promulgated during the boom years. To this way of thinking, the 'roaring twenties' had rendered the laws of economic gravity obsolete, and installed the mere maintenance of collective confidence as sufficient to ensure that the boom never had to come to an end:

> The basic delusion was that we had entered a fourth-dimensional economic world. The wonderful feature of this new world was that all possibilities of increase were infinite. There was no longer any limit upon the rise of common stocks. Since this was obvious to everyone, it followed that common stocks could not fall. How could they fall? There was no reason for people ever to sell them.
>
> *(qtd. in Klein 2001:165)*

In the 1920s, it proved quite possible to be attracted to the 'New Era' sensibility, while simultaneously heeding the doleful lessons of the previous decades of boom and bust. The writer wishing to assay this period of economic change was presented with a complex challenge: to capture what it felt like to be living inside a bubble, and at the same time to signal an awareness precisely that one *was* in a bubble, and incorporate a projection of how the period might come to look in retrospect, after the bubble had burst.

By the spring and summer of 1924, the bubble was formed, and rapidly expanding. It was during these months that the story that would become *The Great Gatsby* took shape in F. Scott Fitzgerald's mind, and steadily on paper, first in Great Neck, Long Island, and then in Valescure in the south of France, from where he forwarded the typescript to New York in October (see Fitzgerald 1991: xi–xv). How finely keyed the novel is to the tenor of these financialized times is clear from its opening pages. Nick Carraway decided to go east, he tells us, to 'learn the bond business,' since 'everybody I knew' was working in the industry (6). Employed at a financial firm headquartered amid the 'white chasms of lower New York' (46), Nick spends his days in such activities as 'list[ing] the quotations on an interminable amount of stock' (120) and an hour each evening studying 'investments and securities' (46). In conversation with Nick, Jay Gatsby himself claims to have lost the large part of a fortune in 'the big panic – the panic of the war' (71); in truth, he is at that very moment raking one in by dealing in stolen securities (129).

Nick works for the Probity Trust, and fiduciary relations – relations of trust, faith, confidence, and credit – are central to the novel's social dynamics. What most distinguishes Gatsby, in Nick's eyes, is his 'extraordinary gift for hope' (6). The 'illusion' Gatsby has built around his lost love possesses a 'colossal vitality': he has 'thrown himself into it with a creative passion, adding to it all the time' (75). At the same time, Gatsby's mysterious past makes him a source of 'romantic speculation' for others (37) In his dealings with his enigmatic neighbor, Nick finds himself veering between 'doubt' and 'incredulity' (52), 'fascination' (53), and 'renewals of complete faith' (101) to the point that he 'believ[es] everything and nothing about him' (79).

While the language surrounding Gatsby resonates with the speculative ethos of the boom years, this connection is explicit in the case of the object of his 'illusion,' Daisy Buchanan. It is Gatsby's curt insight into Daisy's 'thrilling' speech – 'Her voice is full of money' (11) – that allows Nick to account for its singular qualities: its 'fluctuating, feverish warmth' (95); the 'inexhaustible charm that [rises] and [falls] in it' (75), but also how, 'the instant [it breaks] off, ceasing to compel [...] attention [and] belief' (95), 'the basic insincerity of what she ha[s] said' becomes palpable (17). Daisy is 'the golden girl' (95), who 'gleam[s] like silver' (117), but her value is not inherent or innate; rather, as in John Maynard Keynes's analogy between the stock market and a newspaper beauty contest (Keynes 1936: 156), in which the task is not to determine which woman is objectively most attractive, but which one others, on average, will favor, Daisy is 'excitingly desirable' for Gatsby because 'many men ha[ve] already loved her – it increase[s] her value in his eyes' (Fitzgerald 1991: 116).

The novel's atmosphere of carnivalesque exuberance is continually shadowed, though, by disaster, especially in the form of automobile accidents, no fewer than four of which – of varying severity – are described (44–5, 48, 49, 61) before the final, fatal collision that sets the novel's catastrophe in motion. Nick describes the spectacle at Gatsby's parties of eager young Englishmen touting – seemingly interchangeably – 'bonds or insurance or automobiles' (35). In the United States of the 1920s, cars and financial assets were inextricably linked: new issues by the leading motor manufacturers were among the most in-demand investments, while the markets, and the economy at large, were time and again likened to a powerful vehicle surging forward at ever-increasing speed (see Fraser 2005: 342). Nick describes himself as 'slow thinking and full of interior rules that act as brakes on my desires' (Fitzgerald 1991: 48) but the 'careless people' (139) around him seem oblivious to impending crisis. When, in the moments before they encounter the body of the unfortunate Myrtle Wilson, Nick and his girlfriend Jordan Baker (herself a 'rotten driver' [48], whose name is a pairing of two car brands [see Fitzgerald 1991: 184, n.18.15]) are pictured driving 'toward death,' while he contemplates the 'portentous menacing road' that stretches before him, the prolepsis' allegorical dimension is hard to ignore, the vehicle, a vivid figure for a whole economic system approaching a devastating smash (106).

*The Great Gatsby* is one of a trio of modernist novels of 1925 that gauge the climate of excitement and anxiety generated by the turbulent eddies of the stock market. Like *Gatsby*, John Dos Passos's still widely read *Manhattan Transfer* and Nathan Asch's comparatively neglected *The Office* have been identified as anticipating the crash of 1929 (see e.g. McInerney 2000: 7; Becquet 2016: 226), and, as in the case of Fitzgerald's novel, too, these claims can be seen to possess some genuine validity insofar as the texts not only dramatize conditions of intense financial instability, but do so in a self-consciously oracular or prophetic register.

In *Manhattan Transfer*'s panoramic portrayal of New York from the turn of the century to the 1920s, the archetypal 'Metropolis' is a chaotic and dangerous place, a 'City of Destruction,' a modern-day '*Babylon*' or '*Nineveh*,' whose '*millionwindowed buildings*,' crammed '*on the narrow island*,' '*will jut glittering, pyramid on pyramid like the white cloudhead above a thunderstorm*,' as one of the novel's chapter-heading prose poems ominously has it (Dos Passos 2003: 489, 803; italics in original). This sense of acute and unrelenting pressure – of an atmospheric tension always about to break – derives especially strongly from the vortices of the financial markets. Joe Harland, the uncle of one of the major characters, was once among the most prominent 'curbstone' brokers (dealers of shares outside the official jurisdiction of the New York Stock Exchange). This onetime 'King of the Curb' (573) or 'Wizard of Wall Street' (607) reveled in 'romping with the bulls' (646) and seemed 'for a while' (698) to hold 'the whole Curb Market in the palm of his hand' (619). He recalls how he 'played the market [...] for ten years,' and in that time 'only took a cropper three times' – until, that is, 'the last time,' a disaster that saw him reduced to penury, and an 'illustration,' so he asserts in a repeated refrain, of 'the peculiar predominance of luck in human affairs' (607).

The fantasy of taking a 'plunge' (577, 607) in the market and coming up 'with your hands full, pockets full, bankaccount full, vaults full of money' (577–8) is a recurrent one in the novel, but the dangers of such a 'gamble' (577) are all too apparent. When news of war in Europe reaches New York, the first reaction we hear is a businessman's judgment that the 'Street'll go plumb to hell' (671). The 'blowup' comes quickly, with news of 'big failures' and 'panic' on Wall Street and 'crazy' conditions in the Chicago wheat pit filling the air (678, 684) before the New York Stock Exchange is forced to close (as various characters insist it must [671, 684, 689]). Even after the Exchange reopens, 'things' remain 'very unsettled downtown,' such that, in one character's estimation, 'anything's liable to happen' (708). The Depression of 1920–21, which saw a steep fall in equity prices, following an immediate postwar boom, also claims major casualties in the novel. The owner of an ailing company complains that 'there are no markets, there isnt a market in the goddam world that isnt shot to blazes' (769). When the firm finally collapses, another character sees the story in the *Wall Street Journal* – BLACKHEAD & DENSCH FAIL FOR $10,000,000 – and 'abandon[s]' himself to a 'reverie' through which flit baleful terms like 'smash,' 'Economic Depression,' and '[a]fter the war slump' (820).

*Manhattan Transfer*'s final chapter, 'Burthen of Nineveh,' reasserts the connection between the future of New York and those capitals of the ancient world whose annihilation, in retribution for gross corruption, opulence, and hubris, is foretold in prophecies recorded in the Old Testament. Set in the novel's 1920s present day, the chapter centers on an encounter between two boys and a drifter who styles himself after one such prophet, Jonah. Identifying the 'wickedness' of New York as more deserving of 'the Lord God's' retribution even than that of Babylon, Nineveh, or the inhabitants of the tower of Babel, this disheveled and frightening figure describes interceding 'only yesterday' with the Angel Gabriel on behalf of 'the women and children an the little babies that dont know no better' who'll 'all be killed same as the rich people an sinners' when the Archangel 'shake[s] it down with an earthquake an fire an brimstone from heaven.' 'All right Jonah old horse, have it your way,' he reports the angel as replying; 'we wont foreclose on em for a week or two.' 'But it's terrible to think of,' 'Jonah,' continues: 'the fire an brimstone an the earthquake an the tidal wave an the tall buildins crashing together' (816–17). This vision of a moment of reckoning that will not be confined to wealthy and iniquitous men of affairs, but will fall upon all classes, genders, and ages, and its casting of the Angel Gabriel in the guise of an exasperated bank manager itching to 'foreclose' on his mortgagers ('changing your name wont do no good ... they got all the aliases down in the judgment book,' 'Jonah' insists) (817), captures something very real about the panics and recessions of the decades around 1900, and very real anxieties concerning the fallout of any future crisis. A note of genuine financial and economic foreboding resounds, then, from the maniacal tirade to which the novel's apocalyptic mood music steadily builds.

Nathan Asch's *The Office* portrays the world of New York finance in terms very much akin to those of *Manhattan Transfer* (the resemblance between the two novels was noted in early reviews). Asch's experimental opening chapter – titled simply 'Wall Street' – is a portrait of downtown Manhattan's financial district rendered in a succession of discontinuous words and phrases, culminating in the litany 'maelstrom – mix-up – bedlam – pandemonium' (Asch 1926: 12). The following two chapters anatomize the titular office, a brokerage that is both a typical feature of this febrile environment – 'The office is filled with noise, confusion, rallies, panics, downward movements, upward movements, stiffenings, weakenings, voices, shouts, cries, laughs' – and a kind of proxy for the US financial system at large:

> The office is filled with customers, who buy and sell securities which are the blood of the nation's life. [...] The office is the central point of the nation's business. The office is the most important point in the nation. The office is the most feared point in the nation.
>
> *(25)*

The pages identifying the office as a microcosm of the nation's financial and economic life are followed by one with a single, momentous line: '... and then one day the office failed ...' (27). Each of the remaining fourteen chapters traces the response of one member of the firm to its collapse. For one of the partners, the 'failure' is the realization of his own pessimistic projections: 'the thing that he had feared and had imagined as his test had happened; the failure really had come' (206).

Another character, Marc Kranz, is closely modeled on Asch himself, who had a spell as a New York stockbroker before 'going away' – as Kranz resolves to at the end of his chapter – 'to Paris' (104), where he wrote *The Office*. And Asch seems to articulate something of his own ambitions when he describes the broker-poet Kranz's aspiration to be 'a prophet' showing people 'their destinies, their road to the future' (102). A kind of Whitmanian Futurist, he 'dream[s]' of 'see[ing] the entire city, the life of all of it,' of 'sing[ing] of the people that crowd the streets below' and 'of the great buildings downtown' (100). His will be 'a song of speed, of energy, in which [will] be mixed the automobile horns and the tick-tick of the ticker'; it will 'be full of' the 'dance of money' and 'the dance of life' (100–1).

The fact that Asch's own 'prophetic' 'song' of the downtown monetary whirl and of the stock ticker (whose 'tik-tik-tiks' he transcribes in long streams [16–21]) is heavily freighted with expectations of disaster is evident both from his depiction of the 'failure' of the brokerage house that is a metonym for the economy at large, and from the way in which he projects his narrative forward into the aftermath of a future moment of mass crisis. In a key scene, for example, a laid-off employee from the office, identified simply as 'One of the Clerks,' observes a 'bunch of bums' in a lunchroom and imagines that 'maybe their office had failed too, or many offices that they had worked in had failed' and 'they had not been able to live through the failures that had happened' (63–4). In response, he envisages a future moment in which the ranks of the destitute and dispossessed will have swelled to absorb him too: 'He pictured himself coming into this restaurant, not as he was now, although jobless, full of ambition and knowledge of eventual success, but really jobless, friendless, without a penny in the world' (64–5). Striking here – as in a capitalist system driven by what Jens Beckert calls 'imagined futures' and 'fictional expectations' (see Beckert 2016) – is the way in which the clerk's gloomy prognostications alter his beliefs and seem thereby to produce the very reality he fears:

> [H]e became frightened. He began to believe that he was actually friendless and without prospects, began to believe that there was no future for him, that he couldn't get a job if he tried, that he could never get another place again. The picture of himself helpless stuck before him and drowned out the other picture, the picture of ambition. He actually was friendless, was jobless, was without hopes.
>
> *(Asch 1926: 66–7)*

The Great Crash and the Great Depression that followed it – brought about, at least in part, precisely by the ebbing of popular confidence in what Asch calls 'eventual success' – would indeed see joblessness and poverty balloon. Writing in 1931, F. Scott Fitzgerald observed that 'the most expensive orgy in history [...] ended two years ago, because the utter confidence which was its essential prop received an enormous jolt and it didn't take long for the flimsy structure to settle earthward' (Fitzgerald 2005a: 137–8). Looking back amid the changed circumstances of the 1930s, Fitzgerald drew attention to the shades of calamity already present in his work of the previous decade. Even as '[t]he whole golden boom was in the air,' he recalled in 'Early Success' (1937),

> [a]ll the stories that came into my head had a touch of disaster in them – the lovely young creatures in my novels went to ruin, the diamond mountains of my short stories blew up, my millionaires were as beautiful and damned as Thomas Hardy's peasants. In life these things hadn't happened yet, but I was pretty sure that living wasn't the reckless, careless business these people thought.
>
> *(Fitzgerald 2005b: 188)*

Fitzgerald did not coin the term 'the Jazz Age,' but his popularization of it, and of its characteristic mood and manners, made him an emblematic figure of 'the ten-year period that [...] leaped to a spectacular death in October 1929' (Fitzgerald 2005a: 130), and he came to see the decline of his own personal fortunes as inextricable from the epoch's demise, even as he could plausibly claim to have anticipated it. The collapse on Wall Street became a figure for his wife's mental breakdown in 1930 – 'The Crash! Zelda + America' he wrote in his ledger (Fitzgerald 1919–38: 184) – and for his own several years later: the language of over-indebtedness, closed out accounts, and deflated values that runs through the harrowing memoir 'The Crack-Up' and its sequels 'Pasting It Together' and 'Handle with Care' (1936) culminates in the insight that 'my happiness, or talent for self-delusion [...] was not the natural thing but the unnatural – unnatural as the Boom; and my recent experience parallels the wave of despair that swept the nation when the Boom was over' (Fitzgerald 2005c: 154).

The 'unnatural' delusions that the 1920s bull market engendered are well evoked in Fitzgerald's quintessential post-crash story, 'Babylon Revisited' (1931). The protagonist, an American named Charlie Wales, has returned to Paris, where his 'luck in the market' (Fitzgerald 2014: 169) in the closing years of the roaring twenties allowed him and his family to live as 'a sort of royalty, almost infallible, with a sort of magic around' (160) them, until 'the market [...] cleaned [him] out' and he ended up 'flat on [his] back in a sanitarium' (168). Charlie is back in this latter-day Babylon to regain custody of his daughter, who is under the guardianship of his late wife's sister. At the height of his dissipation, Charlie locked his wife out of their house following a row one 'terrible February night,' and she wandered disorientated in a snowstorm (170). Though she 'escap[ed] pneumonia by a miracle' (171), she died soon after, and Charlie's sister-in-law holds him responsible. Charlie acknowledges having 'lost a lot in the crash,' but insists that he 'lost everything [he] wanted in the boom': with these words, 'the memory of those days [sweeps] over him like a nightmare,' and he thinks of '[t]he men who locked their wives out in the snow, because the snow of twenty-nine wasn't real snow. If you didn't want it to be snow you just paid some money' (177). Inside the bubble, where Charlie lived for two 'crazy years' (172), the monetary magic conjured by an ever-rising market rendered the weather as harmless as the snow in a snow globe – or so it seemed.

In *Tender Is the Night* (1934), another story of American expats 'promenading insouciantly upon the national prosperity' (Fitzgerald 2012: 85) in 1920s France, Fitzgerald approaches the crash via a strategy of insistent foreshadowing: as the novel nears its end, ironically upbeat discussions of stock holdings, Wall Street, and the brokerage business proliferate (e.g. 292, 236, 307, 227), ably evoking what the narrator calls a 'whole system sway[ing] and thunder[ing] onward' and, as it does so, 'len[ding] a feverish bloom' to commercial 'principles' that augur 'doom' (66). Fitzgerald was clear in his preliminary notes that the novel's main narrative would conclude in July 1929, three months prior to the Wall Street Crash, but the published text is equally clear in drawing events to a close in July 1930 (see Fitzgerald 2012: xxxvi). This scenario, in which the crash has presumably occurred, and yet, after all its relentless adumbration, goes weirdly unmentioned, seems at once to retain something of Fitzgerald's original intention and heighten its effect, producing an uncanny temporality in which crisis is both necessary (it has already happened) and contingent (perhaps it is still to come – there was no inevitability, after all, to its happening in October 1929 – or has even been contained by an alternate political response). It is a situation in which, as the narrator puts it elsewhere, 'the very march of destiny stop[s]; inevitably [becomes] evitable' (80).

John Dos Passos does something similar in *The Big Money* (1936), the concluding part of his *U.S.A.* trilogy. The prologue to the trilogy asserts that 'U.S.A.' is, among other things, 'a column of stockquotations rubbed out and written in by a Western Union boy on a blackboard' (Dos Passos 1996: 2), and the centrality of finance capital to the life of the nation is especially clear in *The Big Money*, Dos Passos's chronicle of the 1920s. The disastrous final act of the decade that would be played out on Wall Street is presaged by newspaper clippings in the book's 'Newsreel' sections that come laden with dramatic irony ('BOOM YEAR AHEAD,' 'BROKERS LOANS HIT NEW HIGH,' 'MARKETS OPTIMISTIC,' 'nation-wide interest in the stock-market,' [1133, 1159, 1160]); by an extended account of the rise and fall of the mid-1920s Florida land boom; and by the repeated financial reversals – as well as the plane and car crashes or 'crackups' (1038, 1078) – suffered by the aviator-turned-stock ticker obsessive Charley Anderson, whose self-professed 'feeling for the big money' proves to be erratic at best (1069).

The last of the book's short biographical sketches of notable figures of the period, focusing on the financier Samuel Insull, gives the reader a glimpse of events following 'the stockmarket crash,' which revealed 'Insull's companies [to be] intertwined in a tangle that no bookkeeper has ever been able to unravel' (1213). The final 'Newsreel' interlude also suggests the impending panic ('WALL STREET STUNNED,' 'Decline in Contracts,' 'NEW METHODS OF SELLING SEEN' [1205]) but even here there is still evidence of optimism: 'REAL VALUES UNHARMED,' 'PRESIDENT SEES PROSPERITY NEAR' read two headlines, while an advice page letter asks guilelessly, 'Do you think I might buy stocks?' (1207, 1206). Meanwhile, the last of the novel's main chapters stops short of the crash: the mother of the journalist and labor activist Mary French blithely remarks that she and Mary's father 'made big killings on the stockexchange on the same day' and are 'going to Europe on a spree' (1224). In both *The Big Money* and *Tender Is the Night*, then, Dos Passos and Fitzgerald underscore the presentiments of financial crisis that they had woven into their novels of the mid-1920s, stressing how what they had sensed then to be potential had come to be realized; and yet at the same time they suspend the fateful moment of collapse – with its devastating effects on rich and poor alike – and highlight the contingency that coexists with necessity in the rhythm of capitalist crisis.

How the impact of the crash would translate into popular mobilization was the central political question of the 1930s, not only in the United States, but also in the many other nations directly impacted by the financial collapse. The economic historian Harold James has observed that the 'world-historical consequences' of '[t]he crash of 1929' include 'the Great Depression, [and] even perhaps the Second World War' (James 2010: 131), and already, in the 1930s, writers were imagining timelines that led from the chaos on Wall Street through economic blight and Fascist insurgency to future global conflagration. Around the time of the 2016 US presidential election, two American novels of the period, Sinclair Lewis's *It Can't Happen Here* (1935) and Nathanael West's *A Cool Million* (1934), were widely discussed for their portrayals of bellicose authoritarian populists being propelled to the White House by the forces of racism, xenophobia, and mass anger at declining economic prospects. The demagogue characters in the novels lay America's woes at the feet of an unlikely cabal consisting of Jewish Wall Street financiers – allegedly responsible for destabilizing the economy for their own ends – and the 'Bolshevik' labor unions who are supposedly choking off any hope of recovery (e.g. Lewis 2017: 15, 41, 99–100, 140; West 1997: 159, 173–6, 226).

The role of the Great Crash in fueling the rise of Fascism and the march to war is especially clear in *House of All Nations* (1938), one of the major works of the important but neglected modernist and Marxist Christina Stead. Born in Australia, Stead spent the late 1920s and 1930s moving between London, Paris, and New York with her American partner, the broker and author William J. Blake. The Paris bank at which Stead began working with Blake in 1929 provided the model for the Banque Mercure, the disreputable institution at the heart of *House of All Nations*. The great draw for the Banque Mercure's clients – especially the down-at-heel American émigrés who loiter there – is 'the flashing in and out of the prices' as they are relayed from New York, a spectacle that seems to 'picture [...] not only the wild scramble in the exchange so many miles away, but also the heartbeats of Dame Fortune herself' (Stead 1974: 240). As this remark implies, the speculators who work at and trade via the bank are an intensely superstitious group – 'mythomaniacs' (77), as one employee puts it, obsessed with occult methods of divining the future.

In the narrative's early 1930s present, this prophetic mindset is focused most intently on the Nazi Party and the prospect of another European war that its rise portends. The 'war-clouds' and the 'shadow' of 'Hitlerism' hanging over Europe are seen by the bank's suitably mercurial director, Jules Bertillon, as the signal phenomena of a 'history of the world' that has pointed only 'down' since what another character calls 'the expropriation of the American bourgeoisie via the stock market, October 29, 1929' (228, 397, 105). The narrator describes 'the terrifying rise of Hitlerism in the May, 1932, elections' (Stead probably means the July 1932 federal election, when the NSDAP became the largest party in the Reichstag) as the moment when 'the wing of terror spread its shadow over Europe, and the governing classes, in despair since 1929, began to see that Fascism was not simply an expedient [...] but a real salvation for their property' (632–3). The Nazis' decisive ascent occurs late in the novel, and it is striking that the extensive discussions of conditions in Germany that appear beforehand are marked by intense disagreement over the likelihood of such a situation coming to pass. That is, Stead – who completed her novel in 1937 – treats the breakthrough of 'Hitlerism' in the same way that she treats the prospect of war: as a possibility, perhaps even a probability, but by no means a foregone conclusion. Stead's portrayal of political events thus resists what Michael André Bernstein calls 'apocalyptic history,' even as she insists on the inherent crisis-tendencies of capitalism itself – the notion that, as one of her Marxist characters puts it, 'one day everyone crashes' (Stead 1974: 145).

The ongoing value of the novels of the 1920s and 1930s that I have discussed in this chapter lies, then, precisely in their staging of the interplay of necessity and contingency in economic and political life. Such texts make it clear that while the timing, location, severity, and particular characteristics of capitalist crises are indeterminable in advance, crisis itself is an integral feature of the system – which is not to say that crises cannot be curbed, ameliorated, or temporarily forestalled, but only that they cannot be abolished. Yet, the writing of the period also indicates how, in the political field, financial and economic crises at least temporarily open up a set of forking paths – for good or ill. Thus, as the work of Lewis, West, or Stead indicates, it was no more inevitable that in the United States after 1929 the forces of reaction should have been held at bay and the (limited, but significant) progressive gains of the New Deal achieved than that other advanced nations should have been led by the martial beat of Fascism toward the catastrophes of the 1940s. As we have been learning all over again since 2008, capitalism *is* crisis, and it is this fact of capitalism that poses both the most terrible political danger (the danger, that is, of a politics worse than capitalism itself) and the greatest political possibility.

## References


Allen, Frederick L. (1935) *The Lords of Creation*, New York: Harper & Bros.

Asch, Nathan. (1926) *The Office*, London: Robert Holden.

Beckert, Jens. (2016) *Imagined Futures: Fictional Expectations and Capitalist Dynamics*, Cambridge, MA: Harvard University Press.

Becquet, Alexandra. (2016) in Nathan Asch, 'Ford Madox Ford,' in Alexandra Becquet and Claire Davison-Pégon (eds.) *Ford Madox Ford's Cosmopolis: Psycho-geography,* Flânerie, *and the Cultures of Paris*, Leiden: Brill.

Bernstein, Michael A. (1994) *Foregone Conclusions: Against Apocalyptic History*, Berkeley: University of California Press.

Dos Passos, John. (2003) *Manhattan Transfer* in *Novels 1920–1925*, New York: Library of America.

Dos Passos, John. (1996) *U.S.A.*, New York: Library of America.

Fitzgerald, F. Scott. (2014) "Babylon Revisited," in J. L. W. West III (ed.) *Taps at Reveille*, Cambridge: Cambridge University Press.

Fitzgerald, F. Scott. (2012) *Tender Is the Night*, Cambridge: Cambridge University Press.

Fitzgerald, F. Scott. (2005) "Echoes of the Jazz Age," "Early Success," "Handle with Care," in J. L. W. West III (ed.) *My Lost City: Personal Essays, 1920–1940*, Cambridge: Cambridge University Press.

Fitzgerald, F. Scott. (1991) *The Great Gatsby*, Cambridge: Cambridge University Press.

Fitzgerald, F. Scott. (1919–38) *F. Scott Fitzgerald's Ledger*, Matthew J. and Arlyn Bruccoli Collection of F. Scott Fitzgerald. University of South Carolina. Irvin Department of Rare Books and Special Collections. http://library.sc.edu/digital/collections/fitzledger.html.

Fraser, Steve. (2006) *Wall Street: A Cultural History*, London: Faber and Faber.

James, Harold. (2010) "1929: The New York Stock Market Crash," *Representations* 110: 129–44.

Keynes, John Maynard. (1936) *The General Theory of Employment, Interest, and Money*, New York: Harcourt Brace.

Klein, Maury. (2001) *Rainbow's End: The Great Crash of 1929*, Oxford: Oxford University Press.

Lewis, Sinclair. (2017) *It Can't Happen Here*, London: Penguin.

McInerney, Jay. (2000) "Introduction," in John Dos Passos, *Manhattan Transfer*, London: Penguin.

Moore, Charles. (2013) "Baz Luhrmann's *The Great Gatsby*: A Faithful Film – And a Terribly, Terribly Bad One," *Telegraph* [online] (May 19). www.telegraph.co.uk/culture/film/filmreviews/10067605/Baz-Luhrmanns-The-Great-Gatsby-a-faithful-film-and-a-terribly-terribly-bad-one.html.

Stead, Christina. (1974) *House of All Nations*, London: Angus & Robertson.

*The Great Gatsby*. (2013) [Film] Directed by Baz Luhrmann. Screenplay by Baz Luhrmann and Craig Pearce, USA: Warner Bros. Pictures.

Traflet, Janice M. (2013) *A Nation of Small Share-Holders: Marketing Wall Street after World War II*, Baltimore, MD: Johns Hopkins University Press.

Verghis, Sharon. (2013) "Careless People of F Scott Fitzgerald's *Great Gatsby* Have a Modern Equivalent," *Australian* [online] (May 4). www.theaustralian.com.au/arts/review/careless-people-of-f-scott-fitzgeralds-great-gatsby-have-a-modern-equivalent/news-story/741508cb31dc43801a0a7144223a2ac2.

West, Nathaniel. (1997) *A Cool Million: The Dismantling of Lemuel Pitkin*, in Sacvan Bercovitch (ed.) *Novels and Other Writings*, New York: Library of America.

# 14

# FRIEDRICH HAYEK AND THE PLEASURES OF LIBERAL THOUGHT IN THE 'GREAT BOOK' OF MODERN JAPAN

*Brian Hurley*

In 1966, a group of economists and intellectuals from around the world gathered in Tokyo for a special meeting of their international association, The Mont Pèlerin Society. Founded in 1947 by the Austrian economist Friedrich Hayek (1899–1992), the Society formed as a force on the right that opposed what its members viewed as the "collectivist" principles of socialism, fascism, and communism, and that advocated instead for liberal ideals that were intended to foster capitalist competition and celebrate the freedom of the entrepreneurial individual. Hayek's address in Tokyo revolved around defining liberalism in terms of "a self-generating or spontaneous order in social affairs," an order which he believed excessive government control and centralized economic planning threatened to obliterate (Hayek 1966a: 2). But at the conclusion of the lecture, Hayek suggested that beneath the sorts of straightforward declaratives that made up his argument lay a more sensuous reckoning with liberty as a distinctly negative ideal whose true substance could never be fully articulated in language. Instead, Hayek implied, liberty was akin to an ineffable atmosphere that naturally precipitated in the place of its evaporated opposite—coercion.

Making this point, he ended his Tokyo remarks with a literary allusion apparently intended to connect his philosophy of liberty to ideas more familiar to his interlocutors in East Asia:

> Is this all so very different
> From what Lao-Tzu says
> In his fifty-seventh poem?:
> If I keep from meddling with people
> They take care of themselves,
> If I keep from commanding people,
> They behave themselves,
> If I keep from imposing on people,
> They become themselves.
> *(Hayek 1966a: 15)*

Another presenter at the Tokyo meeting of the Mont Pèlerin Society continued this line of inquiry. The scholar Nishiyama Chiaki—who had been one of Hayek's students at the University of Chicago and later translated Hayek's *The Road to Serfdom* (1944) and Milton

Friedman's *Free to Choose* (1980) into Japanese—claimed in his lecture at the Tokyo meeting that "the Japanese" had an instinctual understanding of what Hayek described as the negative ideal of liberty because Japanese thought was founded on "the assertion of our traditional negation of reason or of intellect and of our age old perception of 'nothingness'"(Nishiyama 1966: 3). He argued that

> for us, the Japanese, it is thus not all so difficult to tread the steps to the center of the Hayekian world. We can, in fact, even claim to Professor Hayek that it was really us, the Asians, who realized first the inescapable limitation of our intellect and that it is precisely from this realization that the sense of freedom emerges.
>
> *(4)*

Nishiyama added that even though "the Japanese" were not yet "naturalized as respectable citizen[s] to the world of Professor Hayek," they had long intuited the sorts of negative ideals associated with liberalism by more poetic names, such as "the Way":

> Does this mean, then, that we ["the Japanese"] have now a passport to the world of Professor Hayek or of the Mont Pèlerin Society? I believe that the answer is affirmative. How much better it would be to have Rao-Tzu [Lao-Tzu] as our fellow citizen in a free society than the creep called technical economist.
>
> *(6)*

Taken in isolation, the idea that the Taoist "Way" was simply another name for the "spontaneous order" of liberal society might be less than convincing. But in the context of this essay, what matters in these statements is the glimpse they give us of prominent economists speaking to each other about reverberations they themselves had felt between literary language and liberal economic ideas. Read this way, these excerpts from the proceedings of the 1966 Tokyo meeting of the Mont Pèlerin Society open up to the central problematic of this essay: namely, that one way of considering the connections linking literary writing and economic thinking is to observe how the ideological atmospherics of liberal sensibility have interloped into more poetic discursive territories, where economic ideas that would seem to bear no trace of literary implication have made their appeals under the cover of aesthetic innocence. In making this argument, I draw on aspects of the interpretive paradigm developed in a different context by the scholar of Japanese literature Alan Tansman, who reminds us that "those creations of the imagination most resistant to political readings" can sometimes best reveal the aesthetic workings of a political formation, for "it is through the products of the imagination that ideology is most effectively diffused, even as those works absorb the ideological atmosphere in which they are created." (Tansman 2009:1)

This essay explores these connections in the course of reading a novel from Japan that was translated by one of Hayek's students at the University of Chicago in the mid-1950s. I argue that the novel allows us to consider how the hard edges and concrete closures of ideological conviction can dissolve into more delicate moments of open-ended literary pleasure. As we read a novel that was originally translated and received within the nascent neoliberal imagination at Chicago in mid-century, we can consider how the literary invites liberal economic thought old and new to drift beyond its own ideological horizons, and to attune to seemingly unrelated aesthetic atmospheres more often associated with pleasure than politics.

## Edwin McClellan's translation of Natsume Sōseki's *Kokoro*

In 1957, Edwin McClellan published his English translation of Natsume Sōseki's *Kokoro* (1914), the title of which might be rendered as "the heart of things." It would go on to become one of the most widely read Japanese novels available in English translation. McClellan himself would later teach at the University of Chicago and Yale University, becoming one of the most influential scholars of Japanese literature of his generation.

But this can make us forget that he actually completed the *Kokoro* translation as a labor of love in a "previous life," so to speak, during which he crossed paths with some of the most prominent figures on the Cold War American right. In fact, he worked on the translation while he was still one of Hayek's graduate student advisees on the Committee on Social Thought at the University of Chicago, preparing it as a companion to his dissertation on Sōseki, one of the most celebrated writers of modern Japan. This reminds us that in the 1950s, McClellan was more of an insider to a segment of the academy studying the intellectual history of liberalism than he was to the academic field of "Japan Studies" we know today—which, after all, did not yet exist when he translated *Kokoro*. Reflecting on himself as something of an outsider to the field of "Japan Studies," McClellan remarked in a 1998 lecture that before translating *Kokoro*,

> My education itself had very little to do with this [Sōseki and Japanese literature] because I went to a Scottish university [St. Andrews], which was the birthplace of the Scottish reformation, and my special subject was the Scottish reformation. And then when I went to study with Hayek and David Grene, what was I doing? I was reading Tocqueville.
>
> So my choice to do Sōseki finally or, rather, translate *Kokoro* was, in a sense, an attempt to persuade two men whom I really thought very highly of, who knew nothing about Japanese literature, to persuade them to accept the next step in what I wanted, which was to write about Sōseki. And if they were going to say yes they would have to be shown a novel by Sōseki which I thought might have a chance of touching them.
>
> *(McClellan 2000: 15)*

Ironically, then, the translation which would become a foundation of "Japan Studies" in the American academy originally had nothing to do with "Japan Studies" at all, and was, in fact, first conceived and received within a liberal imagination that organized in closer relation to what it believed were globally relevant social scientific, economic, and philosophical forms of knowledge. The crux of the matter presently comes into view: what was it about *Kokoro* that made it the novel from modern Japan with the best chance of "touching" Hayek and the liberal imagination at mid-century Chicago?

By the time Hayek read *Kokoro*, he had long been at the center of a movement to revive liberal sentiments in the aftermath of the Great Depression. The historian Angus Burgin has observed that

> [i]n the midst of the Great Depression, market advocates were acutely aware that the social philosophy of the free market inspired little support within either academic institutions or popular politics. They sought to overcome their isolation by establishing networks of sympathizers who could work in conjunction to reexamine the philosophical foundations of their ideas and reconstruct the public presentation of their arguments.
>
> *(8)*

Hayek's frequent interlocutor John Maynard Keynes had declared "The End of Laissez-Faire" in 1926, stating that "[f]or my part, I think that Capitalism, wisely managed, can probably be made more efficient for attaining economic ends than any alternative system yet in sight, but that in itself it is in many ways extremely objectionable"(321). During the interwar years to come, Hayek would watch with horror as authoritarians in fascist Italy and Nazi Germany rose to power, promising to overcome the crises of capitalism with the illiberal measures of state planning and government control. Hayek believed that the collectivist turn during the 1930s was symptomatic of a moment in which the powers of the state expanded so greatly that civilization itself was presently on the brink of irredeemable destruction. In response, he convened the Mont Pèlerin Society in 1947, which, as Burgin has observed, provided "an international gathering place for leading philosophers, economists, journalists, politicians, and philanthropists who supported the market mechanism," and which "has long been cited as a progenitor of the social philosophy that has become known as 'neoliberalism'"(8). The gravity of the midcentury moment came through in the "Statement of Aims" drafted by the Society in 1947, which began by stating that "[t]he central values of civilization are in danger. Over large stretches of the Earth's surface the essential conditions of human dignity and freedom have already disappeared."

McClellan came of age at around the same time that Hayek formed the Mont Pèlerin Society. He was born to a Japanese mother and a Scottish father in Kobe in 1925, and used both English and Japanese as native languages. He later studied at St. Andrews, in Scotland, and it was there that he first came into contact with Russell Kirk, who was then completing research for what would become *The Conservative Mind* (1953). McClellan became Kirk's graduate advisee at Michigan State, and later joined the Committee on Social Thought at the University of Chicago, where his doctoral advisor was Hayek. In the same year that he graduated, 1957, McClellan published his *Kokoro* translation with Henry Regnery Company, a prominent press on the American right that had earlier published William F. Buckley Jr.'s conservative classic *God and Man at Yale* (1951).

Soon after the *Kokoro* translation appeared, Hayek hired McClellan to polish the prose style of his own manuscript of *The Constitution of Liberty* (1960). When Hayek petitioned Relm Foundation years later, in 1966, for funding to hire McClellan to edit another manuscript—*Law, Legislation and Liberty*—he wrote:

> I believe that it is important that when the book comes out it should be fairly polished in exposition. If *The Constitution of Liberty* has been fairly successful, this is in a large measure due to what Edwin MacClellan [*sic*] did to my original draft.
>
> *(Hayek 1966b)*

Hayek would later rejoice at McClellan's willingness to collaborate on the manuscript of *Law, Legislation and Liberty*, exclaiming:

> [T]o my equal surprise and gratification Edwin McClellan declared himself willing to do for my forthcoming book what he did for the Constitution of Liberty. Since he writes the kind of English I would like to write and is, of course, now thoroughly familiar with my ideas, this seems to me greatly preferable to any other solution.
>
> *(Hayek 1966c)*

## Pleasure and politics

Hayek might have first sensed the appeal of McClellan's prose style in the course of reading *Kokoro* in translation. McClellan has written that he showed the translation to Hayek and his other advisor at Chicago, the classicist David Grene, in 1956, and that he was overjoyed at their responses to the novel, recalling:

> I have never forgotten and shall never forget the generosity of feeling of those two men, the Irish classicist [Grene] and the Austrian economist [Hayek], when without any reserve they told me how moved they had been by the novel.
>
> *(McClellan 1999: 204)*

But taken at face value, *Kokoro* would not seem to have much in common with the intellectual historical contexts which related to the efforts of Hayek and others to rehabilitate "free market" ideas at mid-century. The first half of *Kokoro* is the first-person narrative of an alienated university student who is about to graduate but has no idea what he wants to do with his life. He tells the story of meeting an enigmatic older man known only as "Sensei," who seems to have penetrating insight into the loneliness of the modern world, but whose full biography and true lessons are shrouded in mystery. The narrative perspective in the latter half of the novel shifts to Sensei himself, and is told in the form of a letter that he writes to the student. In the letter, Sensei tells the story of his life, explaining that as a university student himself, he had betrayed a more virtuous friend (known as "K") in order to win the hand in marriage of the woman who would become his wife. Sensei writes that he has lived with shame and regret over his betrayal of K ever since. The letter and the novel end with Sensei's declaration that he will atone for his egotism by committing suicide.

To be sure, the links between *Kokoro* and the liberal mind are not unfathomable. Most obviously, the novel dramatizes the promise and peril of self-interested individualism in the modern world, and these themes are familiar refrains in the canon of liberal thought, too. The prominent literary critic and philosopher Karatani Kōjin has even written that "[i]n a way, Natsume Sōseki was an English liberal, as can be seen in his lecture 'Watakushi no kojinshugi' [My individualism]. It can perhaps be said that Sōseki's philosophical standpoint was that of Hume" (108). But as a moving novel, *Kokoro* goes further than merely recapitulating the classic conundrums of liberal individualism that had already been explained in philosophical exposition. After all, the most interesting thing about *Kokoro* is not the content of its narrative, but its form and feel as a piece of fiction we encounter in the sensuous realm of the aesthetic. It is a novel of gentle sensibility whose complex structure loops back onto itself like a Mobius strip, dissolving any simple linearity of relation between beginnings and endings, causes, and effects. If the expository writings of intellectuals like Hayek convey arguments and information, *Kokoro*, as a novel, gives us the chance to drift into undulating moments of affective resonance that would seem to bear no trace of ideological implication, nor any inclination toward argumentative instrumentalism. The themes of loneliness and alienation are obvious in the novel, and the trials to the soul bred by egotism are unmistakable, but *Kokoro* is the opposite of doctrinaire because it does not insist on any one reading, meaning, or message in particular.

The trouble with linking Sōseki's novel to Hayek's thought only deepens in considering that the last person who would have argued that *Kokoro* had anything to do with Cold War neoliberalism might well have been McClellan himself. His favorite moments in *Kokoro* would seem to have had nothing to do with politics at all. In the same 1998 lecture cited earlier, for example, he pointed to the atmospheric passage below as an example of the poetic power and rhythmic cadence of Sōseki's language:

> Among the things that Sensei said, what interested me most was his remark that no man was immune to temptation. I knew, more or less, what Sensei meant, of course. But I wanted Sensei to talk more about the matter.

After the departure of the dog and the children, the large garden became quiet once more. We sat still for a moment or two, as though made immovable by the silence around us. The beautiful sky began slowly to lose its brightness. And before us, the delicate, green maple leaves, which looked like drops of water just about to fall from the branches, seemed to grow darker in color. From the road below, the sound of cart wheels reached our ears. I imagined that a man from the village had loaded his cart with plants or vegetables and was on his way to some fair to sell them. Sensei stood up, as though the sound had aroused him from his meditation.

"Let us go home," he said. "The days are becoming longer, but dusk seems to fall quickly when we are sitting about lazily like this."

*(Sōseki 1957: 62–63)*

McClellan lauded this passage:

What I see is a scene where the young friend, unbeknownst to himself—though he as an older man, remembering and telling the story of their friendship, is much wiser in retrospect—begins to hear sounds and see things as he had never heard and seen before, that is, with the awareness of a new melancholy. The breaking of the silence around them, first by the sound of the cart-wheels, then by the very ordinary, almost banal remark made by Sensei, increases the sadness and our awareness of the silence. It is this new awakening to sorrow on the part of the young man that shaped my timing, diction, and voice.

*(McClellan 2000: 5)*

The poetics of rhythm and voice with which McClellan himself was so taken commune with a readerly mood that would seem to be incompatible with the polemics associated with the controversial term "neoliberalism" that is sometimes attached to the influence of Hayek and the Mont Pèlerin Society. This tells us that the connections between McClellan's translation of *Kokoro* and Hayek's liberal thought at mid-century cannot be fully understood by insisting on any straightforward correspondence at the level of content. The novel did not simply say the same thing that Hayek did, and neither did the translation reveal Hayek's "influence" on McClellan. Somewhat paradoxically, though, what makes the reading of McClellan's *Kokoro* translation in the context of Hayekian thought a matter of aesthetics is actually the fact that the novel seems to make no political argument whatsoever. Its literary style, aesthetic ambience, and pathos are far more arresting than its intellectual historical conditions of possibility—so arresting, in fact, that the translation's connections to Hayek have rarely been noted.

But connected they were. One way of thinking through their relation is to consider the place of pleasure in the politics of ideology. In particular, we might link the readerly enjoyment of McClellan's literary translation of *Kokoro* to the liberal economic and philosophical standpoint of Hayek by observing that although the experience of reading the novel is distinct from (and even opposed to) the closed conclusion of ideological conviction, it might also be true that for this very reason, Sōseki's novel (more than Hayek's arguments) allows readers to commune with the more open-ended, free-floating enjoyment of what might be called a "pre-ideological" form of liberal pleasure. This formulation adapts aspects of Slavoj Žižek's argument in *The Sublime Object of Ideology*, where he explained that although the "discursive" elements of ideological formation can be understood through deconstructive "symptomal readings" which expose the artificiality of ideological constructs, the forms of pleasure that more subtly undergird ideological realities call for a different sort of critique, one which "aims at extracting the kernel of *enjoyment*, at articulating the way in which—beyond the field of meaning but at the same time internal to it—an ideology implies, manipulates, produces a pre-ideological enjoyment structured in fantasy"(140). Focusing on the pleasures of the text as a piece of literature first and foremost draws us into the aesthetic part of the imagination that is attracted to Sōseki's narrative and McClellan's prose style beyond any question of cognitive agreement with an argument or premise. And in so doing, this approach also opens up to literary pleasures which are not ideologically irrelevant if they remind the liberal imagination of its own fascination with the spontaneity and plurality of an undesigned world. For the skeptical reader already distrustful of the strict structures of ideological discursivity, the gentle currents of sentiment and the looping structure of *Kokoro* promise relief from the ruse of reification itself, and access to a spontaneous literary pleasure capable of enchanting the liberal imagination only all the more.

Several aspects of the novel itself open up to this sort of reading experience. For example, the words "kokoro" and "sensei" in McClellan's translation might be read as floating signifiers that evoke (without disclosing) a kind of untethered meaning: insofar as the novel is about a "sensei" who is defined by his insights into "kokoro," and insofar as the novel figures "kokoro" as something to be understood through the "sensei," these untranslated signs become in McClellan's English-language text the cumulative referents of the entire novel without ever being explicitly defined. Like the word "liberty" itself—which Hayek understood to indicate a negative ideal that could never be positively defined, nor philosophically summed up—the words "kokoro" and "sensei" conjure the alluring and elusive nature of a modern world structured more by unintended effects, spontaneous orders, and invisible hands than any overt design or irrefutable logic. In a liberal imagination that doubts the powers of the rational mind to completely explain society, "kokoro" and "sensei" enchant as floating signifiers that communicate a form of enjoyment that seems to bear no trace of ideological implication.

Several moments in the narrative commune with the free-floating pleasures promised by the signs of "kokoro" and "sensei." Early in the novel, we are told that the very bond between the student and Sensei is only possible in the absence of systematic analytical thought (*kenkyū*; "research," "analysis")—the kind of thinking, that is, which locks signs into a stable regime of conclusive signification. In one scene, Sensei's mysterious behavior and terse statements confuse the student. But even so, the student takes for granted that questions will never lead to answers:

> I thought his behavior very strange. But I did not visit Sensei with the purpose of studying [*kenkyū*] him. And I decided to think no more about it. My attitude towards Sensei then is one of those things that I remember with a certain amount of pride. Because of it, I believe, we were able to become so close to each other. Had I been curious in an impersonal and analytical [*kenkyūteki*] way, the bond between us would surely not have lasted. I was, of course, not aware of all this at the time. I hate to think what might have happened had I acted differently. Even in his relationship with me, he was in constant dread of being coldly analyzed [*kenkyū sareru*].
>
> *(13–14)*

What McClellan translated as "we were able to become so close to each other" appears in the Japanese original in language that might be rendered less literarily as "we were able to have a warm relationship as human beings" (*ningenrashii atatakai tsukiai*). In this context, the systematic meanings produced thorough analysis and explication (*kenkyū*) are figured as the antithesis of humane (*ningenrashii*) feeling.

The opposition between totalizing "analysis" and spontaneous "humanity" appears at several other points in the novel, too. When the student approaches Sensei about his graduate thesis, for example, Sensei intimates to him that the more you study something, and the more you try to exercise your explanatory power over it, the less human you become. Sensei, then, is not only a man who does not wish to be studied, he is also a man who has become alienated from those who do study—that is to say, from scholars. This comes out in Sensei's response to the student's academic striving:

> The topic that I had chosen [for my graduation thesis at the university] was closely related to Sensei's field of specialization. When I asked Sensei whether he thought such a topic was suitable, he said that it would probably be all right. I was in a state of panic, and I soon rushed back to Sensei to ask what books I should read. He willingly gave me all the information he could, and then offered to lend me two or three books that were necessary for my work. But he steadfastly refused to give me any further guidance. "I have not been reading very much lately. I am not acquainted with up-to-date scholarship. You should ask the professors at the university."
>
> When Sensei said this, I remembered the remark his wife once made to me that though Sensei was once an avid reader, he had since lost his old interest in books. Forgetting my thesis for the moment, I said to Sensei:
>
> "Why is it, Sensei, that you are not as interested in books as you once were?"
>
> "There is no particular reason...Well, perhaps it is because I have decided that no matter how many books I may read, I shall never be a very much better man than I am now. And ..."
>
> "And?"
>
> "This is not very important, but to tell you the truth, I used to consider it a disgrace to be found ignorant by other people. But now, I find that I am not ashamed of knowing less than others, and I am less inclined to force myself to read books. In short, I have grown old and decrepit."
>
> *(54)*

One of the most poignant moments in the novel comes soon after this scene, when the student finally finishes his thesis, graduates from university, and dines with Sensei and his wife in what is supposed to be a celebration:

> "Congratulations," Sensei said, and raised his saké cup to me. The gesture did not make me particularly happy, partly because, by then, I was not in such high spirits about having graduated, and partly because Sensei's tone of voice did not seem to invite a merry response from me. True, he grinned at me when he raised his cup, and I did not detect any irony [*aironī*] in his grin. But neither did it convey happiness for my success. His grin seemed rather to say, "It is, for some strange reason, considered proper to congratulate people on such occasions as this."
>
> *(70)*

To the student's ear, the spontaneity of Sensei's voice reverberates with an intuitive truth liberated from the stultifying formulae of congratulation. And that truth is that universities, diplomas, graduations, and professors are all tainted by their association with "analysis" (*kenkyū*) and the inhumane reifications that follow from it. In the scene above, this is conveyed by the subtle sound of Sensei pronouncing a single word—"congratulations" (*omedetō*)—in a way that means the opposite of what it says without becoming ironic. As the waves of sound spoken by Sensei dissolve the tethered meaning of the commonplace "congratulations," the floating signifiers "kokoro" and "sensei" momentarily cohere, each becoming synonymous with the other in currents of mutual attunement unburdened by the fixity and closure of systematic signification. In a moment that is as mundane as it is magical, the kokoro of the sensei endows a meaningless word with the aura of truth.

These sorts of moments remind us that the reverberations between McClellan's *Kokoro* and Hayek's thought resonate in the negative spaces where each evokes something in excess of itself without ever fully articulating what that something is. As I have noted, Hayek himself described "liberty" as a negative ideal the true substance of which could never be completely enumerated in positive terms:

> It is often objected that our concept of liberty is merely negative. This is true in the sense that peace is also a negative concept or that security or quiet or the absence of any particular impediment or evil is negative. It is to this class of concepts that liberty belongs: it describes the absence of a particular obstacle—coercion by other men. It becomes positive only through what we make of it. It does not assure us of any particular opportunities, but leaves it to us to decide what use we shall make of the circumstances in which we find ourselves.
>
> *(Hayek 2011: 69–70)*

Hayek implied that the closures of concrete rhetoric, and the limitations of explicit definition, were at odds with the more nebulous workings of the invisible hand of the marketplace, the spontaneous orders of liberal society, and the vastness of the liberal horizon. In *The Constitution of Liberty*—the prose of which McClellan himself polished soon after completing the *Kokoro* translation—Hayek posited that "the scientists tend to stress what we do know; but in the social field, where what we do not know is often so much more important, the effect of this tendency may be very misleading"(73). He blamed an "erroneous intellectualism" for the misplaced faith in the human mind to precisely explain the undesigned features of an incalculably complex world (75). Hayek sensed that more explanation, and more prose, could have the opposite of their intended effect, as he argued in 1945 at the end of "Individualism: True and False":

> What individualism teaches us is that society is greater than the individual only in so far as it is free. In so far as it is controlled or directed, it is limited to the powers of the individual minds which control or direct it. If the presumption of the modern mind, which will not respect anything that is not consciously controlled by individual reason, does not learn in time where to stop, we may, as Edmund Burke warned us, "be well assured that everything about us will dwindle by degrees, until at length our concerns are shrunk to the dimensions of our minds."
>
> *(Hayek 1948: 32)*

However paradoxically, the open-ended structure of *Kokoro* might have been congruent to the indefinable ideal of liberty that Hayek believed was always marked by an ineffable surplus beyond language, narrative, and the specificity of all human designs. After all, *Kokoro* is a novel that ends by looping back on itself, and in the century since it first appeared, it has opened up to any number of readings and rereadings without ever insisting on, nor fully conforming to, any one interpretive line in particular. Which is to say that *Kokoro* is a novel that "refuses to shrink to the dimensions of our minds."

## Literature and the liberal imagination in mid-century America

This essay has examined moments in *Kokoro* which do not disclose any obvious alignment with a particular political position. I have suggested that nevertheless—and perhaps all the more—these sorts of seemingly nonideological, apparently apolitical moments in the novel enchant the part of the liberal imagination that is taken with the mysterious movements of invisible hands, and the undesigned formations of spontaneous orders. In closing, I would draw this perspective into dialogue with Lionel Trilling's suggestion in *The Liberal Imagination* (1950) that the literary is a necessary supplement to the more conventionally defined terrain of intellectual history because the literary delivers the imagination to a space of unresolved possibility that doctrinaire convictions and straightforward arguments threaten to destroy. In particular, Trilling wrote that "[t]o the carrying out of the job of criticizing the liberal imagination, literature has a unique relevance, not merely because so much of modern literature has explicitly directed itself upon politics, but more importantly because literature is the human activity that takes the fullest and most precise account of variousness, possibility, complexity, and difficulty" (xxi).

To be sure, we may wonder just what notion of "liberal" Trilling had in mind in writing *The Liberal Imagination*, and Louis Menand has observed that in all likelihood, he was "treating all liberals alike" whether left or right, collectivist or individualist (viii). But what matters in the context of the current analysis is that for Trilling at mid-century, the literary rendering of "varoiusness, possibility, complexity, and difficulty" was in short supply in the more "patently" political literature of the time:

> If we now turn and consider the contemporary literature of America, we see that wherever we can describe it as patently liberal and democratic, we must say that it is not of lasting interest. I do not say that the work which is written to conform to the liberal democratic tradition is of no value but only that we do not incline to return to it, we do not establish it in our minds and affections. Very likely we learn from it as citizens; and as citizen-scholars and citizen-critics we understand and explain it. But we do not live in an active reciprocal relation with it. The sense of largeness, of cogency, of the transcendence which largeness and cogency can give, the sense of being reached in our secret and primitive minds—this we virtually never get from the writers of the liberal democratic tradition at the present time.
>
> *(301)*

For Trilling, then, the "patently" ideological novel could have only diminished literary force because it would overwhelm the imagination with the closures of conviction, and because it would convey to readers no "sense of being reached in our secret and primitive minds."

In this light, we begin to see why the liberal force of McClellan's *Kokoro* gathered not in any doctrinaire appeal, but in the open-ended pleasures of the novel that reverberated with the contingencies of a still-forming intellectual episteme that gradually emerged from the efforts of Hayek and the Mont Pèlerin Society to renovate liberal culture and thought at mid-century. As Hayek and his colleagues in the intellectual sphere breathed new life into what they believed had become a deteriorated liberal tradition riven with crisis, they struggled against the contingencies of their own time and the contradictions of their own dialogues. This is why historians of economic thought have emphasized the place of indeterminacy in narrating the intellectual history of "neoliberalism," pointing to its plurality and complication rather than treating its eventual rise as a foregone conclusion.

But Trilling would suggest that it would have been the very open-endedness of the formulation of a new liberalism that availed its intellectual discourse to the sort of moving literary distribution that I have argued coalesced in McClellan's *Kokoro*. Trilling believed that the convulsions of thought in its moment of becoming would be just the thing to reinvigorate the dialogue between literature and ideas in mid-century America:

> [I]f we … think of ideas as living things, inescapably connected with our wills and desires, as susceptible of growth and development by their very nature, as showing their life by their tendency to change, as being liable, by this very tendency, to deteriorate and become corrupt and to work harm, then we shall stand in a relation to ideas which makes an active literature possible.
>
> *(303)*

As an indeterminate novel which is not "patently" ideological, McClellan's *Kokoro* appealed to the liberal imagination at mid-century not as a pedagogical manual of citizenship, nor through the closed circuits of doctrinaire conviction, but as a "great book" of the human condition available for continual interpretation. This is why readers may "live in an active reciprocal relation with it," and "incline to return to it," whether or not they agree with (or even acknowledge) the ideas and arguments that surrounded its original context of production and reception.

## Acknowledgment

I would like to thank the estate of Friedrich Hayek for granting permission to quote from materials held in the Friedrich A. Von Hayek Papers, Hoover Institution Archives. I have also written about this topic elsewhere (see Hurley 2014, 2016), as has Aida Hirotsugu (see Aida 2008).

## References

Aida Hirotsugu. (2008) "Sōseki, Haieku, Etō Jun: Kokoro no kizuna," *Bungei Shunjū* 86: 334–41.
Burgin, Angus. (2012) *The Great Persuasion*, Cambridge, MA: Harvard University Press.
Hayek, Friedrich. (2011) *The Constitution of Liberty: The Definitive Edition*, Chicago, IL: University of Chicago Press.
Hayek, Friedrich. (1966a) "The Principles of a Liberal Social Order," Friedrich A. von Hayek papers, Box 85, Folder 9, Hoover Institution Archives.
Hayek, Friedrich. (1966b) Correspondence To Richard Ware (March 2), Friedrich A. von Hayek papers, Box 17, Folder 37, Hoover Institution Archives.
Hayek, Friedrich. (1966c) Correspondence To Richard Ware (October 23), Friedrich A. von Hayek papers, Box 17, Folder 37, Hoover Institution Archives.
Hayek, Friedrich. (1948) *Individualism and Economic Order*, Chicago, IL: University of Chicago Press.
Hurley, Brian. (2016) "*Kokoro* Confidential: Edwin McClellan, Friedrich Hayek and the Neoliberal Reading of Natsume Sōseki," *Representations* 134: 93–115.
Hurley, Brian. (2014) "Seishokusha to yogensha: Sōseki no kigo o yomu," *Bungaku* 57: 114–57.
Karatani Kōjin. (2005) "Overcoming Modernity," Richard Calichman (trans.), in Richard Calichman (ed.) *Contemporary Japanese Thought*, New York: Columbia University Press.
Keynes, John Maynard. (1932) "The End of Laissez-Faire" in *Essays in Persuasion*, New York: Harcourt, Brace, & Co.
McClellan, Edwin. (2000) "Edwin McClellan on Natsume Sōseki and Shiga Naoya" in Donald Richie (ed.) *Words, Ideas, and Ambiguities: Four Perspectives on Translating from the Japanese*, Chicago, IL: Imprint Publications.

McClellan, Edwin. (1999) "'The Photographer': An Essay by Soseki; Prefatory Remarks by the Translator" in Todd Breyfogle (ed.) *Literary Imagination, Ancient and Modern: Essays in Honor of David Grene*, Chicago, IL: University of Chicago Press.
Menand, Louis. (2008) "Introduction," in Lionel Trilling, *The Liberal Imagination*, New York: New York Review of Books.
Natsume Sōseki. (1957) *Kokoro*, Edwin McClellan (trans.), Washington, DC: Regnery Publishing Inc.
Nishiyama Chiaki. (1966) "Arguments for the Principles of Liberty and the Philosophy of Science," Friedrich A. von Hayek papers, Box 85, Folder 9, Hoover Institution Archives.
Tansman, Alan. (2009) *The Aesthetics of Japanese Fascism*, Berkeley: University of California Press.
Trilling, Lionel. (2008) *The Liberal Imagination*, New York: New York Review of Books.
Žižek, Slavoj. (1989) *The Sublime Object of Ideology*, London: Verso.

# 15

# FREE TRADE MASCULINITY AND THE LITERATURE OF NAFTA

*Stephen M. Park*

In her 1987 book, *Borderlands/La Frontera*, Gloria Anzaldúa famously remarks that the US–Mexico border is "*una herida abierta* where the Third World grates against the first and bleeds" (25). To be sure, the border has served as a site of the colonial violence of US expansion and the state-sponsored violence against Mexican Americans. It has been, as Anzaldúa also observes, a site of linguistic terrorism and gender-based violence where entrenched patriarchy keeps women in roles of limited mobility and where, in the time since the publication of Anzaldúa's book, women in Juaréz and all along northern Mexico have been brutalized and killed. The centuries-long history of the border provides no single explanation for the complex relations of coloniality, gender, and power that unfold daily between the US and Mexico, but an important site of intersection for all these is the economic violence of the border. Within the field of Border Studies, there has been a sustained interest in the cultural impact of the North American Free Trade Agreement (NAFTA) (see Saldan~a Portillo 2005; Carroll 2017), but by beginning with Anzaldu'a I hope to frame NAFTA as a new phase in a longer history of economic violence. Her image of violence, of the Third World grating against the first, is a reminder of how global economic forces have local consequences and how abstractions become material.

For these reasons, the era of the NAFTA in the mid-1990s provides a useful case study for thinking about the economic violence along the US–Mexico border precisely because the agreement's attempt to make illegible the inequalities that it creates. The subtle violence of NAFTA is that its abstractions and promises construct a work of fiction, one in which the border disappears or, at the very least, its problems can be ignored. But of course, the fantasy of "free" trade as it pertains to the US–Mexico border is always full of contradictions. The border is the place where trade barriers for goods and services come down and where walls are simultaneously fortified to stop the movement of people. The bizarre fantasy constructed by NAFTA is reflected in Carlos Fuentes' collection of stories, *La frontera cristal* (1995), where these global economic forces have transformed the border into a metaphorical "crystal frontier" or "glass border." In the titular story, Leonardo Barroso, a wealthy *maquila* owner from Northern Mexico, quickly adapts to the fictions of free trade:

> Apenas aprobado el Tratado de Libre Comercio, don Leonardo inició un intenso cabildeo para que la migración obrera de México a los Estados Unidos fuese clasificada como "servicios," incluso como "comercio exterior."

> En Washington y en México, el dinámico promotor y hombre de negocios explicó que la principal exportación de México no eran productos agrícolas o industriales; ni maquilas, ni siquiera capital para pagar la deuda externa (la deuda eterna), sino trabajo. Exportábamos trabajo más que cemento o jitomates. Él tenía un plan para evitar que el trabajo se convirtiera en un conflicto. Muy sencillo: evitar el paso por la frontera. Evitar la ilegalidad.
>
> *(Fuentes 2013: 617–18)*
>
> As soon as the North American Free Trade Agreement had gone into effect, Don Leonardo had begun lobbying intensively to have the migration of Mexican workers to the United States classified as "service," even as "foreign trade."
>
> The dynamic promoter and businessman explained, in Washington and Mexico City, that Mexico's principal export was not agricultural or industrial products, not assembly-line products, not even capital to pay the external debt (the eternal debt) but labor. Mexico was exporting more labor than cement or tomatoes. He had a plan to keep labor from becoming a conflict. Very simple: simply avoid the frontier. Prevent illegality.
>
> *(Fuentes 1997: 167)*

Barroso's plan for avoiding the border is both physical (he flies his workers directly from Mexico City to New York) and legal (he arranges it so that his workers have no status as workers under the US law). The legal fiction that the men working for him are not "workers" is of course absurd, but Barroso is merely operating within the rules of NAFTA, which is itself a fiction built on the abstractions of the free market rather than the economic realities of North America.

It is a situation like this one that makes literature a useful tool for understanding economics and the ways in which it permeates our culture. Both *La frontera cristal* and NAFTA itself are "economic fictions," a term I use to capture the textual and narrative interplays of literature and economics. My interest in the intersection of literature and economics has been motivated, as is true of many of the authors in this volume, by recent works by literary scholars as well as the growing subdiscipline of economists who are engaged in the analysis of economic discourse itself. Walter Benn Michaels laid much of the important foundation for literary scholars attempting to theorize textual relationships with economics (see Benn Michaels 1987; Osteen and Woodmansse 1999). A small but growing subdiscipline of economics has been devoted to an analysis of the rhetoric used in economic writing itself. This critical work, with its emphasis on the metaphor and other literary devices employed by economists, has also informed my notion of "economic fictions" (see McCloskey 1998). However, my notion of economic fictions draws more specifically from sociologist Daniel Bell's observations on economic discourse. Of the idealized economies often described in works of economic theory, Bell remarked:

> an economic *system* is not an economy; it is an analytical abstraction, an ideal, closed world where resources flow freely in response to price, where comparative advantage dictates a shift of resource utilization, where labor is not people but units of skill (or lack thereof), where there are no political boundaries, and where machinery, capital, and commodities distribute themselves to maximum benefit of 'mankind.'... In short, economic theory is a convenient fiction.
>
> *(Bell 1981: 69–70)*

Since economic theory does not *describe* as much as *invent* economic systems, I would submit that the discourse around free trade in North America has been yet another "convenient fiction." Though it is now part of the reality of everyone living on the continent, NAFTA is itself a work of fiction in that it constructs a new world based on an idealized free-market setting; it redefines the meanings of words according to its own abstractions (e.g. "workers" become "foreign trade"), and it places all stories within the ur-narrative of classical economics in which "rational choice" explains every character.

Fuentes' *La frontera cristal* is also a work of economic fiction, but not only because it meditates on the economic realities of the US and Mexico. Beyond that, the book uses its own form to explore the fundamental narratives of free trade. While the rise of the *maquila* industry and the exploitation of workers have become familiar narratives in the last twenty-five years of NAFTA's implementation, Fuentes' focus on Leonardo Barroso and his numerous doppelgangers throughout the book suggest another, unexplored plotline of free trade. In Fuentes' hands, trade becomes something that is less about law or policy details than about the performance of machismo. In economic terms, this entails risk taking. This is the bravado required to live in a world where the free market is taken to its absurd extremes, and where there are no guarantees for the future. Fuentes' stories in this volume simultaneously celebrate such a world and expose its shortcomings. Attending to the underlying economic narratives of these stories offers us a new way of understanding free trade, and it ultimately reveals the potential for using literature to understand the unstated narrative drives of economic theory.

## Free trade and literary form

Since NAFTA was first debated and implemented in the early 1990s, it has provoked responses from literary figures as well as political reimaginings of the North American landscape, which were themselves works of fiction. Early proponents, including economists and politicians, portrayed the agreement as the beginning of an economic utopia for the continent. At the signing ceremony in December of 1993, Bill Clinton remarked: "I believe we have made a decision now that will permit us to create an economic order in the world that will promote more growth, more equality, better preservation of the environment, and a greater possibility of world peace." But Clinton was not alone in his optimism. Mexican poet Octavio Paz famously declared that the trade agreement presented opportunities for Mexico. "NAFTA," he wrote, "will be important for Mexicans because it is finally a chance for us to be modern" (Fox 1999: 19). For a Nobel-winning poet to weigh in on the potential of the free trade agreement suggests the ways in which NAFTA pushed the conversation around free-market economics into the literary imagination. Numerous writers and artists weighed in on the policy. Canadian writer Margaret Atwood contributed an essay to the 1993 book, *The Case Against Free Trade*. There she notes the trade agreement's provisions for copyright law and the arts, which Atwood claimed would wreck the Canadian film and publishing industries. Simply, she states, "I believe the free trade issue has the potential to fragment and destroy the country as nothing else has succeeded in doing" (92). This apocalyptic tone has come to dominate many of the literary representations of NAFTA.

What's more, NAFTA has been the explicit or implicit subject of numerous literary works since the 1990s, even to the point of defining a transnational corpus of texts. For instance, Karen Tei Yamashita's novel, *Tropic of Orange* (1997), which takes place primarily in a multinational in Los Angeles, features a wrestling match between performers named "Super-NAFTA" and "El Gran Mojado." David Foster Wallace's *Infinite Jest* (1996) features the parodic O.N.A.N. (The Organization of American Nations), which has realigned North America into a continental political and economic structure. The characters observe "Interdependence Day" and mark time in years that are now sponsored by the multinational corporations that run their lives. And, of course, Fuentes' *La frontera cristal* is another example of a literary text which engages explicitly with NAFTA—his characters discuss the agreement and deal with its consequences in settings ranging from the assembly line of the *maquila* to the crystalline skyscrapers of Manhattan, where Mexican workers have been imported. These books taken together raise the important question—what does literature have to say about NAFTA? And, to arrive at the broader questions of the present volume, how do the disciplines of literature and economics inform one another? I submit that the texts mentioned earlier are more than simply literary texts *about* NAFTA. To be sure, each makes its own overt comment on free trade and its consequences, but the literary form provides another kind of analysis that goes beyond the editorial response. As I will show with *La frontera cristal*, the literary text responds not just to economic policy but to the ways in which the logic of economics has come to inform every aspect of life in North America. When the implicit *stories* of economics—the story of rational, individual choice, the story of competition, and the story of market value as the only value—become the dominant narratives of everyday life, literary texts are precisely the terrain on which to contest those underlying narratives of economics.

The implementation of NAFTA in 1994 is but one moment in a longer history of neoliberal economics, a body of thought that has had increasing political and social influence since the 1970s. The implementation of these extreme free-market ideas has reached far beyond economic policy and led to, as David Harvey has put it, "the financialization of everything" (33). As the work of extreme free-market economists like F. A. Hayek and Milton Friedman entered the political mainstream with the ascendency of Margaret Thatcher and Ronald Reagan, this had consequences not just of government policies but also for the very ways in which life was viewed. This is the era in which Michel Foucault formulated his notion of governmentality whereby, in a world in which competition between individuals is prized above all, there are no guarantees for the security of one's life. Building off of Foucault in her book, *Undoing the Demos*, Wendy Brown has argued that neoliberalism is something "other than a set of economic policies, and ideology, or a resetting of relations between state and economy." She goes on to explain:

> As a normative order of reason developed over three decades into a widely and deeply disseminated governing rationality, neoliberalism transmogrifies every human domain and endeavor, along with humans themselves, according to a specific image of the economic. All conduct is economic conduct; all spheres of existence are framed and measured by economic terms and metrics, even when those spheres are note directly monetized. In neoliberal reason and in domains governed by it, we are only and everywhere *homo oeconomicus*.
>
> *(9–10)*

Brown's observations suggest that literary texts need not focus on specific policies to serve as meditations on economics. In a culture where all human behavior is explained according to economic drives and evaluated according to economic metrics, analyses of character and narrative—traditional purviews of literary studies—become fundamental economic questions. Indeed, Brown's allusion to *homo economicus*, economic man, reveals the way in which literary structures are deeply embedded in neoliberal economics.

*Homo economicus* is a frequent, if often silent, character in economic theory, reflecting the concept of methodological individualism which lies at the foundation of neoliberal economics (especially within the Austrian School of Hayek and Ludwig von Mises). This concept, as one economist has defined it, is "the doctrine that all social phenomena (their structure and their change) are in principle explicable only in terms of individuals—their properties, goals, and beliefs" (Hodgson 1994: 409). Of course, free-market thinking imagines a particular kind of individual—one who is rational and completely self-interested—and it extends this vision of the individual to argue that communities work best when individuals pursue their own interests. However, as feminist economists such as Susan Feiner have pointed out, figures like *homo economicus* are based on an implicitly male gaze. In orthodox economic models, Feiner writes, "the traits of economic actors map (too perfectly to be coincidental) onto traditional notions of masculinity" (Osteen and Woodmasse 1999: 194; see also Ferber and Nelson 1993). Once the implicit narrative of classical economics is exposed, free trade can then be understood as an extension of its male-centered premise. NAFTA is in many ways the most extreme assertion of this vision.

## Carlos Fuentes and the machismo of risk

It is a male-centered world of economic competition and violence along the border that Carlos Fuentes had in mind as he composed *La frontera cristal*. In an interview just after the book's publication in Mexico, the author remarked:

> En *La frontera de cristal* se da la prueba clarísima de que podemos ser gobernados por fuerzas totalmente fuera de la ley. Es una visión espantosa de un futuro en el que nadie queda exento de la violencia. Muchas veces he hablado de la universalización de la violencia y de ésta como el único pasaporte a la identidad del siglo XX
>
> *(Fuentes 1999: 259)*
>
> In *The Crystal Frontier* the proposition that we can be governed by forces completely outside the law is clearly tested. It is a frightening vision of a future in which no one is exempt from violence. Many times I have spoken of the universalization of violence and of this as the only passport of the 20$^{th}$ century.

While this observation can be understood as a response to realities of Northern Mexico at the time, particularly in Juárez, Fuentes' ideas on violence also grow out of his understanding of economics. An economy that moves away from regulations and protections looks increasingly like extralegal economies, where transactions are high in risk and where there are no guarantees.

The intricacies and contradictions of risk have preoccupied theorists within and without economics for some time. Anthony Giddens and others have theorized risk as a particularly modern phenomenon, distinct from the hazards of premodern life (see Giddens 2006; Giddens 1990). One of the other main theorists of risk, Ulrich Beck, has argued that the modern world is moving away from a concern with economic inequality and toward a focus on avoiding risk (see Beck 1992). However, in Fuentes's formulation, the opposite occurs. Taking risk is what is valued, even when (and perhaps *especially* when) there is no safety net. Far from Nietzsche's "last man," who works toward safety and small comforts, Fuentes presents late twentieth-century capitalism as a macho performance. Life has always been hazardous, and this does not change in the modern era. Instead, the separate notion of risk refers to things that we can supposedly manage and control. And, of course, risk has the potential to be profitable. To take just the example of Columbus's voyages, which preoccupied Fuentes for many years in *Cristóbal Nonato* (1987) and *El naranjo* (1994), risk was a kind of investment which could command great returns. In applying the framework of risk to NAFTA, what *La frontera cristal* makes clear is that one's experience within the market depends very much upon whether a person has *chosen* to take on risk (for which they will conceivably be rewarded) or been made vulnerable to the hazards through the very structures of free trade. For Fuentes, and the fictional world he creates, Northern Mexico has been a site of violence precisely because NAFTA has reduced worker protections, incentivized risk, and therefore created the vacuum of protection in which *caudillos* thrives.

Throughout the collection of stories, Leonardo Barroso is emblematic of this strong-man figure. Early on, the reader is told (and Barroso agrees) that "El dinero era él. El poder era él" (515) ("He was money. He was power" [19]). In the opening story, "La capitalina," which puns on "capitalista," Barroso seduces his own goddaughter (the eponymous "Capital Girl" from Mexico City). She is from an old family that is now in decline, making them economically vulnerable and therefore dependent on the daughter, Michelina, to benefit from her connection to Barroso. The fact that the family's aristocratic history is out of place in the new consumer society of Mexico is made clear early in the story through Michelina's grandmother: "doña Zarina Ycaza de Laborde se refugió en la curiosa ocupación de coleccionar triques, chunches y sobre todo revistas" (506) ("Doña Zarina Ycaza de Laborde took refuge in the curious hobby of collecting junk, bits and pieces of things, and, most of all, magazines" [7]). This is nothing more than an eccentricity for the eighty-four-year-old woman until "una compañía norteamericana de memorabilia le compró su edición completa de las revistas *Hoy*, *Mañana* y *Siempre* por cincuenta mil dólares" (507) ("an American company specializing in memorabilia bought her complete collection of *Today*, *Tomorrow*, and *Always* magazines for something like $50,000" [7]). These objects with no use value are transformed suddenly, indeed magically, into valuable objects. Thus, the American company brings the world of commodity fetishism into the family and into the story.

Beyond the grandmother's junk, however, they have no means of adapting to this new economic landscape and thus turn to a more traditional form of accessing wealth—marriage. At the urging of Barroso, she marries his reclusive son in a sham marriage that will allow her to cement the financial ties between the two families while still serving as Barroso's mistress. As he proposes this deal, he makes clear to Michelina all that she will gain:

> No quería alardear, pero ella sería todo el dinero, todo el poder, ahora sólo veía el desierto encuerdo, pero su vida podía ser como esa ciudad encantada del otro lado de la frontera, torres de oro, palacios de cristal…
>
> Sí, le dijo ella, lo sé, lo acepto.
>
> Leonardo frenó bruscamente, saliéndose de la recta carretera del desierto. A lo lejos, los vigilaban los túmulos de piedra catedralicia, ahora dibujados como frágiles siluetas de papel en el atardecer.
>
> *(514–15)*

> He didn't want to brag, but she would get all the money, all the power; now she was seeing only the naked desert, but her life could be like that enchanted city on the other side of the frontier: golden towers, crystal palaces.
>
> Yes, she said, I know, I accept it.

> Leonardo slammed on the brakes, exiting the straight desert highway. In the distance, the monuments of cathedral-like stone, which seemed now like fragile paper silhouettes, watched over them.
>
> *(19)*

This opening story makes clear the links between money and sex that ripple through the collection of stories. Everything about the relationship between Leonardo and Michelina is transactional and it is dependent on the economic context in which they find themselves. The decline of Michelina's family is emblematic of the economy of no guarantees. Once upon a time, their old wealth, symbolized by the stone buildings that are now "como frágiles siluetas de papel," would have protected them. However, in the Mexico of 1990s, where the shifting economic terrain of peso devaluation and free trade continues to expand the ranks of the economically vulnerable, Don Leonardo's power is all that can save them. This is why her family made him her godfather in the first place and why they are willing to look the other way as he seduces her now. It is the "palacios de cristal" that he promises, with its nearly invisible wealth, that will symbolize, throughout Fuentes' book, the power of the new economy.

This also evokes the famous Crystal Palace of London's Great Exhibition of 1851. Karl Marx was in London at the time of the event and the structure, and the objects inside, served as a perfect illustration of his ideas on the fetish of the commodity. As Giorgio Agamben has written of Marx's reflection on the exhibition,

> the transfiguration of the commodity into *enchanted object* is the sign that the exchange value is already beginning to eclipse the use-value of the commodity. In the galleries and the pavilions of its mystical Crystal Palace, in which from the outset a place was also reserved for works of art, the commodity is displayed to be enjoyed only through the glance at the *enchanted scene*.
>
> *(38, emphasis in original)*

This is precisely the image that Fuentes is playing on with his vision of El Paso as a "ciudad encantada" on the other side of the border. It is the site of commodity fetishism and it has enchanted Barroso, Michelina, and, by extension, all of Mexico. The image of crystal, with all of its Marxist connotations, continues throughout the stories of *La frontera cristal* as an important touchstone for the book's comment on the new economic realities and unrealities of the border.

In the title story, "The Crystal Frontier," we meet one of Leonardo's many alter egos, Lisandro Chávez, one of the workers the millionaire flies to New York for the weekend to wash the windows of Manhattan skyscrapers. This was not originally the plan for Lisandro's life, which began with private schools and annual trips to Houston during his childhood. But, because of the failure of his father's business, the family is now as economically vulnerable as Michelina's. As the plane takes off, Lisandro reflects on his circumstances and those of his country:

> Ya no había país, ya no había México, el país era una ficción o, más bien, un sueño mantenido por un puñado de locos que alguna vez creyeron en la existencia de México... Una familia como la suya no iba a aguantar veinte años de crisis, deuda, quiebra, esperanzas renovadas sólo para caer de nueva cuenta en la crisis, cada seis años, cada vez más, la pobreza, el desempleo.
>
> *(620, ellipsis in original)*

> There was no homeland anymore, no such thing as Mexico; the country was a fiction or, rather, a dream maintained by a handful of madmen who at one time believed in the existence of Mexico... A family like his was not going to be able to withstand twenty years of crisis, debt, bankruptcy, hopes raised only to fall again with a crash, every six years, more and more poverty and unemployment.
>
> *(170–1, ellipsis in original)*

The notion that Mexico itself is "a fiction" suggests the evaporation of all the traditional forms of security. The aristocracy that once guaranteed the future of Michelina's family is gone, and beyond that the nation state that once provided some safety net for Lisando's family is also gone. The only guarantee is now the largess of Leonardo Barroso. Michelina depends on him as her godfather and lover, Lisandro depends on him for the job in New York, and characters in other stories look to him as their financial savior. In "Pain," Juan Zamora relies on him to pay for his tuition at Cornell, and the four women of "Malintzin of the Maquilas" depend on the factory he owns for their paychecks. More than any other element connecting the nine stories of *La frontera cristal* is the characters' shared financial dependence on Barroso. In the absence of social safety nets and reliable work, those at the bottom have to choice but to remain dependent or to embrace the economy of risk. This, according to Fuentes, is what NAFTA is all about.

## NAFTA and the Bet

During the initial debates around NAFTA, in the US and Mexico, Fuentes was especially vocal in his public support for the agreement. In 1993, he published numerous editorials in both English- and Spanish-language newspapers. These articles range from the straightforward pro-NAFTA argument based on employment statistics and projections to a strange comedic dialogue in which Fuentes serves as the straight man to a fictional Mexican analogue to Ross Perot, millionaire businessman "Ruiz Poroto." Although he is from a different nation than Perot, Poroto espouses equally anti-NAFTA, protectionist views which allow Fuentes' more "reasonable" pro-trade positions to shine through. (For instance, when confronted with the fact that Mexican consumers may want to buy US-made toys for their children rather than Poroto's toys on which children have cut their hands, the Mexican millionaire replies, "Let them bleed for their country!"[Fuentes 1993b].) Apart from Fuentes' overt engagement with popular economic debates, another aspect of Fuentes' economic thinking emerges. This is the centrality of the bet, of risk taking not just as a signifier of masculine bravado but also a driving economic and narrative force. In one article, he frames his entire discussion of NAFTA within a bet he has made with the writer Jorge Castañeda: if NAFTA was approved, Castañada would buy him dinner; if it wasn't approved, Fuentes would buy dinner (Fuentes 1993a). Furthermore, once the US Congress approved the agreement, Fuentes wrote that this was not just a political victory for Mexico's President Salinas but a kind of gambling win, as well. In December 1993, Fuentes wrote: "Criticized for putting all his eggs in one basket, President Carlos Salinas di Gortari bet the house and won. When you gamble that big and win, you win big" (Fuentes 1993c). In Fuentes' imagination, then, the free trade agreement is transformed into a continental hand of poker, and Salinas has displayed the bravery necessary to be a political and economic winner.

This take on NAFTA reemerges indirectly in Fuentes' story "The Bet," the penultimate story in *La frontera cristal*. The story's twin narratives begin worlds away from one another, in Mexico and Spain, and converge in the violent aftermath of a single bet. One narrative focuses on Leandro Reyes, a dispirited middle-aged man who makes his living driving tourists from Mexico City to Cuernavaca and offering them a grudging tour of the sights. In his frustrations and insecurities, Leandro serves as the foil to Don Leonardo, who is confident and in command of every situation. Indeed, Leandro's flaws all stem from his performance of hyperaggressive masculinity as a way to offset his own failures. His childhood memories of his father working as a waiter, acting with what Leandro understands to be servility, make him hypersensitive to his own service job. He resents the work so much that he ignores and insults his customers and drives wildly, getting a minor thrill out of scaring his passengers. One of the tourists he drives to Cuernavaca, a Spanish woman named Encarnación who is also a tour guide in her home country, plainly tells Leandro: "¡Ya deja de comportarte como un machito de mierda y ven a cumplir con tu obligación, hijo de puta!" (637); "Why don't you stop trying to be a fucking he-man and do your job, you son of a bitch!" (196). Encarnación's candor disarms Leandro, softens his rudeness and aggression, and they begin a love affair in Mexico before she returns home to Spain. After a months-long correspondence, Leandro takes up a job with none other than Leonardo Barroso who, as luck would have it, needs a driver to accompany him to Spain.

Once in Asturias, their relationship continues the process of stripping away Leandro's gender performance. Encarnación "lo hizo reír, sin rubor, sin machismo, sin complejos, sin resentimiento o desconfianza" (647); "made him laugh without shame, without machismo, without anxiety, without resentment of skepticism" (210). But, as Don Leonardo's driver, he cannot escape the shadow of the millionaire or avoid mimicking his macho performance. While Barroso is away in Rome, Leandro borrows the car to take Ecarnación for a weekend in Madrid. In a brief moment of contentment, Leandro absorbs Don Leonardo's persona:

> Era una espléndida carretera y Leandro conducía el Mercedes de su jefe de prisa, con una sola mano. Con la otra apretaba la de su Enarca y ella le pedía ir más despacio, Jesús, que no la asustara, se trataba de llegar vivos a Madrid, pero él que ni modo, por más que ella lo suavizara, él tenía costumbres y reacciones de macho que no iba a dejar de un día para otro, además el Mercedes ronroneaba como un gato...
>
> *(649)*

> It was a splendid highway and Leandro drove his boss's Mercedes quickly, with one hand. With the other he squeezed his Encarna's, and she asked him to slow down, Jesus, not to scare her—let's get to Madrid alive. But no matter how she softened him, he had his macho habits and responses he wasn't going to give up over night; besides, the Mercedes was purring like a cat...
>
> *(213)*

This moment is meant to echo an earlier scene in "La capitalina," in which Don Leonardo drives with Michelina ("Manejaba con una mano. Con la otra, apretaba la de Michelina" [514]) and then tells her that she can have anything she desires as they look out to the crystal palaces of the north. Leandro thus mimics his boss's life and for one brief moment in his car shares the power and security of Barroso himself. However, even though Leandro is a reformed macho, this moment of bliss is torn apart by the violent machismo of other characters in the story.

Meanwhile, in the second plotline of "The Bet," a group of Spanish thugs torments an intellectually disabled character, Paquito, who lives on his own next to the town square. The group takes turns stealing from him and assaulting him, challenging each other with petty bets to go further and further until the main character finally beats him severely. In response, Paquito's father appears in the square and challenges the attacker to a high-stakes game of chicken. He has accumulated two hundred thousand pesetas, and "Ahora la apostaba. La apostaba. Todo lo que tenía" (646) ("Now he was betting it. He was betting it all. Everything he had" [208]). The terms of the bet are that the attacker and Paquito's father will each drive the wrong way through a tunnel, opposing traffic, and that the survivor will get all the money. At the story's end, however, the ultimate losers are Leandro and Encarna who are driving through the tunnel when the attacker's car strikes them head on. As different as these two plotlines are, Fuentes suggests that both Leandro and the anonymous attacker are both products of the same culture of machismo, so that Leandro is ultimately the victim of the logic of his own macho performance. Before he accepts the bet, the narrator addresses Paquito's attacker:

> No es que tuviera que forzarlos. Todos estaban preparados para asumir una apuesta, ya lo sabías. En eso te criaste. En eso vivían tú y tus amigos. Pero este ser casi sobrenatural que los recibió sorpresivamente en el desván donde vivía Paquito, les puso muy alta la postura, les comprometió la vida y el honor en su desafío.
>
> *(645)*

> It's not that he had to force them. They were all prepared to take a bet—you already knew that. That's how you grew up. That's how you and your friends lived. But this almost supernatural being who received them so unexpectedly in the shack where Paquito lived, raised the stakes very high, he held their lives and honor up to question with his challenge.
>
> *(207)*

While accepting this bet is irrational, within the logic of this character and his friends it becomes inescapable. This is because the bet is about more than the money. It's about performance and bravado and, as Fuentes says of Carlos Salinas, the need to "bet the house" when everyone is looking.

The bet, so crucial to this story and to Fuentes' conception of NAFTA, is a fundamentally illogical behavior for classical economics, but it is nevertheless a highly symbolic economic activity. Anthropologist Clifford Geertz has famously theorized the bet in his essay on Balinese cockfighting, "Deep Play." Geertz takes this term from Jeremy Bentham, who had used it to describe high-stakes betting which was of little utility to the individual or society and should therefore be prohibited. As Geertz frames this opposition, "For Bentham and those who think as he does (nowadays mainly lawyers, economists, and a few psychiatrists), the explanation is... that such men are irrational—addicts, fetishists, children, fools, savages, who need only to be protected against themselves"(70). Economists, the kind who rely on the behaviors of *homo economicus* to demonstrate the rationality of the market, cannot account for the bet and therefore dismiss it. However, despite the seeming irrationality, Geertz finds that in such bets, "money is less a measure of utility... than it is a symbol of moral import, perceived or imposed" (70). It is in this way that for Fuentes, the "deep play" of both his characters and of the Mexican president becomes a symbolic way of understanding the irrational world that has been constructed by the supposedly rational policies of free trade.

Risk economies are inherently illogical, but, Fuentes suggests, they are the fundamental condition of the free trade economy. This is the landscape of North America under NAFTA, where everyday life becomes a high-stakes game with economic as well as symbolic consequences, and where workers have few rights and no guarantees. As much as Fuentes praised Carlos Salinas for his gamble in promoting NAFTA—he "bet the house and won. When you gamble that big and win, you win big"—this metaphor conveniently elides those who lost big in NAFTA. The losers have not been those at the center of the bet, those with the most to win, but rather those who are ill-suited for a risk economy. It is not Leonardo Barroso, after all, who dies as a result of the fictional bet in *La frontera cristal* but instead his pale imitation, Leandro Chávez, who had nothing to gain. Despite his public promotion of NAFTA in 1993, Fuentes' fiction betrays the promises of free trade for a continent of workers who could never afford to "bet the house."

## References


Agamben, Georgio. (1992) *Stanzas: Word and Phantasm in Western Culture*. Minneapolis: University of Minnesota.

Anzaldúa, Gloria. (1987) *Borderlands/La Frontera: The New Mestiza* (2nd ed.). San Francisco, CA: Aunt Lute.

Atwood, Margaret. (1993) "Blind Faith and Free Trade" in Ralph Nader (ed.) *The Case Against Free Trade: GATT, NAFTA, and the Globalization of Corporate Power*. San Francisco, CA: Earth Island Press.

Beck, Ulrich. (1992) *Risk Society: Towards a New Modernity*. London: Sage Publications.

Benn Michaels, Walter. (1987) *The Gold Standard and the Logic of Naturalism: American Literature at the Turn of the Century*. Berkeley: University of California Press.

Brown, Wendy. (2015) *Undoing the Demos: Neoliberalism's Stealth Revolution*. New York: Zone Books.

Carroll, Amy Sara. (2017) *ReMEX: Toward an Art History of the NAFTA Era*. Austin: University of Texas Press.

Carroll, Amy Sara. (2012) "Global Mexico's Coproduction: *Babel*, *Pan's Labyrinth*, and *Children of Men*," *Journal of Transnational American Studies* 4.2: 1–30.

Clinton, Bill. (1993) "Remarks on the Signing of NAFTA," Reprinted at the Miller Center, University of Virginia. http://millercenter.org/president/speeches/speech-3927.

Daniel Bell. (1981). "Models and Reality in Economic Discourse" in Bell and Irving Kristol (eds.) *The Crisis in Economic Theory*. New York: Basic Books.

Ferber, Marianne A. and Julie A. Nelson. (1993) *Beyond Economic Man: Feminist Theory and Economics*. Chicago, IL: University of Chicago Press.

Fox, Clair F. (1999) *The Fence and the River: Culture and Politics at the U.S.–Mexico Border*. Minneapolis: University of Minnesota Press.

Fuentes, Carlos. (2013) *Cuentos completes*. Mexico, DF: Fondo de Cultura Económica.

Fuentes, Carlos. (1999) *Carlos Fuentes: Territorios del tiempo: Antología de entrevistas*. México, DF: Fondo de Cultura Económica.

Fuentes, Carlos. (1997) *The Crystal Frontier*. New York: Farrar, Straus and Giroux.

Fuentes, Carlos. (1993a) "Bet on It: U.S. and Mexico Will Benefit from NAFTA," *Chicago Sun-Times* (July 18).

Fuentes, Carlos. (1993b) "Mexicans Fear 'Giant Crunching Sound' of NAFTA," *Chicago Sun-Times* (November 14).

Fuentes, Carlos. (1993c) "NAFTA's Wake: Mexico Needs Political and Economic Reform," *Seattle Post-Intelligencer* (December 3).

Geertz, Clifford. (2005) "Deep Play: Notes on the Balinese Cockfight," *Daedalus* 134.4: 70.

Giddens, Anthony. (2006) "Fate, Risk, and Security" in James Cosgrave (ed.) *The Sociology of Risk and Gambling Reader*. London: Routledge.

Giddens, Anthony. (1990) *The Consequences of Modernity*. Palo Alto, CA: Stanford University Press. Harvey, David. (2005) *A Brief History of Neoliberalism*. Oxford: Oxford University Press.

Hodgson, Geoffrey M. (1994) "Hayek, Evolution, and Spontaneous Order" in Philip Mirowski (ed.) *Natural Images in Economic Thought: "Markets Read in Tooth & Claw."* Cambridge: Cambridge University Press.

McCloskey, Deirdre N. (1998) *The Rhetoric of Economics* (2nd ed.). Madison: University of Wisconsin Press.

Osteen, Mark and Martha Woodmansse. (1999) *The New Economic Criticism: Studies at the Interface of Literature and Economics*. London: Routledge.

Saldaña-Portillo, María Josefina. (2005) "In the Shadow of NAFTA: *Y tu mamá también* Revisits the National Allegory of Mexican Sovereignty," *American Quarterly* 57.3: 751–77.

# PART III

# Principles

# 16
# ASYMMETRIC INFORMATION

*Andrew Kopec*

Neoclassical economics assumes that individual choices express one's preferences. Allying itself with rational choice theory, the neoclassical social scientist further believes that "in acting rationally, an actor is engaging in some kind of optimization." This individual enjoys complete freedom of choice, exhibiting, as Milton Friedman puts it in an influential treatise *Capitalism and Freedom* (1962), a "belief in his own responsibility for his destiny" (1). For the purposes of this chapter on nineteenth-century American fiction and information asymmetries, this model makes a related key assumption: consumers can best pursue profit-maximization "through voluntary exchange" (13) precisely because they possess all relevant information that allows them to take "action that maximizes the differences between benefits and costs" (Coleman and Fararo 1993: xi). As this model of economic behavior presumes, in order to maximize profits—or, alternately, in minimizing costs—free individuals act under conditions of perfect information.

And yet imperfect information exists in exchanges with such imbalances precluding optimization. Challenging the primacy of the assumptions enumerated earlier, some modern economists pursue the idea of *information asymmetries*: the reality that one party to a transaction can have access to better information than another one. In 2001, the economists George Akerlof, Michael Spence, and Joseph Stiglitz jointly received the Nobel Prize in Economics for what the *Royal Swedish Academy* called "their analyses of markets with asymmetric information." Economists specify information asymmetries in two ways: *adverse selection* and *moral hazard*. To illustrate these two principles, they often conjure scenarios about car insurance markets. In the case of adverse selection, in which one party lacks information during the negotiation of a contract, a hypothetical high-risk driver knows more about his driving style than the insurer. The driver might know, but the coverage provider might not, for instance, that he prefers to drive 40 miles per hour in residential neighborhoods rather than the posted 25 miles per hour. As for moral hazard, according to Nobel Laureate in Economics Paul Krugman, it implies "any situation in which one person makes the decision about how much risk to take, while someone else bears the cost if things go badly" (63). In this case, then, a different driver increases her risk taking—she now drives 50 rather than 30 miles per hour in residential neighborhoods—precisely because she has negotiated a contract with the insurance company that relieves her liability.

As narrative fictions unfold from beginning to end, they rely on asymmetric information, exploiting diagetic gaps in order to develop themes, subplots, and morals. Narrative fiction, this is to say, can first model the asymmetries at the heart of information economics and then use them to achieve some effect. Literary criticism, it follows, is especially suited to studying these information asymmetries in relation to fiction. While a narratologist might track how an implied author creates some greater or lesser distance between narrator and reader, a psychoanalytic critic might find instead how information asymmetry among characters reflects the formation of human identity. In an admittedly selective survey of the nineteenth-century novel, my chapter pursues, instead, the conjunction of business and marriage plots in both romantic and realist novels. In her feminist anthropology of marriage, Gayle Rubin demonstrates how women emerge as the object of exchange between father and husband. In this reading, the institution of marriage achieves significance as a site of negotiation: a competitive market (see Rubin 1975; Michie 2009). The novels studied below reveal how nineteenth-century fiction imagined women as both empowered by and objectified within the marriage system, signaling ways that fiction could prime young people (and their parents) in negotiating—and reflecting on—the terms of marriage itself. Hence, the marriage plot, pervasive in the nineteenth-century Anglo-American literary field, offers fertile ground on which to see how and why authors use information asymmetries to complete—or upend—marital transactions.

American fiction of the long nineteenth century tends to criticize the values of an era in which "capitalism takes command," affirming virtue over ambition (see Kornblith and Zakim 2011). In *The Theory of Moral Sentiments* (1759), Adam Smith tackles this very polarity, helping us figure these impulses as countercultural. Exploring why people tend to respect "the rich and the great" rather than the "wise and virtuous," Smith explains how commercial societies offer "[t]wo different characters … to our emulation; the one, of proud ambition and ostentatious avidity; the other, of humble modestly and equitable justice" (73). The nineteenth-century marriage plot finds in this dilemma a dramatic occasion, typically representing a heroine's (in Friedman's idiom, seemingly voluntary) choice as one between virtue and wealth.

If they were to traverse marriage markets with perfect information, the heroines of early sentimental novels might well reach the most efficacious individual, and thereby the best social, outcomes. Imagining a society founded on more than just gender relations by recommending woman as a rational actor, the early American proto-feminist Judith Sargent Murray affirms in her *Gleaner* (1797) instances of *"female capability."* Women "have a talent," she writes, which needs to be "cultivated" so as to give them a "more rational prospect of tranquility" (39). And yet, this imagined agent, freed to maximize her utility, yielded to her opposite in much of the era's fiction. Indeed, in ubiquitous seduction plots, many young women's fates hinge on information asymmetries within the market, a narrative fact that portrays how such imperfections obstruct optimizations, and how women often maximize costs instead of utility.

Anonymously authored *Amelia: or the Faithless Briton* (1787) tackles the challenge asymmetric information poses to efficient marriage outcomes, evincing anxieties over the stability of marriage as an institution managed by men. This particular seduction narrative does so by explaining the typical rake's behavior to exploit information asymmetries. *Amelia* names its seducing rake Doliscus, "most likely," the novel's modern editors write, "extend[ing] *dolus*, meaning deceit or trickery" (4n). Doliscus's crime thus becomes wrongfully circumventing the negotiation between men that Gayle Rubin locates at the center of the traffic in women through marriage. Like most rakes from early sentimental novels, Doliscus masks his true licentiousness when speaking to his love object, but in nudging Amelia to "sacrifice ... her honour" he undertakes "the detestable agency of perfidy and fraud." More particularly, Doliscus overcomes Amelia's aversion to "the scandal which the world imputed to clandestine marriages, and the fatal consequences that might arise from obscurity of the transaction," and achieves what the narrator terms a "fictitious marriage" in a "privately repeated" ceremony (6). *Amelia* thus vilifies Doliscus for perpetrating a moral hazard whereby he leaves Amelia to bear the costs of his lust. Abandoning a pregnant Amelia, Doliscus affects that he does "not perfectly comprehend the meaning of some expressions you have employed" (7) in her accusations. Even as Amelia, having boldly followed him across the Atlantic to Great Britain, "demanded a public and unequivocal acknowledgement of their marriage," Doliscus continues to deny her, refusing to be "thus duped or controuled" by her pretended snare (9).

More to the point, in order to ruin Amelia, Doliscus must defraud her unsuspecting father Horatio: a presumptive equal party to the marriage transaction. A "respectable inhabitant of the state of New-York," Horatio begins the novel retired from a successful mercantile career. When the Revolutionary War begins, lacking in the "passions which rouse men to opposition, and qualify them for enterprize," he "withdrew from public clamour, to a sequestered cottage, in the interior district of Long-Island" (3). Horatio eventually follows Amelia to Great Britain, but the novel faults him for forsaking his duty to traffic his daughter efficiently. Rakes can prevent marriage markets from clearing, no doubt: they leave potentially socially useful women to wither in ruin. So too, however, can kindly but aloof fathers impede optimizations—not by exploiting information asymmetries in negotiations but failing to seek information in the first place.

Published later in the early national period, Rebecca Rush's novel *Kelroy* (1812) portrays the marriage market not through the eyes of an information-averse father but, rather, through those of an information-savvy mother. Left indebted by her late husband, formerly of "immense wealth" (2), Mrs. Hammond imagines her two daughters, the materialistic Lucy and the virtuous Emily, as assets by which to restore her wealth (15). To achieve her goal, Mrs. Hammond moves from Philadelphia to the country, preparing her daughters for marriage on their coming of age. While Horatio Blyfield removes his family from the city to the country for his own study, Mrs. Hammond, under "the pretence that she was incapacitated by grief from enjoying ... the pleasures of society," does so for her own gain. To this plot, "[t]he good-natured world" remained "ignorant of her real motives," applauding her "delicate respect" for her late husband (3).

In terms of information asymmetries, Mrs. Hammond's behavior throughout *Kelroy* approximates *adverse selection*. On returning to the city "at the expiration of four years" (5), indeed, she endeavors to negotiate marriage contracts while hiding the knowledge that her daughters are penniless. "Trusting to their beauty, and her own experience," she urgently seeks husbands for Lucy and Emily as the remnants of her estate dwindles. In one last-ditch effort to win suitors, Mrs. Hammond throws a ball, eventually achieving the success she covets: a propertied Englishman, Mr. Walsingham, becomes infatuated with Lucy, and the couple is married. While Mrs. Hammond's managerial acumen secures Walsingham's wealth for Lucy, at the same time, though, the Englishman threatens Mrs. Hammond's plans for the virtuous Emily who becomes infatuated with Walsingham's noble but impecunious friend Edward Kelroy. Imagining a high opportunity cost in this attachment, Mrs. Hammond fears that Walsingham plays the same game as herself, suspecting Walsingham of a "scheme to assist Kelroy in attempting to better his circumstances" (57).

While initially Walsingham "judged only from appearances, and was a stranger to the hidden motives which actuated this selfish, imperious woman" (66), he eventually confronts Mrs. Hammond's bad faith negotiations. Puzzled by the incongruity between Mrs. Hammond's apparent financial stolidity and her eagerness for Emily to marry a distasteful but rich man Mr. Marney, Walsingham and Kelroy conclude "the report of her wealth to be merely an invention of her own" (122–3). In order to promote Kelroy's love for Emily, then, Walsingham presses his mother-in-law for repayment of a prior loan, aiming to draw out the truth of her relative poverty. Having achieved information parity with Mrs. Hammond, Walsingham endeavors but nonetheless fails to effect Emily and Kelroy's union founded in love. For in an unexpected plot twist, Mrs. Hammond wins a "fifty thousand dollar prize … in the lottery" (193). Newly solvent, Mrs. Hammond withdraws once more to the country, where she commits a final fraud, duping her daughter and Kelroy (who has gone to India in search of fortune) into breaking their engagement. Although contentedly married to a new suitor, Mr. Dunlevy, Emily Hammond eventually discovers her mother's falsification of Kelroy's fate and dies. Kelroy, on learning of Mrs. Hammond treachery, in turn dies at sea.

Compared to *Amelia*'s straightforward critique of information asymmetry among male negotiators, as the foregoing plot overview suggests, *Kelroy*'s insights seem more complex. If Mrs. Hammond's materialistic values are loathsome, why does the lottery prize allow her to escape consequences? Why does the prize allow her to overcome Walsingham's efforts to subdue her behavior, giving her the freedom to effect Emily's union with the rich Dunlevy? And yet in response to these dilemmas, the novel nevertheless offers an economy of pain whereby the romantic Emily, finally achieving information parity, dies. Where *Kelroy* begins by describing Mrs. Hammond's behavior as adverse selection, pathologizing her as a market negotiator, then, it concludes by demonstrating her scheme as moral hazard. Freed from debt by the lottery, she assumes risks that only her daughter's life will settle.

The centrality of information to optimization takes dramatic form in early American sentimental narratives, which address the behaviors of more or less free individuals. Often incorporating the conventions of popular fiction for rhetorical effect, nineteenth-century slave writings complicate this theme by situating the bondservant within information economies. Since the eighteenth century, male slave narratives, while mostly avoiding any mention of marriage, have criticized the information economics at the heart of the slave system. In his *Interesting Narrative* (1789), Olaudah Equiano explains in gripping detail his transformation from tribal prince to transatlantic commodity. Through a powerful defamiliarization, he demonstrates the irony of information asymmetry from the commodity's perspective, describing his "astonishment, which was soon converted into terror" (54), at being involuntarily shipped across the Atlantic. In perhaps the most alluring display of information asymmetry, Frederick Douglass claims his right to control information. Reversing the logic of moral hazard, Douglass refuses to disclose the particulars of his escape from the South so as to prevent risking future beneficiaries of the Underground Railroad. "I deem it proper," he declares to the reader, "to make known my intention not to state all the facts connected with the transaction." Such discipline becomes a virtue in Douglass's powerful rhetoric:

> It would afford me great pleasure indeed, as well as materially add to the interest of my narrative, were I at liberty to gratify a curiosity, which I know exists in the minds of many, by an accurate statement of all the facts pertaining to my most fortunate escape. But I must deprive myself of this pleasure, and the curious of the gratification which such a statement would afford.
>
> *(65)*

Most significant for my purposes, Harriet Jacobs's *Incidents in the Life of a Slave Girl* (1862) explicitly examines information economics in relation to marriage. Long misread as a sentimental novel, Jacobs borrows the tradition's pathos-driven appeals to white middle-class readers. In the chapter "The Lover," Jacobs's narrator Linda Brent wonders, "Why does the slave ever love? Why allow the tendrils of the heart to twine around objects which may at any moment be wrenched away by the hand of violence?" (37). Here, Brent evinces angst over the slave's right to self-directed love. Like Douglass, however, rather than accept that the slave has no power in such negotiations, Brent claims information asymmetry as her own. Hiding in her grandmother's attic for seven years, she undertakes a campaign of misinformation, having letters sent to the South from New York so as to further confuse her master Dr. Flint's efforts to rescue his property. Through Brent's observations, indeed, the reader delights as Flint's anger grows over his exclusion from the transaction. Despite her control of information, however, Linda Brent's story does not end "in the usual way with marriage" (201). At narrative's end, like and unlike the heroines of seduction narratives, Brent both suffers outside the institution of marriage and inside the world of work where she labors to secure a middle-class life for her children. Having waged a successful misinformation campaign against her master, she finds that in the free North, racism obstructs markets from clearing as well.

Early sentimentalists from Rush to Jacobs explore the relation between information and marriage markets in more or less abstract ways. While narrators might offer specific figures—for instance, the $900 that Walsingham loans to Mrs. Hammond or the $50,000 that she wins in the lottery prize—the mechanics of these transactions are not always crucial to their literary projects. In his numerous novels from the antebellum era, the writer, editor, and leading temperance advocate Timothy Shay (T.S.) Arthur bucks this trend, offering readers a deluge of narratives that link (but also conflate) the public sphere of business transactions with the private one of romantic love. Especially active in the 1840s and 1850s, Arthur's business-related fiction espouses middle-class values by offering cautionary but realistic tales about one's relation to information in business transactions.

In Arthur's works, the business world exists as a relatively confined sphere where personal relationships matter (see French 1958). Given this restricted spatiality, Arthur's narratives tend to structure themselves in Manichean pairs that revolve around conflicts between a virtuous professional—a merchant, a lawyer, or doctor—and a ruthlessly materialistic counterpart. As such, Arthur's business novels achieve a relentless moral clarity whereby the man who overcomes the values of the age prospers and the one who typifies them fails. More subtly, though, in developing this strident moralism, Arthur attends to the information (a)symmetries that obtain within his characters' professional networks.

The 1848 novel *Debtor and Creditor; A Tale of the Times* offers a case in point. The narrator introduces the reader to a newly humbled merchant, Mr. Coleman, coming to terms with the fact that "overtrading and losses" "had so crippled him that, in the whole time, he had not once laid his head upon his pillow without an oppressive weight of care on his bosom" (5). Citing this constant worry, the narrator excuses Coleman for not declaring bankruptcy sooner, a delay that thereby sacrificed for his creditors a larger dividend. His business acts, this is to say, while unsuccessful in financial terms were not "really dishonest in themselves" (6): not intended, that is, to defraud his associates. Hence, Arthur's *Debtor and Creditor* differentiates Coleman's behavior—at its core, a form of *moral hazard*, since he extends his credit while knowingly insolvent—from outright fraud. Inevitably, Coleman's affairs come to a "crisis" when a creditor, Turner, demands "satisfactory information" on the state of his business affairs. Necessarily causing pain for a network of people, this crisis nevertheless enables

Coleman to make a full account: not to shrink away from inconvenient facts but to offer free and accurate information. In "making the fullest acknowledgment of his affairs," Coleman not only protects himself legally, then. Rather, his behavior permits Arthur to model a proper relation to information in business. Information symmetry in business, the novel implies, diminishes moral, social, and financial harm.

I might proliferate examples from Arthur's *oeuvre* that place information symmetries at the heart of business ethics. The novel *Rising in the World; A Tale for the Rich and Poor* (1857) typifies much of these works by opposing the virtuous man Dunbar and the materialistic one Hudson, but I single it out for its explicit meditation on the relation between information and marriage markets. While both men hail from humble origins, in his haste for wealth, Dunbar evinces the go-aheadism typical of the era: in the words of his mentor, "Shrewd, acute, ardent, and ambitious; there is nothing in the way of his rising in the world" (17; for a history of "go-aheadism" see Sandage 2005). Not only using his business acumen to extend his legal career, he also brings it to bear on his approach to marriage. Initially captivated by an idealized woman, Mary Lee, Dunbar eventually breaks his engagement for material reasons: "Mary was poor; she could not … aid him in his upward struggle by the strong elevating power of wealth" (Arthur 1857: 32). Slowly becoming "conscious of a change" (44) in Dunbar, Mary Lee frees him from the contract.

Obsessed with rising as quickly as possible, Dunbar undertakes an "iniquitous scheme" (73) whereby he conspires with opposing counsel at the expense of his client. This misdeed will prove Dunbar's undoing, for after he agrees to damage his reputation at the expense of his unwitting client, Dunbar pursues "a matrimonial speculation": an orphaned heiress from Baltimore, Henrietta Gay, "said to be worth sixty or seventy thousand dollars"(87–8). In turning to the anthropology of marriage, Arthur's narrative thus ironicizes the negative implications of information asymmetry, for, as luck will have it, the trustee of Gay's estate is Mr. Harrison, the defendant with whom Dunbar conspires. Shortly after marrying Gay, Dunbar seeks the particulars of his wife's estate, going to Harrison for "all information on the subject" (167). Here, Harrison reveals why, on paying Dunbar a bribe related to the legal conspiracy of $30,000, he made the lawyer accept a receipt for payment. When Dunbar demanded the estate's value—$30,000, as it turns out—Harrison claims to have already paid him, forcing Dunbar to expose his own fraud in demanding his wife's estate. Like an arch detective, Harrison foresees all the moves to be played, triumphantly halting Dunbar's rise. Both the perpetrator and the victim of information asymmetry, Dunbar, the novel declares, receives an appropriate comeuppance for a businessman eager to exploit any advantage for his own rapid gain.

By the end of the nineteenth century, novelists working intentionally under the rubric of realism after the US Civil War further explored marriage in increasingly rigorous economic terms. Indeed, while Arthur represents the relatively confined world of merchants, lawyers, and doctors, novelists like Henry James and Edith Wharton examine capital's global reach. In James's *The Portrait of a Lady* (1880), investment capital provided by Daniel Touchett, "a shrewd American banker" (18), sets into motion the heroine Isabel Archer's marriage plot. With his substantial gift to his niece, Touchett and his son Ralph put some "wind in her sails" (160), a power meant to relieve her of the burden of marriage negotiations. And yet, as the pernicious Madame Merle puts it, characters seek to "profit by… knowledge" at Archer's expense, and James's heroine falls prey to bad-faith marriage negotiations undertaken so as to secure her inherited "seventy thousand pounds" (206). Presuming to choose her life's path, indeed, she marries a mercenary man incapable love. In doing so, she pays for Osmond's indifference with the immense opportunity costs of not only more suitable matches with an

English nobleman (Lord Warburton) or an American industrialist (Caspar Goodwood) but also of her "one ambition—to be free to follow out a good feeling" (293).

For Milton Friedman, in *Capitalism and Freedom*, the neoclassical model imagines the individual as responsible for "his own destiny." James strikes a similar note in the Preface to the New York Edition of *The Portrait of a Lady* (1908), where he remembers that the "corner-stone" of his novel became "the conception of a certain young woman affronting her destiny" (8). James's novel ultimately represents how others vitiate the extent to which one controls her destiny. Even in the midst of her marital woe, Archer, who likens herself to a "free agent," believes that "the sole source of her mistake had been within herself." "There had been no plot, no snare," she naively affirms. And yet she in fact suffers from a plot, a snare: an information asymmetry that she realizes too late. Her "ruin," however, occasions no moralizing from James as it does in *Amelia*, *Kelroy*, *Incidents in the Life*, and *Rising in the World*. Friedman explains that the economist "has nothing to say about what an individual does with his freedom"—that is the "realm of individual ethics and philosophy" (12). Yet even though he does not moralize explicitly, James nevertheless maps how information asymmetries lead markets to fail, imputing an almost unrepresentantable cost to rational but ethically bankrupt snares.

James's contemporary Edith Wharton likewise dramatizes marriage negotiations among the elite in the 1890s. Her realist novel *The House of Mirth* (1905) represents corresponding financial and social worlds in which access to information dictates whether one rises or falls. Trafficking in the "mysterious Wall Street world of 'tips' and 'deals'" (65), the novel's most informed character, the stock speculator Sim Rosedale, "was making his way through the dense mass of social antagonisms," "placing Wall Street under obligations which only Fifth Avenue could repay" (188). Possessing a patience that T.S. Arthur might appreciate, "[w]ith … slow unalterable persistency" (188), Rosedale exploits information asymmetries so as to make inroads into Fifth Avenue society.

While Wharton remains agnostic about Rosedale's truck with information, she values Lily Bart's renunciation of the materialism of the "house of mirth." As such, *The House of Mirth* synthesizes elements from many of the texts discussed earlier. Like *Amelia*, the heroine Lily Bart dies in the prime of her life; like *Kelroy*, Bart is groomed by a managerial mother who views her beauty zealously as a financial "asset" for the marriage market; and even like *Incidents in the Life of a Slave Girl*, Bart's position is likened to that of a bondwoman, her thwarted romantic interest Lawrence Selden seeing her bracelets as "manacles chaining her to her fate" (Wharton 1990: 8). Perhaps not surprisingly, then, a strident anti-materialism pervades the novel's ending. Early in the novel, in order to secure financial breathing room, Bart embraces an information asymmetry that might benefit her: she has a loathsome character, Gus Trenor, managing her portfolio so as to benefit from Rosedale's "tips." Unsure of the "exact nature of the transaction" with Trenor, Lily wishes for its "vagueness" to "diminish its indelicacy" (65). Ignorance, she reasons, is power, and "[t]he first thousand dollar cheque which Lily received … strengthened her self-confidence" (68). At the novel's end, however, like T.S. Arthur's debtor Coleman, Bart makes a full account of her financial status, and in her final act, "She then wrote out a cheque for Trenor" (249). No longer seeking to profit from those precious Wall Street "tips," she finds such transactions too costly and closes her account: just prior to overdosing on chloral, Lily Bart removes the debt before she "would slip into the gradual tolerance" (249) of it, severing all ties with the rewards of information asymmetries.

The nineteenth-century novel in the United States, from its sentimental beginnings to its high-water mark in realism, consistently imagines how information asymmetry hinders optimizations. In doing so, it exposes, rather than further obscures, how markets operate, more particularly imagining in marriage how markets are not always efficient, just, and equitable. In criticizing materialism, haste, and ambition, then, nineteenth-century novelists interested in the relation between markets and information anticipate a recent work of *non*-fiction that clarifies what Wall Street insiders insist cannot be clarified. I am thinking here of Michael Lewis's book *Flash Boys: A Wall Street Revolt* (2014), which offers insight into the world of high-frequency trading, a financial practice that exploits an information asymmetry about the bid or offer price of a financial security. With a temporal advantage measured in microseconds (one millionth of a second), high-frequency trading firms drive security prices up or down at will, reaping enormous profits at the expense of "slower" investors in the process. The hero of Lewis's book, a Canadian trader named Brad Katsuyama, undertakes a public campaign to reduce the investors' ignorance about this information asymmetry, and Lewis's prose assumes the same project. Perhaps expectedly, then, they have been denounced by the industry as "novelists": "to me," financier Manoj Narang writes, Lewis's book "is fiction masquerading as journalistic exposé." *Flash Boys*, in this man of business' damning phrase, reads like a "novel."

Narang's terms—fiction, novel—return us to the early republic, an era in which sentimental novels like *Amelia* emerged in environs hostile to fiction. And yet, as we have seen, fiction writers tend to demonstrate how markets work, how information circulates within them, by mapping their rules, logics, and values through imaginative projections. In an Information Age, one cannot help but wonder if "novels" are precisely what we need to imagine a just life under late capitalism. One cannot help but wonder, that is, if literary thinking—creative and critical—can help overcome the information asymmetries that some experts in finance and economics presume to be insuperable.

## References

Anonymous. (2015) *Amelia; or the Faithless Briton*, Duncan Faherty and Ed White (eds.) http://jto.common-place.org/wp-content/uploads/sites/2/2013/01/Amelia-1787-with-headnote.pdf.

Arthur, Timothy Shay. (1849) *Debtor and Creditor: A Tale of the Times*, New York: Baker & Scribner.

Arthur, Timothy Shay. (1857) *Rising in the World: A Tale for the Rich and Poor*, New York: Baker & Scribner.

Coleman, James S. and Fararo, Thomas J. (1993) *Rational Choice Theory: Advocacy and Critique*, London: Sage Publications.

Douglass, Frederick. (1997) *Narrative of the Life of Frederick Douglass*, New York: Norton.

Equiano, Olaudah. (2002) "The Interesting Narrative of the Life of Olaudah Equiano" in Henry Louis Gates (ed.) *The Classic Slave Narratives*, New York: Signet.

French, Warren G. (1958) "Timothy Shay Arthur: Pioneer Business Novelist," *American Quarterly* 10.1: 55–65.

Friedman, Milton. (1962) *Capitalism and Freedom*, Chicago, IL: University of Chicago Press.

Jacobs, Harriet. (2000) *Incidents in the Life of a Slave Girl*, Cambridge, MA: Harvard University Press.

James, Henry. (1995) *The Portrait of a Lady*, New York: Norton.

Kornblith, Gary J. and Zakim, Michael. (2011) *Capitalism Takes Command: The Social Transformation of the Nineteenth Century*, Chicago, IL: University of Chicago Press.

Krugman, Paul. (2009) *The Return of Depression Economics and the Crisis of 2008*, New York: Norton.

Michie, Elsie B. (2009) "Rich Woman, Poor Woman: Toward an Anthropology of the Nineteenth-Century Marriage Plot," *PMLA* 124.2: 421–36.

Murray, Judith Sargent. (1995) *Selected Writings of Judith Sargent Murray*, New York: Oxford University Press.

Narang, Manoj. (2014) "A Much-Needed HFT Primer for 'Flash Boys' Author Michael Lewis," *InstitutionalInvestor.com* (April 7). www.institutionalinvestor.com/Article/3328158/Banking-and-Capital-Markets-Trading-and-Technology/A-Much-Needed-HFT-Primer-for-Flash-Boys-Author-Michael-Lewis.html#/.WHziW2QrKfV.

Rubin, Gayle S. (1975) "The Traffic in Women: Notes on the 'Political Economy' of Sex" in Rayna Reitner (ed.) *Toward an Anthropology of Women*, New York: Monthly Review Press.
Rush, Rebecca. (1812) *Kelroy*, Philadelphia, PA: Bradford and Innskeep.
Sandage, Scott. (2005) *Born Losers: A History of Failure in America*, Cambridge, MA: Harvard University Press.
Smith, Adam. (2002) *The Theory of Moral Sentiments*, Cambridge: Cambridge University Press.
Wharton, Edith. (1990) *The House of Mirth*, New York: Norton.

# 17
# BLACK MARKETS

*Sharada Balachandran Orihuela*

"Black Markets" posits that the piratic, which refers broadly to possessory acts that exist outside the law, constitutes both a poetics and a model for understanding how persons who have been left outside the restrictive and exclusive categories of citizen resist the regulatory powers *of* and demand redress *from* the liberal state. Indeed, it is because rights in a liberal tradition are considered to be a type of property, and the protection of property has been a cornerstone in the creation and protection of the liberal person that property is the subject of this inquiry. This chapter emphasizes the underbelly of this liberal story: it looks to the place of unlawful ownership as a means of challenging the dispossessions facilitated by the state. By analyzing or even participating in forms of property ownership that exist outside what is legally permissible, this chapter suggests that dispossessed populations imagine and help to and create new social, political, and economic communities.

More specifically, "Black Markets" turns to John Brougham's burlesque *Columbus, El Filibustero!* (1858) and Eligio Ancona's *El Filibustero: Novela Historica* (1864), texts that center on pirates and piracy, to signal the importance of the piratic in the creation of exceptional American property regimes. By turning my attention to these two mid-nineteenth-century texts, one written by an American dramatist and the other by a Mexican historian, I demonstrate how American authors across the hemisphere use the figure of the pirate, a subject who participates in unlawful property ownership, to narrate the story of independence, the creation of American property regimes, and the formation of the normative personhood. As these texts dramatize, the story of the Americas is a piratic tale. Indeed, one way to understand American property regimes, themselves a response to restrictive and undemocratic English land laws (such as tenurial obligations, primogeniture, fee tail, and coverture), is to understand them as piratic in that American property rights are purportedly more expansive and democratic. Moreover, given colonial rule is understood as a type of dispossession in these works, both Ancona and Brougham suggest that American independence, and its attendant expansive property regimes, requires that colonial subjects participate in unlawful property acquisition. And yet, later nineteenth-century writers also begin to use allegories of the piratic to tell the story of rampant speculative economic growth, seen as an extractive "business" led by rogue and outlaw railroad tycoons and Wall Street financiers, or modern-day pirates. For this reason, the pirate reappears in nineteenth-century American literature as a figure critical of the very liberal property regimes she/he it helped to create. In so doing, these property outlaws demonstrate the failures of the liberal promise of economic and political freedom.

Given the diverse treatments of piracy in literature, this chapter proposes approaching the piratic as a poetics for reading imaginative literature about dispossessed persons. In addition to providing a framework for understanding rights and independence as types of property that must be unlawfully acquired, piracy also allows for a more expansive model for reading about dispossessed persons in literature. This mode of reading and exegesis not only accommodates the ways in which unlawful property ownership is represented in American literature and what it represents to dispossessed persons engaging in these unlawful propertied regimes, but also remains attentive to those transactions and populations that might otherwise be left out of most literary and historical accounts. For this reason, the piratic is a type of recuperative reading and serves to elucidate those persons and transactions that might otherwise remain in the shadows.

## The promise of property: the person and the citizen

Property is critical to the creation of liberal person. In his seminal work in liberal philosophy, John Locke asserts that,

> every man has a *property* in his own *person* … the *labour* of his body, and the *work* of his hands, we may say, are properly his. … Whatsoever then he removes out of the state that nature hath provided, and left it in, he hath mixed his *labour* with, and joined it to something that is his own, and thereby makes it his *property*.[1]

This aspect of Locke's work, called possessive individualism, refers to the condition of the person as the sole owner of the property of one's skills and one's laboring body. As critics have argued, possessive individualism "borrows from property law an almost spatial sense of the bounded self- of what in the eighteenth century were called the 'fences' that constituted the liberties of free men."[2] Indeed, for Locke as for other liberal thinkers, the self-possessed body is itself the primary property entitled to the person, and possession of the property of the self is a precondition for liberal personhood.

More importantly, the "property which men have in their persons as well as goods" is foundational to the fulfillment of desire and lies at the very core of civil society, because it is only after acquiring property that the subject feels the need to relinquish the freedom he experienced in the state of nature for the safety and protections attached to belonging to a civil or political society.[3] Locke therefore confidently asserts that "government has no other end but the preservation of property."[4] For Locke as for other liberal philosophers, the property of the inalienable self-possessed body, while primary and which enables the ownership of other alienable properties, is most important because it ensures a range of protections and freedoms that are in part guaranteed by the state when it protects property. After all, in Locke's view, life, liberty, *and* property are interdependent, and identify those inalienable rights which ensure that neither person nor state can interfere with one's survival.

However, the interdependence of property and person is not limited to liberal philosophy, but rather, is codified in legal and political discourses. In the U.S., property has always been central to the creation and maintenance of normative conceptions of belonging, or citizenship. Even after the removal of property restrictions from enfranchisement in 1792, state constitutions, such as those of Massachusetts, Iowa, and California limited the "privileges and immunities" that free citizens enjoyed to exclude "paupers, vagabonds, and fugitives from justice" from the enjoyments of citizenship.[5] These populations were excluded from citizenship because they were seen to be incapable of participating in the regime of property ownership, thus demonstrating the primacy of property in the creation of citizenship.

Moreover, limitations to property were not limited to material goods, but also included immaterial properties such as whiteness, which underwrote the exclusion of African Americans from citizenship.[6] Both the *Dred Scott* (1857) and *Heirn v. Bridault* (1859) Supreme Court decisions, for example, demonstrate the entanglements of citizenship (and whiteness) and claims to property. While the former decision legally institutionalized the exclusion of black persons from the category of the citizen, the latter, lesser-known decision centered on the right of a free black woman to inherit property from the white man with whom she had lived. Indeed, *Heirn v. Bridault* legally codified the exclusion of black persons from all forms of property ownership, not simply the property of citizenship, as was the case with *Dred Scott*. Because Mrs. Bridault was unable to naturalize as a U.S. citizen, and was to be a perpetual alien, it was decided by the courts that she was incapable of inheriting this property.[7]

The equivalence of property and person is echoed in the language of American independence and is integral to the establishment of the American state. "Life, liberty, and property" is borrowed directly by the framers of the Declaration of Independence who change "property" to "pursuit of happiness." And yet, the phrase "life, liberty, and property" is included verbatim in the Fifth and Fourteenth Amendments, amendments that address the rights and privileges of national membership—that is, the rights to due process, and citizenship and equal protection, respectively. The Fourteenth Amendment, for example, which ensured that formerly enslaved persons would be welcomed into the folds of citizenship and forbade the state from denying anyone the equal protection of their "life, liberty, and property," expresses the entanglements of material properties and the symbolic properties of citizenship. By recognizing and protecting their property, as well the property of their bodies, a formerly dispossessed population was afforded citizenship by the state. For this reason, property has been seen as the cornerstone of liberal philosophy's production of freedom, rights, citizenship, and government, as well as of modernity's subject.

Given the centrality of property, both material and immaterial, in understanding the modern person and the American citizen (even before the formal existence of the latter), one must ask, what do we do with property ownership that exists outside of these limitations? Moreover, as in the case of *Heirn v. Bridault*, when property ownership directly tests and conflicts with the status of the Black body *as* property, I ask, what kinds of property can those persons who cannot legally hold property claim to have? Finally, how might a person's unlawful claims to property help us imagine forms of inclusion and representation for persons that have been formerly excluded from experiencing these privileges? To answer these questions, I propose that we read unlawful propertied behaviors as piratic, in that the range of unlawful forms of property ownership in which dispossessed persons participate unsettle the naturalized relationship between possession and citizenship.

## Piratic properties

Piracy has historically been defined simply as an act of robbery on the high seas that would be considered a felony if committed within the bounds of a single sovereign nation-state. Because piracy is committed outside the domain of any single sovereign state and thus cannot be punished easily, piracy was considered to be a crime so severe and unsettling that it was punishable by death from the sixteenth to the nineteenth centuries.[8] The act of piracy, in other words, has always been a crime that tests the jurisdictional territory and powers of the nation-state: it is an exceptional crime. In U.S. federal law, the pirate is a figure that is neither an enemy, for which the pirate would be affiliated with another nation-state, nor a political belligerent, for which he would be recognized as a lawful member of the U.S. nation-state. Instead, at certain moments in American legal history, piracy has been interpreted as a behavior akin to treason. The Crimes Act of 1790, for example, which defined federal crimes and their punishment, included the crimes of treason, piracy, and counterfeiting as crimes punishable by death.

Moreover, piracy refers as much to crimes that include acts of robbery in ungovernable spaces as it does to conspiring behaviors that attempt to undo and unmake the state altogether. Indeed, the pirate occupies an oppositional and hostile position to the very idea of the state: the pirate, in other words, is a figure that more closely resembles a terrorist than an enemy. For this reason, Rediker calls pirates "villains of all nations." Indeed, the etymology of "pirate" derived from the Greek *peirates* is defined as the one "who attacks" or who "makes a hostile attempt." Yet, the subject of the pirate's "hostile attempt" or "attack" is left unclear: seemingly, the pirate concurrently attacks property, the person, and the state. It is this indeterminacy regarding the pirate's true crime that makes the pirate a dangerous, as well as an exciting figure in law, as well as in literature: a figure with the potential to disrupt and reshape the meanings of property as well as the properties and powers of the state. And yet, as much as piracy is antithetical to the state, it has also been seen as instrumental in the expansion of state power. In her work, Jody Greene has written that the pirate is the "constitutive exception, the extralegal figure without whom [a body of international legal thinking] would not have been able to delimit itself in the first place."[9] For Greene, the pirate occupies an "exceptional but exceptionally productive status in law, in culture, and in language."[10] Piracy, in other words, is a propertied crime that helps to legitimate a range of punitive measures against undesirable populations and warrant state growth, as well as exclude certain populations from protections of the state.

These diverse treatments of piracy suggest that piracy helps to expand upon the complicated position of the individual's relation to the state. For example, rather than call the smuggler an individual violator of the law, Adam Smith blames the "corrupted governments" for producing the figure of the smuggler as "not many people are scrupulous about smuggling, when, without perjury, they can find any easy and safe opportunity of doing so."[11] Thus, for Smith, any interruption of free trade by the state is liable to produce the smuggler because the individual's natural rights to property and to trade are being infringed upon by the state: a state whose only role is to protect that individual's property.

In this view, the enslaved subject who has been denied all claims to property and is therefore excluded from any state protections has no other recourse but to become a smuggler. Moreover, because the slave has no rights to property, including the property of his/her own body, for the enslaved person to own property would mean that s/he always owns property in an unlawful way. For example, in the event of escaping slavery and transporting his/her body outside the reach of the slaveholder, the enslaved person expresses a form of unlawful ownership of the primary property of the self. The enslaved subject becomes *out*law for several different reasons. Firstly, s/he is breaking the law, and secondly s/he exists outside the protections of the law. For this reason, the shadows function as a place where dispossessed persons lacking the properties of state protection and recognition can become propertied subjects.

The "piratic" borrows from extant scholarship on piracy, but includes a wider range of unlawful propertied behaviors (theft and smuggling, for example) that serve as the basis for new forms of social organization.[12] As Marcus Rediker writes, "illegality had become an accepted part of seamen's daily lives, a means of expression in a society whose institutions and customs seemed in many ways planned to worsen their very difficult lot."[13] Shared participation in the unlawful behavior of piracy is a response to the limitations imposed by the state on the individual on his/her full expression of personhood, and the high seas were a location where novel forms of community could exist outside the control of the state. The piratic, in other words, functions as a demand for reparation and redress from the state, and can help to form more just systems because it lays bare the interrelationship of property, person, and the state. Moreover, because it includes a fuller range of unlawful propertied behaviors, the piratic allows for a deeper understanding of behaviors that test, trouble, and contest the exclusion of certain populations from the regime of property ownership as a means of excluding them from personhood altogether. In the event of being denied the rights to property and thus participating in unlawful forms of property ownership, subjects who have no recourse to the state become instrumental in contesting and challenging the authority of the state. Piratic behaviors, I stress, are critical in undermining the state's exclusive power in creating and legitimating the liberal person, as well as central to imagining and creating new forms of belonging for populations that face dispossession.

## The piratic: an American case

To illustrate the importance of the piratic in imagining novel forms of personhood and community, I turn my attention to John Brougham's comedy, *Columbus, El Filibustero!* and Eligio Ancona's *El Filibustero: Novela Historica*, two texts that look to the central place of piracy in the creation of the Americas. These texts represent the anticolonial pirate as the nascent American subject par excellence in that these early "American" pirates unsettle extant regimes through their expressions of new forms of governance and property relations. Set in the early eighteenth century, Ancona's historical romance, *El Filibustero: Novela Historica*, follows its young protagonist, the poor Leonel, as he transforms into the notorious pirate Capitán Barbilla (a play on the name of the infamous pirate Blackbeard, who terrorized the Atlantic Ocean during the same period). Leonel begins his life as an orphan left on the steps of Don Gonzalo de Villagómez's hacienda. He is, in other words, an archetypal pirate: a man who lacks inherited property and a family name, and one who is critical of the colonial structures that exclude him from the properties of personhood altogether. Indeed, his desire for equality and personhood is informed by his education from the Franciscan priests in Yucatán, Fray Hernando de Plasencia in particular. Plasencia provides Leonel with an education steeped in Rousseau's ideals of democratic citizenship and social empowerment found in *Discourse on Inequality* (1755). Having read Rousseau's treatise, Leonel is enlightened about his marginalization and dispossession from claiming and expressing his rights as a full citizen.

Realizing that he will be unable to enter into the possession of those properties and that he will always be excluded from the category of full person due to his propertyless origins, Leonel leaves Villagómez's hacienda in order to seek his fortune on the high seas. Not only does Leonel leave in search of his wealth, but he also leaves to find his patrimony. Leonel notes that he is in search of a name "that I create with my own merits, not the one borrowed from strangers."[14] Therefore, Leonel falls into piracy because it is an act that breaks with the mores, codes, and rules of a repressive and innately unjust civil society, which, as Ancona describes, is hierarchal and structured on an inherently repressive and paternalistic colonial order. Leonel's desire for personhood outside the constraints of his lineage is in many ways the quintessential "American" break from aristocratic, European social and economic hierarchies. His alter ego, Barbilla, pursues piracy not only in order to find autonomy and wealth, but his piratic pursuits ultimately come to be motivated by a pursuit of justice and a desire for redistribution and restitution for impoverished, indigenous Mexicans. Indeed, the novel's denouement describes Barbilla's fortune being used to support the dispossessed inhabitants of a small village in the Yucatán.

And yet, as I want to underscore, Barbilla's desire for the redistribution of property and the unsettlement of colonial governance can most immediately be understood as an anticolonial activity. Looting, as Barbilla frames it, rivals and contests the piratic exploitation of the colonies by the Spanish government. The introduction to the text, for example, equivocates "the government agent, the friar, the governor, the bishop, [and] the pirate," all participating in the exploitation of the powerless.[15] Thus, Barbilla's response is to disrupt the operations of a Spanish colonial regime by kidnapping governors and stealing Spanish goods, thereby upsetting the continued dispossession of colonial Mexicans by governors and agents of the Catholic Church. Indeed, Barbilla's piratic activities upset a range of different regimes, from the familial to the colonial state. For this reason, Barbilla is unlike the stateless pirates mentioned alongside "the bishop and the governor." Instead, he is a subject that seeks justice through a propertied redistribution, a propertied redistribution that, as the ending to the novel dramatizes, is critical in the creation of a new community: a postcolonial state which is comprised of formerly dispossessed persons. Ancona represents piracy as a behavior that allows Yucatecs, generally, to achieve autonomy and independence, and Barbilla's "piracy" can be interpreted as an allegory for Mexican independence.

While Ancona's view of the historic interrelation of Spanish colonization, colonial independence, and piracy is not unique to his work, it is one of the more explicit expressions of what is to be gained from the piratic as an anticolonial behavior. Ancona's use of the piratic helps to underscore the propertied autonomy that is unique to American life, an autonomy that Americans pursue in the face of restrictions and limitations imposed by colonial regimes, themselves representative of purely extractive and exploitative administrations. Moreover, Ancona underscores the importance of expanded property rights for postcolonial Americans, and expressions of propertied and commercial autonomy in the fulfillment of the promises of independence. In sum, Ancona represents how American pirates can be instrumental in the creation of possession in a state intent on dispossession.

However, because this piratic figure is the one who, through his very existence, critiques exclusionary and dispossessive state practices, it is no surprise that this archetypal American piratic figure should eventually turn his critical stance on the expansive power of the U.S. state. Authors later in the nineteenth century use the pirate to critique the American state and its unfettered pursuit of possession and acquisition . To make this case, writers compare piracy to colonization. For example, in *Moby Dick* (1851), Herman Melville censures the imperialist expansionist projects of the U.S. state Ishmael discusses Columbus's appropriative act, saying,

> What was America in 1492 but a Loose-Fish, in which Columbus struck the Spanish standard by way of waiting it for his royal master and mistress? What was Poland to the Czar? What Greece to the Turk? What India to England? What at last will Mexico be to the United States? All Loose-Fish. What are the Rights of Man and the Liberties of the World but Loose-Fish? What all men's minds and opinions but Loose-Fish? What is the principle of religious belief in them but a Loose-Fish? What to the ostentatious smuggling verbalists are the thoughts of thinkers but Loose-Fish? What is the great globe itself but a Loose-Fish? And what are you, reader, but a Loose-Fish and a Fast-Fish, too?[16]

This passage addresses the predatory commercial and propertied behaviors that undergird American life. In this view, colonization lies on a continuum of predatory and shadowy appropriative behaviors, some of which, as John Brougham underscores in *Columbus, El Filibustero!*, are piratic. Ishmael discusses colonial appropriation, not only by transitioning between the territorial conquest and the conquest of intellectual property by the "smuggling verbalists," but also by framing everything, both material and immaterial ("men's minds and opinions"), as open to possession and appropriation. Piracy, Melville suggests, has a long after life as demonstrated in American expansionism.

Brougham's comedy, *Columbus, El Filibustero!*, depicts the creation of the Americas as a piratic act, and thus follows Melville in his representation of the piratic afterlife of American colonization.[17] Brougham's dramatic conceit is that the discovery of the Americas, structured on the unlawful appropriation of property, has created a nation-state deeply corrupted as demonstrated in its unfettered economic growth and territorial expansion in the mid-nineteenth century. The comedy, set in fifteenth-century Spain as well as nineteenth-century New York, includes a cast which comprises King Ferdinand, described as an aggressive monarch; Don Christoval Colon (or Columbus), "a clairvoyant voyager, whose filibustering expedition gave rise at the time to a world of speculation"; Columbia, a national debutante; and "Members of Reception Committee, Aldermen, Discontented Politicians, Independent Voters, and other natural curiosities by Competent Representatives. Full-grown States, Juvenile Territories."[18] Given that Brougham's play is a burlesque, a satirical or parodic drama with roots in popular theater from the late eighteenth century, it relies on "comic exaggeration, mockery of high culture, and cross-dressing … [and] resembled minstrelsy in its obsessive use of puns, malapropisms, and other comic wordplay, and in its reliance on topical humor" to highlight the absurdity of colonization and unfettered state growth, as well as the exploitative and predatory behaviors endemic to nineteenth-century finance capitalism.[19] Reading Brougham's work in the context of other nineteenth-century American literary treatments of piracy such as Ancona's reveals that piracy is at the heart of the American national story.

Brougham casts Columbus as the first in a long line of successive piratical figures that unlawfully and unjustly seize property that reaches its apogee with the nineteenth-century financier. The language of piracy, in other words, permeates the play as colonization is reduced to low-investment/high-yield marketing, at best, and get-rich-quick schemes, at worst (the "profits enormous, and the outlay small").[20] For example, Columbus's first interaction with King Ferdinand is a conversation about taxes, stocks, bonds, shares, and Wall Street. Ultimately, *Columbus, El Filibustero!* represents filibustering as a failed activity that has long-lasting effects on the economic well-being of an American body. The play ends with an apocalyptic premonition of revolt:

> The plethora of wealth
> Corrupt and undermine the general health,
> I see vile madd'ning fumes incite to strife,
> Obscure the sense and whet the murderer's knife.
> I see dead rabbits—[21]

This vision of maddening fumes and dead rabbits, Brougham seems to insist, is the "return" on Spanish "investment" in the Americas. The fraud and corruption that Brougham critiques is indebted to Columbus's inaugural act of piracy, and yet the quote above suggests that a slightly more optimistic ending to the American story where piracy still results in the creation of a revolutionary state. If the expansion of property rights is a cornerstone of

American notions of the liberal person, then the elimination of property restrictions and unfettered access to property has created the unhealthy and toxic economic climate which Brougham critiques.

Brougham's comedy, unlike Ancona's novel, demonstrates how the fulfillment of the promises of property can have a disastrous effect on the health of the nascent nation-state. The piratic, in other words, is as creative as it is destructive: the piratic helps us trace the creation of new propertied subject and is seemingly instrumental in the creation of an autonomous nation-state founded on the expansion of property rights. However, the demands for commercial and political autonomy allegorized in imaginative literature might indeed result in financial crisis, as demonstrated in Brougham's suggestion that the very piratic sentiment that undergirds demands for independence can very easily slip into the proliferation of damaging unfettered speculative exchange. These contradictions represent the piratic at play: the piratic is neither purely a propertied expression that helps to trouble the powers of the liberal state, nor a lawless behavior in pursuit of private gain. Therefore, regardless of whether the revolutionary American origin story is the one that exists *in response to* unjust, exploitative, and extractive colonial regimes, or a story about the creation of an economically corrupt state *because of* extractive colonial regimes, the American story is a piratic one because it is a story about the creation of a social and political system rooted in ownership of property, as well as in unlawful appropriations of this property.

## Piratic methodologies and poetics

The piratic serves as a model for understanding why certain forms of unlawful property ownership can become the vehicle for personhood and representation. And yet, reading American literary and legal history for instances of unlawful property ownership in which dispossessed persons participate produces complicated and contradicting approaches to the topic of the piratic. For this reason, I want to underscore the importance of the piratic as both a hermeneutic and poetics that helps us reread and reinterpret a range of different written materials, in addition to elucidating the meanings of unlawful properties in the creation of the nation and its normative citizen. As a hermeneutic, the piratic responds to the scant materials present in the archive regarding unlawful propertied and commercial behaviors. After all, the successful unlawful act leaves no trace. Therefore, as a hermeneutic, the piratic requires that we read as much for what is included as what is left out. Though this hermeneutic might echo what we literary critics call "suspicious reading" popularized by Paul Ricoeur, a piratic reading requires that we read a text for how it represents property as well as the subject's attachments to property. In the face of a scant archive about persons who lack the properties of citizenship, putting a piratic hermeneutic into practice helps us read the strategies employed by these populations for reparation and remediation in the face of dispossession.

Literature is particularly adept at making space for imaginative expressions of propertied subjects when they have yet to exist legally and politically. Literature imagines the networks of belonging and recognition for dispossessed populations that exist outside the official channels of the liberal state. Thus, this hermeneutic looks to the gaps and the fissures in literary and historical accounts of personhood, as much as of property, which mimic the gaps one experiences when looking for accounts of the life and afterlife of the black market. In these gaps, a piratic hermeneutic reveals the modes of survival employed by those that lack legal rights and protections by the state. However, reading with this hermeneutic in mind—which looks to gaps, omissions, and fissures within a text's representation of persons who lack rights, recognition, and claims to full membership within a national community—also surfaces a poetics.

As a poetics, the piratic looks to the creative power of literature: it looks to the animative power of unlawful property ownership for populations who have been left out of a narrative of the liberal state, as well as out of literary accounts of persons expressing their strategies for survival in the face of exclusion or even erasure. The piratic is more than a figurative expression of redress for the dispossessed: it is also a mode of reading literature that encourages us to see those propertied behaviors that would otherwise be unaccounted for as demands for redress from the state. This poetics reveals the forms of reproduction, cooptation, elision, and mobility that structure the procedures as well as the styles of illegal property ownership in literature. This poetics also reveals the imaginative practices taking place within literature to create a new propertied community when accounts of these populations are scant. It is in literature that persons left out of the category of liberal person are represented *as* liberal and *as* propertied persons in their defiance of the state. As a poetics, therefore, the piratic surfaces the numerous ways in which subjects are created through literature and a range of different discursive strategies. In this way, by animating persons who have yet to exist legally through a dramatization of how and why certain populations break the law, literature anticipates and imagines the propertied behaviors that can produce long-lasting social and political changes.

## Notes

1 John Locke, *Second Treatise of Government*, ed. C.B. Macpherson (Indianapolis, IN: Hackett, 1980), 19.

2 Hendrik Hartog, "The Constitution of Aspiration and 'The Rights That Belong to Us All,'" *Journal of American History,* 74.3 (1987): 1021.

3 Locke, *Second Treatise of Government*, 90.

4 Ibid., 46, 50.

5 Kunal Parker, "Citizenship and Immigration Law, 1800–1924: Resolutions of Membership and Territory," in *The Cambridge History of Law in America. Volume II: The Long Nineteenth Century*, ed. Michael Grossberg and Christopher Tomlins (Cambridge: Cambridge University Press, 2008), 174.

6 Cheryl I. Harris, "Whiteness as Property," *Harvard Law Review* 106.8 (June 1993): 1707–91.

7 Ibid., 183.

8 In a tradition dating back to Edward Coke, *Institutes of the Lawes of England* (1628), piracy can only be committed in locations where a nation's common law has no jurisdiction. This is echoed in American law in the *Crimes Act of 1790* (*An Act for the Punishment of Certain Crimes against the United States*). According to the Crimes Act, acts of piracy include "murder and robbery," mutiny, and the "felonious" theft of any ship or vessel, as well as the "reception, entertainment, or concealment" of piratically taken goods (Gales, "Article 8 and Article 11," 2275). However, as demonstrated in the judicial interpretation in the Supreme Court case, *United States v. Palmer* (1818), the Crimes Act was too specific and limited piracy to crimes committed against U.S. citizens on U.S. vessels harming U.S. citizen bodies. In 1847, Congress passes the *Act to Provide for the Punishment of Piracy in Certain Cases* which finally expands the scope to include "any subject or citizen of any foreign State, who shall be found and taken on the sea, making war upon the United States, or cruising against the vessels and property thereof" (Minot, *The Statutes at Large and Treaties of the United States of America*, 175). It also includes acts of war or acts threatening the property of the nation-state.

9 Jody Greene, "Hostis Humani Generis," *Critical Inquiry* 34.4 (Summer 2008): 683–705, 695.

10 Ibid.

11 Ibid.

12 Janice Thomson, *Mercenaries, Pirates and Sovereigns: State-Building and Extraterritorial Violence in Early Modern Europe* (Princeton, NJ: Princeton University Press, 1994). Shannon Lee Dawdy and Joe Bonni, "Towards a General Theory of Piracy," *Anthropological Quarterly* 85.3 (2012): 673–99. Hans

Turley, *Rum, Sodomy, and the Lash: Piracy, Sexuality, and Masculine Identity* (New York: New York University Press, 1999). Marcus Rediker, *Between the Devil and the Deep Blue Sea: Merchant Seamen, Pirates and the Anglo-American Maritime World, 1700–1750* (Cambridge: Cambridge University Press, 1987). Marcus Rediker, *Villains of All Nations: Atlantic Pirates in the Golden Age* (Boston, MA: Beacon Press, 2004). Marcus Rediker, *Outlaws of the Atlantic: Sailors, Pirates, and Motley Crews in the Age of Sail* (Boston, MA: Beacon Press, 2014).

13 Rediker, *Between the Devil and the Deep Blue Sea,* 251.

14 No es el nombre de mis padres el que voy a buscar en ese tiempo, puesto que cuando mis padres me lo negaron, es que no me creyeron digno de llevarle. Voy a buscar, señora, el nombre que satisface más al justo orgullo del hombre. Voy a buscar el nombre que se forma por los propios méritos, no el que se toma prestado de los ajenos. Eligio Ancona, *El Filibustero: Novela Historica* (Mérida: Editorial Yucatense "Club del Libro", 1950), 30.

15 Ibid., v.

16 Herman Melville, *Moby Dick, or the White Whale* (Boston, MA: C.H. Simonds, 1892), 375.

17 John Brougham, *Columbus, El Filibustero! A New and Audaciously Original Histrico-plagaristic, Ante-national, Pre-patriotic, and Omni-local Confusion of Circumstances, Running through Two Acts and Four Centuries* (New York: Samuel French and Son Press, 1858).

18 Brougham, *Columbus, El Filibustero! A New and Audaciously Original Histrico-plagaristic,* Cast.

19 The numerous forms of piracy represented in the text include filibustering and privateering, as well as more modern uses of the term piracy to mean copyright infringement on texts, i.e. plagiarism.

20 Brougham, *Columbus, El Filibustero! A New and Audaciously Original Histrico-plagaristic,* 1.1.9.

21 Ibid., 1.1.10.

# 18
# CLASSICAL ECONOMICS

*Eleanor Courtemanche*

Classical economics—usually understood to mean the British laissez-faire school of political economy from Adam Smith's *The Wealth of Nations* (1776) up to John Stuart Mill's *Principles of Political Economy* (1848), including the works of Jeremy Bentham, Thomas Malthus, James Mill, and David Ricardo—has an interestingly complicated relationship to its literary-critical afterlife. First of all, literary writers in the nineteenth century responded to the new prestige of what was then called 'political economy' with fascinated ambivalence, admiring its imaginative scope while deploring the aspects of its abstract social theory they found dehumanizing. Though many authors (like Maria Edgeworth and Harriet Martineau) integrated classical economic ideas into their storylines, others (notably Charles Dickens, under the influence of Thomas Carlyle) declared more-or-less open warfare on its aspiration to calculate human happiness in the aggregate. Second, this hostility to classical economic theory that became identified with literary values was adopted wholesale into much twentieth-century literary criticism, which took it upon itself to defend the worth of the individual imagination against economic values considered harsh and reductive, and against the vulgarity of mass consumer culture. After WWII, this hostility to classical theory was echoed somewhat in the Marxist cultural critique of capitalism, which originated in the nineteenth century in close dialogue with British political economy—but some Marxists, such as Raymond Williams, also saw the literary aversion to economic theory as a bourgeois dismissal of economic concerns. In the West, the Cold War clearly shaped the literary-critical response to classical economics, since the defense of classical economics became increasingly associated with the militant conservative ideology of Friedrich Hayek and Milton Friedman, who sought to extend the realm of economic calculation unboundedly into all areas of public life. (Confusingly, these revivals of classical economics are called 'neoclassical economics'—a school that extends from William Stanley Jevons's *Theory of Political Economy* (1871) and Alfred Marshall's *Principles of Economics* (1890) to Gary Becker and beyond—while the postwar political implementation of these ideas is often called 'neoliberalism,' and is inspired by nineteenth-century political liberalism, which was pro-capitalist.) This perceived combination of philistinism, cruelty, and alliance with compromised political power made classical economic theory an easy straw man for literary critics, who adopted some Marxist critiques of capitalist life while generally ignoring the economic turmoil of the Communist societies of the Second World.

With the collapse of the Soviet Bloc and the end of Cold War around 1990, literary critics turned a renewed critical eye on classical economic theory, this time from a more historicist perspective. The 'New Economic Criticism' (identified in a 1999 anthology edited by Mark Osteen and Martha Woodmansee) called on critics to read economic works with a literary eye as complex cultural documents embedded in their historical moment. While the 2008 Great Financial Crisis might be seen as the end of the Reagan-Thatcher-era revival of laissez-faire that began in 1979, cultural critics continue to refer back to classical economic theory in search of an intellectual origin point for current neoliberal political alignments.

## Classical economic theory: 1776–1848

There was economic theory before Adam Smith (consider the management of the polis in Aristotle's *Politics*, the seventeenth-century mercantilism of Jean-Baptiste Colbert, and the pamphleteers of the eighteenth century), but Smith's publication of *The Wealth of Nations* in 1776 is considered the beginning of what Joseph Schumpeter calls 'the classical situation' (52). Only in the late eighteenth century, according to Schumpeter, does the 'stock of factual knowledge and conceptual apparatus that had slowly grown, during the centuries, in the studies of philosophers' combine with 'the stock of facts and concepts that had been accumulated by men of practical affairs' (52) to reach the 'status of a recognised field of tooled knowledge' (143). Smith, a Professor of Moral Philosophy at the University of Glasgow, was inspired by Newtonian cosmology and French physiocracy to create a unified conceptual system of what we would today call 'social science' that included ethics and jurisprudence as well as economics. His *Theory of Moral Sentiments* (1757) is a must-read for scholars of eighteenth-century sentimentality and the ethical foundations of the realist genre (see, for instance, Greiner 2012). Smith's *Wealth of Nations* was a sustained attack on the mercantilist argument that nations create wealth by forcibly attracting money to a nation-state, either by taxing foreign trade or by resource extraction from colonies. Smith argued that the source of value was not a favorable balance of trade, but human labor—the so-called 'labour theory of value' that was later adopted by Karl Marx. Greater efficiencies in production through the 'division of labour' could create wealth, as in his story of the pinmaker who, working on his own, 'could scarce, perhaps, with his utmost industry, make one pin in a day'—but who, when joined with nine other workmen focused on simple tasks ('One man draws out the wire, another straights it, a third points it,' etc.) could produce 'forty-eight thousand pins in a day' (I, 14–15). Therefore, wealth was not a zero-sum struggle to be settled by tariffs and armed combat, but could actually grow on its own if governments were only to leave industry in peace to maximize its efficiency. Though he wrote before the rise of the industrial revolution in Britain, Smith's famous pin-factory anecdote was later seen as foreshadowing the innovations of industrial manufacturers, which led to the accumulation of vast wealth.

As for the morality of this 'system of natural liberty' (II, 687), Smith borrowed from Bernard Mandeville's satirical *The Fable of the Bees* (1714) the paradoxical idea that prosperity flows from vice. But where Mandeville mocked the vice of luxury spending, the more genial Smith saw the 'system of natural liberty' as harmonious with the wishes of Providence. Smith's suggestion that the system transformed selfish behavior into prosperity as if 'by an invisible hand' (I, 456) provided an elegant, if metaphysically ambiguous, solution to the moral problem of reconciling mercantile greed with public welfare (see Courtemanche 2011: 24–5 for an analysis of this 'troublesome' and 'incautiously vivid' but appealingly 'utopian' metaphor). But Smith's essentially optimistic take on the idea of a natural economic law turned darker as Thomas Malthus, among others, wrestled with the question of resource scarcity. Karl Polanyi argues in *The Great Transformation* (1944) that early political economy can be starkly divided between Smith's Francophile rationalism and the obsession with the failure of the Speenhamland system of outdoor poor relief that characterized every thinker after Malthus, up to the 'scientific cruelty' (86) of the 1834 Poor Law Act. In his *Essay on the Principle of Population* (1798, revised 1803), Malthus sketched out a bleak future in which every increase in resources contributes to even greater increases in human population, leading ultimately to a population crash. Starting from an assumption that both food and 'the relation between the sexes' (12) are necessary for humans, and observing that '[p]opulation, when unchecked, increases in a geometrical ratio. Subsistence only increases in an arithmetical ratio' (13), Malthus concludes that the human population has been kept in check throughout history chiefly by misery and the threat of starvation. (This calculus of subsistence and misery later inspired Charles Darwin to argue that extinction, and not a Lamarckian striving for excellence, is the motor of evolutionary change; see Vorzimmer 1969.) Therefore, the only way of avoiding misery is to delay marriage until a couple collects enough resources to raise children. Although Malthus recommended abstinence for the poor, the suspicion that a 'preventive check' (31) might involve birth control made the *Essay* quite controversial, especially since Malthus was an Anglican clergyman. The stockbroker David Ricardo took a similarly dark view of economic law in his *On the Principles of Political Economy and Taxation* (1817), which argued that rent on fertile land increased as ever-more-inferior land is brought into cultivation, requiring ever-greater labor to extract its value, so that profit is ultimately brought to a standstill. Though Ricardo's work is sometimes seen as a moment when the previously broad and humanist scope of political economy narrows into a more mathematical and deductive doctrine, his depiction of the competing interests of laborers and landlords is also considered one of the roots of Marx's theory of class conflict. Ricardo's theory of 'comparative advantage' (248), in which countries profit by trading commodities in which they naturally excel—the principle 'that determines that wine shall be made in France and Portugal, that corn shall be grown in America and Poland, and that hardware and other goods shall be manufactured in England' (114)—is still influential as a theory of international trade.

Another strand of classical political economy is linked with Jeremy Bentham, famous for his rationalist approach to ethics—including, in the *Introduction to the Principles of Morals and Legislation* (1789), a formula for calculating the total amount of pleasure derived from any action that his supporters later called the 'felicific calculus.' Benthamite philosophy's most 'fundamental edict,' as stated in the *Fragment on Government* (1776), was that 'it is the greatest happiness of the greatest number that is the measure of right and wrong' (93)—a claim greeted as both amoral and dangerously democratic. Bentham was not specifically a free trader, but his work was amalgamated into the growing stream of early nineteenth-century political economy that became known as Philosophical Radicalism, associated with the *Westminster Review*. These Radicals joined with the Whigs in passing a series of rationalistic legislative reforms through Parliament after the passage of the First Reform Bill in 1832. A key figure in the new synthesis of rationalism and laissez-faire that made up classical political economy was James Mill, a vocal ally of Bentham who was also a friend of Ricardo, and whose 1821 treatise on the *Elements of Political Economy* was indebted to the work of both men. Mill was perhaps most famous at the time for his *History of British India* (1818), but later generations know him more vividly as the father of John Stuart Mill, who became a utilitarian philosopher like his father, and whose severe intellectual upbringing is depicted in his *Autobiography* (1873).

Mill's *Principles of Political Economy* became the standard economic textbook until Alfred Marshall's *Principles of Economics* supplanted it in 1890, and can be considered a final synthesis of the classical position, though it also points out the limitations of free trade in several passages that anticipate the rise of socialism later in the nineteenth century. Mill's emotional break from the limitations of his father's strict utilitarianism, as outlined in his *Autobiography*, began in 1826 when, at the age of 20, the young philosopher fell into despair that any of his philosophical contributions would contribute to his personal happiness, and was only rescued from depression by reading William Wordsworth's poetry and Samuel Coleridge's social philosophy. (Mill's later essays 'Bentham' and 'Coleridge' thoughtfully balanced the contributions of these contrasting thinkers.) At this time, he wrote, 'my eyes were opened to the very limited and temporary value of the old political economy, which assumes private property and inheritance as indefeasible facts, and freedom of production and exchange as the dernier mot of social improvement' (100). However, Mill's *Principles* is still grounded in utilitarian principles and the scientific method, though enlarged by inductive observation and flavored by some of the sensitivity to historical conditions that would later mark the late nineteenth-century historical school of economic theory associated with Gustav von Schmoller and Max Weber. *Principles* includes a suggestion that a 'stationary state' of economic development might be a possible 'improvement on our current condition' (113), and rejects paternalist approaches to the plight of the working class, suggesting in language influenced by Saint-Simonian socialism that future improvements will come from 'the association of the labourers themselves on terms of equality, collectively owning the capital with which they carry on their operations, and working under managers elected and removable by themselves' (133). Mill's anti-paternalism extends here to women, arguing that they should not be banned from 'independent industrial employment' (325), a theme he elaborated in his groundbreaking feminist essay *The Subjection of Women* (1869).

## The nineteenth-century literary response to political economy

It is perhaps too simple to claim that all Victorian literary writers reacted with horror to the cold doctrines of political economy, but the Lake Poets' critique of economic materialism became assimilated to many Victorian cultural positions. The radical William Blake attacked 'dark Satanic Mills' (161) in the 1804 preface to 'Milton: A Poem' as a poetic symbol of industrial inhumanity, and though Wordsworth and Coleridge evolved away from their early political radicalism, they continued to attack the Mammonism and cruelty of the dawning age in a mood that was taken to indict the new economic science. In the 'The old Cumberland beggar' (1798), Wordsworth chides the implicitly Malthusian 'Statesman' who 'has a broom still ready in your hands/ To rid the world of nuisances' (51), asking that the worthy mendicant be supported by his neighbors' charity rather than being sent to a workhouse: 'May never House, misnamed of industry / Make him a captive' (54). Wordsworth's lament in the 1806 sonnet 'The world is too much with us' that 'Getting and spending, we lay waste our powers; / Little we see in Nature that is ours' (270) contrasts empty profit-seeking behavior with a deified and spiritually restorative Nature, as opposed to the economic fusion of natural law with the wealth of nations.

Wordsworth's fellow Lake Poets were even more explicit in their distaste for the new science, with Robert Southey describing it as a 'rank, noxious, putrescent, and pestilential' philosophy (Connell 2001: 8), and Coleridge eventually proffering the idea of an elite humanist 'National Clergy' (45) or 'Clerisy' (49) in *On the Constitution of Church and State* (1830) as counterbalance against the monied interests of the state. In his careful intellectual history of this period, Philip Connell warns against reading the Victorian and modern opposition between Romantic 'culture' and Philistine 'commerce' back too rigidly into the early years of the century, when individual authors' loyalties to the leading figures of political economy were often more tangled. For example, Percy Bysshe Shelley famously attacked political economy in his *Defence of Poetry* (1821)—arguing 'we have more scientific and economical knowledge than can be accommodated to the just distribution of the produce which it multiplies. The poetry in these systems of thought is concealed by the accumulation of facts and calculating processes' (695)—and yet he increasingly admired Bentham himself as a fellow 'rabid anti-cleric' (Connell 2001: 217). Many literary writers also embraced the new political economy, most notably in the children's economic fables of Maria Edgeworth, the Anglo-Irish author of *Castle Rackrent* (1800) and *The Absentee* (1812), Jane Marcet's *Conversations on Political Economy* (1816), and Harriet Martineau's *Illustrations of Political Economy* (1832–34) (see also Lana Dalley's 'Women's Writing and the Mainstreaming of Political Economy').

The intellectual fault line between political economy and Coleridgean intuitionism was visible enough to be parodied in Thomas Love Peacock's *Crotchet Castle* (1830) through the figures of the economist Mr. Macquedy and the poet Mr. Skionar. But the most influential expression of reaction against the presumed alliance between calculating philosophers, personal selfishness, and the social disarray of industrialism came from Thomas Carlyle. In 1829, his *Edinburgh Review* essay 'Signs of the Times' cited utilitarianism and political economy as two symptoms of the new 'Mechanical Age' (465), a desperately chaotic but metaphysically thin era in which 'we hope to comprehend the infinitudes of man's soul under formulas of Profit and Loss; and rule over this, too, as over a patent engine, by checks, and valves, and balances' (476). His tone of prophetic moral outrage and social despair struck a responsive chord among Victorian literary writers, especially Charles Dickens. Carlyle's extended essay *Past and Present* (1843) was organized around a scathing comparison between the well-run twelfth-century monastery depicted in Jocelin of Brakelond's *Chronicles* and a contemporary England suffering under the dark 'Enchantment' (7) of unemployment and unreason. Carlyle saw laissez-faire as not just an economic principle but also as a sign of the ruling classes' criminal dereliction of their duty in the face of suffering. Instead of leading to universal prosperity, political economy had become a destructive ideology that reduces every human tie to financial advantage: 'Behold! Supply-and-demand is not the one Law of Nature; Cash-payment is not the sole nexus of man with man—how far from it! Deep, far deeper than Supply-and-demand, are Laws, Obligations sacred as Man's Life itself' (187)—obligations to labor and care for others. (The idea that Carlyle criticizes capitalism for reducing all human relations to a 'cash nexus' is derived from this volume and from Carlyle's 1839 'Chartism,' though Carlyle does not use that exact phrase.) The reductive creed of political economy engenders destructive social apathy, permitting great poverty to persist in the midst of riches—so the nation is cursed like King Midas, who turned everything to gold but was then unable to eat his metallic food.

Since the time of Adam Smith, England had become the world's foremost industrial power, leading to great wealth but also atrocious working conditions and such pressing social inequality that terrified observers feared a violent upheaval—possibly a revolution like the one that had ripped France apart in 1789. However, the 'Condition of England Question' was an intellectual response to a completely new kind of social inequality in human experience—not the product of an entrenched aristocracy as in France, but derived from an employer-employee relation supposedly based on free contract, which led to the rise of a nouveau riche class of industrial magnates. Though this conflict would soon play itself out all over the world, leading to global industrialization and upheaval, it was, of course, completely new to British observers, and they increasingly found the legacy of classical political economy inadequate to their complex and turbulent society. *Past and Present* outlines one possible reaction to this intellectual and social crisis: turning to the past in search of models or moral guides to help envision a new path forward. Carlyle rejected Chartism, utilitarianism, reform movements, and in fact democracy itself as merely mechanical contrivances, fake 'Morrison's Pill[s]' or cure-alls (28), calling instead for a resurgence of moral heroism by the 'new Sovereignty, Industrial Aristocracy' (248). At roughly the same time, the ex-Prussian soldier Friedrich Engels, sent by his parents to manage their Manchester sewing-thread factory, followed Carlyle in deciding that classical political economy held the key to understanding the industrial age—though he came to a rather different conclusion. Early in 1844, Engels enthusiastically reviewed *Past and Present* for the journal *Deutsch-Französische Jahrbücher* (a journal that also published the young Karl Marx, though they were not yet collaborators), declaring it 'the only [English book] which is worth reading' of the whole past year, 'the only one which strikes a human chord, presents human relations and shows traces of a human point of view' (444). But he finds Carlyle's conclusions unsatisfying, showing 'On the one hand vestiges of Tory romanticism and humane attitudes originating with Goethe, and on the other sceptical-empirical England' (461) without actually discovering the cause of the nation's violent inequality. Engels notes wryly that 'In all Carlyle's rhapsodies, there is not a syllable mentioning the English Socialists,' and while he agrees with Carlyle that democracy is an unsatisfying goal, he suggests that it should be viewed instead as 'a transitional stage ... towards real human freedom' (466). Engels's own extended analysis of the great dynamism but damaging inequality of industrial England was published that year in German (later translated as *The Condition of the Working Class in England in 1844*), and four years later, he and Marx proposed their own solution to what Carlyle called the 'Sphinx-riddle' (18) of industrial misery in *The Communist Manifesto* (1848).

Thus, Charles Dickens sometimes sounds to modern readers like a Marxist, with his outraged condemnation of urban poverty and distress—but in fact he was influenced by Carlyle, whose energetic denunciations probably had their own separate impact on the Marxist tradition. Dickens's early novel *Oliver Twist* (1838) had already attacked several effects of political economy, including the Whig-Radical New Poor Act of 1834, which required every recipient of parish charity to move into a workhouse made deliberately as unpleasant as possible to discourage shirking. The depiction of the workhouse as viciously inhumane to children is not only darkly funny—little Oliver's pathetic 'Please, sir, I want some more' (15) being followed by a wildly punitive overreaction—but a powerfully sentimental rebuke to the utilitarian idea that efficiency should be the main goal of charity. A leering conversation between the coffin-maker Mr. Sowerberry and the burbling beadle Mr. Bumble adds to the mood of black humor: "Well, well, Mr. Bumble, [says Mr. Sowerberry] ... there's no denying that since the new system of feeding has come in, the coffins are something narrower and more shallow than they used to be; but we must have some profit, Mr. Bumble" (28). Mr. Bumble, showing off a Good Samaritan badge that he in fact earned by letting a pauper starve to death on the workhouse doorstep, responds that his enemies '"haven't no more philosophy or political economy about 'em than that," ... snapping his fingers contemptuously' (30). *Oliver Twist's* narrator blames political economy's elevation of the principle of self-interest (the motor of Adam Smith's 'invisible hand') for the wardens' coldheartedness, depicting an organized scheme of child exploitation and starvation, from baby farming to apprenticeship, that works perfectly well for the adults concerned, and is functionally congruent with the thief Fagin's motto of looking out for 'number one' (360).

Carlyle and Dickens became friends in the 1840s, and the Scottish prophet's influence on Dickens is probably most visible in two novels: *A Tale of Two Cities* (1859), which drew heavily on Carlyle's *The French Revolution* (1837), and *Hard Times* (1854), which depicts economic theory as an enemy not only of love, childhood, and moral behavior, but also of the imagination itself. *Hard Times* describes the northern industrial city of Coketown as a miserable town allegorically ruled by principles of efficiency and profit—the narrowest axioms of rational secularism combined with the saddest asceticism of Dissent—to an absurdly exaggerated degree. Leona Toker describes the novel as an early intimation of totalitarian dystopia, defined by 'censorship,' 'reality control,' 'regimentation,' and 'surveillance' (468–71). The town is effectively run by the well-meaning but rigid utilitarian ideologue, Mr. Gradgrind, and his evil shadow Mr. Bounderby, a bloated, bullying factory owner who lies about being a self-made man, oppresses his employees, and abuses his much younger wife. Gradgrind loves his children, but is blinded by his habit of reducing every human relation to mathematical 'Facts' (5) and pushes his daughter Louisa into a loveless marriage with Bounderby by quoting aggregate statistics to her about May–December marriages. Political economy is represented as the core of a seamlessly degraded way of life: a way of depriving children of fantasy and play that leads to ennui and eventually crime (as in the case of young Thomas Gradgrind); a way of lying about the need for factory regulations (the local manufacturers threaten to 'pitch their property into the Atlantic' (86) at the least sign of legal action); and a way of building dangerous walls between the classes, as when Louisa realizes that she had never met a worker in person, but had been taught that he was simply '[s]omething to be worked so much and paid so much, and there ended; something to be infallibly settled by the laws of supply and demand' (120). The alternatives to this powerful dark world are, as so often in Dickens, not truly up to the job of grappling with evil, consisting mostly of a traveling circus that imparts the spirit of play to sentimental heroine Sissy Jupe, and Bounderby's accidental death from 'a fit' (221).

Of the other industrial novels that engage intellectually with economic conflicts—Raymond Williams lists Charles Kingsley's *Alton Locke* (1850), Charlotte Brontë's *Shirley* (1849), Elizabeth Gaskell's *Mary Barton* (1848), Benjamin Disraeli's *Sybil* (1845), and George Eliot's *Felix Holt* (1866) (Williams 1983: 87)—probably Gaskell's *North and South* (1855) most explicitly addresses the tenets of political economy. This novel, serialized in Dickens's journal *Household Words* directly after the serialization of *Hard Times*, resembles Jane Austen's *Pride and Prejudice* (1813) rewritten as a novel of ideas about factories and strikes. The heroine Margaret Hale, forced by her cleric father's apostasy to relocate from rural Helstone to smoky Milton-Northern, discovers that she vehemently disagrees with the rough, hardworking factory owner Mr. Thornton about his harsh economic principles. When he argues, on 'sound economic principles,' that 'as trade was conducted, there must always be a waxing and waning of commercial prosperity; and that in the waning a certain number of masters, as well as of men, must go down into ruin, and be no more seen among the ranks of the happy and prosperous,' she rebels against his assumption that 'this consequence [is] so entirely logical, that neither employers nor employed had any right to complain if it became their fate'—'as if commerce were everything,' she thinks, 'and humanity nothing' (152–3). Margaret and Mr. Thornton have long debates, barely masking their sexual tension, about the role of Christian paternalism in management, and the narrative action climaxes in a violent strike in which employers and employees pointlessly inflame each other with disastrous results. The story tries hard to represent each side fairly—Margaret is playfully called a 'democrat' and 'socialist' for what she claims is 'standing up for the progress of commerce' (323). Yet it is clear that fiction itself is increasingly seen as a supplement and corrective to the new economic ideas: either as an ally of romantic Nature, as in Dickens's suggestion that fiction and fantasy lead to greater moral truth than narrow rationality, or as an implicit contrast between rigid economic laws and the density of observation and accident afforded by the form of a realist novel, and, by extension, human experience itself. Following in Carlyle's footsteps, later Victorian sages like John Ruskin and William Morris increasingly articulated an angry resistance to the alliance of classical economics and the manufacturing class.

## Classical economics in hibernation: modernist literary criticism

Laissez-faire policies achieved their peak influence in Britain with the 1846 repeal of the 1815 agricultural protectionist Corn Laws, a great victory for a temporary alliance of manufacturers and the working class, and one that split the government of Conservative leader Robert Peel. But thereafter, the political power of the classical economic tradition was complicated by new movements such as the rise of trades unions, Joseph Chamberlain's 1880s 'municipal socialism,' and Chamberlain's pro-imperialist and protectionist Tariff Reform movement in the early 1900s. The 1880s saw the growth of new socialist movements such as Henry Hyndman's Social Democratic Federation, the Fabian Socialist ideas advanced by George Bernard Shaw and Sidney and Beatrice Webb, and William Morris's more pro-Marx Socialist League. In economic theory, classical political economy gave way to neoclassical theories of value based on consumer demand instead of labor in the 'marginal revolution' led by Stanley Jevons in Britain, Carl Menger in Austria, and Léon Walras in France. Meanwhile, economists in quickly industrializing countries like the United States and Germany (following Alexander Hamilton and Friedrich List) tended to favor protectionist policies to protect their 'infant industries.' Laissez-faire was so far out of intellectual fashion by the 1920s that liberal economist John Maynard Keynes, in his essay 'The End of Laissez-Faire,' confidently swept away all the philosophical underpinnings of the tradition:

> It is not true that individuals possess a prescriptive "natural liberty" in their economic activities. There is no "compact" conferring perpetual rights on those who Have or those who Acquire. The world is not so governed from above that private and social interest always coincide. It is not so managed here below that in practice they coincide. *(312)*

Though novels like E.M. Forster's *Howards End* (1910) continued to stage the clash between money and culture (with the cultured Schlegels asserting primacy after the self-destruction of the philistine Wilcoxes), modernist cultural criticism generally defended the moral worth of high culture against the low realms of mass culture, advertising, and anything having to do with economic thought. F.R. Leavis's *The Great Tradition* (1948) champions novelists who provided 'a challenge to an unusual and sustained seriousness'—George Eliot, Henry James, and Joseph Conrad—and dismisses most of Dickens as the melodramatic work of 'a great entertainer' (19). However, he allows *Hard Times* into his canon in a separate chapter—mostly for its formal unity, but also for its diagnosis of the conflict between utilitarianism and 'vital human impulse' (231), raising it to the status of 'a completely serious work of art' in which 'the inhumanities of Victorian civilization are seen as fostered and sanctioned by a hard philosophy, the aggressive formulation of an inhumane spirit' (227–8). For Leavis, the only morally serious response to political economy is one of relentless opposition to its inhumane premises.

Raymond Williams's analysis of *Hard Times* in *Culture and Society* (1958) strikes a quite different note. As a socialist, Williams is interested in reintegrating the study of economic thought in general back into literary critique, and rejecting the singularity of the 'romantic artist' who is 'indifferent to the crude worldliness and materialism of politics and social affairs'

(30). Although there has been a 'subsequent dissociation of interests,' readers should not forget that 'Wordsworth wrote political pamphlets, that Blake was a friend of Tom Paine and was tried for sedition, … that Byron spoke on the frame-riots and died as a volunteer in a political war' (30–1). Instead of setting up nineteenth-century utilitarianism as the opposite of moral sentiment, Williams sees it in retrospect as an engine of democratic reform and a precursor to state socialism. Implicitly attributing to Leavis the classist feeling that to the 'twentieth-century intellectual … trade, as such, is gross' (93), he chides Dickens for inviting readers to

> condemn the kind of thinking … that in fact promoted a large measure of social and industrial reform. One wonders, for example, what a typical Fabian feels when he is invited to condemn Gradgrind, not as an individual but as a type.
>
> *(94)*

Williams's analysis of the mid-Victorian industrial novels paved the way for much of the skeptical left-historicist criticism of the late twentieth century.

## The new economic criticism

In the 1970s and 1980s, classical economic theory enjoyed an ideological revival in the Anglo-American political sphere. The return to laissez-faire by the governments of Ronald Reagan and Margaret Thatcher was celebrated by a fetishization of all things Adam Smith, but the new policies were more politically aggressive than those of Smith's day, undertaking to dismantle the intervening century's worth of social protections that had been created at least in part in reaction to the first wave of classical economics. Though they wield the language of anti-statism, neoliberal economies paradoxically depend on the state to protect existing businesses and 'construct' consent (Harvey 2005: 39). The prominence of economic discourse in politics—some would say the replacement of political by economic language—was one of the factors contributing to a new wave of interest in economic theory among cultural critics. Osteen and Woodmansee list the return to historicist methods, the 're-emergence of cultural studies,' and growing interest in economic rhetoric among economists such as Deidre McCloskey, along with the increasing 'public attention' paid to political economy in the 1980s, including 'discussions of interest rates, stock market speculation, takeovers, leveraged buy-outs, and so on,' as influences on what in the introduction to their 1999 anthology they term 'the new economic criticism' (4). Rather than assuming that opposition is the only thoughtful response to classical political economy, the new historically-inflected critics teased apart various strands of classical and neoclassical economic theories that had previously been left to economics departments. Note the contrast between Igor Webb in 1981—

> although Smith perceived labor as the source of value, it was difficult for him fully to realize the implications of this perception, because he could not, at heart, think in any terms but those of sales, prices, purchases, and gold,
>
> *(31)*

which is a crude caricature of Smith's social theory—and Regenia Gagnier and John Dupré's more subtle 1999 argument that classical political economy had included 'insight into social relations,' care for the 'negative consequences of the division of labour,' and a disinclination to accept markets as 'the end of history' that were erased from economic theory with the turn to neoclassicism (402–3).

Other important New Historical, new economic, or post-Foucauldian responses to the heritage of classical economic theory include Gagnier's *The Insatiability of Human Wants* (2000), Mary Poovey's *A History of the Modern Fact* (2005), and Catherine Gallagher's *The Body Economic* (2005), as well as Connell's *Romanticism, Economics, and the Question of 'Culture'* (2001). In a parallel movement, Victorianist scholars reclaimed the liberalism and skeptical epistemology of John Stuart Mill as part of a reconsideration of the Victorian realist novel in works such as Amanda Anderson's *The Powers of Distance* (2001) and Lauren Goodlad's *Victorian Literature and the Victorian State* (2003). Since the New Economic Criticism is premised on the desire to overcome the concern that 'most literary critics' knowledge of economics begins and ends with Karl Marx' (Osteen and Woodmansee 1999: 12), and is very much a post-Cold-War attempt to think beyond the twentieth-century opposition between capitalism and communism, it will be interesting to see how much of that historicist mood persists into the post-2008, post-Great Financial Crisis critical moment, which has seen a resurgence of interest in Marx and Marxist economics.

## References

Bentham, Jeremy. (1891). *A Fragment on Government*. Oxford: Clarendon Press.

Blake, William. (2008). *Selected Poetry*. Oxford: Oxford University Press.

Carlyle, Thomas. (1965). *Past and Present*. Boston, MA: Houghton Mifflin.

Carlyle, Thomas. (1869). "Signs of the Times" in *Critical and Miscellaneous Essays, Vol. 1*. New York: Lovell, Corvell.

Coleridge, Samuel Taylor. (1839). *On the Constitution of the Church and State: According to the idea of each*. London: Pickering.

Connell, Philip. (2001). *Romanticism, Economics, and the Question of 'Culture'*. Oxford: Oxford University Press.

Courtemanche, Eleanor. (2011). *The 'Invisible Hand' and British Fiction, 1818–1860: Adam Smith, Political Economy, and the Genre of Realism*. Basingstoke: Palgrave Macmillan.

Dickens, Charles. (2001). *Hard Times, for These Times*. New York, Norton.

Dickens, Charles. (2003). *Oliver Twist, or, the Parish Boy's Progress*. Harmondsworth: Penguin.

Engels, Friedrich. (1975). '*The condition of England: Past and present* by Thomas Carlyle, London, 1843' in *Karl Marx Frederick Engels Collected Works, Vol. 3*. New York: International Publishers.

Gagnier, Regenia, and John Dupré. (1999). 'Reply to Amariglio and Ruccio's "Literary-Critical 'economies', economic discourse, and the question of Marxism"' in Mark Osteen and Martha Woodmansee (ed.) *The New Economic Criticism: Studies at the Interface of Literature and Economics*. London: Routledge.

Gaskell, Elizabeth. (1995). *North and South*. Harmondsworth: Penguin.

Greiner, Rae. (2010). *Sympathetic Realism in Nineteenth-Century British Fiction*. Baltimore, MD: Johns Hopkins University Press.

Harvey, David. (2005). *A Brief History of Neoliberalism*. Oxford: Oxford University Press.

Keynes, John Maynard. (1963). 'The end of laissez-faire' in *Essays in Persuasion*. New York: Norton.

Leavis, Frank Raymond. (1948). *The Great Tradition: George Eliot, Henry James, Joseph Conrad*. New York: G.W. Stewart.

Malthus, Thomas. (2004). *An Essay on the Principle of Population*. Oxford: Oxford University Press.

Mill, John Stuart. (1969). *Autobiography*. Boston, MA: Houghton Mifflin.

Mill, John Stuart. (1970). *Principles of Political Economy: Books IV and V*. Harmondsworth: Penguin.

Osteen, Mark and Martha Woodmansee. (1999). *The New Economic Criticism: Studies at the Interface of Literature and Economics*. London: Routledge.

Polanyi, Karl. (2001). *The Great Transformation*. Boston, MA: Beacon.

Ricardo, David. (1922). *Principles of Political Economy and Taxation*. London: Bell and Sons.

Schumpeter, Joseph A. (1954). *History of Economic Analysis*. New York: Oxford University Press.

Shelley, Percy Bythe. (2003). "The defence of poetry" in *The Major Works*. Oxford: Oxford University Press.

Smith, Adam. (1979). *An Inquiry into the Nature and Causes of the Wealth of Nations*. 2 vols. Oxford: Clarendon Press. Reprinted Indianapolis, IN: Liberty Fund.

Toker, Leona. (2001). '*Hard Times and a Critique of Utopia: A Typological Study*' in *Hard Times*. New York: Norton.
Vorzimmer, Peter. (1969). "Darwin, Malthus, and the theory of natural selection." *Journal of the History of Ideas* 30.4: 527–42.
Webb, Igor. (1981). *From Custom to Capital: The English Novel and the Industrial Revolution*. Ithaca, NY: Cornell University Press.
Williams, Raymond. (1983). *Culture and Society: 1780–1950*. New York: Columbia University Press.
Winch, Donald. (1970). "Introduction" in *Principles of Political Economy: Books IV and V*. Harmondsworth: Penguin.
Wordsworth, William. (2008). *The Major Works: Including The Prelude*. Oxford: Oxford University Press.

# 19

# CONSUMPTION

## Cultures of crisis, overproduction, and twenty-first-century literature

*Alden Sajor Marte-Wood*

Cultural Marxism, by which I mean a materialist mode of analysis "founded on a rejection of economism" that emphasizes "the autonomy of culture and ideology in social life,"[1] has erroneously privileged an independent account of consumption. In his introduction to Wolfgang Fritz Haug's *Critique of Commodity Aesthetics* (1986), the cultural Marxist Stuart Hall argues for an analysis of the "impact of commodity production on the sphere of culture"[2] and the development of "a discourse which connects with and transforms 'the sensual awareness' of modern consumer society" (4). Such analyses that examine "the distinctive rituals of consumption"[3] view individual and collective consumption as mere meaning-making within the symbolic economy of, redundantly put, "consumer capitalism" – as if each individual consumer were making meaning external to and autonomous from a socially imbricated economic system. The microeconomic focus here on consumption and its relationship to the symbolic economy ignores its structural locus within the real macroeconomy of capitalist development. Consumption, divorced from its economic function in the reproduction of capitalist relations, wrongly becomes an isolated, epiphenomenal object of study within cultural Marxism's account of consumer society.

Mistakenly privileging the autonomy of consumption by occluding its relation to production and circulation encourages a reactionary form of literary studies that has persisted into the contemporary moment. Such limited accounts find solace in the ability of the "contemporary North American novel" to "mobiliz[e] the powers of literary form to capture an indivisible present."[4] Pieter Vermeulen argues that this form tries "to imagine a continuity between the world it describes, the process of description, and its consumption by the reader" (15). By granting political agency to consumption and commending the "provocatively affectless notation" of contemporary novels like Tao Lin's Alt Lit manifesto *Taipei* (2013) and its dehistoricized "commitment to [a] present [...] that is rigorously disarticulated from any past or future that is more than a few seconds away" (19), readings like Vermeulen's inadvertently valorize the capitalist realist compression of historical time within the age of secular stagnation.[5] Against such analyses, I claim that accounts of consumption should be understood within the more totalizing context of capitalism's "permanent reproductive crisis."[6] The stagnant consumer worlds of specific twenty-first-century literary movements like the New Sincerity, Alt Lit, and post-irony[7] cannot, as a review of *Taipei* in *The Guardian* claims, "breathe new life into literature."[8] These literary developments instead embody a stultifying commitment to the consumption of capital's "indivisible present." This commitment reflects the inability of an autonomous cultural politics to account for the shift from signal crisis to terminal crisis[9] within the twenty-first-century capitalist world-system. Part of this inability arises from the dehistoricized separation of consumption from capital's more expansive circuit of reproduction.

In Hall's dismissal of a "more classical 'political economy' of culture,"[10] he actually defines, by way of denunciation, the very position I argue a renewed economic criticism of literature must adopt, as that which

> insists that the economic processes and structures of cultural production are more significant than their cultural-ideological aspect: and that these are quite adequately caught in the more classical terminology of profit, exploitation, surplus-value and the analysis of culture as commodity.
>
> *(70–1)*

Hall argues that within such a resolutely economic framework, the "specificity of the effect of the cultural and ideological dimension once more tends to disappear" (71). Hall's characterization discounts the underlying unity of capitalist totality and the inherent contradictions therein. According to the Marxist crisis theorist Samezō Kuruma, capitalist development advances toward "the concentrated explosion of all of the contradictions of capitalistic production."[11] Understood this way, through a conception of crisis at the level of material totality and *not* symbolic autonomy, the contradictions immanent to production, consumption, and circulation (exchange) conjointly constitute capital's tendency toward reproductive crisis. The focus solely on consumption produces demand-side myopia, which forecloses the perception of contradiction. A determinedly economistic approach to literature only becomes possible (and necessary) when the perceived autonomy of consumption encounters its limit in the "permanent reproductive crisis" of capital, which is also to say that culture can only be stripped of its false autonomy and resituated within capital's more expansive contradictions when material conditions have pushed global capital accumulation toward terminal crisis.

In *Fictions of Capital* (1990), Richard Godden asserts: "consumption cannot be divorced from production."[12] Citing the commodity fetish of Marx's *Capital Vol. I* (1867), Godden continues: "Just to look from the viewpoint of exchange compounds cultural commodification, turning 'the social relations between men [sic]...[into] the fantastic form of a relation between things'" (6). Following Godden's logic here, I claim that a symptomatic interpretation of consumption's aesthetic representation necessitates not only an account of the circuits of "cultural production," but also an account of the mercurial productive relations within the macroeconomy more generally. Georg Lukács provocatively claims that

> in periods when capitalism functions in a so-called normal manner, and its various processes appear autonomous, people living within capitalist society think and experience it as unitary, whereas in periods of crisis, when the autonomous elements are drawn together into unity, they experience it as disintegration.[13]

In other words, for Lukács, in moments when the underlying unity of the capitalist system should be most obvious, the experience of crisis obscures that inherent totality. The post-1973 "long downturn" in the capitalist world-system is now affectively experienced in the twenty-first century as secular disintegration. Economistic literary criticism therefore emerges – both as possibility and necessity – as a *historically specific* mode of perception capable of seeing literature produced during the contemporary moment of capital's globalized "permanent reproductive crisis" as Lukácsian unity. As the literary expression of this historically specific experience of unitary disintegration, twenty-first-century North American fiction harrowingly depicts a new affective and economic culture of crisis: the totalizing contemporaneity of capitalist overproduction.

Colson Whitehead's debut novel, *The Intuitionist* (1999), registers the affective response to crisis in an explicitly historical mode. Combining elements of speculative fiction and the historical novel, Whitehead creates a narrative in which an alternative past consistently gesturing toward a utopian future runs up against the limits of our own increasingly dystopic contemporaneity. In contextualizing *The Intuitionist* as a "main archive" of "the historical present," Lauren Berlant asserts that the novel is "constituted by catching up to a crisis already happening in worlds that are being shaped by a collectivity that is also caught up in making and apprehending the present moment."[14] The historical attenuation of crisis-as-event gives way to a conception of protracted catastrophe that becomes commonplace. Berlant argues that the contemporary historical novel expresses an "intuitive sense of the historical present in scenes of ongoing trauma or crisis ordinariness" (846). Explicitly, Whitehead's novel depicts a profound allegory of the prolonged crisis of American race relations and the subsequent racialization of labor.[15] Implicitly, it allegorizes the crisis ordinariness of contemporary capitalism. Thus, building on Berlant's claim that the contemporary historical novel attempts to locate the "present's origins in the past" (849) by self-reflexively contextualizing its own constitution within "the global culture of disseminated production and localized consumption" (850), I argue that *The Intuitionist* successfully historicizes the present. It indexes the affective ordinariness of contemporary economic crises, precisely by depicting the interpenetration of capitalist production and consumption. Whitehead's novel illustrates twenty-first-century literature's ability to represent and see beyond the demand-side myopia of consumption. By contrast, Alt Lit like Tao Lin's *Taipei* shows that contemporary literature is equally capable of becoming mired in a solipsistic fantasy of autonomous consumption, thoroughly interpellated[16] by the capitalist realist logic of overproduction.

Borrowing from the noir genre, *The Intuitionist* is set in motion by a singular crisis occurring early in the narrative: "An elevator has fallen."[17] In what is ostensibly an alternative postwar New York City after a summer of riots, Whitehead's protagonist, Lila Mae Watson, the first female African-American in the city's prestigious Department of Elevator Inspectors, believes that she has been framed for the malfunction and sets out to determine the cause of the crash. In what follows, Whitehead creates a complex narrative in which antagonistic philosophies of assessment, Empiricism and Intuitionism, attempt to account for the central crisis. Thus, given that "last summer's riots" (23) allude to the Harlem riot of 1964 and Whitehead's leitmotif of elevation and verticality clearly allegorizes W.E.B. Du Bois's ideology of racial uplift, *The Intuitionist*'s foundational crisis is inherently racialized. Yet, to assert that Whitehead's novel is only an allegory for racial tension and nothing more ignores how racialized subordination is constitutive to the development of capitalism itself. Against such reductive isolationism, Chris Chen argues for an "account of the relationship between 'race' and the systematic reproduction of the class relation"[18] that ultimately rejects "an understanding of capitalism as an increasingly inclusive engine of racial uplift" (223). Thus, while the rise and fall of Whitehead's elevators locate the "present's origins in the past" by metaphorizing the uplift of post-Reconstruction sociality and the eclipse of the Du Boisian "brief moment in the sun"[19] by way of Jim Crow, the cycles of ascent and descent also symptomatically suggest crises at the structural level of the economic.

When the novel's narrator, in free indirect style, writes that the "accident resounds in [Lila Mae] still, the final notes of the crash the new background music of her mind" (239), crisis, at the explicit level of affective reception, now permeates experience as the new ordinary. In a novel where "prosperity is an index to verticality" (246), "the future is in how high you can go" (16), and the cycle of "[i]nnovation and regression" (20) is inevitable, the rise and fall of Whitehead's elevators symbolically register the everyday ordinariness of economic boom and bust – the "background music" of Sismondi's business cycles, Kondratiev's waves, Arrighi's systemic cycles of accumulation, and Kuznets's long swings. Yet, such accounts of the oscillation between innovation and regression encounter the limits of descriptive capacity insofar as they are non-teleological. Conversely, the crash of elevator Number Eleven expresses a clear telos precisely in the cessation of the cyclical up and down movement heretofore defining its nature; a conclusive end to constant crises becomes possible only through the destruction of the elevator and the economic mode of production it represents. Determined to understand the implications of Number Eleven's crash, Lila Mae inadvertently generates a theory of crisis.

The Empiricists and the Intuitionists compete to explain the nature of the elevator catastrophe in a definitive manner, analogous to the economic debates between underconsumptionist and overproductionist accounts of capitalist crisis. The Empiricist school of elevator inspection figuratively mirrors the underconsumptionist position of demand-side economics, insofar as the Empiricists are blinded by rationalized logic. The corrupt head of the Department of Elevator Inspectors, an Empiricist, attacks Intuitionism and claims "sometimes the old ways are the best ways" and "Empiricism has always been the steering light of reason" (27). Empiricism is associated with the "rise of safety regulation, safety device innovations, [and] the search for a national standard" (45). The "business of Empiricism" is predicated "on what things appear to be" (239). Empiricism's constricted field of vision, a form of rationalized blindness, recalls Adorno and Horkheimer's caution against the instrumentalization of Enlightenment reason. Whitehead's Empiricists attempt to explain the elevator crash according to a standardizing logic of rational regulation; they are unable to comprehend the crisis at a structural level because their reasoning operates only at the level of appearance. Demand-side economics makes a similar error in attempting to account for capitalist crises as crises of underconsumption.

A precursor to the Keynesian emphasis on the lack of effective demand as a central cause for economic crisis, underconsumptionism emerges out of the Mercantilist tradition, and is most closely associated with the Swiss classical political economist Jean-Charles-Léonard Simonde de Sismondi. Against the tendency toward general equilibrium posited by Jean-Baptiste Say and David Ricardo, Sismondi, in *New Principles of Political Economy* (1819), claims "productivity can decline" when "consumption itself [...] is lessening and thereby is calling for a diminished reproduction."[20] Sismondi's privileging of demand-side economics and locating crises of reproduction in an "inability to consume" (75) later appears, in augmented form, within Keynesian justifications for increasing aggregate demand by way of governmental deficit spending. Marxist crisis theory argues that while Sismondi's approach appropriately moves well beyond the deficiencies of Say and Ricardo, underconsumptionism nonetheless remains confined within an empiricist logic that only apprehends the surface of the structural contradiction within capitalist reproduction. Sismondi's account of crisis suffers from demand-side myopia as it focuses entirely on circulation and consumption, and thus does not intuit a more holistic approach integrating the supply-side economics of production. Marx claims that Sismondi "forcefully criticizes the contradictions of bourgeois production but does not understand them, and consequently does not understand the process whereby they can be resolved."[21] Marx argues that one must move beyond the empirical realm of appearance, the "noisy sphere" of exchange "where everything takes place on the surface and in full view of everyone," and delve "into the hidden abode of production."[22]

Against the Empiricists, Whitehead's Intuitionist school of elevator inspection acknowledges that "there [is] a truth behind" mere appearance (239). Intuitionism's eccentric founder, James Fulton, is described as "hope's last chance against modernity's relentless death march" (238). The Intuitionist approach is depicted as "postrational, innate [...] Human" (238). Intuitionist inspectors like Lila Mae, merely enter an elevator, ride it up and down, and *feel* its current state. Understood metaphysically, "Intuitionism is about communicating with the elevator on a nonmaterial basis" (62). Against the confines of rationalizing empiricism, the utopian Intuitionists understand that there "is another world beyond this one" (63). By the conclusion of *The Intuitionist*, Lila Mae ascertains that the crash of Number Eleven was not due to sabotage or human error; instead, the "total freefall" (228) was simply a "catastrophic accident" (227). Lila Mae finally understands that such catastrophes are not aberrant incidents. The ordinariness of catastrophe becomes intrinsic to modernity itself. On the inevitability of Number Eleven's crash, Whitehead writes: "It's not even probability because it's beyond calculation. It's fate" (228). The Marxist crisis theory of overproduction shares this inherent fatalism.

Unlike underconsumptionism, overproduction theory understands the lack of effective demand to be merely one component within a more holistic account of economic crisis, not its determining cause. Due to the inherent tendency toward intensifying intercapitalist competition, the drive to increase capital accumulation results in the continual overcapacity of productive forces and the overproduction of commodity capital. Underconsumption predates the capitalist mode of production, whereas overproduction is entirely unique to capitalism. Because labor is never remunerated for the surplus value it produces, overproduction eventually encounters a lack of effective demand. In *Capital Vol. II* (1885), Marx claims "society's total product, and thus its total production process, breaks down into two great departments."[23] Department I is the production of the means of production: the fixed capital of machinery and raw materials to be reinvested in the productive process. Department II is the production of consumer goods: commodities understood in relation to individual consumption. The distinction between the two departments is crucial in accounting for economic crisis insofar as the increasing demand within Department I on the part of competing individual capitalists intensifying their productive processes paradoxically results in an increasing general overproduction of consumer goods in Department II which subsequently decreases effective demand. Thus, overproduction drives underconsumption and therefore capitalist economic crises do not originate in the sphere of circulation, but in the "hidden abode of production."

The vertical urbanism depicted in *The Intuitionist* is an overproduced "affirmation of modernity" (14) saturated with "lots of stuff, 360 degrees to choose from and the generous illusion of choice" (17). The overproduction of modernity's crisis ordinariness is mediated by the "generous illusion of choice" within consumer society, or as James Fulton writes: "We conform to objects, we capitulate to them. We need to reverse this order. [...] Nothing we create works the way it should" (38). The need for "a renegotiation of our relationship to objects" (62) implicitly acknowledges the destructive consequences for a consumer society predicated on obfuscated social relations inherent within the commodity fetish. Whitehead suggestively links the advent of the modern elevator with the birth of modern consumer society. In a fictionalized account of Elisha Otis's introduction of the modern elevator to the world at the 1853 Exhibition of the Industry of All Nations, the U.S. Vice President first addresses the crowd with optimistic visions of capitalist modernity:

> We are living in a period of most wonderful transition, which tends rapidly to accomplish that great end to which all history points – the realization of the unity of mankind. [sic][…] The products of all the quarters of the globe are placed at our disposal today and we have only to choose which is the best and cheapest for our purposes, and the powers of production are entrusted to the stimulus of competition and capital.
>
> *(80–1)*

Over a century later in the fictive present of Whitehead's 1960s, the unbridled optimism of a consumer society "entrusted to the stimulus of competition and capital" has disintegrated into the paradoxical rationalization of an inherently irrational system of social organization. Lila Mae ultimately "pierce[s] the veil of this world" (100) and intuits that the singular event of Number Eleven's crash is not the crisis as she initially contended. Instead, the crisis *is* the very ordinariness of a modernity defined by exploitative capitalist relations, gendered subjugation, and racialized oppression.

Lauren Berlant argues that Lila Mae can be understood as a citizen of

> the contemporary US world of economic, gendered, and racialized violence, torture, and death; of secreted political, military, and economic power whose processes are open secrets, and yet whose opening to knowledge does not make them any more vulnerable to contestation or transformation.
>
> *(849)*

Yet, Lila Mae's utopianism is not diminished, as *The Intuitionist* ends with her attempting to finish James Fulton's incomplete last volume, a radical synthesis that moves dialectically beyond both rationalized Empiricism and institutionalized Intuitionism. Against Berlant's crisis ordinariness, Lila Mae affirms that the possibility of another world is not yet foreclosed.

In their introduction to the collection, *Reading Capitalist Realism* (2014), Alison Shonkwiler and Leigh Claire La Berge argue that there "can be no doubt that the economic events" in the aftermath of the Great Recession "have generated space for the creation of new economic knowledge and representation."[24] Expanding on Mark Fisher's characterization of capitalist realism as based in "the widespread sense that not only is capitalism the only viable political and economic system, but also that it is now impossible even to *imagine* a coherent alternative to it,"[25] Shonkwiler and La Berge argue that "the relationship between capitalist realism and narrative and visual representation demands recognition of their mutual imbrication in current conditions of crisis and contradiction" (10). The crisis that ties the ideological conceptualization of capitalist realism and representation into structural conditions of contradiction is ultimately an economic crisis of overaccumulation and overproduction.

Robert Brenner argues that the "long downturn" in global manufacturing profitability initially stems from the contradiction between intercapitalist cost-cutting competition and the vulnerability of fixed capital (the fixed assets within the means of production such as factory buildings, equipment, and technology).[26] Within economies of scale, investment in fixed capital requires significantly large outlays of venture capital that are realized only after a relatively expansive period of time. Brenner asserts that due to the constant technological reorganization of production processes inherent to intercapitalist competition, existing manufacturing firms "tend to find it difficult to adopt specific inventions without significantly altering or entirely transforming their layout" (32–3). Thus, Marx's concept of the real subsumption of labor under capital should be understood not in a teleological sense, as a finite moment in capitalist development, but as an inherently perpetual, crisis-laden process.[27]

Since transforming a firm's productive capacity may not be economically feasible due to the trapped investment in outmoded fixed capital, Brenner claims that older manufacturing firms coalesced into "partly self-conserving blocs" are especially prone to "dangers which arise with the advent of new blocs of interrelated productions at higher levels of productivity, or simply lower costs" (33). When some older firms choose, instead of abandoning inefficient fixed capital, to maintain market share by reducing prices to the average rate of profit set by newer firms with lower-cost output, "the result is to consolidate the situation of generally reduced aggregate rate of profit in the affected lines at a kind of new equilibrium" (35). Thus, the tendency toward overcapacity and overproduction within manufacturing paradoxically reproduces reduced aggregate profitability.

The capitalist realist disavowal of an *other* to the capitalist mode of production results in modes of representation predicated upon, according to Shonkwiler and La Berge, our "interpellat[ion] as economic subjects of various sorts: as consumers, producers, and debtors, and as spectators and as casualties" (7). Thus, twenty-first-century North American literature can be understood as a mode of cultural representation where the interpellation of economic subjects is totalizing and self-recursive. Given that capitalist realism, according to Shonkwiler and La Berge, "denotes the site upon which the limit of the imaginary is constructed" (6), when interpellated economic subjects encounter this representational limit, they recursively turn back into themselves – reproducing and strengthening the ideological conviction that no alternatives to contemporary capitalism exist. This process of normalization depends on capitalism as a mode of impersonal domination obfuscating the structural contradictions resulting in individuation, reification, and alienation. Capitalist realism normalizes the corresponding crises of economy and affective ordinariness.

Perhaps no other contemporary literary tendency embodies the fatalistic, demand-side myopia of the self-recursive consuming subject in capitalist realism more harrowingly than the so-called Alt Lit community. Having emerged in the wake of the Great Recession, Alt Lit is most closely identified with authors and poets such as Tao Lin, Megan Boyle, Mira Gonzalez, and small press publishers like Muumuu House, Civil Coping Mechanisms, and Boost House. *Artforum* claims that Alt Lit, as a distinct expression of social media and Internet culture, "manifests itself not in discrete, re-readable texts but status updates, tweets, digital collages, PDFs that are opened once and then lost among desktop clutter" and it "prizes not motion but the animated stasis of sitting at a keyboard with distant friends and strangers, accruing digital ephemera that occupies space on some remote server."[28] As a genre that privileges animated stasis over motion, Alt Lit epitomizes the age of secular stagnation. At the level of the affective, Alt Lit's animated stasis expresses nongrowth, flat affect, and the perils of self-recursive signification producing multiple "versions" of the commodified self. Alt Lit's economic subject remains fractured, disseminated, reproduced, and mediated by social media networks. Alt Lit is therefore thoroughly and self-reflexively informed by self-promotion, self-publication, self-mediation, and self-consumption. Thus, as opposed to the redemptive speculative–historical fiction of Colson Whitehead, the hypermediated Alt Lit community paradoxically consumes its own ideological overproduction of the interpellated, capitalist realist self.

Tao Lin's novel *Taipei* best expresses the capitalist realism of Alt Lit. The novel's twenty-something protagonist, Paul, aimlessly floats through a flattened representation of twenty-first-century hyperconsumption. The novel is set in the interchangeable, transnational spaces of advanced capitalist consumer society. The haute couture of curated artisanal consumption fuses with Big Box Americana and Taiwanese shopping, as the Whole Foods, Urban Outfitters, American Apparel, Barnes and Noble, Target, and Best Buy stores of New York City and other urban metropoles become indistinguishable from Taipei's Ximending consumer district. To the ire of Lin's many critical detractors, relatively little happens in *Taipei* by way of plot, as Paul's experiences over the course of a year are condensed into a meager past-tensed to do list: "hid in his room, gone on a book tour, gotten married, visited his parents."[29] The nearly continuous consumption of uppers such as cocaine and prescription amphetamines punctuates this negligible year of boredom as the synthetic attempt to stimulate Paul, a writer, out of ennui-laced lethargy. Yet, these attempts never succeed. Instead, *Taipei* depicts the depressingly stagnant temporal experience attendant to the postindustrial shift in U.S. labor market composition toward more precarious forms of service-sector employment – a shift Richard Florida has mistakenly lauded as the so-called "rise of the creative class."[30]

Lin's representation of temporality flattens into the trope of animated stasis which characterizes much Alt Lit. Paul often feels "passively committed to not moving" (11), and when he and the other "depleted" (162) Millennial hipsters of the novel actually simulate movement they unresponsively observe: "we still kept moving at the same speed, when we had no goal" (83). During one of Paul's many uninspired musings on the increasing interrelationship between technology and contemporary life, it occurs to him that "memories [...] were images, which one could crudely arrange into slideshows or, with effort, sort of GIFs, maybe" (118). The GIF (Graphics Interchange Format) becomes a metaphor for life within the ideological confines of Lin's capitalist realism. Ubiquitous across different social media platforms, the GIF bitmap image format compresses, pixelates, and infinitely loops brief seconds of visual representation. Such recursive compression recalls David Harvey's claim, elaborating on Fredric Jameson, that the "other side to the loss of temporality and the search for instantaneous impact is a parallel loss of depth."[31] Thus, Paul's analogy between human memory and GIFs expresses the capitalist realist representation of time as nonlinear, ahistorical, instantaneously immanent, and recursively immediate. The horizon of the future, and the utopian impulse it heralds, recedes into the static compression of the present. Paul thinks

> how forty or fifty years, like windows on a computer screen, maximized on top of each other, could appear like a single year that would then need to be lived repeatedly, so that one felt both nearer and withheld from death.
>
> *(53)*

Here, contemporary life loses affective depth through its infinite regression and compression into a singular moment of atemporality. The life-as-GIF leitmotif repeats throughout *Taipei* as Paul consistently feels "like he'd already experienced this exact situation" (49) in his "self-consciously repetitive life in America" (16).

At the level of economic representation, *Taipei*'s self-recursive life-as-GIF leitmotif symptomatically expresses what Jeffrey Sklansky has called capital's "financial turn."[32] The turn to finance informs an attempt, as Shonkwiler and La Berge state, to "search for new pathways of growth in the face of a declining rate of profit" (4). Overproduction and the declining aggregate profitability in the global manufacturing sector instantiate the privileging of fictitious capital circulation during the "long downturn." The turn to financialization occludes fictitious capital's structural dependence on the future returns of productive labor.[33] Like the looping GIF, fictitious capital's idealized self-valorization as an illusory, closed system of self-reflexivity operates in a fundamentally ahistorical register where the future is consistently postponed and the present is wholly overproduced.

*Taipei* instantiates the capitalist realist logic of overproduction, as Paul obsesses over "increases [in] productivity" (182) and the manic avoidance of "zero productivity" (52). Significantly, he terms his use of ecstasy containing methylenedioxyamphetamine, a psychoactive that enhances empathy, "overdrive" as it overproduces affective desire to the point where he cannot "feel pleasure, to any degree, as if lacking the concept" (203). An acquaintance of Paul's likens Adderall to ecstasy, but "without the euphoria" and claims "[i]t's good for doing work [...as it] helps you focus" (86). Paul's preoccupation with productivity reflects the anxiety of an increasingly precarious labor force within the emergent twenty-first-century "gig economy." Paul's position as a writer with a "lack of [...] long-term projects" (74) expresses the precarity associated with the restructuring of labor within the ideological moment of capitalist realism – a moment where "94% of net job growth in the past decade was in the alternative work category."[34] The reader comes to understand Paul's "nearly continuously high levels of internet activity" (91) as central to the casualization of his labor process.[35] Thus, Paul's fragmented labor becomes an indistinguishable conflation between consumption and production.

The passive consumption of the hypermediated spectacle of contemporary Internet culture and social media paradoxically reproduces the spectacle's very existence. Paul, as an interpellated economic subject, simultaneously produces and consumes himself through the mediation of the Internet. Paul dreams "something about his cube-shaped room being a storage facility in which he'd been placed by an entity that believed in his resale value" (53). This feedback loop, the animated stasis of life-as-GIF, precludes the existence of an outside. As a product so profoundly of the Internet, Alt Lit is a uniquely capitalist realist form of contemporary literature. Its closed system of consumption forms the recursive conditions for its production. While earlier literary representations of indifferent consumption, such as Bret Easton Ellis's *Less Than Zero* (1985), also express passive nihilism, only the literature of capitalist realism, and its totalizing mediation by the Internet, ideologically engages in the paradoxical overproduction and hyperconsumption of the interpellated self.

Berlant insists on "capitalism's refusal of futurity in an overwhelmingly productive present."[36] Alt Lit, as a capitalist realist literary movement, represents this refusal through the valence of an apathetic, self-destructive, consumer society mediated by the Internet and structured by overproduction. Here, capitalist realist subjects produce and consume their interpellation within the macroeconomic "imbalances of production and consumption, which underlie the tendency to crisis."[37] Yet here we encounter the limits of capitalist realist ideology insofar as its culture of crisis is never completely normalized or stationary. Such foreclosed despondency only exists within the determinate space of cultural–ideological production and the symbolic economy. As Whitehead shows, the reproductive crisis immanent to the contradictions within the twenty-first-century capitalist mode of production can also generate a space for emancipatory potentiality. Instead of occluding the utopian horizon, crisis sets it in stark relief. Capitalist realism shares with *Taipei*'s protagonist an "inability to recognize anything" which subsequently begins "to feel like a failure of imagination" (34). Crisis ordinariness is, in fact, precisely a failure of the utopian imagination. Accounts of twenty-first-century literature that move past the demand-side myopia of consumption and the concomitant stasis of ideological overproduction can therefore gesture beyond the illusory limits imposed by capitalist realism.

## Notes

1 Dworkin, Dennis. *Cultural Marxism in Postwar Britain: History, the New Left, and the Origins of Cultural Studies*. Duke UP, 1997, p. 4.
2 Hall, Stuart. Introduction. *Critique of Commodity Aesthetics: Appearance, Sexuality and Advertising in Capitalist Society*, by Wolfgang Fritz Haug, Polity Press, 1986, p. 2.; hereafter cited parenthetically.
3 Hebdige, Dick. *Subculture: The Meaning of Style*. Routledge, 1979, p. 103.
4 Vermeulen, Pieter. "How Should a Person Be (Transpersonal)? Ben Lerner, Roberto Esposito, and the Biopolitics of the Future." *Political Theory* Original Manuscript (2016): 1–23, p. 4; hereafter cited parenthetically.
5 The term, first put forward by the Keynesian Alvin Hansen following the Great Depression and subsequently repopularized by Larry Summers, denotes the normalization of negligible or nonexistent economic growth.
6 Vishmidt, Marina. "Permanent Reproductive Crisis: An Interview with Silvia Federici." *Mute*, 7 March 2013, http://www.metamute.org/editorial/articles/permanent-reproductive-crisis-interview-silvia-federici.
7 For a comprehensive account of the New Sincerity and post-irony see: Hoffmann, Lukas. *Postirony: The Nonfictional Literature of David Foster Wallace and Dave Eggers*. Transcript, 2016. For Alt Lit, see the anthologies: *40 Likely to Die Before 40: An Introduction to Alt Lit* (Civil Coping Mechanisms, 2014) and *The Yolo Pages* (Boost House, 2014).
8 Holloway, Dan. "Why Tao Lin's *Taipei* can Breathe New Life into Literature." *The Guardian*, 13 June 2013, https://www.theguardian.com/books/2013/jun/13/taipei-tao-lin-new-life-literature.
9 In *The Long Twentieth Century* (1994), Giovanni Arrighi borrows from Gerhard Mensch and defines a "signal crisis" as the "time that the leading agency of systemic processes of accumulation begins to switch its capital in increasing quantities from trade and production to financial intermediation and speculation. [...] This crisis is the 'signal' of a deeper underlying systemic crisis, which the switch to high finance none the less forestalls for the time being" (220/221). Arrighi goes on to define "terminal crisis" as "the eventual supersession of the still dominant regime of accumulation by a new one [...that marks] the end of the long century that encompasses the rise, full expansion, and demise of that regime" (221).
10 Hall, Stuart. "Cultural Studies: Two Paradigms." *Media, Culture and Society* 2 (1980): 57–72, p. 70; hereafter cited parenthetically.
11 Kuruma, Samezō. "An Overview of Marx's Theory of Crisis." *Marxists.org*, August 1936, www.marxists.org/archive/kuruma/crisis-overview.htm.
12 Godden, Richard. *Fictions of Capital: The American Novel from James to Mailer*. Cambridge UP, 1990, p. 6; hereafter cited parenthetically.
13 Lukács, Georg. "Realism in the Balance." *Aesthetics and Politics*. Ed. Ronald Taylor. Verso, 1980, 28–59, p. 32.
14 Berlant, Lauren. "Intuitionists: History and the Affective Event." *American Literary History* 20.4 (2008): 845–60, p. 846; hereafter cited parenthetically.
15 For clarifying accounts of the novel's racial allegory see: Selzer, Linda. "Instruments More Perfect than Bodies: Romancing Uplift in Colson Whitehead's 'The Intuitionist.'" *African American Review* 43.4 (2009): 681–98; and Saldívar, Ramón. "The Second Elevation of the Novel: Race, Form, and the Postrace Aesthetic in Contemporary Narrative." *Narrative* 21.1 (2013): 1–18.
16 The term "interpellation" was popularized by Louis Althusser in his famous 1970 essay "Ideology and Ideological State Apparatuses." For Althusser, individuals recognize themselves or are interpellated as subjects through ideology, which is the set of practices or institutions that sustain the subject's imaginary relationship to her material conditions of existence.
17 Whitehead, Colson. *The Intuitionist*. Anchor Books, 1999, p. 10; hereafter cited parenthetically.
18 Chen, Chris. "The Limit Point of Capitalist Equality." *Endnotes 3: Gender, Race, Class and Other Misfortunes*, 2013, 202–23, p. 203; hereafter cited parenthetically.
19 Du Bois, W.E.B. *Black Reconstruction in America*. The Free Press, 1935, p. 30.
20 Simonde de Sismondi, J. C. L. *New Principles of Political Economy*. (Vol.1, Books 1 & 2 only). Trans. John S. Vertegaal, 1819, p. 75; hereafter cited parenthetically. www.vcn.bc.ca/~vertegaa/sismondi.pdf
21 Marx, Karl. *Karl Marx: Selected Writings*. Ed. David McLellan. Oxford UP, 2000, p. 449.
22 Marx, Karl. *Capital Volume I*. Trans. Ben Fowkes. Penguin Books, 1990, p. 279.

23 Marx, Karl. *Capital Volume II*. Trans. David Fernbach. Penguin Books, 1992, p. 471.
24 Shonkwiler, Alison and Leigh Claire La Berge. *Reading Capitalist Realism*. University of Iowa Press, 2014, p. 7; hereafter cited parenthetically.
25 Fisher, Mark. *Capitalist Realism: Is There No Alternative?* Zero Books, 2009, p. 2.
26 Brenner, Robert. *The Economics of Global Turbulence: The Advanced Capitalist Economies from Long Boom to Long Downturn, 1945–2005*. Verso, 2006, p. 32; hereafter cited parenthetically.
27 Marx defines the formal and real subsumption of labor under capital in "Results of the Direct Production Process" (1864). The distinction, between formal and real, is initially temporal in Marx's definition: when capital first takes over existing labor processes, this is formal subsumption. Real subsumption occurs when capital transforms social relations and labor processes in its own image to suit its own needs. Here, the change from formal to real is seen as perpetual and crisis-laden.
28 Droitcour, Brian. "Brian Droitcour." *Artforum*, 9 Dec. 2012, www.artforum.com/slant/id=37709.
29 Lin, Tao. *Taipei*. Vintage, 2013, p. 237; hereafter cited parenthetically.
30 Florida, Richard. *The Rise of the Creative Class*. Basic Books, 2012.
31 Harvey, David. *The Condition of Postmodernity*. Blackwell, 1989, p. 58.
32 Sklansky, Jeffrey. "Labor, Money, and the Financial Turn in the History of Capitalism." *Labor: Studies in Working-Class History* 11.1 (2014): 23–46.
33 Against accounts that claim financialization is an inherently new, post-1970s phenomenon, I follow Giovanni Arrighi's claim in *The Long Twentieth Century* (1994) that "financial expansions are taken to be symptomatic of a situation in which the investment of money in the expansion of trade and production no longer serves the purpose of increasing the cash flow to the capitalist stratum as effectively as pure financial deals can" (8–9). Such moments of expansion signal the shift from a production-centered (material) phase to a circulation-centered (finance) phase within one Arrighian systemic cycle of accumulation (SCA).
34 Krueger, Alan as quoted in Dan Kopf, "Almost All the US Jobs Created since 2005 are Temporary." *Quartz*, 5 Dec. 2016, http://www.qz.com/851066/almost-all-the-10-million-jobs-created-since-2005-are-temporary/. I am indebted to Annie McClanahan for bringing this article to my attention.
35 Lin and Mira Gonzalez published a literary collection in 2015 titled: *Selected Tweets* (SF/LD Books).
36 Berlant, Lauren. *Cruel Optimism*. Duke UP, 2011, p. 189.
37 Clarke, Simon. "The Marxist Theory of Overaccumulation and Crisis." *Science & Society* 54.4 (1990/1991): 442–67, p. 454.

# 20
# CORPORATE SPACE

*Robbie Moore*

The incorporated joint-stock company, ancestor of the modern corporation, developed slowly and unevenly in Victorian Britain. Its emergence as a business form and as a legal form was controversial, contested, and not at all inevitable; it was not the product of an emergent liberal–capitalist consensus, nor an urgent economic necessity (Ireland 2010; Loftus 2009; Taylor 2006). In 1844, there were only 947 joint-stock companies in England, and by 1885, after decades of corporate law liberalization, such companies only represented between 5% and 10% of all English business organizations (Johnson 2006, p. 219). Nonetheless, the incorporated joint-stock company was a persistent source of cultural anxiety. As an impersonal vehicle for transacting business beyond the boundaries of a knowable community, the incorporated joint-stock company collaborated in the incomplete and fitful disentanglement of business from personal relationships, personal character, and personal responsibility.

One dimension of this disentanglement was spatial. Corporate space – or architecture financed and managed by joint-stock companies – marked a decisive break from the small-scale, local, and domestic architectural forms of an earlier business paradigm. From inn to hotel, shop to department store, banking house to grand banking hall, and domestic office to city office block, joint-stock capital was contributing to the specialization, rationalization, and densification of British urban environments in the middle decades of the nineteenth century. What was new about these spaces was not only their occlusion of the domestic, their scale, their capital intensity, their urban presence, and their frequent adoption of a cellular and departmentalized plan: corporate spaces were also a new form of self-representation for Victorian businesses. Mark McGurl (1996), writing on interwar American radio and film corporations in a very different period of corporate history, argues that architectural self-representation 'was a way for the corporation to lay visible claim to a privileged, indeed dominating, place on the landscape,' as well as 'a way to quell the corporation's anxieties about its odd identic status as a legal fiction.' Architecture provided a means for the 'body of business, corporeal but invisible, to convince itself of the "reality" and sturdiness of its own existence.' But the materialization of fictional corporeality was accompanied by an 'anxiety of embodiment. To be visible is, after all, to be … a glaring target: of public criticism, or federal antitrust legislation, or the actions of organized labor.' (p. 417)

The politics and ontological anxieties of the interwar corporation were distinct from their Victorian predecessors, especially because of the developing legal definition of corporate personality. But the nascent Victorian corporation, gradually coming into focus as a legal person, also labored under an identity crisis, with its political status, its legality, and its morality called into question. Corporate spaces furnished the Victorian corporation with a concrete form and identity. In turn, Victorian culture apprehended the corporation through the architectural spaces it built. Investors, customers, legislators, and critics all read the corporation through its spaces. And space allowed writers of fiction to materially figure the tensions and contradictions of the corporate form. This chapter considers Dickens's navigation of corporate space, and the way in which corporate space challenged the meaning-making apparatus of the novel itself.

Pre-corporate capitalism was a family affair: small partnerships and family firms predominated, particularly in manufacturing. By law, partnerships were regarded as voluntary associations of individuals rather than as singular corporate entities. These individuals were bound together in relations of mutual obligation. The partnership doctrine of mutual agency meant that any partner could sign a contract that was binding on all partners; any partner could take and use the property of the partnership without consultation; and all partners were liable down to their 'last shilling and acre' for the debts incurred by all. One could not be a passive *rentier* in a partnership without submitting to the risk of bankruptcy if the firm failed. Private wealth, as well as personal reputation, could be stripped away for one's public misdeeds and misfortunes. The intention, at least, was to provoke careful vetting, active involvement, and personal responsibility by all members (Ireland 2010, pp. 840–1). Operating within local networks, partnerships and family businesses were grounded on personal relationships and personal character. Transactions were underpinned by the perception of one's 'moral collateral' (Collini 1991, p. 106). During the 1853–4 Royal Commission on limited liability, Commissioner Kirkman Daniel Hodgson reiterated the common trope linking character to credit-worthiness: 'It must always be recollected that the capital of a house is only one ingredient in the credit it enjoys; conduct, prudence, character … are all included in the phrase "in first rate credit"' (p. 36). In the first decades of the nineteenth century, 'character,' 'responsibility,' and 'liability' were all double-edged terms: simultaneously moral and economic, they expressed a continuity between private and public activities (Miller 1994, p. 143). The 'character' of a business, then, was the sum total of the character of its individual owners. As Davidoff and Hall have suggested, 'the personality of the entrepreneur, or partners, *was* the firm' (2002, p. 200).

Just as these partnerships assumed a continuity between private and public selves, so places of business were not clearly distinguished from domestic spaces. Purpose-built offices only began to appear in the City of London from the 1830s. The architect and surveyor Edward I'Anson, a major figure in the Victorian remodeling of the City, noted that when he

> first began to build on the new London Bridge approaches, previous to 1840, city offices as now constructed were not thought of; the houses were built as shops and dwellings, or as warehouses, and it was the same in Moorgate Street.
>
> *(1873, p. 43)*

The Bank of England, for instance, remained the only purpose-built banking establishment in the Moorgate financial zone until the joint-stock London and Westminster Bank opened its headquarters in 1838 (Black 2000, pp. 358–9). Before purpose-built offices, an office 'still usually referred to kitchens and outbuildings, the working part of an estate or large house,' and a merchant's 'counting house' was merely a room attached to their dwelling (Davidoff and Hall 2002, p. 232). Even nominally commercial buildings doubled as domestic quarters:

> men in clerical or managerial positions were often expected to live above or behind the office, guarding the premises as well as being available around the clock. Their wives would be responsible for cleaning and running the buildings and often prepared the midday meal for the senior partners.
>
> *(Davidoff and Hall 2002, p. 267)*

Businesses thereby reproduced and reinforced familial social relations. Business rooms themselves were inflected with the familial: before the 1830s, London's private 'banking houses' resembled discreet Georgian town houses, with everyday business taking place at the shop counter, and personal business taking place in private parlors modeled on domestic drawing rooms (Black 2000, pp. 356–7). The drawing room, a traditionally feminine space that mediated between private domesticity and public sociability, was here deployed as a means of privatizing the circulation of capital, of welcoming it indoors, away from the masculine tumult of publicity. Black argues that the modesty and domestic scale of these spaces were allegorical expressions of the private banker's discretion and prudence. For Taylor, too, private banking houses were 'in several ways expressive of the personality of the banker' (2006, p. 35). The built environment therefore acted as a means of projecting private values into the public sphere, while drawing public business back into the moral realm of the interior.

The rhetorical continuity between public and private, space and character, and character and credit, began to founder in the 1830s and 40s, with the growing visibility of joint-stock companies. These companies, in their mature form, were associations composed of a relatively large number of members with more or less freely transferable shares (Ireland 1996, p. 42). They were officially prohibited before 1825: the Bubble Act (1720), passed in response to the speculative exuberance of the South Sea Bubble, made it illegal to raise, transfer, or assign transferable stock, or to act as a corporate body, without approval from parliament or the Crown. Nonetheless, unauthorized joint-stock companies began to bubble up in the first decades of the nineteenth century, led by banking and insurance schemes (Taylor 2006, pp. 94–105). In this period, they often traded as unincorporated companies, still technically subject to the law of partnership. Some were legitimate enterprises undertaking real economic activity, but the haziness of the law encouraged dubious promoters and outright scams, including a series of high-profile insurance frauds in the early 1840s.

The company law reforms of 1825 (repealing the Bubble Act) and 1844 (the Joint-stock Companies Act, allowing joint-stock companies to incorporate through registration) were designed to bring joint-stock companies into the light and to set them on a firmer legal footing (Taylor 2006, pp. 135–43). The upshot of these Acts was that the *economic* form of the joint-stock company coalesced with the *legal* form of incorporation, to produce an impersonal entity with transferable shares – the ancestor of the modern corporation (Ireland 1996, pp. 42–5). Separating ownership from management, such companies no longer required intimate bonds of trust as the basis for investment. Investors could step in or out at will. Unlike a partnership, which could be wound up upon the death or bankruptcy of a partner, incorporated companies enjoyed perpetual succession, or the ability to outlive any changes to its membership.

In extending the privilege of incorporation, the 1844 Act was animated by a desire to undergird the connection between character and credit. The reforms tried to distinguish and make visible the good and bad characters of legitimate and fraudulent firms for the benefit of vulnerable shareholders – or as *The Times* phrased it, 'to preclude the growth and to detect the knavery of those fictitious and scheming adventures, which, under the guise and name of trading companies, are continually being devised' ('Parliamentary Intelligence' 1844, p. 4).

But this distinction was increasingly difficult to make. In early joint-stock ventures, the lack of regulation, the anonymity and fluidity of directorship, and the proliferation of nominal partners and passive investors with little personal knowledge of the company's organization precipitated a crisis in the traditional hermeneutic mode devoted to the revelation of a business's 'character.' As the report of the Select Committee on Joint-stock Companies states, fraudulent and illegitimate businesses

> adopt, as far as possible, the outward characteristics common to those of the best kind. They exhibit an array of Directors and officers,—announce a large capital,—adopt the style and title of a company,—issue plausible statements, intimating excellent purposes,—... use some conspicuous place of business, in a respectable situation,— and employ throughout the country respectable agents and bankers. But many of these characteristics are fictitious. The Directors have either not sanctioned the use of their names, or they are not the persons they are supposed to be. Not only is there no capital, but neither subscribers nor deed of settlement.
>
> *('First Report' 1844, p. 4)*

Many witnesses and committee members argued that the hermeneutic mode and its associated system of values could be preserved. John Connell, a solicitor and parliamentary agent, suggested that 'a knowledge of the names of the directors and other partners would lead to a pretty accurate knowledge of the character and responsibility of the company' ('First Report' 1844, p. 73). And indeed, registration of the names, occupations, and addresses of company promoters was one of the major provisions of the subsequent Joint-stock Companies Act – a provision that proved, during the 'railway mania' of the mid-1840s, to be manifestly inadequate. A dissenting opinion was raised during the Select Committee by the solicitor Edward Smith Bigg. When asked about the viability of a public board that could test the character of managers and trustees, Bigg demurred: 'I do not put it altogether upon the test of character, but I take it that money is the ground-work of all the rest; money is the test' ('First Report' 1844, p. 98). The answer was a reflection of an emerging economic reality, articulated by Marx in the *New York Tribune*: that 'in joint-stock companies it is not the individuals that are associated, but the capitals' (2008, p. 185). Whole new ways of imaginatively apprehending the business firm, and apprehending the agency and responsibility that adhered in it, were required. What emerged in these decades was a discourse of 'trust' – or 'the dependence of individuals not on other individuals, but on abstract principles' (Miller 1994, p. 143) – which uneasily coexisted with a residual discourse of personal character.

The hermeneutic crisis precipitated by joint-stock companies extended to the interpretation of business spaces. The Select Committee looked into the most notorious fraud of the period, the Independent West Middlesex Fire and Life Assurance Company: a teetering proto-Ponzi scheme with no paid-up capital and no shareholders, but with 'handsome' offices in Baker Street, London, and with further offices (at least, according to their advertising) in Edinburgh, Glasgow, and Dublin ('The Joint-stock Company Act' 1844, pp. 28–9). The Committee asked Connell, who had visited the Baker Street office, whether the space was 'likely to cause deception to the public': he replied, 'Certainly; if I had had no suspicion, I should have taken the company to be respectable, from the appearance of the office' ('First Report' 1844, p. 72).

Charles Dickens's *Martin Chuzzlewit* (1842–4), serialized in the wake of West Middlesex's collapse, explores the strategic logic of these kinds of joint-stock office spaces. Dickens's 'Anglo-Bengalee Disinterested Loan and Life Insurance Company' is similarly built on fraudulent documents and on fraudulent architecture. Company founder and petty thief Tigg Montague has a grand architectural vision: 'provided we did it on a sufficiently large scale, we could furnish an office and make a show, without any money at all' (pp. 371–2). The interior accouterments of the Anglo-Bengalee offices are arranged to catch the eye of impressionable investors. These objects stand in for, and signify, absent capital, much as a promissory note stands in for legal tender:

> Business! Look at the green ledgers with red backs, like strong cricket-balls beaten flat; the court-guides, directories, day-books, almanacks, letter-boxes, weighing-machines for letters, rows of fire-buckets for dashing out a conflagration in its first spark, and saving the immense wealth in notes and bonds belonging to the company; look at the iron safes, the clock, the office seal — in its capacious self, security for anything. Solidity! Look at the massive blocks of marble in the chimney-pieces, and the gorgeous parapet on the top of the house! Publicity! Why, Anglo–Bengalee Disinterested Loan and Life Insurance Company is painted on the very coal-scuttles. It is repeated at every turn until the eyes are dazzled with it, and the head is giddy.
>
> *(p. 373)*

What is revealed here is a new strategic logic underpinning a new kind of architectural space. For joint-stock companies, whether fraudulent or legitimate, it was no longer imperative to reify personal character in the built environment. While London's private bankers projected discretion and prudence through domestic-scaled architecture, these moral values were almost entirely irrelevant to joint-stock businesses as they tried to drum up willing speculators. The success of joint-stock companies, and indeed the success of scam enterprises, relied on confidence, publicity, and spectacle. They needed to make themselves visible in the marketplace in order to attract and persuade potential investors (Taylor 2006, p. 35). From the 1830s, joint-stock banks like the National Provincial Bank of England, with greater capitalization than most private banks, invested in monumental banking halls in London's financial district (Black 2000). A joint-stock venture like this

> was a speculative venture – a product of the commercial aspirations of several hundred proprietors with no common link between them. The readiest advertisement, the greatest cohesive factor, the most satisfactory source of corporate identity, was a purpose-built bank of some pretension.
>
> *(Booker 1990, p. 50)*

If credit traditionally resided in character, now luxury and extravagance became, in Marx's words, 'a means of credit': 'The actual capital that someone possesses, or is taken to possess by public opinion, now becomes simply the basis for a superstructure of credit' (Marx 1981, p. 570; Taylor 2006, pp. 35–6). Credit-worthiness was losing its moral complexion and becoming instead a public performance of capital accumulation. This new imperative could be seen in the sudden development of 'grandiose headquarters' for London's joint-stock insurers: 'Between 1836 and 1843 the Atlas in Cheapside replete with pedimented cornices, the Globe, the Alliance, the Sun, were all testimony to a belief in the reassuring properties of uncompromising physical solidity' (Kynaston 1996, p. 139).

Following this logic, the Anglo-Bengalee office refuses to signify the continuity of private and public values, or to project moral values into the public sphere. It refuses to allegorize the corporation as a human character. The values exclaimed by this space ('Business!',

'Solidity!', 'Publicity!') are resolutely public and impersonal, referring to economic functions, to the accumulation of capital, and to its visibility in the public sphere. The office does not signify business as the work of individuals, but business as a system. Unattended by human hands, the gleaming technology for weighing, timing, accounting, and filing creates the illusion of the office as an autonomous mechanism. Meanwhile, the office is wiped clean of personal imprints. It is blank, generic, antiseptic: 'newly plastered, newly painted, newly papered, newly countered, newly floor-clothed, newly tabled, newly chaired' (p. 372). This is an aesthetic of corporate impersonality: fittingly, the space imprints the corporate name on every visible surface.

The confusion caused by the West Middlesex and Anglo-Bengalee offices makes visible what Poovey describes as the modern credit economy's 'problematic of representation.' This problematic emerges in moments of social crisis, like market panics, when the 'authenticating ground' upon which the economy is built seems to evaporate from below, calling the concept of value radically into question (Poovey 2008, pp. 1–7). For Dickens, as for members of the Select Committee, personal character provided that authenticating ground and the increasing redundancy of that concept became a source of existential uncertainty.

In *Hard Times* (1854), architectural space helps to figure contemporary anxieties about the indistinct line between personal and corporate agencies. *Hard Times*, of course, is frequently read through the filter of industrial politics, but it could equally be read through contemporaneous political debates about corporate liability which were unfolding in parliament, journals, and debating societies. This is, nonetheless, to read the novel against the grain. Bounderby is a 'banker, merchant, manufacturer, and what not' (p. 19), and his businesses (identified only as 'Bounderby's mill' and 'Bounderby's Bank') are private rather than corporate concerns. In fact, Dickens goes out of his way to render Bounderby as the sole owner and operator. Though his Bank has a 'managerial board-room,' (p. 107) it never appears to be used; actual work is almost entirely occluded in this vast, empty edifice. This arrangement is economically untenable and historically improbable, doubly so, as private banks had been losing ground to joint-stock banks since the 1820s (Cassis & Cottrell 2015, pp. 147–50). The fictional setting of the novel, Coketown, is loosely based on the industrial powerhouse of Preston, and at the time Preston's central financial institution was the joint-stock Preston Banking Company, which boasted twenty-nine manufacturers as partners (Dutton and King 1981, p. 88). Bounderby is therefore a blatant artifice, an improbable condensation of human and corporate functions designed to personify industrial capital.

It is this condensation that links Bounderby to contemporary discourses of corporate identity. Bounderby exists, like a corporation, as a legal fiction: constructed as a single person, yet composed of many. As a personification, the construction of Bounderby is analogous to the process whereby dispersed investors are personified as a corporate entity. This link between the corporate form and personification has been elucidated by Mark Neocleous. Neocleous builds on Marx's concept of personification – the idea that individuals in capitalist societies relate to each other not as individuals but as 'social representatives' personifying different factors of production. Neocleous argues that this process can happen in reverse: that 'personification enables *things* to appear as *non-human persons*.' This process, he suggests, has been 'fundamental to the consolidation of the social power of corporate capital' and came into being via developments in Victorian company law (2003, p. 78). We can read Bounderby in similar terms as a thing rendered as a person, whose ontological status as human is repeatedly undermined. As a businessman becoming corporation, he is an ideal allegory for the transformations underway in mid-century corporate law.

Early Victorian legal scholars were already considering the implications of corporate personhood. The idea of the corporation as a legal person was articulated by the barrister John William Smith in 1834:

> A corporation... consists of several individuals, united in such a manner that they and their successors constitute but one person in law, a person distinct from that of any of the members, though made up of them all ...; for all the individual members that have existed from the foundation to the present time, or that shall ever hereafter exist, are but one person in law; as the river Thames is still the same river, though the parts which compose it are changing every instant.
>
> *(p. 39)*

Yet as Paddy Ireland argues, at this stage, the legal person of the corporation was still perceived as an amalgam of bodies (or a stream of droplets) rather than a separate, singular entity. Nonetheless, this began to shift: first with the Royal Commission into limited liability (1853–4) and the debates surrounding the Limited Liability Act (1855) and the Joint Stock Companies Act (1856). With the introduction of limited liability, each shareholder bore only limited personal responsibility for the company's debts – only up to the value of their personal shareholdings. Liability was no longer moral and existential; it was something that could be traded away with the disposal of one's shares. The legislation, as Poovey notes, 'severed the link between business failure and personal ruin.' In doing so, it finally 'stripped the economic domain of its theological overtones,' since imprudent investors no longer suffered the divine retribution of a debasing bankruptcy (Poovey 1995, p. 23). Importantly for discussions of corporate personhood, limited liability also marked a more definitive division between shareholder and company, by removing the assumption that investors should apply themselves as active agents in company affairs. The company was becoming, by law, separate from its members.

Amidst these legal developments, the language used to describe corporations in legal judgments began to subtly shift. It became less common to refer to a corporation as a 'they,' as a group of people coming together to form an enterprise, and more common to use a singular pronoun, rendering the corporation as a bodiless 'it' (Ireland 1996, pp. 46–7). The Victorian corporation was being defined, according to Neocleous, as a nonhuman person or a 'special legal subjectivity for capital'; a persona allowing 'disparate capitals or investors to act as a unity on the juridical stage' (2003, pp. 80–2). For Paddy Ireland, the Victorian corporation emerged not as a subject but as a reified object: 'not merely an entity with an independent legal existence from its shareholders but an *object* which has been effectively cleansed of them' (1996, p. 41). The implications of this special legal subjectivity were profound: 'In thinking through a new correspondence between institutional activity and personal responsibility, participants in the debate revealed problems within available notions of autonomy and accountability' (Miller 1994, p. 140). This was also a representational question for Victorian novelists: as Tara McGann argues, 'the impersonal agency driving financial markets not only renders the literary figure of the financial villain obsolete but also displaces the individual moral agent and even human agency' (2007, p. 156).

*Hard Times*, published on the threshold of these transformations during the debates surrounding limited liability, reflects some of these circulating ideas about the corporate person in its depiction of Bounderby. Bounderby is an assemblage: his character, in Katherine Kearns's words, is 'dependent ... on localized and temporalized metonymies for the substance by which it displays itself' (1992, p. 869). Dickens draws spatial analogies between Bounderby's bank, his home, and his body: he is at once a self, a space, and a company. Both Bounderby's house and his bank are redbrick structures, which recall Bounderby's own 'great red countenance' (p. 103); both have the same shutters, the same black front door and white front steps, and the same 'brazen door-plate' and 'brazen door-handle' (p. 70), recalling Bounderby's 'metallic laugh' (p. 31) and 'brassy speaking-trumpet of a voice' (p. 19). 'BANK' is written on the bank (p. 154); 'BOUNDERBY (in letters very like himself)' is written on the brazen door-plate of the house (p. 70). The doubleness of 'brazen' – being a category of metal as well as a quality of human personality – suggests that both Bounderby and his buildings announce themselves in tones that are simultaneously thing-like and human. And the human is not necessarily a privileged category in this assemblage: the bank might be considered an expression of Bounderby's personality, but equally Bounderby might be an expression of the bank's architecture.

Bounderby is surrounded in this novel by a Baroque excess of mirroring and doubling. Its effect is to disrupt the moral coordinates of Victorian political economy. Bounderby's private life and business life, too, are mirror images of each other. The bank contains apartments in its upper levels, and Bounderby pays for a shadow family to inhabit them: the widow Mrs Sparsit, who occupies a liminal zone between housekeeper, private secretary, and shadow-wife, taking tea in the evening among empty rooms of office furniture, and Bitzer, who acts as a security guard, spy, and shadow-son, and sleeps outside the bank vault. Bounderby's relationships with both his wife and his shadow-wife break down; only his shadow-son remains at the end of the novel. In delineating these two spaces, the private house is not privileged as the original in relation to the bank's copy; the bank came first, with Bounderby gaining possession of the house when the bank foreclosed the mortgage of an indebted manufacturer. Nor is Bounderby's domestic relationship with his wife, Louisa, more real or profound than his professional relationship with Mrs Sparsit. It is possible to read this as a moral critique of business's diminution of the private self – much as Julian Wolfreys argues that Dombey's home in *Dombey and Son* becomes a department of his business operation: 'the idea of home has been elided, occluded even, by the "House" of business' (Wolfreys 2010, p. 30). But Bounderby troubles these categories, and takes us further away from the certainty of the character-credit dyad. That dyad posits character as the authenticating ground upon which capital circulates: capital is anchored by the human. But now the location of the ground is uncertain: perhaps capital, a *thing*, is the ground upon which the human is built. The ambiguity of Bounderby, flickering between person and object, name and body, recalls the ambiguous form of the Victorian corporation.

Dickens offers two contradictory endings for Bounderby, Inc. On the one hand, Bounderby's humanity is stabilized: he is revealed to have a past and to fit into a web of familial relationships; his mechanical self-descriptions are revealed to be bluster. But on the other hand, his final act in the novel is resolutely post-human. Bounderby draws up a will that endows twenty-five new Bounderbies, fabricating new human as well as architectural representations of himself into perpetuity:

> a vain-glorious will, whereby five-and-twenty Humbugs, past five and fifty years of age, each taking upon himself the name, Josiah Bounderby of Coketown, should for ever dine in Bounderby Hall, for ever lodge in Bounderby buildings, for ever attend a Bounderby chapel.
>
> *(p. 272)*

Turning away from the familial, Bounderby engages in asexual reproduction of the self through the investment of financial capital. The descendants of Bounderby, fittingly, will be persons and things. Their incarnation of 'Bounderby' will be deathless, disembodied, corporate: a precognition of the future.

## References


Black, I S (2000) 'Spaces of Capital: Bank Office Building in the City of London, 1830–1870', *Journal of Historical Geography*, vol. 26, no. 3, pp. 351–75.

Booker, J (1990) *Temples of Mammon: The Architecture of Banking*, Edinburgh University Press, Edinburgh.

Cassis, Y & Cottrell, P L (2015) *Private Banking in Europe: Rise, Retreat, and Resurgence* (Vol. 1). Oxford University Press, USA.

Collini, S (1991) *Public Moralists: Political Thought and Intellectual Life in Britain, 1850–1930*, Clarendon Press, Oxford.

Davidoff, L & Hall, C (2002) *Family Fortunes: Men and Women of the English Middle Class 1780–1850*, 2nd edition, Routledge, Abingdon.

Dutton, H I & King, J E (1981) *Ten Per Cent and No Surrender: The Preston Strike, 1853–1854*, Cambridge University Press, Cambridge.

Dickens, C (1844) *Martin Chuzzlewit*, ed. M Cardwell, 1982, Oxford University Press, Oxford.

Dickens, C (1854) *Hard Times*, ed. Paul Schlicke, 2006, Oxford University Press, Oxford.

'First Report of the Select Committee on Joint Stock Companies; together with the Minutes of Evidence (taken in 1841 and 1843), Appendix, and Index', *House of Lords Papers*, vol. 20.

I'Anson, E (1873) 'On the Valuation of House Property in London', *Papers Read at the Royal Institute of British Architects: Session 1872–73*, pp. 39–54.

Ireland, P (1996) 'Capitalism without the Capitalist: The Joint Stock Company Share and the Emergence of the Modern Doctrine of Separate Corporate Personality', *Journal of Legal History*, vol. 17, no. 1, pp. 41–73.

Ireland, P (2010) 'Limited Liability, Shareholder Rights and the Problem of Corporate Irresponsibility', *Cambridge Journal of Economics*, vol. 34, pp. 837–56.

Johnson, P (2006) 'Market Disciplines' in P Mandler (ed.), *Liberty and Authority in Victorian Britain*, pp. 203–223, Oxford University Press, Oxford.

Kearns, K (1992) 'A Tropology of Realism in *Hard Times*', *ELH*, vol. 59 no. 4, pp. 857–81.

Kynaston, D (1996) *The City of London Volume 1: A World of its Own 1815–1890*, Pimlico, London.

Loftus, D (2009) 'Limited Liability, Market Democracy, and the Social Organization of Production in Mid-Nineteenth-Century Britain', in N Henry & C Schmitt (eds.), *Victorian Investments New Perspectives on Finance and Culture*, Indiana University Press, Bloomington.

Marx, K (1981) *Capital: A Critique of Political Economy, Volume Three*, Penguin, London.

Marx, K (2008) 'The French Crédit Mobilier [III]' in J Ledbetter (ed.), *Dispatches from the New York* Tribune: *Selected Journalism of Karl Marx*, pp. 183–8, Penguin, London.

McGann, T (2007) 'Literary Realism in the Wake of Business Cycle Theory: *The Way We Live Now* (1875)' in F O'Gorman (ed.), *Victorian Literature and Finance*, pp. 133–56, Oxford University Press, Oxford.

McGurl, G (1996) 'Making It Big: Picturing the Radio Age in *King Kong*', *Critical Inquiry*, vol. 22, no. 3, pp. 415–45.

Miller, A H (1994) 'The Discourse of Liability in the Joint Stock Companies Act of 1856 and Gaskell's *Cranford*', *ELH*, vol. 61, no. 1, pp. 139–57.

Neocleous, M (2003) *Imagining the State*, Open University Press, Maidenhead.

'Parliamentary Intelligence' (1844), *The Times*, July 4, 1844, p. 4.

Poovey, M (1995) *Making a Social Body: British Cultural Formation, 1830–1864*, University of Chicago Press, Chicago, IL.

Poovey, M (2008) *Genres of the Credit Economy: Mediating Value in Eighteenth- and Nineteenth-Century Britain*, University of Chicago Press, Chicago, IL.

Smith, J W (1834) *A Compendium of Mercantile Law*, Saunders and Benning, London.

Taylor, J (2006) *Creating Capitalism: Joint-Stock Enterprise in British Politics and Culture 1800–1870*, Royal Historical Society, London.

'The Joint-stock Company Act' (1844), *The Law Magazine and Review*, vol. 2, no. 2, pp. 24–57.

Wolfreys, J (2010) *Literature, In Theory: Tropes, Subjectivities, Responses and Responsibilities*, Continuum, London.

# 21
# CURRENCY

*Kimberly Hall*

As early as eighteenth-century Scottish Enlightenment writer David Hume's essay, "On Money," economists have emphasized the idea that currency is, at its core, a social contract (1742). One that is not simply between the government and its people, but between people themselves. We have agreed that pieces of paper, or strings of code, are a mutually agreeable method of discharging debts and purchasing goods. But because of the fallibility of this social construct, the materiality and nature of currency has also long been a source of anxiety. Whether it's the recent spike in the value of Bitcoin, or the twenty-first-century decision to detach the dollar from the gold standard, questions of authority and authenticity are the permanent shadow of currency.

This tension inherent to currency as a social structure is at the core of three recent speculative fiction novels, *Super Sad True Love Story* by Gary Shteyngart (2010), *Ready Player One* by Ernest Cline (2011), and *The Circle* by Dave Eggers (2013). All present a recognizable near-future world in which currency has become solely digital, and in which the economy is deeply intertwined with forms of social media. *Super Sad True Love Story*, the comic novel by Gary Shteyngart, imagines a dystopian world in which global politics is unstable and digital media rules every facet of individual lives. The United States is involved in murky and ill-fated military operations in Venezuela and the dollar is pegged to the Yuan, emphasizing the economic and political instabilities of the state. At the same time, individuals are publicly projecting nearly every metric of their life, from net worth to emotional states, and even sexual desirability. Although the metrics of measurement seem to differ greatly, the reason for this display is always the same: to capture the attention of someone else, thus increasing one's status and value. The protagonist, Lenny Abramov, longs for the stability of analogue media and interpersonal dynamics, and fights to maintain his moral integrity and burgeoning relationship with Eunice Park as the world they have known disintegrates around them.

The world of *Ready Player One* is also familiar, but in this dystopian vision of a near-future reeling from environmental and economic decimation, anything of any real value takes place in the OASIS, the virtual reality world developed by a mysterious coder and avid gamer, James Halliday. Part Internet and part Second Life, the OASIS operates through avatars and imagined worlds that require OASIS credit to access and navigate. In a quest for an unrivaled fortune, the impoverished protagonist Wade Watts, AKA Parzival, along with nearly every other denizen of the virtual world, is competing in "the contest," a series of hidden challenges left in the OASIS by Halliday before his death. Every aspect of the hunt is made public and faithfully followed by those jacked into the system, changing every aspect of Wade Watts' life when he becomes a celebrity as a result of his skill in the contest.

Similarly, in *The Circle* by Dave Eggers, information and attention have become the most important forms of currency in a future dominated by a search and social media company known as The Circle. The protagonist, Mae Holland, quickly rises through the ranks of the company due to the popularity of—and her enthusiasm for—the livecasting of her every move. Although this transparency has painful consequences for her friends and family, Mae equates the availability of all possible information about individuals as the truest form of both freedom and security. In his reimagining of the total surveillance society first anticipated in George Orwell's novel *1984*, Eggers presents a vision of the potentially totalizing effects of a fully functional attention economy.

Each of these dystopian reflections of our own society imagines the economy and digital culture to be deeply and inextricably intertwined. The consequences of such an entanglement are nearly always negative, primarily resulting from a positivist faith in the power of technology. The recurring trope of instability and crisis expresses a cultural anxiety over what counts as real or authentic in a world that is completely mediated. What each narrative asserts is that the real currency of a fully immersive, ever-present digital world is attention, as quantified by a range of different metrics. Attention is significant because it is an inherently scarce resource and requires that the individual becomes a commodity in order to compete in this marketplace. In an attention economy, the marker of value is authenticity, which becomes the site of authority for this currency. Yet each novel also illustrates how such a currency demands forms of proof, validation, and testing because the marker of value and authority has become both decentralized and ethereal, and those demands result in the deformation of the social relationships that underpin the attention economy. This chapter reads these three contemporary novels alongside monetary theory to consider how the transition of currency signaled in these narratives reflects a larger cultural transition in which authenticity and authority become both the most valued and the least stable metrics of the attention market and require a renegotiation of the social contract.

## The attention economy

In each of these three recent novels, there is a distinct emphasis on the transition away from a fiat currency, a currency that has been issued and backed by a government and centralizes authority, authenticity, and distribution, which results in instability. This destabilization is reflected formally in the fragmented and polyvocal narrative structures, which, like the worlds they construct, transition between a variety of voices and forms in order to compete for the reader's attention. All of the novels rely, to some degree, on the epistolary form—reinvigorated for the digital age—and include on-screen conversations, text messages, and emails within the narrative. This genre directly engages questions of authority and authenticity, which it seeks to answer through its multivalent structure.

*Super Sad True Love Story* is the most directly epistolary novel, and the narrative unfolds primarily through the diary entries of Lenny Abramov and the email and text exchanges of Eunice Park. While Lenny's entries utilize the familiar date and address, "Dearest Diary," Eunice's contributions always begin with the title "From the Globalteens Account of Eunice Park" and are similarly dated, but the format varies. Many are email exchanges between Eunice and her best friend, but they also include text message exchanges between Eunice and her mom, or Eunice and her sister. This epistolary format breaks up the novel into short, snappy chapters that keep the narrative unfolding with a frenetic energy. This structure creates gaps in the chronology as it switches from one narrator to the next that the reader has to work to fill in. At the same time, the epistolary structure also provides a variety of perspectives on the same subject, the relationship between Lenny and Eunice, and creates rich, complicated characters for whom each diary entry or email exchange takes on increasing value as a form of stability in a world being completely upended.

Both *The Circle* and *Ready Player One*, on the other hand, deploy the epistolary form much more sparingly, and their narratives are therefore much more controlled in their pacing. *The Circle* uses third-person narration and a chronological structure, but the narrative is punctuated with email exchanges and messages, which are often offset in italics. Because these messages are interruptions, they create a sense of immediacy and urgency. They are often responses to moments of perceived crisis, such as when Mae's friend Annie leaves Mae nine text messages to ensure that she didn't misinterpret a harmless comment about a colleague (113–4), which results in a reinterpretation of a situation that had unfolded just hours earlier. This technique emphasizes the instability of meaning within the narrative, and the power of any character to use personal perspective to completely recast a situation. The effect is unsettling, but also much more intimate, as these conversations typically employ first-person narration and reveal much more about the characters than is revealed about them in the flow of the third-person narration.

*Ready Player One* also uses the epistolary form much more sparingly, and often to illuminate the relationship between characters. Because much of the narrative takes place within the virtual reality of the OASIS, the dialogue flows naturally between characters as it would in person. But because it is a mediated world, there are also screen messages, emails between players, and lists of the high scorers in the contest for Halliday's fortune, many of which are set off by bold type. Cline's novel utilizes first-person narration, so the message interruptions remind the reader that this world is highly mediated, a fact reinforced by the structure of the novel itself. Like *Super Sad True Love Story*, *Ready Player One* uses short, swift chapters to propel the narrative, but the novel is divided into three much longer sections, which are referred to in title pages as "Levels," evoking the ludic nature of the videogame world. Each Level begins with an epigraph that questions the nature of reality and social norms. The Level One epigraph, for instance, from OASIS creator James Halliday's autobiography reads, "Being human sucks most of the time. Videogames are the only thing that make life bearable" (12). The novel uses such techniques to call attention to its status as a constructed world, dividing a reader's attention between the diegetic and extradiegetic levels of the narrative.

The epistolary form in these novels mirrors the functioning of the attention economy by aestheticizing the flow of attention within the narrative worlds. And these worlds are deeply mediated, reflecting on the increasingly large role of networked sociality by utilizing its primary forms of communication. In this way, both overtly and implicitly, these are novels about the economy, and all three imagine the most important economy of the near future to be an attention economy. As Michael Goldhaber frames it in his early theoretical article on the attention economy, "attention can ground an economy because it is a fundamental human desire and is intrinsically, unavoidably scarce," noting that the Internet is a particularly rich site in which to witness the operation of the attention economy because it "affords new opportunities for capturing attention that might otherwise dissipate" (1997). In other words, networked sociality is so powerful because it is both the site and the record of transactions within the attention economy, just as the novelistic reflection of this economic flow renders them as digital epistolary exchanges.

One of the critiques of this theory of the attention economy is that attention cannot be equated to currency because it cannot be stored and transferred to discharge debts as can other forms of currency. But as Goldhaber notes, money is not obsolete in an attention economy, it is simply secondary; "Below this primary exchange will flow the less important exchange of goods and materials" (1997). Meaning that fiat currency, such as the dollar, still plays a role in the attention economy, but attention is more valuable precisely because it isn't issued from a central authority, such as the state, but flows and accrues among and between individuals and corporations, making it the more accurate marker of value. This reordering of the role of currency is also echoed in monetary theory, which works to call attention to the nature of money and markets as social structures. As philosopher Georg Simmel asserts, "we live in a world of values which arranges the content of reality in an autonomous order," suggesting that markets are such powerful metaphorical tools because values shape reality to its form (2004: 57). And as David Hume notes, "Money is nothing but the representation of labour and commodities, and serves only as a method of rating or estimating them" (1742: 285), highlighting the fact that currency is simply a visible marker of perceived value, just as records of attention are within the attention economy.

## Authority

Although the workings of the attention economy have become somewhat normalized, both in our current moment and in narrative representation, there is also a corresponding anxiety about forms of authority within this economy because it operates outside of, or in addition to, a fiat system of currency in the flow of authority When dealing with a fiat currency, such as the dollar, the bill is backed or guaranteed by the United States government and is minted in government-controlled facilities so that when it is in circulation, that currency becomes a guarantee of the authority and the authenticity of the government that issued it. As economist Georg Knapp notes, "money is a creation of law…it is a creation the legislative activity of the State, a creation of legislative policy" (1924: 40). Currency, then, doesn't simply serve an economic function; it has a significant legislative and social function. By issuing the currency that can be used to discharge debts, the government becomes the guarantor and authenticator; it is through this currency that all obligations must be fulfilled.

But even fiat currencies have been the site of deep anxiety about authority. For instance, when President Franklin Delano Roosevelt first took the United States off the gold standard in 1933 for national transactions, and then President Nixon abandoned the gold standard internationally in 1971, these moments marked a change not only in the measurement of value, but in the authority of the currency to stand, on its own, as a marker of value (Bell 2001: 153). Similarly, the 2002 adoption of the Euro as the legal currency of nearly every member country of the European Union was initially met with skepticism and reservations, but an organized and methodical transition relying heavily on banks and merchants allowed the abolition of former currency as quickly as February 2002 (Lotz and Rochteau 2002: 582–3). In terms of Modern Money Theory, these moments of transition, although wracked with doubt and uncertainty, succeeded in no small part because of the state authority from which such a transition was demanded.

What the transitions in currency signify is a change in the site and marker of authority within a larger social system. In the contemporary moment, such a material change is underway as well. As Benjamin Cohen notes in 2001,

> as electronic commerce (e-commerce) expands, it seems only a matter of time before various innovative forms of money, based on digital date and issued by private market actors, begin to substitute in one way or another for state-sanctioned banknotes…as customary means of payment.
>
> *(2001: 197–8)*

Even in this Web 1.0 moment, Cohen predicted that it was consumer preferences, rather than government policy, that would give way to a new currency, as has occurred with the meteoric rise in value of cryptocurrency, such as Bitcoin (Matonis 2013). As earlier transitions illustrate, the introduction of new forms of currency was driven by macroeconomic policy demands and supported by orchestrated government efforts.

Within the attention economy, currency is even more complex, because, as the novels make clear, fiat currency still serves a crucial function, but money is not the direct mode of exchange between a viewer and a content producer. Instead, there is a different system in place that makes visible the credits and debts system, and that is the metrics of engagement. In social media, this is signified by views, hits, likes, retweets, or shares. Because attention is the commodity that all producers are competing for, some signification of that attention in these visible, public, and easily quantifiable metrics represents currency. While it would be easy to argue that because "likes" can't be spent in the same way that money can, it is an unsuitable comparison. As economists such as A. Mitchell Innes insist, currency emerges when "the state (or any other authority able to impose an obligation) imposes a liability in the form of a generalized, social unit of account used for measuring the obligation" (Wray 2016: 9). Within this framework, then, money is not an end in and of itself; rather, it is a visible and authorized method of measuring the obligation between two parties. Obligation might be a term that unsettles the direct comparison to social media, yet engagement does result in an obligation of response, a form of repayment in kind that suggests a functioning system of currency.

The site of authority and its relationship to attention is represented differently in the three novels, but all suggest a smaller, more distributed locus of authority within the attention economy. In *The Circle*, Mae's authority as an influencer is the result of the visible cumulative effect of her social interactions. As Mae's co-worker, Gina, explains, top Circlers have "accumulated enough credibility that their followers trust their recommendations implicitly, and are deeply thankful for the surety in their shopping" (250). Here, the consumer owes a debt to the content producer—the Circler—for both entertaining her and saving her valuable time in her shopping. Instead of weighing her options, the consumer can just purchase what Mae recommends because the social nature of their relationship has endowed Mae with credibility and authority. The consumer is rewarded with more free time and a sense of trust in her purchasing decisions. In return, she makes visible her engagement with Mae's recommendation, creating the loop of debt and discharge through attention.

In *Super Sad True Love Story*, the functions of the attention economy often highlight Lenny Abramov's sense of alienation, because he questions the structure of this new social and economic order:

> Just then, passing by the ochre grandiosity of St. Mary's, I saw a pretty woman, a little chunky and wide of hip, cross herself in front of the church and kiss her fist, her Credit ranking flashing at an abysmal 670 on a nearby Credit Pole. I wanted to confront her, to make her see the folly of her religion, to change her diet, to help her spend less on makeup and other nonessentials, to make her worship every biological moment she was offered instead of some punctured deity. I also wanted to kiss her for some reason, feel the life pulsing in those big Catholic lips, remind myself of the primacy of the living animal.
>
> *(Shteyngart 2010: 80–1)*

The credit poles are visible public markers of an individual's net worth, and although Lenny is a High Net Worth Individual, in this scene he recognizes the different forms of authority competing with net worth. Whether it is religion or fitness, the individual is ranked and rated in this attention economy, and an individual's scores are what garner and guarantee attention. And yet Lenny questions the authority of these markers, and longs to move past them to a more primal authority, to a sense of physical connection that obliterates these other forms of attention. The novel highlights the fallibility of forms of authority within the attention economy to highlight their nature as social constructs.

Similarly, *Ready Player One* also decentralizes authority, and instead of focusing on how players within the OASIS, the virtual reality within which most individuals spend their time, are garnering attention, the attention economy rewards those who *pay* attention effectively. Wade Watts is so successful at the contest because he meticulously reviewed Halliday's popular culture interests, from video games, to music, to television shows, so that every time he is navigating one of the "gates" in the challenge, he is able to draw upon this vast store of knowledge to make the right decision in the game (63–5). His intense attention to the life and interests of Halliday reward him when he is the first player to successfully complete the challenge, garnering him an overwhelming fortune and control over the future of the OASIS. Here, the repayment of attention is delayed, but it is direct and it overtly imbues engagement with authority.

## Authenticity

Although authority is a key site of anxiety for both monetary theory and the novels, it is not the only one that emerges in an attention economy. One question common to both currency and digital culture, as the novels make clear, is how a market can guarantee authenticity, the affective foundation of currency. The fear of the counterfeit haunts not simply paper money, but the metrics of attention, or even the object of attention. And this fear is not new. As literary scholar Mary Poovey argues, the transition to paper money, in the form of the bank note, at the end of the bullion era in eighteenth- and nineteenth-century England sparked an enormous debate about the authenticity of this new currency, detached as it was from gold and silver (2008: 3–4). In fact, Poovey notes, the dominant metaphor critics used to describe this new currency was that of "fiction" (2008: 77). And as Kevin McLaughlin illustrates of the nineteenth century, "even before the disappearance of convertibility or of the gold standard...the paper of paper money is virtual" (2005: 4) meaning that the paper on which money is printed doesn't exist as a value in and of itself, it disappears in its representational value, it becomes a metaphor, valuable because of its ability to validate that which it stands in for. What both Poovey and McLaughlin chart is the transition to nonconvertible paper money as fiat currency. This legislative transition further signifies the transition in information currency. With lowered paper costs and rising literacy rates throughout England in the eighteenth and nineteenth centuries, paper became the material by which information circulated and thus became reality. But the adoption of paper money, as Poovey and McLaughlin illustrate, requires the cultural adoption of not simply the economic advantages of the new materiality, but also the vulnerabilities. Forgery, counterfeiting, and overproduction were all cited as potential drawbacks, and very real threats to paper currency.

In a reversal of the recession of materiality in the face of representation, currency in the digital age must rise to the level of visibility, presenting a paradoxical problem. The anxiety surrounding authenticity is no less charged, but the methods for resolving it in a non-fiat economy must be similarly distributed. The novels all highlight how the attention economy attempts to resolve this anxiety by anchoring authenticity to the individual, who becomes the inviolable guarantor of a genuine transaction. *The Circle* deals with this trope most directly by introducing extreme forms of transparency into the culture in order to guarantee authenticity. So complete is the dominance of The Circle that it eventually supersedes companies like Facebook and Google in popularity and use. Over the course of the novel the company goes on to revolutionize the economy and the government through the enforcement of its radical transparency. This is all achieved through a system called "TruYou" which aggregates all personal information into a single public profile. TruYou is the operating system built by Circle founder Tyler Gasparov and it promises,

> one account, one identity, one password, one payment system, per person. There were no more passwords, no multiple identities. Your devices knew who you were, and your one identity—the *TruYou*, unbendable and unmaskable—was the person paying, signing up, responding, viewing and reviewing, seeing and being seen.
>
> *(Eggers 21)*

In this formulation, the flow of attention is authenticated through the vast social network of The Circle, and questions of veracity and authenticity are rendered moot because they are guaranteed by a system connected to the identity of an individual. The self thus becomes the site of authority and authenticity, even as the system requires constant engagement and verification in order to maintain that authority and authenticity. In such a system, the novel asserts, to be visible is to create a credit, whereas privacy is an undischarged debt akin to stealing from the credit marketplace created by total transparency. The demands placed on Mae for total and all-encompassing transparency are the trade-off that enables her, and other Circlers, to obliterate any chance of "not knowing," the thing that Mae identifies as the blockade to true freedom and happiness. What the novel suggests is that in the attention economy, obtaining currency—and thus value—requires increasing amounts of visibility, vulnerability, and accessibility.

Similarly, the conclusion of *Super Sad True Love Story*, reveals that the epistolary exchanges that have constituted the novel the reader has just completed are eventually published within the diegetic world as a novel, bringing Lenny the attention he has long desired, but only after he has lost his girlfriend and been forced to live as an expatriate (327–31). Ironically, the habit that made him so undesirable in the direct attention economy makes him a hero to the culture that emerges from the economic downfall of the United States. And what appeals so strongly to the new generation rediscovering the power of the written word is "a real interest in the world around her" evident in Eunice's entries. Because her writing is less than perfect, and worse than Lenny's, hers is prized as more authentic, even "alive" in a way that Lenny's more polished prose is not (327–8). Throughout the novel, visible metrics for an individual have attempted to stand in for authenticity, but as the novel returns to text in its conclusion, it suggests that authenticity does not emerge from the individual, as *The Circle* posits, but from the relationship between individuals, from messy sociality itself because it creates a record of the attention transactions that form the basis of both relationships and the economy.

*Ready Player One* similarly concludes with a return to a predigital state as the most genuine form of attention. After Wade Watts, as Parzival, has completed the last contest, the avatar of creator James Halliday shares his most important insight with him:

> I need to tell you one last thing before I go. Something I didn't figure out for myself until it was already too late…as terrifying and painful as reality can be, it's also the only place where you can find true happiness. Because reality is *real*.
>
> *(364)*

Halliday was a recluse who lived most fully in his engagement with other media, but in his final words, he urges Watts to live outside of any mediation and to connect, for better or worse, with others. Watts follows this directive immediately, leaving the OASIS to finally meet Art3mis, the woman he'd fallen in love with in the OASIS, but had never met in person. The novel concludes with Watts musing that he had no desire, for the first time in his life, to return to the OASIS (372). Despite the fact that the bulk of the narrative occurs within virtual reality, the novel concludes in the "real" world, suggesting that authenticity can only be verified outside of mediation, just as the relationship between Parzival and Art3mis can only be validated once they have met in person. Such a resolution implies that mediated attention is merely a chartal for "real" connections between people that must be validated outside of mediation. In this continuum of verification, then, the novels demonstrate that while authenticity is a problem central to the attention economy, there is no one solution for its resolution.

In bringing the attention economy to the level of representation and imagining its social and individual consequences, these three novels illustrate how currency theory infuses speculative fiction and also offers valuable insights into questions central to narrative. Theories of the attention economy further suggest that these novels are not merely speculative, but they are reflective of changes already under way in our own cultural moment. At the same time, each of these novels is set in a dystopian future, and the three protagonists struggle with the demands for transparency and accessibility placed upon them within this marketplace. They assert that the consequences of the attention economy will be nearly constant surveillance, the loss of privacy, and the increasingly blurred line between the worlds of work and leisure. What their resolutions indicate is that rather than moving away from the attention economy, individual identity will continue to become increasingly entangled with the demands for authority and authenticity necessitated by this mediated economy.

## References


Bell, S. (2001) "The Role of the State and the Hierarchy of Money," *Cambridge Journal of Economics* 25, 149–63.

Cline, E. (2011) *Ready Player One*, New York: Broadway Books.

Cohen, B. (2001) "Electronic Money: New Day or False Dawn?" *Review of International Political Economy* 8.2, 197–225.

Eggers, D. (2013) *The Circle*, New York: Alfred A. Knopf.

Goldhaber, M. (1997) "Attention Shoppers!" *WIRED Magazine*, December 1, accessed November 2017.

Hume, D. (1742) *Essays: Moral, Political, and Literary* [1985], New York: Cosimo Classics.

Knapp, G. (1924) *The State Theory of Money* [2013], Eastford, CT: Martino.

Lotz, S. and Rochteau, G. (2002) "On the Launching of a New Currency," *Journal of Money, Credit and Banking* 34.3, 563–88.

Matonis, J. (2013) "Bitcoin Obliterates 'The State Theory of Money,'" *Forbes*, April 3, accessed November 2017.

McLaughlin, K. (2005) *Paperwork: Fiction and Mass Mediacy in the Paper Age*, Philadelphia: University of Pennsylvania Press.

Poovey, M. (2008) *Genres of the Credit Economy: Mediating Value in Eighteenth- and Nineteenth-Century Britain*, Chicago, IL: University of Chicago Press.

Shteyngart, G. (2010) *Super Sad True Love Story*, New York: Random House.

Simmel, G. (2004) *The Philosophy of Money*, D. Frisby (ed.) T. Bottomore and D. Frisby (trans.), London: Routledge.

Wray, L. R. (2016) "From State Theory of Money to Modern Money: An Alternative to Economic Orthodoxy," in D. Fox and W. Ernst (eds.) *Money in the Western Legal Tradition: Middle Ages to Bretton Woods*, Oxford: Oxford University Press.

# 22
# LITERATURE AND ENERGY

*Imre Szeman*

Energy is a fundamental element of human life.[1] It is what gives societies the capacity to undertake all of the varied activities that occur within them—what, in a word, makes societies and the individuals in them "go," and not only in a basic, material sense, but socially and culturally, too. To take but one example: energy is required for the modern system of transportation to function; what makes that system "go" is not only the raw stuff of fossil fuels (and, to a much lesser degree, electricity), but also the ideas and ideals driving everything from global trade to individual mobility—the "freedoms" associated with neoliberal economics and the ability to travel when and where one wants.[2]

If the first point might seem obvious—human societies require energy if they are to function at all—the latter point—that there is a connection between energy and culture—has only recently come to the fore of critical attention.[3] For too long, energy has been treated as a largely neutral input into societies—a necessary element of social life, but not the one that has any significant, defining impact on its shape, form, and character. The history of modernity, for instance, has been figured in relation to novel developments in literary culture, scientific discovery, the birth of cities, the expansion of individual political freedoms, the structures and strictures of colonialism, and the creation of the global nation-state system. It has seldom been narrated in relation to the massive expansion of socially available energy (and energy of a specific form: fossil fuels, which are easy to transport and store) and the concurrent redefinition of social practices, behaviors, and beliefs occasioned by this historically unprecedented explosion of access to energy.[4] Leaving energy out of our picture of modernity (and indeed, out of any period of history) has meant that we lack a full understanding of the forces and practices animating not only its politics and economics, but also its social and cultural life. Energy names the material force that makes societies go. But energy is also a social relation, animating through its specific form the character and capacities of the societies we inhabit and the practices that shape them. As we attempt to address the consequences of modern petrocultures and to transition beyond them, we need to include energy in our account of any and every aspect of the social and cultural landscapes we inhabit. Without doing so, we remain stuck, imagining techno-utopian solutions to our environmental crisis instead of getting to work redefining our existing social relations, structures, and behaviors (Szeman 2007).

What does this mean for the study of literature and of culture more generally? Environmental scientist Vaclav Smil, who has repeatedly drawn attention to the broad historical and social significance of energy, has written "timeless artistic expressions show no correlation with levels or kinds of energy consumption: the bison in the famous cave paintings of Altamira are not less elegant than Picasso's bulls drawn nearly 15,000 years later" (Smil 2004, 559). This view of the relationship between energy and cultural production is sustainable only if one imagines the aesthetic as falling completely outside history—as in fact "timeless" in the way suggested here. This is in fact contradicted by Smil's own comments elsewhere in "World History and Energy" about the depth of energy's impact on the development of the forms taken by societies throughout history.[5] Smil's claims about the lack of a relationship between art and energy come in the final section of his essay, in which he cautions against a too simple "energy determinism" in relation to historical development. One of the significant challenges of introducing energy into cultural and social analyses is to figure out exactly how to plot its impacts and effects. While adding energy to the study of literature and culture might not constitute something akin to a "final" explanation of these practices and their symbolic significance (as if energy were a substitute for the economic base, "in the last instance" determining *both* the character of the economic base and the superstructure connected to it), it is equally problematic to write energy out of the picture, as having no significance at all, and so requiring none of our critical and conceptual attention when we engage in the study of literature and culture.

An energy determinism is unsustainable. The claim that energy has no impact on literature and culture is equally unsustainable, whether we understand this impact in a narrowly material sense—in the very substance of the acrylic paints used on modern canvases, the stock used to shoot films (see Bozak 2011), or in the electricity required to run printing presses and generate cable signals—or socially, through its figuration of social capacities and expectations. How might one begin to add energy to cultural analysis in a way that captures its force and impact, without deferring to either one of these extremes? This is the question that I want to take up, specifically in relation to how energy might add to our accounts and understanding of world literature. Does making a link between a specific energy system and a literary period (or movement, or form) open up a new way of analyzing texts? Or does it unnerve not just the how but the *why* of literary studies? Given the significance of energy for societies, we need to begin to add energy to our literary and cultural analyses. But just what does it mean to do so, especially in our accounts and understanding of world literature?

* * *

The history of energy is constituted by forms of energy giving way to other forms of energy—for instance, the dominance of water and wind in the UK in the early nineteenth century moving to coal by the mid to late part of the century (Malm 2016).[6] One of the ways in which it might thus be possible to grasp the impact of energy on literary and cultural production is by engaging in a process of periodization—refiguring literary history around eras defined by wood, tallow, coal, whale oil, gasoline, and atomic power, as in the title of Patricia Yaeger's provocative *PMLA* editor's column on literature and energy (Yaeger et al. 2011).

The aim and intention of Yaeger's loose periodization of energy is to begin a conversation about the material and social impact of energy within literary studies. Such broad energo-cultural periodizations are rendered immediately problematic by the real character of energy systems. In our own energy period, it can be easy to overstate the degree to which oil or fossil fuels are in fact the dominant form of energy (Jones 2016). To begin with, the forms of energy used at any given moment in history are inevitably mixed and changing. As new forms of energy are discovered and added to the mix, energy systems become more and more diverse and complicated; contemporary energy systems are made up of an array of energy forms—hydro, nuclear, solar, wind, and more in addition to fossil fuels. The introduction of nuclear energy in the period following World War II has done very little to offset levels of fossil fuel use, and while the use of fossil fuels since 1850 has decisively reshaped the sources of energy used,[7] the specific mix of the types of fossil fuels used (coal, gas, and oil) shifts and changes year in and year out. In an era that I've come to describe as a "petroculture" (to try to stress the ultimate importance of oil), the use of coal continues to grow, and not only in the developing world.[8]

What might further trouble any easy definition of energy periods are the vast differences in levels and forms of energy use around the world. This is true both between developed nations, and even more so between developing and developed nations. Canada and Germany are both members of the G8 and are among the group of the world's most developed nations. However, the mix of energy forms that they use and the level of energy employed per capita makes it difficult to easily figure them as part of a period of single petroculture: Germany has a far greater proportion of sustainable energy than Canada as part of its overall energy use, and uses about half of the energy per capita as Canada.[9] When the comparison is made between developed and developing countries, the direct link between access to energy and levels of development becomes all too clear. Per capita energy use in Canada is *twenty-five* times greater than that in the Democratic Republic of Congo, and close to *twenty* times that in Benin and Haiti. These differences in energy use are connected to histories of colonialism, underdevelopment, and global political and economic power; even in petromodernity, large swathes of the planet are still powered by animal labor and the labor of bodies.

Finally, the assertion of a single petroculture obscures the huge differences of access to power *within* nations. Elites everywhere use more energy per capita than poorer members of societies. While some elites have no doubt transitioned from fossil fuels to solar power on their homes in wealthier neighborhoods, the use of animal energy, wood, and coal continues to fuel societies around the world.[10] Does this admixture of energy forms render the task of energy periodization confusing and pointless, unable to provide analytic insight into the impact of energy on culture?

Despite the complex map of energy use at the present time, it seems to me that energy periodization *can* open up new ways of figuring and analyzing literature in relation to the world in which it is produced. To begin with, where and what kinds of energy are used, and how much is used and by whom, provides a map of power, privilege, control, and dispossession. There is a strong correlation between energy use and GDP; increases in energy use per capita inevitably lead to economic growth and higher living standards. The politics of colonialism and postcolonialism were shaped by race and ethnicity, military power, and control over the trade of goods (with colonial powers benefiting at the expense of the colonies they controlled). Colonialism was also a period animated by access to energy, and the search for and struggle to control evermore energy. Access to fossil fuel energy—first coal, and then oil and gas—was essential to managing and maintaining colonial control; the struggle over energy remains a largely untold story within postcolonial literary studies and in the study of world literature, which has focused on other aspects of the combined and uneven development that has characterized modernity (Ghosh 2016). At a minimum, tracking levels of energy use can be used to identify nodes of power in the world, and to consider the impact of these differentials of power in relation to cultural production. Indeed, one could argue that the "world" announced by the category of "world literature" doesn't in fact come into existence until the beginning of the era of fossil fuels: the production of the imaginary named "world" is fueled by the presence of energy sources, including coal and oil, that make the space of the globe increasingly available and accessible to travel, trade, and political power.[11] A global map of energy, one that also captures differences of energy use within nations, highlights the ways in which power is actively materialized, with inevitable impacts on social and cultural capacity and sensibility.

With few exceptions—Saudi Arabia and the Emirates stand out today as not just producers of energy but also as enormous energy consumers—a map of energy power is, however, not unlike our already existing understanding of power and privilege, from colonialism through to the postcolonial, neoliberal present. The strong connection between energy and political power, between levels of per capita energy use and socioeconomic status, means that existing narratives of global power tell us a great deal about the sociocultural impact of energy use, even if the specific importance of energy is rarely named. Can we thus do without critical appeals to energy, assuming that its force and social import will show up in the political, economic, and military structures and forces that it has fueled?

It seems clear to me that this would be a mistake. While it may be the case that there is a strong correlation between existing narratives of culture and power, the specific role of energy in shaping both cannot just be passed over, nor can the specificity of the experiences, social sensibilities, and cultural imaginaries produced by distinct energy systems. There is also a strong political rationale for foregrounding fossil fuels in the analysis of cultural production. Given the strong link between expanded energy use and development, countries in the global South will, of necessity, need to use more and more energy per capita in order to give citizens in their nations the social capacities and opportunities that high levels of energy use have afforded in the global North. Whatever forms development might take, it means using more and more energy (Klare 2016). The environmental consequences of doing so, and the social and political pressures this will generate at a global level, promise to extend existing colonial and postcolonial struggles deep into the twenty-first century, and do so in reference to an issue to which we barely paid any attention—energy.

Despite the mixed and uneven use of energy around the world at the present time and throughout modernity, it *is* possible to speak meaningfully of a period of petromodernity. Petroleum is the *hegemonic* form of energy at the present time. The claim that something has become hegemonic is intended to capture an organizing principle or a shaping dictate of a period: what is hegemonic about immaterial labor at the present time, for example, is not that the majority of people are involved in such forms of work, but that it places demands on all forms of labor to "informationalize, become intelligent, become communicative, become affective" (Brown and Szeman 2005, 109). It is in this sense that fossil fuels are hegemonic and that we live in a petroculture. Energy use remains mixed, both in terms of the forms of energy use and the amounts used by individuals around the world. However, our cities have not been shaped around nuclear energy or hydropower. The fantasy of suburban living and the freedoms of highways owe nothing to wind farms and solar power, and no country imagines that the way forward in their development is to shape agricultural systems around plow and oxen as opposed to mechanical farming and fertilizers. The enormous, unprecedented energy of fossil fuels has shaped (and continues to shape) our cultural and social imaginaries in profound ways, including the character of our political structures, and, as Timothy Mitchell (2011, 109–43) points out, the principles and rationales of our economic practices and decisions. Being alert to the differences and distinctions in energy use that I've already pointed to is essential. My intent in claiming that we understand modernity as a *petro*modernity isn't to flatten out these differences, in a manner akin to the way that the

Anthropocene has been critiqued for eliminating a more nuanced history of the human impact on the environment.[12] It remains important to identify the dominant rationales or logics that have shaped the world in which these differences and distinctions exist, including those connected to the forms of energy in use.

In "Conjectures on World Literature," Franco Moretti argues that we need to understand the world literary system as "one, and unequal: *one* literature (*Weltliteratur*, singular, as in Goethe and Marx)...but a system which is different from what Goethe and Marx had hoped for, because it is profoundly unequal" (2000, 56). So, too, with the system of energy use: one petroculture, but a profoundly unequal one. Moretti's essay provides a quick articulation of and justification for his system of "distant reading," which is intended in part to identify dominant logics that have structured the world literary system. For him, the system of *Weltliteratur* is organized by a triangle of forces: "foreign form, local material—and *local form*" (2000, 65). Moretti cites the Brazilian literary critic Roberto Schwarz, who provides an example of what the inequality of world literature produces at the level of content: "Foreign debt is as inevitable in Brazilian letters as in any other field... it is not simply an easily dispensable part of the work in which it appears, but a complex feature of it" (Schwarz in Moretti 2000, 56). One might imagine inequalities not only of financial power (which generates debt) but also of energy form and capacity to be figured differently at center and periphery, shaping and forming what Moretti calls "local materials" in a strong and profound way. Jennifer Wenzel's "Petro-Magic-Realism" (2006) offers an example of literary analysis that foregrounds the impact of energy on literary form at the periphery. In order to offer further specificity and analytic density to the widely used literary category of "magic realism," Wenzel argues that the "political ecology" of Nigerian literature is better described as "petro-magic-realism,"

> a literary mode that combines the transmogrifying creatures and liminal space of the forest in Yoruba narrative tradition with the monstrous-but-mundane violence of oil exploration and extraction, the state violence that supports it, and the environmental degradation that it causes.
>
> *(456)*

Such mappings of specific encounters between aesthetics and politics via the position of literature within petromodernity are essential; there are all too many oil encounters about which the whole story has yet to be told. If I had to assign a tendency that has emerged in literary critical attention to energy systems, and especially to the petrocultural system that has shaped the colonial encounter and the experience of the modern, it is the attempt to identify the sites and spaces in which the specific configuration of form and content names not only a political tension but also a tension animated by energy differentials (unlike Marxist critics such as Masao Miyoshi, Fredric Jameson, and Nicholas Brown whose attention stays more squarely in the realm of political economy). But the inclusion of energy inequality as an axis of analysis is hindered by one major problem—a defining aspect of oil in relation to culture that has to be placed at the center of any conceptualization of energy as an analytic tool within the study of world literature. *The importance of fossil fuels in defining modernity has stood in inverse relationship to their presence in our cultural and social imaginaries*, a fact that comes as a revelatory surprise to almost everyone who engages in critical explorations of energy today.

The arts of a world powered by horses and the labor of bodies cannot help but be distinct from the expanded time, space, and power of our own petromodernity. Nevertheless, attention to energy differentials has largely been absent not only from critical investigations of literature and culture, but also from literature and culture itself. Those who have begun to grapple with the cultural absence of oil in a period shaped by and around the substance have scanned literary history to find texts that have confronted oil hegemony, with productive results (Ghosh *Derangement*). But questions remain. Why has it been so difficult to locate a literary archive for what now appears to be so important a social and historical force? And despite this absence or gap, why does it seem necessary and important to do so now?

One of the earliest links between energy and aesthetics was made by Amitav Ghosh in his 1992 essay "Petrofiction: The Oil Encounter and the Novel" (1992). Ghosh's essay is, in part, a review of Abdul Rahman Munif's monumental *Cities of Salt* quintet, which maps the coming-to-be of American petroleum interests in the Middle East and its world-altering impact on those living in the Arabian Peninsula. "Petrofiction" also offers a broader critique of the failure of literary fiction to address what Ghosh names the "Oil Encounter": the intertwining of the fates of Americans and those living in the Middle East around this commodity, a connection that continues to have far-reaching economic, cultural, and political reverberations. In the twentieth century, US power was strongly tied to oil. For the first half of the century, the US was the world's first true oil superpower, and it used its energy riches to develop a consumer culture built around automobiles, suburbs, and malls. The geopolitical crises of the second half of the last century and the first two decades of the current one are the result of the need for the US to continue to have access to oil to fuel to fill the tanks of SUV drivers as well as its larger economy. Given the deep imbrication of the US economy and its politics with petroleum, Ghosh expresses puzzlement that no author has taken up the Oil Encounter as a literary subject. Ghosh's essay is now a quarter-of-a-century old; yet, there are still far too few literary fictions that undertake an exploration of what could well be said to have defined the politics of the period since the discovery of oil in the mid-nineteenth century—the struggle over access to oil. Nor, for that matter, are there very many fictions that have dealt with the social, cultural, and political importance of energy and oil in any way, shape, or form. I'm not suggesting that there are no such fictions—there are, including such one-of-a-kind theory-fictions like Reza Negarestani's *Cyclonopedia: Complicity with Anonymous Materials* (2008) and recent postcolonial narratives such as Helon Habila's *Oil on Water* (2011).[13] Very often, however, the presence of oil in a fiction is little more than shorthand for wealth and power, which could have other sources and be just as well figured in other ways.

Ghosh's insight regarding the absence of oil and the Middle East from modern US fiction has resonated with critics and theorists who have attended to the representational challenge presented by fossil fuels. As the planet's hegemon during the height of petromodernity, we might well expect to find it difficult for US fiction and culture to figure, directly and unfalteringly, one of the principle sites and sources of the nation's power. From the perspective of the US, oil is simply what makes the country "go," and in a way that doesn't necessitate comment or concern; as a result, it gets lost to the background of the physical apparatus within and against which social, culture, and political life is played out, no more worthy of comment than furniture or the asphalt covering its streets—indeed, less so.

One of the distinctive elements of oil as an energy source is that, unlike coal energy (which does enter into Victorian-era writing; see MacDuffie 2014), it is a resource whose consumption is disassociated from its extraction. The historian Christopher Jones (2014) points out that from the very beginning of the establishment of the oil pipeline system, "the users of oil gained benefit of cheap energy without assuming responsibility for its environmental damage" (143). This ethical dissociation also speaks to its place in the cultural and social imaginaries—it vanishes to the background, invisible to narrative and so, too, to critique. What Munif's *Cities of Salt* (1987) captures so perfectly is the blind sense of entitlement of those engaged in extracting oil, and a sense of puzzlement by those native to the land whose space and culture have been invaded. Even more powerfully, it shows how the world made by oil can only be seen by those foreign to it. *Cities of Salt* manages to transform oil modernity into the science fictional time and space that it is: occupied by creatures of steel and asphalt that are animated by the liquid remains of plants millions of years old, and whose imperatives and rationales seem so out of joint with the physical environment of the Earth that it is hard to believe that they are not from elsewhere in the universe. "What new era had begun—what could they expect of the future? For how long could the men stand it? The night had passed, but what about the nights to come?" (222). The fear and uncertainty that Ibn Rashed and his community experience in *Cities of Salt* are justified. The dissociation that enlivens the Americans is infectious; their appearance in the Middle East to hunt for the substance that fuels them is felt by the Arab community as a rupture in time with unknown consequences.

Munif and other postcolonial writers have managed to grasp some of the social power of oil as a result of imaginative openings that the periphery provides. Just as the colonial system and the mechanisms of postcolonial power are evident to those who have to endure them, one might imagine that the significance of energy for shaping modernity is readily apparent in those spaces where petroculture has yet to take hold. Munif's *Cities of Salt* shows the critical openings that the gap between center and periphery can provide. And yet, the representational challenges posed by oil are deeper and more complex than this. Ghosh's interest in Munif's work arises in part because it stands as an exception: it is not only US fiction that fails to name oil as a key element of the human drama of the twentieth century, but much of postcolonial fiction as well. For the most part, despite their evident sociohistorical importance, fossil fuels have in fact played a very small role in artistic and literary expressions during the fossil fuel era. In this case, the exceptions—those texts that have been examined by literary critics working in the energy humanities—definitely prove the rule.

I suggested earlier that whether or not it was used everywhere in the world to same degree (or indeed, whether it was used at all in some places), oil has to be seen as hegemonic—as an energy source that organizes life practice in a more fundamental way than we've ever allowed ourselves to believe. What this means is that despite the absence of fictions that take up oil or the oil encounter directly by making it a part of narrative, form, or both,[14] that *any and all* examples of cultural expression in the era of oil have in fact been crucially figured by it. In their introduction to *Oil Culture*, Ross Barrett and Daniel Worden (2014) write that "oil culture encompasses the fundamental semiotic processes by which oil is imbued with value within petrocapitalism… the symbolic forms that rearrange daily experience around oil-bound ways of life" (xxvi). It is a point echoed by Frederick Buell in his overview of the framing cultural and social narratives of the fossil fuel era: for him, "[energy] (especially oil) remains an essential (and, to many, *the* essential) prop underneath humanity's material and symbolic cultures" (70). Might we thus read all of modern literature as a petroliterature, and so, too, make energy a necessary component of literary analysis?

The literary critic Graeme Macdonald (2013) has offered answers to these questions in his provocative and compelling overview of the key issues that have arisen for critics as they have begun to grapple with the entwined histories of energy and culture. For Macdonald,

> fiction, in its various modes, genres, and histories, offers a significant (and relatively untapped) repository for the energy-aware scholar to demonstrate how, through successive epochs, particularly embedded kinds of energy create a predominant (and oftentimes

> alternative) culture of being and imagining in the world; organizing and enabling a prevalent mode of living, thinking, moving, dwelling, and working.
>
> *(4)*

His article unfolds the implications of what fossil fuels have meant for being in and imagining the world, and what they have meant, too, for the fictional forms that have developed in relation to this world shot through with "narrative energetics" and "psycho-social dynamics" linked to oil's force and power.

Macdonald argues that the inclusion of energy in literary analysis allows us to better grasp the ways in which distinct forms of energy help to make possible distinct modes of being and imagining. It is thus tempting—and the results are interesting enough to try it out—to map specific moments of literature in relation to developments in energy history. Modernism can be read in relation to the dissociation that is a central part of the history of fossil fuel use, identifying in the key dates of 1870 (the moment when more energy is extracted from fossil fuels than from photosynthesis) and 1890 (the year in which more than half of global energy comes from fossil fuels) significant moments in the history of energy with resonances in literature and culture. Or one might consider postmodernism in relation to the 1973 OPEC crisis, a moment in which narratives of petromodern futures and US hegemony were deeply unnerved, and so, too, the self-certainties of narrative and the Western subject. Or read postcolonialism as an affirmation of a new era of colonial power linked to the fact that the moment of decolonization was also one in which the mantle of the biggest producer of fossil fuels was being passed from the United States to Saudi Arabia, Venezuela, and other producers in the global South. To do so would undeniably enrich the vocabulary of literary and cultural analyses, and do so in a manner that forces us to increasingly recognize the significance of fossil fuels in the shape taken by modernity *and* to ask questions about how and why energy has for too long been a "nothing" in our assessments.[15]

But while we might thus enrich the critical literary vocabulary, the addition of energy here hasn't truly added an analytic element that helps us to better understand it. In each of the above examples, the work of analysis confers the sociocultural significance of developments in the world of energy by indexing it to changes we already know about: reconfigurations of energy did not produce modernism, nor create postmodern style, nor bring about the end of colonialism—which is not to say that they were insignificant. The challenge as we begin to figure energy into literary and cultural analyses is to know how to explain the precise social impact of a force whose significance is indexed in part by the fact that in much of the culture produced over an extended period, its import was not figured in culture. Macdonald is right: all of modern culture is a petroculture; we might also say that world literature is a world petroliterature. But in identifying world literature as the literature of an oil era, are we doing anything more than asking that we now pay attention to the ways in which literature can be used as a space that can be mined for insight into the character of this petro-era, presumably for other purposes, i.e. so that we might upend petroculture and bring it to an end?

Ian Baucom (2014) has written:

> Although I have for some time accepted the force of Fredric Jameson's dictum that 'we cannot, not periodize,' until very recently it would not have occurred to me that postcolonial study, critical theory, or the humanities disciplines in general needed to periodize in relation not only to capital but to carbon, not only in modernities and postmodernities but in parts-per-million, not only in dates but in degrees Celsius.[16]

Is it productive or meaningful to undertake such a periodization? One could quibble with Baucom's choice of carbon or temperature as the measure of a new periodization,[17] while still understanding the rationale for it: to reimagine literature and culture in relation to environmental concerns. A periodization developed around energy and forms of fuel used captures something which Baucom's proposed periods could never do: changes to social capacities and possibilities, to the ways in which access to energy—or equally, lack of access to it—creates a predominant way of being and imagining that we usually describe as being modern. Despite all of the caveats, qualifications, and warnings I've provided about reading world literature as a petroliterature—as a literature that has to exist within a system organized around the capacities, fantasies, and desires, the imaginative and physical possibilities of oil—reading energy into literature and into the world *does* provide us with critical, political resources we might otherwise lack, even if care must be taken with precisely how we figure literature in relation to energy.

There is one final connection between energy and literature that needs to be addressed. I asked at the outset: does including energy into literary studies unnerve not just its how, but its *why*? Environmental historians McNeill and Engelke (2014) describe the period since 1945 as the "Great Acceleration"—a period that "unfurled in the context of a fossil fuel energy regime and... exponential growth in energy use" (2). It is also, they point out, "the most anomalous and unrepresentative period in the 200,000-year-long-history of relations between our species and the biosphere" (5) and a period that is unlikely to continue. Shouldn't we see literature as a key aspect of this period of Great Acceleration—as a practice that not only gives us insight into the period, but also a category and an activity (writing, reading, and interpreting) that is an outgrowth of fossil fuel use? I'm not suggesting here that literature is synonymous with the fossil fuel era—a claim that comes across as absurd given the historical range of texts studied in any literature department. What I'm proposing is that we think more seriously about the links between the expansion of socially available energy and the coming-into-being of a general social capacity for literary activity—i.e. a segment of mass culture that emerged with expanded force and power at the turn of the twentieth century just as fossil fuels became more abundant (more energy for more people means more culture: a missing piece of the puzzle in Thorstein Veblen's assessment of the rise of mass culture).

There is a largely unarticulated, widely accepted, liberal narrative of literature, which links it to a developmental account of social capacity: more literature means more narrative which means more freedom and more social possibilities—as if world literature were, in the end, a policy of the World Bank.[18] One of the chief insights we gain by adding energy to world literature is that it allows us to see that all culture is petroculture because our understanding of culture is linked to oil's initial promise of unending abundance. It is always supposed to be better for there to be evermore culture, evermore energy. In recognition of modern culture's deep ties to energy, the link between literature and energy that critics and theorists have begun to make with ever greater frequency raises questions about the material and ecological weight of literature itself. To date, literature has avoided imagining its relationship to energy through units such as watts/hour or kilojoules/year, seeing itself as a medium that generates no environmental burden even as it proliferates awareness about the catastrophe of climate change. Figuring this meta-relationship of literature to energy might well generate an important and original ecological relationship to the apparatuses and objects of modern petroculture, and might do so in a manner that would help undo the damaging self-certainties of the culture of liberal capitalism as well.

A different version of this essay was published under the title "Conjectures on World Energy Literature" in *Journal of Postcolonial Writing* 53.2 (2017).

## Notes

1 I recognize that energy is not a physical thing, but a force—a property of objects that cannot be created or destroyed. As is a common practice in English, I use energy as a substitute term for fuels, i.e. as an umbrella term to capture all of the fuels used today.

2 In "On Ideology," the final chapter of *On the Reproduction of Capitalism*, Louis Althusser writes:

> the subjects 'go', they recognize that 'it's really true,' that 'this is the way it is,' not some other way, that they have to obey God, the priest, De Gaulle, the boss, the engineer, and love their neighbor, and so on. The subjects go, since the have recognized that 'all is well' (the way it is), and they say, for good measure: *So be it!*
>
> (197)

For Althusser, what makes subjects "go" are the Ideological State Apparatuses, which makes them "go all by themselves" without (for the most part) the need of Repressive State Apparatuses.

In the same chapter, Althusser writes: "One can say that every social formation 'functions on ideology,' in the sense in which one says that a gasoline engine 'runs on gasoline'" (200). When I say that energy makes society and subjects "go," the connection to Althusser is deliberate. While I don't have the space to elaborate this here, it is worth drawing attention to the way in which fossil fuels are like ideology—absolutely essential to the operations of the social, but also largely invisible to their operations. A missing element in accounts of social reproduction to date has been an analysis of the process by which energy has come to be an element of ideology. "The subjects go, since they have recognized that 'all is well' (the way it is)" (197), even if what makes them go is quickly bringing the environmental systems in which they live to an end. See Althusser, *On the Reproduction of Capitalism*, trans. G. M. Goshgarian (New York: Verso, 2014).

3 See, for instance, Ross Barrett and Daniel Worden, eds. *Oil Culture* (Minneapolis: University of Minnesota Press, 2014); Imre Szeman and Dominic Boyer, eds. *Energy Humanities: An Anthology* (Baltimore: Johns Hopkins University Press, 2017); Imre Szeman, Jennifer Wenzel, and Patricia Yaeger, eds., *Fueling Culture: 101 Words for Energy and Environment* (New York: Fordham University Press, 2017); and Sheena Wilson, Adam Carlson, and Imre Szeman, eds. *Petrocultures: Oil, Politics, Culture* (Montreal-Kingston: McGill-Queen's University Press, 2017).

4 J.R. McNeill and Peter Engelke point out that by 1870, human beings were already using more energy from fossil fuels than the annual amount of energy produced by all photosynthesis on the planet; since 1860, there have been *one trillion* barrels of oil used. See McNeill and Engelke, *The Great Acceleration: An Environmental History of the Anthropocene Since 1945* (Cambridge, MA: The Belknap Press, 2014), 8.

5 Smil notes that "only a few coastal societies collecting and hunting marine species had sufficiently high and secure energy returns (due to seasonal migrations of fish or whales) such that they were able to live in permanent settlements and devote surplus energy to elaborate rituals and impressive artistic creations (for example, the tall ornate wooden totems of the Indian tribes of the Pacific Northwest)" (550). At a minimum, art as a social practice necessitates "surplus energy," which means that varying levels of surplus energy, in conjunction with broader changes in society animated by shifting forms of energy, would produce distinct modes of art practice as well as alter the social significance of art. In all of the changes that Smil narrates in relation to energy, his identification of art as "timeless" speaks more to his own unwillingness to figure art in relation to energy than to art's apparent ability to sidestep the historical shifts generated by changing forms and levels of energy.

6 Though there is a tendency to imagine societies as having evolved "naturally" to evermore energy-intensive systems and infrastructures, studies of the transition to fossil fuels highlight the political and social struggles that took place to make this happen. See Bob Johnson, *Carbon Nation: Fossil Fuels in the Making of American Culture* (Lawrence: University Press of Kansas, 2014); Christopher Jones, *Routes of Power: Energy and Modern America* (Cambridge, MA: Harvard University Press, 2014); and Andreas Malm, *Fossil Capital: The Rise of Steam Power and the Roots of Global Warming* (New York: Verso, 2016).

The most acute analysis of the significance of energy transitions for politics remains Timothy Mitchell's *Carbon Democracy*. Mitchell describes the emergence of modern forms of mass democracy in conjunction with the use of coal: striking workers could easily impede the energy source on which nineteenth-century economies depended by blocking the rail lines that led from mines to factories and cities. In turn, the emergence of pipelines transporting oil has impeded such mass actions, while helping to animate the biopolitical practices of contemporary nation-states. See Mitchell, *Carbon Democracy: Political Power in the Age of Oil* (New York: Verso, 2011).

7 Edward Renshaw points out "animals contributed 52.4 per cent of total work output in the United States in 1850; human workers, 12.6 per cent; wind, water, and fuel wood, 27.8 per cent; and fossil fuels, 6.8 per cent. In 1950, work animals are estimated to have contributed only 0.7 per cent of total work output; human workers, 0.9 per cent; wind, water, and fuel wood, 7.8 per cent; and fossil fuels, 90.8 per cent" (284). See Renshaw, "The Substitution of Inanimate Energy for Animal Power," *Journal of Political Economy* 71.3 (1963): 284–92. (Thanks to Jeff Diamanti for bringing this article to my attention).

8 Christophe Bonneuil and Jean-Baptiste Fressoz point out that "If, in the twentieth century, the use of coal decreased in relation to oil, it remains that its consumption continually grew; and on a global level, there was never a year in which so much coal was burned as in 2014." Bonneuil and Fressoz, *The Shock of the Anthropocene* (New York: Verso, 2015), 101.

9 According to the International Energy Association, in 2013 Canadians used 7,202 kg of oil equivalent per capita; by comparison, Germans used 3,868 kg of oil/capita. The German figure represents a *decrease* from 1971 levels. See World Bank, "Energy Use Per Capita," *World Development Indicators*. Available at http://data.worldbank.org/indicator/EG.USE.PCAP.KG.OE.

10 For a recent account of the emergence of a new fuel in Madagascar—charcoal—see Norimitsu Onishi, "Africa's Charcoal Economy is Cooking. The Trees are Paying." *New York Times*, 25 June 2016. Available at: www.nytimes.com/2016/06/26/world/africa/africas-charcoal-economy-is-cooking-the-trees-are-paying.html?_r=0. According to the United Nations Food and Agricultural Organization, over the past twenty years, charcoal production in Africa has doubled; today, it accounts for 60% of total global production. The UN also predicts that demand for charcoal in Africa will double or triple by 2050, in large part as a result of population increases on the continent.

11 The dates are about right: Goethe claims in 1827 that a world literature is "beginning," while Marx speaks famously in 1848 in the *Communist Manifesto* of a "world literature" arising out of the "the many national and local literatures." If these comments predate the oil era, they speak to the capacities and possibilities that are emerging as coal begins to be used to generate an increasingly larger part of the energy used in Europe and the UK. In their "Introduction" to *Marxism and the Critique of Energy*, Brent Bellamy and Jeff Diamanti argue "Marxism's methodological and theoretical development in the 1840s occurs not despite but within the contemporaneous surfacing of the theory of energy across Britain, Prussia, and France… Marxism's historical materialism discovers itself in the industrialization of energy, and energy therefore was and remains central to historicizing the fissures of a planet reverberating against the fault lines of an exhausted stack of capital today (ix)."

12 See, for instance, Claire Colebrook, "Not Symbiosis, Not Now: Why Anthropogenic Climate Change Is Not Really Human," *The Oxford Literary Review* 34.2 (2012): 185–210; and Donna Haraway, "Anthropocene, Capitalocene, Chthulucene: Making Kin" *Environmental Humanities* 6 (2015): 159–65. Critics of the concept of the Anthropocene are far more common than defenders of it; one exception is Dale Jamieson's argument for an "ethics" that emerges from the concept of the Anthropocene. See Jamieson, *Reason in Dark Time: Why the Struggle against Climate Change Failed and What It Means for Our Future* (Oxford: Oxford University Press, 2014), 185–92.

13 In *Cyclonopedia*, oil possesses qualities well beyond those we normally assign to it. Negarastani describes it as nothing less than a "satanic sentience" that "possesses tendencies for mass intoxication on pandemic scales (different from but corresponding to capitalism's voodoo economy and other types of global possession systems)" (26).

14 The most compelling account of the impact of energy on literary form remains "The Work of Art and the Work of Nature at the Dawn of Oil," the first chapter of Jeff Diamanti's PhD thesis, *Aesthetic Economies of Growth: Energy, Value, and the Work of Culture After Oil*. See Diamanti, 72–117.

15 Macdonald writes: "if *all* fiction is potentially energetic, valorizing energy use, then how do we kinetically assert our claims and configure our readings to make it more apparent?" (19).

16 Ian Baucom, "History 4°: Postcolonial Method and Anthropocene Time, "*Cambridge Journal of Postcolonial Literary Inquiry* 1.1 (March 2014): 125.

17 "A carbon focus is reductionist, possibly the greatest and most dangerous reductionism of all time: a 150-year history of complex geological, political, economic, and military security issues all

reduced to one element—carbon." See Thomas Princen, Jack P. Manno, and Pamela L. Martin, "The Problem," in Princen, Manno, and Martin, eds., *Ending the Fossil Fuel Era* (Cambridge, MA: The MIT Press, 2015), 6.

18 See Amitava Kumar, ed. *World Bank Literature* (Minneapolis: University of Minnesota Press, 2002).

## References

Althusser, Louis. *On the Reproduction of Capitalism*. Trans. G. M. Goshgarian. New York: Verso, 2014. Print.

Barrett, Ross and Daniel Worden, eds. *Oil Culture*. Minneapolis: University of Minnesota Press, 2014. Print.

Baucom, Ian. "History 4°: Postcolonial Method and Anthropocene Time." *Cambridge Journal of Postcolonial Literary Inquiry* 1.1 (2014): 123–42. Print.

Bellamy, Brent and Jeff Diamanti. "Introduction." *Marxism and the Critique of Energy*. Chicago, IL: MCM' Press 2018: ix–xxxvii. Print.

Bonneuil, Christophe and Jean-Baptist Fressoz. *The Shock of the Anthropocene*. Trans. David Fernbach. New York: Verso, 2016. Print.

Bozak, Nadia. *The Cinematic Footprint: Lights, Camera, Natural Resources*. New Brunswick, NJ: Rutgers University Press, 2011. Print.

Brown, Nicholas. *Utopian Generations: The Political Horizon of Twentieth-Century Literature*. Princeton, NJ: Princeton University Press, 2005. Print.

Brown, Nicholas and Imre Szeman. "What Is the Multitude? Questions for Michael Hardt and Antonio Negri." *Cultural Studies* 19.3 (2005): 372–87. Print.

Buell, Frederick. "A Short History of Oil Cultures: Or, the Marriage of Catastrophe and Exuberance." *Journal of American Studies* 46.2 (2012): 273–93. Print.

Colebrook, Claire. "Not Symbiosis, Not Now: Why Anthropogenic Climate Change Is Not Really Human." *The Oxford Literary Review* 34.2 (2012): 185–210. Print.

Diamanti, Jeff. *Aesthetic Economies of Growth: Energy, Value, and the Work of Culture after Oil*. PhD Thesis. Department of English and Film Studies. University of Alberta, 2015. Print.

Ghosh, Amitav. *The Great Derangement: Climate Change and the Unthinkable*. Chicago, IL: University of Chicago Press, 2016. Print.

———. "Petrofiction." *New Republic* (2 March 1992): 29–34. Print.

Habila, Helon. *Oil on Water: A Novel*. New York: W.W. Norton & Company, 2011. Print.

Haraway, Donna. "Anthropocene, Capitalocene, Chthulucene: Making Kin." *Environmental Humanities* 6 (2015): 159–65. Print.

Hardt, Michael and Antonio Negri. *Empire*. Cambridge, MA: Harvard University Press, 2000. Print.

Jamieson, Dale. *Reason in Dark Time: Why the Struggle against Climate Change Failed and What It Means for Our Future*. Oxford: Oxford University Press, 2014. Print.

Johnson, Bob. *Carbon Nation: Fossil Fuels in the Making of American Culture*. Lawrence: University Press of Kansas, 2014. Print.

Jones, Christopher. "Petromyopia: Oil and the Energy Humanities." *Humanities* 5.2 (2016). Web.

Jones, Christopher. *Routes of Power: Energy and Modern America*. Cambridge, MA: Harvard University Press, 2014. Print.

Klare, Michael. "Hooked! The Unyielding Grip of Fossil Fuels on Global Life." *TomDispatch.Com*, 14 July 2016. Web.

Kumar, Amitava, ed. *World Bank Literature*. Minneapolis: University of Minnesota Press, 2002. Print.

Lord, Barry. *Art & Energy: How Culture Changes*. Chicago, IL: The AAM Press, 2014.

Macdonald, Graeme. "The Resources of Fiction." *Reviews in Cultural Theory* 4.2 (2013): 1–24. Print.

MacDuffie, Allen. *Victorian Literature, Energy, and the Ecological Imagination*. Cambridge: Cambridge UP, 2014. Print.

Macdonald, Graeme. "Research Note: The Resources of Fiction." *Reviews in Cultural Theory* 4.2 (2013): 1–20. Print.

Malm, Andreas. *Fossil Capital: The Rise of Steam Power and the Roots of Global Warming*. New York: Verso, 2016. Print.

McNeill, John Robert and Peter Engelke. *The Great Acceleration: An Environmental History of the Anthropocene Since 1945*. Cambridge, MA: The Belknap Press, 2014. Print.

Mitchell, Timothy. *Carbon Democracy: Political Power in the Age of Oil*. New York: Verso, 2011. Print.
Moretti, Franco. "Conjectures on World Literature." *New Left Review* 1 (2000): 54–68.
Munif, Adbul Rahman. *Cities of Salt* (Cities of Salt Trilogy, Vol. 1). New York: Vintage Books, 1987. Print.
Negarestani, Reza. *Cyclonopedia: Complicity with Anonymous Materials*. Melbourne: Re.Press, 2008. Print.
Princen, Thomas, Jack P. Manno, and Pamela L. Martin, eds. *Ending the Fossil Fuel Era*. Cambridge, MA: The MIT Press, 2015. Print
Sinclair, Upton. *Oil!* New York: Grosset & Dunlap, 1927. Print.
Smil, Vaclav. "World History and Energy." *Encyclopedia of Energy* (Vol. 6), ed. J. Vutler Cleveland. Amsterdam: Elsevier, 2004. 549–61. Print.
Szeman, Imre. "System Failure: Oil, Futurity and the Anticipation of Disaster." *South Atlantic Quarterly* 106.4 (2007): 805–23. Print.
Szeman, Imre and Dominic Boyer, eds. *Energy Humanities: An Anthology*. Baltimore, MD: Johns Hopkins University Press, 2017. Print.
Szeman, Imre, Jennifer Wenzel and Patricia Yaeger, eds. *Fueling Culture: 101 Words for Energy and Environment*. New York: Fordham University Press, 2017. Print.
Wenzel, Jennifer. "Petro-Magic-Realism: Towards a Political Ecology of Nigerian Literature." *Postcolonial Studies* 9.4 (2006): 449–64. Print.
Wilson, Sheena, Adam Carlson and Imre Szeman, eds. *Petrocultures: Oil, Politics, Culture*. Montreal-Kingston: McGill-Queen's University Press, 2017. Print.
Yaeger, Patricia, et al. "Editor's Column: Literature in the Ages of Wood, Tallow, Coal, Whale Oil, Gasoline, Atomic Power, and Other Energy Sources." *PMLA* 126.2 (2011): 305–310. Print.

# 23
# FINANCIALISATION

*Christian P. Haines*

'If we were arriviste /we'd have arrived already. / Securities speak. / They say, "Take comfort." / Money cancels criticism.' (97) writes Alissa Quart in her collection of poetry *Monetized* (2015), which asks after the condition of poetry in a society saturated by finance. *Monetized* offers a phenomenology of financialisation, or an account of the affective and experiential textures that emerge from the increasing dominance of finance capital and financial techniques over everyday life. In doing so, it suggests that there may be no space left for lyric experience, and no margin of critique in which poetry can speak truth to power. If poetry, at least since the Romantic period, has frequently articulated itself as critical of the reigning social order, financialisation would appear to saturate existence with a calculability – a fiscal accountability – that denies this position of alterity. 'Money,' Quart writes, 'cancels criticism': the very place of the speaking subject, or lyric person, is usurped by securities who speak in 'our' place. In this world of speculation, criticism ages without grace, crumbling like those long-ago abandoned factories that litter the U.S. rust belt.

At the same time, the critical value of Quart's poem is predicated on the prosopoeia that it seeks to contest: it can call financialisation into question only by repeating a fiction that finance tells about itself, namely, that finance capital belongs to another ontological level, that it is free of mere existence, untethered from the concrete labour that reproduces capitalism – in short, that finance speaks for itself, to itself, in a place of its own making. Quart recapitulates the hegemonic discourse concerning finance, shared both by the proponents of high finance and its critics, according to which finance creates and circulates abstraction and complexity as opposed to the concrete and simple facts of the 'real' economy. As Leigh Claire La Berge argues, this arrangement of dichotomies – captured by the colloquial synecdoche that pits 'Wall Street' against 'Main Street' – is a ruse insofar as it obfuscates the actual functioning of class power: invocations of complexity and abstraction do as much to short-circuit considerations of the social practices and political struggles that constitute finance as they do to elucidate it.[1] They conceal the mutual imbrication of fictitious capital (i.e. capital that derives profits in a manner not immediately tied to commodity production) and productive capital (i.e. capital invested in the production of commodities), reinforcing belief in the transcendence of finance over the social domain of labour. The critical power of poetry, I would suggest, is not a matter of opposing concrete authenticity to abstract semblance but of reckoning with the social, political, and discursive implications of the distinctions between the abstract and the concrete, the complex and the simple. My argument is thus not that Quart's poetry is simply ideological, nor that it should be understood as purely derivative of the dominant social formations identified with finance. Instead, in its struggle and failure to achieve critical autonomy from financialisation, Quart's *Monetized* articulates a space in which the critical act of social mediation can occur, or in which the opposition between the abstract and the concrete comes to be replaced by a lyric thinking of social genres of abstraction and concretion. In short, lyric poetry in the age of finance offers one manner of thinking through the entanglements of social life with financial abstraction.

Quart's is only one among a number of responses to finance in the contemporary landscape of poetry. This essay does not attempt to survey every one of these responses. Rather, it enquires into two matters: first, the capacity for poetry to maintain a critical stance in respect to financialised capitalism; second, the manner in which the lyric subject of recent poetry has adapted to the financialisation of capitalism. It concerns itself especially with the overlap between these matters, with the question of how a transformation of the lyric subject might herald a new critical power. My point of departure for this account is Theodor Adorno's well-known essay 'On Lyric Poetry and Society,' which asserts that the 'lyric work hopes to attain universality through unrestrained individuation' (1991, p. 38). Adorno continues:

> The universality of the lyric's substance, however, is social in nature. [E]ven the solitariness of lyrical language itself is prescribed by an individualistic and ultimately atomistic society, just as conversely its general cogency depends on the intensity of its individuation.
>
> *(1991, p. 38)*

Adorno suggests that the genre of lyric poetry involves a constitutive paradox: it utters the universal only insofar as it creates a private style. At the same time, Adorno insists that lyric poetry's pretensions are inherently social; they are a consequence of capitalism insofar as

> [t]he lyric spirit's idiosyncratic opposition to the superior power of material things is a form of reaction to the reification of the world, to the domination of human beings by commodities that has developed since the beginning of the modern area, since the industrial revolution became the dominant force in life.
>
> *(1991, p. 40)*

Originally published in 1957, Adorno's essay surveys modernist poetry as it grapples with a moment of capitalism (Fordism, monopoly capitalism, imperialism) in which individuality itself becomes mass-produced and universality amounts to the crushing weight of the capitalist social totality.[2] The poetry on which Adorno focuses dramatises the impossibility of aesthetic autonomy, even as it painfully longs for the transcendence of capitalist existence. In a dialectical manner, it is not the reconciliation of capitalist contradictions but the intensification of contradiction to a point of crisis that measures the success of the poem. Adorno discovers critical power in poetry that strives to overcome capitalist social relations, but that in the process of doing so shatters apart, leaving behind the ruins of poetry's utopian longings. These ruins are not only traces of failure but also testaments to a refusal of resignation – signs of hope, however, faint.

That being said, the contemporary moment of capitalism does not correspond to the situation about which Adorno was writing. The story of the transition to this moment (late capitalism, post-Fordism, postmodernity, etc.) is a familiar one. Fredric Jameson's account remains the most canonical version, with its dialectical apprehension of the replacement of depth by surface, emotion by affect, the atomistic individual by the fragmentary schizoid, and modernist pursuit of aesthetic autonomy by postmodern revelry in pastiche (Jameson 1991). In the North American context, this moment sees the emergence of poetry that does not so much abandon the critical impulse as shift its energies towards pluralistic, reader-oriented, and populist experiments in linguistic invention. The Language poets, the New York School, and a diverse array of multi-ethnic traditions buck the desire that Adorno identified in modernist poetry – the desire for a quasi-religious transcendence of mere existence – in favour of sometimes militant, sometimes playful, interventions into everyday life. This narrative is reductive, little more than an analytical fiction, but it at least indicates the historical distance between an earlier modernist moment and the present. Yet, as Christopher Nealon has argued with reference to recent poetry, postmodernism may no longer adequately account for the relationship between capitalism and culture.

Nealon identifies a poetry whose 'stance' consists of a 'camp messianism.' These poets 'have struck a kind of camp posture toward the "damage" of late capitalism, in a way that borrows from but reinterprets both the messianism of Adorno and Benjamin and the subcultural (especially queer) trajectory of camp' (Nealon 2004).[3] Nealon elaborates this in terms of a distinction between the Language poets (qua paradigmatic postmodern poets) and what follows in their wake:

> We might say that where the Language poets discovered a reserve of uncapitalised materiality in the lively, 'aspectual' character of language – so that the open-endedness of texts might outpace their superscription by languages of power – the post-Language poets battered by another generation's-worth of the encroachments of capital, are not so ready on those aspectual reserves. They can discern them in language, of course, and in material objects, but it's not their focus; instead [...] they expend their considerable talents on making articulate the ways in which, as they look around, they see *waiting*.
>
> *(2004, p. 588)*

Less a messianism without a messiah, in Derrida's sense, Nealon finds in recent poetry a stubborn persistence in attending to the ruins of the enclosures, foreclosures, and deindustrialised wreckage wrought by capitalist accumulation since the 1990s. In terms of this essay's concerns, Nealon indicates the ways in which poetry has constituted a record of creative destruction, a mode of bearing witness to the concrete consequences of financialisation, to the territorialised ruination coextensive with deterritorialised flows of speculative capital.

At this point, it is necessary to precisely define the term financialisation. Financialisation suggests at least two historical transformations. First, it refers to the increasing role of financial operations in corporate governance and corporate revenue streams, or as Greta Krippner defines it,

> a pattern of accumulation in which profits accrue primarily through financial channels rather than through trade and commodity production. [...] 'Financial' refers here to activities relating to the provision (or transfer) of liquid capital in expectation of future interest, dividends, or capital gains.
>
> *(2005, pp. 174–5)*

The crucial index for Krippner's argument is the extent to which 'non-financial firms derive revenues from financial investments as opposed to productive activities' (2005, p. 182).

Companies open divisions devoted to financial activity that are relatively autonomous in respect to both the factory floor and the commodities produced. As Krippner explains, this kind of financialisation begins in the 1970s, accelerating in the 1980s and 1990s, in large part because it constitutes a compensatory mechanism for declining profits: financialisation substitutes purely financial gains for the profits lost to economic stagnation.[4] From this perspective, finance capital does not replace manufacturing but rather supplements it.

The second understanding of financialisation designates the proliferation of financial practices and attitudes in everyday life. The increasing role of finance in corporate governance goes hand in hand with the increasing role of finance in the household, not least because of the rise in consumer credit (credit cards, student loans, etc.). Randy Martin describes this state of affairs as follows:

> Financialisation integrates markets that were separate, like banking for business and consumers, or markets for insurance and real estate. It asks people from all walks of life to accept risk into their homes that were hitherto the province of professionals [i.e. investment bankers or brokers]. Without significant capital, people are being asked to think like capitalists.
>
> *(2002, p. 12)*

If the first understanding of financialisation implies the privileging of liquidity (the availability of cash and its financial equivalents) over material assets, the second understanding imagines the liquidisation of society, or the conversion of material means of life into flows of money easily available for investment. As Martin argues, this desire for liquidity requires a new kind of economic subject, one defined not by the protestant work ethic that Max Weber identified as the spirit of an earlier moment of capitalism (an ascetic subject willing to diligently forgo the pleasures of the moment in favour of long-term labours and rewards) but by an ethos of opportunism:

> Financialisation promises a way to develop the self, when even the noblest of professions cannot emit a call that one can answer with a lifetime. It offers a highly elastic mode of self-mastery that channels doubt over uncertain identity into fruitful activity.
>
> *(2002, pp. 10–11)*

The idea of progress gives way to a mode of short-term thinking that privileges instantaneous profits over long-term prosperity. The evaporation of sustained career trajectories, for example, leads to the multiplication of temporary jobs contingent upon a willingness to take on risk, to improvise, and to reshape the self in response to new conditions.

While ideologies of financialisation promise a transcendence of work, the material realities of financialisation have actually involved the extension of labour hours and the reduction of wages – in large part due to the ratcheting up of pressure on managers and employees by the shareholder-value model: the revolution in corporate management privileging immediate returns for investors over the long-term health of a corporation. As Dick Bryan, Martin, and Mike Rafferty articulate it: 'Derivatives markets and securitisation discipline capital to deliver high productivity and profitability or face a write-down of asset values. Demands for increased productivity, longer hours of work, and lower real wages follow accordingly' (2009, p. 470). It is tempting to read this situation as a textbook example of ideological mystification in which the fantasy of capital without labour, or profit without cost, cloaks the material reality of increased exploitation. This reading is correct, but it does not adequately account for the practical realities of financialisation as an ideological apparatus. It does not account either for the libidinal compensations offered by finance or for what might be called the biopolitical dimension of financialisation: the crossing of the abstract and the concrete so that financial techniques become lived experience. Although Michel Foucault did not have financialisation specifically in mind, his theory of neoliberalism as 'a social fabric in which precisely the basic units would have the form of the enterprise' ('*homo œconomicus* as entrepreneur of himself, as being for himself his own capital') implies this biopolitical dimension (2010, p. 226). Mystification – the illusion that financialisation entails greater, more immediate, and easier to obtain rewards – inheres in a practical rationale that traverses the economic and the political, reorganising social relations according to the model of the enterprise. In short, the ideologies of financialisation issue promissory notes that cannot be fulfilled, at least not on a mass scale, but these nonetheless transform the conducts of subjects and the qualities of social relations, substituting risk management and debt maintenance for critique, protest, and revolt.

Camp messianism constitutes a response to financialisation, not only surveying the wreckage that financialisation leaves in its wake (empty factories, increased unemployment, declines in physical and mental health) but also preserving the hope that another world is possible. Quart's *Monetized* certainly belongs to this school of camp messianism, but I want to build on Nealon's insights by calling attention to camp messianism's position within a spectrum of comportments in respect to financialisation. I have named these comportments 'the speculative sublime,' 'pragmatic accounting,' and 'social movement ecstasy' for reasons I will explain below. These comportments share in common a transformation of the lyric subject into a figure either besieged or exhilarated by financial risk. More often than not, the lyric subject performs a vanishing act, evacuated by the incursions of capital. In some cases, the lyric subject does not so much disappear as strip itself of personhood so as to become a placeholder for a social movement. In all of these comportments, we find the hope for a mode of existence irreducible to, if not altogether free from, capitalism. One could name this desire a longing for autonomy, but it would have to be of a rather different kind than the modernist version – autonomy as the effect of a refusal of the market, rather than as an innate property of the work of art/medium (Brown 2012).

Rae Armantrout's collection *Money Shot* (2011) exemplifies the comportment of the speculative sublime in respect to finance.[5] Armantrout turns towards money directly, towards the point at which the abstractions of finance become tangible not as objects but as beckoning voices. 'Soft Money,' for instance, alternates between the second-person and the third-person plural, constructing a relay race of desire in which the solicitation of a sexy non-thing ('They're sexy/because they're needy,/which degrades them.//They're sexy because/they don't need you.') inverts itself to become a frustrating paradox: 'They want to be/the thing-in-itself//*and* the thing-for-you –//Miss Thing–//but can't.//They want to be you,/but can't,//which is so hot' (Armantrout 2011, pp. 37–8). The pronominal shifts in the poem deny a place where ends would meet, generating instead a series of missed connections. The Kantian distinction between appearance and the thing itself thus becomes less an epistemological than a libidinal matter. The wry invocation of 'Miss Thing' speaks to pure frustration, as the repetition of 'but can't' strips the last vestiges of content away to culminate in a strange conjunction of spare form and pure desirous intensity ('so hot'). If there is content to the poem, it is signalled by the title, alluding as it does to the wash of unaccounted-for campaign contributions pervading U.S. politics. However, even this possibility devolves into intangible abstraction, for the sheer anonymity of these funds does not lend itself to identifiable political narratives.

Another poem in the collection, 'Money Talks,' transports readers to a realm in which the sublime intensity of finance capital itself reveals its autocratic power of command. Here is the poem:

> 1
> Money is talking
> to itself again
>
> in this season's
> bondage
> and safari look,
>
> its closeout camouflage.
>
> Hit the refresh button
> and this is what you get,
>
> money pretending
> that its hands are tied.
>
> 2
> On a billboard by the 880,
>
> money admonishes,
> 'Shut up and play.'
> *(Armantrout 2011, p. 73)*

The single 'you' in the poem reaches out to the reader only to the extent that it introduces a mass muteness: money can be loquacious only because those subject to it 'shut up.' Money is palpable, here, a clothed figure with a 'look' – even if that look is fleeting, always ready to be replaced by the push of 'the refresh button.' Finance capital enters Armantrout's lines, as capital in its purest, most counterfeit form, as money that commands without respect, feigning that 'its hands are tied,' knowing no limits, hearing only its own voice. Monetary circulation approaches a point of pure circularity, without the interruption of material concerns, or, more precisely, with matter (the commodity, the labourer) reduced to a spectator whose presence is barely tolerated. The poem is, in short, a parody of the financial fantasy of profits freed from the material necessity of labour, of circulation unloosed from production.

Armantrout's poems transmit monetary exaltation within a critical frame that marks finance as an imposter, an emperor with no clothes. In contrast, John Ashbery's collection *Planisphere* (2009) relates to financial speculation through a strange mixture of curiosity and anxiety. The poems constitute an atlas of global space that has been mortgaged off, and sold to financial powers that will not rest until the very idea of the future has been subsumed by capital. As Joshua Clover puts it, 'There is no lyrical leap to ecstasy, to someplace beyond the capacious Ashberian land. Time itself is the worldly country, and there is no other'; and this sense of worldliness is not innocent, for 'what is a mortgage, after all, but the exchange of thirty years for a plot of land now, the conversion of time into space?' (2010). The titles of the poems speak to this anxiety over a mortgaged-off future, so many of them signalling the tenuous quality of time in the contemporary period: 'Attabled with The Spinning Years,' 'The Foreseeable Future,' 'I Didn't Know What Time It Was,' 'A Penitence.' The poems suggest a tardiness endemic to the present, a sense of having arrived after the fact, in a twilight period. 'Stress Related' begins, 'You don't see so much of these anymore,/not so much of this'; 'Lost Sonnet' laments, 'They grow up too fast/these days'; and 'Working Overtime' asks,

'Where is Rumpelstiltskin when we need him?'[6] There is a regretful quality to these words. Written in the years immediately preceding the financial crash of 2008, Ashbery writes the housing bubble as a loss in advance of possession: time takes its place in the poems but only in retreat; objects come forward only to spin away. No poem captures this coming and going better than 'The Logistics,' which opens 'Then tomorrow? Then tomorrow,' goes on to trace an itinerary in which the first-person plural subject nostalgically recalls a Fordist vision of the industrial city ('To come back for a few hours to/a city of 20,800 people,/all good citizens,/stout in work in doing/washed over by a wave,/they keep ducking,/imagining') but concludes by finding the premises vacated: 'And the people? They've left too, wedged in a fucking dream' (51–2).

Ashbery dramatises the dialectically intertwined processes of financialisation and deindustrialisation, or the way in which the rise of finance capital entails a wasteland of abandoned factories, decrepit infrastructure, and empty housing. Matter does not disappear, but it does become dysfunctional, stripped of purpose, unemployed. In this context, time is not a luxury, it is a dream: the fantasy of a moment when work still carried meaning, when one could still be 'stout in work in doing.' The titular logistics of Ashbery's poem designates capital's management of the circulation of life, but it also names poetry's manoeuvring alongside capital, its doubling of capital in a margin of critical, or at least questioning, commentary.[7]

Ashbery adopts a speculative posture in *Planisphere*, lamenting the loss of time only insofar as he gathers the future into the present of his poems. In contrast to Armantrout, Ashbery relies on the durability of lyric subjects to make this loss felt; the first-person singular and plural regularly appear, and these pronominal figures do not simply feel the loss of time, they also speculate on time, on what remains of it, on what could come of it. However, in both Armantrout and Ashbery, capital threatens to usurp the place of the lyric subject. The lyric person in these poems comes with a stamp indicating that its date of expiration was years ago.

The speculative comportment acknowledges the sublime power of finance, but another comportment of contemporary poetry, what I term pragmatic accounting, adopts a different critical stance. This comportment is no less aware of the damage wrought by capitalism, but instead of speculation, it takes account of the merger between subjectivity and finance in an incremental manner. It shifts its attention from the presence or absence of the material subject to processes of materialisation and dematerialisation.[8] It does not ask whether subjects can exist but rather how they manage to survive in tenuous times. Examples of this comportment include Cathy Park Hong's *Engine Empire* (2012), Jena Osman's *Corporate Relations* (2014), and Timothy Donnelly's *Cloud Corporation* (2010). Whereas the speculative comportment maintains a melancholic attachment to Adorno's vision of the lyric as utopian vocation, this strand of poetry pragmatically negotiates the mingling of aesthetics and finance. It does not seek the realisation of the universal in the particular but admits that the universal has already been realised, for better or worse, in the practical form of capitalist circulation. In other words, this comportment acknowledges that there is no aspect of social life not coloured by capitalism, without, however, equating the financialisation of personhood with subjectivity's extinction.

Donnelly's *The Cloud Corporation* reads as if it were a treatise on the cosmology of financialised capitalism written in the margins of a corporation's ledger. Allusions to divine beings effortlessly morph into corporate planning strategy. The titular poem conducts a meteorological enquiry into financialised capitalism, charting the movement of capital as cloud formations guiding the conduct of the humans below: 'The clouds part revealing an anatomy of clouds/ viewed from the midst of human speculation, a business/ project undertaken in a bid to acquire and retain/ control of the formation and movement of clouds' (2010, p. 30).

Donnelly's cosmological bent speaks to a situation in which capital has sunk so deeply into existence that it has subsumed even the heavens. This poetry, however, does not seek to transcend this situation but to repurpose financial attitudes, lexicons, and practices towards other ends.[9] The poem 'To His Debt' negotiates the mutual imbrication of finance and personhood by accounting for the doubling of life by debt. The first four, of thirteen, couplets read:

> Where would I be without you, massive shadow
> Dressed in numbers, when without you there
>
> behind me, I wouldn't be myself. What wealth
> could ever offer loyalty like yours, my measurement,
>
> my history, my backdrop against which every
> coffee and kerplunk, when all the giddy whoring
>
> around abroad and after the more money money
> wants is among the first things you prevent.
>
> *(Donnelly 2010, p. 7)*

The critical power of the speculative comportment revolves around the elision of the lyric subject, or the sense that capital threatens to annihilate subjectivity. In contrast, here, the lyric subject comes to be doubled by its debt, the 'massive shadow/Dressed in numbers' guaranteeing that there is no getting free of one's financial obligations. This poem parodies fiscal responsibility. Its playful plosives ('kerplunk') and quirky repetitions ('around abroad'; 'money money') suggest that this situation should not be understood in binary terms but as a gradation between liberty and servitude. Debt is what assures a certain stability, a limitation to the liquidity of selfhood, in the form of a 'backdrop' or 'measurement' against which one's actions and person make (financial) sense. However, debt is also what makes living difficult, propagating an internal heteronomy according to which one's life is and is not one's own: 'there you are, supernaturally/redoubling over my shoulder like the living// wage I never make, but whose image I will always/cling to in the negative, hanged up by the feet//among the mineral about me famished like a bat/whose custom it is to make much of my neck' (8). The division of 'living//wage' over the course of two enjambed lines is a perfect image for the comportment of pragmatic accounting. It not only conveys a sense of economic and existential misery but also implies the precise extent of this comportment's critique: the living wage does not abolish capitalism but it does ameliorate its pernicious effects. Pragmatic accounting pushes back against the ideological apparatus of fiscal responsibility (or 'responsibilisation': the process of disciplining subjectivity to conform to state- and corporate-sanctioned financial norms), sketching the horizon not of a post-capitalist society but of a more livable capitalism.[10]

The final comportment to which I turn is that of social movement ecstasy: a poetry in which the instability of the lyric subject is not an effect of speculative capital's incursion but of participation in political struggle. Financialisation is no less in the atmosphere, but this poetry's tone is militant, beginning from the premise that a post-capitalist society is desirable. This poetry links up to recent social movements, including but not limited to #Occupy, #BlackLivesMatter, and environmental justice demonstrations. It asks what the place of poetry is within struggles to communise or otherwise reappropriate private property for the sake of the commons. Recent poetry by Fred Moten (*The Feel Trio*[ 2014]), Joshua Clover (*Red Epic* [2015]), and Rob Halpern (*Music For Porn* [2012] and *Common Place* [2015]) engage in a salvage project that has less to do with preserving the possibility of lyric experience than with gathering materials for revolt. This poetry recuperates the Adornian vocation of poetry – to achieve the universal in the particular – but it does so in the name of a society to come, as if the choreographies of the riot, the occupation (in the #Occupy sense), and the blockade (blockades of highways in the name of social justice for Black life) were not simply portents but tentative material bases for new ways of life.[11] The Oakland-based publisher Commune Editions is a hothouse for this poetic production, not only publishing Clover's *Red Epic* but also Jasper Berne's *We Are Nothing and So Can You* (2015), Ida Börjel's *The Sabotage Manuals* (2016), and Julianna Spahr's *That Winter the Wolf Came* (2015).

These collections reflexively reckon with the political economy of the present; they treat lyric poetry as a medium whose power resides in the linkages that it enables between the personal and the political, the individual and the social, immediacy and futurity, feeling and (critical) thought. The publisher itself proudly includes the following notice in its books, under the copyright information: 'we encourage the sharing of this book and everything else: *omnia sunt communia*.' The shared ethos of this poetry is the overcoming of capitalist relations through a commoning of language. Language becomes a space of political contestation, a domain in which the social and political determinations of the subject can be exposed to social, formal, or linguistic possibilities that exceed the parameters of entrepreneurship, risk management, and private property in general.

Spahr's *That Winter the Wolf Came* is an exemplary instance of social movement ecstasy. The poems situate themselves within a polluted landscape in which oil spills are less accidents than the necessary consequence of capital's control over ecology.[12] The collection alternates between prose poetry and more conventional line structures, but there is always a looseness to the form, a tendency to spill over the borders of lyric poetry as a genre. 'It might be that only through the minor we can feel enormity,' one poem reads:

> It might be that there is nothing to epiphany if it does not hint at the moment of sweaty relation larger than the intimate. For what is epiphanic song if it doesn't spill out and over the many that are pulled from intimacies by oil's circulations?
>
> *(Spahr 2015, p. 14)*

These lines conserve the idea of the poem as a linguistic event, as momentary transport to spiritual heights (the epiphany), but they do so only while at the same time replacing transcendence with the sweaty mess of bodies inextricable from capital's spills. Revolt becomes a spilling over and against the capitalist spill; it is not the assertion of concrete bodies against the abstraction of capital but the provisioning of relations among bodies no longer based on accumulation in terms of private property.[13] The most compelling version of this struggle comes in the penultimate poem of the collection, 'It's All Good, It's All Fucked,' which narrates the aftermath of revolt as if it were a break up with a former lover. This analogy between revolt and romance might appear to neutralise the political dimension of the struggle, but, in fact, the poem does the reverse: it exposes intimacy to political contestation; it interrogates libidinal attachments in terms of the conditions with which they are bound up; it reorients affection away from possession towards something more communal. The poem, however, does not name this former lover 'revolution' but 'Non-Revolution,' in the sense not of negation but of prelude:

> I knew going into it that it never lasts with Non-Revolution. I never thought it would. I just knew I wanted it in whatever moment I could get it. If it did not end, if it became Revolution, I knew that would be hard. That was an entirely different lover, one I was not sure I was ready for and yet longed for so much that they often showed up in my

> dreams and led me by a hand into an incredible sadness and a high so intense that the personal sadness would become incidental to the possibility. I mean I will take that hand and be lead to whatever room when it comes because oh my god, the body of Revolution is something magnificent.
>
> *(Spahr 2015, p. 71)*

Recalling the centrality of the sonnet in the tradition of lyric poetry, with its habit of apostrophising lovers, Spahr's writing cannot help but perform a double intervention: it reorients love and desires away from those possessive forms that dovetail with the reproduction of capitalism; and it redefines the poetic vocation, shifting from the individual voice as appeal to higher feelings to the individual voice as a vehicle for an anonymous uprising. Spahr does not simply put the lie to the supposed opposition between libidinal intensity (ecstasy) and political struggle (organising). She recites the joys of revolt ('a high so intense') as a way of troubling the lyric subject, of forcing it to acknowledge that its permeability to material spills implies not only the corruption of capital but also 'something magnificent': some way of being in the world beyond the dictates of finance, not science fiction but the ecstasy of belonging to something larger than oneself, something spilling over into a post-capitalist future. Although I do not have the space to elaborate on the matter, this comportment is ecopolitical insofar as it predicates the possibility of new kinds of collective relationships on a transformation of the social metabolism of human and non-human natures (what Donna Haraway terms 'naturecultures').[14]

This survey of contemporary U.S. poetry's responses to financialisation should not be understood as exhaustive. It does, however, indicate the range of such responses, as well as the persistence of lyric poetry's power for critique. The three comportments that I have articulated can be read as permutations of the critical vocation that Adorno identifies in lyric poetry, that is, poetry's capacity to register the damage wrought by capitalist social relations and to hold out hope for a redeemed world. The speculative sublime rehearses the failure of the lyric subject in respect to the intensity of capital's presence; the evacuation of the lyric subject from the poem constitutes a death knell for the aesthetic dimension; yet, the lyric word continues to sound out, a lonely voice in a post-apocalyptic wilderness of abandoned factories and rusting machinery. In contrast, pragmatic accounting adopts a less apocalyptic mode, reintroducing lyric personhood as a doppelganger of fiscal responsibility: the aesthetic dimension becomes coextensive with, if irreducible to, risk management; the desire for a living wage – for a kind of entente in respect to financialisation – substitutes for the utopian impulse. Finally, social movement ecstasy co-opts the speculative power of finance in the name of revolt, reimagining the lyric subject as a mediating figure between capitalist contamination and a society to come. What each of these comportments share in common is the knowledge that poetry's only hope of exceeding the dictates of finance is not pure transcendence but the transformation of subjects in the here and now – less risk management than a learning to dwell otherwise within the ruins.

## Notes

1 See La Berge (2014).
2 The most relevant text regarding this moment of capitalism, for my purposes, is Max Horkheimer and Theodor Adorno's *Dialectic of Enlightenment* (2002). Adorno's essay on lyric poetry offers a utopian salve of sorts in response to the *Dialectic*'s bleak vision.
3 Nealon has elaborated on this account more recently, though not under the label of 'camp messianism' (2011).

4 Krippner's focus, it should be noted, is on the United States, but her argument can be extrapolated in respect to global capitalist conditions, provided that one reckons with a global division of labour in which specific nations and international organisations (the IMF, the World Bank, etc.) wield financial power. Giovanni Arrighi performs such an analysis (1994).
5 Alison Shonkwiler articulates the concept of the financial sublime but in reference to Don DeLillo's prose work (Shonkwiler 2010).
6 John Ashbery, *Planisphere*, pp. 104, 54, 146. Further references cited parenthetically in the body of the essay.
7 Deborah Cowen, Alberto Toscano, and Jasper Bernes have recently argued for the centrality of logistics in the reproduction of contemporary capitalism (Bernes 2013; Cowen 2014; Toscano 2011).
8 Christopher Breu describes financialisation in terms of processes of materialisation and dematerialisation (Breu 2017).
9 This comportment of pragmatic accounting is notably similar to the social practice aesthetics that transform debt into medium as described by Leigh Claire La Berge (2015).
10 Maurizio Lazzarato offers an incisive critique of responsibilisation as a manner through which power operates in neoliberal regimes (Lazzarato 2012, 2015). For another reading of Donnelly's poem, see Annie McClanahan (2016), pp. 91–5.
11 Joshua Clover's recent book-length study of riots considers the reemergence of riots, as well as blockades and occupations, as definitive of the contemporary moment of capital (2016).
12 Spahr has written with Joshua Clover regarding the inextricability of capitalism and ecology (2014, 2016).
13 I make this distinction in part as a response to Franco Berardi's provocative, but quite narrow, conception of poetry as sensuous revolt against capitalist austerity measures (2012). Berardi does not adequately account for the productive uses poetry makes of abstraction.
14 On the term 'naturecultures,' see Haraway (2008). In another essay, I hope to show how Juliana Spahr participates in a project to revitalise the commons as an ecological project, one which contests the financialisation of the life-world. In addition to Spahr, see Nick Dyer-Witheford (2006), Jason W. Moore (2015), and Kim Stanley Robinson (2017).

## References

Adorno, T. 1991. 'On Lyric Poetry and Society,' in *Notes to Literature*, Vol. 1, pp. 37–54. Columbia University Press, New York.

Armantrout, R. 2011. *Money Shot*, Wesleyan University Press, Middletown, CT.

Arrighi, G. 1994. *The Long Twentieth Century: Money, Power, and the Origins of Ourt Times*, Verso Press, New York.

Ashbery, J. 2009. *Planisphere*, HarperCollins, New York.

Benjamin, W. 2006. *The Writer of Modern Life: Essays on Charles Baudelaire*, The Belknap Press of Harvard University Press, Cambridge, MA.

Berardi, F. 2012. *The Uprising: On Poetry and Finance*, Semiotext(e), Cambridge.

Bernes, J. 2013. 'Logistics, Counterlogistics, and the Communist Prospect,' *Endnotes*, vol. 1, no. 3. Available from: https://endnotes.org.uk/issues/3/en/jasper-bernes-logistics-counterlogistics-and-the-communist-prospect. [10 September 2016]

Breu, C. 2017. 'Of Markets and Materiality: Financialization and the Limits of the Subject,' in S. Grattan and C. Haines (eds), *Cultural Critique*, Special Issue: 'What Comes After the Subject?' no. 96 (Spring, 2017).

Brown, N. 2012. 'The Work of Art in the Age of its Real Subsumption under Capital,' *Nonsite*. Available from: http://nonsite.org/editorial/the-work-of-art-in-the-age-of-its-real-subsumption-under-capital. [13 September, 2016]

Bryan, D., Martin, R. and Rafferty, M. 2009. 'Financialisation and Marx: Giving Labour and Capital a Financial Makeover,' *Review of Radical Political Economics*, vol. 41, no. 4, pp. 458–72.

Clover, J. 2010. 'The Bubble and the Globe,' *The Nation*, 25 February. Available from: www.thenation.com. [10 September, 2016]

Clover, J. 2016. *Riot Strike Riot: The New Era of Uprisings*, Verso, New York.

Clover, J., and Spahr, J. 2014. *#Misanthropocene: 24 Theses*, Commune Editions, Oakland, CA.

Clover, J. and Spahr, J. 2016. 'Gender Abolition and Ecotone War,' *South Atlantic Quarterly*, vol. 115, no. 2, pp. 291–311.
Cowen, D. 2014. *The Deadly Life of Logistics: Mapping Violence in Global Trade*, University of Minnesota, Minneapolis.
Donnelly, T. 2010. *The Cloud Corporation*, Wave Books, New York.
Dyer-Witheford, N. 2006. 'Species-Being and the New Commonism: Notes on an Interrupted Cycle of Struggles,' *The Commoner*, vol. 11, pp. 15–32.
Foucault, M. 2010. *The Birth of Biopolitics: Lectures at the Collège de France, 1978–1979*, trans. Graham Burchell, Picador, London.
Haraway, D. 2008. *When Species Meet*, University of Minnesota Press, Minneapolis.
Horkheimer, M. and Adorno, T. 2002, *Dialectic of Enlightenment*, Stanford University Press, Stanford, CA.
Jameson, F. 1991. *Postmodernism, or, the Cultural Logic of Late Capitalism*, Duke University Press, Durham, NC.
Jobst, A. 2008. 'What Is Securitisation?' *Finance and Development*. Available from: www.imf.org/external/pubs/ft/fandd/2008/09/pdf/basics.pdf. [16 September, 2016]
Krippner, G. 2005. 'The financialization of the American economy,' *Socio-Economic Review*, vol. 3, no. 2, pp. 173–208.
La Berge, L. 2014. 'The Rules of Abstraction: Methods and Discourses of Finance,' *Radical History Review*, vol. 118, pp. 93–112.
La Berge, L. 2015. 'Wages against Artwork: The Social Practice of Decommodification,' *South Atlantic Quarterly*, vol. 114, no. 2, pp. 571–93.
Lazzarato, M. 2012. *The Making of Indebted Man*, trans. Joshua David Jordan, Semiotext(e), Cambridge.
Lazzarato, M. 2015. *Governing by Debt*, trans. Joshua David Jordan, Semiotext(e), Cambridge.
Martin, R. 2002. *The Financialisation of Daily Life*, Temple University Press, Philadelphia, PA.
McClanahan, A. 2016. *Dead Pledges: Debt, Crisis, and Twenty-First Century Culture*, Stanford University Press, Stanford, CA.
Moore, J. 2015. *Capitalism in the Web of Life: Ecology and the Accumulation of Capital*, Verso, New York.
Nealon, C. 2004. 'Camp Messianism, or, the Hopes of Poetry in Late-Late Capitalism,' *American Literature*, vol. 76, no. 3, pp. 579–602.
Nealon, C. 2011. 'Bubble and Crash: Poetry in Late-Late Capitalism,' in *The Matter of Capital: Poetry and Crisis in the American Century*, Harvard University Press, Cambridge, MA.
Quart, A. 2015. *Monetized*, Miami University Press, Miami.
Robinson, K. 2017. *New York 2140*, Orbit.
Shonkwiler, A. 2010. 'Don DeLillo's Financial Sublime,' *Contemporary Literature*, vol. 51, no. 2, pp. 246–82.
Spahr, J. 2015. *That Winter the Wolf Came*, Commune Editions, Oakland, CA.
Toscano, A. 2011. 'Logistics and Opposition,' *Mute*. Available from: www.metamute.org/editorial/articles/logistics-and-opposition. [22 September 2016]

# 24

# GLOBALIZATION

## Everything in chains; the aesthetics of global capitalism

*Kyle Wanberg*

> The deepest meaning conveyed by the idea of globalization is that of the indeterminate, unruly and self-propelled character of world affairs; the absence of a centre, of a controlling desk, of a board of directors, of a managerial office.
>
> —*Zygmunt Bauman (1998: 59)*

> Capitalism is a system of relationships, which go from inside to out, from outside to in, from above to below, everything is in chains. Capitalism is a condition both of the world and the soul.
>
> —*Franz Kafka (Janouch, 90)*

In 1993, Mary Louise Pratt identified three major historical trends in the academic study of literature and culture that would define the changes taking place at the end of the twentieth century: globalization, democratization, and decolonization. She defined globalization as "the increased integration of the planet, the increasingly rapid flows of people, information, money, commodities, and cultural productions, and the changes of consciousness which result" (Bernheimer, 59). At the time she was writing, decolonization and democratization imbued globalization with critical possibility. Yet, it is also clear that these interpenetrating processes are susceptible to reversal and backlash. And while certain changes in consciousness have accompanied increased mobility of populations, information, and finance, they have not wrought the desired emancipatory nor democratizing effects.

Drawing attention to the way its utterance on certain lips suggests entitlement, while on other's, a source of misery, Zygmunt Bauman argues that "globalization" is fast becoming a shibboleth (1998: 1). Globalization means something different to those who are in a position to gain from these flows, and those who are fixed, degraded, and immobilized by them. While it has indeed allowed for greater mobility for certain individuals, those who belong to the class devoted to tourism, finance, and investment, globalization has caused others to grapple with the movement of jobs and capital elsewhere. As Bauman suggests, the increasing separation and bifurcation of the populace has an effect of introducing a certain sense of insecurity into the ranks of those who have something to gain from the continuing processes of globalization (Bauman, 1998: 2). This insecurity has led to the criminalization and policing of those who do not benefit, imposing "safety" measures upon increasingly immobilized groups. Equally policed are the large-scale migrations of economic and humanitarian refugees that are increasing as corporate raiding and global monetary instruments have weakened the political and governing structures in the regions from which they are fleeing.

One of the problems with developing a clear understanding of globalization is that its material effects can be cited in abundance and in multifarious ways; yet, its own definitions and representations remain difficult to pin down. The lack of consensus in critical writings on globalization abounds. Indeed, some writers seem to identify it as more or less coextensive with the present (Szeman) or with the period following the Cold War (Appadurai; Bauman, 1998). Others, such as Immanuel Wallerstein, take a long view of globalization, describing it as a process that has been at work since at least the fifteenth century. Walter Mignolo offers a compromise between these views, exploring globalization as a process that has been ongoing for the past 500 years but one which has acquired a new character over the last half-century (279). Other critics emphasize what Vilashini Cooppan has called the cultural axis of globalization over the economic, tending to focus on elements such as interconnectivity, space-time compression, virtual contact between people across the globe, greater opportunities for cultural exchange, and the emergence of worldwide media and technologies. In other words, the term comes to signify differently in different critics' hands. Indeed, for this reason, both Imre Szeman and Emily Apter have called it "an amorphous term" (Szeman 4; Apter 71). Hence, there is an urgent need for a reevaluation of globalization, its forms, effects, and implications for aesthetics.

Calling to mind the ubiquity of Starbucks and Google mapping systems, globalization is both underdeveloped and overdetermined as an idea. As Robert Reich has suggested, "Globalization is one of those words to have gone from obscurity to meaningless without any intervening period of coherence" (Reich). Likewise, the principle upon which it draws, the global, does not declare a clear or fixed paradigm. Rather, the term gestures to uncertain and fluctuating sets of relations in the world. These relations include the history of colonialism, modern-day transnational capitalism, digital interconnectivity, and international politics. The global is used to describe everything from European imperialism, to the aspirations of finance capital, to the vast networks of information and exchange that are part of everyday life in the twenty-first century.

While scholars have spent decades investigating and criticizing the effects of globalization, recently it has been taken to task in the political arena by forms of xenophobic nationalism. In Europe with the Brexit decision, and in the US with the 2016 election, the aesthetics of globalization took center stage. In what seemed to be a break with tradition, the conservative candidates and politicians expressed the greater hostility to global trade pacts. This seeming reversal, which has been unfolding slowly over the past thirty or forty years, in fact suggests that beneath its claims to integration and making space for multiculturalism, the idea of globalization and the global has always been haunted by nationalist specters. Moreover, these traces can be found in the aesthetics of the globe itself and the history of aesthetics in areas of cultural production like literature. Therefore, rather than thinking of these new developments in Europe and the United States against globalization as some kind of radical opposition, might they be seen as embedded in the project of globalization itself? In order to continue with any sustained critique of globalization and the exclusionary, nationalistic co-optation of that critique, the aesthetics of globalization must be interrogated, to look for alternate ways to frame this history and the aesthetic and political forms it has produced.

My argument in this chapter assumes that globalization has an aesthetic dimension which may be teased out of its various processes, representations, and effects. Its aesthetic implications are not limited to constructions of space-time, the possibilities for continued life on the planet, digital and surveillance technologies, or the deregulation of global markets or their effects. It also has an important impact on the critical imagination. The process of globalization entails a form of becoming that is perpetually incomplete. This is part of the reason why the term carries such semantic instability. It is why so many efforts to resist the economic forms of oppression implied within the term have produced analogous, but distinct concepts, such as oneworldedness (Apter), *mondialité* (Glissant), border gnosis (Mignolo), worldliness (Said), and planetarity (Spivak). Such concepts mirror the universality of the global while developing its potential for critique.

This chapter explores how the idea of globalization is disseminated in overlapping but distinguishable ways across historical moments, aesthetic forms, and economic analytics. It traces the idea at the root of globalization, the global, from earlier iterations that predate the term itself to its contemporary ubiquitous usage as a form (the global), a process (globalization), and a policy program (globalism). From an aesthetic perspective, I explore how these interrelated ideas are represented, critiqued, and mobilized and explore whether the dissemination of this relatively young term really signifies something new for aesthetic and literary productions.

## From the world to the global

The widespread adoption of the term "the global" is symptomatic of the growing interconnection among universities, financial agencies, and consumer culture as flows of capital and transnational economic exchange increase on an international scale. Switching from an earlier focus on the "world," politicians and journalists alike have started heralding the contemporary era as a "global" one. Writers and critics working within literary studies and adjacent fields have had to grapple with the defamiliarizing effect this has on them and their sense of place and time. There is an expectation that scholars must come to terms with the "global context." This relatively new demand to situate academic scholarship by mapping it within this paradigm has a decisive, if ambiguous, effect on twenty-first-century literary history. It also has a significant impact on anticolonial discourse and analysis.

Yet in spite of its widespread usage, "the global" is a term that somehow alludes to nearly everything without necessarily clearly denoting anything in particular. The concept in English is relatively young, from a term that described the shape of a sphere in the seventeenth century; "the global" had been transformed into a concept of universality that remained in rare usage by the end of the nineteenth century. It gained traction in the 1960s and 1970s as critics of cultural and economic processes sought new ways of describing interconnectivity and worldwide scenarios of war and disaster during the Cold War era, such as global nuclear war and global environmental impact and devastation. During the same period, countercultural critics and environmental activists drew inspiration from the "Blue Marble" photograph of the planet and other similar photographs of the earth seen from space, raising popular consciousness of the fragility of the earth in the cosmos. In the years following, the "global" semantically changed from a modifier used to describe specific sets of phenomena (i.e. "the global village" or "global warming") to something much more general. By the end of the twentieth century, the concept graduated to become one that circulates ubiquitously but without requiring conceptual moorings. A major shift in representation in the way human beings think and talk about themselves in relation to the world was taking place, as the global was invested with aesthetic and semantic significance.

This emerging universality betokens a radical kind of equivocality. In the United States, the global has crept into the rhetoric around international politics and determinations about foreign policy. By 1975, Henry Kissinger was discussing the birth pangs of a "truly global society" (Qtd. in Curtis), and in 2003, Donald Rumsfeld declared the existence of a "global war on terror" (Rumsfeld). While "globalism" became associated with a political program to deregulate trade and impose austerity measures in the wake of the 2008 financial crisis, the deterritorializing processes expanding the frontiers of capitalism are not narrowly reflected in any single political platform or set of policies. There is a dangerous tendency to identify the protection of borders and the mobilization of nationalism as counterpoint or even anathema to globalism, rather than being part and parcel of the dynamics by which certain forms of global capital expand themselves.

This dissociative logic seems to forget the long and complicated history of contradictions subsumed under the equivocity of universal forms, beginning long before the contemporary usage of "globalism" and the "global," in which the ascendency of nationalisms and their proscription alternate and create friction. While the discursive formation of the "global" from Kissinger to Rumsfeld seems to imply that national boundaries are on the verge of fading away, this is a calculated illusion. Its futurity can be seen reflected in earlier cosmopolitan conceptions of the world. For example, debates in literary studies over the tradition a work exemplifies reflect analogous forms of vacillation. In Renaissance Europe, the recognition of national literary traditions—and, as a result, national rivalries—came into existence along with the formal establishment of national borders and modern European statehood (Casanova, 5). Nations represented the universal framework against which culture would be imagined (Anderson). Literary production held a special place in the formation of national identities and characters, and the nation represented the totality of aesthetic imagination. Thus, literature has an important role to play in communicating and promoting nationalisms, as well as their sublimation and critique. These contradictions are contained and entwined within the genealogy of the modern nation-state. Moreover, the world form is itself limited and tends to privilege certain geographies and forms of knowledges over others. Hence, the cosmopolitanism of "world literature" is not separate from the national rivalries across literary traditions.

Goethe's ideas about *weltliteratur* represent an important shift in perspective from the projects set forth by European nations to promote discourses that enshrined their own literatures. This shift entailed a change of the dominant lens through which to understand cultural and aesthetic achievements. The limited purview of the nation-state was said to give way to the all-embracing scope of the world. Yet, it is important to remember that while world literature has come to be seen as a cosmopolitan form of literary aesthetics, and one that is not entirely circumscribed by the nation form or a single linguistic tradition (the idea of *weltliteratur* as considered by Marx and Engels in *The Communist Manifesto:* a newly emergent intellectual commodity with its own circuits of production, translation, marketing, and consumption), Goethe never renounced the kind of factional competition that characterized national literary perspectives. In the same breath that he introduces the concept of world literature, remarking that "the epoch of world literature is at hand," Goethe singles out and addresses his fellow Germans, insisting that they develop their literary endeavors through wider reading practices for the enhancement and progress of German literary culture alone (Goethe, 165).

The international perspective Goethe was offering sought to shore up German modernity by edifying German literature. Perhaps this is why, despite Goethe's assertion of the incoherence and anachronism of national literature, or his conviction that poetry had become the "universal possession of mankind" (165), world literature has not actually supplanted national literary traditions. Indeed, as the Editors of *n*+1 have recently suggested, "the big story since Goethe's proclamation of the imminence of world literature, in other words, has been, until recently, the *nationalization* of literatures" (*n*+1).

One of the legacies of Goethe's great cosmopolitan vision for world literature is that the spaces where colonialism and other imperial ambitions have thrived are marked as peripheral even where they have been central to these ambitions. The worldly perspective Goethe put forward allowed Europeans greater access to non-Western literary traditions, but this was framed as being wholly in the service of the expanding of a European enlightenment consciousness. The defining characteristic of this expansive consciousness was not its sensitivity to the cultures for which European imperial projects had dire consequences, but rather its capacity to adapt and expand, and to appropriate other cultures under the banner of universalism. Underlying this consciousness are narratives maintaining Europe's ascendency over the rest of the world that gave license to the uneven international markets that emerged and the colonial regimes established to manage them. Just as nationalism continued to haunt the world in the era of the Enlightenment, when culture was imagined as having universal import and as colonialism disseminated it in homogenized forms, so the global is haunted by its earlier universalistic ideologies in the guise of world and nation.

In 1975, the Greene report on professional standards, submitted to the American Comparative Literature Association, spoke of a dizzying widening of intellectual horizons that marked a transition from world literature to global literature. It states that "a new vision of *global* literature is emerging, embracing all the verbal creativity during the history of our planet, a vision which will soon begin to make our comfortable European perspectives parochial" (Bernheimer, 30). But is it true that the transition between these frameworks, of world and globe, really leaves behind the residues of European provincialism?

## The aesthetics of an ongoing process

Globalization entails a set of processes that create peripheries dependent upon centers where capital is amassed. Contrary to ideas that these processes automatically signal greater equality or mark the effacements of old colonial centers of power (c.f. Pirie; Coy), rather, they are perfectly in line with the history of colonial expropriation. This is why critics such as Wallerstein and Mignolo have discussed globalization as coterminous with colonialism, as a process that began 500 years ago. From the latter half of the twentieth century to the present, global processes have continued to build upon historical forms of extractive economic rationality, further expanding the system described by David Harvey as "accumulation by dispossession" (Harvey). Indeed, Arjun Appadurai argues that today, globalization is "characterized by disjunctive flows that generate acute problems of social well-being" (6). Yet, the overestimation of powers administered under the aegis of different historical rubrics, such as colonialism and globalization, opens up the processes indicated by these rubrics to exposure and attack. Thus, we can see new opportunities for friction, reflection, and subversion of the forms of dominance and oppression at hand through an exploration of the way globalization is imagined.

As the processes of globalization develop, forms of communication and information join in the commodification process and require circulation just like material goods. Not surprisingly, these flows often take place in the same economic networks that have been developed and secured by the material–capital exchange markets. Under the broad rubric of the global, these networks generate new peripheries that become increasingly neglected and opaque. These broadly political concerns with globalization set the stage for thinking about aesthetic production because its power works through the very institutions and spaces where literature and art are studied. Globalization in this sense is eminently relevant to how works of literature and aesthetic production are imagined, evaluated, and disseminated.

Achille Mbembe warns that globalization has facilitated the potential destruction of populations deemed superfluous. He calls the formation of political control that administers this population control "an economy of coercion" (Mbembe in Appadurai, 51). Within this economy, politics signals an end to the age of humanism. It means, as Mbembe writes, that reason and facts do not matter, only the perception of winning, of achieving triumph over one's competitors within the market of politics. As he writes, "In this context, the most successful political entrepreneurs will be those who convincingly speak to the losers, to the destroyed men and women of globalisation and to their ruined identities" (Mbembe). The interpenetration of politics and aesthetics is realized in this cynical embrace of the disenchantment of the world.

If this is among the effects of the processes of globalization, there are certainly grounds not only for developing a critique of these processes, but also of looking elsewhere for liberatory politics and possibilities. Claire Colebrook, for example, suggests that the globe itself is a conceptual and figural trap, a kind of dead-end for ethical thinking. She argues that "now is the time to think non-globally" (32), since the global imagination, that figure of an ecological and organic whole, is essentially defective and suicidal. It is imagined as an object that can be sacrificed to destructive forces of globalization deemed beyond human control. As she writes, "the globe or earth as the planet that was blessed with the contingency of life, including the human species whose global imagination has done so much to create destructive systems beyond its own power and comprehension, cannot be saved" (Colebrook, 38).

Yet, Colebrook's exhortation comes without a definite alternative. Gayatri Spivak has long been a vocal critic of the effect of globalization on the humanities. Referring to her proposal of the planetary as a critical alternative to the global, she describes a problem with the contemporary fixation on globalization:

> Globalization is achieved by the imposition of the same system of exchange everywhere. It is not too fanciful to say that, in the gridwork of electronic capital, we achieve something that resembles that abstract ball covered in latitudes and longitudes, cut by virtual lines, once the equator and the tropics, now drawn increasingly by other requirements—imperatives?—of Geographical Information Systems. The globe is on our computers. It is the logo of the World Bank. No one lives there, and we think that we can aim to control globality. The planet is in the species of alterity, belonging to another system; and yet we inhabit it, indeed are it. It is not really amenable to a neat contrast with the globe.
>
> *(Spivak, 338)*

Distinguishing the planetary from the virtual network of lines that constitute the framework of electronic capital, Spivak offers a visualization of the processes in action that are designated under the rubric of contemporary forms of globalization. Innovations in the speed of financial exchanges, racing along lines made up of fiber-optic cables, within electronic information systems of virtual exchange, ensure their recursion as systems of exchange forever imposing themselves on ways of life and forms of representation. This is the image of the network under the aegis of the new status quo. Its self-replicating logarithms lull viewers into falsely imagining that these virtual technologies, with their mapping and security systems, contribute to some sense of total control. Impugning economic discourses with the hubris to declare the regularity of systems of exchange on the basis of these models, Spivak is signaling other ways of considering the problem. According to her, the planet does not simply offer a model. This "species of alterity" does not belong to the reiterating sets of lines making up the gridwork of globalization, but rather is indistinguishable from the collectivity inhabiting it. Such responses to the aesthetics of globalization offer alternatives to the impact of the global on our ways of thinking.

They highlight the fact that there is nothing inevitable about globalization, and that only by finding an alternative aesthetics that is both planetary and noneconomic, we can challenge this sense of inevitability. The misleading conceptualization of the global as an unavoidable and fatalistic form of progress is what I turn to in the following section as "globalism."

## Policy as sleight of hand

Globalism refers to that feature of contemporary globalization that has been sanctioned as the correct (or only) practice and policy of government: to allow the market to regulate itself, to create conditions for competition to determine winners and losers, and to prioritize financial capital over labor capital in the workforce. In political and cultural criticism, globalism is often entwined with the ideology of neoliberalism.

Neoliberalism emerged in the postwar period in the United States as an objection to both the logic of Keynesian or social democratic statecraft on the one hand and fascism on the other. Coined at a meeting in Paris in 1938, the term is often associated with the theoretical writings of F. A. Hayek, promoting the freedom of the market and economic theory in determining policy decisions. The ideas of neoliberalism succeeded in becoming policy starting in the 1970s and 1980s in the US and the UK, as the protections of the liberal democratic state built upon the ideas of Keynes were rigorously and systematically dismantled. More recently, the European Union has undergone similar reforms under the rubric of "austerity." As George Monbiot writes:

> After Margaret Thatcher and Ronald Reagan took power, the rest of the package soon followed: massive tax cuts for the rich, the crushing of trade unions, deregulation, privatisation, outsourcing and competition in public services. Through the IMF, the World Bank, the Maastricht treaty and the World Trade Organisation, neoliberal policies were imposed – often without democratic consent – on much of the world. Most remarkable was its adoption among parties that once belonged to the left: Labour and the Democrats, for example (Monbiot).

The policies of neoliberalism are ongoing and diffuse, encouraging the unrestricted and unregulated operation of the market conceived as the tautological progression of the globe itself. It takes form in administrative policy strategies, from the elimination of financial laws to disrupting the power of unions.

As opposed to the more ambiguous periodization of globalization, neoliberal globalism is a relatively discrete period. The recent imposition of neoliberal reform as governmental policy tends to be cloaked in the guise of globalization because it offers a totalizing aesthetic of an overwhelming and inevitable progression. As Immanuel Wallerstein states, "we are told that there is no alternative to globalization, to whose exigencies all governments must submit" (ix). In other words, globalism is premised upon such ideas of its own inevitability and of its character as a natural phenomenon. This conception has been dealt a series of blows. Recently, public discourse espousing nationalism and protectionism has been escalating, through which politicians on the right candidly express their "hostility" to globalization. As a rhetorically specific but politically diffuse target for these groups, globalization allows them to appeal to the anger of those disenfranchised by globalist policies, while avoiding any true confrontation with the processes driven by neoliberalism underlying them. In other words, it presents an opportunity for political dissimulation, while effectively allowing the economic systems to continue unaltered. These politicians draw upon this nation-centered vision, which was never fully eradicated or eclipsed in the global form to begin with.

During the 2016 election in the United States, Hillary Clinton, a candidate who came to represent the unchecked program of globalism, was pitted against Donald Trump. Trump challenged the freedom of the press and endorsed xenophobic reactionary policies. His rallies became frenzied caldrons of anti-immigrant fervor and massive demonstrations of public dissatisfaction with the results from decades of neoliberal policies. In a surprise victory, Trump carried the election, without, however, winning the popular vote. In the wake of these events, Cornel West suggested that Trump's victory signaled the death knell of the ideology of globalism. In his article "Goodbye, American Neoliberalism: A New Era is Here," he writes that "the neoliberal era in the United States ended with a neofascist bang" (West). Of course, West is suggesting that the era of globalism where deregulated commerce was protected by Democrats in the United States has given way to a more authoritarian form of politics that aims to dispense with basic civil liberties. Yet, West's idea that Trump's authoritarianism is incompatible with the continued proliferation of neoliberalism seems to underestimate the problem. Neoliberalism never was democratic. In fact, Bauman argues that its covert dismantling of social liberalism is what led to Trump's rise. In so doing, he suggests that the "decisionist" rule of authoritarians like Trump draws upon the politics of identifying and excluding "foreigners" and of attacking the vaguely defined 'establishment.' These politics, identified with the will of the strong leader, are imagined as a quick fix to problems endemic in a country which has endured thirty to forty years of neoliberal hegemony (Bauman, 2016).

The 2016 election was staged as a choice between authoritarian xenophobia and neoliberal globalism. This is a false aestheticization of political alternatives in a global system: either disavow cultural interconnection or endorse economic globalization. It precludes a critical alternative. This is why thinking alternatives to the aesthetics of globalization as a predetermined eventuality is important. One of the surreptitious consequences of neoliberalism is to transform politics into economics, resulting in the hollowing out of democracy. Its economic rationality has an important impact on culture in that it atomizes collectivity, atrophying constructions of critical citizenship and consciousness. Moreover, one of its most overt effects is the impact it has on the imagination, and hence on the study of aesthetics. The economic logic of neoliberalism is applied as a universal so that there appears no way out, no alternative models for thinking, and no escape hatch. This economic rationality is globalism's hallmark, one with dire consequences for human beings and their continued survival on the planet. Moreover, it manufactures apathy in response to the radical disequilibrium caused by accumulation by dispossession and its attendant forms of securitization.

The antidemocratic element within neoliberalism is not simply the way it naturalizes itself or paints its progression as inexorable. There is something even more insidious here. Zygmunt Bauman sees the tripartite motto of liberalism (Egalité, Fraternité, Liberté) as hanging in a delicate ideological balance in the modern state form. Neoliberalism actively seeks to dismantle this axiomatic confluence of ideas, particularly by obliterating the element of Egalité (Bauman, 2016). And Wendy Brown has argued that the logic of neoliberalism, which pervades all dimensions of existence, presents a basic challenge to democratic elements within society at large, having already eroded liberal democracy from within. As she writes:

> The neoliberal solution to problems is always more markets, more complete markets, more perfect markets, more financialization, new technologies, new ways to monetize. Anything but collaborative and contestatory human decision making, control over the conditions of existence, planning for the future; anything but deliberate constructions of existence through democratic discussion, law, policy.
>
> *(Brown, 221–2)*

If this logic frames globalization and its impact as an economic tautology, then it not only signals the erosion of liberal values such as equality or democratic contest, but also the degeneration of the imaginative possibilities that are as yet politically unrealized. To confront this crisis of imagination, an analysis of globalization must therefore also consider the aesthetic reframings and subversions of this logic.

## Aesthetics of the global

Democratic efforts to disrupt this logic are critical. With regard to aesthetics, globalism has an ambivalent significance. The contrapuntal effects of criticism, organization, and activism may create conditions necessary for finding alternatives to the self-replicating and naturalizing processes of globalization. In fact, it is possible that the attention that globalization has received, taken together with its equivocacy, may offer an opportunity to think about the global in ways that are antithetical to the economic and ideological trends that have been identified as characteristic of globalization. As Imre Szeman suggests, "the wide-ranging debate in the academy over the precise meaning of globalization might point to the fact that it is a concept open to re-narration and re-metaphorization" (8).

Another lesson could be taken from the way cosmopolitan and nationalistic perspectives have been entwined within world literature, especially in light of the history of European colonialism and the liberation movements across the globe to end colonial oppression. In these struggles, nationalism takes on a new significance, but so too do efforts to read across anticolonial traditions for a politics and aesthetics of opposition and critique. By overturning certain aesthetic hierarchies that are reinforced by established markets of world literature, many of the old values and structures that were created during and in the service of colonialism may be dismantled. This would require not simply an opening up of the literary discipline but toppling its naturalized economic forms of rationality, and examining aesthetics from a nonhierarchical position. As Mignolo suggests, globalization has contradictory effects, both in line with forms of colonialist suppression, as well as drawing attention to linguistic diversity outside of the framework of the nation form. As he writes:

> Globalization made possible both massive migrations and the visibility of local social movements. By the same token, it made possible the resurgence of indigenous languages suppressed by colonial and imperial expansion and by the surge of fractured imperial languages within and outside national territories.
>
> *(Mignolo, 255)*

Such contradictory effects point both to the stifling atmosphere of the aesthetics of globalization and the liberatory potential that a future global aesthetics may have.

Perhaps the imagination of the global can be turned against the consequences of globalization and the entrepreneurial ethos to exploit heretofore untapped resources and populations, but only if we recognize the history of the global and its various ideological entanglements with neoliberalism and world literature. Historically, globalization has reinforced widespread neglect of non-written sources and demonstrated a predilection for works originating in dominant European languages. As a counterpoint to the aesthetics of globalization, global aesthetics might offer ways to study works of cultural production inspired by creolization, folklore, performance, and song. It may also offer a way to explore the confrontation staged between the colonial metropole and its peripheries as a way of reflecting back on the imperial center its own image in a critical and subversive light.

## References


Anderson, Benedict. *Imagined Communities: Reflections on the Origin and Spread of Nationalism.* New York: Verso Books, 2006.

Appadurai, Arjun (Ed.). *Globalization.* Durham, NC: Duke University Press, 2001.

Apter, Emily. *Against World Literature: On the Politics of Untranslatability.* Brooklyn, NY: Verso, 2013.

Bauman, Zygmunt. *Globalization: The Human Consequences.* New York: Columbia University Press, 1998.

Bauman, Zygmunt. "How Neoliberalism Prepared the Way for Donald Trump" in *Social Europe,* November 16, 2016. Web.

Bernheimer, Charles. *Comparative Literature in the Age of Multiculturalism.* Baltimore, MD: Johns Hopkins University, 1995.

Brown, Wendy. *Undoing the Demos: Neoliberalism's Stealth Revolution.* Brooklyn, NY: Zone Books, 2015.

Casanova, Pascale. *The World Republic of Letters,* trans. from the French by M. B. DeBevoise. Cambridge, MA: Harvard University, 2004.

Colebrook, Claire. "A Globe of One's Own: In Praise of the Flat Earth" in *SubStance,* 41.1 (30–9).

Cooppan, Vilashini. "World Literature and Global Theory: Comparative Literature for the New Millennium" in *Symplokē,* 9.1/2 (15–43), 2001.

Coy, Peter. "A Cheerleader for Globalization Has Second Thoughts" in *Bloomberg.* June 14, 2016. Web.

Curtis, Adam. "Baby It's Cold Outside" segment in *The Power of Nightmares: The Rise of the Politics of Fear.* BBC Documentary Film 2004.

Editors of *n+1.* "World Lite: What is Global Literature?" in *n+1,* 17, Fall 2013.

Glissant, Édouard. "Le divers du monde est imprevisible" in *Keynote Address at the Conference Beyond Dichotomies.* Stanford University, Stanford, CA, May 8–10, 1998.

Goethe, Johann Wolfgang von. *Conversations of Goethe with Johann Peter Eckermann,* trans. from the German by John Oxenford. Da Capo, 1998.

Harvey, David. "The 'New' Imperialism: Accumulation by Dispossession" in *Socialist Register,* 40, 2004: 63–87.

Janouch, Gustav. *Conversations with Kafka.* New York: New Directions Books, 1971.

Marx, Karl. "Manifesto of the Communist Party" in *Later Political Writings,* ed. by Terrell Carver. Cambridge University Press, 1996.

Mbembe, Achille. "The Age of Humanism is Ending" in *Mail & Guardian.* 22 December 2016. Web.

McLuhan, Marshall. *The Gutenberg Galaxy: The Making of Typographic Man.* Toronto, Canada: University of Toronto, 1962.

Mignolo, Walter. *Local Histories/Global Designs: Coloniality, Subaltern Knowledges, and Broder Thinking.* Princeton, NJ: Princeton University Press, 2012.

Monbiot, George. "Neoliberalism: The Ideology at the Root of All Our Problems" in *The Guardian.* April 15, 2016. Web.

Pirie, Madsen. "Ten Very Good Things 9: Globalization" in *Adamsmith.org.* October 12, 2012. Web.

Reich, Robert. Speech given on October 3, 2013, "Robert Reich explains how globalization, technology, and natural resources are reshaping global economy" in *The Georgia Straight.* Online news source, October 4, 2014. Accessed April 2, 2016.

Rumsfeld, Donald H. "Global War on Terrorism" qtd. in full in "Rumsfeld's War-on-Terror Memo" *USA Today,* Washington/Politics section, 20.05.2005. Accessed May 29, 2014 (memo dated from 2003).

Said, Edward. *The World, the Text, and the Critic.* Cambridge, MA: Harvard University Press, 1983.

Spivak, Gayatri. *An Aesthetic Education in the Era of Globalization.* Cambridge, MA: Harvard University, 2012.

Szeman, Imre. "Imagining the Future: Globalization, Postmodernism and Criticism" in *Frame: Journal of Literary Studies,* 19.2. Utrecht: 2014.

Wallerstein, Immanuel. *World Systems Analysis: An Introduction.* Durham, NC: Duke University Press, 2004.

West, Cornell. "Goodbye, American Neoliberalism: A New Era is Here" in *The Guardian.* November 17, 2016. Web.

# 25
# INFLATION

*Joseph Jonghyun Jeon*

Released by Columbia Pictures in 1984, just two years after *E.T.* and Reese's Pieces inaugurated (according to orthodoxy) a golden age of product placement that has not yet abided, and more significantly, two years after Columbia was acquired by the Coca-Cola Company, *Ghostbusters* might be read as a giddy celebration of early 1980s corporate branding logics. Recall that in 1982, the same year of the merger, the soft drink conglomerate also released Diet Coke, the first spin-off of its most famous product since the original recipe was invented 1886. We might note that the initial red and white design of the new product, which is conspicuously placed at the Ghostbuster's headquarters when Dana Barrett (Sigourney Weaver) enters, echoes very strongly the Ghostbuster's own logo, which is not only affixed on the side of their signature automobile (a refurbished 1959 Cadillac ambulance/hearse that rivals Marty McFly's Delorean as the most iconic filmic car of the 1980s), but also emblazoned on T-shirts waved (and not even worn) by the adoring crowd after the team has triumphed, near-apocalypse being the perfect time for pushing merch. Even such minor sleuthing, however, becomes unnecessary after the appearance by Ray Parker, Jr. (who wrote and recorded the hit theme song) in a 1985 Diet Coke commercial that emphasized his connection to the film. His appearance laid bare the extent to which *Ghostbusters* was a sales blitz in an era of corporate rationalization.[1]

So putting the details of Gozer the Gozerian aside, an examination of the corporate logics at work in the film might prompt an alternate focus on the film's depiction of the meteoric growth of a small business, backed by highly leveraged financing in the form of Raymond Stantz's (Dan Aykroyd) third mortgage at the usurious rate of 19%. He takes the loan after the trio of scientists are fired from Columbia University, which, though of course private, serves in the film as a stand-in for the frustrations of blinkered and ineffective public institutions in the same genus and species as the EPA, with its barky figurehead, Walter Peck (played by smarm-master William Atherton), serving as the epitome of regulatory stupidity and governmental emasculation (they joke about him having "no dick"). After all, the university does share its name with a studio bought out by a soft drink company. This convergence is in fact echoed in the film's opening credits, in which the title of film appears superimposed on a rear view of the statue of Athena at Columbia University, a statue featuring a raised scepter in Athena's right hand that, in this context, powerfully echoes the torch-bearing woman styled in Roman garb of Columbia Pictures' logo. The fact that our heroes occupy an abandoned fire house and wear uniforms in homage to public sanitation employees feeds nicely then into a complementary story about the push toward public service privatization in the period, which takes as its adversary the small-minded taboos of public oversight.

But brands not only emerge as the *sine qua non* of these privatizing urges, they also combine and proliferate, and thus reflect the accelerating mergers and acquisitions activity in the period. The only thing worse than crossing the streams, it turns out, is not crossing the streams (and here we must be speaking about revenue streams), especially in times of distress (and here we must be speaking about economic recession). "Ghostbusters" is a made-up brand name in a film that puts an entire supernatural world inside Sigourney Weaver's refrigerator just so Bill Murray can later display prominently placed Coke cans that occupy it in its non-haunted mode; and it is one of two brands in the film that do not exist in real life, the other "fake" brand being Stay Puft Marshmallows, memorably represented in the film's climax by the Stay Puft Marshmallow Man (hereafter the SPMM). In fact, Dan Akroyd's explanation for his failure to keep his mind blank in a crucial moment turns out to rehearse the logic of the brand itself: "I couldn't help it. It just popped in there."[2]

Turning our attention to the SPMM, the preoccupation with corporate branding practices in *Ghostbusters* in a period of corporate transition might here serve as an index for a broader transition in the deindustrializing political economy of the period, in which U.S. firms, including motion picture studios, reached outside of their traditional spheres in order to seek profits under the looming threat of secular stagnation. Particularly after the 1970s in which high inflation threatened to devour the purchasing power of capital, inflation targeting in particular became an important component of U.S. monetary policy, increasingly geared toward the needs of finance. A figure of inflation if there ever was one, the colossal figure of the massive inflated marshmallow man foregrounds this concern at the climax of *Ghostbusters* by representing inflation as a catastrophic spectacle. This is a fitting trope for a U.S. economy emerging out of the Volcker Shock years beginning in 1979, when the U.S. Federal Reserve Bank under the direction of Paul Volcker kept interest rates high to combat runaway inflation, and in the process sounded the death knell for U.S. heavy industry.

Though inflation is, in a sense, just how you make marshmallows, the SPMM's monstrosity specifically inheres in the fact of its out-of-scale, monstrous growth. What was a beloved memory from Ray Stantz's childhood, "something that could never ever possibly destroy us," now terrifies Egon "beyond the capacity for rational thought."[3] It's not just that the SPMM is monstrously large; it's monstrous *because* it is large, and would not be so in a smaller proportion. Like macroeconomic inflation (i.e. the relative value of money in relationship to goods and services), the SPMM is quite lovable when more modest.[4] The ideal rate of inflation for the U.S. Federal Reserve Bank is approximately 2%. If inflation is too low, there is an incentive to hoard capital and not invest. And to parry charges of reading too much into things, I refer you to a 2000 IMF seminar paper written by none other than Andrew Haldane, now Chief Economist and Executive Director of Monetary Analysis and Statistics at the Bank of England, entitled "Ghostbusting: The UK Experience of Inflation Targeting,"[5] a paper that examines the practices of global banks in response to the ghosts of inflationary pressures. Quite significantly, as in the movie, the force of ghosts is both to mark the passing of industrial capitalism and to face us with the monstrosity of inappropriate growth in a financialized era. In this context, it is worthwhile to note that the SPMM is both ghost and monster: Not translucent like other ghosts in the film or able to fly, the SPMM is rendered as Godzilla-like, as a building-sized brute that threatens urban space. Ghosts as such are figments of our imagination that turn out to be quite dangerous; and contemporary modern monetary policy in OECD countries is often focused on preventing monstrous forms of inflation, for which the SPMM offers a literal figure.

The fear of inflation manifested in the SPMM triggered practices of inflation targeting that outlasted the crises of the 1970s, first in the western postindustrial economies and then, more broadly, as a primary protocol of American empire, now in an economic mode late in its reign as a global hegemon. While in the 1970s, governments were responding to extremely high rates of inflation, inflation targeting gradually became a key part of a larger strategy geared toward reshaping sub-imperial economies, like that of the Republic of Korea (the exemplary case in this paper). This strategy was tied to the desire for more flexible labor markets, a strategy which not uncoincidentally suited American corporate interests as well as the neocolonial ambitions of Washington Consensus American empire. Inflation targeting was thus a manifestation of empire that operated less in the explicit mode of the colony, and more in the subtler mode of global finance. Furthermore, because these impositions were offered not so much as acts of aggression, as in military occupation (though the massive global presence of the U.S. military should not be understated), but rather as sound financial protocol, they masked the extent to which they facilitated the extraction and redistribution of capital from the client state to the hegemonic power. Understood to be disinterested, protocols are supposed to be neutral rules that govern interactions. In the account of late U.S. empire offered in this chapter, however, protocols are rather part of the wide-ranging attempt, reflected in cultural production, by the Washington Consensus to construct an asymmetrical system of global capital circulation that favors western firms.[6]

We will return to this scene of danger, in which inflation threatens global economic stability for Haldane and human existence in general for *Ghostbusters*, but not before a quick survey of the history of inflated art and design, obliquely indexed by the SPMM. Inflated art often expressed utopian, if vexed, sensibilities and by reconjuring it, I can contextualize the specific confluence of inflation aesthetics and political economy manifested in the SPMM. I fast-forward somewhat through the early history of the hot air balloon in the eighteenth century, continuing to the interwar airship, and to the present-day blimp as an eye-in-the-sky at major sporting events, pausing to note the persistence of populist underpinnings in this trajectory, a legacy of its initial reception in revolution-era France, which celebrated the fact that a view from up high could now be enjoyed, at least in the abstract, by prince and pauper alike.[7] I also note, quickly, the history of the inflatable doll, associated with commercial and sexual forms of fetish. Here, exemplary figures might be Bibendum, a.k.a. the Michelin Man—a figure that coincides with that company's invention of the removable pneumatic tire in 1889 (just three years after the birth of Coca Cola) and surely an ancestor of the SPMM—and Woody Allen, who featured various inflatable sex dolls and other similar objects in his early 1970s films, as in, for example, *Bananas* (1971), *Everything You Always Wanted to Know about Sex* (1972), and *Sleeper* (1971).[8]

But we should slow down as we near midcentury avant-garde art and design practices, particularly at the end of this period, as western industrial capitalism stands on the precipice of collapse. Especially in Europe, after idealistic modernist principles became disconcertingly manifest in the brutal concrete structures of postwar reconstruction, some of a younger generation of artists and architects turned to inflatable objects for an aesthetics that celebrated the airy and impermanent over the heavy and monumental. Critics have even floated the periodizing moniker, "The Inflatable Moment," to refer to this turn toward ephemeral and often kitschy structures and objects.[9] If pressed for a more specific date, I would give March of 1968 when the Utopie group, consisting of architecture students at the École des Beaux-Arts, organized an exhibition entitled *Structures Gonflables* (*Inflatable Structures*) in Paris that consisted of over a hundred pneumatic objects of various kinds, foregrounding an aesthetic that at least one critic has smugly branded "the shock of the pneu."[10] Commenting on the *longue durée* of inflatable art beginning with hot-air ballooning in revolution-era France to a very different moment of upheaval in 1968, Marc Dessauce writes of its double, self-canceling movement:

> All pneumatic scenes produced the same exaltation. Each time the effortless mediation of the inflated volume, rather than its ascensional or virtualizing effect, was at work. The daze of slow motion, as on the assembly line, the optimism of the forms and their fragile monumentality, concurred to dissipate the apprehension of the wind of change which they made visible. The virtue of pneumatics is to bear the shadow in euphoria; or even, like the king enjoying the spectacle of his vanishing privilege, to earn consent from that which is not to survive its passage.[11]

Both representing progress and its shadow, the inflated objects at the 1968 show indulged in a kind of false populism that recurs in the history of inflatable design. Focusing on the spaces of bourgeois life (inflatable sitting rooms) and the objects that might fill it (inflatable furniture), *Structures Gonflables* offered a vision of the new as quite literally full of hot air, a gleeful signature of an industrial logic at the moment of its imminent death. If the Volcker Shock meted the death blow to the western industrial economy, *Structures Gonflables* celebrated its demise. Structures that weren't structures at all seemed to burst with life while simultaneously bursting at the seams (or at least slowly leaking)—these were shadows in euphoria indeed.[12]

The year 1968 is of course a watershed for many reasons, but for our purposes, the other key event that year in this quick history of inflation is the March publication (the precise month that *Structures Gonflables* opened) of "The Role of Monetary Policy" in *The American Economic Review* by Milton Friedman, which was the transcript of his presidential address to the Eightieth Annual Meeting of the American Economic Association in Washington, D.C. at the end of the previous year.[13] In this essay, Friedman lays out his notion of the *natural rate of unemployment*, a concept that fixes the ideal rate of unemployment in relation to inflation. As such, Friedman's concept is an example of what Joseph Vogl calls the "physicalist" tendency of economic discourse through which "the history of political economy is punctuated at key moments by ideas of economic functioning that are directly modeled on natural laws."[14] To protect us from monstrous ghosts, monetary policy for Friedman should be based on an equilibrium principle designed to produce stability in currency valuation, keeping marshmallows from becoming monsters.

Friedman's thinking became hugely influential, verging on ideologically fundamental. Most fully realized in the NAIRU (Non-Accelerating Inflationary Rate of Unemployment) and a refinement of the classic Phillips Curve, the idea is that low unemployment, crossing the NAIRU stream, would bring about perilous monetary conditions, and thereby threaten us with the ills of previous eras of stagflation (increasing inflation, decreasing growth).[15] This relationship became crucial to Washington Consensus monetary policy, which was then forcefully spread to OECD countries, like the Republic of Korea. Crucially in Korea, it provided the intellectual justification after the IMF crisis for the rapid increase and controversial proliferation of flexible labor. Instruments like NAIRU ultimately became protocols for late-empire U.S. financial hegemony, and protocols which maintain their global influence because they create ideal conditions for capital mobility,[16] despite ample scholarship debunking the premises on which they stand.[17] Casting Keynesian maneuvers toward full employment as overly euphoric, inflation for Friedman becomes the unacknowledged shadow; and whatever satisfaction we might derive from low unemployment is like the king enjoying the spectacle of his vanishing privilege. Higher unemployment becomes a necessary condition for low inflation. Friedman thus provided intellectual basis for the worldwide implementation of structural adjustments in vulnerable economies that benefited neocolonial enterprises.[18]

We might then think of the inflatable armchair featured in *Structures Gonflables* and NAIRU, as transitional figures, as the shadows of endings that inhere in beginnings. As in the finale of Chris Marker's 1962 time travel film, *La Jetée*, both treat us with the spectacle of our own deaths. Following Giovanni Arrighi, they are signatures of the signal crisis; like the Reagan era in Arrighi's account, moments of what seem like economic optimism after this point are flames brightening the moment before they dissipate.[19] Or following Robert Brenner, they mark the crisis of profitability at the end of the U.S.-dominated postwar economy and the accompanying urgent need to expand profitability in financial sectors,[20] a correlating set of pressures that set the scene for Coke to buy Columbia in 1982. Lower inflation and higher unemployment become key to strategies of capital extraction and redistribution in a global economic environment in which asset bubbles, whose specific pneumatic implications I'll address below, become the new normal.[21]

The late work of Yayoi Kusama offers a series of figures that resonate powerfully with the SPMM, at least as presented here, specifically in her *Dot Obsession* series (begun in 1997), and her work might also serve to figure the realized synthesis of the two streams that I have staged: aesthetic and economic forms of inflation which coalesced in 1968 and re-emerged in analogous forms in the contraction after the Japanese asset bubble burst in 1991. Kusama's signature phalluses were originally smaller and more multiple in earlier work, conceived as they were under different economic regimes. In *Dot Obsession*, they are grotesquely inflated instead of stuffed as they were in earlier times, producing a "sense of precariousness that troubles the terrain in which they are situated."[22] Their intumescence then seems more monstrous than vital, and more comically pathological than animated, a fitting figure for Japan's lost decade(s), a period of rampant inflation and diminished growth. In some ways then, we might think of Kusama's *Dot Obsession* figures as the SPMM's transnational cousins.

The spread of inflation-targeting monetary policy in OECD countries like South Korea manifests then not just in structural reforms, as in the kind demanded in the 1998 IMF bailout of the South Korean economy, but also in Korean cultural forms as well. And indeed, we might trace in such forms a kind of posthumous transnational itinerary for the SPMM, which might then be understood as a subtle itinerancy of empire. The 2009 Showbox/Mediaplex production *The Scam (Jak Jeon)*, for example, not only demonstrates the confluence between aesthetic and economic practices, but also instantiates the hegemonic relation that the SPMM both exemplifies and haunts. *The Scam* chronicles the misadventures of former gangsters who become white-collar criminals and try to pull off a pump-and-dump scheme in the milieu of Korea's growing day-trading economy. We might note that though sometimes used vulgarly to describe the sexual practices of one-night stand artists, the origin of "pump and dump" is pneumatic, and their scheme, though it does not operate at quite this literal level, is to inflate the value of securities before selling them to unsuspecting investors unaware that the rise in price is an artificially orchestrated phenomenon.

Before they initiate the plan, the film offers a scene of info-dumping, in which a supposedly complicated financial maneuver has to be explained to a newbie, who serves as proxy for film's uninitiated audience.[23] In the scene, seasoned traders, Min-hyeong (Kim

Mu-yeol) and Brian (Jun-seong Kim), describe to neophyte Hyun-soo (Park Yong-ha) how their pump-and-dump scheme will work. Though a series of precisely timed "matching transactions" designed so that one conspirator might pass off a parcel of securities to the next without letting anyone else in the market buy, they are able to artificially inflate the security's price and raise to a fever pitch the desire of the "ants," the Korean slang term for individual day traders, on whom they will dump the overvalued securities before running off with their bounty. To demonstrate, Min-hyeong translates finance into the objects of Korean masculinist drinking culture. He fills a large tumbler with whiskey saying "Let's assume that this is the value of the stocks we own," and then pours in a little more, "Now I raise the price a little and hand it to Brian," who suavely downs it. The glass is passed around the trio of men, each time filled a little higher until Min-hyeong swaps it for a pint glass and initiates another round: "The stocks keep rising as it goes around between us. The ants will go crazy wanting to buy it, but they can't." After Hyun-soo gulps down his full pint with a decided strain, Min-hyeong then empties out a bucket for Hyun-soo to fill, and invites back into the room one of the hostesses who had earlier been interested in extracting a stock tip from the men. It's a timely interruption because she gets quickly cast for the role of the ant. "Now the ants swarm in and go after whatever we sell," explains Min-hyeong, a point which Brian, a bilingual Korean American, punctuates in English, "Pump and dump, baby!"

A pump-and-dump scheme might be thought of as an asset bubble in miniature. And thought the logic of the asset bubble is not identical to that of inflation, they are connected by a generalized fear of pneumatic inertia. This is a cultural anxiety, now getting refigured to reflect an economic reality marked not by hyperinflation but by repeated crises/bubbles. In a pump and dump, the security is overinflated such that it cannot sustain the price that it trades for under manipulated conditions; it doesn't have that kind of underlying valuation because it's not worth that much. We know, of course, that asset bubble inflation and macroeconomic inflation of the sort that concerned Friedman and Haldane are not the same thing. The former relates to the prices of a much narrower group of assets—tech stocks, housing, etc.—while the latter measures cost of living more generally, with a more comprehensive basket of goods and services, ranging from food to health care. But as in the case of the collapse of the Japanese real estate bubble in the late 1980s, not only can macroeconomic inflation follow from the bursting of an asset bubble,[24] perhaps more pertinently, this fear abides in contemporary economies regardless of any causal relation. *The Scam* in fact references a specific bubble, the Korean credit card crisis in 2003, which is when Hyun-soo began his career in securities speculation using credit cards as a source of capital. When this lending bubble burst, inflation rose to dangerous levels and Hyun-soo contemplated suicide.[25] It is an apt reference to the larger context developed in this paper because the 2003 crisis and the sharp increase in consumer debt that caused it was a ripple effect of the larger political economic changes brought on by the 1997–1998 Asian Financial Crisis, a moment when the belated (and uneven) developmentalism of a number of Asian economies began to experience the same deindustrializing pressures experienced by the west a few decades earlier.

Against this figure of the runaway inflation and unrestrained pneumatic pressure, we see a moment of restraint when the young hostess, offered a million won by Brian (about $900), attempts to drink the bucket full of whiskey. In the context we have developed, Brian's offer fixes a monetary value to an object (a full bucket of whiskey) that is already a metaphor for money. This tautological relation, the price of a price, the value attributed to money, seems to index the relation implicit in inflation. Standing, Hyun-soo attempts to intercede, "That's enough," he says. Min-hyeong tells the hostess that she doesn't have to drink the whiskey if she doesn't want to, but doubles the reward. As she pauses to contemplate, Hyun-soo leaps across the table and attacks Min-hyeong in a moment of self-righteousness and belated chivalry. But what is Hyun-soo's real motivation here?

His attempt to halt the proceedings, after having participated in them for some time, seems to stem not from a reaction to the material circumstances in the room, but to a more inchoate, general sense of moral indignation that seems more rote than driven by any specific feelings, say, for the hostess, who very much wants to earn the stakes. It's worth remembering here that inflationary fear in the present is less a reaction to an imminent disaster, as it was in the 1970s, and more about rehearsing learned behavior. In the 1970s, inflation rates topped 10% in the U.S. and 30% in the Republic of Korea. Since the year 2000, inflation has rarely reached 5% in either national economy, so more recent forms of inflationary fear are less about stemming a monstrous tide. Inflationary fear is more notional than in the past; the training has been in a sort of caution that no longer necessarily extends from the urgencies of everyday life, but rather from the assumptions of a hard-earned knowledge. But fear of inflation is also a form of precaution that prescribes moderation instead of systemic overhauls; it underwrites the logics of a financialized bubble economy even as it cautions against its excesses. In the present scene then, it is more a nebulous sense of caution that raises Hyun-soo's ire than anything concrete. When he pushes back which at last, with "that's enough" (which we may regard as the rallying cry of inflation targeting itself), it comes much too late, against the momentum of the system that he has helped create.[26] Inflation control here is a protocol, a compulsory form of behavior that one enacts as learned behavior; or as Alexander Galloway and Eugene Thacker have defined it, "an apparatus that facilitates networks and a logic that governs how things are done within that apparatus."[27]

The specific illustration of inflationary pressure as whiskey drinking reminds us of earlier naturalist accounts of capital accumulation as the bodily ingestion of inappropriately large amounts of food, drink, or other substances, against which someone must cry "that's enough." Indeed, the connection between excessive drinking and pneumatic inflation is at least as old as Bibendum (iconographically, the SPMM's ancestor), whose rotund figure was originally created for and rejected by a German brewery, and, as a result, is in fact named after alcohol consumption. In his rendering for the brewery, the French cartoonist Marius Rossillon (a.k.a. O'Galop) had quoted Horace's phrase "Nunc est bibendum" or "Now is [the time for] drinking." The image and motto appealed to the Michelin brothers, and so Rossillin tweaked the image, remaking the figure into one made out of tires, and adding the clarifying advertising copy "That is to say, to your health. The Michelin tire drinks up obstacles." We might say that *The Scam* carries through this historical logic of Bibendum by rendering drinking as identical to inflation.

Another point of comparison is *Rogue Trader* (1999)—the Pathé biopic about Nick Leeson, the notorious derivative trader in Asian-tiger-era Singapore whose reckless activity bankrupted Barings, the storied English merchant bank that financed the Louisiana Purchase. Nick's over-the-top drinking is meant to correlate to his daredevil trading style. In *The Scam*, the scene of drinking as objective correlative for cutthroat finance is preceded by a scene in which Brian makes everyone drink a cocktail called, "Dracula," consisting of vodka and red wine, which one is supposed to gulp down messily allowing the red liquid to spill down one's face and onto one's clothing. The alcohol, equated with security price in the other scene, here becomes associated with blood. Coming full circle to a kind of nineteenth-century naturalism at least as old as Bibendum himself (he is about a decade older than *Dracula*, which Stoker published in 1897),[28] the point of this connection among pump-and-dump schemes, sport drinking, and bloodlust is to reimagine finance in relation to insatiable bodily appetites and urges (to be filled with large amounts of food, liquids, or air, none of which the body requires, at least in such amounts, for sustenance), against which the only possible advice seems to be caution.

As the drinking metaphor obtains explanatory power, the composition of the pump-and-dump scene simultaneously suggests finance's resistance to human understanding. The slick editing of the pump and dump is organized by frequent cuts and a series of split-screen wipes that slide on and off the screen, to and from its edges. The shots are fairly tight, and there is, for example, very little panning to establish relations of physical proximity of the characters in the room. In this respect, the scene is reminiscent of Han's Richter's short 1928 film, *Inflation*, which represents the milieu of its subject matter as a chaotic onslaught of images, with rapid cuts and sustained bleeds, accompanying a series of rapidly increasing numbers. An "essay film" presently "by solely formal means," as Marion Von Hofacker explains, *Inflation* employed what were regarded at the time to be "new photographic and technical skills, such as extreme boom shots, zoom shots, enlargements, photo montage, extreme angles, transparency, and negative and multiple exposures."[29] The sum effect is dizzying, and that's the point. The film presents inflation as if it challenged our capacities for apprehension, and film editing techniques attempted to reproduce materially these daunting challenges. The pump-and-dump scene in *The Scam* is not likely homage, though we do see a picture of a pile of money to the right of Brian that is reminiscent of Richter. Rather, it's that both films seem to intuit the potential in film editing to represent the supposed complex sociality of finance and the ostensibly disorienting complexity of macroeconomic effects that can only be represented, it seems, in such muddled arrays that, in turn, require the guidance of natural laws like NAIRU to assuage our anxieties. Against such ostensibly inchoate foes, the protocols of inflation targeting come to seem identical and as necessary as the common sense caution in Hyun-soo's interdiction, "That's enough."

Inflation targeting in *The Scam*, as it is in avant-garde aesthetics and monetary theory post-1968, is implicitly offered up as a kind of *a priori* protocol, simultaneously part of a metaphor where finance correlates with bodily experience and at the same time stylized as exceeding the limits of human apprehension. Protocol here indicates that which blurs the line between signal and infrastructure and hardwires ideological positions into material apparatuses. It takes the form of a moral ethos, in which we learn to pragmatically forego overly idealist aspirations to full employment for the common good of currency stability and to regard financialization as a form of fiscal responsibility. These logics, in turn, scale to transnational relations in an era in which the economic regime shift in the West from industrial to financialized modes compels client states downstream to follow suit. In this context, I want to suggest that these examples from 1968, both the Utopie show and the Friedman essay, do not mark the persistence of inflation as an abiding transhistorical concern, but rather, the emergence of inflation discourse in a modulated form, one in which the pneumatic and the macroeconomic are not so different after all. In a period characterized by recursive asset bubbles (and fears of their bursting), in which valuation gets determined by operations not all that different from pump and dump, we are caught in an echo chamber as we continue to search for metaphors to make sense of inflationary ghosts, less because the procedures are complicated (the supposed complexity of financial instruments is crucial to their mythology), and more because we need to give form to air. In our financialized moment with its ubiquitous monetary ideology and constant cycles of asset bubbles, culture senses the scam at the heart of protocols.

The point is less to critique inflation targeting as such, but rather to call attention to what happens when such protocols take on the force of natural law. Friedman's vision of inflation is ultimately, like that of his contemporaries the Utopie group, utopian, by which I mean not just future-oriented idealism, but also that it marks the transition between regimes of accumulation. If the SPMM, as the monstrous incarnation of a fake brand in *Ghostbusters*, signals a broader political economic shift of the American economy from one oriented to production to one dominated by circulatory practices (i.e. fake brands are not produced, and thus can do nothing but circulate), then inflation targeting becomes a protocol for the containment of the monsters necessarily engendered by that turn to a fictitious economy (which we must remember are never actually fictitious). In the meantime, ideal conditions for financialized capital accumulation emerge for those who are positioned to take advantage of a situation where inflationary fear is offered up as a form of knowledge, ultimately through a kind of bait and switch that is not unlike the pump-and-dump scheme in *The Scam*. We come to fear inflation, just as we do giant marshmallow men, based on, not in opposition to, the economic science, which has more in common with art than it might care to admit.

## Notes

1 A bizarre counterpart to *Ghostbusters* as described here might be the Australian film, *The Coca-Cola Kid* (1985), which narrates the exploits of a Coca Cola executive's attempt to open a small rural market in Australia to his company's products against the wishes of a local soft drink producer, who controls the area. Though taking the form of free market triumph over protectionist provincialism, the film in its profound weirdness ultimately represents such strategies of corporate expansion as pathological and not as motivated by the reasonable moral stance it purports to assume.

2 *Ghostbusters*, directed by Ivan Reitman (1984; Culver City, CA: Sony Pictures Home Entertainment, 2006), DVD.

3 Ibid.

4 To respond to low inflation, the Japanese central bank recently adopted negative interest rates in order to encourage investment and to disincentivize saving. Negative interest rates mean that you have to pay to save. According to the logic, a proper level of inflation encourages the brisk circulation of capital. Jonathan Soble, "Japan's Negative Interest Rates Explained," *The New York Times*, September 20, 2016, www.nytimes.com/2016/09/21/business/international/japan-boj-negative-interest-rates.html?_r=0.

5 Andrew Haldane, "Ghostbusting: The UK Experience of Inflation Targeting," paper presented at the IMF Institute Seminar, "Implementing Inflation Targets," March 20–21, 2000 (Washington, DC: International Monetary Fund, 2000).

6 See Bruce Cumings, "The Korean Crisis and the End of 'Late' Development," *New Left Review* 231 (1998): 43–72.

7 See Sean Topham, *Blowup: Inflatable Art, Architecture, and Design* (New York: Prestel, 2002), 17–30.

8 Ibid., 10–13, 30–1. See also Marc Dessauce, "On Pneumatic Apparitions," in *The Inflatable Moment: Pnuematics and Protest in '68*, edited by Marc Dessauce (New York: Princeton Architectural Press, 1999), 17–18.

9 Some of these critics are collected in Marc Dessauce, ed., *The Inflatable Moment: Pneumatics and Protest in '68* (Princeton: Princeton Architectural Press, 1999).

10 See Sean Topham, *Blowup: Inflatable Art, Architecture, and Design*, 80–119.

11 Marc Dessauce, "On Pneumatic Apparitions," 25.

12 It should be noted that *euphoria* is often used as a semi-technical term in economic discourse to describe the process through which asset bubbles develop.

13 Milton Friedman, "The Role of Monetary Policy," *The American Economic Review* 58.1 (1968): 1–17.

14 Joseph Vogl, *The Specter of Capital*, translated by Joachim Redner and Robert Savage (Stanford: Stanford University Press, 2015), 38.

15 There are, of course, important distinctions among the Phillips Curve, the Natural Rate of Unemployment, and the NAIRU, but the point here is less to parse the specifics of theory and policy, but rather to think more generally about the effects of such organizations of economic knowledge, specifically as a equilibrial relationship between labor and money, from the later 1960s to the present.

16 Bill Dunn, *The Political Economy of Global Capitalism and Crisis* (London: Routledge, 2014), 116 and Anwar M. Shaikh, "Explaining Inflation and Unemployment: An Alternative to Neoliberal Economic Theory," in *Contemporary Economic Theory*, edited by Andriana Vachlou (London: MacMillan, 1999), 102.

17 See Servaas Storm and C.W.M. Naastepad, *Macroeconomics Beyond the NAIRU* (Cambridge: Harvard University Press, 2012), 1.

18 See Jason Hickel, *The Divide: A Brief Guide to Global Inequality and its Solutions* (London: William Heinemann, 2017).

19 Giovanni Arrighi, *The Long Twentieth Century: Money, Power, and the Origins of our Times* (London: Verso, 2010), 325.

20 Robert Brenner, *The Boom and the Bubble: The U.S. in the World Economy* (London: Verso, 2002), 7–47.

21 See Michael Hudson, "The Transition from Industrial Capitalism to a Financialized Bubble Economy," working paper, Levi Economics Institute, October 2010 and Robert Brenner, *The Boom and the Bubble.*

22 Mignon Nixon, "Infinity Politics," in *Yayoi Kusama*, edited by Frances Morris (New York: Distributed Art Publishers, 2012), 188.

23 *The Scam (Jak Jeon)*, directed by Lee Ho-jae (2009; Seoul, ROK: Showbox/Mediaplex, 2009), DVD.

24 Shigenori Shiratsuka, "Asset Price Bubble in Japan in the 1980s: Lessons for Financial and Macroeconomic Stability," Institute for Monetary and Economic Studies, Bank of Japan, Dec. 2003, 1–27.

25 The question becomes: What happens when the scale of the asset bubble becomes so large (as in 2008) that macroeconomic consequences become inevitable? This kind of analysis anticipates the moment when the asset bubble becomes the model for the global economy writ large.

26 One might argue here that he identifies with Joo-hee as a powerless ant oppressed by a rigged system. This is somewhat true, but his indignation is less that he is a victim and more that he is on the wrong side of the rigging.

27 Alexander R. Galloway and Eugene Thacker, *The Exploit: A Theory of Networks* (Minneapolis: University of Minnesota Press, 2007), 29.

28 See Franco Moretti, "The Dialectic of Fear," *New Left Review* 136 (1982): 73. "The money that had been buried comes back to life, becomes capital and embarks on the conquest of the world: this and none other is the story of Dracula the vampire."

29 Marion Von Hofacker, "Richter's Films and the Role of the Radical Artist, 1927–1941," in *Hans Richter: Activism, Modernism, and the Avant-Garde*, edited by Stephen C. Foster (Cambridge: MIT Press, 1998), 129.

# 26
# KEYNES AND KEYNESIANISM

*Matt Seybold*

On New Year's Eve 1965, the cover of *Time* magazine featured a rather unflattering portrait of John Maynard Keynes, making the economist a *de facto* "man of the year" two decades after his death. The headline to the cover story was "We Are All Keynesians Now." The resonance of this phrase, which has its own Wikipedia page, is evidenced by dozens of reappropriations in the aftermath of the 2008 economic meltdown by publications as disparate as *The Boston Globe*, *The Daily Telegraph*, *The Wall Street Journal*, and *Time* itself. In 1965, *Time* attributed the "We Are All Keynesians" quote to Milton Friedman, then the most prominent opponent of Keynesian policies. Friedman was eager to clarify that what he actually said was, "In one sense, we are all Keynesians now; in another, nobody is any longer a Keynesian" (Friedman 1966: 15). Such is the lasting paradox of the eponym.

Part of the persistent confusion about what it means to be a Keynesian stems from the fact that Keynes managed to maintain complicated but convivial relationships with a diverse cross section of economists throughout his lifetime. Though he was certainly capable of scathing critique, Keynes also viewed even his most entrenched antagonists as colleagues and potential converts. He patiently endured their long circular arguments in private correspondence, read and responded generously to tedious misrepresentations of his work, and made sure the prestigious journal which he edited included ample dissent. In public writings, his habit was to lead with praise, however faint, and charitably rationalize error. Such magnanimity, combined with the nuance and dynamism of his positions, contributes to disagreements about where Keynes fits in contemporary economic debates which are frequently characterized by reductive political partisanship and *ad hominem* personal disputes. Cornell West (2011) attributes to the Clinton and Obama administration an economic philosophy of "Keynesian neoliberalism" (100) which to readers of Michel Foucault's *Birth of Biopolitics* (2008) might seem a contradiction in terms. According to Foucault, what unifies the disparate neoliberalisms of Europe and North America is their "main doctrinal adversary, Keynes, the common enemy" (79). In *Undoing the Demos* (2015), Wendy Brown defines neoliberalism as "a historically specific economic and political reaction against Keynesianism" (21), but also argues that "its worms live in the bowels of a hegemonic Keynesianism" (51).

Difficulty clarifying the political and technical traits of Keynesianism may explain why literature scholars, even those focusing on modernist writers Keynes counted as personal friends and intellectual allies, habitually ignore his influence. Keynes does not appear in

Leslie Fiedler's *Waiting For The End* (1964), Hugh Kenner's *The Pound Era* (1971), Marshall Berman's *All That Is Solid Melts Into Air* (1982), Michael Levenson's *Genealogy of Modernism* (1984), or Louis Menand's *Discovering Modernism* (1987). Not until Jennifer Wicke's "Mrs. Dalloway Goes To Market" (1994) were there any sustained readings of Keynes in the context of literary modernism. In the decade following Wicke's essay, and usually with direct allusion to it, there was a flurry of engagement with Keynes from literary scholars, highlighted by Michael Szalay's *New Deal Modernism* (2000), Michael Tratner's *Deficits & Desires* (2001), Paul Delany's *Literature, Money, & the Market* (2002), and Jed Esty's *A Shrinking Island* (2004). These scholars treat Keynes's writings, particularly *The General Theory of Employment, Interest, and Money* (1936), and *The Economic Consequences of the Peace* (1919), as texts in the modernist canon which emerged from interbellum Britain. This canon is, as Menand argues, characterized by ideological heterodoxy, the priority of interpretive agency, and the promise to challenge and innovate. During his mature phase, Keynes explicitly urges his readers to conceive of economics as a textual art, and this is an oft overlooked but essential aspect of comprehending his work.

Careful attention to Keynes's actual writings is necessary, in part, because Keynes is not a Keynesian. A very visible subset of pseudo-disciples, including John Hicks and Paul Samuelson, erected a programmatic economics which bore Keynes's name but was frequently openly hostile to substantive portions of his actual work (see Turgeon 1996). Treating his work, particularly *The General Theory*, as an axiomatic expression of macroeconomic law requires ignoring much of what Keynes actually wrote. He came up with numerous, often humorous, ways of saying something relatively obvious: that because an economy is made up of people, who behave inconsistently and unpredictably, relationships between economic forces are "not homogenous through time," and thus economic policies, and the theories which inform them, cannot aspire to permanence and positivism. Among the more famous expressions of this is:

> We assume that the present is a much more serviceable guide to the future than a candid examination of past experience would show it to have been hitherto...I accuse the classical economic theory of being itself one of these pretty, polite techniques which tries to deal with the present by abstracting from the fact that we know very little about the future.
>
> *(Keynes 1973c: 114–15)*

Keynes insisted with increasing urgency over the final two decades of his life that the preferred methods, conventional presumptions, and professional habits of economists needed to be drastically altered if economics was ever going to be able to achieve what Keynes insisted was its point: making the world better by degrees.

## While there is peace, there is peace

Keynes read W. H. Auden's occasional poem, "Spain," while recovering from a heart attack in the summer of 1937. Though he worried about Auden's propensity for chewing his fingernails, Keynes had found the "youthful" poet "altogether delightful" upon meeting him the previous year (Skidelsky 1992: 628). Keynes offered to produce Auden's anti-fascist play, *On The Frontier* (1938), co-authored with Christopher Isherwood, even though he agreed with his old friend, T. S. Eliot, when he remarked "I'm afraid that Hitler is not the simpleton the authors make him out to be" (Skidelsky 2001: 38).

Keynes described "Spain" as a "moving, yet serene expression of contemporary feeling towards the heart-rending events of the political world" (Keynes 1982b: 61). He regarded Auden's call to arms – his imperative to "Intervene. O descend as a dove or / A furious papa or a mild engineer, but descend" – as potentially unsettling the public's pervasive predisposition toward pacifism which Keynes still celebrated as the "dominating factor" (57) in British foreign policy. Auden "teaches us, as a poet should, how we should feel," Keynes wrote for the *New Statesman*, but, playing the role of jaded diplomat to Auden's romantic revolutionary, Keynes felt it necessary "to question whether he rightly directs how, at this moment at least, we should act" (61). In his editorial, Keynes appropriates both the language and the organizational premise of Auden's poem, which is structured by stanzas which begin "Yesterday," "To-morrow," and "To-day." Keynes highlights his own vision of past, present, and future by quoting Auden's own lines in the opening, closing, and middle paragraphs of the essay, a hat-tip to the modernist habit of using allusion to reinforce argument and create poetic structure.

Keynes's rich and rigorous, if at times archaic, vocabulary is on display when he characterizes Britain's embattled Foreign Secretary, Anthony Eden, as well as himself, as *cunctators*, committed to the inevitably unpopular policy of delaying direct engagement with an aggressive enemy. "The task of the cunctator is always a thankless one" (64), Keynes says, precociously anticipating the resignation of Eden the following year under attack from both Prime Minister Chamberlain and an increasingly hawkish Winston Churchill. But Keynes maintains that "cunctation is one of our most powerful and characteristic national weapons" and "our age-long instrument against dictators" (63). By repeatedly invoking this strange word, he is practicing yet another characteristic tactic of modernist poets, recontextualizing an allusion in a manner which confuses and contradicts its conventional ideological signification. *Cunctator* enters English specifically as the epithet for Roman General Fabius Maximus, namesake of the Fabian Society, the most influential socialist organization in interbellum Britain. Thus, in the process of good-naturedly disagreeing with Auden, he also lays claim to a socialist icon. Keynes doesn't need to explicitly perform this etymology. The significance of his nomenclature is driven home to the audience for whom it is intended when he writes, "Since Fabius Maximus there has scarcely been a stronger case for cunctation than there is today" (63), thus implying Fabian Socialism's irrelevance and futility, a position he makes explicit in an 1939 interview, when he referred to the "outworn creed mumbling moss-grown demi-semi-Fabian Marxism" (Keynes 1982a: 495). In the *New Statesman*, however, his dismissal is more gentle, in part because he regarded Fabian followers as future converts to his own cause.

Keynes is convinced that Auden represents "the splendid [raw] material of the young amateur Communists" who, in their "ultimate maturity," will be "the heirs of eternal liberalism" (495–6). Keynes was interested in "young members of the Left who toyed with Marxism" (Keynes 1982b: 27) because they demonstrated an admirable tendency toward altruism and asceticism. "When Cambridge undergraduates take their inevitable undergraduate trip to Bolshiedom, are they disillusioned when they find it all dreadfully uncomfortable?" he asked in 1934, "Of course not. That is what they are looking for" (35). Marx appealed to the melodramatic self-immolation of those who did not, like Keynes's generation, remember the Great War. The romanticization of violence was a refuge only for those whose lives contained no violence. Keynes fixated on the phrases "deliberate increase in the chances of death" and "conscious acceptance of guilt in the necessary murder" (61) from Auden's "Spain." The poet was "speaking for many chivalrous hearts," but Keynes insisted, it was an "illusion" to believe war would "settle" the "moral issues" undergirding fascism. "At best we should be back to where we were," said Keynes, who had coined the phrase "Carthaginian Peace" to describe the Treaty of Versailles, "Victory, as usual, would be useless, and probably pernicious" (62).

Keynes expected Auden's generation to outgrow Marxism when they comprehended that the egalitarian society it promised was uncertain, while the violence required to achieve that society was not. But the consummate cunctator was in no hurry for them to learn this lesson. In the *New Stateman* editorial, Keynes quotes himself, from *A Tract on Monetary Reform* (1923) – "it is a disadvantage of 'the long run' that in the long run we are all dead" – but qualifies that

> I could have said equally well that it is a great advantage of 'the short run' that in the short run we are still alive…If we are at peace in the short run, that is something. The best we can do is put off disaster, if only in the hope, which is not necessarily a remote one, that something will turn up.
>
> *(62)*

This hope, that "something will turn up," Geoff Mann calls "the radical kernel at the heart of Keynesianism" (Mann 2017: 395) which emphasizes the uncertainty and unpredictability of "the long run." Keynes believes that both Marxists and libertarians indulge that same delusion, that on the other side of their self-inflicted suffering lies utopia. He hopes to dissuade them.

Keynes "bid Auden…to pass by on the other side…be patient and unheroic" (Keynes 1982b: 65). The cunctators, Keynes promises, will "claim the benefit of the first part of one of Auden's stanzas" – "to build a just city" – while leaving to Marxists the "the suicide pact, the romantic / Death" (63). In the conclusion to his editorial, the unabashedly bourgeois economist appropriates the words given Spain's "poor in their fireless lodgings," turning them against the communist poet, assuring him that "Time the refreshing river" is preferable to a "Fumbled and unsatisfactory embrace before hurting." "It is silly and presumptuous to say that war is inevitable; for no one can possible know," Keynes chides, "The only conclusion which is certain is that we cannot avoid war by bringing it on." He takes solace in a tautology worthy of Gertrude Stein: "While there is peace, there is peace" (62).

This humble appreciation of horizons of intelligence, and the danger of overestimating the predictive potential of prior experiences and professional expertise, must be central to any estimation of Keynesianism which aspires to include Keynes himself.

## Flavors of Keynesianism

Most of the postwar economists we now identify as Keynesian are Neo-Keynesians or New Keynesians or, as Joan Robinson calls them, "Bastard Keynesians." They are associated with the Keynesian synthesis, which means that they selectively translate Keynes's ideas into quantitative models which can be integrated into an orthodox economic formalism which retains most of the neoclassical theory he was explicitly attempting to invalidate. The Keynesian models popularized by Hicks, Samuelson, and others Neo-Keynesians – most notably the Hicks–Hansen (or IS–LM) model – are now the primary, if not the only, way professional economists engage with Keynes's thought. Neo-Keynesians, conditioned by orthodox economics pedagogy, generally believe that Keynesianism has eclipsed Keynes. Only a small fraction of professional economists read Keynes's *General Theory*, or any canonical works in the history of economic thought, for that matter. On the question of "What Keynes Really

Meant," Neo-Keynesians take the view bluntly expressed by Paul Krugman (2012): "I don't care...If where you take the idea is very different from what the great man said somewhere else in his book, so what? This is economics, not Talmudic scholarship." Neo-Keynesians are to Neoclassicals what New Democrats were to Reagan Republicans. Their differences are mostly theatrical.

A second, smaller group of Political Keynesians, also frequently called *Post-Keynesians*, include Robinson, John Kenneth Galbraith, Robert Skidelsky, and Hyman Minsky. Based on more comprehensive interpretations of Keynes's work, Political Keynesianism is, as Mann argues, a Hegelian dialectical synthesis of what Keynes regarded as equally dangerous Utopian delusions: Marxism and laissez-faire capitalism. Political Keynesians propose flexible, pragmatic safeguards against imminent apocalypse, threatened by both Marxist revolution and sociopathic libertarianism. Keynes argues that what he calls the "catastrophism" of Lenin and the anarchism of Ludwig von Mises, though they define themselves by ideological opposition, are indistinguishable in practice, both depending on an absurd "Benthamite calculus" which reduces the range of human experiences to a singular "economic criterion" (Keynes 1972b: 446). In a world torn between such ludicrous extremisms, the only rational position is a centrist one.

Neo-Keynesians and Post-Keynesians are both recognized subgroups of economists (like, say, New Historicists and Deconstructionists are in literary studies). There are ongoing feuds between them, but also common ground, and, undoubtedly, resistance to categorical distinctions like those I am making. But these categories, howsoever conceived, appear with regularity in professional debates (see Foley 2014; Mann 2017). The remainder of this chapter is dedicated to an alternative, emerging brand of Keynesianism which I call Cultural Keynesianism because, though it is not native or exclusive to cultural studies, it is naturally attractive therein. Cultural Keynesians, who often, but not always, share with Political Keynesians a predisposition to moderation and creative response, are foremost defined by their emphasis on three aspects of Keynes's thought which are altogether ignored by Neo-Keynesians and infrequently prioritized by Post-Keynesians: (1) his aversion to mathematical economics; (2) his reverence for the unknown, uncertain, and unquantifiable psychological forces; and (3) his analysis of how financialization exacerbates the volatility of such forces.

Keynes believed that economics had spent "a full hundred years in an artificial groove" (Keynes 1972b: 87), fruitlessly chasing the mirage of mathematical elegance and the prestige of natural science. He believed that his legacy was not the techniques he innovated, the models he built, or the principles he described, all of which he regarded as fleeting by nature, but rather changing the professional culture such that "economists could manage to get themselves thought of as humble, competent people, on the level with dentists" (Keynes 1972a: 332) instead of as distilled and defunct voices who made slaves of both "practical men" and "madmen in authority" (Keynes 1973a: 383). He stated unequivocally that economics was "not a natural science" (Keynes 1973c: 297) and that "the pseudo-analogy with the physical sciences leads directly counter to the habit of mind which it is most important for the economist to acquire" (300). Obviously, this perspective on the profession, though pervasive in Keynes's mature thought, is anathema to contemporary orthodox economists, including many, like Krugman, who self-identify as Keynesian.

## The dream of beetles

On Sunday, March 7th, 1915, Bertrand Russell hosted a small brunch at his Cambridge flat. The purpose was to introduce D. H. Lawrence to John Maynard Keynes. "When I saw

Keynes that morning in Cambridge it was one of the crises of my life," Lawrence wrote the following month, "It sent me mad with misery and hostility and rage." He said the visit "made me dream of beetles" and he decided if "people like this" were his best chance for intellectual fellowship, he would "rather be alone." Of the Cambridge Apostles, he pronounced, "They are cased each in a hard little shell of his own and out of this they talk words. There is never for one second any outgoing of feeling and no reverence, not a crumb or grain of reverence" (Keynes 1972b: 431).

Reading these words decades later provoked Keynes to seek an explanation for why Lawrence, who he admired, viewed him with such animosity. His soul-searching yielded an essay, "My Early Beliefs," which remains probably the most earnest memoir of the Bloomsbury Group's intellectual origins. The essay, written while Keynes was defending his *General Theory*, also provides unique insight into his economics at its maturity. The foundational achievement of the Cambridge Apostles, as Keynes sees it, is the rejection of Utopianism. "Utopians," Keynes claimed,

> believe in the continuing moral progress by virtue of which the human race already consists of reliable, rational, decent people, influenced by truth and objective standards, which can be safely released from the outward restraints of convention and traditional standards and inflexible rules of conduct, and left, from now onwards, to their own sensible devices, pure motives and reliable intuitions of the good.
>
> *(Keynes 1972b: 447)*

This rejection of Utopianism "served to protect the whole lot of us from the final *reductio ad absurdum* of Benthamism known as Marxism" (446). There is no denying that Keynes dismissed Marx too easily. A contemporary reader who happens upon his assertion, to George Bernard Shaw, that "Marx's picture of the capitalist world, which had much verisimilitude in his day is unrecognizable, with the rapid flux of the modern world" (Keynes 1982b: 32) justifiably cringes. Keynes, at least to a degree, misjudged Marx because he conflated Marxism with the "catastrophism" of Soviet communism in the 1920s, in part because he projected his evergreen hatred of David Ricardo onto Marx, who adopted Ricardo's labor theory of value (though not as wholesale as Keynes assumes). But Marxist critics also frequently ignore the qualifications that almost always follow Keynes analysis of Marx. After denigrating the "Marxist delusion" in 1921, he nevertheless states that "cynical conservatism is a far greater danger of the near future than revolutionary socialism" (Keynes 1977: 270). Though he frequently pejoratively characterizes Marxism as a religion, he also admits "Capitalism too is a religion" (Keynes 1981: 441) and regards those "who are completely satisfied by Christian capitalism or egoistic capitalism" (Keynes 1972a: 257) as equally laughable zealots. When he asks, "How can I accept a doctrine which sets up as its bible, above and beyond criticism, an obsolete economic textbook which I know to be not only scientifically erroneous but without interest or application in the modern world?" (258), he is likely thinking of Ricardo's *Principles of Political Economy* (1817), as foundational for the Marginal Revolution as it was for the Marxist. "Egoistic and altruistic systems," he realized, "work out in practice to the same conclusions" (Keynes 1972b: 447). The Utopian end, whether it followed from faith in the invisible hand or state control of the means of production, is but a mirage, and pursuing it is a Faustian bargain which leads instead to widespread poverty, demagoguery, and war.

While the Marxists and Neoclassicists view each concurrent economic event through the lens of its relationship to an unrealized equilibrium, the achievement of which is both the responsibility and the reward of every economic actor, Keynes is untroubled by anything but the active investigation of present circumstances and the persuasion of economic agents, particularly representatives of the state, to take actions which serve the most immediate and transparent needs of the system, including, perhaps most importantly, the prevention of its self-destruction. The actions cannot be prescriptive, because economic circumstances are not homogenous across territory and time. Short-term motives are prioritized because the relationships between macroeconomic forces are always evolving. Persuasion is, therefore, along with sober analysis of present circumstances, the primary tool and talent of Keynes's ideal economist.

The second precept of his Cambridge education to which Keynes held fast, the paradigm of his tutelage under G. E. Moore, was "a method of discovery by the instrument of impeccable grammar and an unambiguous diction" (Keynes 1972b: 440). Keynes was convinced, despite his substantial talents as a statistician and symbolic logician, that only language, and only language unrestricted by exclusionary vernaculars, was remotely adequate to macroeconomic representation. Like the economy, language is an unstable and organic system. It is nonhomogenous through time. Its development is predicated upon both conscious and subconscious actions by human agents, who produce it by both social negotiation and individual choice. It provides endless opportunities for increased comprehension, but full comprehension remains permanently elusive. As a conceptual tool, it is equally functional for both the most accurate accounts of reality and the most ambitious flourishes of pure imagination.

Keynes's celebration of linguistic precision in "My Early Beliefs" might seem at odds with the contemporaneous reviews of *The General Theory* by some of his peers, like Arthur Pigou, who accused Keynes of carelessly disregarding economics rigorous disciplinary vocabulary (see Pigou 1936). Keynes was only too happy to argue semantics, as Friedrich Hayek had discovered in 1931. Hayek reviewed Keynes's *Treatise on Money* (1930) in *Economica*, fatally admitting that though "it is not at all easy to detect the flaw in the argument," he was sure Keynes was wrong (Keynes 1973b: 244). Unable to articulate a substantive disagreement, Hayek chose, as Keynes put it, "to pick over the precise words I have used with a view to discovering some verbal contradiction or insidious ambiguity" (244). Keynes was all too willing to "show that most of my alleged terminological inconsistencies are either non-existent or irrelevant" (244), and, moreover, to return the favor, exposing Hayek's *Prices and Production* (1931) as such "a frightful muddle" (252), Hayek himself ended up admitting that Keynes's was "obviously a better terminology" (258). "Dr. Hayek has seen a vision," Keynes wrote, "and though he woke up he has made nonsense of his story by giving the wrong names to the objects which occur in it" (252).

Even knowing "how thick a bank of fog still separates his mind from mine" (256), Keynes engaged in lengthy debates, realizing that even if he could not convert Hayek, by exposing the inanity of his critique, he would convert others. But his private correspondence with Hayek is equally lengthy. He told Piero Straffa after months of letters with Hayek, "the abyss yawns – and so do I. Yet I can't help feeling there *is* something interesting in it" (265). Keynes stated and restated his arguments across dozens of settings, rarely recycling material, because he was always searching for sharper articulations, more lucid metaphors, and compelling examples, not only for his various interlocutors and audiences, but also for himself.

Many Political Keynesians, notably Galbraith and Robinson, consciously emulated Keynes by developing a rich body of prose works and emphasizing the persuasive elements of economic practice. Galbraith's work is even more radically absent of quantitative evidence and complicated mathematical theorems than Keynes's was. There are many modern economists, philosophers, and critical theorists who are embracing the rhetorical style informed by Cultural Keynesianism without consciously recognizing the debt to Keynes. Nassim Nicholas Taleb, for instance, lionizes Keynes for his far more formalist *Treatise on Probability* (1921) rather than for the *General Theory* that "tweed-clad leftists love to quote" (49), as well as for keeping "skin in the game" as an active trader. Taleb claims to regret that Keynes "ventur[ed] into the murky field of political economy" (49), even as he is following him down that path, embracing political iconoclasm, public intellectual discourse, and the difficult project of improving our awareness of the unquantifiable, the uncertain, and the unknown.

## The dangerous charlatanism of mathematical economics

In "My Early Beliefs," Keynes makes a virtue of the words which emerged from the "hard little shells" Lawrence disparaged. The essay was written while he was grappling with the methods of economists who were trading words for numbers. After publishing *The General Theory*, Keynes maintained his active program of correspondence and publication, particularly in *The Economic Journal*, where his byline appeared at least once in every issue from December 1937 until September 1940. In these contributions, Keynes consistently focuses on critiquing econometrics, and other subfields of what he dubs "mathematical economics." In *The General Theory*, he had warned, "too large a proportion of recent 'mathematical' economics are merely concoctions...which allow the author to lose sight of the complexities and interdependencies of the real world in a maze of pretentious and unhelpful symbols" (Keynes 1973a: 298).

In 1939, he reviewed the work of econometrician Jan Tinbergen. Keynes was fond of Tinbergen personally and believed in his good intentions, but told correspondents that Tinbergen's work was "charlatanism" (Keynes 1973c: 305) and "dangerous" (288). According to Keynes, mathematical methodologies belonged exclusively to microeconomics because they depended "on the economist having furnished, not merely a list of significant causes... but a *complete* list" (308). The creators of quantitative models were naturally inclined to be "influenced by what statistics are available" and to ignore "vital factors...because they are statistically intractable or unprocurable" (287). Most importantly, there was no place in econometrics for "non-numerical factors, such as inventions, politics, labor troubles, wars, earthquakes, financial crises" (287) and many other "important influences which cannot be reduced to statistical form" (295). In summation, according to Keynes, "the method cannot prove or disprove a qualitative theory," "it cannot give a quantitative guide to the future," and "it is not a very lucid way of describing the past" (315). Tinbergen, he feared, was "much more interested in getting on with the job than in spending time deciding whether the job is worth getting on with" (307) and, faced with criticism, Keynes predicted, "his reaction will be to engage another ten computers and drown his sorrow in arithmetic" (318). In a letter to Tinbergen, he asked, "Who, the economist or the statistician, is in the saddle and who is the patient ass?" (319).

Keynes's assault on Tinbergen was an extension of his increasing discomfort with the neoclassical habit of applying hard science methodology to economics. Keynes found this to be absurd, because of the human composition of all the objects of economic observation and all the forces of interaction between those objects. When it came to the operative forces in physics – like gravity – once a formula for measurement was contrived, the work was done. But in economics, desire, prudence, mania, fear, and confidence were the operative forces.

Even if there were a formula for their measurement, it would not be the same two days in succession. For the increasingly popular analogy with physics to function, he told R. F. Harrod, it would be

> as though the fall of the apple to the ground depended on the apple's motives, on whether it is worth while falling to the ground, and whether the ground wanted the apple to fall, and on the mistaken calculations on the part of the apple as to how far it was from the center of the earth.
>
> *(300)*

In 1969, when the Swedish Academy began awarding the Nobel Prize in Economics, the first recipient was Jan Tinbergen. Keynes had prophetically declared, "I think it is very dangerous for a collection of responsible economists to give [him] any sort of *imprimatur*" (304). Now Tinbergen had the profession's highest accolade. The econometric bubble had begun to inflate. Professional economics is now closely associated with the creation, retrieval, and analysis of financial metrics and with the self-consciously deceptive algebraic alchemy which has produced, among other things, mortgage-backed securities and "black-box" derivatives. As Keynes suspected would be the case, there is still no evidence econometrics provides any basis for prediction and policy. Econometrics provides some insight into what has happened, no insight into what will happen, and minimal insight into what is happening. Even so, the mainstreaming of econometrics might be perfectly legitimate if only its practitioners were willing to concede the methodology's apparent limitations and accept that, for the purposes of analysis and instruction, econometrics is no more exacting than any of the other Social Sciences or Humanities methodologies. To the contrary, however, the illusion of predictive positivism promoted by mathematical economics has been essential to the expanding enrollments and budgets of business schools and, as Donald MacKenzie has shown, to the placement of finance at the center of nearly all discussion of economic theory and policy (see MacKenzie 2006). The Disciples of Utopians like Friedman, Larry Summers, and Alan Greenspan came to believe too heartily that their present experience was a fixed blueprint for the future. Candid examination of the evolving economic organism ceased and economic policy became predetermined and predictable. It was comforting to believe that for the attainment of permanent prosperous equilibrium, deregulation was always the answer. This answer was seductive in part because the preponderance of contemporary economists has been trained to think of the economy as an algorithm and deregulation as the elimination of is superfluous factors. For most of the last three decades, mainstream economics has been pretending to find Euclidian grace in a quantum world.

## The state of confidence

In his letters to Tinbergen and to other economists under his sway, Keynes asks, over and over again, some version of the same question: What about the state of confidence? This is, he believes, the single most significant factor which can never be quantified, but is always relevant to macroeconomic questions. The state of confidence is the predominant factor in the state of long-term expectation, to which Keynes dedicates Chapter 12 of *The General Theory*, which is often summarized by his quip therein: "We devote our intelligences to anticipating what average opinion expects average opinion to be" (Keynes 1973a: 156). The state of confidence is the foremost of Keynes's "animal spirits," the unquantifiable and uniquely human forces which have the potential to overpower rational expectation and make economies unpredictable and unstable.

I believe the most underappreciated principle in *The General Theory* is that the greater the proportion of macroeconomic activity which depends on financialization, the more the volatility incumbent to securities markets permeates the larger economy, and the more susceptible the economy becomes to swings in the state of confidence produced by cultural forces. "In the absence of securities markets," Keynes explains, the farmer cannot "remove his capital from the farming business" on a whim and "reconsider whether he should return to it later in the week," but "the Stock Exchange revalues many investments every day and these revaluations give frequent opportunity to individuals to revise commitments" (151). At the exchange, one can buy corn, even when corn is not in season, or a stake in a building, even when no tenants are moving in or out. Securities can be invented, amalgamated, contracted, and split. When properties are subject to constant revaluation, confidence becomes an essential consideration because pricing is necessarily fluid and value may be driven by absent, incoherent, or misleading information.

Securities prices frequently reflect merely "the mass psychology of a large number of ignorant individuals" (154). "In abnormal times in particular," Keynes writes, "the market will be subject to waves of optimistic and pessimistic sentiment, which are unreasoning and yet in a sense legitimate" (154). Under such conditions, any person or institution with the capacity to persuade the populace to alter their economic behavior has the power to radically unsettle (or calm) the marketplace. Mass media outlets became the most direct means of affecting the state of confidence, for good or ill. As has been discussed in books by Ron Suskind (1994) and George Soros (2010), using the media to "talk up the market" was an explicit component of President Obama's economic recovery strategy in 2009. His advisors, borrowing from the economists George Akerlof and Robert Shiller (2009), nicknamed Obama's telegenic charisma "the confidence multiplier." They considered it a source of fiscal stimulus which, conveniently, did not require the cooperation of Congress. Drawing upon their interpretation of President Roosevelt's Fireside Chats, they postulated that the confidence of the executive begets the confidence of the constituency. And confident constituents were more likely to become confident consumers and investors.

Keynes argues that the simultaneous emergence of mass media and organized finance turns popular culture into a countervailing power which harnesses the animal spirits (see Keynes 1973a; Houck 2001; Seybold 2014). As technological and institutional innovations increase the speed, variety, and accessibility of both information and investment, classical economic binaries – labor and capital, supply and demand, public and private, even profit and loss – can be disrupted and even usurped by popular sentiment. Persuasive narratives, given sufficient saturation, have direct and drastic influence on securities prices, lending practices, liquidity preferences, and mass economic behavior. Potent storytellers and prominent publishers can, purposefully or inadvertently, cause bankruptcies, inflate asset bubbles, determine regulatory burdens, and instigate banking panics. For all intents and purposes, the media is the market.

With few exceptions – notably, Shiller and McCloskey – scholars trained in economic departments are unwilling to accept the implications of this facet of Cultural Keynesianism, in part because, to do so exposes most of their colleagues as, to borrow McCloskey's metaphor, "drunks searching for economic truth under a lamppost, instead of out in the dark where it is do be found" (McCloskey 1996: 33). But many literary figures, including several who precede Keynes, recognized the failure of orthodox economics to meaningfully account for cultural countervailences. For instance, the media montages and other genre-mixing techniques in John Dos Passos's *U.S.A.* novels draw attention to the fragmentary, memetic, atrophic, and cacophonous foundations from which modern narratives and ideologies often coalesce. In Dos Passos's narratives, ideas and their expression, independent of merit, have exceptional material power. The circulations of ideas through diverse mediums is unmanageable and unpredictable, liable to produce unintended consequences and contradictory interpretations.

Keynes was both a direct product of the neoclassical revolution, trained at the institution most central to it, and its antithesis, dedicating much of his career to debunking neoclassical principles and demythologizing their architects (see Regina Martin's "Neoclassical Economics"). Like Adam Smith and John Stuart Mill before him (see "Introduction"), Keynes emphasized the role of language and culture in both the functioning of the economy he studied and the methods of his analysis. He consumed the literature of his era at least as rapaciously as Marx had, unabashedly inserting himself into cultural debates seemingly unrelated to his primary expertise, and, to a greater extent than Marx ever could, directly ingratiated himself to the literary community by acts of fiscal patronage and charismatic sociability (see Walsh 2008; Goodwin 2011). Indeed, Keynes was regarded by many of his contemporaries as the most titanic member of the Bloomsbury–Cambridge–London system, around whom iconic literary figures orbited (see Goodwin 2011; Seybold 2017). Considering his biographical associations with numerous writers, the cultural and rhetorical claims of his own writings, and the fact that he was not only present for epochal world-historical events like the Versailles Treaty, Crash of 1929, New Deal, and World Wars, but also significantly contributed to the record of those events, it is surprising that there is not, as yet, a more codified Cultural Keynesian analogue to Marxist Literary Criticism. Keynes viewed Economics is a method of imagining the world beyond the portions of it which we can reliably measure and observe. He believed precise and persuasive language was its principle and compulsory tool, and via this tool, he contended, it had the potential to "revolutionize…the way the world thinks" (Keynes 1982b: 42). In other words, Keynesian economics is a literature, not that there's anything wrong with that.

## References


Akerlof, George and Shiller, Robert. (2009) *Animal Spirits: How Human Psychology Drives the Economy, and Why It Matters for Global Capitalism*, Princeton, NJ: Princeton University Press.

Anonymous. (1965) "We Are All Keynesians Now." *Time* 86.27 (Dec. 31): 74–82.

———. (2008a) "We Are All Keynesians Now." *Boston Globe* (Nov. 25): A18.

———. (2008b) "We're All Keynesians Now." *Wall Street Journal* (Jan. 18): A12.

Berman, Marshall. (1982) *All That Is Solid Melts Into Air: The Experience of Modernity,* New York: Verso Books.

Brown, Wendy. (2015) *Undoing the Demos: Neoliberalism's Stealth Revolution*, Brooklyn, NY: Zone Books.

Clemmer, Dick. (2009) "Was Keynes a Keynesian?" *Daily News* (Nov. 1).

Conway, Edmund. (2009) "Like It or Not, We Are All Keynesians Now." *Daily Telegraph: Blogs* (Jan. 10). http://blogs.telegraph.co.uk/finance/edmundconway/8070247/Like_it_or_not_we_are_all_Keynesians_now/

Delany, Paul. (2002) *Literature, Money, and the Market, from Trollope to Amis*, Basingstoke: Palgrave Macmillan.

Esty, Jed. (2004) *A Shrinking Island: Modernism and National Culture in England*, Princeton, NJ: Princeton University Press.

Fiedler, Leslie. (1964) *Waiting For The End,* New York: Stein & Day.

Foley, Duncan K. (2014) "Varieties of Keynesianism." *International Journal of Political Economy* 43.1: 4–19.

Foucault, Michel. (2008) *The Birth of Biopolitics*, New York: Palgrave Macmillan.Friedman, Milton. (1953) *Essays in Positive Economics*, Chicago, IL: University of Chicago Press.

Friedman, Milton. (1962) *Capitalism & Freedom*, Chicago, IL: University of Chicago Press.
Friedman, Milton. (1966) "Friedman and Keynes." *Time* 87.5 (Feb. 4): 15.
Goodwin, Crauford D. (2011) "The Bloomsbury Group as Creative Community." *History of Political Economy* 43.1: 59–82.
Houck, Davis W. (2001) *Rhetoric as Currency: Hoover, Roosevelt, and the Great Depression*, College Station: Texas A&M University Press.
Kenner, Hugh. (1971) *The Pound Era,* Berkeley: University of California Press.
Keynes, John Maynard. (1972a) *The Collected Writings of John Maynard Keynes, Vol. IX: Essays in Persuasion*, London: Macmillan St. Martin's.
Keynes, John Maynard. (1972b) *The Collected Writings of John Maynard Keynes, Vol. X: Essays in Biography*, London: Macmillan St. Martin's.
Keynes, John Maynard. (1973a) *The Collected Writings of John Maynard Keynes, Vol. XII: The General Theory of Employment, Interest, and Money*, London: Macmillan St. Martin's.
Keynes, John Maynard. (1973b) *The Collected Writings of John Maynard Keynes, Vol. XIII: The General Theory & After, Part I: Preparation*, London: Macmillan St. Martin's.
Keynes, John Maynard. (1973c) *The Collected Writings of John Maynard Keynes, Vol. XIV: The General Theory & After, Part II: Defense & Development*, London: Macmillan St. Martin's.
Keynes, John Maynard. (1977) *The Collected Writings of John Maynard Keynes, Vol. XVII: Activities 1920–1922*, London: Macmillan Cambridge University Press.
Keynes, John Maynard. (1981) *The Collected Writings of John Maynard Keynes, Vol. XIX: Activities 1920–1929*, London: Macmillan Cambridge University Press.
Keynes, John Maynard. (1982a) *The Collected Writings of John Maynard Keynes, Vol. XXI: Activities 1931–1939*, London: Macmillan Cambridge University Press.
Keynes, John Maynard. (1982b) *The Collected Writings of John Maynard Keynes, Vol. XXVIII: Social, Political, and Literary Writings*, London: Macmillan Cambridge University Press.Krugman, Paul. (2012) "Minsky and Methodology." *The New York Times* (Mar. 27). https://krugman.blogs.nytimes.com/2012/03/27/minksy-and-methodology-wonkish/
Levenson, Michael. (1984) *A Genealogy of Modernism: A Study of English Literary Doctrine, 1908–1922*, Cambridge: Cambridge University Press.
Mann, Geoff. (2017) *In The Long Run We Are All Dead: Keynesianism, Political Economy, and Revolution*, New York: Verso.
McCloskey, Deirdre N. (1996) *The Vices of Economists – The Virtues of the Bourgeoisie*, Amsterdam: Amsterdam University Press.
MacKenzie, Donald. (2006) *An Engine, Not a Camera: How Financial Models Shape Markets*, Cambridge, MA: MIT Press.
Menand, Louis. (1987) *Discovering Modernism: T. S. Eliot & His Context*, New York: Oxford University Press.
Pigou, Arthur Cecil. (1936) "Mr. J. M. Keynes's General Theory of Employment, Interest and Money." *Economica* 3.10: 115–32.Seybold, Matt. (2014) "The Rhyme of Crisis: Speculative Euphoria, Confidence Multipliers, and Intellectual Bubbles." *Western Humanities Review* 68.2: 11–17.
Seybold, Matt. (2017) "The End of Economics." *Los Angeles Review of Books* (July 3). https://lareviewofbooks.org/article/the-end-of-economics/
Skidelsky, Robert. (1992) *John Maynard Keynes: The Economist as Savior, 1920–1937*, London: Macmillan.
Skidelsky, Robert. (2001) *John Maynard Keynes: Fighting for Freedom, 1937–1946*, New York: Viking.
Soros, George. (2010) *The Soros Lectures at the Central European University*, New York: PublicAffairs.
Suskind, Ron. (1994) *Confidence Men: Wall Street, Washington, and the Education of a President*, New York: Harper.
Szalay, Michael. (2000) *New Deal Modernism: American Literature and the Invention of the Welfare State*, Durham, NC: Duke University Press.
Taleb, Nassim Nicholas. (2004) *Fooled By Randomness: The Hidden Role of Chance in Life and in the Markets,* New York: Random House.
Tratner, Michael. (2001) *Deficits & Desires: Economics and Sexuality in Twentieth-Century Literature*, Palo Alto, CA: Stanford University Press.
Turgeon, Lynn. (1996) *Bastard Keynesianism: The Evolution of Economic Thinking and Policymaking since World War II*, Westport, CT: Greenwood Press.
Walkom, Thomas. (2009) "What Would Keynes Do? Keep an Open Mind." *Toronto Star* (Jan. 10): ID1.

Walsh, Justyn. (2008) *Keynes and the Market*, Hoboken, NJ: Wiley.
Wapshott, Nicholas. (2011) *Keynes Hayek: The Clash That Defined Modern Economics*, New York: Norton.
West, Cornell. (2011) "Prophetic Religion and the Future of Capitalist Civilization," in Eduardo Mendieta and Jonathan Vanantwerpen (eds.) *The Power of Religion in the Public Sphere*, New York: Columbia University Press.
Wicke, Jennifer. (1994) "Mrs. Dalloway Goes to the Market: Woolf, Keynes, and Modern Markets." *NOVEL* 28.1: 5–23.

# 27

# NEOCLASSICAL ECONOMICS

*Regina Martin*

George Gissing's *New Grub Street* (1891) is a particularly apt novel for an essay in a *Companion to Literature and Economics* because it poses a question implied by the juxtaposition of the words "economics" and "literature": what does economics *do* to literature? Gissing's novel presents an ensemble cast of aspiring literary men and women who are trying to make a living out of writing literature and literary criticism. And it satirizes what it depicts as a literary marketplace driven by a logic of quantity over quality and of commercial tastes over a more cultivated sensibility. The novel's answer to the question posed above is a straightforward one: economics takes the literary out of literature—that is, when literary production becomes subject to the economic forces of the market, the product is no longer literature *per se*. In this sense, the novel anticipates what Andreas Huyssen would a century later describe as modernism's "great divide" between high and commercial cultures, and it participates in the gradual process, described by Raymond Williams, of delimiting the word "literature" to mean "imaginative" works of a "certain quality" whose right to the label is assessed by professional literary critics (48–51). Though the novel's answer to the question of what economics does to literature is by now a fairly well-worn one, its depiction of *how* economics takes the literary out of literature is much more interesting as it registers two interrelated historical processes taking place during its writing: the development of neoclassical economics and the growth of the professional classes.

In the late nineteenth century, Alfred Marshall and others who came to be known as neoclassical economists distinguished their approach to economics from that of classical political economy by developing theories of marginal utility. Marshall defines marginal utility thus:

> each several want is limited, and that with every increase in the amount of a thing which a man has, the eagerness of his desire to obtain more of it diminishes; until it yields place to the desire for some other thing.
>
> *(167)*

In other words, as we get more of something, we desire a little less of it until our desire is satisfied and we turn our sights toward something else. In the case of a consumer good, we are willing to pay less for it as we acquire more of it, or, in the case of money, as we become wealthier, each unit of money becomes less valuable to us, and we are willing to part with it more easily. The concept of marginal utility made it possible for economists to theorize market equilibrium: the marginal price of a good represents the point at which a market is supplying just enough to satisfy demand. Therefore, marginal utility has become the foundation for modern mainstream economics' central (albeit controversial) premise: the assumption that free markets "tend toward a long-run equilibrium in which resources are allocated efficiently" (Bateman 2006: 472).

Theories of marginal utility represented a break with a foundational principle in classical political economy: the labor theory of value, in which labor was conceived of as the primary source of value production in an economy (see also "Classical Economics" by Eleanor Courtemanche). Theories of marginal utility thereby effected a shift in focus from production to consumption, and John Dupré and Regenia Gagnier argue that with this transition, "The concern for the well-being of workers... ceased to be considered relevant to economics" (179). Within neoclassical economics, individuals came to be defined by and valued for their insatiable desires as consumers instead of their labor potential. Yet, the very first page of Marshall's *Principles* announces that it is indeed centrally concerned with the life of workers. Marshall writes,

> the business by which a person earns his livelihood generally fills his thoughts during by far *the* greater part of those hours in which his mind is at its best; during them his character is being formed by the way in which he uses his faculties in his work, by the thoughts and the feeling which it suggests, and by his relations to his associates in work, his employers or his employees.
>
> *(1–2)*

This passage suggests that a core premise of Marshall's study is the notion that individuals are defined by the work they do for a living. However, the worker at the heart of Marshall's *Principles of Economics* (1890) is not the debased and exploited factory worker of classical political economy; instead, Marshall's worker is a well-educated and ambitious man of business. I use the generic masculine when referring to Marshall's text because, for Marshall, the man of business was decidedly a man. He is a member of the growing ranks of the professional classes, for whom work is not merely a means to a living; it is a source of identity, pleasure, and intellectual stimulation. Marshall writes,

> much of the work by which people earn their living is pleasurable in itself... Indeed even business work, that seems at first sight unattractive, often yields a great pleasure by offering scope for the exercise of men's faculties, and for their instincts of emulation of power.
>
> *(84)*

The notion that work should be enjoyable would have been a fairly radical one to the classed society of Victorian England. The working classes would have objected for obvious reasons, and the claim would be inscrutable to the middle and upper classes whose social status relied on claims to leisure. But Marshall developed his economic theories during the nascent stages of what Harold Perkin would later describe as *The Rise of Professional Society* (1989), when the professional classes, made up of civil servants, private sector administrators and managers, bookkeepers, office workers, doctors, lawyers, teachers, and other nonmanual workers, began to grow in number and influence. Indeed, Marshall, whose father was a cashier at the Bank of England, grew out of this class, and Marshall continued in its ranks as a professor at Cambridge (Groenewegen 2006: 3). Neoclassical economics and its marginal revolution may have come to view the consumer as the primary actor in the drama of economics, but as I will demonstrate, Marshall looks to the professional businessman, and makes him the hero of an epic journey to address what Sylvia Nasar identifies as "the central paradox of modern society" (63): why does poverty endure among so much prosperity (see Gagnier 2000; Schleifer 2018).

If Marshall stands out against a backdrop of classical political economy for placing workers from the professional classes front and center in his treatise, *New Grub Street* stands out for similar reasons. Professional class characters are uncommon protagonists in the Victorian novelistic tradition, which, when Gissing was writing, was still very much attached to the continued social and political power of the leisured upper and middle classes. These classes, as Perkin explains, continued to translate their wealth into the status markers of leisure and land, while the professional classes embraced "human capital" as their "dominant form of wealth" (6). Indeed, one of Gissing's aspiring literary men admonishes his fellow writers "to write of the wealthy middle class" (202) if they want to sell their work (see Severn 2010). But *New Grub Street* breaks with its character's advice and instead organizes its narrative around professional class characters, and the interwoven plots of the novel turn on the successes and failures of the characters in the literary marketplace.

Though the literary profession along with complex markets for the production and distribution of literature have existed since the eighteenth century, it is not until the late Victorian period that literary professionals became part of a social class with distinctive features (see Benedict 2004; Severn 2010: 169–70). Reading Gissing's novel through the lens of Marshall's depiction of the businessman in his *Principles of Economics* transforms Gissing's novel from a facile denigration of the literary marketplace into an examination of how theories of marginal utility impact the literary profession. The novel imagines a new professional mode of subjectivity whose relationship to literature is necessarily vexed and whose identity is tied to the way, according to Marshall, professionals, as a class, produce economic value by reducing marginal costs and creating new economic efficiencies.

## Alfred Marshall's man of business

Marshall's abandonment of the labor theory of value in favor of marginal utility reflected the changing world around him. The classical political economists were writing at a time when the primary capital-generating institution was the owner-operated manufacturing firm that pitted labor against capital, so the major actors in their economic story were the working classes, merchants, and the capitalist or manufacturing classes. But by the time Marshall wrote his treatise, the investor-owned (or joint-stock), limited-liability, vertically integrated corporation had been legalized and deregulated, and it was quickly displacing the owner-operated firm as a more efficient mode of capital production and accumulation (see Arrighi 1994: 159–238; Kornbluh 2013; Martin 2015). The multilayered structure of corporations required a complex network of managers and technical experts, "who formed the backbone of Britain's [emerging] professional culture" (Severn 2010: 169), and also the backbone of Marshall's economic treatise.

The growth of the professional classes created new forms of remunerated labor that did not produce value in the same way as manufacturing labor. According to Marshall, this new kind of labor posed a problem for economists: "It is comparatively easy to find out the wages of bricklayers" but "the adjustment of supply to demand in the case of business ability is somewhat hindered by the difficulty of ascertaining exactly what is the price that is being paid for it in any trade" (689). Although "business" is now a common profession, in the Victorian context that gave shape to Marshall's and Gissing's texts, the businessman was a new class of worker whose attributes and status had yet to be defined (see Chandler 1977). One of my arguments in this essay is that Marshall's *Principles* and Gissing's *New Grub Street* participate in the theoretical and cultural works of creating and defining the new profession of business that we now take for granted. Indeed, as I will argue in my conclusion, Marshall's ideal businessman becomes the standard bearer for all professions.

The businessman was so new during Marshall's time that it was not clear to him how the processes of supply and demand would determine his wages. Importantly for my argument, he illustrates the problem by drawing an analogy to the art world, which will bear on my discussion of Gissing's novel below:

> There never was a time at which moderately good oil paintings sold more cheaply than now, and there never was a time at which first-rate paintings sold so dearly. A business man of average ability and average good fortune gets now a lower rate of profits on his capital than at any previous time; while yet... a man exceptionally favored by genius and good luck can... amass a huge fortune.
>
> *(Marshall 1898: 773)*

Although the professional classes are, like the working classes, subject to the laws of supply and demand in determining wages, there are exceptions to this rule: geniuses in art and geniuses in business. But there is an important difference between artistic genius and genius in business implicit in this passage: The artistic genius produces a salable commodity whose value is still determined by laws of supply and demand. The artistic produce of an artistic genius is in such low supply that it can demand a high price. But what does Marshall's genius in business produce?

The answer begins with this strange claim:

> Man cannot create material things. In the mental and moral world indeed he may produce new ideas; but when he is said to produce material things, he really only produces utilities; or in other words, his efforts and sacrifices result in changing the form or arrangement of matter to adapt it better for the satisfaction of wants.
>
> *(132)*

This passage is a clear example of how thoroughly manufacturing labor is relegated to the margins in Marshall's *Principles*. Laborers do not create things; they only reorganize material resources into utilities. The only *things* humans can actually create are *ideas*, and it is in the trade of ideas that Marshall's genius of business demands his high income.

To encourage the creation of new ideas, Marshall advocates spreading education to the masses:

> For by this means many, who would have died unknown, are enabled to get the start needed for bringing out their latent abilities. And the economic value of one great industrial genius is sufficient to cover the expenses of the education of a whole town; for one new idea, such as Bessemer's chief invention, adds as much to England's productive power as the labour of a hundred thousand men.
>
> *(296)*

The use of Sir Henry Bessemer as an example of education's potential is illustrative of what Marshall really has in mind when he speaks of the creation of ideas. The value of Bessemer's invention, the Bessemer converter, did not derive from the production of the converter itself (though Bessemer and others did get plenty rich off of its production). Rather, its greater value lies in the new *efficiency* it created in the production of steel. Bessemer did not so much create a new utility as increase the speed and reduce the marginal cost at which a highly desirable utility could be produced, thereby making it more affordable for a larger number of people.

While discussions of efficiency are rare in classical political economy, the word is ubiquitous in Marshall's *Principles*, which participated in what Thomas C. Leonard refers to as the "cult of efficiency" at the turn of the twentieth century (119). For example, Marshall identifies efficiency (not natural resources or other forms of material property) as the foundation of prosperity: "personal wealth," he argues, are "those energies, faculties, and habits which directly contribute to making people industrially efficient" (126). Increased efficiency is the means by which Alfred Marshall imagines that free markets and competition will lead to increased prosperity for all. Thus, the hero of Marshall's narrative is the striving businessman, who has the ability, not necessarily to create new commodities or utilities, but to create new efficiencies and thereby decrease marginal costs making more things more affordable for more people.

## The business of literature in *New Grub Street*

A trio of Gissing's characters—Jasper Milvain, an aspiring and ultimately successful "literary man," Edwin Reardon, a novelist who has achieved moderate critical success but little pecuniary gain, and Whelpdale, the only character to get rich from his literary ambitions—form a complex of foils whose contrasting approaches to the "business" of literature illustrate the problems a world evaluated through the marginal utilities of neoclassical economics creates for literature and its professionals. I enclose "business" in quotation marks because throughout the novel, literature is pointedly and repeatedly referred to as a business instead of an art form. For example, the first chapter establishes the contrast between Jasper and Edwin by identifying their different attitudes toward the "business" of literature. While Edwin "is the old type of unpractical artist" (6), who "can't keep up literary production as a paying business" (4), Jasper declares himself to be "the literary man of 1882" who sees literature as "a trade" and has set out to "learn" the "business" (6). According to Jasper's characterization, Edwin's inability to earn an income by writing is caused by his refusal to view the production of literature and literary criticism as a business; he views it as an art. He is so concerned with the quality of his literary production that he is unable to produce enough literature to make a living. But Jasper's explanation oversimplifies the situation. Edwin's failure is not just an inability to produce more literature; it is a failure to understand the production process as a problem of efficiency.

Like Marshall, *New Grub Street* distinguishes between the moderately good artist and the artistic genius as well as the moderately good businessman and the business genius, who, as I argue above, achieves the designation by creating new efficiencies that reduce the marginal prices of goods. But while Marshall's exploration of the overlap between the two spheres of art and business is, at most, ancillary, this overlap is *New Grub Street's* chief concern (see Marshall 1898: 168; Beech 2015). In the same breath that Jasper calls literature a "trade" and insists that "your successful man of letters is your skillful tradesman," who "thinks first and foremost of the markets," he identifies an exception: "men of genius, who may succeed by mere cosmic force" (6). Shortly after this speech, Jasper makes a similar exception when he is debating the role of merit in the literary world. His sister wants to believe that "really good work will sooner or later be recognized" regardless of market forces, but Jasper points out that the timeline will likely be "Later, rather than sooner" and in the meantime the author may "starve" (25). *But* he adds the following caveat: "You understand that I am not speaking of genius; I mean marketable literary work" (26).

Jasper, the novel's cynical voice of pragmatic market values, twice extracts genius from market equations. Genius can produce great works of literature *and* receive remuneration enough to sustain bodily integrity, but the novel is curiously silent on how. In Marshall's text, the answer is clear: artistic geniuses can command more for their paintings because they are in short supply in a market of high demand. Marshall's artistic genius very much functions within market forces. Gissing's readers could likely speculate about how markets might reward literary genius, but the more interesting observation to make about these passages is that a novel so attuned to how market forces shape literature and its profession points to "cosmic force" as its (non)explanation for the pecuniary success of literary genius. By refusing to attribute the success of literary genius to market forces, the novel delineates a social space for the existence of a mode of literature that articulates a kind of value (aesthetic, moral, etc.) whose greatness exceeds or offers an alternative to market accountability.

John Ruskin insists that "no good [art] in this world was ever done for money" (61). It is not my purpose to wade into the thicket of debates about the existence of such a mode of literature (see, for instance, Attridge 2004); my aim is to simply observe that *New Grub Street* participates in a long and continuing tradition in those debates to extricate the literary (or artistic or cultural) from the economic. It should be no surprise to readers that we never meet one of these geniuses; instead, we become intimately familiar with the plight of Edwin Reardon who is not a genius but is nevertheless haunted by the specter of the literary. Upon the death of his father, who had only moderate success as a professional photographer in a provincial town, Edwin inherited "two hundred pounds" and promptly moved to London "To become a literary man, of course" (52). *New Grub Street* is exhaustingly attentive to the economics of its characters' literary production, and this is most certainly true of Edwin. The novel's depiction of Edwin's economic situation suggests that financial stability is anathema to aspirations toward literary genius (when one is not actually a genius). After arriving in London, Edwin lived frugally on the "two hundred pounds" left by his father while educating himself into the literary profession (52). When that money ran out, he had to take a position as a clerk, during which time he began writing novels in the evenings. His first two novels received some critical acclaim but were not financially successful. But then Edwin receives an unexpected legacy from his grandfather of "four hundred pounds" (56). This financial windfall allowed him to quit his job as clerk and devote himself to writing full-time. His third novel, which he wrote under these conditions, "was a great improvement on its predecessors, and the reviews were generally favourable" (57).

Notably, Edwin produced his most critically acclaimed work while paying his bills with inherited wealth. In other words, his mode of literary production resembled that of the leisured Victorian middle classes instead of the professional classes. Indeed, the phrase "mode of production" is an inappropriate descriptor for the conditions under which Edwin wrote because he was not so much producing a commodity as participating in the leisured activity of meticulously composing a novel. His leisured activity just so happened to translate into some modest pecuniary gain, which Edwin used to engage in another privileged activity of the leisure classes—"he spent six months travelling in the south of Europe" (57)—instead of using his income from the novel as a source of capital to reinvest in the advancement of his profession. Thus, Edwin is not just old-fashioned in his commitment to the literary, per Jasper's diagnosis at the beginning of the novel; he is also old-fashioned in the sense that his horizons of expectations continue to be shaped by the still socially and politically dominant Victorian middle classes for whom leisure *and* the literature it makes possible designates social status. But Edwin does not possess the inherited wealth to maintain either leisure or the literary, which, through his character, the novel depicts as two inextricably related social distinctions delineating the Victorian middle class as a class.

Eventually, Edwin gives up on the possibility of producing anything with literary merit, and he settles down to write a novel with marketable appeal. When he does so, his working habits begin to resemble those of a factory worker. He "tick[s] off his stipulated quantum of manuscript each four-and-twenty hours" (110) as if he were engaged in the repetitive motion of screwing a nut onto a bolt hour after hour and day after day. At one point, he even compares himself to a "machine... earning so much money a week... until the day of final breakdown" (329). And finally, to punctuate Edwin's descent from a brief membership in the Victorian middle classes into the Victorian working classes, the novel tracks Edwin's progress with a "a workhouse clock clanging its admonition at the poet's ear" (115).

While Reardon is cowering under the dual threat of literary failure and the workhouse clock, Jasper explains how he spends his days as a "literary man":

> I got up at 7.30, and whilst I breakfasted I read through a volume I had to review. By 10.30 the review was written—three-quarters of a column of the Evening Budget.... At eleven I was ready to write my Saturday causerie for the Will o' the Wisp; it took me till close upon one o'clock, which was rather too long. I can't afford more than an hour and a half for that job. At one, I rushed out to a dirty little eating-house in Hampstead Road. Was back again by a quarter to two, having in the meantime sketched a paper for The West End. Pipe in mouth, I sat down to leisurely artistic work; by five, half the paper was done; the other half remains for to-morrow...
>
> *(168–9)*

Like Edwin, Jasper is also very concerned about producing a certain amount of writing in a specific amount of time, but his labor looks much more like that of a business manager than that of a factory worker. He is more concerned with the process of production as a problem of efficiency than he is with the quality or even quantity of the product. He has carefully considered which publications will earn him the most money, which of them he can produce quickly, and which will take longer. Moreover, he has assessed how his body can be used most effectively and efficiently to accommodate the writing he needs to do. For Jasper, the roles of "literary man" and manager of business go hand in hand, making him an example of Marshall's man of business whose market value derives from his ability to identify and leverage efficiencies in modes of production and in the market rather than just from the production of utilities themselves.

Though Jasper may be an example of Marshall's man of business, he is not Marshall's *genius* in business. That role in Gissing's novel is reserved for Whelpdale. Like Edwin and Jasper, Whelpdale has literary ambitions, but his first novel is a failure, and he is otherwise unable to earn a living by his writing. However, instead of abandoning his literary ambitions, he invents a new kind of literary business. He gives himself the title of "literary advisor" and places an ad in a literary journal advertising his services: "To Young Authors and Literary Aspirants... Advice given on choice of subjects, MSS. read, corrected, and recommended to publishers. Moderate terms" (152). Edwin dismisses Whelpdale's business as a "swindle," but Jasper points out that he "made six guineas in the first fortnight" (152). Moreover, his invention of the literary agent adds a new element of efficiency to the business of literature. While Jasper had to spend the early days of his career getting to know the right people, Whelpdale does that work on behalf of an aspiring writer. Later Whelpdale, "fertile in suggestions of literary enterprise," gets together enough capital to buy a failing journal called "Chat." He alters the name to "Chit-Chat" and stipulates that "No article in the paper is to measure more than two inches in length, and every inch must be broken into at least two paragraphs" (429). Whelpdale's new magazine not only transforms the production of literature into a much more efficient process, it also lends efficiency to the consumption of literature, so that readers will be able to read and digest the content of the magazine while in transit from home to work on the London Underground. At novel's end, Whelpdale's "noble new development of journalism" has "triumphed" by providing "the quarter-educated... with literature to their taste" and, one might add, to the level of their income (445). Whelpdale's magazine reduces the marginal cost of literature making it accessible to a greater number of people. But then, of course, a character like Edwin would not call the contents of Whelpdale's invention literature. Thus, the novel posits an intrinsic conflict between this thing we call literature and a reduction of its marginal costs, as if to suggest that the rising levels of prosperity Marshall attributes to the reduction of marginal costs may not include increased accessibility to literature, whose definition in this novel depends on its remaining a rarified form of writing (see also Ryle 2005).

## Conclusion: A society of Henry Bessemers and Whelpdales

Throughout *Principles*, Marshall maintains a distinction between "business" and what he calls the "learned professions" (372). He laments the fact that some professionals, like "a physician or a solicitor manages... his own business" because "much valuable activity is wasted" by a class of people who

> have not the special aptitude required for obtaining a business connection; they would be better paid, would lead happier lives, and would do more good service for the world if their work could be arranged for them by some sort of middleman.
>
> (372)

Certainly, Edwin Reardon, who suffers from this problem, and Whelpdale, who gets paid to be that middleman, would agree. Marshall's desire to maintain the professions as a sphere of activity whose economics is managed within the separate sphere of "business" plays to the same logic upon which the notion of a celebrated category of the literary is based. But Marshall's blueprint for solving the problem that motivates his interest in economics in the first place—the reality that grinding poverty continues amidst plenty—depends on the transformation of the professions into sources of new efficiencies. In other words, according to Marshall's rationale, there can be no separate spheres of economic and noneconomic activities if all are to enjoy relative prosperity.

Robert W. Butler identifies Marshall's proposal that education is the means by which new efficiencies are invented as a "desire to make the working class over into middle-class gentlemen" (97). However, the nomenclature of "gentlemen," which implies a man of learned leisure, is inappropriate to Marshall's vision for the working classes. Marshall's advocacy for an education program that "develop[s] the faculties" instead of just teaching "technical" skills (288) is not intended to endow the working classes with cultural capital that would make them presentable in a Victorian middle-class drawing room; Marshall wants to transform the working classes into a class of Henry Bessemers, or "geniuses in business," whose critical faculties are directed toward the creation of new ideas and most importantly, new efficiencies. In other words, Marshall's blueprint for raising prosperity involves transforming all members of society into sources of new efficiencies. Gissing's novel points out that this aim must also include the "learned professions." In *New Grub Street*, economistic measures of value engulf every activity, including what the novel casts as literary endeavors. At the end of the novel, Edwin Reardon has perished along with his commitment to the literary, and Jasper Milvain and Whelpdale stand triumphant, not so much as "literary" men but as men of business, a new kind of professional whose expertise lies not in producing the literary but in transforming the literary along with the cultural capital it represents into an evermore efficient moneymaking venture.

## References


Arrighi, Giovanni. (1994) *The Long Twentieth Century: Money, Power, and the Origins of Our Times*. New York: Verso.

Attridge, Derek. (2004) *The Singularity of Literature*. New York: Routledge.

Bateman, Bradley W. (2006) "Speculation" in *The Elgar Companion to Alfred Marshall*, Tiziano Raffaelli, Giacomo Becattini, and Marco Dardi (ed.). Northhampton, MA: Edgar Elgar.

Beech, Dave. (2015) *Art and Value: Art's Economic Exceptionalism in Classical, Neoclassical and Marxist Economics*. Boston, MA: Brill.

Benedict, Barbara M. (2004) "Readers, Writers, Reviewers and the Professionalization of Literature" in *The Cambridge Companion to English Literature*, Thomas Keymer and Jon Mee (ed.). New York: Cambridge University Press.

Chandler, Alfred. (1977) *The Visible Hand: The Managerial Revolution in American Business*. Cambridge, MA: Harvard University Press.

Dupré, John and Regenia Gagnier. (1999) "The Ends of Economics" in *The New Economic Criticism: Studies at the Intersection of Literature and Economics*, Martha Woodmansee and Mark Osteen (ed.). New York: Routledge.

Gagnier, Regenia. (2000) *The Insatiability of Human Wants: Economics and Aesthetics in Market Society*. Chicago, IL: University of Chicago Press.

Gissing, George. (1997) *New Grub Street*. New York: Everyman.

Groenewegen, Peter D. (2006) "Life and Activities" in *The Elgar Companion to Alfred Marshall*, T. Raffaelli, G. Becattini, and M. Dardi (ed.). Northhampton, MA: Edgar Elgar.

Huyssen, Andreas. (1986) *After the Great Divide: Modernism, Mass Culture, and Postmodernism*. Bloomington: Indiana University Press.

Kornbluh, Anna. (2013) *Realizing Capital: Financial and Psychic Economies in Victorian Form*. New York: Fordham University Press.

Leonard, Thomas C. (2009) "American Economic Reform in the Progressive Era: Its Foundational Beliefs and Their Relation to Eugenics." *History of Political Economy* 41.1: 109–41.

Marshall, Alfred. (1898) *Principles of Economics* (4th ed.). New York: Macmillan.

Martin, Regina. (2015) "Absentee Capitalism and the Politics of Conrad's Imperial Novels." *PMLA* 130.3: 584–98.

Nasar, Sylvia. (2011) *Grand Pursuit: The Story of Economic Genius*. New York: Simon & Schuster.

Ruskin, John. (1926) *Unto This Last and Other Writings*. New York: Dutton.

Schleifer, Ronald. (2018) "A New Sense of Value: Literary Modernism and Economics" in *Bloomsbury Companion for Modern Literature*, Ulrika Maude and Mark Nixon (ed.). London: Bloomsbury.
Severn, Stephen E. (2010) "Quasi-Professional Culture, Conservative Ideology, and the Narrative Structure of George Gissing's *New Grub Street*." *Journal of Narrative Theory* 40.2: 156–88.
Perkin, Harold. (1989) *The Rise of Professional Society: England Since 1880*. New York: Routledge.
Ryle, Martin. (2005) "'To Show a Man of Letters': Gissing, Cultural Authority, and Literary Modernism" in *George Gissing: Voices of the Unclassed*, Martin Ryle and Jennie Bourne Taylor (ed.). Burlington, VT: Ashgate.
Williams, Raymond. (1977) *Marxism and Literature*. New York: Oxford University Press.

# 28
# NEOLIBERALISM

*Alissa G. Karl*

While this chapter aims to illuminate 'neoliberalism' as a concept and historical phenomenon, we should begin by acknowledging that there is no narrowly correct use of the term. 'Neoliberalism' applies to a range of referents, including 'the transformations capital underwent at the turning point of the 1970s and 1980s' (Duménil and Lévy 2004: 1); an economic dogma concerned with the cultivation of capitalist markets and competition; a philosophy of radical self-interest that emerges out of classical liberalism; protocols for governmental policy including the deregulation and privatization of industry and the weakening of organized labour; the proliferation of contingent and insecure labour conditions via the subcontracting and outsourcing of labour contracts, freelancing, and zero-hour arrangements; and the current stage in the history of capitalist accumulation.

Many commentators also stress that the tendencies and doctrines that we identify as neoliberal are often irregular and inconsistent; David Harvey calls it an 'unstable and contradictory political form' (Harvey 2005: 13). And John Comaroff (2009) prefers 'the adjective, "neoliberal"... since it may be taken to describe a tendency, a more-or-less realized, more-or-less articulated, unevenly distributed ensemble of attributes discernible in the world' (46). Furthermore, 'neoliberalism' is used so frequently and widely that it risks becoming an 'evacuated term... [that] signals the absence of a specific political economic, historical, or cultural critique' (Elliott and Harkins 2013: 2). The challenge of talking about 'neoliberalism' thus stems from the variety of concepts and practices for which it is a label, as well as the frequency of its application in critical discourse. And yet, it is that very extent of neoliberalism's reach that makes it such a compelling and important object of study. In political theorist Wendy Brown's oft-cited formulation, '[n]eoliberal rationality... *involves extending and disseminating market values to all institutions and social action*' (Brown 2005: 29–30). While Brown's claim that neoliberal priorities are somehow 'everywhere' might exemplify the concept's overexposure, it also demands that we understand the historical specificities of neoliberal philosophy, economic doctrine, and political policy such that we can fathom this pervasive rationality of our times.

## Neoliberalism's precursors

The term 'neoliberal' combines 'Neolclassical' and 'Liberal,' and intellectual neoliberalism incorporates features of each of these nineteenth-century schools of political and economic thought. For instance, in 1947, a group of academic economists and philosophers who were followers of Austrian economist Friedrich von Hayek (who is often positioned as the counterpoint to John Maynard Keynes, the British economist whose prescription of managed state economic interventionism was essentially the rule in high-GDP capitalist countries from the 1930s through the 1970s) formed the Mont Pelerin Society (1947) through which they prescribed a combination of market and personal freedoms (see also Brian Hurley's essay 'Hayek and the Pleasures of Liberal Thought in the "Great Book" of Modern Japan'). In the society's founding statement, the group laments a 'decline of belief in private property and the competitive market; for without the diffused power and initiative associated with these institutions it is difficult to imagine a society in which freedom may effectively be preserved.' These early neoliberals claim that the individual freedom that is at the core of nineteenth-century *Liberal* political thought can best be promoted through the unrestrained competitive markets advocated by later nineteenth- and early twentieth-century *Neoclassical* economic theory (see also Regina Martin's 'Neoclassical Economics').

The application of Neoclassical principles to Liberal individualism presents a distinct evolution of the notion of personal freedom. Starting in the later nineteenth century, Neoclassical economists (including William Stanley Jevons, Léon Walras, and Alfred Marshall) replaced the classical labour theory of value (which held that value derived from the labour that contributed to an item's making) with their own 'marginal' theory of value, in which value consists in an item's usefulness to the consumer. Jevons (1957) calls economic science 'a calculus of pleasure and pain' whereby 'the object of Economics is to maximize happiness by purchasing pleasure, as it were, at the lowest cost of pain' (23). Neoclassicists like Jevons thus position individualism at the core of their theory by predicating all economic activity and value upon the desires of individual people such that economics becomes a study of personal choices (Mirowski 2013: 24). And much like their classical predecessors, neoclassical economists contend that through acts of choice, the self-interested pursuits of individuals ultimately comprise markets that adjust and balance themselves to accommodate everyone's desires.

Where nineteenth-century Liberal thought enshrines the pursuit of self-interest and personal freedom, and where Neoclassical theory makes personal desire and choice the basis of all economic activity and value, neoliberal doctrine evolves the concept of self-interest even further. Joseph Vogl (2014) points out: 'whereas the market once fulfilled the (liberal) natural law of self-interest, it now follows the (neoliberal) idea or form… of competition' (37–38). In a neoliberal paradigm, competition in the markets becomes the primary means through which individuals can pursue their self-interest, assert their choices, and exercise their freedom—hence Wendy Brown's aforementioned claim that neoliberal rationality involves the submission of all spheres of life to a model of the market and her further assertion that today's neoliberalism is an extension and mutation of nineteenth-century Liberalism (see Brown 2015). Others, like David Harvey, see neoliberalism as an outcome of historical developments within capitalist economies, and in particular a response to dwindling accumulation from industrial capitalism of the early and mid-twentieth century, and the next section describes some of the changes to capitalist profit-making since the 1970s that are now identified as neoliberal modes of accumulation. It is worth pointing out, though, that whatever a commentator's designation of neoliberalism within intellectual or economic history, currently the term itself is most often used by those who are critical of it—unlike early neoliberals for whom it named a distinct economic and philosophical lineage.

## 1971: floating currencies, financialization, and the rise of the derivative

At the conclusion of the Second World War, forty-four countries established the Bretton Woods system to stabilize international currency markets and financial relations. Under the system, the values of currencies were 'pegged' or indexed to the US Dollar, which itself was convertible to gold—initially at 35 dollars per ounce. Such a managed monetary system constrained the circulation of capital and currency around the world, and individual countries had to maintain a disciplined balance of their imports and exports. All of this changed in 1971, when the increased conversion of US Dollars into gold by foreign central banks made the Dollar's gold convertibility rate impossible to maintain; President Richard Nixon effectively nullified the Bretton Woods system by suspending the Dollar's convertibility to gold. By 1973, all of the former Bretton Woods currencies were off the exchange rate standard and became fiat, or freely floating currencies. The end of exchange rate controls meant an increased volume of capital circulation around the globe, and that currencies became more volatile, which spawned two financial effects: currency speculation (for those who sought to profit from exchange rate fluctuation) and the rise of financial derivatives (financial contracts designed to ensure against the risks of financial speculation). Those derivatives then become objects of trade and speculation themselves.

As Richard Godden puts it, the reintroduction of fiat currencies in 1971 'upp[ed] the ante on money's function as lubricity rather than mean' (Godden 2011a: 854). Rather than tethering economic activity within a stipulated web of value relationships (under managed exchange rates), fiat currency enables the proliferation of financial transactions, speculation, and a whole financial system that has very little to do with other kinds of industrial or economic activity. This is not to say that financial markets are unique to the late twentieth century; indeed, Giovanni Arrighi offers a detailed history of the centuries-old oscillation of capitalist economic activity between productive and financial cycles (see Arrighi 1994). But with the newly floating world currencies entailed by the end of the Bretton Woods system, 'the fulcrum of power and profit beg[ins] to shift from the production of commodities to the circulation and capital' (LiPuma and Lee 2004: 67).

Developments in finance since the 1970s that were enabled by the demise of the Bretton Woods system mark new methods of capitalist accumulation that are mainstays of today's neoliberal world system. While in the immediate decades after the Second World War, labour and capital (that is, the interests of those performing productive labour and those of the owners and upper management of firms) are said to have reached a 'Keynesian compromise' whereby capital restrained its impulses to generate greater profits in exchange for relative stability in the labour force, in the early 1970s, the release of capital and currency controls helped sever this unspoken pact. Finance and production became increasingly divorced from one another through a number of means: an increase in the volume and type of financial products, contracts, and trades; industries and profits that are not tied to material production or assets; and the prioritization of a firm's 'shareholder value'—its value on financial markets via share price and other financial indicators. Harvey describes the climate of financial capitalism since 1973 as spectacular for its speculative and predatory style:

> Stock promotions, ponzi schemes, structural asset destruction through inflation, asset-stripping through mergers and acquisitions, and the promotion of levels of debt incumbency that reduce whole populations, even in the advanced capitalist countries, to debt peonage, to say nothing of corporate fraud and dispossession of assets… by credit and stock manipulations – all of these are central features of what contemporary capitalism is about.
> *(Harvey 2003: 147)*

Harvey's laundry list of financial transactions and schemes characterizes contemporary capitalism's attempt to replace accumulation from productive sources by maximizing profit solely through 'speculative and predatory' means. Furthermore, under the trend that Randy Martin calls *The Financialization of Daily Life* (2002), individual profit-maximization has become a key priority for average people. So while financialization is a topic of critical scrutiny and theorization in its own right and while the financial turn since the 1970s is not identical to the rise of neoliberalism, finance since the 1970s has prompted many of the economic transformations that have come to be called 'neoliberal'—in particular, the creation of markets that are divorced from labour and material production, and that would seem to locate all potential for value within those markets themselves.

Although financial crashes and crises are not unique to neoliberal capitalism, any discussion of neoliberalism and financialization would be incomplete without some mention of the worldwide financial crash of 2008. As one commentator puts it, 2008 'was the year the neo-liberal economic orthodoxy that ran the world for 30 years suffered a heart attack of epic proportions' (Mathiason 2008). Many have claimed that the seeds of the 2008 crash were sown in the 1980s with the deregulation of the financial industry under Margaret Thatcher and Ronald Reagan (more on which in the following section) or even earlier, in Joshua Clover's (2012) view:

> [w]e might say that the crisis began … with the 1973 recession, the oil shocks, the final collapse of the Bretton Woods agreements, the meteoric ascent of the finance sector, driven by new markets in derivative assets and by the need to replace fading industrial profits.
>
> *(113)*

The vast fallout of the 2008 crisis includes the insolvency, government bailout, or engineered takeover of major financial institutions in the US, Europe, and worldwide. State and municipal governments, pension funds, and even national governments (like that of Iceland) found their assets wiped out due to exposure to shaky financial investments. The causes of the 2008 crisis are debatable, but also manifold; they include the exposure of banks to 'subprime' debt that was unlikely to be repaid and the over-leveraging of financial speculations (that is, too much exposure to risk for the amount of underlying assets to cover losses). Though the scope of the 2008 crisis can't be covered here, it evidences certain developments of the neoliberal era, such as the simultaneous *separation* of financial from labour or production values (via financial derivatives), and the exhaustive *exposure* of everyday people to those financial markets that redirect the latter's assets 'upwards' and into the coffers of finance capitalists, bankers, speculators, and investors.

## 1979–1980: Thatcher, Reagan, and the neoliberal state

While academic and intellectual neoliberalism had been simmering for decades, and while dramatic neoliberal economic reforms had been implemented elsewhere before (as in the wake of General Augusto Pinochet's military coup in Chile in 1973), the elections of Margaret Thatcher's Conservative Party in Britain in 1979 and of Ronald Reagan to the US Presidency in 1980 were highly visible—and vigorous—turns towards neoliberal economic and social policies in two large and influential economies. In both cases, the new governments sought to move the collective functions of the state or social institutions into the markets, and to promote markets as the sole means of achieving prosperity—indeed, perhaps the main achievement of neoliberal statecraft has been the redefinition of national prosperity *as and only as* economic growth. Margaret Thatcher is famous for claiming: 'There is no such thing [as society]! There are individual men and women.' As the UK Prime Minister from 1979 to 1990, Thatcher promoted competition and entrepreneurship at corporate and individual levels—and hence dismantled the major pillars of the post-war British economic regime of a robust welfare state and strong labour unions. Thatcher's government privatized major industries (including British Airways, British Rail, the Royal Mail, telecommunications, electricity, and gas); weakened local municipal councils and the welfare programmes that they administered; and deregulated financial markets. In outlasting a year-long strike by the National Union of Mineworkers (NUM) in 1984–5, Thatcher not only forced reforms to the coalmining industry but more generally realigned economic life around the individual rather than collective institutions like the state or organized labour.

At the core of so many of Thatcher's initiatives (often influenced by her advisor, MP and neoliberal ideologue Keith Joseph) can be glimpsed a belief that individual enterprise generates competition and returns net benefits for all. As Stuart Hall (1979) observed on the eve of Thatcher's first election,

> in the doctrines and discourses of 'social market values'—the restoration of competition and personal responsibility for effort and reward, the image of the over-taxed individual, enervated by welfare coddling, his initiative sapped by handouts by the state—'Thatcherism' has found a powerful means of popularizing the principles of a Monetarist philosophy.
>
> *(17)*

Hall's linkage of the economic policy of Monetarism with the philosophical inclination towards individualism is characteristic of the combination of policy and philosophy that neoliberalism often presents. Monetarism, which is the economic policy prescription for government manipulation of the money supply to control inflation and promote economic growth, is most often associated with the US academic economist of the University of Chicago, Milton Friedman, and with the economic policies of Ronald Reagan in the 1980s.

Regan undertook a number of economic reforms similar to those of Thatcher in his deregulation of US industry (including airlines, telecommunications, and finance), corporate tax cuts, and confrontation of organized labour—most famously in his breaking of the air traffic controllers' union (PATCO) strike in 1981. But the application of Monetarism is perhaps the most notable of Reagan's neoliberal interventions, particularly in the policy shift initiated by the then Chair of the US Federal Reserve, Paul Volcker. Beginning in 1979 before Reagan took office, Volcker sought to spur growth in the US economy when he dramatically raised interest rates by Federal Reserve decree; Volcker's intervention created a deep recession with high unemployment, especially in manufacturing sectors. When Reagan followed the so-called 'Volcker shock' with financial deregulation and tax cuts on investment profits, he helped deepen the divide between finance capital and labour, as investors sought higher rates of return in other regions and countries, and away from sites of traditionally organized labour (see Harvey 2005: 25).

The promotion of market-based initiatives and competition under Thatcher, Reagan, and countless other subsequent governments worldwide presents a key paradox of neoliberalism's involvement with the state: in order to promote the market as the sole site of individual and collective life, the state must intervene in the affairs of citizens and of the market. And in the course of cultivating 'freedoms... [that] reflect the interests of private property owners, businesses, multinational corporations, and financial capital' (Harvey 2005: 7), the state has arguably undermined its own sovereignty through the very entities that it promotes. As Brown puts it,

> nation-state sovereignty has been undercut... by neoliberal rationality, which recognizes no sovereign apart from entrepreneurial decision makers (large and small), which displaces legal and political principles (especially liberal commitments to universal inclusion, equality, liberty, and the rule of law) with market criteria, and which demotes the political sovereign to managerial status.
>
> *(Brown 2010: 22)*

Or, as Joseph Vogl has it, theorists of capital have routinely implied that self-interest begets effective social organization, but only *absent* state intervention. Vogl claims that capitalist economic orthodoxy from the classical period forward has assumed that 'trade and market forces creat[e] a milieu in which the desires and interests of *homo economicus* regulate and control themselves,' and that '[c]ivil society... has been created by [this] agency' (28).

So whether one follows Brown in claiming that the state has been usurped by the logic of the market, or whether one sees a trend, as Vogl does, in the articulation of the liberal state as an outcome of self-interested competitive behaviour, neoliberal states today routinely embrace privatized competition and managerial behaviour when it comes to the provision of state services. Case in point was No Child Left Behind Act of 2001, which instituted performance-based, competitive funding standards for public schools in the United States—effectively de-funding or closing 'underperforming' schools that typically serve the least advantaged students. And at the same time that the state behaves as a profit-maximizing manager, market-based choice is conflated with liberal democracy, and the neoliberal consumer with the democratic citizen.

## Neoliberal labour

The so-called 'globalization' of labour, production, and business over the past few decades has entailed significant changes to the experience of workers worldwide. Under the trade agreements of recent decades, workers are 'freed up' to compete with one another on a global scale (and, in much more limited ways, to migrate in search of work), just as corporations can pursue labour contracts around the world. The breaking of the aforementioned 'Keynesian compromise' and the separation of financial from production values have influenced the development of such conditions, as employers seek low-cost labour, and often seek to avoid union or other labour regulations, to increase their bottom lines. The scenario of contemporary labour thus conforms to a neoliberal paradigm in which workers everywhere are free, competitive agents enabled by evermore exposure to global markets. On the other hand, today's labouring classes have very little protection from the tides of competition that should theoretically enrich them.

Technological capacities have helped generate the dynamic, often insecure labour scenarios that prevail under neoliberal capital. Beginning with the scanner at your local grocery store, the ability to gather, store, and analyse data about consumption patterns has created the demand for a highly agile supply chain. 'Just-in-time' production makes goods available at short notice and avoids stockpiling excess inventory, but it also requires a surplus of available labour that can be deployed at short notice. So-called 'zero hours' contracts place employees on call, often not knowing when or how many hours they will work in a given week. With short-term and temporary contracts, employers need not maintain large payrolls when such a volume of labour is not needed. As such, the 'outsourcing' and 'subcontracting' of labour from high- to low-GDP countries doesn't just entail hiring workers in another place, but has seen the renovation of labour conditions and the wage contract worldwide.

Judith Butler calls the above the

> arbitrary and violent rhythms of being instrumentalised as disposable labour: never knowing the future, being subjected to arbitrary hirings and firings, having one's labour extensively utilized and exploited and then enduring stretches of time, sometimes indefinite, in which one has no idea when work might come again.
>
> *(Butler and Athanasiou 2013: 148)*

Yet, the precarity that Butler describes is often presented as an asset: Sarah Brouillette (2014) explains that for today's professional and creative class, 'commit[ment] to constant indeterminacy and self-evolution… converges with the neoliberal image of the flexible creative worker whose career is her primary site of self-discovery' (14). Under a neoliberal paradigm that enshrines individual choice, the worker who is unencumbered by long-term contracts or collective bargaining agreements is free to innovate in her workplace and to deploy her capacities as she sees fit. And yet, the requirement that labour be perpetually available and flexible means that, practically, workers are deeply insecure in their 'freedom' to surf the labour market. And as Jane Elliott points out, neoliberal freedom

> is obviously not the neutral framework for free choice it purports to be, [and] the unacceptability of the choices it offers does not render them illusory or without import — quite the opposite: the choices between gas or childcare, illegal immigration or destitution, prostitution or starvation, are so significant and so painful precisely because they are so unjust.
>
> *(Elliott 2013: 87)*

When paired with the increasingly precarious conditions of work and the roll-back of welfare safety nets, the neoliberal refrain of personal freedom ultimately leaves the individual worker responsible for whatever conditions she might find herself in, given that they technically are a result of her own choices. Neoliberal labour protocols likewise reveal deeper assumptions about personhood: that people are first and foremost free and competitive, that individuals are responsible for optimizing their worth as workers and as people, and as Brown contends, have evolved from the *homo economicus* of classical economics to neoliberal 'human capital' to be cultivated in the markets (Brown 2015: 34).

## Neoliberalism and literary studies

While it may be the case that neoliberalism 'risks becoming and evacuated term' if it is used excessively or imprecisely, the concept remains salient in contemporary literary studies in a number of ways. By way of conclusion, we'll outline a few of these.

### *Periodization and postmodernism*

From the historical sketch above, it is clear that the age of neoliberal theory and policy overlaps with the literary period of postmodernism, which is often identified by its formal fragmentation, irony, self-awareness and irreverence, and in recent years scholars have started to make connections between the two. In 1984, Fredric Jameson famously defined postmodernism as the 'cultural logic of late capitalism' and argued that we should consider 'postmodernism' not primarily as an aesthetic category, but as a phase of capitalism in which the social and cultural realms have taken on the tendencies of the economic such that there is no point 'outside' of capital from which it can be viewed, much less critiqued. As Jameson (1991) puts it, 'the possibility of the positioning of the cultural act outside the massive Being of capital... has very precisely been abolished in the new space of postmodernism' (48). Though Jameson doesn't theorize the term neoliberalism specifically, he prompts us to re-read postmodern 'freedom' as an iteration of, or as having been co-opted by, neoliberal logic. As Jeffrey Nealon (2012) says of Jameson's version of postmodernism/late capitalism:

> [I]t's one logic, smeared across a bunch of discourses, and... you can't quite so easily or naively cherry-pick and affirm the stuff you like (say, the Yale School of literary criticism), while you simply denounce the stuff you don't like (say, the Chicago School of economics). Or, to put it more precisely, you can't unproblematically say that the logic of one of those things (American deconstruction, in this example) somehow inherently subverts or resists the logic of the other (neoliberal capitalism).
>
> *(23)*

In Mathias Nilges' account of the relationship between postmodernism and neoliberalism, on the other hand, the latter emerges out of the former, as neoliberalism instantiates postmodernism's cultural critique of the socio-economic order into a fully blown 'social and cultural regulation' of, well, everything. As Nilges puts it: 'postmodernism's wishes were granted—by neoliberalism,' such that postmodernism ultimately prepared us for neoliberalism's rise (375). There are, of course, other models of the interface between postmodernism and neoliberalism; suffice it to say here that the prominence of the former as a literary category demands accounting for by those who would deploy neoliberalism in literary studies.

## Value and representation

The free-floating currencies and proliferation of financial derivative values of the post-1971 economic order are remarkably similar to the poststructuralist take on language, with its endless plays of signification and refusal of unitary 'meanings' (see Tratner 2003). Yet where the deconstruction of language tends to be underpinned by anti-establishment and anti-authoritarian sentiments, as we have seen, the neoliberal financial order has decidedly consolidated wealth and power upwards, in the hands of the capitalist class. Literary scholars who have been trained in the intricacies of poststructuralist theories of language are deploying their insights onto the realm of high finance and the global economy, enquiring into the ramifications of immaterial, endlessly perpetuating techniques of financial acquisition. Some aim to use an enquiry into financial value to offer a diagnosis of our crisis-prone financial system and political culture for, according to Joshua Clover, 'the inability to think value in terms adequate to the critique of political economy—to grasp the moving contradiction of the value form, of use and exchange, production and circulation—prove[s] a near-absolute limit to understanding the historical situation' (113). Others aim to trace the labour and social relations that are effaced by current financial regimes of value. Richard Gooden asks:

> [g]iven that the financial sector works in a medium—speculative capital—that systematically seeks to avoid uncomfortable collisions with the more material practices of the economy, how might such an immaterial mask be rendered expressive of the social relations that give rise to it?
>
> *(Godden 2011b: 413)*

The production/finance schism discussed earlier, then, points to a larger set of quandaries about signification and value that literary studies are especially poised to investigate.

## Genres and tropes

Due to neoliberalism's range as referent, from matters of policy to those of personhood, literary scholars are also invested in how neoliberal economies and culture arise and are addressed within literary texts. The novel has been of particular interest, given its historical association with the rise of liberal capitalism. If, for example, novels of the eighteenth and nineteenth centuries established norms of personhood in line with the requirements of bourgeois capitalism, then how might the contemporary novel refigure the individual for neoliberal times in line with our notions of human capital and creditworthiness, and cultures of debt? (see McClanahan 2014). How have novelistic genres, like the crime novel or the *Bildungsroman*, evolved to register the new domains of personhood under neoliberal logics of self-government and entrepreneurship, and neoliberal conditions of insecurity and fraught globalism? (see Christensen 2013; Johansen 2015). How has the novel's formal and narrative cohesion responded to the temporal and spatial compression and intensification of neoliberal labour and consumer markets? (see Karl 2015; Nilges 2015).

In a well-known thesis on the neoliberal novel, Walter Benn Michaels (2009) insists that the motifs and preoccupations of the contemporary US novel obscure economic inequality in a particularly dangerous way. By focusing on matters of identity—racial, ethnic, gendered—and dramatizing the family, the US novel today contests some forms of inequality (again, racial, ethnic, and gendered) while apparently consenting to economic inequality. As Michaels puts it: 'increasing tolerance of economic inequality and increasing intolerance of racism, sexism and homophobia—of discrimination as such—are fundamental characteristics of neoliberalism' (11). By training the reader's eye on matters of anti-discrimination, the novel allows economic inequality not only to proceed unchecked, but ultimately reproduce it.

Whether literature is one component of a larger capitalist economic and cultural system, or whether it has bought the stories that neoliberalism tells, literary critics are concerned with whether and how neoliberal rationality can be critiqued, circumvented, or supplanted—not just a the level of economic practice, but of culture and personhood as well. Indeed, the shift from liberal humanism to what Brown has called 'human capital' has provoked soul-searching on the part of readers and scholars of literature. Some see this turn as the death knell of the humanities as the studies of that which defines and enriches our humanity are replaced with those that can or increase our currency in economic and social markets. Others, however, see critical potential in literature, claiming that it can provide alternate sets of priorities and values. Literary studies' fundamental emphasis on reading and interpretation—from whatever methodological angle—would seem to offer two paths, one imperilled and one hopeful: our tasks as readers can be thwarted by the quandaries of representation and narrowing of perspective that neoliberalism presents (deceptively, through a focus on 'freedom' and openness that would appear to offer the contrary); or, they can situate us in critical postures from which we can begin to identify the compulsions and contradictions of neoliberal life.

## References


Arrighi, Giovanni. (1994) *The Long Twentieth Century: Money, Power, and the Origins of Our Times*, London: Verso.

Brouillette, Sarah. (2014) *Literature and the Creative Economy*, Palo Alto, CA: Stanford University Press.

Brown, Wendy. (2005) 'Neoliberalism and the End of Liberal Democracy' in *Edgework: Critical Essays in Knowledge and Politics*, Princeton, NJ: Princeton University Press.

Brown, Wendy. (2010) *Walled States, Waning Sovereignty*, New York: Zone Books.

Brown, Wendy. (2015) *Undoing the Demos: Neoliberalism's Stealth Revolution*, New York: Zone Books.

Butler, Judith and Athanasiou, Athena. (2013) *Dispossession: The Performative in the Political*, Cambridge: Polity Press.

Christensen, Matthew. (2013) 'African Popular Crime Genres and the Genres of Neoliberalism,' *Social Text* 31.2: 103–21.

Clover, Josh. (2012) 'Value I Theory I Crisis,' *PMLA* 127.1: 107–14.

Comaroff, John. (2009) 'The End of Neoliberalism?' *The Johannesburg Salon* 1: 46–9. bwww.jwtc.org.za/the_salon/volume_1.htm

Duménil, Gerard and Lévy, Dominique. (2004) *Capital Resurgent: Roots of the Neoliberal Revolution*, Cambridge, MA: Harvard University Press.

Elliott, Jane. (2013) 'Suffering Agency: Imagining Neoliberal Personhood in North America and Britain,' *Social Text* 31.2: 83–101.

Elliott, Jane and Harkins, Gillian. (2013) 'Introduction: Genres of Neoliberalism,' *Social Text* 31.2: 1–17.

Godden, Richard. (2011a) 'Fictions of Fictitious Capital: *American Psycho* and the Poetics of Deregulation,' *Textual Practice* 25.5: 853–66.

Godden, Richard. (2011b) 'Labor, Language and Finance Capital,' *PMLA* 126.2: 412–21.

Hall, Stuart. (1979) 'The Great Moving Right Show,' *Marxism Today* (Jan.): 14–20.

Harvey, David. (2003) *The New Imperialism*, Oxford: Oxford University Press.

Harvey, David. (2005) *A Brief History of Neoliberalism*, Oxford: Oxford University Press.

Jameson, Frederic. (1991) *Postmodernism, or, the Cultural Logic of Late Capitalism*, Durham, NC: Duke University Press.

Jevons, William S. (1957) *The Theory of Political Economy*, New York: Kelley Millman.

Johansen, Emily. (2015) 'The Banal Conviviality of Neoliberal Cosmopolitanism,' *Textual Practice* 29.2: 295–314.

Karl, Alissa. (2015) 'The Zero Hour of the Neoliberal Novel,' *Textual Practice* 29.2: 335–55.

LiPuma, Edward and Lee, Benjamin. (2004) *Financial Derivatives and the Globalization of Risk*, Durham, NC: Duke University Press.

McClanahan, Annie. (2014) 'Bad Credit: The Character of Credit Scoring,' *Representations* 126: 31–57.

Martin, Randy. (2002) *The Financialization of Daily Life*, Philadephia, PA: Temple University Press.

Mathiason, Nick. (2008) 'Banking Collapse of 2008: Three Weeks that Changed the World,' *The Guardian* (Dec. 28). www.theguardian.com/business/2008/dec/28/markets-credit-crunch-banking-2008

Michaels, Walter B. (2009) 'What Matters,' *The London Review of Books* (Aug. 27): 11–13.

Mirowski, Philip. (2013) *Never Let a Serious Crisis Go to Waste: How Neoliberalism Survived the Financial Meltdown*, London: Verso.

Mont Pelerin Society. (1947) 'Statement of Aims.' www.montpelerin.org/statement-of-aims/

Nealon, Jeffrey T. (2012) *Post-Postmodernism, or, The Cultural Logic of Just-in-Time Capitalism*, Palo Alto, CA: Stanford University Press.

Nilges, Mathias. (2015) 'Neoliberalism and the Time of the Novel,' *Textual Practice* 29.2: 357–77.

Tratner, Michael. (2003) 'Derrida's Debt to Milton Friedman,' *New Literary History* 34.4: 791–806.

Vogl, Joseph. (2014) *The Specter of Capital*, Palo Alto, CA: Stanford University Press.

# 29

# REAL-ESTATE CONFESSIONS

## Moral realism in a risk economy

*Alison Shonkwiler*

In his memoir *American Sucker* (2004), film critic and New Yorker writer David Denby chronicles his obsession with the market of the late nineties alongside an account of his failed marriage. In *Busted: Life Inside the Great Mortgage Meltdown* (2009), business journalist Edmund L. Andrews narrates his experience covering the subprime mortgage crisis for the *New York Times* as well as his own mortgage and marriage troubles.[1] The result in both cases is an interestingly vexed form of financial confession that reveals the conflicts between moral and structural accounts of the market. Asserting that they are well-informed observers familiar with the risks of speculation, these memoirists struggle to account for their susceptibility to market seduction (Andrews begins with the assertion "If there is anyone who should have avoided the mortgage catastrophe, it is me"). Conceiving of the market in terms of personal behavior and moral responsibility, in which individuals are always subject to temptations and desires, becomes a way to make sense of its structural misalignments. Committing themselves to a moral economy of character, these texts inadvertently show something more complicated and disavowed about economic selfhood: how realist modes of "character" and "agency"—and our training in reading according to these modes—help to uphold a moralizing distinction between real and unreal financial economies.

It is no accident that a genre of economic narratives centered on the home arrives at a moment of accelerated financialization driven by real-estate speculation and mortgage debt. I argue that these texts deserve to be read as linking the crisis of value exemplified in the bubble markets of the 1990s and 2000s together with a crisis of neoliberal selfhood which demands that the individual exerts financial agency without being reduced to a "purely" economic actor. The booming economy appears to offer a tempting new site of self-realization, as narrated in these confessions. But grappling with the failure to become a successful *homo economicus* subsequently becomes a way of asserting a "real" self that exists outside the market and is able to hold its excesses to moral account.

If memoir is a literary form that anchors the fragmented, postmodern subject-in-crisis, real estate appears similarly in the economic domain to offer ballast in a sea of unanchored values. As the most speculative and least speculative commodity at once, real estate represents the promise of a tangible real in an economy in which value seems abstract, unstable, and un-locatable. Real estate investment is one of the primary drivers in a postindustrial world of FIRE circulation (finance, investment, real estate) that has overtaken industrial production. But it is also an asset whose value, as realtors like to insist, is not reducible to price. Houses, fundamentally associated with use value, are the site of emotional (over)investment, linked to intimate desires, needs, and attachments. Moreover, in a flexible, mobile economy, in which selfhood is no longer anchored by a secure work identity, demands on the individual for continuous self-expansion and adaptability are subsidized, quite literally, by rising property values. The house becomes a site, both financial and affective, for individuals to speculate with their own modes of existence.

For middle-class Americans, real estate is where finance becomes domesticated. To an extent, this has always been true; cultural anthropologist Constance Perin has argued that "America's most widespread cottage industry is the house itself as small business, the household's credit rating providing for each generation's economic well-being, the location for the children's public education, and its eventual resale and profit-taking for the parents' future."[2] But under conditions of everyday financialization, the "cottage industry" of homeownership becomes even more important both as security *against* the market and as a point of access *into* the market. We might call the house a site of entrepreneurial speculation and wealth concentration for beginners. As the U.S. economy has transformed from a Keynesian, "consensus" economy based at least nominally on concerns of social distribution to a neoliberal economy based on risk management and the protection of wealth, the house offers both a hedge against this transformation and a wedge into it. Homeownership represents—along with a college degree—one of the sites at which the middle class clings to privileges that have elsewhere been hollowed out. It is in this sense that real estate now functions as the "primary economic vehicle of neoliberalism at the local scale."[3] As profits become rent, as capital gains become ascendant over earnings, and as production is transformed into services and information, homeownership becomes a material link to all the processes of financialization that underlie these structural–economic shifts and are driven by them.

In both of these memoirs, a house or apartment represents the desire for a stabilizing bulwark against a volatile market and/or a crumbling marriage. Trying to protect this asset from divorce or foreclosure spurs each writer's desire to become the kind of person who can thrive in a risk economy. Each writer also reflects on getting "suckered" by this desire. In this sense, the confession becomes an ideal performative genre for an unreal economy in which the work of self-representation mimics the work of financial representation. When successful, the work of self-production ends in self-commodification, e.g. through the sale of a book. At the same time, however, the confessional as a genre tends to disavow the examination of structural relations in favor of moral self-scrutiny. Therefore, even as it contributes to the production of the entrepreneurial selfhood that is endemic to the survival genres of neoliberalism, the financial confession posits a guilty relation to the market. The writer has taken advantage of (or at least fallen for the hype of), something *not real.* In this sense, the realism of the confessional—its reference to real persons and events, its attention to everyday, domestic scenes—performs the logic of financialized capitalism and compensates for it. It invests in the production of entrepreneurial selfhood, but it also atones for it by returning to the "reality" of the shamed self.

An analysis of the confessional's drive to impose moral clarity on the representation of structural change can be extended beyond the genre of memoir. In the arena of fiction, the confessional narrative's inward and retrospective focus potentially even more strongly affirms a misalignment between moral and structural narratives of finance. Comparing the memoirs above to a realist novel—Jane Smiley's *Good Faith*—helps to demonstrate the ways that "character," in the literary as well as the moral sense, gets used as an index for historical change. *Good Faith* helps to explain how, in an economy of abstract balance sheets, the reliance on character as a mode of reading becomes stronger than ever.[4] To the novel's narrator, the Reaganomic transformations of the 1980s become legible *through* the types of characters they produce. Even as the novel offers some of the historical material necessary for reading structures, not persons, as the primary text of American social distribution, its confessional narrator demonstrates the persistence of cautionary moral realism as a lens for understanding an economy in which nothing seems real anymore.

For a brief, exhilarating period of the late nineties, the "money hunger" takes over Denby's life. He reads the *Wall Street Journal*; watches CNBC and CNN; rubs elbows with Internet analysts, venture capitalists, and entrepreneurs; and tracks the opinions of Federal Reserve chairman Alan Greenspan. He is fascinated with a seemingly new ethos of self-definition: "The pitch for the service, the Web site, the venture capital company, came so fast and unapologetically that it felt less like a hustle than like a new, entirely candid way of presenting oneself" (45). He describes "these New Economy people" as having

> something fine and free about their manners. They exuded enthusiasm; they were open, generous with themselves, not guarded or haughty in the old big-business style. Like revolutionaries everywhere, they were fervent and self-propelling and they wanted to erase all doubts in their listeners.
>
> *(47–8)*

Denby is eager to have his doubts erased. "I asked myself the same question that many Americans were asking: Was risk something I could any longer afford to avoid?" (17). Left by his wife, and determined to buy her out of their shared apartment, he sees the booming stock market as the solution not only to his money troubles but also to his midlife sense of missed opportunities. "One had to keep making moves. I was sure of it, because I had not moved in the past." (30). The only limit to self-realization, it seems, is a willingness to seize risk. "Expanding, you would be rewarded. Stay where you were, and you slipped behind" (66).

Denby's focus on character traits is a way of making structural forms of risk into personal choices. He ruminates on the nature of greed, for instance, and asks whether the moral language of sins and passions, desires and temptations, anger and guilt is still relevant to the modern economy. "How deadly a sin *is* greed?" he wonders. What about the positive side, when it joins with ambition and creativity to get things done?

> Liberals like me had watched with surprise as their residual distaste for capitalism slipped away, turning to grudging tolerance, and then, by degrees, to outright admiration. Some of the tech entrepreneurs and CEOs, men like Bill Gates, Andrew Grove (Intel), and Henry Nicholas (Broadcom), created products and new markets, employed thousands of people. I couldn't pretend I didn't admire them.
>
> *(18)*

He seeks out inspiring models to profile such as Sam Waksal (a gregarious entrepreneur and founder of ImClone) and celebrated stock analyst Henry Blodget. Denby admits, "I enjoyed being with these people, *of* them for an hour or two, indulging my private fantasy. I was a financier, a man of money, making deals" (59). The "free" manners and "generous" selves of the *Fast Company* set appear to put the lie to literary models of entrepreneurialism. Reading Theodore Dreiser's 1912 novel *The Financier*, Denby rejects the fictional main character, Frank Cowperwood, for his "freezing egotism and nihilistic selfishness" (120). He decides that Dreiser's representation of the financier as focused amorally on accumulation fails to capture the creative energy of late twentieth-century technocapitalism.

Unsurprisingly, Denby's real-life heroes disappoint once the promises of the New Economy begin to unravel. After the crash of ImClone stock, Denby follows Sam Waksal's fall all the way through the CEO's indictment, trial, and conviction. He tries throughout to reconcile the seeming contradictions between Waksal's unethical actions and his affable personality. Similarly, Denby interviews disgraced stock cheerleader Henry Blodget after the analyst's reputation and career are in ruins over his misleading predictions (and Blodget's employer, Merrill Lynch, has offered one disgruntled investor a $400,000 settlement). Denby struggles to make sense of Blodget's explanation that his stock recommendations were never "keyed to the ordinary investor." Unable to sort out good faith from bad, he concludes that his only recourse is to psychologically "let go" of Blodget. As exhibits of New Economy hubris, Waksal and Blodget ultimately force Denby to the disappointed conclusion that "greed dissolves the foundations of character" (88).

Even if Denby is put off by Dreiser's financier, therefore, his focus on character development borrows strongly from literary models. The realist/naturalist tradition's close attention to relations among action, intention, and outcome is echoed in Denby's narration of opportunities he has missed:

> "There's this stock," I said, holding a piece of sushi between sticks. "Microsoft. It makes the operating system for IBM and all the clones."
>
> "Never heard of it," our broker said, dipping his vegetable tempura in sauce. If his right hand had been free, he might have written down the name of the company. But it wasn't, *his right hand wasn't free*, and the moment passed. I ate my salmon roe and failed to insist that he follow up, even though at some level I *knew*.
>
> *(30)*

Everything could have turned out differently if not for a bite of sushi. Denby's lost opportunity is a matter of accident, or a whim of fate. Yet, a seemingly Dreiserian moment of chance, in which outcomes depend on the play of unknowable contingencies and random forces, becomes harder to sustain later in the narrative when Denby pursues the market more vigorously. Trying to get in on the IPO of a fiber-optics company, on a day when he is driving upstate to visit his son at a summer camp, he keeps pulling over the car to call his broker:

> Oh, but it was hard.... More than ever I felt like an outsider. How do you crack this game if you're just a single, small-time investor? The opening price was first announced as between $12 and $14. Then at $36 I was beginning to understand how the game worked: The underwriters wanted to do a favor for certain clients and made shares available to them before the stock was publicly traded. Once the stock was actually traded, it could be "flipped," or dumped... at enormous profit. As an outsider, you could get burned very badly if you bought the stock near the end of opening day.
>
> *(170)*

If the Microsoft stock was a dropped lottery ticket, the IPO is more clearly an insider event. Denby's frustration at being shut out of the action comes in part from the assumption that he is no ordinary outsider. An educated knowledge-worker—a media critic no less—should be qualified to take risks in an information- and communication-based economy. The IPO becomes a tightly controlled game designed to take advantage of newcomers who still believe in the myth of the open market.

But it is the presumption of insiderness that makes Denby's narrative a confession in the first place; if he were not privileged from the start, there would be no drama in his failure. Losing money in the market becomes a shameful inability to capitalize on his existing privilege. For instance, it is clear that Denby and his ex-wife are already members of the asset class. Early in the book, he observes, "In the fall of 1999, I realized we would increase our assets that year (on paper, anyway) more from capital gains than from salaries and royalties. An extraordinary realization" (16). Benefitting from the rise of the asset economy, he does not consider the other side: the increased economic inequality that the relative stagnation of the wage economy is likely to produce. His moral division between "winners" and "suckers" substitutes for any systemic analysis of the "unreal" economy, in which the professional and creative classes are already being lofted upward by inflating stock portfolios and skyrocketing apartment values. Despite being on the verge of acknowledging an unequal playing field, Denby's continued focus on the problem of greed, and the "erosion" of the self, allows him to avoid a structural critique of his own position.

In his 2009 memoir, Edmund Andrews, an economics reporter for the *New York Times*, integrates two approaches to the story of the subprime mortgage crisis: a journalistic explanation of events leading to the credit crisis and a personal account of how the threat of foreclosure damaged his life and marriage. Again, the downward spiral begins with real estate. Eager to start domestic life with a new wife, Andrews is surprised to discover that he can easily qualify to buy "a lovely little house in a cozy neighborhood" (6), using a "don't ask, don't tell" loan that does not require disclosure of his steep alimony and child support obligations. Three years later, during a *Times* interview with Alan Greenspan on the mortgage crisis, Andrews blurts out the confession that he is personally close to defaulting. "Shouldn't the Fed or some other government regulator have stopped [the lender] from lending to someone like me?" he asks the Fed Chairman (6). Greenspan weighs the question and responds that since Andrews has already gone more than three years without defaulting, and being the kind of responsible borrower who would try to avoid default at all costs, he has probably already validated the lender's calculation of risk. ("I bet they've made money on you already.")

For Andrews, the drama of his story comes from the discovery that no fraud was involved with his loan. Digging into the numbers, he is amazed that he was allowed to take on such risk. He writes:

> Yes, I had borrowed huge piles of money without documenting my ability to keep up with the payments. But I hadn't defrauded anybody and nobody had defrauded me. It had all been perfectly legal. ... In fact, I had been assisted by a long chain of enablers and promoters—loan officers, underwriters, banks, Wall Street firms, and rating agencies.

Like Denby, Andrews fails to become a successful economic actor—not because he cannot enter the market, however, but because nobody restrains his irrational actions.

In contrast to Denby's inward moral scrutiny, Andrews seems more prepared to recognize systemic aspects of the crisis. He argues, "Blaming the mortgage meltdown on fraud ignored the rot and corruption in the whole system, up to and including policy makers like Greenspan" (5). Andrews is even forced to recognize that the uneven distribution of risk is precisely what the system has been designed to achieve. For instance, he compares his loan profile with that of another applicant who obtained the same kind of mortgage from the same lender at the same time. He and "Laura" had similar credit scores, earnings, employment records, and homeownership histories. They started with the same interest rate. Laura even put down a higher down payment, 25% compared to Andrews' 10%. Andrews flounders to come up with an explanation for the $1,000 difference in their monthly payments. "It seemed irrefutable," he says. "The lenders stuck her with a more expensive loan" and told her that it was the only loan she could qualify for. Maybe they knew they could get away with it because "women were more trusting" (197), or maybe something else. At any rate, "as a white man who had grown up in a secure home and gone to a good college," he concludes, "I had been oblivious to this market-based form of discrimination. … I had been clueless about how much I had benefited from discrimination myself."

Being confronted with this instance of his structural privilege, Andrews admits, deepens his perspective on issues that he covers as a reporter. Writing about redlining and race-based lending patterns for the *Times*, he more seriously questions the mortgage industry's official story that disparities in credit rates reflect objectively different risks between white and nonwhite borrowers (193). He questions the fairness of the risk assessment that is hidden in the industry's hazy area of credit profiling. Since credit profiling is a system of subjective assessment camouflaged in objective-seeming data and statistics, it indexes and reinforces all the other ways persons are profiled, such as by race, gender, location, education, income, consumption habits, etc.[5] Andrews realizes that he benefits by belonging to a group that is rated higher (white professional men) precisely because other groups are rated lower, even when individuals from different groups share exactly the same personal circumstances.

Even as the book arrives at some measure of insight about financial inequality, however, it does so not because the author experiences the market as discriminatory but because he experiences it as excessively permissive. He is not blocked from becoming a market actor; instead, he has complete freedom to fail to become one. With no line drawn between irresponsible lending and irresponsible borrowing, Andrews discovers what it means for the consumer to bear the entire responsibility of acting according to Greenspan's doctrine of enlightened self-interest. It goes without saying that this experience, like Denby's, is highly raced and gendered. The implication is that if even an educated white professional in the suburbs cannot objectively judge risk, how can those from less privileged groups do better? Andrews' confession is ultimately an appeal to the fact that the author himself does not match the public face of foreclosure. The confessional is thus revealing of both writers' social entitlement (in raced, classed, and gendered terms) and of their deflection away from an analysis of structural inequities and privileges. The *failure* to become an economic man does not occasion a critique of the uneven demands of neoliberalism across differently positioned selves. Instead, it occasions the writers' return to the "reality" outside the market. The self that has failed in financial and credit-based terms turns to the confessional form to recuperate its self-coherence in more traditionally foundational, i.e. moral, terms.

Here, I argue, is where a work of fiction can bring into sharper focus the conflict between moral "realism" and a more expansive, structural canvas. Jane Smiley's novel *Good Faith* demonstrates that the shift toward financial modes of accumulation, away from a "real" capitalism based on production of goods and services, doesn't reduce the pressure on moral character as a basis for predicting, evaluating, and understanding individual behavior. In fact, financial abstraction presses notions of character into greater service. Even as character becomes a less stable or reliable index to economic legibility, the interpretive demands made upon economic "virtue" persist and even strengthen.

"This would have been about '82," begins the narrator. Starting with the effort to figure out when the '80s began, the novel ends on the eve of the S&L crisis when one of the main characters absconds with a suitcase of cash and leaves behind a legal and financial mess for everyone else to clean up. If *Good Faith* allegorizes how ordinary Americans got suckered in the 1980s, then the narrator's retrospective point of view is implicitly a confessional, as he reflects on his own degree of culpability for a tangle of bubble enthusiasm and fraud.

The narrator, a small-town realtor, meets Marcus Burns, a would-be real estate developer, who is a cheerleader for financial risk-taking. Marcus refers to "what's happening in Washington" and the "recent election" to support his prediction of a coming business revolution. "Experience doesn't count anymore," he argues. "It's just a drag on you, because if you make decisions according to your experience, you will have no idea what is happening in this country" (76). He foresees a coming flood of investment capital:

> It's all changing! I'm telling you, this time last year I was reading income tax returns. It's like reading the book of the future, to read income tax returns all day. There's money everywhere. Money money money! You know what they say at the IRS? Reported income is like cockroaches. For every dollar you see, there are a hundred more in hiding. And it's looking for a home! Don't you understand how things work? There's a lot more money than there are good investments, or even investments at all, even bad investments.... Money these days is like water. It can't stop looking for a place to go. It's filled up all the places it usually goes, and now it's lapping at the shore and seeking out other nooks and crannies.

Marcus's prediction of a gold rush in the housing market aligns perfectly with the actuality of 1980s speculation as investment dollars seeking high-return markets found their way to real estate.[6] With the deflationary crises of the late 1970s in the past and deregulation in full swing, capital's search for opportunities for risk and safe places to "park" generated explosive growth in U.S. financial centers such as New York and Boston. Real estate became the face of the shift from production to finance, with domestic anxieties about American economic competitiveness articulated, most famously, around the sale of Rockefeller Center to Japanese investors in 1989.

The novel bypasses these global processes of financialization, however, to focus on the local level, through changing landscapes and cultural demographics of a semi-rural mid-Atlantic American town. The domestic ripples of global real-estate speculation are channeled through the local savings-and-loan bank. "They're going to let S and Ls develop properties now," Marcus informs Joe. "It looks to me like they're going to let them do just about anything they want" (177). Standard accounts of the growth of S&Ls in the 1980s emphasize their contribution to a process of financial emancipation from local economies. After the industry was deregulated in 1982, small-town lenders could begin to operate more like other kinds of global investors, by amalgamating local funds and funneling them upward and outward. But the process of extraction runs in two directions, and the novel highlights the other side, as finance becomes more *local*. The small town is reorganized by the same processes of "disembedding" as cities undergoing urban renewal. With branch offices and new housing developments springing up ("A savings-and-loan branch and a few tasteful and convenient stores and some office space would brighten the area up, is what I think"), the local landscape becomes a kind of social text of the ramping up of otherwise hard-to-figure forms of restructuring.

A former IRS employee, Marcus has also developed far-reaching economic predictions based on changing population demographics: "And here's the key. More people means scarcer resources, scarcer resources mean inflation, and inflation means property and interest-bearing capital have a higher value and work has a lower value. It's as simple as that" (147). This statement articulates an entire paradigm shift in which property widens the divide between laboring and asset classes. "You know what I hate?" Marcus asks Joe. "I hate paying taxes." The simplest way to avoid paying taxes, he argues, is to live on borrowed money. Debt requires "no cheating and no creative bookkeeping and passes every audit." The only requirement is that property values keep rising. Marcus' hatred of paying taxes corresponds not only to the expansion of mortgage debt but also to the rise of anti-tax sentiment in the 1980s. Critics describe a growing resistance to taxes among middle-class homeowners not as a result of neoliberal ideologies at work but as anticipating and softening the ground for Reagan supply-sideism to come.[7] Various property-tax resistance movements, it has been argued, constitute a form of rent seeking *concealed* in the language of property protection.[8] Together, debt-financing and tax protectionism provided a cornerstone of the domestic architecture of neoliberalism. Rising property values, joined with downward pressure on real-estate taxes, offset the increasing instabilities of a risk-driven economy. Homeownership became one of the tradeoffs that made Reaganomics politically sustainable, counterbalancing the destabilizing effects of deregulation, anti-union policies, and declining real wages.

Catherine Jurca, in a study of the literature of the postwar American suburb, has argued against the critical commonplace that home and market operate as separate and opposed spheres. Instead of the home as a sentimental space that protects and compensates individuals from the injuries of the commercial space, postwar suburban fiction posits "a beneficial fluidity between homes and businesses...an affinity" that is not based on "an outworn tension between home and market."[9] In the late twentieth and early twenty-first centuries, however, it is insufficient to call the home inseparable from the market: it has now become a primary site for managing the mixed symptoms of class security. Consumers embrace "everyday" financialization through personal debt, investment retirement plans, and the leveraging of homeowner equity.[10] Even at times when the housing market is clearly no haven against the vicissitudes of the stock market, the demands of risk-taking and the anxieties of class positioning under neoliberalism continue to ensure that property ownership and property values serve as twin anchors of social entitlement. Economist Jan Toporowski argues that "in an era of financialization, the mass of the middle class is sedated and deprived of the need to think by escalating property values."[11] What we might call contemporary homestead economics enables—and provides cover for—the generalized wealth transfer that David Harvey calls the "class project" of neoliberalism, and that leads Fredric Jameson to observe that in the era of finance, the "guiding thread of all contemporary politics seems much easier to grasp, namely that the rich want their taxes lowered."[12]

Which brings us back to the problem of character. The suspense in Smiley's novel is never whether Marcus is a good guy; his salesman's grandiosity makes his betrayal predictable.

> [Marcus] "So he started out as a teller when he was twenty-two, putting money in a drawer and taking it out, and he's been thinking small for fifteen years. The S and L business has hardly been high-risk."
>
> "God forbid," I said.
>
> Marcus laughed, a loud, hearty laugh. Then he said, "Look, why don't you stay away from Crosbie? I'll do the talking."

Marcus's hearty laugh, I suggest, signals a crisis of character reading. To the reader, the hearty laugh represents the substitution of a familiar typological abstraction—the con man—in place of realism's particularization of personality and motivation. It indicates a resistance to "developed" realism in favor of generic flattening. With the word "hearty," Joe submits Marcus to analysis of what Leo Bersani calls the "expressive function" of character ("the relation of a narrative surface to a typological deep structure") in which the "most casual word, the most trifling gesture, the most tangential episode all submit easily to the discipline of being *revealing* words, gestures and episodes."[13]

"An investment in character can teach us about the character of investment," writes Sara Ahmed.[14] This investment refers to an affective attachment to an idea of selfhood that tends to prevail even when contradicted by actual evidence. It is this idea of consistency—a set of expectations or a sense of genre—that makes it possible to judge what is "in character." It allows us to distinguish how a character is like or unlike itself, or how it evolves over time. A change of character is the opening of a space between one set of expectations and another, a space that demands a new way of reading. Joe's "investment" in character, in Ahmed's sense, is that of a realist reader who seeks to penetrate the surface to assess the true interior and to assign values and responsibilities:

> [Marcus] "Crosbie is the real villain, you know why?"
>
> [Joe] "Why?"
>
> [Marcus] "Because a big loan is an asset. All those deposits he's got, those are the liabilities, and those loans are assets. Crosbie's new. He came in to transform the savings and loan from money loser to moneymaker, and he's got to make the books look good, so he's making big loans, which go on the asset side and cover old loans that aren't making any profit."
>
> *(149–50)*

The word "villain," again drawing from the typology of melodrama, marks the incoherence of the demand for structural realism and for moral clarity at the same time. The villain is summoned into existence by a structural imperative ("he's got to make the books look good"). Of course, it can also be read as a retrospective displacement of the narrator's guilt. But either way, the typologization papers over a shortfall in character-based realism that cannot achieve a full survey of accounts ("the books"). The rise of typological and allegorical characters such as villains and suckers becomes a way of navigating the structural abstraction of risk.

In other words, even a synoptic novel of changing demographics, consumer aesthetics, and real-estate speculation that appears to seek a landscape-oriented mode of reading rather than a portrait one exposes how attached to portrait modes we remain. Novel theorists have argued that character always operates dialectically, arbitrating between the allegorical and the representational.[15] Extending this insight, we might say that financialization is the field within which this ongoing dialectical tension of character is now to be historicized and within which personhood becomes socially legible. The confessional text expresses the contradiction of this moment in which the structural "unreal" is thrown back into personified terms of virtue, agency, and intentionality—particularly in a representational economy that encompasses speculative representations of the self.

Arguments have been made elsewhere about the characteristics of personality demanded and rewarded by flexible capitalism. The point is not that personality has changed in an era of finance, as Denby imagines it has, but about our limited ability to escalate ways of reading beyond the inside/outside dimensions of character. Economic realism may not be what we typically associate with the confessional genre. But in texts discussed here, the confessional represents in the narrative domain what real estate represents in the financial domain: a putatively stabilizing form and a place to secure value. The confessional's located subject compensates for anxiety about the unstable self. Houses become stand-ins for reality in an economy that rewards not "real" labor but representational value. And when the work of becoming a risk-taker in the neoliberal economy goes wrong, the result is an effort to recuperate some degree of representational coherence through the moral terms of shame and failure. When routed through the confessional's dialectics of inadequacy and entitlement, narratives of the "unreal" economy become class-marked cautionary tales about the mismanagement of a wayward self, rather than an examination of the neoliberal demands that produce it. The persistence of a moral-realist mode of inward and outward alignments of the self suggests some of contemporary narrative's difficulty in accommodating a world of structural change.

## Notes

1 David Denby, *American Sucker* (Boston: Little, Brown, 2004). Edmund L. Andrews, *Busted: Life Inside the Great Mortgage Meltdown* (New York: Norton, 2009).

2 Constance Perin, *Everything in Its Place: Social Order and Land Use in America* (Princeton 1989), 129.

3 Jason Hackworth, *The Neoliberal City* (Ithaca, NY: Cornell University Press, 2007), 78. Urban sociologist Hackworth argues that real estate becomes a "quasi autonomous" form of capitalist development in the post-1970s economy, replacing the mid-twentieth "spatial fix" that "likely had petered out by the mid-1990s" (78). Hackworth characterizes three aspects to the neoliberal city: (1) inner city gentrification, (2) inner suburban devalorization, and (3) continued physical expansion of metropolitan areas (80–1).

4 Jane Smiley, *Good Faith* (New York: Knopf, 2003).

5 See Annie McClanahan, "Bad Credit: The Character of Credit Scoring." *Representations* 126.1 (Spring 2004), 31–57.

6 See George Sternlieb and James W. Hughes, *America's New Market Geography: Nation, Region, and Metropolis* (New Brunswick, NJ: Center for Urban Policy Research, Rutgers University, 1988).

7 I discuss this point in reference to California's "Proposition 13" in a longer discussion of *Good Faith* in *The Financial Imaginary: Economic Mystification and the Limits of Realist Fiction* (Minneapolis: University of Minnesota Press, 2017).

8 Sociologist Isaac William Martin writes that the mortgage-interest deduction for homeowners is a social giveback so significant that it is no less than an entire "invisible welfare state" to the middle class (15). "On the eve of the tax revolt [in California]," Martin writes, the mortgage deduction "was providing more benefits than any other social policy in America, except for the twin blockbusters of the federal budget, Social Security and Medicare" (9–10). Isaac William Martin, *The Permanent Tax Revolt: How the Property Tax Transformed American Politics* (Stanford 2008).

9 Catherine Jurca, *White Diaspora: The Suburb and the Twentieth-Century American Novel* (Princeton 2001).

10 See Randy Martin, *The Financialization of Daily Life* (Philadelphia: Temple University Press, 2002). See also Max Haiven, "Finance Depends on Resistance, Finance Is Resistance, and Anyway, Resistance Is Futile," *Mediations* 26, no. 1–2 (Fall 2012/Spring 2013). Haiven argues that the working class's embrace of "financialization" is also a form of resistance to neoliberalism.

11 Jan Toporowski, "The Wisdom of Property and the Politics of the Middle Classes," *Monthly Review* 62, no. 4 (2010): 15.

12 Fredric Jameson, "Culture and Finance Capital," *The Cultural Turn: Selected Writings on the Postmodern, 1983–1998* (London: Verso, 1998), 247.

13 Leo Bersani, *A Future for Astyanax: Character and Desire in Literature* (Boston, MA: Little, Brown, 1976), 52–3. John Frow describes a similar view that "behavior and action in the novel *exemplify* moral and psychological qualities which it is then the reader's task to retrieve (to put a name to, finding what was there to be found)." John Frow, "Spectacle Binding: On Character," *Poetics Today* 7, no. 2 (1986): 236.

14 Sara Ahmed, "Willful Parts: Problem Characters or the Problem of Character," *New Literary History* 42, no. 2 (2011): 231.

15 Deidre Lynch argues that the allegorical and the representational work in dialectical fashion such that "allegorical typifications are both drawn from and fed back into the social text". Lynch quotes Ian Hunter on the need for attention to alterations of "the historical surfaces on which the content of a text can appear" (140). Deidre Shauna Lynch, *The Economy of Character: Novels, Market Culture, and the Business of Inner Meaning* (Chicago: University of Chicago Press, 1998).

# 30
# REPRODUCTION

*Nicky Marsh*

The 2015 film *Waffle Street* tells the real story of Jim Adams, an ex-Hedge Fund manager, who seeks redemption for his role in the financial crisis through 'real' work: clocking up 1,000 hours in a fast food restaurant in order to fulfil a condition of its purchase. The literalism of this narrative of restitution extends to its gender politics. Jim's manual labour gives him access to the blue-collar pride of his forefathers and allows him to enter their paternal ranks: his abrupt sacking from 'Alpha Finance' followed his admission that he and his wife are 'trying for a baby' and his first evening of unemployment includes a seduction scene that implies success. The film's narrative arc conflates productive masculine capital with productive feminine bodies right through to its conclusion: a disruption in Jim's ability to reproduce capital (a rejected credit card) is simultaneous with a disruption in his wife's ability to reproduce at all (she collapses with a failing placenta) and it is only after the intervention of no less than three father figures that the couple, and the financialised economy, can recover, as Jim does not open a restaurant but a financial advice service in the home they share with their new son.

The film literalises one of the dominant motifs of post-crash popular culture – a narrative apparent in different ways through films such as *Wall Street: Money Never Sleeps* (2010), *Wolf of Wall Street* (2013) and *Arbitrage* (2012), and novels such as John Lanchester's *Capital* (2012), Alex Preston's *This Bleeding City* (2010), Sebastian Faulk's *A Week in December* (2010) and Jess Walter's *The Financial Lives of Poets* (2009) – in which bad bankers struggle to become better fathers as they are repeatedly taught, but only partially learn, that their illicit sexual and financial appetites need to be rerouted towards the normative service of the home and the productive economy if money is to recover. This conflation of a faltering in biological and economic reproduction was not new and it can be traced through a longer history of literary representations of money. In the early twentieth century, for example, an economic anxiety about hoarding, the withdrawal of capital by both the working and middle classes, was represented by a crisis in fertility, in a storyline that is apparent in the ghostly baby cradled by Lily Bart when she is belatedly spent at the end of Edith Wharton's *House of Mirth* (1905), in the hoarder Trina's weeping for the loss of her gold as 'other women weep over a dead baby's shoe' (175) in Frank Norris' *McTeague* (1899), and in the 'still-born' (23) tear shed by the secreted away, wittily named, Kismine, in F. Scott Fitzgerald's *The Diamond as Big as the Ritz* (1922). The conflation is, of course, a deeply ambivalent one. On the one hand, the use of female reproduction as an analogue for financial reproduction warns of the dangers of the unproductive use of capital and heralds the need to re-embed money in the meaningful life of the social in order that both can be reproduced. It is a defence of an economy that calls upon the properties of the *oikos*, the realm of domesticity and the good life in the Classicists' terms, in contrast to the deforming dangers of *chremastics*, the realm of money and exchange. Yet, such warnings, like Aristotle's own assumption that the *oikos* requires mastery of wife and slaves before anything else, normalise a set of deeply masculinist assumptions, specifically the need to consolidate familial wealth in accordance with the heterosexist logic of inheritance which, as Thomas Piketty has made clear, has returned us at the start of the twenty-first century to a restricted system of patrimonial capital (see Hawkes 2016: 8; Piketty 2016).

I want to make sense of the ambivalence that this gendered parallel between a financial and a reproductive economy implies by examining the ways in which female sexuality operates as both a gift and a commodity within it. In the first stage of the argument, I follow the ways in which female sexuality underpins exchange in the two traditions that these terms most obviously respond to: as I trace the origins of the New Economic criticism of the 90s through the twin trajectories associated with the gift economy theorised by Marcel Mauss and Claude Levi Strauss and the money economy theorised by Karl Marx and Georg Simmel. I suggest that an attention to the parallel ways in which gendered reproduction is treated in these two traditions, and in their contemporary afterlives, suggests an intersection between them that complicates their more frequently assumed polarities, something that the similarities between the economic writing of second-wave feminists as ostensibly different from one another as Gayle Rubin and Luce Irigaray similarly demonstrate. In my conclusion, I briefly explore how these parallels are critically re-imagined in Jacques Derrida's writing about money, as it attempts to negotiate the dual inheritance of Mauss and Marx, in order to clarify what cultural work these recurring symbols of female sexual reproduction, that occur not only through the language of maternity but through the policing of its limits that the virgin and whore dyad enact, play in our understanding of money. Finally, I want to suggest that we need to begin to formulate a critical practice for bringing the significance of money's gendered politics to the fore in critical discussions.

One of the most ubiquitous models for analysing the relationship between money and literary cultures is that provided by 'New Economic Criticism' which was

> predicated on the existence and disclosure of parallels and analogies between linguistic and economic systems. Thus any adequate theoretics of literary economics must begin with the axioms of Saussurean linguistics and post-structuralist theory - that all signs are arbitrary and related syntagmatically – and then address the similarly fictive or constructed nature of money and finance.
>
> *(Osteen and Woodmanssee 1999: 14)*

This was an approach that can be traced most obviously to texts such as Marc Shell's *The Economy of Literature* (1978) and Jean Joseph Goux's *The Coiners of Language* (1994) but, preceding even these, was Derrida's 1974 essay 'White Mythology' which productively connected the 'truth' effaced by Nietszche's coin to the structural 'value' realised by Saussure's coin to suggest a theory of difference that could deconstruct the material/immaterial dyad of metaphysics. Yet, the lapsarian loss that this critique seemed to imply for some critics, as a crisis in the gold standard was repeatedly correlated with a crisis in referentiality, extended to gender, specifically to the reliability of paternity. In the work of Jean Joseph Goux, for example, the questioning of the value of 'money and language' means that

> the value of paternity, and all other values that regulate exchanges, are questioned. Gold, father, language, phallus: continually serving as mutual metaphors for each other, these structurally homologous general equivalents, with their respective functions in measurement, exchange and reserve, simultaneously undergo a fundamental crisis.
>
> *(Goux 1994: 4)*

For those invested in the material histories of money, New Economic Criticism's assumption of the parallel between money and language, that implied a shift from a materially realised and socially meaningful exchange of gold or goods to the dematerial and socially alienating exchange of an abstract money form, was problematic. For economic anthropologists, the move omitted money's social and material meanings, the fact that money is a 'social relation, a symbolic system, and a material reality' (Maurer 2006: 34), and for economic historians and sociologists, it erroneously assumed that money's origins lay in gold and barter (and, as Walter Benn Michaels asserts, the gold standard is closer to barter than money), rather than in its historically documented ability to tabulate debt (Benn Michaels 1987). Yet, the anxiety about paternity, and the shadowing of the exchange of money with the exchange of women that it implies, is still present in the work of those literary critics that read paper money as a symbol of debt and reciprocity rather than one of loss and absence. John Forrester explains Lacan's account of money, for example, in which the 'symbolic debt to the father' that produces the subject is also the 'register of money. For can we forget that among the most common uses of the polysemic debt are those linked to money and the system of finance?' by pointing to the way in which Lacan's language for money follows 'Strauss and Mauss' in moving towards 'the movement of women, objects and signifiers' and that, moreover, this is 'a movement which reflects the inverse movement at the unconscious level of debt' (Forrester 1997: 136): suggesting the presence of a debt that, unlike a financial one, cannot be simply annulled by the restitution money provides.

Implicit in Forrester's evocation of Strauss and Mauss, of course, is their analysis of a system that made the centrality of the secure exchange of women entirely central to its remit. Mauss's *The Gift* (2000: 18) infamously begins by noting that 'everything—food, women, children, property, talismans, land, labour services, priestly functions, and ranks—is there for passing on, and for balancing accounts' and the role of the exchange of women in marriage was central to Levi-Strauss' (Strauss 69: 18) analysis of the work. In Strauss' reading, the category of woman exceeded its structural abstraction, as he suggested that although the 'emergence of symbolic thought must have required that women, like words, should be things that were exchanged' that woman could never be reduced to 'just a sign and nothing more, since even in a man's world she is still a person, and since in so far as she is defined as a sign she must be recognized as a generator of signs' (24). It is this generative capacity, the gift's ability to produce a surplus that the money economy denies, that is key to the ambivalent role that female sexuality and reproduction play in this alternative economy. It is an assumption that continues into a contemporary theoretical archive for money, even one that is well-versed in a feminist critique. Lewis Hyde's influential account of the gift, for example, tellingly illustrates the contrast between a 'commodity' that 'is truly "used up" when it is sold' and a gift that 'can support an affluence of satisfaction' as it moves from 'plenty to emptiness' with an image of a metaphysical reproduction that makes clear the base passivity attributed to femininity in this mode: 'The Lord says, "All that opens the womb is mine," for it is He who filled the empty womb' (Hyde 2006: 23).

Clearly, the exchange of women is central to the anthropological tradition of Mauss and Strauss in a way that it is not of Marx and Simmel and yet the former's anxiety about the relationship between female reproduction and paternity is also evident in the latter. The story of money as the universal equivalent that is told in the third chapter of *Capital Vol. 1* is a familiar one: it is

> because all commodities, as values, are realised human labour, and therefore commensurable, that their values can be measured by one and the same special commodity, and the latter be converted into the common measure of their values, *i.e.*, into money.
> *(Marx 2011: 106)*

Yet, Marx's vocabulary for describing the tensions within the commodity form, between its material use value and its abstracted exchange value, takes a gendered form. He most notoriously illuminates this duality within the commodity, for example, by suggesting that it 'differs in this respect from Dame Quickly, that we don't know "where to have it"' and the contrast metonymically associates the bawdy prostitute from Shakespeare's *Henry IV* with the 'coarse materiality' of use value that negatively illuminates the abstraction of exchange value in the commodity form where 'not an atom of matter enters into its composition' (55). The baseness of the prostitute's body is used again, via another quote from Shakespeare, as the obscenity of money's levelling of the 'moral order of things' is illustrated with an excerpt from *Timon of Athens* which names money as that which can 'knit and break religions; bless the accursed [...] / makes the wappen'd widow wed again' because it is nothing less than the base and 'common whore of mankind' (148fn). The baseness of money and prostitution, as both embody the sale of that which should not be sold, is reiterated when the quote is followed with a reference to the commercialisation of the 'bones of saints', but this time the accompanying footnote references virgins rather than whores and it points to the 'despoiling' of the sanctity of the 'Delphic Temple' by the Phoenicians who purchased the virginity of young women (148fn).

The move from the virgin to the whore implies that money traduces not simply because it allows for the exchange of that which should not be exchanged but because in doing so, it allows women, not only whores but also virgins and widows, a moment in which they can take charge of their *own* exchange. What is obscene in the example of the Delphic Virgins is not that they should be understood as a form of currency (the contents of these temples are described as 'sacred banks') but that they have withdrawn their own value and have *themselves* offered 'to the goddess the piece of money they received' for it. The remarriage of the 'widow' is similarly abject because it disrupts the proper purpose of the inevitable exchange of women: she is tempted to marry for money even though she is 'wappen'd' – exhausted – and thus presumably no longer fertile. One way of reading the danger of these examples of woman's wresting control of her own value is, like trope of the virgin and the whore itself, that it is so dangerous because it threatens the paternal system that is implicitly assumed in the metaphorical dyad of virgin and whore. As Vladimir Tumanov (2011) has argued, it is a binary that speaks of an anxiety about paternity: 'Mary is an eternal virgin, symbolically allaying all fear of paternal uncertainty' as she makes 'it possible for the male psyche to have its reproductive cake and eat it too' whereas Eve 'represents not just female sexuality but specifically female sexual choice—the real source of masculine anxiety' (507–21).

The exchange of women, and specifically the need to defray the possibility that woman's entry into the economy would allow them to take possession of their *own* exchange in ways that might deny or defraud paternity, continued to underpin the structuralist analysis of money and economics that emerged at the start of the twentieth century. It was apparent, for example, in Georg Simmel's *The Philosophy of Money* (1900) which combined Marx's critique of money's destruction of the social with Saussure's comparison of money and language as relational forms. So, as Nigel Dodd explains, for Simmel money's ability to realise an abstracted and objective form involved the sublimation not of labour but of desire, requiring a 'mutual sacrifice' between 'two owners of objects, each of whom wants or needs what the other possesses' (Dodd 2014: 28). Both the sacrifice and the objective relations it produces are presented in deeply gendered terms through this work. At its end, most obviously, Simmel uses the 'ominous analogy' between money and prostitution to assert both money's corruption and women's exclusion from objectivity, suggesting that the impact of prostitution's 'mutual degradation' is asymmetrical because sex 'employs only a minimum of the man's ego but a maximum of the woman's' because men are 'individualized' whereas women 'are more closely and deeply rooted in the dark, primitive forces of nature [...] their most essential personal qualities must also be rooted in those natural universal functions that guarantee the uniformity of the genus' (Simmel 1978: 409).

Yet, as with Lewis Hyde's gendered language for the theories of the gift, these assumptions about money and gender persist into contemporary analyses. The philosopher Ole Bjerg's scathing account of money's deformation of the social, for example, functions through a contrast with the gift that shares Simmel's assumptions about the passively naturalised feminine. Bjerg represents the eighteenth-century shift from the Physiocratic economy of Francois Quesnay to the neoclassical economy of Adam Smith as a shift from a land-based real economy which had understood nature to be the 'kick-starter of the economy providing an initial gift of the real' (79) to a monetary-based symbolic economy in which 'the invisible hand' had usurped 'mother nature' as a source of earthly divinity (72–3). It is a contrast that Bjerg seeks to now reverse, as he critiques second-wave feminism's complicity with the 'capitalist criteria of the market' and calls for what he considers a more 'truly subversive feminism' that would 'call for the preservation and regeneration of the productive and reproductive capacities of the "household" economy' (Bjerg 2016: 187).

What Bjerg and Lewis overlook, of course, are the feminist critiques of women as both the commodity and the gift that emerged in the late seventies, which drew on both Mauss and Marx and provide a frame for reading these parallels between economic and sexual reproduction. Gayle Rubin's reading of Strauss provided one of the most obvious touchstones in this context as it finds the 'genesis' of Marx's 'historical' context that makes 'a "wife"' one of the 'necessities' that a worker requires in anthropology (Rubin 1978: 164). For Rubin, gift kinship, that has marriage and the exchange of women at its heart, is the structure that transforms 'males and females into "men" and "women"' 'as complimentary wholes' in ways that produce the sex–gender system from which the socially constructed 'organization of human sexuality', including the 'incest taboo, obligatory heterosexuality and an asymmetric division between the sexes' follows (186). The possibility that the non-monetary characteristics of these exchanges may offer a route to disrupt these relations is an empty one: the exchange of women in a gift economy does not necessarily imply 'objectification' since the gift remains 'imbued with highly personal qualities' but the 'relations of such a system are such that women are in no position to realize the benefits of their own exchange' (174).

It is this sense of women as being unable to realise the value of their biological productivity that was at the core of Luce Irigaray's less well-known 1977 essay 'Women on the Market'. In this essay, Irigaray appropriates the Marxist vocabulary of the commodity in order to explain an anthropological notion of exchange, arguing that women's fertility is the commodity from which the possibility of all other commodities depends. She transposes the distinction between use and exchange value into gendered terms, arguing that 'the commodification of women' produces a '*schism that divides them into the* categories of usefulness and exchange value' in ways that produce 'two irreconcilable bodies: her natural body and her socially valued, exchangeable body' (176). For Irigaray, this is a distinction most obviously embodied by the dyadic language of female sexuality: the virgin is 'pure exchange value. She is nothing but the possibility, the place, the sign of relations among men. In and of herself, she does not exist' whereas the prostitute is pure use value, her body is 'valuable because it has already been used. [...] because its nature has been "used up", and has become once again no more than a vehicle for relations among men' (185–7). The figure of the mother, which stands between the two, 'cannot circulate in the form of commodities without threatening the very existence of the social order' because her 'responsibility' is to ensure that her 'products are legal tender' by marking them with 'the name of the father' (185).

So both Marx's language of the commodity and Mauss' language of the gift can be read through the assumption of the exchange of female sexuality. For Irigaray and Rubin, the only way to realise what both hesitantly call a feminist 'utopia' is by withdrawing from these gendered roles but for neither is this act coded in terms of a feminised economy: Rubin rejects the possibility of a matriarchal inversion, what she calls an Amazonian 'elimination of men', and Irigaray also suggests that 'it is out of the question' for women to 'go to "market" on their own, enjoy their own worth among themselves, speak to each other, desire each other' within this structure. Hence, Rubin aspires to an 'androgynous and genderless (although not sexless) society' (204) and Irigaray to the possibility of 'exchanges without identifiable terms, without accounts, without end....without additions and accumulations... without sequence or number' (197).

I want, finally, to conclude by returning to the precepts of New Economic Criticism to offer a reading of Derrida's contribution to these debates in order to explore one of the potential ways in which Irigaray and Rubin's demand for an economy that can resist the inevitably gendered demands of exchange, one that can function 'without additions and accumulations', has been imagined in contemporary theory. Derrida's contribution to these debates appeared in the early nineties: his reading of Mauss and the gift, *Given Time: I. Counterfeit Money*, was published in 1992 (although based on a series of lectures that were given in the late seventies) and was followed in 1994 by *Specters of Marx: The State of the Debt, the Work of Mourning and the New International*. The two works share an attempt to theorise the possibility of an exchange that could defy its own terms, that could be given *without* producing the expectation of a return or the demand for a restitution, and they offered an important contribution to the methodological assumptions of New Economic Criticism, suggesting new ways of bringing a materialist political vocabulary into conversation with a post-structuralist textual practice. It is the way in which a critique of the politics of gender is embedded into this analysis, and the limitations that become apparent when it isn't, that I want to conclude by examining.

Derrida's reading of Mauss in *Given Time* deconstructs the dyadic assumptions about female sexuality that underpin the gift in order to produce a more radical, supplementary, reading of it. The work's conceptual conceit is a reading of Jean Baudelaire's short story 'Counterfeit Money', in which a man gives a false coin to a beggar in an attempt to win what is scathingly described as 'paradise economically' (82). The paradoxes that this implies are used to complicate the distinctions between money and the gift and the real and the counterfeit in order to locate the 'supplementary' that the relinquishment of the demand for return will entail. Derrida casts the 'poetics of narrative' (28) that this possibility involves as a form of time (time share the gift's 'aporetic paralysis', as it is that which we can never be in but never out of) and his description of its eventual realisation as 'at term' at the 'now meaningfully delayed "due date"' (40), both evokes and complicates the familiar biological metaphors of reproduction that attend upon the language of gift kinship.

The epigraph to the work encapsulates both this critique of the language of gender, and its overall argument, through the impossible words of Madam Maintenon – 'the King takes all my time: I give the rest to Saint-Cyr, to whom I would like to give it all' – and provides it with two readings. In the first, Derrida uses the contradictions of Madam Maintenon's historical positioning to erase the distinction between the real and the counterfeit: she is the secretly married wife of Louis XIV, she is the Calvinist-born protestant who led him back to the Catholic Church, she is both 'an outlaw and the very figure of the law' and 'everything in her life' bears the 'most authentic stamp of counterfeit money' (2). In the second, he extends this contradiction to the radical time of the ungifted gift: the King 'takes all' of her time and yet she still has time that can be 'given' to her charity; indeed, she would like to 'give it all' and it is this given surplus that marks the possibility of the outside of an exchange economy for Derrida. Yet, the feminisation of this surplus of the gift is productively problematised by the ways in which Derrida identifies Madam Maintenon with the overdetermined twin poles of female sexuality. The time 'taken' by the King is eroticised outside of the conventions of marriage and reproduction, as she is both the married whore and the childless mother: legally his wife but denied inheritance and title rights, formerly his mistress but introduced to him by a previous mistress as the governess of their illegitimate children. Yet, the time that the queen herself 'gives' away is entirely the opposite. Although 'Saint Cyr', Derrida notes, sounds like it may be Madam Maintenon's 'lover' it is actually 'above all *not* masculine [...] it is a – very feminine – place, charity, institution' (4), a foundation for 'young virgins' who have fallen on hard times. So Madam Maintenon encapsulates both the pure whore and the sullied Virgin and in occupying the contradiction so intently, she collapses the dichotomy upon which their exchange rests.

This desire for a time of exchange that can exceed the constrained expectations of return also underpins *The Spectres of Marx* as Derrida reads Marx through *Hamlet* in an attempt to recast the determinism of the paternal debt in a hauntological light. Derrida rejects 'the body of Marxist doctrine' and its 'supposed systemic, metaphysical, or ontological totality' (110) whilst making clear the connections between deconstruction and the 'spectralizing disincarnation' of Marx's account of the 'bodiless body of money' which produces only 'a life without personal life or individual property. [...] the general property of money neutralizes, disincarnates, deprives of its difference all personal property' (51). Derrida's description of the logic that underpins Marx's account of money aspires, like his reading of Mauss' gifts, to replace an assumed desire for 'calculable equality', a justice 'that would be limited to sanctioning, to restituting', with a notion of justice that corresponds to the 'singularity of the an-economic ex-position to others' and he traces this possibility through the paradoxes that are revealed in Marx's reading of Shakespeare as it highlights the structural logic of disavowal, the redoubling of a desire that Marx's reliance on a spectral logic that 'does not like ghosts [..] does not want to believe in them' but actually 'thinks of nothing else' (57), reveals.

Yet, the gendering of this logic goes curiously uncommented upon even though Derrida's examples of Marx's reading of Shakespeare touch once more on the metaphorical language of female sexuality. The obscenity of the 'madam who would give up even her whores for money', that Derrida finds in Marx's reading of *Timon of Athens*, for example, is read as evidence of the 'absolute double bind on the subject of the *bind*', of the 'paradoxical hyperbole' of that which 'enslaves itself to what is betrayal itself, perjury, abjuration, lie and simulacrum. Which are never far from the spectre' (55) but the specific assumptions about female sexuality that are enabled in this vocabulary, that are so nimbly deconstructed in

Derrida's reading of Madam Maintenon, pass without comment. Yet, this logic of disavowal is clearly connected to money and gender in the play. Gertrude uses the paradoxical ironies of fiat money – that the less real it is the more it needs to be believed in – to depict Hamlet's wavering mental state, and thus to both assert and undermine his claim upon the throne, as his shared descriptions of his father's ghost are cast as false money, merely the 'coinage' of his 'brain and thus a 'bodiless creation ecstasy', whereas the remorseful 'madness' that he exhibits after killing Polonius is 'ore / Among a mineral of metals base, / Shows itself pure'. Hamlet himself amplifies this logic as he simultaneously calculates and dismisses calculation, wishing that this 'too too sullied flesh would melt, thaw, and resolve itself into a dew' because the world has become 'flat and unprofitable' and measuring his love for Ophelia by rejecting the very possibility of measurement by others, 'Forty thousand brothers / Could not with all their quantity of love / Make up my sum' (V.i). This latter move locates Ophelia as an object between the two families, a status confirmed by Polonius when he declares that Hamlet's 'vows are brokers' that his daughter should not trust because they are 'not of that dye which their investments show' and Polonius' extended pun on 'tender' – warning Ophelia that she has foolishly 'ta'en these tenders for true pay, / Which are not sterling. Tender yourself more dearly' makes it clear that it is his own value that is at stake – 'else you'll tender me a fool' (I.iii). Again, it is a position only confirmed by Hamlet as he alternates between casting Ophelia as a whore, with 'country matters' (III.ii) on her mind, and a virgin whose dowry should 'be thou chaste as ice, as pure as snow, thou shalt not escape calumny' (III.i).

It is hardly surprising, of course, that Derrida should use literary analogues to deconstruct the ways in which the exchange of female reproduction is implicit in the writing of Mauss but not of Marx: it is clearly central to the former in the ways in which it is not in the latter. Yet, the language of female sexuality and the threats to paternity that it poses appear as a latent shorthand in the critical vocabulary for Marxism that I have sketched here, from Marx, Simmel and through even to Derrida's example of *Hamlet*, where it casts the material-abstract dialectic through the gendered language of reproduction. So, to return to my opening examples, the recurrent use of the language of female sexuality in narratives of financial crisis, the parallels between biological and economic reproduction evident in the recurring displacement of anxieties about money onto the female reproductive body, cannot be simply read as either an alternative to, or a confirmation of, the conditions of money in the crisis. It is not simply that the schema is too broad; it is, rather, that these recurrent metaphorical tropes need to be examined in their own terms, and the feminist critiques of Irigaray, Rubin and Derrida offer a starting point, because they reveal the ways in which the language of money is also always underpinned by a language of gender.

## References


Bjerg, Ole. (2016) *The Parallax of Growth: The Philosophy of Ecology and Economy*, London: Polity.

Derrida, Jacques. (1992) *Given Time: I Counterfeit Money*, Chicago, IL: University of Chicago Press.

Derrida, Jacques. (1994) *Specters of Marx: The State of the Debt, the Work of Mourning and the New International*, London: Routledge.

Derrida, Jacques and Moore, F. C. T. (1974) "White Mythology: Metaphor in the Text of Philosophy," *New Literary History* 6.1: 5–74.

Dodd, Nigel. (2014) *The Social Life of Money*, Princeton, NJ: Princeton University Press.

Fitzgerald, F. Scott. (2008) *The Diamond as Big as the Ritz*, London: Juniper Press.

Forrester, John. (1997) *Truth Games: Lies, Money and Psychoanalysis*, Cambridge, MA: Harvard University Press.

Goux, Jean-Joseph. (1994) *The Coiners of Language*, Norman: University of Oklahoma Press.

Hawkes, David. (2016) *Shakespeare and Economic Theory*, London: Bloomsbury.

Hyde, Lewis. (2006) *The Gift: How the Creative Spirit Transforms the World*, Edinburgh: Canongate Books.
Ingham, Geoffrey. (2004) *The Nature of Money*, London: Polity.
Irigaray, Luce. (1985) *This Sex Which Is Not One*, Ithaca, NY: Cornell University Press.
Levi-Strauss, Claude. (1969) *The Elementary Structure of Kinship*, Boston, MA: Beacon Press.
Marx, Karl. (2011) *Capital, Volume One: A Critique of Political Economy*, New York: Dover Books.
Maurer, Bill. (2006) "The Anthropology of Money," *Annual Review of Anthropology* 35: 15–36.
Mauss, Marcel. (2000) *The Gift*, New York: W.W. Norton.
Norris, Frank. (2015) *McTeague*, London: CreateSpace.
Piketty, Thomas. (2016) *Capital in the Twenty-First Century*, Cambridge, MA: Harvard University Press.
Osteen, Mark and Woodmanssee, Martha. (1999) *The New Economic Criticism: Studies at the Intersection of Literature and Economics*, Routledge: London.
Rubin, Gayle. (1978) "The Traffic in Women: Notes on the Political Economy of Sex" in Rayna Reiter (ed.) *Toward an Anthropology of Women*, New York: Monthly Review Press.
Shakespeare, William. (1973) *The Tragedy of Hamlet Prince of Denmark*, New York: Signet Classics.
Simmel, George. (1978) *The Philosophy of Money*, London: Kegan Paul.
Tumanov, Vladimir. (2011) "Mary Versus Eve: Paternal Uncertainty and the Christian View of Women," *Neophilologus* 95: 507–21.
*Waffle Street*. (2015) [film] Eshom Nelms and Ian Nelms (dir.) USA: MarVista.

# 31

# SECULAR STAGNATION AND THE DISCOURSE OF REPRODUCTIVE LIMIT

*Annie McClanahan*

A specter is haunting mainstream economics—the specter of secular stagnation. In 2013, former Treasury Secretary and current hedge fund managing partner Larry Summers gave a speech at the IMF in which he began by congratulating his colleagues on the "great achievement" of resolving the financial crisis of 2008. And yet in the four years since the end of the recession, he went on to observe, neither unemployment nor GDP had improved measurably. Given this, Summers said, it seemed possible that "a set of older ideas" were relevant once again:

> I always like to think of these crises as analogous to a power failure...The network would collapse. The connections would go away....And we would understand that... when there wasn't any electricity there wasn't really going to be much economy. But then you'd expect that once things normalized, you'd get more GDP...not that four years later, you'd still be having substantially less than you had before. So there's something odd about...[this] continued slow growth.[1]

Despite Summers' relatively phlegmatic tone of curiosity about this "something odd," his prediction caused economists and observers to pretty much freak out. The *Economist*, *Wall Street Journal*, and *Time* all covered secular stagnation, while Ben Bernanke debated it with Summers, and Paul Krugman grumped that he had been saying the same thing for a while.[2] And Summers himself has not only continued to make the argument, but in fact made it even more forcefully in the years since 2013.

So what *was* Summers saying, and why did it cause such a stir? Put simply, he was resurrecting an argument that had long been considered moribund by bourgeois economists: the idea of secular stagnation, first discussed under that name by Keynesian economist Alvin Hansen in 1938. In an address titled "Economic Progress and Declining Population Growth," Hansen predicted that the world economy would tend toward a permanent and intractable condition of low growth and high unemployment—and, more specifically, that such a condition might well be heralded by a postcrisis period characterized by "weak and anaemic...recoveries which die in their infancy."[3] The possibility that this was the situation of the US economy, whose growth has been historically slow even after the official end of the recession in 2009 despite a monetary policy designed to encourage growth (historically low interest rates and multiple rounds of "quantitative easing"), and whose strength or lack thereof had global consequences—since, as Summers notes, the integration of global capital markets meant that it was "likely to be a contagious malady"—was thus understandably worrisome as a prediction about the stability of the US and global economy. Moreover, and as Summers' reference to "a set of older ideas" that, he admits, were "pretty firmly rejected" by his own mentors and teachers already begins to suggest, the secular stagnation prognosis also threw into doubt a number of axiomatic principles of economic thought, including not only technical theories pertaining to monetary policy and the unemployment rate, but also much more fundamental ideas about the naturalness of economic equilibrium, the inexhaustibility of technological innovation, the infinitude of nature, and the inevitability of generational upward mobility.

In this essay, then, I want to consider a few of the all-too-few moments in bourgeois economic thought when the conventional belief in capitalism's limitless growth faltered. I want to note that both prior to and alongside neoclassical and developmentalist theories of perpetual improvement and expansion, there were alternative predictions of economic enervation and decline. Indeed, I want to suggest that rather than reading these grimmer predictions as marginal cases or as superseded moments of heterodoxy, we might instead read them as a crucial, if hidden, undercurrent in the history of economic thought, either as explicit challenges to orthodoxy from within orthodoxy, or as the coded articulation of the anxieties and uncertainties that haunt an otherwise confidently positivist discipline. I make this argument primarily by reading a kind of latent continuity in the metaphorical language used to describe both growth and stagnation, both development and stasis, both infinite expansion and stillborn reproduction: that is, I suggest that we can trace the influence of the theory of (or at least the anxiety about) stagnation by observing that both the pessimistic Malthus and the optimistic Smith represent the outer limit of economic growth as natural and natal; that both confident Keynes and his more fatalistic student, Hansen, use the figure of birth to describe the regeneration of the economy; and that the otherwise sanguine predictions of ideologues like Joseph Schumpeter and Frances Fukuyama—as well as contemporary theorists of stagnation like Summers and Robert Gordon—are troubled by the awareness that the lives of the next generation might be worse than those that came before them. As these examples already clarify, two clusters of metaphorical language seem to recur again and again in the discourse around economic development from the eighteenth century to the twenty-first: representations of economic growth (or decline) through organic or biological images of liquid circulation and change (or stagnation and stasis); and representations of economic development through images of reproductive vitality, population growth, birth, and generational improvement (or reproductive enervation, population decline, stillbirth, and generational decline).

The limits of space in this particular essay mean that I take up the first of these only glancingly, as part of what should be a larger argument about economists' occasional attunement to natural limit. I explore the language of reproduction and generationality in somewhat more depth, and the conclusion of this essay argues that by tracking a relationship between this language and the contemporary crisis of reproduction, we are better prepared to understand the present, and better able to draw a connection between the ideological mystifications of economic orthodoxy and the challenges of Marxist-feminist materialism.

## Economic development and the stationary state

A range of scholars, from literary critics to intellectual historians, have observed that Classical Political Economy (CPE) tends to naturalize economic development and growth, producing what Catherine Gallagher terms a form of "bioeconomics," in which value is a vital energy that moves through both nature and the body.[4] Inspired by new anatomical science—especially William Harvey's mid-seventeenth-century treatise "On the Motion of the Heart and Blood"—Smith describes the circulation of currency as analogous to the circulation of blood, and thus as necessary to the health of the social and economic body.[5] Whereas this vitalist discourse of monetary "circulation" implies a perpetually animated natural economy, however, the discourse of economic "stagnation" evokes precisely the limits or inertia of the natural word. This sense of the inertial economy is most apparent in Smith's account of the "stationary state," which he represents as the inevitable endpoint of economic development.[6] For Smith, the economy was both national and natural, and economic development meant that the national container was slowly filled to its brim with natural resources: once the nation was "fully stocked" (with wealth) and "fully peopled," the economy could grow no further.[7] Yet although Smith saw the stationary state as natural, he also thought it was far from desirable. Rather, for Smith "The progressive state, while the society is advancing to the further acquisition, is in reality the cheerful and the hearty state," whereas "the stationary economy which has acquired its full complement of riches is dull."

Smith's fear of the decline that would inevitably follow from abundance had a lot to do with his fear of China, for him the purest example of the stationary state. Comparing China to the nascent economies of North America, he argued that whereas the open territories of the colonies had great potential for growth, China—already so rich, so abundant, and so populous—could not possibly grow further. And yet although Smith's account often reproduced a familiar Orientalism, one perfectly content to claim that the Chinese eat carrion and kill their infants, it also refused to represent China as lagging or delayed (as Marx would later do). Arguing that it "stands still, but it does not go backward," Smith suggested that China was the future of Britain, too: that *all* nations, once having "acquired [their] full complement of riches," were destined for such a condition of deathly stasis. Thus although we tend to associate Smith with the view that history operates in a series of virtuous cycles (high demand for goods begets higher wages which begets more workers which begets higher demand), in fact Smith argues that the long-term tendency of growth is toward intractable and permanent poverty. Suggesting that history moves in the direction of material decline and moral decay, Smith's writings on the stationary state thus anticipate the development of late nineteenth-century concepts like entropy as well as *fin de siècle* anxieties about cultural degeneration.[8]

The prediction that economies inevitably tend to fall into stasis, or at least are always in danger of doing so, was common to much of CPE: in *Principles of Political Economy,* J.S. Mill notes the common belief among political economists "that all progress in wealth is but a postponement of [the stationary state], and that each step in advance is an approach to it."[9] Smith's ambivalence about economic development puts him intellectually as well as chronologically somewhere between Thomas Malthus, whose "dismal science" held that economic decline was inevitable as well as baleful, and Mill, whose optimistic theory of a salutary stationary state was heterodox even among his contemporaries.[10] In any case, CPE's theory of economic finitude was itself not long for this world, done in by the pyrotechnic growth of the world economy that happened in the latter half of the nineteenth century.[11] Smith's and Malthus' belief that economic growth was limited because *land* was limited made sense in the "organic economy" of the preindustrial period, in which productive capacity depended on how much energy one could store or command, but less sense in the wake of the Industrial Revolution. Thus aside from heterodox Marxists like Rosa Luxemburg, from the mid-nineteenth century until the Great Depression, economic theory refused to imagine any ultimate or immanent limits to capitalism."[12] It is to that refusal that my next section turns.

## From the stationary state to endless innovation

Transformations in the economy transformed the conversation about growth, but so did transformations in economic thought itself. At the end of the nineteenth century, "political economy" became "economics," and specifically microeconomics, with its characteristic focus on the smaller scales of individual consumption at the expense of the *longue duree* of global development. And yet, the early twentieth century did produce at least one hugely important account of stasis versus change, namely that of Joseph Schumpeter. Like his classical predecessors, Schumpeter's idea of the stationary state was routed through images of natural circulation: what he terms the "circular flow" economy is a strictly pre-capitalist state of continuous but not expanding activity, an economy "similar to the circulation of blood through an animal organism."[13] We might connect Schumpeter's use of these natural images not only to CPE's "bioeconomics" but also, and more specifically, to what Philip Mirowski calls "the heritage of physical analogy" in all theories of so-called "natural" economic equilibrium.[14] Indeed, Schumpeter initially linked his idea of the "circular flow" economy to the field-founding work of Leon Walras on "general equilibrium," the principle that because supply and demand tend toward a state of balance, overall economic development likewise tended toward an eventual state of stationary equilibrium. Yet unlike Walras and the other equilibrium fetishists that Mirowski describes, Schumpeter ultimately insisted that equilibrium was only the *starting point* of economic development: in order to continue to function, he argued, capitalism must necessarily progress toward disturbance. Only by dispensing with the Walrasian fantasy that there might be a kind of equilibrium entrepreneur who "neither makes nor loses," Schumpeter argued, could one get toward "clear thinking on profits."[15] What is most interesting about Schumpeter's circular flow is thus not only his *refusal* to enshrine stationary equilibrium as the ideal type of economic motion (and the endpoint of economic development), but also his commitment to the necessary disequilibrium produced precisely by the individual entrepreneur: thus, the natural metaphor of water gives way, in Schumpeter's account, to a more heroic individualism, as the entrepreneur "swims against the stream if he wishes to change the channel."[16]

And yet, Schumpeter's entrepreneurial historicism had a darker side too, because the entrepreneur must inevitably hand down his business to his heirs. Although Schumpeter had a social-Darwinist belief that the bourgeois class, "superior as to intellectual and volitional aptitudes," would tend to pass on some of their unique endowments to their children, he also had a remarkably non-Darwinist belief about the inheritability of those traits.[17] Put simply, Schumpeter believed that because the inheritors of wealth "acquire from the fruits of [the entrepreneur's] success a position not immediately dependent on [the heirs' own] personal conduct," there inevitably extends to capitalist growth "a process of decline, of loss of caste, of elimination." Here, then, the very insistence that economic dynamism depends on individual temperament also dooms the economy to stasis. This happens, moreover, because Schumpeter takes Smith's anxieties about demography—about China as an "overstocked" nation where "the hands...naturally multiply beyond their employment"—and transforms them a more individualized and sociological, but nonetheless similarly reproductive anxiety about generational weakening. That is, Smith's anxieties about population as a natural mass that continues to increase despite the finitude of natural resources reappear as Schumpeter's anxiety about the social effects of a generational reproduction that continues despite the persistent decline in the quality of the offspring. "An American adage expresses it," Schumpeter writes pessimistically, "three generations from overalls to overalls." We will have cause to return to precisely this adage.[18]

Schumpeter's rather surprising late career claim that capitalism would eventually collapse as a result of this unavoidable decline notwithstanding; however, optimism about growth defined twentieth-century economic thought. This is true even in the work of twentieth-century economics' most heterodox mainstream economist, J.M. Keynes. Keynes' views on economic equilibrium are complicated, as is the relationship between Hansen's thesis and the predictions of his mentor, but in a rather strange polemical essay titled "Economic Possibilities for Our Grandchildren," Keynes explicitly refutes what he describes as his moment's "bad attack of economic pessimism." Attempting to contravene this pessimism, Keynes offers an encomium to the virtues of naturally increasing returns: after "sleeping for many generations," the power of "accumulation by compound interest," he says, has been "reborn and renewed its strength." Channeling the possibility of infinite accumulation, Keynes here falls prey to the fantasy of a self-reproducing capital that generates interest "just as a pear tree bear[s] pears," as Marx put it with brittle irony.[19] If the seeming endlessness of generational reproduction causes Smith to worry over population growth, and Schumpeter to balefully propose that the stronger and richer the parent, the weaker and poorer the child, Keynes uses metaphors of birth and generation to suggest the infinite abundance of nature itself: for the moderns, he suggests, nature is a "new-found bounty."[20]

Although he was Keynes' student, Alvin Hansen bristled at this idea of the economy's natural abundance, claiming instead that "The classicals were quite right when they argued that the economy [would move] to the point at which there would be no net investment."[21] For Hansen, *declining* population growth would lead to a fall in investment. Barring the perpetual development of radically transformative technology, and even with the help of public investment, he argued, long-term structural factors would inevitably slow the American economy. As Hansen's emphasis on the finitude of technological innovation suggests, his account was based on a reading of economic history as a series of expanding and contracting frontiers of possibility, one that economic historians Roger Backhouse and Mauro Boianovsky have suggested was indebted to Frederick Jackson Turner's argument that the closing of the geographical frontier at the end of the nineteenth century presaged a baleful future of American decline.[22] Thus although Hansen's concern was with population decline rather than population growth, like Smith he insisted on a set of basically natural limits to economic vitality. More important to Hansen than simply the *mass* of the population, however, was the employment *rate*, which he argued tended to become a problem as capitalism modernized and as investment in what he calls the "technical coefficient" of capital (what Marx might call the "fixed capital" of stock and machines) increased at the expense of labor. Through this partly external, partly immanent account of capitalism's limits, Hansen thus offered a starkly pessimistic diagnosis, arguing that "the great era of growth and expansion" is over and predicting that "We are moving swiftly out of the order in which those of our generation were brought up."[23]

Smith's naturalization of economic limits appears in metaphors of water and blood, land and the birthrate, whereas in Keynes, the refusal to imagine limit appears as a discourse of natural fecundity. In Hansen, by contrast, we find a vexed relationship between exogenous, natural explanations (like demographics or the limits of physical space) and endogenous, immanent explanations (like rising unemployment), and this ambivalence becomes visible in Hansen's metaphors themselves, especially those relating to the body and—as, again, in Smith, Schumpeter, and Keynes—to birth. In the most frequently cited lines from his essay, for instance, Hansen describes secular stagnation as "weak and anaemic...recoveries which die in their infancy and depressions which feed on themselves and leave a hard and seemingly immovable core of unemployment." Here, the naturalization of the body economic exists uneasily alongside a sense that this is no longer a healthy body. Rather, it is one that is not only on the way to a steady decline but that is coming into that state uncannily too early, dead in childhood and unnaturally "feed[ing] on itself." Against Keynes' fantasy of autochthonous growth, Hansen asserts, "a vigorous recovery is not just spontaneously born from the womb of the preceding depression."[24] Hansen's almost Malthusian—and certainly richly, even excessively metaphorical—images of reproductive morbidity are suggestive both of Hansen's anxiety about stagnation and of what I have been describing here as a larger anxiety visible across the history of economic thought. That is, the presence of vividly connotative language in a text that otherwise eschews rhetorical flourish indicates the moments of stress and contradiction within Hansen's account: like the infant emerging from the womb, the causes of stagnation are both inside *and* outside of the economic body; the economy is both constitutionally weak *and* attacked from without by an exogenous sickness. Moreover, when traced across the history of economic thought, such language of economic stagnation as reproductive enervation (notable, again, in a discipline that tends to see itself as largely empiricist rather than interpretive) allows us to locate Hansen's work both within and against a discourse of reproductive and generational decline, and thus to see the historical intensification of this discourse as a way of responding to emerging and intensifying crises within capitalism itself. If Keynes imagined a bright future for "our grandchildren" while Schumpeter's cyclical belief in "overalls to overalls" was phlegmatically pessimistic, Hansen's much grimmer account of what awaits the next generation would haunt the thinkers of twenty-first-century secular stagnation.

Of course, Hansen's Depression-era prediction was invalidated by the miraculous postwar recovery, so that as the twentieth century drew to a close, and despite many signs to the contrary, economists became even *more* committed to the narrative that capitalism could grow forever. The most interesting example of this thesis is Francis Fukuyama's "end of history." Positing two mutually constituting "logics" of historical development—natural science, technology, and the fight for survival on the one hand; freedom, democracy, and the fight for individual recognition on the other—Fukuyama argues that history has effectively "ended" in the successful synthesis of these two in the form of liberal capitalism. And yet although we tend to remember Fukuyama's account as implausibly optimistic, in fact (and especially in the shorter, earlier essay version of the argument) he predicts something remarkably like Smith's enervated stationary state: "The end of history will be a very sad time, the end of the worldwide ideological struggle that called forth daring, courage, imagination, and idealism....In the post historical period there will be [only] centuries of boredom."[25] Curiously, moreover, the explanation he offers for this attenuation of vital energy is a kind of reversal of Smith's and Malthus's arguments about the problem of satisfying growing demand for basic, and naturally limited, human subsistence. That is, Fukuyama argues that the final achievement of the first of those historical logics is certain: we have effectively conquered nature and perfected our capacity to innovate economically and technologically, such that our bodily survival—the satisfaction of what Fukuyama identifies as our natural "appetite"—is guaranteed. The end point of the liberal democracy, on the other hand, is somewhat less certain: our spirited *thymos*, or willingness to *risk* our own survival, perhaps cannot be satisfied by the relatively bloodless rationality of the modern state. While the "dismal science" of Smith and Malthus worried over man's ability to produce enough to satisfy his consumption needs and thus over his very capacity to physically survive, Fukuyama—who, ironically, writes at precisely the moment at which nature's infinitude seems less guaranteed than ever—worries that our "endless" consumption and guaranteed bodily reproduction can never satisfy our more fundamental need to risk our life.[26]

In the end, however, Fukuyama steps back from the potentially bleak conclusions of his own argument, choosing instead to promote the fantasy of endless technological development even as the innovations he describes suggest in their very triviality the slowing down of a truly dynamic economy: in one exemplary moment, for instance, we see him attempt to get excited about innovation even in "prosaic areas like the marketing of hamburgers and the creation of new types of insurance."[27] Fukuyama's end of history prediction thus at once inherits and rather unsuccessfully represses the existential melancholy of Smith's stationary state. And yet, his contemporaries lacked even this ambivalence. As the massive bubbles of the late twentieth- and early twenty-first-century economies made it appear as if capitalism had launched itself free of any remaining tendency to contraction or stasis, a Noble-Prize economist argued, "This expansion will run forever."[28] And then, into this muddle of ideology, bad historicism, and wishful thinking, the crisis of 2008 came striding into town.

## The return of secular stagnation

What happened in 2008 had surprised mainstream economists. But what happened *after* the crisis was in the end the more shocking problem. What happened *after* 2008 was exactly what Hansen describes: a "sick recover[y] which die[d] in its infancy." Surely, economists predicted after the official end of the recession in 2009, the stalled economy was *just about* to shudder into revitalized motion. And yet today, even though the US has not been remotely austere, average annual per capita GDP growth in the US has fallen to less than 1% in 2015. Thus, Summers writes, "the overall potential of the US economy has been revised downward by 5 percent," noting further that "this is not a temporary but a sustained, long-term decline."[29] In 2015 alone, three major works of economic theory agreed: Robert Gordon's *The Rise and Fall of American Growth* argues that the US economy is in a period of permanent stasis; finance expert Satyajit Das claims that "the central illusion of the age of capital—endless economic growth—is ending"; and economist Mohamed El-Erian rejects his own 2009 prediction of restored growth and forecasts instead total global stagnation.[30] As a *New York Times* article put it, "if something doesn't change, the twenty-first century will be a gloomy one."[31]

In various ways, I have suggested, Smith, Hansen, and their more recent interlocutors offer us a language for imagining capitalism as terminating *neither* in end of history abundance, *nor* in a radical transition to a new economic arrangement. If all of these accounts are characterized, in various ways, by a troubling organicism, they are also attuned to capitalism's limits in a manner resonant with contemporary understanding of ecological crisis: their organicism itself thus has a kind of double valence, naturalizing the development of capitalism and drawing on a vitalist conception of human physiognomy while also resisting the fantasy of a natural world and a human body without limits. They suggest that what Fred Magdoff and John Bellamy Foster have termed the "growth imperative of capitalism" is constitutive not only of the capitalist mode of accumulation but also of mainstream economic thought under capitalism, and they do so precisely by wondering what would happen if this imperative was not satisfied or this conceptual axiom proved false.[32] Refuting the fantasy that capitalism infinitely and effortlessly reproduces itself, an emphasis on decline and diminishment provides a powerful figure for the limits of natural resources, the unavailability of new territories for expansion, and the inevitable slowing of technological innovation.

We also find, in all of these thinkers—as, remarkably, in thinkers more uncertain or skeptical about the inevitability of stagnation like Schumpeter and Keynes—the discourse of specifically reproduction, both literal (as an anxiety about population) and figurative (as a metaphor for a development stillborn or a generation impoverished). The conclusion of this essay wants to think about what this language of reproduction means in the context of the present. Lee Edelman has urgently argued that what he terms "reproductive futurism" undergirds a nationalist and heteronormative ideology.[33] Yet, the ambiently anxious language of generational inheritance that characterizes so much stagnation discourse, from Schumpeter's "overalls to overalls" to Robert Gordon's 2015 prediction that today's young people will be the first generation worse off than their parents, also has an acutely diagnostic power. What it diagnoses, I want to argue, is the fact that capitalism is now in what feminist political economist Sylvia Federici has termed a "permanent reproductive crisis."[34] This means capitalism can no longer guarantee the reproduction of the livelihood—and ultimately the life—of the worker herself, producing a crisis in what the collective Endnotes describe as "the ongoing production and reproduction of the commodity labour-power."[35] Thus in the US, de-investment in labor took the form of both wage stagnation and rising un- and underemployment starting in the 1970s: given the simultaneously rising price of basic necessities like health care, housing, and education, households turned to credit, from mortgages and credit cards to student loans and even more dramatically exploitative forms of debt like payday loans. When housing values began to fall in 2007 and the payments on adjustable rate mortgages began to climb, households could no longer continue to support themselves through debt, revealing the underlying crisis in the wage and employment rate. Since the crisis, 95% of new jobs added have been temporary, part-time, or contract work—this statistic not only indicates the utility of a concept like the "feminization of labor" (naming the qualitative change where the features typically associated with women's work, especially precariousness and low wages, become common conditions of work across formerly gender differentiated spheres), it also suggests that the "recovery" has done little to make the lives of working-class households more stable. The ongoing reproductive crisis is arguably at its most extreme in the global South where, as Farshad Araghi argues, a regime of "underreproduction" or "forced underconsumption" has allowed capital to "transgress the normal limit" of the human body by pushing individual consumption down below the level "necessary for restoring and regenerating labor power": noting that a crisis of global value relations currently expresses itself as "the end of cheap food," Araghi also allows us to connect the limit of the worker's body to the limit of natural resources described earlier.[36]

The language of both generational decline and stillborn reproduction may thus be understood as a crystalline expression of an epoch in which the reproduction of workers themselves is uncertain, and in which the economic futures of their children under capitalism appear unrelentingly bleak. It is also an expression of the particular conditions in which capital, desperate for new sources and sites of profitability, reenters the very domestic sphere it formerly abandoned: as Gonzalez puts it, having ensured that "social relations and forms of everyday life [are] subordinated to the prerogatives of capital's own reproduction"—that is, having depressed wages to such a degree that workers can only feed and house themselves by going into debt, or having forced them into conditions of underreproduction—capital then begins its "coercive unification of these spheres within the logic of capital," capitalizing on household crises through mechanisms ranging from subprime loans to microcredit schemes.[37]

Finally and most urgently, the work of feminist scholars like Gonzalez and Federici allows us to show both what is revealed and what is repressed by the persistent language of biological reproduction that I have read across the history of both classical political economy and neoclassical economics. It exposes the fact that capital accumulation depends materially on the "natural" abundance of both land and the female body, which then serve as metaphorical figures for the mystical or metaphysical vitality of capitalism as a system. As Federici notes, for both Smith and Marx, population increase appears not as a "social, historically determined activity, invested by diverse interests and power relations" but rather as merely the "natural effect" of economic growth. That is, the body and land share not simply a capacity to be depleted, but also a tendency to appear as natural givens, their organic fertility a "free gift" from which profit might inexhaustibly spring. Moreover, and as critics like Federici have urgently argued, by occluding the fact that "the production and reproduction of the worker is…a source of capital accumulation," capitalist ideology also makes this reproduction appear entirely *outside of* capitalism.[38] That is, not only have both orthodox and heterodox economists systematically ignored the interests which organize biological reproduction under capitalism, but capitalism itself has separated the spheres of factory production and domestic reproduction in order to command—but never to wage—the reproductive labor of women. Breaking through these repressions, the anxious, overdetermined discourse of biological reproduction—whether it appears as manifest content (in Smith's concern over population, or Gordon's more recent worry over generational downward mobility) or as trope (in Keynes' utopian fantasy of the autochthonous fertility of compound interest or Hansen's weakened infants)—can thus be read as a sign of intractable crisis, indicating a realization that the supposedly unlimited capacities of land and of producing and reproducing bodies are in fact finite, indicating that the formerly concealed power sources of capital's dynamic circuit have become instead the site of impasse, stall, and terminal stagnation.

## Notes

1 Lawrence Summers, Speech at the International Monetary Fund Research Conference in Honor of Stanley Fischer, Washington, DC, 13 November 2013. Transcript accessed at http://larrysummers.com/imf-fourteenth-annual-research-conference-in-honor-of-stanley-fischer/.

2 Ben Bernanke, "Secular stagnation," *Brookings Institution blog*, March 31, 2015, www.brookings.edu/blog/ben-bernanke/2015/03/31/why-are-interest-rates-so-low-part-2-secular-stagnation/; Paul Krugman, "Secular Stagnation, Coalmines, Bubbles, and Larry Summers," *New York Times* blog, November 16, 2013, http://krugman.blogs.nytimes.com/2013/11/16/secular-stagnation-coalmines-bubbles-and-larry-summers/.

3 Alvin Hansen, "Economic Progress and Declining Population Growth," *The American Economic Review* 29.1 (March 1939): 1–15.

4 See Catherine Gallagher, *The Body Economic: Life, Death, and Sensation in Political Economy and the Victorian Novel* (Princeton, NJ: Princeton University Press, 2008).

5 On Smith and Harvey, see Richard Sennet, *Flesh and Stone: The Body and the City in Western Civilization* (New York: W.W. Norton, 1996), 256. For Smith on liquidity and circulatory fluids, see *An Inquiry into the Nature and Causes of the Wealth of Nations*, Project Gutenberg ebook, book 4, chap. 7, www.gutenberg .org/ebooks/3300.

6 Smith, *Wealth of Nations,* book 1, chap. 8.

7 See Giovanni Arrighi, *Adam Smith in Beijing* (London: Verso, 2007): 40–68; Erhun Kula, *History of Environmental Economic Thought* (London: Routledge, 1998): 14–21.

8 See Robert Heilbroner, "The Paradox of Progress: Decline and Decay in *Wealth of Nations*," *Journal of the History of Ideas* 34.2 (April–June 1973): 243–62. I owe the point about Smith's anticipation of later developments in physics to a provocative footnote in Philip Mirowski, *More Heat than Light: Economics as Social Physics, Physics as Nature's Economics* (Cambridge: Cambridge University Press, 1989), 419.

9 John Stuart Mill, *Principles of Political Economy with some of their Applications to Social Philosophy*, Library of Economics and Liberty ebook, book 1, chap. 11, www.econlib.org/library/Mill/mlP.html#.
10 See E.A. Wrigley, "The Limits to Growth: Malthus and the Classical Political Economists," *Population and Development Review* 14 (1980): 30–48.
11 See E.A. Wrigley, *Continuity, Chance, and Change: The Character of the Industrial Revolution* (Cambridge: Cambridge University Press, 1990).
12 See Rosa Luxemburg, The Accumulation of Capital, Trans. Agnes Schwarzschild (New York: Routledge Classics, 2003 [1913]).
13 Joseph Schumpeter, *The Theory of Economic Development: An Inquiry into Profits, Capital, Credit, and the Business Cycle*, trans. Redvers Opie (London, UK: 2010 [1934]), 61.
14 Mirowski, *More Heat than Light*, 238.
15 See Richard Arena, "Schumpeter on Walras," *The Contribution of Joseph A. Schumpeter to Economics*, ed. Richard Arena (London: Routledge, 2002), 56–9.
16 Schumpeter, *Theory of Economic Development*, 79–80.
17 Qtd. in David Reisman, *Schumpeter's Market: Enterprise and Evolution* (London: Edward Elgar, 2004), 106.
18 Schumpeter, *Theory of Economic Development*, 156–7.
19 Karl Marx, *Capital Volume III*, trans. David Fernbach (London: Penguin Classics, 1993 [1894]) 516.
20 John Maynard Keynes, "Economic Possibilities for Our Grandchildren," *Revisiting Keynes: Economic Possibilities for Our Grandchildren*, eds. Lorenzo Pecchi and Gustavo Piga (Cambridge, MA: MIT Press, 2008 [1930]), 17, 19, 23.
21 Qtd. in A.C. Pigou, "The Classical Stationary State," *The Economic Journal* 53.212 (Dec. 1943), 343.
22 Roger Backhouse and Mauro Boianovsky, "Secular Stagnation: The History of a Macroeconomic Heresy" (May 5, 2015), https://papers.ssrn.com/sol3/papers.cfm?abstract_id=2602903.
23 Hansen, "Economic Progress," 1.
24 Hansen, "Economic Progress," 4, 11.
25 Francis Fukuyama, "The End of History?", *National Interest* (Summer 1989). Accessed October 2016 at www.wesjones.com/eoh.htm, n.p.
26 See Fukuyama, *The End of History and the Last Man* (New York: The Free Press, 1992), *passim*. For an especially rich account of these paradoxes in Fukuyama's text, see Joseph Mcarney, "Shaping Ends: Reflections on Fukuyama," 1.202 (Nov–Dec 1993).
27 Fukuyama, *End of History*, 93.
28 Rudiger Dornbusch, "Growth Forever," *Wall Street Journal* (30 July, 1998).
29 Lawrence Summers, "US Economic Prospects: Secular Stagnation, Hysteresis, and the Zero Lower Bound," *Business Economics* 49.2 (2014), 66.
30 Robert Gordon, *The Rise and Fall of American Growth: the US Standard of Living Since the Civil War* (Princeton, NJ: Princeton University Press, 2015); Satyajit Das, *The Age of Stagnation: Why Perpetual Growth is Unattainable and the Global Economy is in Peril* (New York: Prometheus Books, 2015); Mohamed el-Erian, *The Only Game in Town: Central Banks, Instability, and Avoiding the Next Collapse* (New York: Random House, 2015).
31 Neil Irwin, "We're in a Low-Growth World. How Did We Get Here?" *The New York Times* blog (August 6, 2016), n.p. Accessed at www.nytimes.com/2016/08/07/upshot/were-in-a-low-growth-world-how-did-we-get-here.html?login=email&_r=1
32 Fred Magdoff and John Bellamy Foster, *What Every Environmentalist Needs to Know About Capitalism* (New York: Monthly Review Press, 2011).
33 Lee Edelman, *No Future: Queer Theory and the Death Drive* (Durham: Duke University Press, 2004).
34 Sylvia Federici and Marina Vishmidt, "Permanent Reproductive Crisis: An Interview with Sylvia Federici," *Mute* (March 7, 2003).
35 Endnotes, "The Logic of Gender on the Separation of Spheres and the Process of Abjection," *Endnotes* 3 (September 2013), n.p. I should also note here that describing the contemporary crisis as a crisis of reproduction does not necessarily imply a purely "underconsumptionist" theory of crisis: rather, the most urgent and accurate accounts of the contemporary reproductive crisis frame the problem of the reproduction of labor power as the *effect* of an ongoing crisis of profitability, overaccumulation, and/or overproduction, but an effect that also intensifies those crises both materially and culturally/politically.

36 Farshad Araghi, "Accumulation by Displacement: Global Enclosures, Food Crisis, and the Ecological Contradictions of Capitalism" *Review (Fernand Braudel Center* 32.1 (2009).
37 Maya Gonzalez, "Notes on the New Housing Question," *Endnotes* 2 (April 2010), https://endnotes.org.uk/issues/2/en/endnotes-notes-on-the-new-housing-question, n.p.
38 Sylvia Federici, *Caliban and the Witch: Women, The Body, and Primitive Accumulation* (New York: Autonomedia, 2004).

# 32
# SOCIAL WANT

*Howard Horwitz*

In a 1931 radio address, attempting to counter the austerity policies of the British government, John Maynard Keynes exhorted his listeners to be, as it were, stimulative. "[B]e in a mood of expansion, of activity—to do things, to buy things, to make things." Consumers tend to spend less during economic downturns, and both the British government and the Hoover administration advised citizens to save, but Keynes advocates consumption: "if you buy goods, someone will have to make them"; "if you do not buy goods,... some one will be thrown out of work" (Keynes 1932: 153, 152). Keynes does not view commercial activity as the work of isolated individuals with no concern for or allegiance to other citizens. He characterizes consumer activity as a collective enterprise, whereby individuals ideally understand what Thomas Paine might have called the "reciprocal blessings" of their transactions (66).

> ... oh patriotic housewives, sally out to-morrow early into the streets and go to the wonderful sales which are everywhere advertised. You will do yourselves good—for never were things so cheap, cheap beyond your dreams. Lay in a stock of household linen, of sheets and blankets to satisfy all your needs. And have the added joy that you are increasing employment, adding to the wealth of the country because you are setting on foot useful activities, bringing a chance and a hope to Lancashire, Yorkshire, and Belfast.
>
> *(Keynes 1932: 152)*

Keynes's optimistic narrative of commerce exemplifies the way social theory involves narratives of social intercourse, which ultimately are narratives of subjectivity, of our experience of our relation to events, social phenomena, and others. Keynes's narrative is a fable of conscious social affiliation. He thinks (or hopes) that we feel a bond with others not only as we shop, but by virtue of shopping. Keynes envisions economic activity as reciprocity, as mutually stimulative activity. As we "satisfy all [our] needs," we make it possible for others to satisfy their needs. The housewives he addresses, likely strapped for cash and in debt, and likely to incur more debt when they purchase the full set of linens fantastically discounted because sales are perilously slow, may not yet feel the consumerist patriotism he boosts, but Keynes expects that the experience of shopping will stimulate in them what Karl Marx in a different context labeled "social want"—"*das gesellsaftliche Bedürfnis*" (*Bedürfnis* means "need," "want," "desire," "wish," "demand")—a collective urge to contribute to a grand, expansive, perhaps transcendent enterprise that constitutes not only society and history but what Georg Simmel called the "processes of sociation" (8), our experience of ourselves through social intercourse. We tend to think of economic statistics like GNP and consumer demand as aggregations of individual wants. Major figures in economic theory, however, craft narratives of sociation in which individual desire and experience generally are functions of social want, serving and, in turn, galvanizing a historical and perhaps ontological demand.

By thinking of economic discourses as narratives of sociation, I am, of course, indebted to the work of Deirdre McCloskey, which launched the rhetoric-in-economics movement. Early in her career, McCloskey treated economic analysis as a kind of narrative gratification. With respect to debates about British economic growth during the Victorian period, for example, "the way of telling stories shape[s] one's opinion about Victorian failure" or Britain's steady economic growth in the period. A scholar's view of the Victorian economy is deeply influenced by the story one "wants to tell" about the supremacy or embryonic decline of the British empire (McCloskey 1990: 45). McCloskey therefore examined the metaphors and narrative structures that make economic narratives credible. She advised scholars to use the different parts of the "rhetorical tetrad"—story, metaphor, logic, fact—to "test" the validity of economic narratives. The consistency or inconsistency among the parts reveals the "aptness" of story and metaphor (4, 84, 90; see also 83, 162). In her later work, McCloskey stresses the discursive mechanisms and effects of economic narratives. The economy is rhetorical, she argues; people must be persuaded to invest labor and resources in particular ways. "People have preferences, matters of discourse and delight, which constitute one side of determining the value of things" (McCloskey 2011: 186). "Ideas," McCloskey declares, "made the modern world" (McCloskey 2016a: 596), and thus the subtitle of her recent *Bourgeois Equality* contends that "ideas, not capital, transformed the world," in particular ideas about liberty (voluntary trade) and dignity (i.e. 11, 20, 24, 26).

McCloskey seeks to sketch, then, the "ideational history" of economic development, the conceptual and discursive conditions in which people heed certain economic (and also ethical) principles rather than others (McCloskey 2015: 62). The theoretical economic narratives I am looking at offer what we might call a more internalized focus than McCloskey's. These economic narratives recount a subjective tendency and principle of sociation, social want, that forms the basis from which we assess ideas and make ethical choices. These narratives presuppose social want as the necessary condition for the interminable growth required of market society.

Keynes's vision of collectively shared social want is not limited to his political liberalism. Milton Friedman, for example, the oft-cited authority of the anti-regulatory and free market approach that arguably has structured much U.S. economic policy since the Jarvis tax revolt of the late 1970s, advisor to Ronald Reagan and Margaret Thatcher, and who earned his Nobel Prize for challenging Keynesian precepts about the relation among price, money supply, employment, and output, eclipses Keynes' optimism that commerce expresses and forms social affiliation. In his 1962 manifesto, *Capitalism and Freedom*, a gospel text of neoliberalism, Friedman imagines citizens freed from the "coercion" of commercial regulation (13), which includes most labor laws and licensing requirements.

> The basic problem of social organization is how to co-ordinate the economic activities of large numbers of people.... Literally millions of people are involved in providing one another with their daily bread, let alone with their yearly automobiles. The challenge to the believer in liberty is to reconcile this widespread interdependence with individual freedom. *(12–13)*

"Central direction" from the state limits the freedom of citizens, Friedman believes, but "competitive capitalism," the "voluntary co-operation of individuals—the technique of the market place"—will coordinate freedom with interdependence. "Exchange can... bring about co-ordination without coercion," he declares (13). Through what Marx called a Robinsonade, so typical of economic treatises (Marx 1993: 83), Friedman fancifully imagines advanced competitive capitalism as an elaborate household economy.

> In its simplest form,... society consists of a number of independent households—a collection of Robinson Crusoes, as it were. Each household uses the resources it controls to produce goods and services that it exchanges for goods and services produced by other households, on terms mutually acceptable to the two parties to the bargain.
>
> *(13)*

A "free economy," he writes, "gives people what they want instead of what a particular group thinks they ought to want" (15), and in the ideal "*the transaction is bi-laterally voluntary and informed*" (13; italics original). If anything, Friedman's economic actors are even more cognizant and enthusiastic than Keynes's shoppers about their reciprocal contribution not only to the welfare but to the liberty of others as well as themselves. In Friedman's story of commerce, social want is shared by all because voluntary and informed, and therefore "bargains" are always mutually satisfactory and beneficial.

If Friedman and Keynes hold contrary views about economic equity and policy, they write strikingly compatible narratives of social want: let's buy and be productive together. Their narrative of sociation is more collective than that of Adam Smith, whose famous defense of self-interest in the *Wealth of Nations* (1776) is an outlier in the model I am trying to sketch. In his 1759 *Theory of Moral Sentiments* (1st edition, 1759; 6th edition, 1790), Smith tries to imagine how we might experience fellow feeling, compassion, sympathy, pity, and so forth, for others, when at the same time we are, he writes in the book's first sentence, "selfish" (11). "Man" requires "the assistance of others," Smith writes, but self-love forestalls the sentiments that incline people to assist others (17). Much eighteenth-century moral philosophy and social discourse posited a conflict between self-love or self-interest and social harmony. In the American context, Thomas Paine thought that our pursuit of self-interest through commerce prompts us "to relax in [our] duty and attachment to each other" (66). And Thomas Jefferson worried that a population pursuing self-interest will become immersed "in the sole faculty of making money" and "will never think of uniting to effect a due respect for... rights" (167). Accordingly, the *Federalist Papers* attempted to market the U.S. Constitution as a tool for tempering the effects of rivalrous and irreducible self-interest.

Contemporaneously, in *Wealth of Nations*, Smith reconciles self-interest and social affiliation by absorbing sociality into self-interest. In a famous passage, Smith says we acquire goods by appealing to the self-love rather than benevolence of merchants like the butcher, brewer, and baker. Here, market behavior is not willingly harmonious, but nonetheless coordinated through contractual agreements. (Contracts distinguish us from other animals; Smith 1937: 13.)

> In civilised society [man] stands at all times in need of the cooperation and assistance of great multitudes, while his whole life is scarce sufficient to gain the friendship of a few persons. In almost every other race of animals each individual, when it is grown up to maturity, is entirely independent, and in its natural state has occasion for the assistance of no other living creature. But man has almost constant occasion for the help of his

> brethren, and it is in vain for him to expect it from their benevolence only. He will be more likely to prevail if he can interest their self-love in his favour, and show them that it is for their own advantage to do for him what he requires of them. Whoever offers to another a bargain of any kind, proposes to do this. Give me that which I want, and you shall have this which you want, is the meaning of every such offer; and it is in this manner that we obtain from one another the far greater part of those good offices which we stand in need of. It is not from the benevolence of the butcher, the brewer, or the baker that we expect our dinner, but from their regard to their own interest. We address ourselves, not to their humanity but to their self-love, and never talk to them of our own necessities but of their advantages.
>
> *(14)*

In this passage, "want" is individual. The agreement sanctioning any transaction—"Give me that which I want, and you shall have this which you want"—is resolutely self-interested. Smith's individuals are indifferent to the concerns and vulnerabilities of others. We calculate others' concerns only in order to make bargains that serve our needs; we feel and express no particular sympathy for others, nor they for us.

Keynes would be dismayed. Yet in Smith's scenario, self-interest does not precipitate rivalry or conflict among individuals, because this perhaps most famous account of market activity omits competition. Smith's commercial world consists of one butcher, one brewer, one baker, and a steady stream of sufficiently funded consumers (the "we" of the passage), who always seem satisfied with the price of goods even though the merchants fear no competitors for market share and therefore can set prices as they wish. Two merchants furnish indispensable staples, and the third brews for leisure activity. Assuming that the baker bakes cakes and desserts as well as bread, social life in Smith's passage consists of artisan merchants servicing a consuming class that enjoys leisure time largely as individuals. Group activity is scarce here and in any event seems not communal in any strong sense of the word, but only formally (contractually) coordinated out of necessity.

Smith's friend Benjamin Franklin—they met around the time of the publication of *Moral Sentiments*—envisions greater integration between self-interest and social intercourse. Beginning in 1729, Franklin wrote a series of pamphlets encouraging the circulation of paper money in the colonies, partly to stimulate immigration and general population growth. The British restricted currency in the colonies in order to stifle investment in colonial manufacture, requiring Americans to purchase British-made items. Franklin countered that British manufacture will benefit as well if Americans have more currency to spend. "*A Plentiful Currency*" increases demand for all goods. Franklin regards goods as an embodiment of "labour," and through money, as "a *Medium of Exchange,*... Labour is exchanged for Labour, or one Commodity for another," and people acquire "that very Thing which they want," ultimately effecting "the Satisfaction of all Parties" (7, 13; italics original). For Franklin, individual want is in principle sociable, whether or not, as in Friedman, individuals contemplate the shared benefits of transactions. Since goods and money represent labor, transactions are ultimately the exchange of labor rather than of goods and money. Thus, commerce exchanges personage, embodied in goods, and identity is itself transactional, formed through exchanges. Sociation, and not just the thing acquired, underlies the satisfaction we derive from commercial exchange.

Because Franklin defines commerce as the exchange of labor, Karl Marx credits him with being "one of the first economists... who saw through the nature of value" (Marx 1906: 59n). Marx, of course, designates labor not only as the first source of value but explicitly as the provenance of identity. Because nature does not spontaneously furnish necessities of survival, labor is "a necessary condition, independent of all forms of society, for the existence of the human race" (50). "[H]uman labour is embodied" in products, as in coats or linen, Marx says numerous times, and value, he writes even more frequently, is the "expression" [*Ausdrück*] of that expenditure (45). Thus, "the value of commodities has a purely social reality... in so far as they are expressions or embodiments of... human labour" (55). Because products must be distributed at least among families, and in any economic system at least some goods are exchanged for others, "man first... recognizes himself... [and] establishes his own identity" through exchange of the products that embody our labor. Identity forms "in *propriâ personâ*" through economic intercourse (61n, 61). Marx's linen, then, is even more integral than Keynes's to the formation of the subject. In Marx, commerce forms the ongoing narrative of the formation and fate of labor, value, and our proper person.

*Capital*, Volume 1, tracks the career and indeed life of capital from its emergence in the form of products and commodities, embodying and expressing labor in abstract form, then in the form of capital, and then as capital accumulates and concentrates. (These stages form the arc of the book.) Capital itself is the main character of this narrative, which reaches its climax in Part Seven on the concentration of capital. Of course, the term "capital" in the volume is metonymy for capitalists, but the term "capital" often figures in Marx's text as an agent itself, often a grammatical agent. Marx at one point, asserts that "the capitalist" has "no right to... historical existence" "[e]xcept as personified capital" (648). Even as the capitalist is the instrument through which capital is "endowed... with consciousness and a will," the capitalist's "actions are a mere function of capital" (649). Just as Charles Darwin in *Origin of Species* (1859), which Marx read carefully, personifies "nature" as a metaphorical agent, selecting traits and species that will survive, Marx's "capital" is the true agent accumulating surplus value, or altering the relation between "constant capital" (generally speaking, capital investment—machinery, brick-and-mortar overhead) and the "variable" element of capital, labor, the tragic victim in this narrative. Capital works incessantly, for example, to produce a surplus, reserve labor force, among other activities. As Marx writes, capital "wants larger numbers of youthful labourers, a smaller number of adults" (704).

Capital's "driving motive and determining purpose" is what Marx calls "self-expansion"—"*Selbstverwertung*" (363; I have rendered a more literal translation of this passage than the Moore and Aveling translation). *Verwertung* can mean utilization, recovery, realization, and so in this model, self is realized through expansion. Capital exhibits "unmeasured passion for self-expansion" (292), which does not merely generate profit, for unless capital expands, it succumbs to competition. As congealed surplus labor, capital, of course, expands itself by increasing the labor force it exploits and exploiting labor power more efficiently. Capital must "employ [any] increase [in the labor force] for its own self-expansion," and laborers must sell "their own labour power... for the self-expansion of capital" (708). As productive capacity expands and "new inventions" abound, "a greater mass of raw material and auxiliary substances enter into the labour-process" and ever more labor is dedicated to producing new machinery and goods (689, 682). Ironically, as Smith and especially David Ricardo noted, the greater efficiency of capital reduces its "marginal productivity" (Piketty 2014: 215), partly because laborers demand higher wages to reflect their contributions amid rising prices (Smith 1937: 112–13). Ricardo outlined this "natural tendency of profits to fall... in the progress of society," "this gravitation as it were of profits." To the relief of employers and investors like Ricardo, "improvements in machinery" and scientific discoveries "enable us to relinquish a portion of labour" (120; see also 118, 122–3). Admiring Smith and Ricardo's sense of the inherent tension between profit and wages, Marx stresses: "the growing extent of the means of production" results "in the diminution of the mass of labour in proportion to the mass of means of production moved by it" (682). Thus, while "increasing [the] productivity of labour," the expansion and concentration of capital "reduce[s] the relative demand for labor," plateauing wages and increasing "pauperism" (682, 689, 707).

Capital's tendency to reduce its outlay to labor creates two related paradoxes. First, even as production employs less labor and curtails wages, population grows, and people must be able to afford the increasing variety and quantity of products becoming produced, or otherwise production collapses (the predicament faced by Keynes). Second, capital must regularly invest in new "constant capital" as processes improve, especially because newer capital, by definition, employs new technology, and even when, inevitably, debt for older machinery remains outstanding. Hence, capital must expand, however costly the process, in order to ensure the "reproduction of the working class" and indeed "a disposable industrial reserve army" (627, 693). Self-expansion is mandatory, interminable, and precarious, and Marx's capital is simultaneously an aggressive and anxious figure.

Capital must expand perpetually to sustain the process that both makes it possible and jeopardizes it. "The continual re-transformation of surplus-value into capital now appears in the shape of the increasing magnitude of the capital that enters into the process of production" (684–85). What Marx labels the "law of the progressive increase in constant capital" mandates "the production of capital by capital" (682, 684). Self-expansion rather than the practical or economic function of any product becomes the ultimate purpose of production. "Every accumulation becomes the means of new accumulation" (685). "The masses of capital… reproduce and augment themselves" (689).

The accelerating concentration of capital defends against the competition it also spawns. As "social capital" grows, "the number of capitalists grows," capital seeking its own concentration in each case (685). The "increasing concentration of the means of production, and of the command over labour," sparks "repulsion of many individual capitals one from another" (686). "[C]ompetition rages" among "antagonistic capitals" (687). Even so, "the repulsion of [capitals] one from another, is counteracted by their attraction" (686). Inexorably, capital centralizes. Here at the onset of the era of monopoly, Marx tracks the "concentration of capitals already formed, destruction of their individual independence," and "transformation of many small into few large capitals." Able to effect greater economies of scale, thereby "cheapening… commodities" and reducing labor costs (enhancing surplus value), "the larger capitals beat the smaller" (686). Ultimately, all "individual capitals" are "amalgamated into one single capital" (688). Think here Standard Oil, Amazon, Google, Citicorp and Wells Fargo, GE, Walmart, Siemens, Microsoft, Apple, and several Chinese conglomerates, like State Grid.

Increasingly anxious about employment and wages, laborers more intensively "turn their labour power into an increasing power of self-expansion of the growing capital" (675). Debunking the myth of free association we find in a Friedman, Marx declares that the "appearance of independence is kept up… by the fictio juris of a contract." In fact, "the wage labourer is bound to his owner by invisible threads" (628), or worse, bound to the product of his labor. In selling labor to capital, laborers "must eternise their dependent relation on their own product, as personified in the capitalists" (675). Nonetheless, even as labor operates more profoundly in the thrall of capital, in Marx's narrative, labor wants this dependent relation, insofar as it wants the concentration of capital. "[T]he expansion of capitalist production," Marx writes, "creates social want [*das gesellsaftliche Bedürfnis*] for those gigantic industrial enterprises, which depend for their realization on a previous centralisation of capitals" (687). Why do we want "the tendency to centralization" that begets multinational conglomerates, which exacerbates our "subjection... to capital" (687, 362)? The term "social want" surely includes the products (or efficiency) afforded by economies of scale. A "product satisfies a social want," Marx writes, or "newly developed social wants" (119, 672). We crave stuff, but if "social wants... are conditioned by the general state of social advancement" (256), social want more generally wants the concentration that seems to be the progressive law of history itself.

Self-expansion is the motivating desire of labor. Like a Darwinian species, laborers possess "instincts of self-preservation and of propagation" (627). Bear in mind that all value, whether it takes the form of commodity or currency, is congealed labor, the germ and prototype of capital. Concentration is the structural principle forming value. Moreover, *Verwertung* connotes expansion because it connotes "recovery" or "realization." For Marx, as for Franklin, people realize themselves through transactions, which are embodiments, or concentrations, of our vital energy, labor. In its very activity, labor propagates itself through concentration, and if labor constantly faces the prospect of constricted wages and replacement either by other workers or by machine, then to propagate, labor must pursue surplus. It must concentrate itself.

Transactions, the activity though which we realize labor, value, and "*propriâ persona*," are, in Marx, as in Keynes or Friedman or Franklin, by definition expansive. Smith thinks an existential "desire of bettering our condition" "animates" us (Smith 1937: 372, 93; also Smith 2002: 61). The cooperative labor in a factory exemplifies the urge to expand. "[T]he fusion of many forces into one single force," Marx writes, "begets in most industries an emulation and a stimulation of the animal spirits that heighten the efficiency of each individual workman" (358). "Emulation" (*Wetteifer*; competitive zeal) is a very specific word here, and ultimately implies interminable competitiveness and dissatisfaction with our present station, which we must always enhance. Smith linked "mutual emulation and the desire for greater gain" to laborers' impulse "to over-work themselves." Without competition, however, "there would be no emulation, and no... industry and ingenuity" (Smith 1937: 94, 163); and in *Theory of Moral Sentiments*, emulation is the psychic mechanism by which we form a moral sense, as we may emulate "humble modesty and equitable justice" as well as ostentatious wealth. Yet even if we just desire praise from an "impartial observer" for an ethical act, "[i]n the race for wealth, and honours," one may "strain every nerve and every muscle, in order to outstrip all... competitors" (Smith 2002: 73, 97).

Thorstein Veblen famously stressed the strain of "pecuniary emulation" in 1899. "Under the regime of individual ownership," we identify ourselves via our relation to the property of others (33). Wealth has become "intrinsically honourable," the basis of "reputability," "self-respect" and "self-esteem" (29). Because we experience ourselves via property relations, we identify ourselves "by an invidious pecuniary comparison with other[s]" (33). Veblen specifies that "pecuniary emulation" is not imitation of others, but "a straining to excel others" (32, 33). We strain not to keep up with the Joneses, but to surpass all possible Joneses, or Rockefellers, in particular ourselves. The "invidious standard" of comparison stretches indefinitely, and can never feel wholly "favourable." "[A]s fast as a person... becomes accustomed to [a] new standard of wealth, the new standard" becomes "the point of departure for a... new standard of sufficiency and a new pecuniary classification of one's self as compared with one's neighbours." We thus "live in chronic dissatisfaction with [our] present lot." No matter our achievements, "this chronic dissatisfaction [elicits] a restless straining to place a wider and ever-widening pecuniary interval between [one]self and [any] standard" (31).

If pecuniary emulation is Veblen's nightmare vision of ceaseless self-expansion, an anxious internalized instinct—which my students always say feels familiar—the emulation Marx notes among workers is fertile, sublated by the visibility of the group labor. Productive efficiency increases as each worker, instinctively obeying stimulated animal spirits, strives to exceed thy neighbor's production in order to outstrip the rate of exploitation. Animal spirits respond to the sheer fact of cooperation. The prospect of a collective product stimulates the individual to augment the collective enterprise. We glimpse in collective efficiency the concentration of our labor, intimation of the fulfillment of history, and thus enhancement of ourselves.

Whether anxiously competitive or potentially sublime, as presented by economic theorists, social want is not reducible to consumer desire but is a constitutive imperative to realize oneself by becoming more than oneself, achieving preservation by propagation, existence by expansion. Marx's term *Bedürfnis* nicely expresses this idea, with its connotation of need and demand as well as desire. Marx does remember the emulative urgency of social want. If Friedman believes that social want expresses our volition, and if Keynes, Friedman, and Franklin think all can achieve satisfaction through exchange, Marx ironizes the idea. Capital's anxious instinct to self-expansion both exemplifies and enlivens social want for indefinite expansion, uniting us in competition with others whenever capitalists seek to augment leverage and exploitation or workers desire wage increases or incur more debt to purchase the latest technological device, or health insurance.

In his seminal volume, *The Long Twentieth Century*, Giovanni Arrighi details the evolution of the mechanics of capital accumulation over different epochs.

> In every phase of financial expansion of the world-economy, the overabundance of money capital engendered by the diminishing returns and increasing risks of its employment in trade and production has been matched or even surpassed by a roughly synchronous expansion of the demand for money capital by organizations for which power and status, rather than profit, were the guiding principle of action.
>
> (232)

As Marx encouraged, Arrighi focuses on the successive crises prompted by the emulative, "successive systemic cycles of accumulation" (354). For Arrighi, economic crises begin with crunches in specific industries, as returns on capital investment decline, partly because of increased competition and partly because labor demands wage increases that acknowledge increased productivity. Laborers' dependence on wages renders them the most vulnerable during economic crises, as in response governments tend to support capital investment and credit instruments. Ricardo understood the irony that laborers should be "stimulated" to "have a taste for comforts and enjoyments" they can scarcely afford. Their expenditure floats the economy; yet, they "are exposed to the greatest vicissitudes and miseries" during economic "calamity" (100–1).

Ricardo anticipates what Marx details, and what we witnessed in the Savings and Loan and junk bond crisis of 1990, the burst of the .com bubble in 2000, and the global credit crisis of 2007–2010. All the while mergers among firms in the same industry and sometimes in disparate industries—to wit, Amazon's 2017 decision to purchase Whole Foods—accelerate. Efforts to concentrate capital intensify, often through debt, until "excessive leverage" outstrips productivity, employment, and consumption, and a contraction ensues (see Saleh 2010: 3–4, 48–50). Hence, scholars like Nouriel Roubini and Stephen Mihm advise readers to prepare for regular financial crises.

Roubini and Mihm's "crisis economics" are fairly typical. They believe that various regulations, like those instituted through the Glass-Steagall Banking Act of 1933, in particular with its segregation of commercial from investment banking, which were permitted to rejoin in 1999, can temper crises and their human costs. Recommendations from across the political spectrum consistently try to moderate concentration: increase capitalization requirements for banks, prohibit banks of a certain size, increase margin requirements on trades, and so forth. Joseph Stiglitz (on the left) and Judge Richard Posner (a defender of the idea of a "rational" market) both suggest, for example, limits on executive compensation, in particular by linking compensation to long-term performance rather than short-term stock gains (Posner 2009: 94, 97; Stiglitz 2010: 8, 13, 270). Robert Shiller, who deprecates the "irrational exuberance" aroused by pecuniary opportunity, triggering bubbles that inevitably burst, intriguingly advises that we "greatly expand the number and variety of markets," to facilitate trading of risky assets, distributing risk more widely (xii, 230).

Shiller's idea to expand markets surely accepts the structural principle of inevitable expansion and its counterparts self-expansion and social want, as does Thomas Piketty's "global tax on capital," which he knows is a utopian wish but which might moderate intensifying income inequality and market volatility and thus stabilize, increase, and smooth global economic growth over time (515, 524–27). For her part, suspicious of regulations that stifle human initiative, and reminding readers that competition for territory, shelter, food resources, and also women and children long predated market life, McCloskey has been advocating in recent work the dissemination of "bourgeois virtues" like "thrift and fair dealing" and "the human connections of the marketplace"—we should "temper[ ] our desires to a thrifty style"—to modulate economic volatility (McCloskey 2006: 48, 456). Wishing more to terminate than mitigate the human cost of "the ongoing crisis of the US regime of accumulation," Arrighi reproaches regulations for preserving the "systemic processes of capital accumulation" and the "competitive struggle" it fosters among nations, sparking military as well as economic violence. Arrighi glimpses the "end... of capitalist history" in the transfer of capital to East Asia, but nations in this region are rapidly the developing the military and administrative structures Arrighi hopes will disintegrate. The "succession of financial expansions" will continue, though with different dominant entities and with suffering and comfort differently distributed (355, 356, 355).

Philip Mirowski blames the need for capital accumulation and thus crises on the modern "banishment of the core unified self," with the self now understood as "a jumble of assets to be invested" (108). Mirowski conjures the end of social want. Marx, Franklin, and my other figures think that the self is transactional, and that what Keynes calls the "innate urge to activity" with others indeed forms the core of subjectivity (Keynes 1964: 163). Keynes and Veblen believe that emulation has become deeply ingrained over time. Marx deems self-expansion a natural instinct: "higher wages stimulate the working population to more rapid multiplication, and this goes on until the labour-market becomes too full, and therefore capital, relatively to the supply of labour, becomes insufficient" (Marx 1906: 699). Smith anticipates Marx's premise here, that any "species of animals naturally multiplies in proportion to the means of their subsistence" (Smith 1937: 91). The working population presumably enjoys more creature comforts with higher wages (and especially with fewer children); yet, it propagates as a first principle, just as capital seeks to propagate. I myself have never quite understood Darwin's idea (stressed more by his followers than by Darwin himself) that members of species "propagate their kind" to perpetuate the species, rendering population growth an evolutionary instinct (175, 80). How could an aggregate, I stupidly wonder, in particular groups incapable of writing and complex communication, recognize the prospect of extinction, and then engage in preemptive family (actually, species) planning? But we have seen that Marx ascribes to laborers "instincts of self-preservation and of propagation" (627). Economists posit a fundamental urge to self-expansion that capital expansion reflects, and if this premise is correct, the pressing problem of political economy would seem to be to manage expansion, to alter its distribution and human costs, and probably we should not just lament it. The calculations are hard, the ethical issues challenging, and political debate about the disposition of capital and the proper means of self-expansion is so often tendentious, self-serving, fruitless, and frustrating.

Keynes thought a primary cause of the Great Depression was "the failure of capital to accumulate" (as if capital accumulates itself; Keynes 1932: 360). At the end of *The General Theory*, Keynes envisions a relatively utopian scenario. Capital accumulation has stabilized at high levels, without the need of stimulation; population growth has plateaued; full employment abides; "the propensity to consume" has adjusted to this relative "equilibrium"; "the struggle for markets" ebbs, obviating international conflict; and individuals can engage in Friedman's ideal, "willing and unimpeded exchange of goods and services in conditions of mutual exchange" (379, 382, 383). Under these conditions, crises do not percolate because accumulation abstains and demand neither slackens nor exceeds equilibrium levels. Social want is suspended. In a 1930 essay, Keynes contemplates the eclipse of social want. Sufficient capital accumulation and technological advance will have solved "the *economic problem*." Basic needs and many comforts will be equitably distributed (Keynes 1932: 366; italics original). If people feel they must labor, fifteen-hour weeks are ample (369). Keynes wonders whether humans can then surrender social customs "promoting the accumulation of capital" (370), such as "love of money" and the urge to "feel superior to our fellows" (369, 365). Released from want, Keynes asks, can we pursue "the highest virtues"? Or should we ask instead if the highest virtues arise as a component of social want?

## References


Arrighi, Giovanni. (1994) *The Long Twentieth Century: Money, Power, and the Origins of Our Times*, London: Verso.

Darwin, Charles. (2008) *On the Origin of Species by Means of Natural Selection, or the Preservation of Favoured Raced in the Struggle for Life*, Oxford: Oxford University Press.

Franklin, Benjamin. "A Modest Inquiry into the Nature and Necessity of a Paper Currency" in *Benjamin Franklin: Selected Writings, Volume 2, Economic and Political Works*, London: William Pickering.

Friedman, Milton and Friedman, Rose D. (1962) *Capitalism and Freedom*, Chicago, IL: The University of Chicago Press.

Jefferson, Thomas. (1999) *Notes on the State of Virginia*, New York: Penguin.

Keynes, John Maynard. (1932) *Essays in Persuasion*, New York: Harcourt, Brace.

Keynes, John Maynard. (1964) *The General Theory of Employment, Interest, and Money*, New York: Harbinger/Harcourt, Brace & World.

Marx, Karl. (1906) *Capital: A Critique of Political Economy*, New York: Modern Library & Charles H. Kerr.

Marx, Karl. (1993) *Grundrisse*, New York: Penguin.

McCloskey, Deirdre N. (1990) *If You're So Smart: The Narrative of Economic Expertise*, Chicago, IL: The University of Chicago Press.

McCloskey, Deirdre N. (2006) *The Bourgeois Virtues: Ethics for an Age of Commerce*, Chicago, IL: University of Chicago Press.

McCloskey, Deirdre N. (2011) "The Rhetoric of the Economy and the Polity," *American Review of Political Science* 14.1: 181–99.

McCloskey, Deirdre N. (2015) "It Was Ideas and Ideologies, Not Interests or Institutions, Which Changed in Northwestern Europe, 1600–1848," *Journal of Evolutionary Economics* 25.1: 57–68.

McCloskey, Deirdre N. (2016a) *Bourgeois Equality: How Ideas, Not Capital, Transformed the World*, Chicago, IL: University of Chicago Press.

McCloskey, Deirdre N. (2016b) "The Great Enrichment: A Humanistic and Social Scientific Account," *Social Science History* 40.4: 583–598.

Mirowski, Phillip. (2013) *Never Let a Serious Crisis Go To Waste: How Neoliberalism Survived the Financial Meltdown*, London: Verso.
Paine, Thomas. (1982) *Common Sense*, New York: Penguin.
Piketty, Thomas. (2014) *Capital in the Twenty-First Century*, Cambridge, MA: Harvard University Press.
Posner, Richard A. (2009) *A Failure of Capitalism: The Crisis of '08 and the Descent into Depression*, Cambridge, MA: Harvard University Press.
Ricardo, David. (1951) *On the Principles of Political Economy and Taxation*, Cambridge: Cambridge University Press, 1951.
Roubini, Nouriel, and Mihm, Stephen. (2010) *Crisis Economics: A Crash Course in the Future of Finance*, New York: Penguin.
Saleh, Nashweh. (2010) *An Anatomy of the Financial Crisis: Blowing Tumbleweed*, New York: Anthem Press.
Schiller, Robert J. (2000) *Irrational Exuberance*, Princeton, NJ: Princeton University Press.
Simmel, Georg. (1971) "How Is Society Possible?" in Donald Levine (ed.) *On Individuality and Social Forms: Selected Writings*, Chicago, IL: The University of London Press.
Smith, Adam. (1937) *An Inquiry into the Nature and Causes of the Wealth of Nations*, New York: Modern Library.
Smith, Adam. (2002) *The Theory of Moral Sentiments*. Cambridge: Cambridge University Press.
Stiglitz, Joseph. (2010) *Freefall: America, Free Markets, and the Sinking of the World Economy*, New York: Norton.
Veblen, Thorstein. (1967) *The Theory of the Leisure Class*, New York: Penguin, 1967.

# 33
# SPECULATION

*Peter Knight*

Speculation has long loomed large in the cultural and legal imagination. Hoarding agricultural commodities to profit from rising prices in times of scarcity was forbidden in ancient Greece and Rome. Likewise in medieval Europe, activities that aimed to interfere with the "fair price" of common goods were condemned, with English common law, for example, prohibiting "engrossing," "forestalling," and "regrating" (Markham 2014: 10–13). However, such practices were not identified as speculation as such, with the word *speculation* only gaining a financial meaning in the late eighteenth century. Adam Smith was the first major writer to identify speculation as an economic as well as a moral problem for society. Smith defined speculation (or "overtrading") as prioritizing short-term opportunities for profit. In Smith's view, speculation became all too tempting in times of boom, but he nevertheless insisted that the government should not intervene in the market to prevent price gouging, trusting that the invisible hand of supply and demand would produce a better solution for society as a whole (Smith [1776] 1999: 105–7). From the eighteenth century onward, most commentators characterized speculation as buying and selling assets to benefit from fluctuations in price in the short term, whereas prudent investment involved making a financial commitment for the long term while receiving a steady income through dividends. However, this distinction was based more on moral sensibility than precise economic definition. What counted as short term? Was risk ordained by providence, or could its probability be calculated and therefore rationalized?

For much of the eighteenth and nineteenth centuries, a great deal of economic writing, both imaginative and factual, sought to make coherent moral and financial sense of the distinctions between speculation and investment. Speculation was frequently equated with gambling, with both condemned on moral and religious grounds. But by the end of the nineteenth century, speculation began to be theorized and dramatized as distinct from gambling, with some writers instead seeing it as a regular, necessary, and even a beneficial element of economic activity. As the nineteenth century progressed, gambling as a way of getting something for nothing remained taboo because it was antithetical to notions of thrift and hard work, and at the same time it was negatively identified as an affliction of the working class. In contrast, speculation was increasingly represented as a respectable form of profit-making through risk, a legitimate part of business. The evil of gambling thus formed a necessary negative analogue to speculation (Fabian 1999; Itzkowitz 2002; de Goede 2005).

Though condemned by the public and populist politicians alike, speculation as a distinct category of financial activity tended to pass beneath the radar of the emerging academic discipline of economics until the tail end of the nineteenth century. In one of the first works to address the topic directly, the anonymously published *Le manuel du spéculateur à la bourse* (1854) [Manual of the Stock Exchange Speculator], Pierre-Joseph Proudhon did not, as might have been expected, mount a moralistic attack on stock market speculation. Instead, he marveled at its capacity as a vital force animating economic expansion, for better or worse. Proudhon recognized that speculation had become divorced from actual labor or material goods, and merely involved making money from money, becoming a self-referential play of signs that seemed to have little to do with the "real" economy (on this reading of Proudhon, see Goux 1997). In the eyes of its critics, however, speculation was attacked precisely for being parasitic on the real work of the economy. In the last decades of the nineteenth century in the United States, for example, farmers complained bitterly about speculation in "wind wheat," as they termed the "fictitious dealing" on the Chicago Board of Trade in future contracts for grain that far exceeded the actual crop being grown (Cowing 1965).

But Henry Crosby Emery, in the first full-length academic treatise on the subject (submitted to Columbia as a PhD in 1896), argued that speculation was not an aberration of free market capitalism but its purest expression. In Emery's account, the rapid, repeated, and unfettered exchange of liquid, intangible assets like corporate shares and commodity futures allowed the true price to be established through the natural laws of supply and demand. Far from distorting the market, speculation in these "frictionless" markets (in the terminology of present-day economic theory) fulfilled a useful economic function by helping make prices more accurately reflect the underlying value of the assets. On this line of thinking, the trade in derivative securities (options and futures) was not merely a shadow of the seemingly more real production of physical commodities, but was a form of production in itself. Price setting was the result of intellectual labor, the product of expertise on the part of stock market operators, coupled with the magic of the invisible hand coordinating supply and demand (on the legal decisions upholding the intellectual property rights of the stock exchanges, see Hochfelder (2006) and Levy (2012)). The speculator thus came to be figured not as a reckless gambler but as a specialist in risk, who contributed to creating rational and efficient markets. Speculation, it was argued, did not necessarily cause wild fluctuations but instead served to stabilize prices. The ability to hedge was claimed to provide a vital form of insurance against an uncertain future for those less able to shoulder the financial risk. Speculation was thus represented as a barometer of the future, helping make economically expansive futures visible. Unlike gambling, whose bets on the future had no effect on the outcome, speculation had the seemingly magical potential to create self-fulfilling prophecies: an optimistic market sentiment could have the effect of kick-starting a boom in the "real" economy, just as a bearish foreboding in the stock exchange could cause the gears of production to come to a grinding halt (Stäheli 2013).

The sticking point for many commentators was that speculation might be tolerated, perhaps even welcomed, if it was confined solely to experts, but increasingly ordinary outsiders – "lambs," in stock market parlance – were getting caught up in speculative frenzies (more at the legally dubious bucket shops than the legitimate exchanges), and in the process creating irrational bubbles. For example, in his landmark 1905 ruling on bucket shops, Supreme Court Justice Oliver Wendell Holmes insisted that speculation carried out "by competent men" involved the rational "self-adjustment of society to the probable" (i.e. through the calculation of probability rather than mere fanciful speculation about possible futures). "Its value," Holmes continued, "is well known as a means of avoiding catastrophes, equalizing prices, and providing for periods of want." For Holmes, it was therefore important to distinguish between "speculation which is carried on by persons of means and experience, and based on an intelligent forecast, and that which is carried on by persons without these regular qualifications" (Board of Trade 1905: 246–9). The political debate therefore revolved around the question of whether amateur speculators should be protected from exploitation, or actively discouraged from participation in trading. Economic theory, however, began to adopt a different approach to the problem. While Emery conceded that a minority of individual speculators might indeed be misguided, he advised against restricting outsiders from playing the markets, because they not only introduced much-needed liquidity, but their aggregated efforts to guess the future tended to converge naturally on the right price. Emery thus anticipated much late twentieth-century economic thinking about speculation based on the belief that the "wisdom of the crowd" ensured that the market was by definition always right.

## Speculative representations

Over the last three centuries, theorists of finance have reframed speculation as a vital element of economic life. But why might literature be interested in speculation? Although at first sight it would seem that creative writing has little to do with the problem of speculation, there is a good reason to believe that there is a close connection between speculative projections and fiction. Jens Beckert, for example, has argued that economic activity proceeds less by rational calculation than by imagination, with the speculative conjuring up of future riches in a world that does not (yet) exist. Literature is therefore best placed to help us make sense of the "fictional expectations" of future-oriented finance, and literary theory is a necessary toolkit for reading the writings of financial capitalism. Beckert shows how imagined outcomes of economic endeavor are sustained by persuasive *narratives* that try to legitimate and make imaginatively and immersively real an uncertain future. Like fiction, speculative projects – and the entire credit economy – manage to create unreal worlds that nevertheless can become self-fulfilling prophecies, helping forge the world they imagine.

Beckert's argument is driven by a historical claim that modern capitalism changed how people thought about the future. Where Max Weber identified delayed gratification, steady accumulation, and worldly success confirming salvation as the engine transforming traditional societies, Beckert highlights a shift from a pre-modern circular view of time to a more linear and future-oriented one. Capitalism might therefore be animated not by the spirit of Protestantism but by the spirit of speculation. Although there might be a deep connection between imaginative and economic speculations, the difficulty with speculative finance is that in recent decades, it has become increasingly abstract, impersonal, self-referential, opaque, and often invisible, despite its outsized effect on society at large. Indeed, there is the question of whether financial speculation can ever be rendered realistically in literature because the seemingly infinite regress of monetary signs circulating in endlessly complex chains of economic substitution is impossible to dramatize. Since the eighteenth century, the credit economy and its paper fictions have periodically pulled away from the "real" economy of products and services to become their own self-sustaining world. This raises the possibility that speculation can only ever be addressed figuratively, or through proxy forms of spectacular financial drama.

So how has British and American literature engaged with speculation in practice? Such a history might begin with Daniel Defoe, who, like other commentators on political economy in the period surrounding the South Sea Bubble (1720), condemned "stock-jobbing" as being like a game of hazard. Although Defoe accepted the necessity of an economic system based not on land but on circulation and credit because it encouraged an attitude of trust that was beneficial to trade more generally, he also deplored the seductive temptations of the fickle "Lady Credit" (Defoe 1706: 17–18). For Defoe, the problem was that the fluctuation of prices in the stock market was less likely to result from rational deliberation than from deception and manipulation (De Goede 2005: 27–35; Stäheli 2013: 30–4). For all that Defoe's nonfiction writing presents a stirring critique of the stock market, his fiction can nevertheless be read as embodying the spirit of speculation, albeit in an ambivalent fashion. Valerie Hamilton and Martin Parker argue that both the novel and joint stock companies are products of the "Projecting Age," in the phrase coined by Defoe in *Essay upon Projects* (1697). The disruptive nature of finance allowed it to undermine traditional aristocratic patterns of wealth and social hierarchy based on real estate. In effect, the Financial Revolution and the speculative projects like the Bank of England it engendered were as radical as the novel in overturning established ways of being and thinking. Just as *Moll Flanders* (1722) permitted readers to experience risky, rip-roaring adventures through the controlled confines of a narrative that convention ensures will turn out for the best, so too did a speculative project like the Bank of England enable investors to engage in risky ventures within the comparatively safe legal structure of a joint-stock company. Both the novelist and the banker are thus "managers of uncertainty" (Hamilton and Parker 2016: 130). Defoe and Paterson (one of the Bank's founders) are chancers, storytellers whose fabulations require a credibility-generating suspension of disbelief from their audiences, but which then come to take on a life and a solidity of their own. Readers of literature, like stock market players, invest their faith in an uncertain future, lending their credit to those projecting a convincing narrative. More generally, the emergence of the novel was shaped by and, in turn, helped forge the rise of financial capitalism, because it conditioned readers to take imaginary worlds represented by paper instruments as if they were real (Sherman 1996).

In its structural form, then, there are important affinities between novel and speculation; yet at the level of content, much writing in the eighteenth century – from melodramatic comedies to political economy pamphlets – remained opposed to risky financial endeavors. Speculation was deplored not merely because it seemed to be gambling by any other name, but also because it destabilized the social order, "weakening government, diverting capital, creating a monopoly, and perversion by luxury" (Preda 2009: 176). In the decades following the Revolution, many American commentators likewise saw the new forms of finance as injurious to the republic and its values, criticizing both private and public indebtedness as a form of effeminizing slavery. Speculation – both land speculation and credit based on paper money – was viewed as the irresponsible building of castles in the air. However, in some writing of the period (by, for example, Cotton Mather, Benjamin Franklin, Royall Tyler, Charles Brockden Brown, and Judith Sargent Murray), debt, and the paper bills that created it, was presented as a positive social good because it fostered national development, cohesion, and trust, all the while reinforcing the bonds of sympathy between individuals (Baker 2005). For some eighteenth-century American thinkers, the market revolution thus did not so much destroy the older bonds of personal sympathy as create them anew by enabling citizens to recognize the connective web of mutual obligation forged by the speculative credit economy.

In the nineteenth century, this Hamiltonian strain in American letters was out-voiced by a moralizing and religious rhetoric opposed to speculation because it led, like gambling, to a state of addiction; to the false hope of getting something for nothing; and to the loss of manly, republican self-control (Weyler 1996; Anthony 2009). To outside observers, though, America was a land of speculation. Harriet Martineau commented in 1837 that in Chicago "the streets were crowded with land speculators, hurrying from one sale to another" to the extent that "it seemed as if some prevalent mania infected the whole people," while the French economist Michael Chevalier found that "[e]very body is speculating, and every thing has become an object of speculation" (Martineau 1837; Chevalier 1839, qtd. in Banner 2017: 7). Yet, the spirit of speculation in the United States was not confined to the frontiersman, the trickster, and confidence artist. Like financial speculation, transcendental philosophy operated by conjecture and abstraction, rhetorically anticipating a future that it tried to make convincingly real. In his prose writings, Emerson, for example, speculatively projects dream-like visions that are in thrall to circulation and speed, the philosophical equivalent of the real estate boosters and financial hucksters of his day (Lawson 2013).

It is also arguable that American realism developed in the antebellum period as a counterweight to the sense of instability and immateriality created by the repeated financial panics. According to this line of thinking, realism creates not a duplicitous illusion of verisimilitude, but an ongoing dialogue with the very question of what constitutes reality in a capitalist economy, in which the world is neither stable nor entirely knowable. The repeated financial panics of the nineteenth century – in particular the Panic of 1837 – led some Americans to question the very nature of social reality, with (as Marx put it) all that seemed solid suddenly melting into air with the proliferation of "fictitious capital" (Lepler 2013; McClanahan 2013). An aesthetic of the concrete and particular rather than the abstract – a "hunger for the real" (Lawson 2012) – was felt most intensely by the lower middle class, whose precarious social situation made them most vulnerable to the rapidly shifting sands of the emerging market economy. Realism in the American context thus emerged not as a simple reflection of economic changes but as a "structure of feeling" (in Raymond Williams's term), and a creative counterreaction to the repeated shocks of finance experienced in the formative years of writers who began to publish from the 1850s onward.

With speculation increasingly presented in the second half of the nineteenth century by Wall Street and City insiders as a scientific discipline rather than a morally suspect melodrama, the world of finance did not seem an obvious topic for novelists. However, some writers came to recognize the potential of the stock market to provide gripping material for stories. In *Extraordinary Popular Delusions and the Madness of Crowds* (1841), the book that introduced the idea of stock market mania to a wide audience, Charles Mackay suggested that, with its rapid twists and turns of fortune, coupled with outbursts of mass hysteria, "the subject is capable of inspiring as much interest as even a novelist can desire" (Mackay 1995 [1841]: 74). By the beginning of the twentieth century, the Wall Street grandee and prolific writer Henry Clews could confidently declare that "[t]here is no more interesting or exciting serial story than the stock-ticker tells, from day to day, to those interested in the stock market, or one that often excites more joy or sorrow, or carries with it more weal or woe, prosperity or ruin" (Clews 1908: 759). An early example of literature's engagement with speculation can be found in the imaginative response by late Romantic writers such as Lord Byron, John Galt, and Walter Scott to the first global stock market panic that began in Britain in 1825. Their self-reflexive works provided allegories of speculation that highlighted its reliance on fictional imagination in a world of contingent futures (Dick 2012; Esterhammer 2017). More broadly, the Victorian novel, in a variety of modes from the silver-fork fiction of the 1840s to the sensation stories of the 1860s and late-century realism, experienced a shift in its economic story line from the inheritance plot to the speculation plot that registered the indeterminacy and instability at the heart of financial capitalism (Wagner 2010).

The realist novel in nineteenth-century Britain thus began to train readers in the new financial reality of an economy fueled by credit and riven by repeated financial crashes that undermined the belief that individuals were solely responsible for their own economic well-being. Fiction provided a safe space of imaginative projection, a speculative realm in which to explore the causes and consequences of financial speculation for both individual characters and the wider society. In Charles Dickens's *Little Dorrit* (1855–7), for example, the inheritance plot is trumped by the speculation plot as the source of reversals of fate. William Dorrit is released from debtors' prison when Arthur Clennam discovers that he is the long lost heir to a considerable fortune, but then Clennam is himself ruined when his investment is lost in the collapse of Merdle's joint-stock company promotion and banking business, and the latter's subsequent suicide. In a further twist, it turns out that Amy Dorrit is herself the heiress to an even larger fortune, but she keeps this knowledge to herself to protect family secrets, enabling her to marry Clennam, whose fortune is restored not by a lost inheritance but by the revival of his partner's business. In its attention to the attractions and dangers of speculation, *Little Dorrit* drew on the "Railway Mania" of speculative stock market investment that gripped Britain in the 1840s, as well as the proliferation of cases of financial misdealings, especially in the summer of 1855, as Dickens began writing the novel, including scandals involving fraud and embezzlement among the partners at the banking firm of Strahan, Paul, and Bates and at the Irish Tipperary Bank, involving the MP and Treasury official John Sadlier, who committed suicide early the following year. Yet, as Mary Poovey argues in her account of how literary writing became separated from economic representation, Dickens downplayed the connection between Sadlier and Merdle, leaving the details of the actual financial practices vague, while the speculation subplot is merely a minor one within the larger story of the redemptive power of love (Poovey 2008: 375).

Speculation invokes a temporal acceleration (the emphasis, after all, is on the attraction and dangers of getting rich quick), and the formal analogue in Dickens's novel is narrative suspense, that leads readers to race forward in their reading for the plot. In contrast, "locating narrative pleasure outside the masculine realm of finance and the frenzy of suspense, *Little Dorrit* stabilizes character by rooting it in the temporality of the domestic" (Jewusiak 2016: 281). Moreover, the ending of *Little Dorrit* suggests a fantasy return to an older, nonfinancial form of commerce with the resurgence of the partnership of Doyce and Clennam that, in turn, permits the resolution of the plot with the marriage of Amy Dorrit and Clennam. Although the collapse of the house of Merdle threatens to ripple ever outward, by contrast in Anthony Trollope's *The Way We Live Now* (1875), the ruin of the banker Melmotte does not bring about a system-wide calamity. In Trollope's novel, speculation is normalized and domesticated, even if not fully embraced in social terms (after all, Melmotte is characterized as an upstart Jewish money lender). The ending, however, goes further than *Little Dorrit* in its recalibration of the social acceptability of speculation, with the marriage between Paul Montague and Hetta Carbury uniting (with their son's future inheritance of Carbury Manor) the landed wealth of the aristocracy with the new money of the City (Lannon 2009).

Toward the tail end of the nineteenth century, American literary realist and naturalist writers also began to address the issue of speculation, albeit in a more ambivalent fashion than their British counterparts. William Dean Howells's *The Rise of Silas Lapham* (1885), for instance, seems to present a straightforward moralistic attack on the dangers of speculation, as it traces the declining economic fortunes of the self-made paint manufacturer as a result of unwise stock market gambles and real estate calamities. At the end of the novel, Lapham has returned to his humble origins on the family farm, to start over again in hands-on production and trade, forsaking the illusory gains of the stock market. Although it might seem that he ends up agreeing with his wife Persis that speculation is no better than gambling, he nonetheless does not renounce business entirely, but instead makes a distinction between good and bad speculative prospects. Howells, in both his fiction and his literary criticism, floated the argument that the realist writer in fact resembles the professional speculator: both use expertise and experience to disclose the underlying reality beneath the surface distractions (Wonham 2016).

As growing numbers of ordinary citizens in both Britain and the US became attracted to stock market speculation in the years about the turn of the twentieth century, fiction writers began to address the world of the City and Wall Street more directly (Zimmerman 2006). In *The Pit* (1903), for example, Frank Norris tells the story of Jadwin Curtis, the arch speculator who attempts to corner the market in wheat. The novel seems to suggest that financial value, as much as aesthetic value, is in the eye of the beholder, with the financier as the genius who understands and is able to control the new world of fungible value. In Norris's account of a speculative economy, "copyist" realism gives way to a kind of epic romance that aims to understand the "elemental forces" of supply and demand that create the global market. Yet, the novel ultimately rejects the semiotics of speculation because it shows how the fluctuating prices on the Board of Trade ignore the resolutely real value of the commodity being traded. The irrepressible fertility of the wheat provides the ultimate material source of value in *The Pit*, and the drama of the produce exchange is merely a sideshow to this inhuman life force (Horwitz 1991). In a related fashion, Dreiser's *The Financier* (1912) pushes the biographical novel to its generic limits. Where other financial fictions are often hazy about the precise monetary and logistical details of speculation, Dreiser's novel overwhelms the reader with its detailed accounting of Cowperwood's hypothecations (Zimmerman 2006). It is less the life history of an individual Napoleon of finance than the biography of speculative capital itself, which threatens to become uncontainable and unrepresentable in the immensely convoluted chains of debt and credit that bind the novel's characters. *The Financier* is thus a far cry from the morality tales of the eighteenth century, and indeed most of the melodramatic Wall Street fictions of the Gilded Age. Speculative capital is the subject – in both senses of the word – of a novel whose determining environment is less the natural world than the amoral and abstract realm of economics.

If literary realism functions partly in reaction to the rise of commodity capitalism, then the abstractions of modernism are, in turn, a response to the abstractions of financial speculation. According to Jean-Joseph Goux, there is a "homological" relationship between the abandonment of the gold standard and the abandonment of realist representation in modernist art and literature, along with the bracketing of the referent – the real, material thing – in structural linguistics. In its formal experiments, modernist literature replicates the shift to forms of value that are both self-referential and free-floating. Thus while a work like *Ulysses* (1922) only fleetingly engages with the problem of speculation at the level of content, its aesthetic innovations are nevertheless shaped by the changing nature of finance capital. Its continual, intertextual displacement of cultural allusions creates, like speculative capitalism itself, a self-referential semiotic economy that threatens to become unmoored from its referent. Likewise, its use of narrative stream of consciousness mimics the ceaseless flow of the stock ticker, a fetishized technology of financial representation which, like modernist art in general, ended up making the medium of communication itself the focus on attention. Yet, as Christopher Kempf argues, the novel ultimately remains wedded to a realist aesthetic of the commodity, resisting the mystificatory *mise-en-abyme* of self-referentiality, and instead looks to the lived personal and political relations of debt that structure Irish society.

Since the 1970s, financialization has become central to the global economy: with the closing of the gold window in 1971, all currencies became free-floating; the source of corporate profit has come increasingly from financial speculation rather than industrial production; with the explosion of new financial instruments, coupled with the dismantling of regulatory mechanisms, the shadow world of derivatives trading now infinitely dwarfs the so-called "real economy." Financialization has saturated everywhere, turning citizens into speculators on their own life prospects (Martin 2002). A number of commentators (Jameson 1997; Taylor 2004; Haiven 2014) have suggested that finance capital has profoundly influenced cultural production, from everyday popular culture to postmodern literature. The question, however, is whether the art, literature, and film produced within the regime of speculative capitalism is capable of critique, or whether it tends merely to replicate a dizzying fascination with the abstraction and semiotic excess of finance. It can at times seem that the contemporary financial system has anticipated much poststructuralist literary theory, thereby defusing its critical potential (Tratner 2004; Clover 2014). Its "semiotic events" – the "play of economic signs" involved in price fluctuations – need to be "read and interpreted" (Vogl 2015: 12–13). With the proliferation of exotic new products of financial engineering such as the $CDO^2$ (a collateralized debt obligation that is itself made up of other CDOs), speculative finance appears increasingly self-referential, a "regime of free-floating signifiers" that create a "crisis of representation," leading potentially to a complete breakdown of meaning (Vogl 2015: 59–61). Yet despite the suspicion that the critical edge of poststructuralist criticism is blunted because it merely replicates in theory what neoliberal capitalism has been instituting in practice, the idea that finance is turning into a semiotic hall of mirrors still presents an important challenge to the myth at the heart of orthodox economics: a rational and efficient market whose prices perfectly represent wider economic reality (Fox 2009).

Since the 2000s, the traditional theatrical spectacle of open-cry trading has been replaced by the anonymous and invisible exchanges between computers using proprietary algorithms, with transactions happening at lightning speed. In a financial world increasingly dominated by High Frequency Trading (HFT), the time frame of transactions is infinitesimally small, beyond human perception, and seemingly beyond human control, with the growing specter of so-called flash crashes. If speculation is distinguished from investment by being short-term, then this is a speculative regime measured in nanoseconds. At the same time, the scale of financial trading in the realm of shadow banking is beyond ordinary imagination (and regulatory oversight). By 2007, a quadrillion dollars worth of derivatives were being traded per year, which is more than ten times the total value of the entire production of global manufacturing over the last century (Stewart 2012). The material reality of algorithmic finance has thus become increasingly posthuman, and seemingly impossible to represent – though Robert Harris's *The Fear Index* (2011), a rewriting of *Frankenstein*, makes a reasonable effort to capture the scary possibility of a posthuman form of machinic agency.

The irony, however, is that the dominant mode of literary responses to the global financial crisis of 2007–8 has seen a return to the familiar tradition of realism, from

Sebastian Faulks's tale of amoral bankers to John Lanchester's self-conscious rewriting of the Victorian state-of-the-nation novel (for a survey of such works, see Shaw 2015). Yet, the turn to realism in both popular thrillers and much literary fiction about finance at times serves to make visible the everyday textures of speculative capitalism, rather than merely repeating the primal scene of the poststructuralist crisis of representation. Capital might be increasingly fictitious, but the real fiction is the fantasy that the world of finance has become completely free-floating and abstracted, separate from all social relations and impossible to understand or critique (Finch 2015). At the same time as the resurgence of realism, however, alternative modes of imaginative engagement with the world made by financialization are also beginning to emerge, including speculative writing – science fiction and fantasy – that is attuned to the posthuman landscape of contemporary speculation (Carroll and McClanahan 2015). Given the increasingly fictitious nature of speculation, literature perhaps needs to become not more mimetic but more self-reflexive about the representational mystifications of contemporary finance (Shonkwiler 2107).

## References

Anthony, David. (2009) *Paper Money Men: Commerce, Manhood, and the Sensational Public Sphere in Antebellum America*, Columbus: Ohio State University Press.

Baker, Jennifer J. (2005) *Securing the Commonwealth: Debt, Speculation, and Writing in the Making of Early America*, Baltimore, MD: Johns Hopkins University Press.

Banner, Stuart. (2017) *Speculation: A History of the Fine Line Between Gambling and Investing*, New York: Oxford University Press.

Beckert, Jens. (2016) *Imagined Futures: Fictional Expectations and Capitalist Dynamics*, Harvard, MA: Harvard University Press.

Board of Trade of the City of Chicago v. Christie Grain & Stock Co. (1905) 198 U.S. 236.

Carroll, Hamilton, and Annie McClanahan. (2015) "Fictions of Speculation: Introduction," *Journal of American Studies* 49 (4), 655–61.

Chevalier, Michel. (1839) *Society, Manners, and Politics in the United States*, Boston, MA: Weeks, Jordan & Co.

Clews, Henry. (1908) *Fifty Years in Wall Street*, New York: Irving.

Clover, Joshua. (2014) "*Retcon*: Value and Temporality in Poetics," *Representations* 126 (1), 9–30.

Cowing, Cedric B. (1965) *Populists, Plungers, and Progressives: A Social History of Stock and Commodity Speculation, 1890–1936*, Princeton, NJ: Princeton University Press.

De Goede, Marieke. (2005) *Virtue, Fortune and Faith: A Genealogy of Finance*, Minneapolis: University of Minnesota Press.

Defoe, Daniel. (1706) *Review of the State of the English Nation*, no. 5, January 10. Repr. Arthur Wellesley Secord, vol. 3, book 6, New York: AMS Press, 1965.

Dick, Alexander. (2012) "Walter Scott and the Financial Crash of 1825: Fiction, Speculation, and the Standard of Value," *Romantic Circles*, www.rc.umd.edu/praxis/forgery/HTML/praxis.2011.dick.html

Emery, Henry Crosby. (1904) *Speculation on the Stock and Produce Exchanges in the United States*, New York: Macmillan.

Esterhammer, Angela. (2017) "Speculation in the Late-Romantic Literary Marketplace," *Victoriographies* 7 (1), 7–24.

Fabian, Ann. (1999) *Card Sharps and Bucket Shops: Gambling in Nineteenth-Century America*, New York: Routledge.

Finch, Laura. (2015) "The Un-real Deal: Financial Fiction, Fictional Finance, and the Financial Crisis," *Journal of American Studies* 49 (4), 731–53.

Fox, Justin. (2009) *The Myth of the Rational Market: A History of Risk, Reward, and Delusion on Wall Street*, New York: HarperBusiness.

Goux, Jean-Joseph. (1994) *The Coiners of Language*, trans. Jennifer Curtiss Gage, Norman: University of Oklahoma Press.

Goux, Jean-Joseph. (1997) "Values and Speculations: The Stock Exchange Paradigm," *Journal for Cultural Research* 1 (2), 159–77.
Haiven, Max. (2014) *Cultures of Financialization: Fictitious Capital in Popular Culture and Everyday Life*, New York: Palgrave.
Hamilton, Valerie and Martin Parker. (2016) *Daniel Defoe and the Bank of England: The Dark Arts of Projectors*, Winchester: Zero Books.
Hochfelder, David. (2006) "'Where the Common People Could Speculate': The Ticker, Bucket Shops, and the Origins of Popular Participation in Financial Markets, 1880–1920," *Journal of American History* 93, 335–58.
Horwitz, Howard. (1991) *By the Law of Nature: Form and Value in Nineteenth-Century America*, New York: Oxford University Press.
Itzkowitz, David C. (2002) "Fair Enterprise or Extravagant Speculation: Investment, Speculation, and Gambling in Victorian England," *Victorian Studies* 45 (1), 121–47.
Jameson, Fredric. (1997) "Culture and Finance Capital," *Critical Inquiry* 24 (1), 246–65.
Jewusiak, Jacob. (2016) "Suspenseful Speculation and the Pleasure of Waiting in *Little Dorrit*," *Victorian Literature and Culture* 44 (2), 279–96.
Kempf, Christopher. (2017) "'Addicted to the lubric a little': Spectacle, Speculation, and the Language of Flow in Ulysses," *Modernism/Modernity* 24 (1), 23–43.
Lannon, Colleen. (2009) "Gambling and/on the Exchange: The Victorian Novel and the Legitimization of the Stock Market," PhD, Boston College.
Lawson, Andrew. (2012) *Downwardly Mobile: The Changing Fortunes of American Realism*, Oxford: Oxford University Press.
Lawson, Andrew. (2013) "An Emotional History of the Business Cycle," *Journal of Cultural Economy* 6 (1), 30–44.
Lepler, Jessica M. (2013) *The Many Panics of 1837: People, Politics, and the Creation of a Transatlantic Financial Crisis*, Cambridge: Cambridge University Press.
Levy, Jonathan. (2012) *Freaks of Fortune: The Emerging World of Capitalism and Risk in America*, Cambridge, MA: Harvard University Press.
Mackay, Charles. (1995 [1841]) *Extraordinary Popular Delusions and the Madness of Crowds*, Hertfordshire: Wordsworth.
Markham, Jerry W. (2014) *Law Enforcement and the History of Financial Market Manipulation*, London: Routledge.
Martin, Randy (2002) *The Financialization of Daily Life*, Philadelphia, PA: Temple University Press.
Martineau, Harriet. (1837) *Society in America*, London: Saunders and Otley.
McClanahan, Annie. (2013) "Investing in the Future: Late Capitalism's End of History," *Journal of Cultural Economy* 6 (1), 78–93.
Poovey, Mary. (2008) *Genres of the Credit Economy: Mediating Value in Eighteenth- and Nineteenth-Century Britain*, Chicago, IL: University of Chicago Press.
Preda, Alex. (2009) *Framing Finance: The Boundaries of Markets and Modern Capitalism*. Chicago, IL: University of Chicago Press.
Proudhon, Pierre-Joseph. (1854) *Manuel du spéculateur à la Bourse* [Manual of the Stock Exchange Speculator], Paris: Marcel Rivière & Cie.
Shaw, Katy. (2015) *Crunch Lit*, London: Bloomsbury.
Sherman, Sandra. (1996) *Finance and Fictionality in the Early Eighteenth Century: Accounting for Defoe*, Cambridge: Cambridge University Press.
Shonkwiler, Alison. (2017) *The Financial Imaginary: Economic Mystification and the Limits of Realist Fiction*, Minneapolis: University of Minnesota Press.
Smith, Adam. (1999 [1776]) *The Wealth of Nations*, Books IV–V, Harmondsworth: Penguin.
Stäheli, Urs. (2013) *Spectacular Speculation: Thrills, the Economy, and Popular Discourse*, Stanford, CA: Stanford University Press.
Stewart, Ian. (2012) "The Equation that Caused the Banks to Crash," *Observer*, 12 February.
Taylor, Mark C. (2004) *Confidence Games: Money and Markets in a World without Redemption*, Chicago, IL: University of Chicago Press.
Tratner, Michael. (2004) "Derrida's Debt to Milton Friedman," *New Literary History* 34, 791–806.
Vogl, Joseph. (2014) *The Specter of Capital*, Stanford, CA: Stanford University Press.
Wagner, Tamara S. (2010) *Financial Speculation in Victorian Fiction: Plotting Money and the Novel Genre, 1815–1901*, Columbus: Ohio State University Press.

Weber, Max. (2002 [1904]) *The Protestant Ethic and the 'Spirit' of Capitalism and Other Writings*, Harmondsworth: Penguin.
Weyler, Karen A. (1996) "'A Speculating Spirit': Trade, Speculation, and Gambling in Early American Fiction," *Early American Literature* 31 (3), 207–42.
Wonham, Henry B. (2016) "Realism and the Stock Market," *Nineteenth Century Literature* 70 (4), 473–95.
Zimmerman, David. (2006) *Panic!: Markets, Crises, and Crowds in American Fiction*, Chapel Hill: University of North Carolina Press.

# PART IV

# Contemporary culture

# 34

# "THE REAL HOME OF CAPITALISM"

## The AOL Time Warner merger and capital flight

*Michael Szalay*

Announced ten days into the new millennium, AOL's $350 purchase of Time Warner, still the largest merger in U.S. history, was by most accounts an epochal affair. *USA Today* called it "one of those rare events that seems to change the world overnight." Tom Brokaw announced, "a whole new universe created overnight."[1] *Business Week* thought that it heralded "a new world order" because "the digital will prevail over the analog, new media will grow faster than old, and the leaders of the Net economy will become the 21st Century Establishment." Roger McNamee, the Silicon Venture Capitalist, told *Time*, "This is the single most transformational event I've seen in my career."[2] Tim Armstrong, then an executive at Google: "I just remember reading the deal and thinking the world had changed." Time Warner CEO Jerry Levin echoed *Business Week* when he offered a what had become a typical account of the implications of that change: "We were emerging from not just old media but from an analog world into a digital world," he said, "and philosophically people were beginning to understand that the digital world was a transformational universe."[3]

In 2000, AOL was a young Internet Service Provider with a big user base. It packaged email software and basic content with dial-up broadband; during the 1990s, it had built up its customer list by mailing millions of CDs to new clients. Time Warner was what would soon be called an "old media" company: among other things, it was made up of film and television studios; book and magazine imprints; and extensive cable holdings, like HBO, CNN, and TNT. The logic behind the merger of the two companies went something like this: heavily reliant on the low-bandwidth twisted copper wires that make up telephone lines, AOL needed a network of coaxial cables, the better to deliver Internet access to its customers. And threatened by the likelihood of readily available free Internet access offered by its competitors, and therefore by the prospect that its wildly inflated share price would come crashing to earth, it needed to buy a corporation with established revenues—ideally one with a library of content deep enough to allow it to continue to justify the access fees it charged. The largest media conglomerate on earth, Time Warner had steady revenues and the nation's second largest network of cable lines, as well as extensive holdings in television, film, music, and print media. It had been chasing hazy dreams of interactive TV for years, and had failed to establish any significant presence on the Internet; its executives, CEO Jerry Levin above all, felt that they needed to make a bold move in digital media. Both companies believed in the magic of synergy. As AOL CEO Steve Case put it in 2001,

> the basic bet is that convergence is going to happen, and it's not just about the TV. It's about knitting together the PC, the TV, the telephone, and the stereo to allow people to be entertained in better ways, to be educated in better ways, to communicate in better ways, to change people's lives.
>
> *(F 227)*

And then there was the heady promise of cross promotion: wanting to secure an advertising deal with Victoria's Secret soon after the merger, AOL approached HBO about airing a Victoria Secret's fashion show (HBO was incensed); and, wait, let's have Mel Gibson record the voice-over that greeted AOL subscribers when they logged on! (Time Warner executives struggled to convince AOL executives that actors didn't directly work for their company) (F 220).

And yet neither Y2K millennialism nor any euphoria over the economic promise of the Internet quite explains the rhetorical grandiosity that surrounded the merger. Whence "the great epiphany-of-life kind of journalism," asked Eduardo Mestre, one of the investment bankers who worked on the financing, that "brought tears to your eyes," and seemed to be about "the second coming of the Messiah"? An answer might begin with Mestre's tendency, shared by many who brokered the deal, to cast the transaction as an exchange not of stock but of different kinds of legal tender. When announcing the merger, Levin was asked how he could justify accepting AOL stock as "legitimate currency," as if he were a head of state who had just decided to accept what some called "Internet wampum" as the coin of the realm.[4] And, in fact, journalists speculated openly that they were witnessing the metamorphosis of the transnational corporation into something like a nation-state. "Were we supposed to regard this as just a business story?" Michael Wolff asked about the news conference that announced the merger.

> Where were the reporters from the national desk? The foreign desk, even?... We're going to miss the meaning of this story, I started to think, because the right desk doesn't exist. Perhaps there should be a corporate-state desk. In that light, the AOL-Time Warner merger might be up there at some Munich Pact-Suez Canal-League of Nations level, or an entirely new kind of corporate historical concept.[5]

Where Wolff saw treaties and accords, Ted Turner, Time Warner's largest shareholder, saw armed conflict. The merger "should pass into history," he later said, "like the Vietnam War and the Iraq and Afghanistan wars"—as "one of the biggest disasters that have occurred to our country."[6] Even conceived as a failure, the merger signaled a newfound parity between state and corporation.

As I will explain below, to many the merger augured the supersession of the former by the latter—the eclipse of a dying order of nation-states by an ascendant order of transnationals. Anthony Sampson might be said to have written the first chapter of this story as it pertains to media and communication firms; in *The Sovereign State of ITT* (1973), he asks how "multinational corporations" like the communications giant ITT "fit in with modern notions of politics and diplomacy? How does it, or should it, relate to the nation-state, the Common Market, or to the models of world trade?" ITT was "everywhere and nowhere"; it was like Melville's white whale,

> a leviathan secretly circling the world, usually detectable only by the turbulence of the water, but suddenly showing one side of its huge strange shape, or spouting dark water,

> first in one corner of the globe, then a few days later at the opposite end—becoming a legend for ubiquity, immortality, and supernatural strength.[7]

Science fiction produced versions of the transnational as all-powerful leviathan, from *The Space Merchants* (1952) to *Blade Runner* (1982), *Neuromancer* (1984), and *Snow Crash* (1992). But these works tended to stress the corporate arrogation of the state's monopoly on violence, and it could not have struck many as plausible that an overleveraged media conglomerate was on the verge of acquiring directly coercive power; however, much of AOL Time Warner threatened control over all culture and information.

Some did speculate that the media company would assume governmental functions when ministering to the public interest. But finally, the exorbitant celebrations of corporate autonomy and transcendence were not a response to any local set of political problems or crises. Nor were they expressions of corporate power generally. Rather, they were efforts to imagine how the combination of old and new media on offer in the AOL Time Warner merger might exploit a global overaccumulation crisis that was producing unprecedented levels of capital mobility. In establishing what seemed a proprietary claim to the Internet, the company seemed poised to become the permanent home of capital on the move. It would do so by sponsoring a transformative production regime that would free capital permanently from the shackles of both the nation-state and the industrial production that once defined capital's relation to that state. The deal "validates the Internet's role as a leader in the new world economy," wrote *CNN Money*.[8] The euphoric celebrations of the deal tended to make a further assertion: because the Internet was *where* that new economy would reside, an old media company controlling access to the Internet would become the sponsor of capitalist spaces allegedly liberated from the territorial space of both the nation-state and the factory floor. In explicit and implicit ways, old media machinery like film and television would henceforth envision this proprietary space; their ideological function would be to naturalize and make audiences feel at home in the miraculous no-place of global capital.

***

The claim that media corporations were on the verge of replacing nation-states was front and center eight days before the merger's announcement, at a CNN roundtable whose participants included CEO Levin; Walter Isaacson, the Editor of *Time Magazine* who was about to become the CEO of CNN; Ken Andersen, an ex-*Time* employee and novelist; Ken Auletta, the *New Yorker*'s media critic; and Robert McChesney, a communications professor. The in-house panel might have seemed an instance of how the press, "much of which would soon be owned," Wolff would point out, "by the merged company," risked becoming "like the Soviet press."[9] But the event was more remarkable for how giddily its participants denounced state power altogether, on behalf of a new imperium. The media transnational would govern the Internet, and by implication all else besides, as a reluctant Cincinnatus called from its core competencies. "We're going to need to have these corporations redefined as instruments of public service," Levin said, "because they have the resources, they have the reach, they have the skill base" and "may be a more efficient way to deal with society's problems than bureaucratic governments." Andersen jumped in, "I agree, that the—sort of the giant corporate—corporations are kind of eclipsing the nation state as the most salient entity." "And maybe that's a good thing," Levin said. Because, at bottom, the media corporation was the only agent trustworthy enough to safeguard the global commonwealth: "who do you feel comfortable with articulating and protecting the public interest?" he asked. "Just tell me where in our society we should look."[10]

Dubbed by *New York Observer* the "philosopher prince of the American media establishment" (F 249), Levin had been spouting sentiments like these for years. He often invoked Henry Luce, who famously insisted that Time Inc. was a "breed apart"; in the words of Nina Munk, the company's "most prized assets included editorial integrity, a commitment to serve the public, and a belief that business was about more than dollars and cents." Luce's will described the company as "an enterprise operated in the public interest as well as in the interests of its stockholders." Years later, William Allen, chancellor of the Delaware Court, agreed: "The mission of the firm is not seen by those involved with it as wholly economic" (L 39). That reasoning resulted in a landmark setback for advocates of shareholder rights. Allen ruled that because of its unique culture, Time Inc. had no fiduciary responsibility to accept the exorbitant price that Paramount was willing to pay for its stock in 1989, and was free instead to merge with Warner Bros. Communications. And so when AOL announced its purchase of Time Warner—ten years to the day after Time Inc. announced its merger with Warner Bros.—the stage was set for a clash between two apparently different visions of the corporation: AOL was oriented toward efficiencies, "the street," and share price, and, putatively, Time Warner was oriented in some significant measure toward public service and noneconomic values.

The terms of that clash recall and yet push to the breaking point the logic of Pierre Bourdieu's cultural field. For Bourdieu, the arena of social struggle bounded by culture is organized by the dynamic between

> the heteronymous principle, favorable to those who dominate the field economically and politically (i.e. "bourgeois art") and the autonomous principle (e.g. "art for art's sake"), which those of its advocates who are least endowed with specific capital tend to identify with [a]degree of independence from the economy, seeing temporal failure as a sign of election and success as a sign of compromise.[11]

The same terms obtain, Bourdieu thinks, in the struggle between small-scale, "restricted [cultural] production" and large-scale mass production. Time Warner certainly thought of itself as a guardian of restricted production and its more literary values. Munk reports that in 2000, "at Time Warner, journalists thought of themselves as artists" (F 220). When AOLers mocked the "higher calling" to which those journalists pretended, they were scorned, in turn, as "not quality people" (F 241, 159). (And of course if "quality" functioned as a sign of gentility, election, and integrity, it also named the aesthetic value of really good TV. Tracing its lineage to the protestant high tones of Time Inc., rather than to the Jewish Warner Bros., HBO coveted the prestige of autonomy.)

But neither Time Warner as a whole nor Time Inc. and HBO in particular were actually small-scale, restricted enterprises. Their autonomy was a curated brand attribute. And even if one were inclined to believe that Time Warner's journalists and artists renounced the "field of power," as Bourdieu thinks autonomous art inevitably does, it would be difficult to say the same of AOL Time Warner as a whole, no matter its culture. If a benevolent AOL Time Warner were to become a "guardian of the global commonwealth," it would do so with hawkish board members like Al Haig and Colin Powell. Commentators regularly overlooked such details; Powell's son Michael was an appointee to the FCC that approved the merger, for instance, and most of the liberal press would fail to note three years later that the FCC, now chaired by Michael Powell, rewarded U.S. news outlets with relaxed cross-platform ownership rules after they lined up behind George W. Bush during the lead-up to the invasion of Iraq.

The essential fact is this: corporations are state-authored legal fictions that shield capitalist property from risk and liability; as such, they are beholden to the states that give them life. One finds nothing in the story of this merger to contradict Althusser's claim that the communications and culture industries are part of an Ideological State Apparatus that indirectly secures the propagation of the relations of production. Whether in concentrated form or not, and whether local or transnational, the media industry is an ideology factory that produces representations of the imaginary relationship of individuals to their real conditions of existence.

And yet, it is also true that corporations are "given such social power," in the words of Joshua Barkan, "that they threaten to undermine the political sovereignty that created them." The relationship between corporations and the state, he adds, typically takes shape as "a kind of *doubling*, in which the fate of state sovereignty and corporate power are conjoined but also in conflict." As Barkan has it, "from the chartered privileges of imperial trading companies to the constitutionally protected rights of contemporary multinationals," corporations have been structured around "legally authorized suspensions, privileges, and immunities from the law." Created by law, corporations are also exceptions to the law's authority—as "private rights held *against the state*."[12] The transnational movement of goods and monies within a single corporation, for instance, is exempt from certain taxes and border controls. And it is with this in mind that Giovanni Arrighi speculates,

> the explosive growth in the number of transnational corporations and the transactions within and between them has become the most critical factor in the withering away of the modern system of territorial states as the primary locus of world power.[13]

Codified in the Treaty of Westphalia following the Thirty Years' War, that system was premised upon "the territorial exclusiveness of states as 'containers of power.'" But the "explosive growth of transnational corporations" has become "the single most important factor in undermining the substance of that exclusiveness," he writes, largely by creating

> a world-scale system of production, exchange, and accumulation, which was subject to no state authority and had the power to subject to its own "laws" each and every member of the interstate system, the United States included. The emergence of this free enterprise system—free, that is, from the constraints imposed on world-scale processes of capital accumulation by the territorial exclusiveness of states—has been the most distinctive outcome of U.S. hegemony. It marks a decisive new turning point in the process of expansion and supersession of the Westphalia System, and may well have initiated the withering away of the modern interstate system as the primary locus of world power.
> *(74–5)*

Arrighi claims further that the ability of transnationals to suspend state sovereignty and to internalize what was once international trade has led to a global network of non-territorial, capitalist spaces. For Barkan, the corporation is "a hinge between capitalism and sovereignty" that is "articulated through a radically different spatial politics than the one associated with the sovereignty of the nation state."[14] In what follows, I elaborate the spatial politics of AOL Time Warner in terms offered by Arrighi, whose work anatomizes how over many centuries European states have competed for capital that has "set itself free" (6) from the commodity form. For Arrighi, "capitalism as a world system of accumulation and rule has developed simultaneously in the space-of-places," where "it triumphed by becoming identified with particular states," and in "the space-of-flows," where "it triumphed by not becoming identified with any particular state but by constructing world-encompassing, non-territorial business organizations" (85). That last distinction is related but not identical to the one Arrighi makes between "capitalism" and "territorialism," which are "opposite modes of rule or logics of power" (34). In the capitalist logic of power, control over territory and population is a means to control over mobile capital; in the territorialist logic, control over mobile capital is a means to control over territory and population.

But in fact, he writes, these logics have rarely operated in isolation from each other, and we might use the wild speculation surrounding the AOL Time Warner merger to delineate the contradictory tensions that governed representations of mobile capital and space during the 1990s. In these representations, capital that has escaped the commodity form and a given state seems both in motion and stalled, both homeless and permanently at home in the "space-of-flows" it inhabits. The phrase "overaccumulation crisis" captures something of these tensions. Confronted with falling rates of profit, capitalists refrain from reinvesting in production. Their profits pile up as the amount of surplus value extracted from the economy as a whole declines. Wealth accumulates, but capital does not: capital exists only in motion, as value in expansion. This means that "mobile capital" is capital proper only if and when it finds outlet in the production of surplus value; it is simply mobile money when routed through, say, the financial sector. But even in that case, money is not piling up, as the phrase "overaccumulation crisis" suggests; rather, it is being loaned and loaned again, to more promising sites of investment—like the media industry, which does not produce surplus value.

Recipients of massive loans during the 1990s, media transnationals represented themselves—whether in their films, video games, or television programming—as the true home of global money on the move. They offered up their insides, we might say, as spaces in which money withdrawn from traditional production might seem both to work and to idle. Arrighi writes of "the difficulties involved in unveiling a capitalist power that is not 'contained' by a state... but encompasses a system of states." He writes of "the bias of our conceptual equipment in favor of the space-of-places that defines the process of state formation and against the space-of-flows of capital that defines the process of capital accumulation" (85). But we also experience a transformation of that bias during overaccumulation crises and their attendant financial turns, as entities like AOL Time Warner sponsor fantasies of territorial transcendence. During such periods, we are encouraged to forget that, as David Harvey reminds us, "capitalist activity is always grounded somewhere. Diverse material processes (physical, ecological as well as social) must be appropriated, used, bent and reshaped to the purposes and paths of capital accumulation."[15]

Along these lines, during the 1990s, we were encouraged to believe that capitalism might be housed within the seemingly non-territorial space of the Internet, which toward the end of that decade concretized the kinds of global capitalist spaces that, *pace* Arrighi, had for some time existed internal to transnational corporations, and that were not, in his terms, "contained by a state." Indeed, as we will see below, the newly formed AOL Time Warner could seem a new kind of stateless, non-territorial entity largely because the Internet had already been celebrated as a safe haven for money in flight from traditional production, a haven in which that money might be put to work in new kinds of "immaterial" production.

***

The AOL Time Warner merger was the culminating folly of the so-called New Economy, and the chief exhibit of that economy's failure either to reverse or compensate for a long decline in U.S. manufacturing. The 1990s had seemed to witness a resurgence of the national economy. An ardent champion of globalization, Bill Clinton, had pushed for the multilateral liberalization of trade and capital movement. For a while, his policies seemed to work, as the "roaring nineties" witnessed the decline of inflation and unemployment and, of course, the massive run-up of the stock market, which would peak in February 2000, just after AOL Time Warner announced their merger. The dot.com bubble would then burst, eventually bringing the new company down with it. Hobbled by $28 billion in debt, AOL Time Warner would write off a $100 billion loss two years later; AOL's stock would eventually fall to less than 10% of its highest share price. There had been warning signs. The second half of the 1990s saw, in Peter Gowan's words, "unprecedentedly high levels of public and household debt, a deep structural imbalance of payments deficit and a business cycle dependent on asset price bubbles." The business cycle was, above all, "deeply dependent upon Wall Street financial markets' ability to maintain inward flows of finance from all over the world."[16] Especially after the liquidity crisis precipitated by the 1997 East Asian meltdown, monetary flows from around the world into the U.S. stock markets accelerated in an unprecedented fashion. Net monies moving into the U.S. in 1998 alone amounted to more than $200 billion.[17]

In the years leading up to the merger, in other words, global monies were flowing into the U.S. as never before; that fact alone might have consolidated the association of state power and capital, rather than weaken it. But the massive flows were achieving a new dynamism and speed, such that national economic policy played out over shorter and shorter intervals, and required increasingly frequent retooling, in its effort to capture mobile capital that could, at any moment, leave for other shores. Robert Brenner identifies the 1985 Plaza Accords and its depreciation of the U.S. dollar as the start of this intensified capital mobility, and the start, also, of a U.S. manufacturing boom that would be ended ten years later by the Reverse Plaza Accords. After 1995, the U.S. would reinflate the dollar, effectively undermining its recently booming manufacturing base, the better to funnel foreign capital into domestic stock markets. The corresponding reduction in German and Japanese interest rates produced by the Reverse Accord prompted still more money to be plowed into U.S. stocks. As did the subsequent dropping of U.S. interest rates, which coincided with the rise of the mortgage-backed securities, collateralized debt obligations, and credit default swaps that figured prominently in the crisis of 2008. In short, then, Brenner describes a post-1985 "hydraulic dynamic" in the world economy, "in which one leading economy or group of them took advantage of reduced exchange rates to undertake manufacturing-led, export driven expansions, but heavily at the expense of others with correspondingly increased exchange rates."[18]

This is a state of affairs in which gold, rather than, say, the dollar, begins to function as a particularly attractive resting place for capital in flight. And, in fact, gold nicely captures the contradictoriness indicated earlier, between capital as still (and therefore not capital) and capital as dynamic. On the one hand, gold is palpably physical as a hoarded store of value. But gold is a valuable safe haven in times of crisis precisely because it is also perfectly liquid, and therefore less potentially risky than raw materials or machines or commodities or even a particular currency—this is why, historically, the gold standard made possible the creation of an expansive global market free from the interventions of national governments. The fin-de-siècle media transnational tended to elaborate this tension in social and spatial terms, and in so doing to ring in a change on how global markets had long been represented.

In ancient Greece, trade developed at the outer limits of the household economy, and markets were thought of as neutral zones best housed at the periphery of or in between settlements (this is why markets adopt Hermes as their patron deity, and why alien merchants were called *metics*, derived from the Greek for "meta-dwelling"). But markets would come to seem far more abstract and placeless with the advent of capitalism centuries later. Marx thus describes

> how the exchange of commodities breaks through all local and personal bounds inseparable from direct barter, and develops the circulation of the products of social labor; and on the other hand, how it develops a whole network of social relations spontaneous in their growth and entirely beyond the control of the actors.[19]

The systematic and generalized exchange of commodities, in other words, created new abstract, nonlocal spaces that would seem to internalize new forms of social life.

Arrighi seeks to give an account of how states have struggled to sponsor and subjugate global versions of those spaces. For Arrighi, new global hegemons, or leaders of the global economy, typically have secured the "general interest" by demonstrating fidelity to both capitalist and territorial spaces: *even as the territorial and material interests of your state align with those of ours*, each new hegemon has declared, *our state pledges to safeguard the interests of global capital as they run in excess of our interests and of the interest of nation-states generally*. Pledging to safeguard capital interests as they exceed state interests has tended to require, in turn, conceiving anew the abstraction layer that for Fernand Braudel sits atop "the favored terrain of the market economy, with its many horizontal communications between different markets." That abstraction layer, or "the zone of the anti-market," is "the real home of capitalism," Braudel writes, where "the great predators roam and the law of the jungle presides."[20] For Arrighi, global hegemony has required postulating more harmonious supranational laws for this jungle. "British free-trade imperialism," for instance,

> established the principle that the laws operating within and between states were subject to the higher authority of a new, metaphysical entity, a world market rule by its own 'laws'—allegedly endowed with supernatural powers greater than anything pope or emperor had ever mastered in the medieval system of rule.
>
> *(56)*

The "free enterprise system" consolidated by the U.S. after World War II, Arrighi claims, reinvents this space under new auspices.

This was possible in part because the U.S. global hegemony that took shape after World War II was itself less exclusively territorial than was the hegemony exercised by previous European world powers. In 1941, Henry Luce dubbed the twentieth century "the American Century" and urged the U.S. to slough off its isolationism and lay claim to a new species of world leadership. Neil Smith notes that Luce's call for a new manifest destiny was striking for "the abstractness, even vacuity, of its geography"; in its embrace of diffuse values and broad imperatives, and in its indifference to concrete global locales, it amounted to "a victory over geography." Wielding a new kind of global power, for Luce, "meant not having to care about the world's geography. Precisely because geography was everything—the American Century was global—it was simultaneously nothing." But Luce could make this claim at all, Smith notes, because

> the emerging American Empire defined its power in the first place through the more abstract geography of the world market rather than through direct political control of territory. Whereas Europeans had accompanied the British East India Company, Dutch East Indies Company, and the Massachusetts Bay Company with settlers, state and civil institutions, and military control, multinational corporations in the twentieth century led with trade, financial, and direct investment agreements while governmental involvement increasingly focused on establishing broad legal and policy conditions rather than direct intervention.[21]

This made it possible for a global network of transnational corporations to constitute much of the world market. This network became the increasingly plausible "real home of capitalism" as the U.S.-led systemic cycle of accumulation waxed and then waned.

During the overaccumulation crises that would mark the waning of U.S. hegemony, media transnationals would represent themselves as that home. The media transnational was itself a newly global entity. "Whereas media systems had been primarily national before the 1990s," wrote McChesney, shortly before CNN's roundtable, "a global commercial media market was emerging in full force by the dawn of the twenty-first century." That global market, he wrote, was linked "to the rise of a significantly more integrated 'neo-liberal' global capitalist economic system."[22] It would be the job of those companies, Jerry Levin later all but declared, not simply to represent that global system, but to offer themselves as the proper resting place of the newly mobile monies then traversing that system—as that money's safe haven. This meant, in effect, offering themselves as sovereign entities capable of replacing traditional territorial powers, and, just as importantly, selling access to non-territorial capitalist space as the space of entertainment. These companies would capture and sell the point of view not simply of money, but of money in flight. Their ideological function inhered precisely in this.

It is here that AOL Time Warner's combination of old and new media would prove decisive. Nothing was then more familiar than the claim that the Internet had become not simply a metaphor for the world market, or a tool for rendering international economic transactions more efficient, but also the place where finance capital went when leaving the confines of the nation-state. The Internet didn't follow in the wake of or make up one part of a global capitalist economic system, as McChesney said world media did; it became that system, in these 1990s claims, as it achieved autonomy from nation-states. It *was* capitalist space freed from territorial shackles. By the early 1980s, Thomas Streeter writes, analogies between the use of networked microcomputers and the individual's economic participation in a global neoclassical market were common. But that participation was understood in literal terms during the 1990s, as attention turned from microcomputers to the increasingly complex global systems that networked them. In the words of John Perry Barlow, co-founder of the Electronic Frontier Foundation, "computers, connected together, had the capacity to create an environment which human beings could and did inhabit."[23] Barlow popularized the term "cyberspace," which he borrowed from novelists like William Gibson, whose *Neuromancer* anticipated countless efforts to imagine in what way humans might enter the non-territorial space of the global economy. In Gibson's novel, the console cowboy jacking into cyberspace gains access not simply to transnational corporations, but to the capital that animates those corporations. That capital is embodied in the novel's two Artificial Intelligences, which in the end unite and take flight from terrestrial to outer space. Smart money was at that moment doing something similar: Gibson wrote just before the Plaza Accords, which is to say just before the precipitous ascent of the yen in 1985, and the corresponding flight of mobile capital out of Japan. His novel thus captures what was when he was writing a flight of capital into Japan, as well as attendant speculations that Japan was replacing the U.S. as the leader of the world economy. But the departure of the AI suggests the radically contingent nature of these capital flows. Seen in this context, Gibson's very old medium, the novel, both announces a new technology and uses that technology to figure the volatile movements of capital at the onset of the hydraulic capital dynamic described by Brenner.

When announcing the historic merger, Steve Case nodded to Henry Luce and called the twenty-first century "the Internet century" (F 187). AOL Time Warner would thus become both an extension and repudiation of U.S. global hegemony. And why not? Already by 1994, the Internet had its own Magna Carta, written by George Gilder and Alvin Toffler, and by 1998, *Wired* evangelists like Kevin Kelly were describing how the web had reshaped "the geography of wealth" on behalf of what he called "the new economic order." Crucially, that new order depended upon a new account of where money was made. "In a country," he wrote, "citizens pay taxes and adhere to laws for the benefit of all. In a network, netizens feed the web for the benefit of all. The network economy is a meta-country." The spatial inversions implicit in this bit of legerdemain went like this: if the web was a country, then the communications that moved through it had internalized and transformed traditional national economies. Thus, Kelly would declare, "Because communication—which in the end is what digital technology and media are all about—is not just a sector of the economy. Communication *is* the economy."[24] Such nonsense—which was akin to Hayek's (nonsense) version of the economy as a massive information-processor—wasn't just a product of the wishful thinking of the tech and media sectors; under this ideological dispensation, wishful thinking itself became the economy's central activity.[25] Claims like Kelly's were at the core of all those New Economy ideologies that stressed capital's newfound liberation from the space of the traditional factory. And such ideologies were the direct counterpart of those that stressed capital's newfound liberation from the territorial space of the nation-state. For just as this period of acute capital mobility precipitated efforts to imagine the location of global liquidity, as something both like and unlike territorial space, so too did this period imagine new kinds of virtual factories lurking within the sphere of circulation.

As Deborah Cowen reminds us, "The entire network of infrastructures, technologies, spaces, workers, and violence that makes the circulation of stuff possible remains tucked out of sight for those who engage with logistics only as consumers."[26] But other networks appear more readily, as fetishes that give fantastic form to money and its imagined social lives. What does finance capital do while pooling as liquidity and waiting for the next productive boom? How does it work while idling, as accumulated debt, say, in a media transnational? During the 1990s, the Internet seemed to promise answers, and a simultaneously spatial and technological fix to the accumulation crisis at hand. Debunking those answers requires a version of the "historico-geographical materialism" described by Edward Soja, which materialism involves

> much more than a tracing of empirical outcomes over space or the description of spatial constraints and limitations on social action over time. It is a compelling call for a radical reformulation of... the many different ways we look at, conceptualize, and interpret not only space itself but the whole range of fundamental relationships between space, time, and social being at every level of abstraction.[27]

This essay is a modest response to Soja's call, insofar as it explains why the emergence of a new kind of media transnational at the start of the twenty-first century, one that controlled significant access to the Internet, seemed to announce a significant new relation between capitalist and territorial spaces—where the latter is the imagined ground both of state sovereignty and traditional manufacturing.

At the dawn of the twenty-first century, in the West's developed economies, decades of uneven deindustrialization and the reformulation of the distinction between work and nonwork had made it possible to believe, in Joshua Clover's words, that the global division of labor had "receded... into the ether of finance."[28] The "productivity miracle" that the U.S. seemed to experience on the back of the Internet during the 1990s lent warrant to that disappearing act, and suggested the coming eclipse of material by immaterial labor. In 1995, the same year that Netscape's IPO kicked off a frenzy for Internet stocks, and the same year that the Reverse Plaza Accords reinflated the dollar and brought to a close the brief reinvigoration of U.S. manufacturing, Allan Greenspan claimed that "in an economy in which the value added is increasingly software, telecommunications, and various means of conveying value to people without the transference of a physical good," businesses should consider money spent on "intellectual services" as capital investments rather than expenses.[29] Advice like this was at the core of Enron's accounting fraud, just as it was at the core of the accounting fraud that AOL concealed right up to the moment the papers were signed on its purchase of Time Warner. Greenspan's advice also led, in less overtly criminal fashion, to the Bureau of Economic Analysis sponsoring "hedonic" adjustments whereby the U.S. GDP was revised upward to reflect perceived increases in the "quality" of domestic products and services (Desai, 211). By these lights, the entire economy might conceivably aspire to the prestige and autonomy of small-batch cultural production. And across the spectrum it went, from claims that software and intellectual services were capital investments, to the claim that quality services produced new kinds of disguised value, to more properly academic claims that under conditions of new connectivity culture and communicative action had become an endlessly renewable source of capital in expansion.

All of this meant that consumers could be entreated to enter the supranational space of the Internet not simply as participatory gamers, but as part of a new kind of workforce. The Internet promised both the traditional imaginative transports of pop culture consumption, in other words, and a putatively revolutionary means of production. Media transnationals would continue to be the ideology factories they had long been considered to be; but now, they might be seen, as gatekeepers of the Internet, to oversee virtual factories in which ideology and indeed information itself became capital. The fact that a single transnational might control both the world's largest cultural library and significant access to the Internet, the principal space in which this new species of ersatz capital was collaboratively made, only upped the ante. "Global media," Levin explained just before the merger,

> will be and is fast becoming the predominant business of the 21st century, and we're in a new economic age, and what may happen, assuming that's true, is it is more important than government. It's more important than educational institutions and non-profits.

Levin thus cast global media, the Internet, and economic growth as self-confirming versions of each other. Media transnationals would enable the unimpeded global flow not simply of information, but of information *as* capital in expansion. Put in Marxist terms, those companies promised a space in which overaccumulated capital would not die, but would instead remain dynamic and continue to expand. Global media would become more important than government, in other words, and liberate itself from the obligation to buttress this or that state ideological apparatus, by becoming the form of appearance of global capital in expansion. As Levin saw it, that capital no longer needed the wage relation or state actors for its furtherance. It was rather by empowering individuals to become not simply consumers, but also (unpaid) producers, he suggested, that the Internet-based media leviathan would become capital's permanent home.

Levin spoke of "the stunning concept" of "disintermediation":

> in the past… because of the more limited nature of the distribution, you always needed some inner position, someone in between you and the material, who, therefore, had gate-keeping control. The elegance of the Internet is that that no longer exists.

Thus could he pretend to resolve a version of "the self-dissolving" contradiction that Marx identified at the core of the joint stock company, that form of "socialized property" still "ensnared in the trammels of capitalism." A form of "private production without the control of private property," the stock company simultaneously intensified and yet failed to overcome what Marx called "the antithesis between the character of wealth as social and as private."[30] One could almost believe, listening to Levin, that Time Warner was about to give up its intellectual property claims, and distribute its stocks and dividends evenly among its workers. Indeed, in Levin's hands, the media transnational could seem to resolve an analogous contradiction between the U.S. state's de facto role as the police force of global capital and its commitment to the ideology of proletarianized global citizenship, which Arrighi thinks central to U.S. hegemony. What did the antithesis between social and private wealth, between citizens and governments, between labor and capital, or even between weak states and strong states, or core and periphery matter now? AOL Time Warner would reconcile the mass "produsage" of the Internet to the hierarchical creative production of the old media industry, and that would itself be evidence of, and the grounds of legitimacy for, a transcendent and momentous evolution of the corporation beyond the narrow state and class interests that once defined it.

## Notes

1 Alec Klein, *Stealing Time: Steve Case, Jerry Levin, and the Collapse of AOL Time Warner* (Simon and Schuster, 2004), 101.
2 Nina Munk, *Fools Rush In: Steve Case, Jerry Levin, and the Unmaking of AOL Time Warner* (Harper Collins, 2009), 180.
3 Tim Arango, "How the AOL-Time Warner Merger Went So Wrong," *The New York Times*, January 10, 2010.
4 Munk, *Fools Rush In*, 128, 180, 181.
5 Michael Wolff, "Happy New Media," *New York Magazine*, January 24, 2000, http://nymag.com/nymetro/news/media/columns/medialife/1837/; accessed 1/9/2017.
6 Bettig, R.V. and Hall, J.L. *Big Media, Big Money: Cultural Texts and Political Economics* (Rowman & Littlefield Publishers, 2012), 54.
7 Anthony Sampson, *The Sovereign State of ITT* (New York: Stein and Day, 1973), 18.
8 "That's AOL Folks," CNN Money: http://money.cnn.com/2000/01/10/deals/aol_warner/; accessed 2/10/2017.
9 Wolff, "Happy New Media."
10 "Special Event: Media in the New Century," CNN Transcripts: www.cnn.com/TRANSCRIPTS/0001/02/se.36.html; accessed 1/14/2017.
11 Pierre Bourdieu, *The Field of Cultural Production* (Columbia, 1993), 40.
12 Joshua Barkan, *Corporate Sovereignty: Law and Governance Under Capitalism* (University of Minnesota Press, 2013), 4, 8, 17.
13 Giovanni Arrighi, *The Long Twentieth Century* (Verso, 2010), 82.
14 Barkan, *Corporate Sovereignty*, 12.

15 David Harvey, *Spaces of Global Capitalism* (Verso, 2006), 78.
16 Peter Gowan, *The Global Gamble: Washington's Faustian Bid to Maintain World Dominance* (Verso, 1999), 123.
17 Economic Report of the President, 2000: 206.
18 Robert Brenner, "What's Good for Goldman Sachs is Good for America," April 18, 2009.
19 Karl Marx, *Capital*, Vol. I: Chapter 3: 2a.
20 Fernand Braudel, *Civilization and Capitalism, 15th-18th Century. Volume 2: The Wheels of Commerce*, trans. Sian Reynolds (New York: Harper and Row, 1982), 230.
21 Neil Smith, *American Empire: Roosevelt's Geographer and the Prelude to Globalization* (University of California Press, 2004), 18–19.
22 Robert McChesney, *Rich Media, Poor Democracy: Communication Politics in Troubled Times* (The New Press, 2000), 27.
23 Thomas Streeter, *Net Romanticism* (NYU, 2011), 120–1.
24 Kevin Kelly, *New Rules for the New Economy* (Penguin, 1999), 1, 72, 5.
25 Streeter points out that well before significant numbers of people ever bought and sold goods over the Internet, which is to say well before the Internet was an actual market of any substance, journalists and tech enthusiasts of all kind encouraged an "associative leap from market metaphor to actual market" (136). The fact that these conceits were all in place before "the explosion of the internet economy" suggests to him that they were an "enactment of hope," and in this were "*anticipatory*" of what "*could happen*" (135). Seen this way, his "net romanticism" names the irrational exuberance that floated the tech bubble.
26 Deborah Cowan, *The Deadly Life of Logistics: Mapping Violence in Global Trade* (Minnessota, 2014), 1.
27 Edward Soja, *Postmodern Geographies* (Verso, 1989), 44.
28 Joshua Clover, *Riot Strike Riot* (Verso, 2016), 124.
29 Desai, *Geopolitical Economy: After US Hegemony, Globalization, and Empire* (Pluto, 2013), 210.
30 Karl Marx, *Capital*, Volume III: Part V: Chapter 27: IV.

# 35

# *HAMILTON*, CREDIT, AND THE AMERICAN ENTERPRISE

*Jennifer J. Baker*

When the Treasury Department decided a few years ago to update one of its bills by replacing a founder's face with that of a historically significant woman, the $10 bill was slated for change. The irony that Alexander Hamilton was deemed dispensable by the very agency he created just seemed to confirm his status as the nation's least celebrated patriarch. Hamilton was never president, and unlike the most beloved non-president founding father, Benjamin Franklin, he did not leave behind handy inventions, scientific speculations, or quaint aphorisms; in fact, with the notable exceptions of the Coast Guard and *New York Post*, Hamilton's legacy consists largely of abstract financial policies.

Lin-Manuel Miranda's *Hamilton* changed all that. The musical that *Rolling Stone* declared "the cultural event of our time" propelled Hamilton into mainstream popularity (Binelli 2016). Ron Chernow's 2004 biography, on which Miranda closely based his libretto, returned to the bestseller lists more than a decade after its original publication, and children began donning powdered wigs to trick-or-treat as the nation's first Treasury Secretary. On April 20, 2016, six months after *Hamilton* opened on Broadway, Treasury Secretary Jacob Lew announced that Hamilton's portrait would stay on the bill (portraits of women suffragists would be added to its reverse side, and Harriet Tubman would replace Andrew Jackson on the $20 bill). In what was surely not a coincidence, Lew had communicated his decision to Miranda in a private meeting at the Treasury Department the month before.

Miranda's recovery efforts are clear in the closing song of the musical, in which James Madison declares, "He took our country from bankruptcy to prosperity. I hate to admit it, but he doesn't get enough credit for all the credit he gave us" (Miranda and McCarter 2016: 280). Madison speaks of the modern neglect of Hamilton, but he also addresses Hamilton's political rivals on stage. In his own lifetime, Hamilton did not always "get enough credit" because building credit, whether personal or national, was itself discreditable and morally charged in elite political circles. Credit schemes were necessitated by a lack of capital or standing, and so they smacked of opportunism and overreaching. They involved a suspiciously strategic deployment of words and self-promotion, inevitably raising the specters of corruption, conflict of interest, and misrepresentations of wealth. Perhaps most controversial, Hamilton's national credit schemes involving banking and paper money did not distribute benefits and burdens evenly, often creating windfalls for profiteers and hitting hardest those without cash in hand or access to inside information. While Hamilton lamented such collateral damage, he considered these credit measures necessary for nation-building.

In many ways, *Hamilton* presents a rosy picture of American capitalism, and some critics have argued that its exorbitant ticket prices ($10-ticket lotteries notwithstanding) are at odds with its egalitarian messages. Nevertheless, Miranda's admiration for Hamilton's fiscal talents is tempered by a clear-eyed and circumspect outlook. Ben Brantley described the musical as "utterly sincere, but without being judgmental or pious," and this qualified celebration of the founders has been most evident to theatergoers in Miranda's racially diverse cast, which ironizes their failure to eradicate slavery even as it earnestly celebrates the power of their liberationist rhetoric to enfranchise, ultimately, people of color (Brantley 2015). I would argue that such circumspection is also evident in Miranda's treatment of Hamilton's economic nationalism. The musical encourages us to see Hamilton as a man whose fiscal ideas were fresh, entrepreneurial, and too readily dismissed by those who could not see past his obscure origins—but, at the same time, it tells the story of a man who made too many compromises for the sake of federal empowerment, committing grave errors in judgment and widespread injury. Organized as it is around questions of value and trust, *Hamilton*'s financial plot grants credit to Hamilton but never with blind faith.

In the details of this financial plot, Hamilton's complicated modernity comes fully into view. His notions of credit reflected a reconceptualization of value in terms of potential rather than tangible material in hand, making possible speculation that was both enterprising and potentially reckless. He saw credit as essential for social mobility—looking forward to the next century, when the rags-to-riches story of someone like Franklin would be embraced—and he rejected the claim that men of landed wealth were above the marketplace and therefore most fit to govern. Hamilton identified self-interest as a universal passion, even if he fancied himself more capable of curbing it than most, and promoted free enterprise even as he worried about a dangerously unregulated marketplace. This understanding of private interest underpinned his thinking on the nation's war debt, currency, and centralized banking. What makes Hamilton such a compelling character in Miranda's hands is not simply that his all-American hustle propels him from lowly origins to statesmanship, but that he works to understand how an individual's pursuit of happiness could both promote and undermine collective welfare.

Although an outlier of sorts among his political peers, Miranda's Hamilton effectively renews the credit of the entire Revolutionary generation for those twenty-first-century Americans who might think of founding fathers as out of touch or un-relatable. Just as Miranda reinvents the American musical by infusing it with hip-hop and rap, he enlivens the founders, reminding us, as one reviewer puts it, that the United States was "built by young risk-takers, not serious old white men who stare out at us from currency about to become obsolete" (Jones 2016). In the story of Hamilton's quest to establish national credit, we also see a figure who is compelling and credible precisely because he is not the subject of hagiography. Miranda's portrait of Hamilton does reaffirm the possibilities of American enterprise, but it also grapples with its inequities and casualties. In the wake of *Hamilton*, the man on the ten-spot, speaking to our optimism, anxieties, and political realities, feels, if nothing else, up to date.

Hamilton's understanding of national credit was shaped by his status as the illegitimate son of a Caribbean merchant. Lacking capital and lineage, this "ten-dollar Founding Father without a father" had to make his own name by wits, words, and deeds, unlike those who were born into wealth or respectability and simply had to maintain it (Miranda and McCarter 2016: 16). Most of Hamilton's political peers viewed such self-accreditation as overreaching. They were suspicious of Hamilton's background and similarly wary of his national financial policies, which aimed to transform the fledgling nation into a good credit risk and encourage individuals to invest in it through the purchase of national bank shares. In addition to stimulating economic growth, Hamilton argued, undertaking debt would help showcase the nation's credibility: just as an entrepreneur might demonstrate his creditworthiness by undertaking debt and paying it off punctually, the nation might use responsible borrowing to inspire the faith of its citizens and other nations. "States, like individuals, who observe their engagements, are respected and trusted," Hamilton wrote in his 1790 *Report on Public Credit* (Hamilton 2001: 532). Through a permanent national debt, the federal government could continually "perform" redemptions and demonstrate its ability to keep its word.

In Miranda's story of Hamilton's youthful wartime experience, debt and credit as indispensable, if precarious, nation-building tools. The Revolutionary War reinforced Hamilton's conviction that nations, like individuals, must undertake necessary risks to exceed the limitations of their capital. In the absence of metal specie, the Continental Congress paid soldiers and military suppliers with government-issued Continental dollars and various IOUs. Hamilton would later call this debt the "price of liberty," an investment undertaken to reap political independence and economic power (533). Because he also witnessed rampant inflation and currency depreciation, the war also taught him the fundamental role that public faith plays in securing the value of credit instruments and the nation's fiat currency. In "Stay Alive," a song of despair during a bleak period of the war effort, Hamilton notes that local merchants will not credit the new nation's currency: they "deny us equipment, assistance" and "only take British money, so sing a song of sixpence" (Miranda and McCarter 2016: 96).

When Hamilton was appointed the Secretary of the Treasury under the new Constitution, those wartime experiences—along with reading in classical economics, trade manuals, and political philosophy—shaped his efforts to use debt as a tool to forge political unity. The controversial first step of Hamilton's plan—and the topic of heated debate in Miranda's first rap-off "cabinet battle"—was his proposed assumption of each state's war debts by the federal government, through which Hamilton hoped to create a single national debt that would shift people's allegiances from the state to the nation. In *Hamilton*, this use of debt to consolidate national power becomes a counterintuitive yet ingenious move. Incredulous but also impressed, Burr wonders, "How does the bastard orphan/ Immigrant decorated war vet/ Unite the colonies through more debt?" (Miranda and McCarter 2016: 152).

In "Cabinet Battle #1," Hamilton argues that the federal assumption of state war debts will transform a loose confederation of states into a politically unified and economically creditable and stable nation: "If we assume the debts, the Union gets a new line of credit, a financial diuretic./ How do you not get it?/ If we're aggressive and competitive/ The Union gets a boost. You'd rather give it a sedative?" (Miranda and McCarter 2016: 161). This diuretic will promote liquidity and the flow of capital and goods. Jefferson, on the other hand, argues strenuously that such a plan will foster political division by favoring states with larger debt burdens and discriminating against those states that have none. In making his case, he reprises a common agrarian argument about the duplicitous and nonproductive nature of market economies and credit-based exchange: "In Virginia, we plant seeds in the ground./ We create. You just wanna move our money around" (161).

While Hamilton famously described a public debt as a "blessing" and "powerful cement" of the union (Hamilton 1961: 635), Jefferson and most founders saw debt as an emergency measure and otherwise something to be avoided whenever possible. Credit systems were morally charged not simply because they enmeshed individuals in market transactions but because they promised a forthcoming payment that did not actually exist at the moment. John Adams declared that every dollar issued beyond the exact quantity of gold and silver in the vaults represented nothing and was, therefore, a "cheat upon somebody" (Adams 1809: 610), and Madison believed "nothing but evil" would spring from "imaginary money" (Madison 1977: 106). Hamilton, by contrast, concurred with Adam Smith's notion that gold and silver languishing in vaults was "dead stock" that could be better put to work in circulation (Smith 1976: 341). He considered a one-to-one correspondence between credit instruments and specie in the vault, in fact, to be a mark of economic stagnation.

In ways both exhilarating and unsettling, Hamilton's personal and national accreditation confirms the power of words in the newly invented nation. Like the protagonists of so many American stories of self-making, Miranda's Hamilton discovers the power of literacy at a young age, and his "skill with a quill" serves him at every turn (Miranda and McCarter 2016: 70). Hamilton's writing is the means by which he manages his public reputation, increasing or preserving credibility in the public eye. Fittingly, Miranda organizes his story around two key scenes of writing: as a teenager, Hamilton writes his way off the island of St. Croix when he publishes an account of a hurricane that convinces local businessmen to finance his journey to New York; twenty-five years later, recalling this youthful self-liberation through the pen, Hamilton publishes a notorious pamphlet admitting marital infidelity in order to clear himself of the charge of financial impropriety.

Writing is equally essential to Hamilton's work to create, manage, and sustain the nation's credibility. He keenly understands that credit instruments are wrought in language and that a pledge of the nation's word in the absence of metal specie can itself constitute value (see Shell 1982; Poovey 2008). Such credit comports with Americans' understanding of the United States as a modern nation deliberately and self-consciously forged through legal documents rather than rooted in genealogy or kinship (see Warner 1992; Looby 1996). Like the authors of the Declaration of Independence and Constitution, who created a nation and national government with strokes of a pen, Hamilton writes "financial systems into existence" (Miranda and McCarter 2016: 232). In addition, other kinds of texts—circulating newspapers, pamphlets, and broadsides—have the power to boost or undermine the public's estimation of the government and its monetary instruments. Hamilton, whom Chernow describes as a "human word machine," solicits public support and manages public perception of the state of the nation through his astonishing output of pamphlets, *Federalist* essays, Treasury reports, and letters and speeches ghost-written for George Washington (Chernow 2004: 444).

In the narrative arc of Miranda's story, Hamilton finds his true calling as a public servant when he decides to wield the quill on behalf of the nation's finances. This vocational crisis requires that he relinquish dreams of military glory and see himself, first and foremost, as a writer. At 12, Hamilton had confided to a friend that he longed for a war because military service might offer a ticket out of poverty and obscurity (Hamilton 2001: 3), and in Miranda's song "Right-Hand Man," an older Hamilton recounts this youthful wish: "As a kid in the Caribbean I wished for a war. I knew that I was poor/ I knew it was the only way to—Rise up!" (Miranda and McCarter 2016: 60). But by the end of that song, Hamilton begins to understand that his legacy will derive not from military service but from the less glorified work of a bureaucrat. In a private conversation with George Washington, Hamilton bristles at the prospect of serving as the general's aide-de-camp, but when Washington confides that the Continental Army has only received a third of the military supplies Congress once promised, Hamilton begins to see how he might earn a name by pushing paper to facilitate the delivery of goods.

Up to this point, Miranda's Hamilton has been careful not to "throw away" his "shot" by taking a clerical position rather than pursue military fame. In this moment, however, he starts to see that such a desk job *is* his shot to serve nation and obtain a name: "I'll rise above my station, organise your information til we rise to the occasion of our new nation" (Miranda and McCarter 2016: 64–5). Although he continues to covet military fame (later admitting to Burr, "I wish I had your command instead of manning George's journal"), Hamilton redefines his purpose in this moment (86). After the war, Hamilton will return to New York and launch a prosperous legal career but soon begin to agitate for an overhaul of the Articles of Confederation because he feels that they do not grant the federal government sufficient power to regulate the nation's finances. New York's economy is "increasingly stalling," he announces in "Non-Stop," and so public service seems to be "calling" (137).

The seeds of this vocational calling lie in an earlier song, "My Shot," a riveting number in which Hamilton similarly contemplates opportunities for advancement and decides finally to take his shot by joining the Revolution. In this song, assorted characters consider the political stakes of colonial rebellion. The Marquis de Lafayette sees rebellion as an occasion to cultivate the ideals of the French Revolution in American soil, and John Laurens hopes to bring French *liberté* to people of color. The tailor's apprentice Hercules Mulligan, on the other hand, sees rebellion as an opportunity to better his social position. Combining these two visions, Hamilton imagines collective political resistance and individual social advancement as mutually reinforcing; accordingly, the mantra "rise up" suggests both colonial agitation and upward mobility. As in "Right-Hand Man," Hamilton considers the sword as a means to achieve elevated social status through public service: "I will lay down my life if it sets us free. Eventually, you'll see my ascendancy" (26). But by song's end, it is clear that his reading in economics and his command of language will be the basis for a newly defined public service aimed at consolidating national economic power. While the skirmishes erupting in the streets are exciting, his own "readin' 'n writin'" has shown him that the nation's future—and his own legacy—will be determined by what happens behind the desk. "We need to handle our financial situation," he declares. "Are we a nation of states? What's the state of our nation?" Now "past patiently waitin'," he looks to the future and begins to envision a strong federal government equipped with powers of taxation and economic regulation (29).

Hamilton's quest to make a name for himself partly inspires this public service, and he needs always to ensure that his own ambition (or the appearance of ambition) does not taint his work or his credibility. Miranda's Aaron Burr offers a model of unchecked ambition detached from any commitment to public welfare, illustrating, by contrast, the way in which Hamilton's aspirations are curbed by principle. In "The Room Where It Happens," a song about the backroom deal Hamilton cut with Jefferson and Madison to get his debt plan passed in Congress, Burr's thirst for power takes center stage. Hamilton is in the room because he has been instructed by Washington to do whatever it takes to break the impasse in Congress and implement his financial plan. Burr, by contrast, wants to be in the room because he craves power in and of itself. As Miranda's Hamilton notes with astonishment, Burr even openly campaigns for president in 1800, embodying "ambition" in the original, pejorative sense of the word (derived from the Latin *ambire* meaning to "walk around" in canvassing for votes). The problem with Burr, Hamilton reasons when he endorses Jefferson for president, is that his ambition is never put to the service of any particular principle.

It is easy to imagine why Hamilton would want to project on to Burr all of the negative qualities associated with unchecked ambition. What dogged Hamilton during his political career was the then-common assumption that a socially mobile individual like himself could never transcend his own interests or govern on behalf of the public good. According to the republicanism of the Revolutionary generation, hereditable landed property removed one from the market place and fostered disinterest. By contrast, members of the mercantile class, no matter how wealthy, were vulnerable to corruption because they were financially entangled and their personal assets were always dependent on the debtors and creditors with whom they did business. The notion that landowners were more fit to govern began to die out at the end of the eighteenth century (though, as the Trump presidency has shown, a businessman-turned-politician still raises concerns about conflicts of interest), and Hamilton's chosen profession of the law was considered a vocation more safely removed from the vicissitudes of the marketplace. Nevertheless, he had to work hard to cultivate a civic personality, taking care to distinguish between his own carefully managed ambition and a thirst for money, power, and glory that knows no bounds.

The Reynolds Affair, the sex scandal that erupts in the musical's second act, makes clear that any suggestion of excessive ambition on Hamilton's part could threaten not simply his own reputation but the public credit he has worked to build. The personal reputations of the nation's leaders will have far-reaching impact on the public perception of government agencies, effectively making personal interests a matter of public concern. When Hamilton's enemies discover that he conducted a years-long affair with Maria Reynolds during his tenure as Treasury Secretary and paid hush money to her husband, James, they immediately suspect financial impropriety. As Chernow recounts in detail, James Reynolds had a long and sordid history of speculation with national securities and went to jail for posing as the executor of a deceased soldier's estate to collect claims against the government (using a list of veterans obtained through illicit means from the Treasury Department). This was not a man with whom a public figure would want to be associated, and Reynolds was happy to implicate Hamilton if he thought he could reduce his jail sentence or obtain more hush money.

Although *Hamilton* does not go into these details, it portrays the scandal as a long-awaited opportunity for Hamilton's opponents to nail him for fiscal misconduct. "An immigrant embezzling our government funds," they sing gleefully, "I can almost see the headlines, your career is done" (Miranda and McCarter 2016: 229). Confident in his verbal prowess, however, Hamilton takes up the pen on behalf of himself and the Treasury he has built. In the song "Hurricane," drawing an analogy between this professional disaster and the Caribbean hurricane of his childhood, he decides to rescue himself yet again through writing. "I'll write my way out/ Overwhelm them with honesty," he says of his decision to publish a 95-page pamphlet admitting to marital infidelity in order to absolve himself of "improper speculation" (233–4). In the musical, this decision to expose his family in order to preserve his public stature is the great mistake of his life. "You and your words," Eliza says angrily as she burns the love letters he wrote her and denounces his eloquence, "obsessed with your legacy" (236). But Hamilton's "legacy" is not simply the personal reputation that will endure after he is gone but also the Treasury and Bank of the United States tied to his name. In writing the pamphlet, Hamilton assumes that sexual indiscretion will be of less importance to the nation's credit rating than his public conduct as Treasury Secretary. Indeed, when Hamilton goes public with the affair, his opponents revel in the fact that he will never be president, but they also breathe a sigh of relief that the fiscal probity of the nation remains intact: "At least he was/Honest with our money!" (136).

The Reynolds Affair is one instance of many in which Hamilton makes ethical compromises in order to maintain the nation's credit rating. This commitment makes him a messy, if compelling, hero. One particularly controversial move, alluded to in the song "Washington on Your Side," is the government's redemption of depreciated credit instruments (in exchange for shares in the new national bank) at near-face value. Historical evidence clearly indicates that while this redemption crucially demonstrated the government's commitment to keeping its fiscal promises, it also rewarded speculators who had bought up certificates for pennies from desperately poor soldiers. Madison, who rightly felt that Hamilton's debt plan was an affront to those men who had risked their lives fighting for the new nation, proposed an alternative plan whereby the government would pay the current billholder only the amount of the resale price and issue the balance to the original billholder. In a decision that destroyed their friendship, however, Hamilton insisted that paying the purchaser anything less than full value would discourage investors from buying national securities in the future. When Hamilton went public with his redemption plan in his *Report on Public Credit*, northeastern speculators, including a Senator and Congressman who were friendly with Hamilton, added insult to injury by sending envoys to southern and western states to buy up discounted certificates before news of their restored value could reach the veterans.

In "Washington on Your Side," Jefferson laments that the soldier-turned-farmer struggling in the countryside is robbed by "Wall Street" looking for "chips to cash in" (Miranda and McCarter 2016: 199). Here, Jefferson's criticism of Hamilton's redemption plan echoes recent concerns about corruption in the financial services sector expressed most forcefully by the Occupy Wall Street movement. Miranda's use of "Wall Street" as shorthand for speculators is a self-conscious anachronism, for what came to be known as "Wall Street" was in 1790 still just a gathering spot under a buttonwood tree for brokers to buy and sell public stock. The anachronism reminds us that our stock market, then as now, favors those who have more disposable income, are better positioned to ride out market fluctuations, and have access to information while others do not. Not until the Securities Exchange Act of 1934, in the wake of the stock market crash of 1929, would trading on inside information become potentially illegal (and then only under certain conditions), and it was not until the STOCK Act of 2012 that legislators and government employees would be explicitly prohibited from profiting off nonpublic information obtained through their positions. These legislative acts, moreover, do not define in sufficiently clear terms what constitutes insider trading, reflecting a long-standing reluctance on Congress's part to inhibit robust enterprise and market liquidity.

Compounding the outrage over Hamilton's redemption plan was his decision to impose steep excise taxes on whiskey, which hit hardest the small-scale distillers, many of them war veterans who distilled their surplus crops for extra income in hard times. *Hamilton* highlights the irony that Hamilton, in his efforts to build public credit, worked to create the very kind of government that colonists had objected to under British rule. Given that Hamilton had complained bitterly about Parliamentary taxes imposed on the colonies, he looked especially hypocritical. As Jefferson warns him, "Look, when Britain taxed our tea, we got frisky./ Imagine what gon' happen when you try to tax our whiskey" (Miranda and McCarter 2016: 161). Equally worrisome is Hamilton's move to double the size of the government for purposes of "[c]entralizing national credit" and "making American credit competitive." (199) In what is obviously a rhetorical question, Madison asks if a large, powerful government had not been the problem that had led the colonies to seek independence.

In an earlier version of the musical, the song "One Last Ride" (revamped when the production moved to Broadway) went even further in detailing the injury done to veterans by Hamilton's revenue policies. The song commemorates Washington's journey on horseback, with Hamilton at his side, to oversee the federal government's suppression of the so-called Whiskey Rebellion by war veterans in western Pennsylvania in response to the excise tax. In this song, the world has indeed turned upside down, as the revolutionaries are now enforcers. "You're outgunned! Outmanned! Outnumbered, outplanned!" Washington warns the rebels, repeating the very words he had previously used to describe his own weak position vis-à-vis the British. Hamilton revels in Washington's muscle-flexing ("*That's* distilled spirit"), and screams at the rebels, "Pay your fucking taxes!" The suppression of the insurrection boosts the new government's clout as a force to be reckoned with, but it is also a menacing display of federal power (Miranda 2016).

Not only did these revenue policies raise ethical questions, but Hamilton's unabashed eagerness to exploit ambition and self-interest for purposes of consolidating national power scandalized his political rivals. Reflecting on his years as the Secretary of State, Jefferson famously described Hamilton as a "singular character" who was "disinterested, honest, and honorable in all private transactions" and yet convinced that "corruption was essential to the government of a nation" (Jefferson 1990: 345). Hamilton worked to imagine how ambition might be productively regulated, through institutional checks and balances, for practical purposes of the nation's economic growth. "Welcome to the present," Miranda's Hamilton says matter-of-factly when Jefferson opposes his debt plan on ethical grounds. "We're running a real nation" (Miranda and McCarter 2016: 161). As he put it in a 1791 report to Congress on manufacturing, there is a "certain fermentation of mind, a certain activity of speculation and enterprise," which if "left entirely to itself" would have "pernicious effects" but if "properly directed" could be "made subservient to useful purposes" (Hamilton 2001: 696). Perhaps most notably, he sought to harness self-interest through the creation of a government-charted national bank that would sell shares to the public: if Americans invested financially in the new nation, Hamilton reasoned, they would have a stake in the future of the nation and want to see the government, and its securities, succeed. Underpinning Hamilton's banking system was a vision of financial investment and patriotism as mutually reinforcing.

As the Bank's first public offering made clear, however, fostering the "fermentation of mind" associated with speculation and enterprise could be treacherous. When Hamilton loosened the credit requirements for purchasing bank shares in order to create investment opportunities for those with limited capital, what followed was a potentially disastrous speculative bubble. Bondholders did not hesitate to use short-term speculation to profit off margins (in one incident, speculators staged fake purchases to drive up the price). Hamilton feared a reprise of the collapse of France's South Sea Bubble in 1720 and so intervened by going on the record about the appropriate price of bank shares. Invoking traditional language used to denounce speculation, he described the announcement as an act necessary to "dissolve the charm," "counteract delusions," and provide the "only secure foundation on which to stand" (Hamilton 1965: 76).

Ultimately, however, Hamilton maintained that such extensions of credit were worth the risks if they created opportunity for those needing a leg up. "If banks, in spite of every precaution, are sometimes betrayed into giving a false credit to the persons described," he had written in his *Report on a National Bank*, "they more frequently enable honest and industrious men of small or perhaps of no capital to undertake and prosecute business with advantage to themselves and to the community" (Hamilton 2001: 585). While his peers worried that speculation would fuel fantasies of upward mobility—in words that bring to mind Hercules Mulligan's frustrations, Jefferson warned Hamilton that after the bubble bursts, the tailor will never again be "content with the slow and moderate earnings of his needle"— in Hamilton's view, the much greater risk was that talented men would be kept from realizing their potential without start-up loans (Jefferson 1986: 74).

Hamilton's encouragement of enterprise no doubt stemmed from his own experience as a poor immigrant, but as many historians have observed, his economic policies favored large-scale manufacturing and necessarily excluded farmers, artisans, and small-scale producers. The recent surge of interest in Hamilton as a historical figure has inevitably brought discredit as well as credit to his name. Some theatre reviewers have criticized *Hamilton* for minimizing its hero's elitism and overplaying his egalitarianism and antislavery convictions. In their analysis of the musical, historians Isaac Kramnick and Jason Frank remind us that Hamilton's vision of American enterprise depended upon "a deferential political underclass to do the heavy work" (Frank and Kramnick 2016). Certainly, Miranda's story overlooks Hamilton's disdain for the lower classes and his antidemocratic sentiments in the years after the Revolution. In the musical's story of Hamilton's quest to maintain public credit, however, we do see the contradictions of his character. In the rich wordplay of Miranda's lyrics, we discover an economic nationalism that benefitted the unscrupulous and exacted an especially high price from select states, Revolutionary veterans, artisans, farmers, and even his wife and children.

*Hamilton*'s story of American opportunity is self-consciously circumscribed not simply by the hero's limited vision of enterprise but also by the different modes of narrative at work in the musical. While it is a story of American self-making, it is also a story—one not at all uniquely American—of irrepressible genius: like the show's prodigious creator, *Hamilton*'s Hamilton is brilliant, verbally acrobatic, and unstoppable. If theatergoers like Hamilton because he showcases the United States as a land of opportunity, they might also recognize the impossibility of extracting from his story any generalization about ordinary American experience because he is so extraordinary and odds-defying. In ways humbling, most of us feel quite keenly that we are *not* like Hamilton (or Miranda, for that matter). The show's dazzling display of talent—both Hamilton's and Miranda's—should prompt theatergoers to consider whether individuals facing social and economic obstacles might only succeed through statistically unlikely combinations of character and talent.

Nevertheless, the story of Hamilton's rise from lowly origins in Miranda's musical gives credence to the American experiment, even as it acknowledges the injustices of slavery and the restricted rights of women. Ironically, Hamilton would not have thought that his meteoric ascent defined him, particularly because such an identification risked accentuating an unseemly ambition. In his view, he was a credit to his nation not because he was a self-made man but because he maintained fiscal probity and helped guide the nation through the financial uncertainty of its birth. He believed that his legacy would lie in the creation of a strong federal government with a good credit rating and wide-ranging fiscal powers. Not coincidentally, the design of the current $10 bill, which depicts Hamilton on the front and the Greek revival façade of the Treasury building on its reverse, dates back to the Great Depression. In designing the bill, the Federal Reserve used "statuesque representations" to "restore faith" in the nation's economic power during "turbulent times" (U.S Department of the Treasury 2016). The design's underlying logic—whereby pictures of an imposing treasury and its custodian might foster trust in the nation and its economy—reveals how thoroughly Hamiltonian is the $10 bill that Miranda's musical helped save.

## References

Adams, John. (1809) Letter to F.A. Vankderkemp (February 16) in *Works of John Adams, Vol. IX*. Boston, MA: Little, Brown, and Company.

Binelli, Mark. (2016) "'Hamilton' Mania! Backstage at the Cultural Event of Our Time." *Rolling Stone* [online] (June 16) www.rollingstone.com/music/features/hamilton-mania-backstage-at-the-cultural-event-of-our-time-20160601 [Accessed 12 December 2016].

Brantley, Ben. (2015) "Review: In 'Hamilton,' Lin-Manuel Miranda Forges Democracy through Rap." *The New York Times* [online] (February 17) www.nytimes.com/2015/02/18/theater/review-in-hamilton-lin-manuel-miranda-forges-democracy-through-rap.html [Accessed 13 April 2017].

Chernow, Ron. (2004) *Alexander Hamilton*. New York: Penguin.

Hamilton, Alexander. (1961) *The Papers of Alexander Hamilton, Vol. 2.* New York: Columbia University Press.
Hamilton, Alexander. (1965) *The Papers of Alexander Hamilton, Vol. 9.* New York: Columbia University Press.
Hamilton, Alexander. (2001) *Writings.* New York: Library of America.
Jefferson, Thomas. (1986) *The Papers of Thomas Jefferson, Vol. 22.* Princeton, NJ: Princeton University Press.
Jefferson, Thomas. (1990) *The Anas, 1791–1806: Selections in Public and Private Papers.* New York: Library of America.
Jones, Chris. (2016) "Review: 'Hamilton' makes the most of its Chicago shot." *Chicago Tribune* [online] (October 20) www.chicagotribune.com/entertainment/theater/reviews/ct-hamilton-chicago-review-ent-1020-20161019-column.html [Accessed 13 April 2017].
Frank, Jason and Kramnick, Isaac. (2016) "What 'Hamilton' Forgets about Hamilton." *New York Times* [online] (June 10) www.nytimes.com/2016/06/11/opinion/what-hamilton-forgets-about-alexander-hamilton.html?_r=0 [Accessed 5 December 2016].
Looby, Christopher. (1996) *Voicing America: Language, Literary Form, and the Origins of the United States.* Chicago, IL: University of Chicago Press.
Madison, James. (1977) *The Papers of James Madison, Vol. 10.* Chicago, IL: University of Chicago Press.
Miranda, Lin-Manuel. (2016) "One Last Ride." *Genius.com* [online] http://genius.com/Lin-manuel-miranda-one-last-ride-lyrics [Accessed 5 December 2016].
Miranda, Lin-Manuel and McCarter, Jeremy. (2016) *Hamilton: The Revolution.* New York: Melcher Media.
Poovey, Mary. (2008) *Genres of the Credit Economy: Mediating Value in Eighteenth- and Nineteenth-Century Britain.* Chicago, IL: University of Chicago Press.
Shell, Marc. (1982) *Money, Language, and Thought: Literary and Philosophical Economies from the Medieval to the Modern Era.* Baltimore, MD: Johns Hopkins University Press.
Smith, Adam. (1976) *An Inquiry into the Nature and Causes of the Wealth of Nations.* Chicago, IL: University of Chicago Press.
U.S. Department of the Treasury. (2016) "History of the $10 Note." [online] https://modernmoney.treasury.gov/history-10-note [Accessed 5 December 2016].
Warner, Michael. (1992) *Letters of the Republic: Publication and the Public Sphere in Eighteenth-Century America.* Cambridge, MA: Harvard University Press.

# 36

# GLOBAL FINANCE AND SCALE

## Literary form and economics in Mohsin Hamid's *How to Get Filthy Rich in Rising Asia*

*Laura Finch*

*Figure 36.1*

In December 2007, the *Financial Times* ran an image of a gleaming cityscape accompanied by the tagline 'World Business. In one place.' (Figure 36.1) The image presents an amalgamation of buildings from financial centres including Shanghai, Kuala Lumpur, Taipei, Yokohama, Hong Kong, Paris, Frankfurt, London, New York, Chicago, and San Francisco.[1] As the centrepiece of the *Financial Times'* campaign, this visual necessarily relies on several widely shared premises about world business: firstly, while this is an image of global finance, it is located on an island whose shape and bristle of ports are more than redolent of Manhattan's financial district; secondly, the scale at which finance should be imagined is the national, which can be metonymically represented by iconic architecture; thirdly (and relatedly), as the glossy impersonal surfaces of the buildings attest to, people are not important in this imagining of finance capital.

While this narrative of finance as slickly homogeneous has held sway since the mid-1970s, it has increased in potency since the 2007–09 credit crisis. In the wake of the collapse, attempts were made to explain the ways that finance had become so abstracted and so impersonal, a 'black box' (Lewis 2014: 3) to even those in charge of it. In the face of contemporary finance's ability to obfuscate its workings and its workings and present an abstract depersonalised account of itself, this essay suggests that literature can be useful in helping us to think finance otherwise; in fact, both *The Economist* (29 April, 2010) and *The Observer* (26 June, 2010) included Anthony Trollope's *The Way We Live Now* (1875) in their lists of non-fiction essential post-crisis reading, claiming that it offered the capacity to move between individual experience and the larger social totality in a way that no factual account could quite manage. On the one hand, Trollope's novel reiterates the idea of finance as the most abstract form of capital: set in the 1870s in an England wracked by financial upheaval, the story revolves around the entrance of 'The Great Financier' Augusts Melmotte into the banking scene. Pitted by the narrative against the embattled landed class of 'traditional England,' Melmotte is distrusted not only as European and Jewish but also as 'a miserable imposition, a hollow vulgar fraud from beginning to end' (Trollope 2005: 26) who has rendered capital yet more abstract than even paper money: 'as for many years past we have exchanged paper instead of actual money for our commodities, so now it seemed that, under the new Melmotte regime, an exchange of words would suffice' (363). On the other hand, as a novel, Trollope's book necessarily engages with finance at the human scale. It has to be said that the financialised human does not fare well: Melmotte commits suicide while the characters who are tasked with responsibly dealing in finance capital take themselves off to North America, finance's new home (See Van 2005). Clearly, finance and the human are not made to coexist in England at the end of its imperial reign.

We find a similarly anti-human imagination of finance in perhaps the two most attended to novels of contemporary US high finance: Bret Easton Ellis's *American Psycho* (1991) and Don DeLillo's *Cosmopolis* (2003). The protagonists of the novels, both young Wall Street traders, exhibit subjectivities that are dramatically eviscerated. Ellis' Patrick Bateman is clear on his dehumanisation: 'there is an idea of a Patrick Bateman, some kind of abstraction, but there is no real me, only an entity...I simply am not there' 'I was simply imitating reality, a rough resemblance of a human being' (1991: 363, 271).[2] Similarly, *Cosmopolis*' Eric Packer is a character thinned out into lines of financial code, who sees future moments of himself on the screen in his limousine before he has lived them and is finally murdered at the conclusion of the book. Packer's statement, 'not that I am interested in description. I am interested in money' (2003: 56) could be taken as the formal concern of the book, which Alison Shonkwiler describes as 'the thinness of the novel's history and the abstractions of its narrative form reflect[ing] precisely this new condition: the sublime imagination of capital does not reach into the thickness of historical material relations' (2010: 254–5). It would be fair to say that *American Psycho* and *Cosmopolis* offer more interesting takes on finance capital than an undialectical reading of the superficiality of their characters. Taken alongside Trollope, we can see that the novel in its very form provides a humanised counterweight – inhumane but not inhuman – to the starkly architectural vision of the *Financial Times*.

## Finance and global scale

Following the 2007–09 credit crisis and subsequent spike in interest in finance in the humanities-oriented disciplines, inroads have been made to finesse and refine the model of finance as monolithic, abstract, and unknowable. The social sciences have paid attention to the actually existing conditions of finance, from the habitus of Wall Street traders to the variety of non-standardised financial networks that exist across various economies, to the differences in urban design of various global financial centres and the racialised effects of finance.[3] Literary studies has brought its own tools to bear on fracturing the smooth surface represented by the *Financial Times'* image. Work has been done to interrupt the assumption that finance is an abstraction away from the 'real' economy (see La Berge 2014) while Randy Martin's work on what he has termed the 'financialization of daily life' (Martin 2002: 9)[4] has gained traction because it provides a framework for studying the ordinary and prosaic lifeworld of finance. While this work re-populates and makes concrete various aspects of contemporary finance capital, we might note that they leave its geography intact. This is partly institutional; these conversations are happening in literature departments structured around national traditions. However, it is also a testament to the power of the image that finance presents of itself as a North American export. The centrality of the US in thinking about finance leads to phrases such as 'capitalism with Chinese characteristics,' as if capitalism was merely a shorthand for 'North American capitalism,' while the labelling of more recently financialising economies as 'informal,' places them in an evolutionary path on the way to true finance.

This chapter's focus on South Asian finance – specifically through a reading of Mohsin Hamid's 2013 novel *How to Get Filthy Rich in Rising Asia* – puts pressure on the model of finance that stems from North America. While critical geography and other humanities-oriented disciplines were increasingly making scale the focus *of* analysis rather than a tool *for* analysis,[5] capital wishes to be excluded from this work. Capital, we are told, telescopes out from the individual to the regional, national, colonial, and global, with ease – Finance hides all kinds of messiness and abuse under its pretence of smooth scalability; it requires a global theory attentive to scale to counter it. In its roughshod riding over scalar differences, financial form pays no attention to location. This would be the very opposite of what Nirvana Tanoukhi describes as the ethics of scale: 'a scale-sensitive procedure – a procedure that 'conceptualizes' by following' (2008: 604).

This scale sensitivity is of increasing centrality in literary studies. On the one hand, the scalar possibilities of our potential to read have shifted with the interest in the capacities of the digital. On the other hand, the object of literary analysis has belatedly turned to the environment where the focus has been on the scale of timeframes: the epochal of the Anthropocene, the geological of deep time, the slowness of particular forms of environmental damage, and the 'massively distributed' timeframe of the hyperobject (Morton 2013: 1). This is not scale as a methodological tool but as scale as an object of inquiry, an object that literature can help to think through; as Marc McGurl writes, 'all literature tries to be functional in this way – to act, that is, as a kind of scaling device, scaling up and scaling down as needed' (2016: 634).

In thinking of scale, studies of finance run up against the same problem as other models for theorising 'global' phenomena that are in fact American exports, such as globalisation, neoliberalism, or American democracy, and the spread of cultural products (e.g. the realist novel) or literary traditions (e.g. modernism). As with these other concepts, the most imperialistic theoretical gesture is to make the 'uncritical habit of conflating epistemological and chronological primacy' (Deckard et al. 2015: 15) and to conceive of finance as a neat package that can be cleanly airlifted into so-called 'emerging' economies. This rhetoric obscures the jagged and grating labour necessary to move between scalar levels that have their own specificity. By acting as if financialisation moves from the Global North to Global South is to be complicit with the logic that underwrites the statement made by British bank *Norwich Union* in 1999 in regard to emerging markets: 'not since the days of the Empire have the British had such an opportunity to profit from the world' (Sidaway and Pryke 2000: 196).

The other alternative to this model is to provide parallel theories of finance for each location, evacuating the model of the ability to describe the relationship among location, time, and the capitalist world system. And in fact, because the vocabulary is always taken from the pre-existing US model, 'value free' descriptors of other forms of finance are labelled as the negative image of the high finance of North American e.g. informal, shadow, black market, emerging economies.[6] Rather than the bad politics of option one or the quietist non-politics of option two, the almost-totality of the capitalist world system demands a global model that includes the combined and uneven development on which capitalism runs. In our 'exorbitantly financialised present' (Baucom 2005: 26), the Global South is not outside finance, waiting in the wings for its moment to step onto the stage of modernity. Rather, development outside the Global North is also 'the development of underdevelopment of maldevelopment and dependent development' (Deckard et al. 2015: 13). The horizon of financial development is not a field emanating from Wall Street but a global process happening synchronically with a wide variety of effects. In order for some countries to live on the profits of financialisation, others must not, and this is an integral part of financialisation. Placing relations of power and inequity front and centre in a comparative analysis prevents a descent into merely cataloguing the difference between global forms in the theoretical equivalent of liberal multiplicity. Rather, it transforms the abstractions of financial scalability into situated assemblages of power, of capital, and of affect.

## Personal finance

Mohsin Hamid's 2013 novel *How to Get Filthy Rich in Rising Asia* is about one man's life in an unnamed South Asian country that Hamid has identified as Pakistan in interviews. The narrative arc follows the protagonist's entrepreneurial ascent from rural poverty to a bicycle delivery boy in a vibrant big city, to a salesman of 'non-expired-labeled expired-goods' (2013: 99), to the creator of a gently fraudulent bottled-water business. The novel ends with the protagonist's death in his seventies, his last words being also the final words of the book, at which point he has lost all the financial gains he had accrued. Hamid's text merges the novel form with the non-fictional genre of the personal finance book. This latter genre ties finance and personal uplift together into one entrepreneurial package and is hugely successful worldwide: Robert Kiyosaki's *Rich Dad, Poor Dad* series holds the title of the bestselling personal finance book of all time and has sold over 35 million copies worldwide in 43 languages. Hamid's short novel takes the protagonist through twelve necessary steps to becoming filthy rich, each enumerated in a new chapter with classically uplifting headings such as 'Work for Yourself,' 'Befriend a Bureaucrat,' and 'Dance with Debt.'

While Hamid's novel deploys a satirical tone throughout, he is far from unsympathetic to the desire to make money in a country steeped in poverty. Part of the attraction to personal finance in a newly financialising market is that it allows access to the financial economy without a formalised relationship to it. Pakistan's most recent alliance with global finance began in the 1990s with a strategic programme to loosen state control of the currency, increase access to foreign exchanges that had been heavily regulated since partition, remove the administration of interest rates, and privatise and deregulate the banking sector (Meenai and Ansari 2004; Abbas and Malik 2010). By 2007, Pakistan was ranked a 'top reformer' by the World Bank, ranking 74th out of 175 countries (World Bank 2007: n.p.) despite the fact that the majority of the population live below the poverty line. While only 10% of adults have an account at a formal financial institution, and this is vastly weighted towards the very richest sectors of the population,[7] if we take 'informal' finance into account (including such activities as lending and borrowing among close relations, neighbours, and friends, suppliers' credit resting on good faith, and rotating saving and credit associations), 50.5% of the population have access to finance (Nenova, Niang, and Ahmad 2009: ix), much of this activity taking place in response to the volatility that has plagued Pakistan's 'formal' economy since 2007. As anthropologist Antonia Settle argues, these Pakistani financial networks are:

> not a digression by which monetary practices return to more simplified, pre-capitalist forms. Not definancialization, or even demonetization in the conventional sense, the practices ... are an expression of global financial integration because they represent new financial strategies that respond to new financial risks that arise with changing financial conditions.
>
> *(2016: 115)*

Settle writes against the narrative of the post-2007 Pakistani economy as a 'return to the traditional social ties of solidarity and obligation' (116). (This ontologisation of behaviour along the lines of national stereotypes can be seen elsewhere: the informal market is labelled a return to *guanxi* [personalised networks] and familial relations in China, and a joyfully subversive anti-market strategy in African countries.[8]) Against the narrative that the 'informal economy' is somehow outside of global finance, Settle argues that it is 'an expression of global financial integration and an alternative, locally constituted version of financialized globalization' (11). The personalised nature of these circuits of debt and credit slots neatly into the self-creation myth of the genre of personal finance, a collision of economy and self that Hamid's novel explores through its genre of satire.

This entanglement of finance and the personal is reiterated and extended in the novel's narrative voice: perhaps the most striking formal feature of Hamid's novel is not its genre but its narration in the second-person singular. This 'you' address is particularly interpellative, or as one wag at the *Washington Post* writes the '[you] constantly reaches off the page and pokes you in the I' (Charles 2013). Through this unusual style, *Filthy Rich* calls on the reader to join in sustaining the narrative of financial ascendancy: 'for our collaboration to work, in other words, you must know yourself well enough to know what you want and where you want to go. Self-help books are two-way streets, after all. Relationships' (77). In cahoots with the reader throughout, the cul-de-sac of the self in a book such as *American Psycho* (where finance leads to increasing social isolation) is replaced by a two-way street of mutual cooperation.

Hamid makes explicit the imaginative labour that the reader must carry out to keep afloat the collaborative project of self-improvement, for books are 'black squiggles on pulped wood or, increasingly, dark pixels on a pale screen. To transform these icons into characters and events, you must imagine. And when you imagine, you create' (97). Referring to reading the novel, this description of mental labour could equally apply to the market-imaginary necessary for the realisation of finance, a cultural animation particularly important for reaching a population that has less access to institutionally maintained financial products. In fact, 'when you imagine, you create' could easily serve as the chapter title in a book of personal finance: Daniel Fridman's ethnography of fans of the *Rich Dad, Poor Dad* series reports the imaginative feats necessary to achieve financial success: as one fan says, 'I have to train my brain to be able to visualize an opportunity and take it. It is a way of fertilizing the soil of my brain to be ready to jump on an opportunity' (Fridman 2016: 97). The work of imagination here is the one that must shuttle between the individual 'you' holding the book and the national/global narrative of finance as the most likely avenue for success in the twenty-first century, suturing the human to the financial in its form.

This cooperative relationship between author and reader is transformed in the opening pages of the novel: the narrator's attention switches from the 'you' of the reader to the more captive 'you' of a character. This shift occurs abruptly between sentences: 'this book is a self-help book,' the reader is told.

> Its objective, as it says on the cover, is to show how you get filthy rich in rising Asia. And to do that it has to find you, huddled, shivering, on the packed earth under your mother's cot one cold, dewy morning.
>
> *(4)*

The accretive bridge of 'and' between the sentences leads the reader into this shift with the belief that it is a continuation of the address to them, only to be confronted by specificity: an infant with a class position, a mother, a time of day, and a location that literally grounds the narrative. This slippery slide between the 'you' of the reader and the 'you' of character is a way of signalling the scales of specificity that literature works between to think and feel through the difficulty of representing both a global system and an individuated experience of it. This individual experience, however, does not have the allegorical purity of a character standing in for a specific economic position (the explicit class position of the characters in Charles Dickens or the position of banker in Trollope, Ellis, or Theodore Dreiser's *The Financier*). Nor is it akin to Gary Shteyngart's *Super Sad True Love Song* (2010), whose characters walk under a cloud of their credit rating, an individuated economic position that reveals the falling away of class consciousness from our identification with the economy.[9]

The closeness of the bond between personal finance and the individual is exhibited by the preternatural knowledge the narrator has about the soon-to-be entrepreneur who is the subject of the narration: 'the whites of your eyes are yellow, a consequence of spiking bilirubin levels in your blood … you're likely to recover. But right now you feel like you're going to die' (4). This narrator is not omniscient: those at the periphery of the narrative of financial uplift remain hazy even at the level of plot: '*maybe* [your mother] doesn't think you're going to die. Then again, *maybe* she does' (4); '*possibly* [your father] exits the compound and makes his way to the ridge… *Possibly* he is alone, or possibly he is not' (6, emphasis added). In these moments, the narrator does not know what these people are doing and he does not care for they will never embody the entrepreneurial drive that personal finance seeks. Similarly, the unproductive years of the protagonist's childhood are swiftly covered until he sets off for the city and becomes a financial and narrative actor.

In line with its genre, the novel teaches 'you' to not only animate finance, but to increasingly identify it. We can see this movement in the embodied forms that finance takes over the course of the novel. The swiftly reached journey to the city is one of the only moments in the novel described in epochal terms:

> You witness a passage of time that outstrips its chronological equivalent. Just as when headed into the mountains a quick shift in altitude can vault one from subtropical jungle to semi-arctic tundra, so too can a few hours on a bus from rural remoteness to urban centrality appear to span millennia… You embody one of the great changes of your time.
>
> *(13–14)*

It is fascinating that this specific moment is granted an expansiveness of scale. Of course, one reason for this is simply that the narrator is leaping over a large distance that is both quantitatively and qualitatively large.

However, I would suggest that the scale of the moment occurs because it is depicting the basic fact of global finance: that of combined and uneven development, even within the space of one country, tying the dynamic of national and global finance to a local instantiation of this globality.[10] The planetary vista we are given is sutured to the specific by the shift from 'witness' to 'embody,' and from observation to experience. This braiding of global and personal finance is given a final binding twist at the conclusion of the book with the narrator's fall from financial power to (relative) poverty and illness. At this point, the narrating financial voice myopically contracts to the scale of the protagonist focusing on his day-to-day existence. In these scenes of decrepitude, why does the narrative voice not discard the protagonist as he drops away from the upward trajectory of the financial storyline? It is because by the end of the novel, finance cannot break away from the personal. As the protagonist falls ill, he succumbs to 'some mad impulse to slough off [his] wealth, like an animal moulting in the autumn … When it is over, [his] financial bones retain only tiny slivers of their former meat' (189). Giving away the remainder of his capital, the protagonist cannot shed finance: in the metaphorical compression of self and economy, the 'financial bones' are indicative of the bodily entanglement of finance. If he previously embodied finance – that is to slip inside the idea of an epochal claim – here the financial bones allow for no such escape.

We have not been acculturated into thinking of finance as a particularly social form of economics. However, by taking the link between the personal and the financial not just at the level of content but as the very basis of how the novel is narrated, Hamid shows that neither side of this two-way street has a choice to disengage. Without the potential for wealth that the narrative of financial uplift offers, the protagonist would have remained in his village; without the creative imagination of the protagonist whose ingenuity makes money, the financial narrative dries up. In the small diegetic slice that *Filthy Rich* offers us, the term financial in the sense understood by the *Financial Times* probably only applies to the protagonist for a couple of decades somewhere between poverty and bankruptcy. However, as an individual living in a rapidly expanding economy, he is embedded and inculcated into finance beyond the moments where he interacts with it. That is to say that even when his life is not directly dealing with finance, he is symbiotically tied to it. The form of finance provides the limiting parameters of his life in capitalism, which is to say, his life. Compared to the violent ends met by financiers in US novels such as *American Psycho* and *Cosmopolis*, Hamid shows a very different intimacy with finance capital. By baking the difficult symbiosis of the global economy and the individual into its form, *Filthy Rich* offers a heuristic for thinking through the collision of finance with life.

## Notes

1 Buildings depicted include the Jim Mao Building and Oriental Pearl Tower in Shanghai, Arche De La Defence in Paris, Petronas Towers in Kuala Lumpur, IFC 2 in Hong Kong, Shurfit-Stone Building in Chicago, Commerzbank Tower in Frankfurt, New York Stock Exchange, Taipei 101, The Gherkin in London, TransAmerica Pyramid in San Francisco, and the Landmark Tower in Yokohama.

2 The critical work has often dwelt on this aspect of the novel. Richard Godden describes this as the 'thin phenomenology of Bateman's experience' (2011: 853). Similarly, Patrick Walter writes that 'each New York setting of *American Psycho* is populated by undifferentiated yuppie stereotypes' (2012: 142), and 'rather than clearly delineated personalities with definite subjective intentionality, characters' names and, most importantly, the name 'Patrick Bateman,' come to signify completely homogenous and replaceable nodes' (143).

3 For ethnographic work on Wall Street traders, see Ho 2009. For non-standardised finance, see Tsai 2002 and Settle 2016. For race and finance in the US, see Been et al. 2009, Dymski et al. 2013, Rosenberg and Rusert 2014, Rugh 2014, and Rugh et al. 2015.

4 For studies of culture, see Aitken 2007, Clark et al. 2004, and Haiven 2011. For work on gender and finance, see Sarto 2010 and Joseph 2013. For work on race and finance in the US, see Been et al. 2009, Dymski, Hernandez, and Mohanty 2013, Rosenberg and Rusert 2014, Rugh 2014, and Rugh et al. 2015.

5 In their forthcoming Special Issue of *MLQ* on scale and value, editors Jim English and Ted Underwood survey the recent focus on scale in literary studies from the 'gigahistoricism' (forthcoming 280) of Pascale Casanova's global literary history to what Mark Seltzer has described as the 'incrementalist turn ... toward the minor and the scaled-down' (2011: 272).

6 The category of 'emerging' contains a strange and shifting geography that includes an 'assorted selection of Asian, African and Latin American countries, two European Union member-states [and] a swathe of central eastern European former communist countries' (Pryke 2000: 195), a collection of nations that is selected based on data from the World Bank and is created by the IFC using data from the World Bank.

7 In comparison, 32% of the population has access to the formal financial system in Bangladesh, and this figure amounts to 48% in India and 59% in Sri Lanka (Nenova, Niang, and Ahmad 2009: ix).

8 This ontologising of non-formal economic structures reiterates racial and ethnic stereotypes that are deeply suspect. 'Taken as authentic features of an essential "Chinese culture," both the Chinese family and *guanxi* particularism have been thoroughly fetishized as objects of cultural analysis by scholars studying overseas Chinese' (Ong and Nonini 1997: 21). For the claims of insurrectionary African economies, see Simone 2008.

9 The 'you' of *Filthy Rich* is more aligned with two recent works that use another unusual narrative voice: Joshua Ferris's debut novel *Then We Came to the End* (2008) and Chang-rae Lee's *On Such a Full Sea* (2014). Both of these novels use the first-person plural to think through the possibilities of navigating a collective voice under the deeply individuated economics of the twenty-first century. For work on *Super Sad* and credit rating, see McClanahan 2014.

10 In this moment, we can also witness a strange metaphorical collapse between time and space: space (a change in ecosystems) is used to better elucidate time (millennia) as though they were separable, although of course the bus journey covers both time and space. This is a signal feature of finance as Joshua Clover reminds us in his reading of Thomas Pynchon's *Against the Day*: finance is a process that 'restlessly pass[es] off time as space' (Clover 2011: 44). That is, after imperial expansion has reached its maximum capacity, money is instead made from finance, a form of capital accumulation that acts as if profit can be made without labour, however is merely the exporting of labour – through space in the expansion of empire, and through a delaying of the necessary labour time during the end of the imperial cycle; thus, 'the financialized formula M-M′ is in fact always the formula M-M′[C].' (44–5). In this moment, 'time is colonized as if it were space. But only "as if" ... This is one way of thinking about capitalist crisis: when a regime of accumulation starts passing time off as space' (45).

## References

Abbas, K. and Malik, M. (2010) Impact of financial liberalization and deregulation on banking sector in Pakistan. *PIDE* Working Articles 64 (2010). n.p. Web.

AbdouMaliq, S. (2008) The last shall be first: African urbanities and the larger African world. In: Huyssen, A. (ed.) *Other Cities, Other Worlds*. Durham, NC: Duke University Press.

Aitken, R. (2007) *Performing Capital: Toward a Cultural Economy of Popular and Global Finance*. New York: Palgrave Macmillan.

Baucom, Ian. (2005) *Specters of the Atlantic: Finance Capital, Slavery, and the Philosophy of History*. Durham, NC: Duke University Press.

Been, V., Ellen, I. and Madar, J. (2009) The high cost of segregation: exploring racial disparities in high cost lending. *Fordham Urban Law Journal*, 36 (3), pp. 362–85.

Charles, R. (2013). Mohsin Hamid's '*How to Get Filthy Rich in Rising Asia*: Life, self help-style. *Washington Post*, [online], Books. Available at www.washingtonpost.com/entertainment/books/mohsin-hamids-how-to-get-filthy-rich-in-rising-asia-life-self-help-style/2013/02/26/0a218216-7abf-11e2-82e8-61a46c2cde3d_story.html [Accessed 17 May 2017].

Clark, G., Thrift, N. and Tickell, A. (2004) Performing finance: the industry, the media and its image. *Review of International Political Economy*, 11 (2), pp. 289–310.
Clover, J. (2011) Autumn of the system: poetry and financial capital. *Journal of Narrative Theory*, 41 (1), pp. 34–52.
Deckard, S., Lawrence, N., Lazarus, N., Macdonald, G., Mukherjee, U., Parry, B., and Shapiro, S. (2015) *Combined and Uneven Development: Towards a New Theory of World-Literature*. Liverpool: Liverpool University Press.
DeLillo, D. (2003) *Cosmopolis: A Novel*. New York: Scribner.
Djankov, S., Mcleish, C., & Klein, M. U. (2006) Doing business. 2007: how to reform: comparing regulation in 175 economies. Washington, D.C., World Bank. http://site.ebrary.com/id/10137789.
Dymski, G., Hernandez, J. and Mohanty, L. (2013) Race, gender, power, and the US subprime mortgage and foreclosure crisis: a meso analysis. *Feminist Economics*, 19 (3), pp. 124–51.
Easton, B. (1991) *American Psycho: A Novel*. New York: Vintage Books.
Ferris, J. (2008) *Then We Came to the End: A Novel*. London: Penguin.
Fridman, D. (2016) *Freedom from Work: Embracing Financial Self-Help in the United States and Argentina*. Redwood City, CA: Stanford University Press.
Godden, R. (2011) Fictions of fictitious capital: American psycho and the poetics of deregulation. *Textual Practice*, 25 (5), pp. 853–66.
Haiven, M. (2011) Finance as capital's imagination?: reimagining value and culture in an age of fictitious capital and crisis. *Social Text*, 29 (3), pp. 93–124.
Hamid, M. (2013) *How to Get Filthy Rich in Rising Asia: A Novel*. New York: Riverhead Books.
Ho, K. (2009) *Liquidated: An Ethnography of Wall Street*. Durham, NC: Duke University Press.
Joseph, M. (2013) Gender, entrepreneurial subjectivity, and pathologies of personal finance. *Social Politics: International Studies in Gender, State and Society*, 20 (2), pp. 242–73.
Kiyosaki, R. (2000) *Rich Dad, Poor Dad: What the Rich Teach Their Kids about Money—That the Poor and Middle Class Do Not!* New York: Warner Books.
La Berge, L.C. (2014) The rules of abstraction: methods and discourses of finance. *Radical History Review*, 2014 (118), pp. 93–112.
Lee, C. (2014) *On Such a Full Sea*. New York: Riverhead Books.
Lewis, M. (2014) *Flash Boys: A Wall Street Revolt*. New York: W.W. Norton & Company.
Martin, R. (2002) *Financialization of Daily Life*. Philadelphia, PA: Temple University Press.
McClanahan, A. (2014) Bad credit: the character of credit scoring. *Representations*, 126 (1), pp. 31–57.
McGurl, M. (2016) "Neither indeed could I forebear smiling at myself": a reply to Wai Chee Dimock. *Critical Inquiry*, 39 (3), pp. 632–38.
Meenai, S. and Ansari, J. (2004) *Money and Banking in Pakistan*. Karachi: Oxford University Press.
Morton, T., 2013. *Hyperobjects: Philosophy and Ecology after the End of the World*. University of Minnesota Press.
Nenova, T., Niang, C. and Ahmad, A. (2009) *Bringing Finance to Pakistan's Poor: A Study on Access to Finance for the Underserved and Small Enterprises*. Washington, DC: World Bank.
Ong, A. and Nonini, D. (1997) *Ungrounded Empires: The Cultural Politics of Modern Chinese Transnationalism*. New York: Routledge.
Rosenberg, J. and Rusert, B. (2014) Framing finance: rebellion, dispossession, and the geopolitics of enclosure in Samuel Delany's Neveryon Series. *Radical History Review*, 2014 (118), pp. 64–91.
Rugh, J. (2014) Double jeopardy: why latinos were hit hardest by the US foreclosure crisis. *Social Force*, 93 (3), pp. 1139–184.
Rugh, J., Albright, L. and Massey, D. (2015) Race, space, and cumulative disadvantage: a case study of the subprime lending collapse. *Social Problems*, 62 (2), pp. 186–218.
Sarto, J. (2010) Note: the disproportionate representation of women in subprime lending: cause, effect, and remedies. *Women's Rights Law Reporter*, 31, pp. 337–67.
Sassen, S. (2009) Cities in today's global age. SAIS Review. 29, 3–34.
Seltzer, M. (2011) The official world. *Critical Inquiry*, 37 (4), pp. 724–53.
Settle, A. (2016) Locating finacialization in a less-developed economy: micro responses to liberalization and volatility in Pakistan. *Competition & Change*, 20 (2), pp. 106–21.
Shonkwiler, A. (2010) Don DeLillo's financial sublime. *Contemporary Literature*, 51 (2), pp. 246–82.
Sidaway, J. and Pryke, M. (2000) The strange geographies of 'emerging markets.' *Transactions of the Institute of British Geographers*, 25 (2), pp. 187–201.

Simone, A. (2008) The last shall be first: African urbanities and the larger African world. In: Huyssen, A. (ed.) *Other Cities, Other Worlds: Urban Imaginaries in a Globalizing Age*. Durham, NC: Duke University Press Books, pp. 99–120.

Tanoukhi, N. (2008) The scale of world literature. *New Literary History*, 39 (3), pp. 599–617.

Tsai, K. (2002) *Back-alley Banking: Private Entrepreneurs in China*. New York: Cornell University Press.

Trollope, A., 2005. *The way we live now*. Broadview Press.

Van, A. Ambivalent speculations: America as England's future in "The Way We Live Now". Novel: A Forum on Fiction, 39.1, pp. 75–96.

Walter, P. (2012) Cyberkill: melancholia, globalization and media terrorism. *American Psycho and Glamorama. Arizona Quarterly: A Journal of American Literature, Culture, and Theory*, 68 (4), pp. 131–54.

World Bank Staff, 2007. *Doing Business in 2007: Understanding Regulation*. World Bank Publications.

# 37

# BEHAVIORAL ECONOMICS AND GENRE

*Michelle Chihara*

In 2008, the failure of almost all economists to predict the financial crisis dealt a blow to the public reputation of the "dismal science." The influential monetarist and Chairman of the Federal Reserve, Alan Greenspan, had famously been a devoted follower of neoclassical economics, the efficient market hypothesis, and the Objectivism of free-market zealot and author Ayn Rand. His legacy was tarnished by his inability to react to or even fully perceive the "irrational exuberance" in the markets before the crash. He was forced to admit, before Congress, that his "ideology" about the infallibility of efficient markets had been proven wrong: "Yes, I've found a flaw," he told Representative Henry Waxman. "I don't know how significant or permanent it is. But I've been very distressed by that fact." (Andrews 2008). Orthodox economic free marketeers like Greenspan had long relied on both an abstraction and a normative prediction about the rational economic subject at the heart of free markets. *Homo economicus*, in aggregate and over time, always acts to maximize utility, based on all available information. He is a crucial component of the theory that markets can and should be efficient. The efficient market hypothesis is, in turn, crucial to the idea that markets are the best way to allocate resources in a society. The stranglehold of *homo economicus* and orthodox economic theory thus loosened at the moment of the crisis, and from within the behavioral sciences and business schools, behavioral economics was poised to position itself as the best new set of explanations. I argue that behavioral economics provided a template for a new genre of narrative in popular culture, which in some ways filled the space left by *The Fountainhead.*

While psychologists Daniel Kahneman and Amos Tversky had been building a movement since the 1980s to incorporate their research into economics, it was during the Obama administration and after the crisis that they would see their efforts come to fruition: Michael Lewis wrote that their "Prospect Theory" paper was "scarcely cited in the first decade after its publication," but that in 2010, it was the second most cited paper "in all of economics." By 2016, when behavioral economist Richard Thaler finished his term as the president of the American Economic Association, "every tenth paper published in economics would have a behavioral angle to it" (Lewis 2017, p. 342). When 2008 and a seeming dearth of explanations arrived, behavioral economics provided templates for a new and different, but still ideological, version of economic common sense in America. In many ways, little changed after 2008 within existing economics-based hierarchies. Instead, as economic historian Philip

Mirowski writes, the crisis provoked a reassertion of power by the orthodoxy along with the "intentional manufacture of doubt and uncertainty in the general populace for specific political motives" (Mirowski and Nik-Khah 2013, p. 280). The crisis exacerbated real economic problems with crushingly real material consequences, and those material consequences shifted the political landscape and contributed to the rise of a global populism. But in the decade that I study, between 2006 and 2016, historically specific economic suffering was often met with further mystification, in a partially manufactured crisis of understanding in which behavioral economics played a crucial role. The behavioral genre both stokes and salves, within literary and popular audiences, a hunger for economic explanation.

The simplest definition of behavioral economics is that it applies psychological research about human behavior to economic models, and by positing that irrational psychological tendencies not only sometimes drive individual actors but also shape the economy, behavioral economics ostensibly unseats *homo economicus*. After 2008, behavioral economists rose to positions of great academic and political power. When President Barack Obama started the Social Behavioral Sciences Team by Executive Order in 2015, he consolidated the existing international trend by ensconcing behavioral economics in the White House (the Behavioral Insights Team in the UK, known as the "nudge unit," had been formed by the coalition government in 2010). I argue that behavioral economics provided a governing set of assumptions for a new genre of economic narratives, across a range of cultural products, with a special emphasis on stories which included an element of economic explanation but were not marketed as conventional "economic" or "business" press. At its most basic, the genre uses behavioral data to explain some aspect of human behavior that seems irrational. I use "genre" to indicate both typified rhetorical actions and systems of expectations, a mode which helps account for how audiences encounter and interpret various texts.

*Homo economicus*, as an abstraction and a normative prediction, was never meant as a complete philosophical account of the human mind. But in aggregate and over time, *homo economicus* is a crucial component of the theory that markets can and should be efficient. He grounds that philosophy. He always acts to maximize utility, based on all available information. Utility could be defined to include subjective preferences, and rational expectations theory and experienced utility could be (and were) used to explain a wide variety of differences among economic actors. Such theories were fundamental to economists' claims of scientific authority for efficient market hypotheses, which were based on utility-maximizing actors, and the efficient market hypothesis (EMH) is crucial to the idea that markets are the best way to allocate resources in a society. Behavioral economics does not challenge economists' overarching emphasis on efficiency, but it does begin with the premise that nonutility-maximizing irrational psychological tendencies profoundly shape the economy, in aggregate and over time. But of course, the faith in free markets is not in itself a rational judgment that arises from logical roots, but an ideology that interpellates subjective notions of freedom and desire. The relatively complete debunking of "trickle down economics" has not rid the culture of its proponents, and I argue that the behavioral genre functions as a new method for the cultural absorption of old economic logics.

The rise of behavioral economics after 2008 was overdetermined, already part of the intellectual self-justification of business schools (Bennis 2005) and also already an answer to orthodox economics' failures of prediction and explanation. I also argue that it was part of the emotional logic of the discourse around austerity, which the Tea Party pushed to the center of their political agenda in the same period. The Nobel-Prize-in-Economics winning and New York Times best-selling behavioral psychologist Daniel Kahneman's account of a two-system decision-making self was foundational to the field of behavioral economics.

Kahneman's *homo moribus*—to coin a term—can be read as an optimistic account of the economic subject's ability to internalize austerity. In Kahneman's optimism, I see good old-fashioned American progressive pragmatism. He believes that the fast, intuitive, often irrational System 1, within the economic subject, often makes irrational mistakes. System 1 can be retrained by the slow, rational System 2. I use the term "emotional logic" to refer to Martijn Konings account of the emotional logic of capitalism. Konings identifies a "distinctively American tradition of pragmatist thought, which was pervaded by optimism regarding the politically progressive potential of America's trajectory of economic modernization." This optimism had at its heart "a vision of an organic connection between the self and its institutional symbols." In this view, when institutions fail, "this problem was generally seen not as embedded in their constitution but as capable of being remedied through pragmatic adjustments" (Konings 2015, p. 69). Behavioral insights were always, in part, an alternative means of better internalizing the same austerity measures that economics has always pushed. So, for example, behavioral economists could step away from the increasingly politically polarized macroeconomic debates around social security, and could simply design nudges that would increase individuals' savings for retirement, in aggregate and over time (this refers to the work of the chair of Harvard's Economics department chair, David Laibson). Narratives that perform *homo moribus*'s organic connection to institutionally mandated economic choices perform both an attraction and a repulsion to the authority behind austerity, without escaping its logic.

Effectively, without challenging the institutional powers that shape the economy and without challenging the logic that posits austerity as a solution, the nudge promised to make pragmatic adjustments go down easy. I argue that behavioral economics' wide public appeal is generated by its attention to the intractable problems that emerge from austerity, like Laibson's attraction to technical solutions near but not for a highly charged politicized issue like social security, combined with the relief of the behavioral economist's politics-free clever fix. Konings writes that center-left progressives often miss the underlying appeal of the neoliberal emotional logic of austerity, which promises to restore an "authentic republican ethos" (Konings 2015). Behavioral economist Richard Thaler says that he believes in a "libertarian paternalism." The behavioral subject is free (liberated) once she has internalized the paternal authority. After the economist's intervention, she has painlessly internalized his ethos. In behavioral economics, individuals can be guided toward economics' demands gently, becoming self-reliant without having to feel the pain of self-denial.

This chapter focuses on this mode of thought in two podcasts, Planet Money and Serial, two of the most successful in the new digital aural medium, both of which are good examples of the genre that I argue comes from behavioral economics—perhaps behavioral realism will fit. In other work, I analyze Gimlet Media's Start Up and Reply All, the books of Michael Lewis even before his book about behavioral economics, the film based on his work *The Big Short*, and apps that formed a behavioral economics cultural narrative like Hello Alfred, Task Rabbit, and Uber. In all of this, I rely on Sianne Ngai's trailblazing definitions in *Our Aesthetic Categories* to argue that what I am calling a genre has, as part of its generic definition, an aesthetic payoff. The behavioral genre relies heavily on the aesthetic judgment of interesting. I argue that the genre functions by reducing or containing the anxiety that political or social issues might otherwise spark in the listener by producing relief when those issues are produced as interesting aesthetic objects. It's possible that my use of "genre" fits entirely inside Ngai's aesthetic category (or that it does not), but by using "genre," I'm able to describe a typified rhetorical mode across a range of cultural products—a set of repeated features, which produce a specific relationship between political concepts and affective responses. In the vein of more recent genre theory, I mean that typified rhetorical actions create socially located systems of expectations, a mode which helps account for how audiences encounter and interpret various texts. Interesting gives the behavioral economic genre its payoff or climax, with the libidinal load that those terms carry. The genre raises the specter of systemic problems around inequality and racism and sexism, performs its attraction to hard-to-solve social problems within its inability to imagine the collective and in thrall to the logic of austerity, and then produces something on a spectrum between affective relief and obsession by repressing the ghosts of history.

Both Planet Money and Serial also index changing conditions in the production and reception of aural media, and in the changing symbolic economies that produce journalistic objectivity and authority. I argue that Planet Money is behavioral realism's answer to the hypermasculine "big swinging dick" authority of financial print culture which Leigh Claire La Berge describes in her literary and cultural history of the 1980s, *Scandals & Abstractions* ("big swinging dick" is Michael Lewis's oft-quoted term from his time on Wall Street). In the aesthetic she locates in *Bonfire of the Vanities* and *Wall Street*, the economic is a genre-defining aspect of realism. "For Wolfe, finance is complicated and therefore difficult to represent; for Stone, finance is exclusive and therefore difficult to represent. For both, the capture of finance, its representation, signals a success of the realist mode" (La Berge 2015, p. 76). Within that, depictions of hypermasculine financial elites became a sign of hard-hitting truth: money men become the economic and the real. After the failure of this type of realism to either prevent or predict its own massive failure, Planet Money stepped in with a promise of "stories" and "fun" packaging economic explanation, a new kind of financial news indexed as a new kind of masculinity. The show began with an acceptance of the idea that finance is complicated and difficult to represent, but instead of pinning its authority on capturing hypermasculine difficulty, the Planet Money host shows his initial intimidation by and distance from that difficulty, and then performs his mastery over his own fear. The Planet Money host commands the real, and his own new masculinity, by not being bullied.

The tagline and promotions for the show read:

> The economy, explained, with stories and surprises. Imagine you could call up a friend and say, 'Meet me at the bar and tell me what's going on with the economy.' Now imagine that's actually a fun evening. That's what we're going for at Planet Money. People seem to like it.

The tone is intimate, almost feminine, gossipy, and informal. The "surprises" make clear that the "stories" are not the same type of narrative as *The Wall Street Journal's* financial stories. The promo assumes that the economy needs to be explained, and that its content is not necessarily "fun." I read Planet Money's new form of financial coverage, and the folksy authority of its hosts, as derived from Kahneman's *homo moribus*. It's as if irrational System 1 needs to be calmed down, and System 2 agreed to meet her at the bar to explain things. As I show in my analysis of host Adam Davidson—the founder of the show—and his interview with Elizabeth Warren, like behavioral economics itself, the behavioral realist has trouble with subjects that are not anxious but angry. Caught between his desire for old journalistic forms of authority and prestige and his desire to upend them, between his anxiety about austerity and his investment in its logics, between his own internalized faith in the old hypermasculine real and his new mode, Adam Davidson basically came apart as a radio host. But the appeal of the genre he helped to create lived on in Planet Money's success.

Planet Money went into production in 2008 just before the crash, and in 2009, it won a Peabody, the most coveted mainstream award in radio, for the episode called "The Giant Pool of Money," which explained the subprime crisis. It shares that award, founding members, and many stylistic tics with *This American Life*. It launched its successful Money brand by explaining the financial crisis to a lay audience, or an audience that did not already have mastery of economic jargon and wasn't necessarily able to follow incremental stories about the financial markets and the institutions that make them up. David Zimmerman wrote in *Panic*! that crisis has offered novelists in the past "an instrument and idiom in which to explore the limits of narratability" (Zimmerman 2006, p. 2). In the face of the un-narratable aspects of the crisis, Adam Davidson, in "The Giant Pool of Money" felt compelled to find a new idiom to describe a crisis which he felt was hard to describe:

> I mean, some strange financial instruments that no one's ever heard of had problems in institutions that no one understands, and suddenly I'm going to lose my job or my cousin just got laid off or we might go into a depression. So the stakes couldn't be higher, but there couldn't be less clarity, less of an ability to understand.
>
> *(Glass and Davidson 2008)*

Davidson speaks with the idiomatic "I mean," a stylistic cue that links Ira Glass's trademark informality and upspeaks to Planet Money's new explanatory mode. When asked to explain how his new show differed from conventional economic news, Davidson said, "I feel like the voice of business journalism is sort of, it's an authoritative voice of God," Davidson said. Planet Money, with its "I means," would not be that voice: "There is no authority," Davidson told the Nieman Narrative Conference in 2009. "It's a process" (Seward 2009).

Just after his claim to have broken free of conventional business press authority, in June of 2009, Davidson interviewed Elizabeth Warren, then the senior advisor on the congressional panel monitoring the Troubled Asset Relief Program (TARP). The TARP panel was intended to oversee the government's dispensation of billions of dollars in relief to the banks. Adam Davidson began the interview in an obviously combative position. The conflict really flamed up when Elizabeth Warren articulated her view that because in her position she oversaw the use of taxpayer money to solve a crisis created by the private sector, she bore some responsibility to make sure the interests of "American families" were represented. Davidson insisted that her role as a monitor for the TARP panel was narrowly defined, that she should have been an economic expert brought in only to save the banks, and that fixing the banks had to take priority over all other interests. She said, "I understand that a banking system is a necessary condition for a functioning economy, but it's not sufficient." Davidson, in return, became even more unfriendly and upset. He interrupted her, snorted loudly, sputtered, and repeatedly talked over her to dismiss her positions as so extreme that he "literally could not name one person" who agreed with her (Davidson 2009).

Adam Davidson had essentially the same reaction that JPMorgan Chase CEO Jamie Dimon had when Senator Warren criticized the banking industry, and Dimon responded by asserting that Warren didn't "fully understand the global banking system." The gendered element in such calls to authority for economic certainty (which Deirdre McCloskey showed were largely narrative in their authority in 1992s If You're So Smart) is also obvious in Adam Davidson's behavior, but part of what's interesting about the intensity of the threat that Davidson perceived to his masculinity was that it derived from his perception that Warren was not sufficiently cowed by the masculine authorities that he too claimed not to be cowed by. He claimed that he was not angry with Warren but with the fact that the TARP oversight panel was not populated with "well-respected economists" and "senior statesmen." These icons of disinterested wisdom and masculine authority are "the kind of people" he talks to "all the time on Planet Money." He finished by claiming that Elizabeth Warren was not journalistically objective, even though she wasn't a journalist, but a politician who might need to think about the consequences of her actions on a variety of constituents. He said that he wanted the TARP panel to be "more public broadcasting, less cable news." Contrast this with his previous claim that "there is no authority," only "process."

It's also striking that in his explanation of his own explanatory mode, Adam Davidson's justifications were not far from very close to Warren's arguments. As when Davidson referred to a connection between strange financial instruments and his cousin losing his job, Warren argued that the TARP had consequences for American families. Like Davidson, she did not accept the godlike authority of the voices that had failed to explain such instruments and their consequences. Like Davidson, she believed that a banking sector is necessary to a "functioning economy." But Warren didn't see her role as a politician (not a journalist) as a simple duty to save the banking sector on the banking sector's terms; she saw her position as a public servant's with a responsibility to the public. The banks' interests weren't necessarily the same as the public's. *The stakes couldn't be higher.* Davidson ostensibly saw this. But new aesthetic approach to financial news was still grounded in the old logic. His host persona was created around raising the social stakes Warren perceived, and then congratulating himself for his own ability to distance himself affectively from those stakes, avoiding anger in favor of anxiety. He knows System 1 is worried, but he came to the bar to show her that System 2 was in control. In a female body, Warren told Davidson bluntly that he was wrong, that she herself was "data driven," and that the American middle class was under assault. While in many ways, Warren openly shared many "data driven" basic assumptions with Davidson about the economy, she both insisted on thinking systemically and on refusing to reduce or contain her own sense of moral urgency. She wasn't interested in fun new ways of thinking about things, and she claimed to have her own explanations. For her, the issues weren't interesting; they were life or death.

Davidson has been paid to speak at marquee financial conferences, like the University of Chicago Booth Management conference, and international conferences on microfinance. He has averred his feelings of intense admiration for Chicago School economists, and in his column for *The New York Times* frequently argued for austerity measures ("It Stinks But The Only Way To Fix The Economy Is To Squeeze The Middle Class" (Davidson 2011)). He had financial and ideological incentives to stand against pro-regulation politicians like Warren. Beyond that, a mini-scandal erupted after the Warren interview, in light of Planet Money's sole sponsorship from Ally Bank, which was the financially troubled GMAC under a new name. GMAC was a financial services company that collapsed in 2008 and received billions of dollars in TARP money. Even *Ad Age* (the advertising industry journal) wrote that for NPR, having such a single sponsor for such a single issue show was unusual: "The close alignment of message and news program is rare" (Ad Age). In the end, it was Davidson who was more vulnerable to charges of bias within traditional public broadcasting norms. This highlights the oddity of his reaction to Warren. He seems to accuse her of bias ("cable news"), but who is she biased toward? The middle class? The affective intensity of his reaction was surprising (particularly to Warren). He reacted from the outset as if she is the one already exhibiting a personal lack of control. In the face of feminine authority, moral urgency (as opposed to anxiety), and an articulated public need, Davidson seemed completely at sea. He immediately reverted to older medium's regime of authority in his search for solid ground. When Warren didn't fit into his new explanatory mode, he reverted to the old tools for discrediting noneconomic authority, in part because his new mode had always been a way of representing his commitment to austerity logic.

Serial is much less obviously about economics, but it is a prototypical example of behavioral realism in the way that it tackles a true crime topic and suppresses a social issue, the role that race plays in the justice system, with the merely interesting. For Ngai, "the hypercommodified, technologically-mediated conditions of production, distribution, and reception" bring "our equivocal aesthetic categories to the fore." The interesting calls up the possibility of its opposite, "disinterestedness," and "oscillates between interest and boredom." In its toggling around interest, "the experience of the interesting can quickly turn into one of obsession" (38). Both Serial and Planet Money use the word "interesting" in promotional materials. When Planet Money sought to hire a reporter in 2016, they posted an ad for a "smart, funny, interesting person to tell smart, funny, interesting stories," and Sarah Koenig and her co-producer on Serial used the word repeatedly to sell their second season. Even in Planet Money's standard promo, notice how quickly the possibility of disinterest is paired with interest: it's "actually" fun and "People seem to like it," but the possibility that it isn't inherently fun or that people maybe don't like it is raised. The same is true of the opening moments of Serial; producer Sarah Koenig begins her show about a murder case with the humdrum possibility of boredom: "I've spent every working day trying to figure out where a high school kid was for an hour after school one day in 1999." (TAL transcript) In covering financial news or in investigating the murder of a young girl, both shows are profoundly unoriginal. Part of the newness of their approach comes from their informality, their disavowal of conventional forms of journalistic authority, and their foregrounding of both the medium and of the process of reporting. They draw attention to the process itself, as interesting. Serial begins with technical details, its theme music plays the pre-recorded message from Global Tel-Link announcing a prepaid call, the company with sole corporate access to phone service for inmates, and the show spends a significant portion of the season going over cell phone technology.

Serial is explicitly concerned with individual perceptions of time, and explicitly disinterested in engaging with the narrative construction of memory or social experiences of time, which might be better described as history. This brings it fully into behavioral realism's inability to mediate between anger and anxiety, and between public and individual needs. Koenig begins Season One, before she describes the murder case, with this:

> Before I get into why I've been doing this, I just want to point out something I'd never really thought about before I started working on this story. And that is, it's really hard to account for your time, in a detailed way, I mean.
>
> How'd you get to work last Wednesday, for instance? Drive? Walk? Bike? Was it raining? Are you sure?
>
> Did you go to any stores that day? If so, what did you buy? Who did you talk to? The entire day, name every person you talked to. It's hard.
>
> *(Serial Transcript)*

This is Koenig's introduction to a story about the violent death of a young woman and the possibility that a young man of color has been wrongly imprisoned for fifteen years. But what behavioral realism finds most interesting is a behavioral question: How do humans account for their time? Not only does this suppress the political scale of the questions raised by the show, but it also directly rehearses questions from some of Daniel Kahneman's most highly circulated and publicized work.

Kahneman's arguments about an "experiencing self" and a "remembering self" were widely covered; he gave an extremely popular TED Talk and multiple articles appeared across lifestyle publications and the business press. Much of his writing discusses behavioral economic challenges in accounting for people's time in a detailed way. He says that the truth of the "experiencing self," which goes to work, drives, and goes to stores, is often lost to time. The "remembering self" uses narrative to not create a database of moments but narrative memories. Particularly in his TED talk (TED itself being part of what I call the behavioral genre), Kahneman claims that "the remembering self is a story-teller." He defines stories as made up of "changes, significant moments and endings" (TED). These moments are unreliable in their very difference, in the fact that they stand out from the numerical bulk of moments. The unquantifiable attributes of moments that have subjective significance grant meaning, but they can be at odds with what he calls in his book the true "quality of the experience." This is in his account of vacations, where the quantifiable number of positive moments as detailed in a journal and daily questionnaire constitutes the true "quality." (389)

In his TED talk, Kahneman says:

> We think of our future as anticipated memories. And basically you can look at this, you know, as a tyranny of the remembering self, and you can think of the remembering self sort of dragging the experiencing self through experiences that the experiencing self doesn't need.
>
> I have that sense that when we go on vacations this is very frequently the case; that is, we go on vacations, to a very large extent, in the service of our remembering self. And this is a bit hard to justify I think. I mean, how much do we consume our memories?
>
> *(TED transcript)*

For Kahneman, the "remembering self" is the self that chooses vacations, and this self tends to choose the vacations that create good memories. On a vacation, the experiencing self gets two weeks of happiness, which is quantifiably (and therefore really) more happiness. But for the remembering self, "two weeks is barely better, because there are no new memories added, you have not changed the story." In the TED talk, it's not clear how serious Kahneman is. But he does suggest that it's irrational to choose a hiking vacation that might have moments of daily discomfort just because it creates good memories. He asserts that vacationers don't "change the story" over one extra week, and that his data might justify shorter vacations, on a policy level. In his book, he writes, "How two selves within a single body can pursue happiness raises some difficult questions, both for individuals and societies that view the well-being of the population as a policy objective," Kahneman wrote in 2011 (Thinking Fast And Slow 14).

I will return to Serial, but it's important here to note that the appeal of behavioral economics is obvious in Kahneman's attention to lived happiness on a policy level, as against the orthodox economist's enshrined focus on greed and self-interest. Refreshingly, and seemingly unlike Greenspan and his colleagues, behavioral economics seemed not to argue that vacations would just appear if we let the market be free. Kahneman encourages policy makers to consider how much happiness is actually being created. He has also spoken publicly about the minimum income that correlates with happiness, which starts to sound a lot like an economic argument for meeting people's basic human needs. At the same time, the other side of the appeal of behavioral economics lies in Kahneman's implicit promise that taking away vacation days (austerity) doesn't have to feel bad.

There are strange moments in Kahneman's TED talk, like when he asks, "How much do we consume our memories?" Even if this is meant as a lighthearted comment, what does it mean? What does it mean to consume a memory? One can imagine an Orwellian scenario where a psychologist with Kahneman's mien threatens to erase memories because they are not being sufficiently or properly consumed. What does time mean, when experienced without our memories? For Kahneman, the remembering self, in its distance from quantitative evaluation, irrationally picks arbitrary moments as significant, instead of relating to time as an ongoing database of commensurable moments. He finds the meaning-making aspect of consciousness to be a tyrant, saying "Time has very little impact on the story," and finding it "hard to justify" that we choose vacations based on narrative significance (TED). From a different humanistic perspective, of course, subjective experience and historic context constitute the self. Time that doesn't impact the story is lost time. One could imagine the entire point of a vacation being the effort to change the larger story that is a life, to bring meaning-making to time spent outside of the wage relation. In this light, behavioral economics' insistence on the synchronic commensuration of emotions and experiences is a final step in the neoliberal colonization of the deepest reaches of the self, as evoked in Randy Martin's *Financialization of Daily Life* (Martin 2002). While for Kahneman, the remembering self's attachment to novelty might justify shorter vacations, that remembering self is also fundamentally irrational. At the same time, in other moments, Kahneman recognizes that differing definitions of "happiness" invalidate much of the data that use measurements of happiness to compare feelings and experiences. The architect of behavioral economics is like a detective, out to find a quantified base on which to ground the remembering self's reality.

The entire Season One of Serial can be described as Sarah Koenig's detective work toward building a better database of Adnan Syed's past, while always suppressing history. She wants to solve or explain a situation, but always with the assumption that the individual is a question she can solve with more information, but never with more subjective context over time. She seeks "experiencing self" information, but not the narrative of the remembering self. Even when she openly realizes that some of the reactions she is trying to elicit from Adnan could endanger his case, she treats the entire story as a question about the nature of his self and memory. How Adnan might have changed over fifteen years in prison, as well as the historically specific context for his case—these strike Koenig as irrelevant, including to her meditations on the nature of sociopathy. Many people believe Adnan to be innocent, believe that he was convicted in large part because he is a Muslim, and believe that he has now spent half his life in prison for a crime he didn't commit. Regardless of whether this is true, Koenig's overt goal is to know Adnan Syed. And yet, her evaluations of him always revolve around an implicit search for a human norm to which she can compare him (perhaps in behavioral psych). What would it mean to have a normal reaction to being incarcerated for a crime you didn't commit for most of your young life? Her show unquestionably helped Adnan Syed's legal case by bringing attention to the case. However, her treatment of Adnan makes the most sense if she is understood as a behavioral economist. The time she spends with Adnan does not create, for Koenig, a narrative between them. She spends large amounts of time on the phone with him; in fact, *Take Part* reported that Global Tek's monopoly on inmate calls means that Serial spent upward of $1,000 on the calls. Of course, the show must have spent more than this on reporting the story, but the prohibitive cost of communication is a measure of how hard it must be for Syed to speak with his actual family and friends on the outside. But while the Global Tek message brands the entire show, Koenig never asks what that corporate message might represent for Syed in the years since the trial. The social question of what it means to isolate inmates and to allow phone companies to profit off that isolation is a social question. These are data, but social data, not behavioral data.

In a show that promised depth and breadth, Koenig also spent more time on relatively unpromising cell phone tower details than on very real concerns about the role that anti-Muslim prejudice played in the trial, as put forward in a letter to the *Baltimore Sun* and signed by the entire South Asian Bar Association. Koenig refused this line of inquiry. Racial tensions would have moved the show's topic away from interesting questions about memory and the individual into the social and political. As with Elizabeth Warren's urgency, Adnan Syed's friend Rabia's intense and politicized urgency about the case embodies a relationship to context and history that clashes with the Serial aesthetic. The show generally makes light of the question of Muslim difference. But at one point, Syed's mother says in no uncertain terms that she is sure that anti-Muslim feeling drove the verdict, "Because we are Muslim, and we are minor in this country. So, that's why they took Adnan." In the audio of the show, you can hear a mother's helpless grief. In the original tape, Sarah Koenig responds, "I don't know, I mean—" again, using the cue for the informality of the behavioral genre as her only direct response. In the edit, she then cuts herself off and performs her distance from the very question of race: "You can hear me not believing her, right?" She gives an affective account of how hard she personally finds it to believe that the cops were motivated by "racism alone." She assumes the listener will find it equally outside the realm of likely that the justice system is systemically unfair to young men of color, but her affect is one of disinterest. Her constant nuanced attention to her own thoughts and everyday experiences, and to the experience of researching Syed's case, is paired with this moment of performative disinterest in the experience of his parents, to the point of cruelty.

This simultaneous investment in a subjective experience with a profoundly reductive account of what subjective experience might be is not only typical of behavioral realism but, I argue, constitutive of its appeal. Serial gained obsessive followers partly because they could try to solve an individual case, and part of the implicit appeal was that this solution would supplant the need to face a social issue—it would grant relief from racial anxiety without having to face or articulate racial anger. Annie McClanahan refers, in her chapter "Behavioral Economics and the Credit-Crisis Novel," to what she writes "may be most interesting about the behavioralist treatment of the economic subject": "its tendency to reduce, flatten, and generalize individual psychology" along with a "deep anxiety about the consequences of this reduction." McClanahan finds in the "surge of popularity" for behavioralism a desire to explain the crisis with "individual feelings" (22). She analyzes credit-crisis novels as "literary laboratories" for "problems of scale and historical causality that haunt behavioral economics" (30). For McClanahan, it was behavioral economics that focused explanations of the crisis on "personal impulses" like "hubris, irrationality, greed, lack of a social conscience" on the part of a number of bad actors.[1] In Serial, there is obviously no explanation of the crisis. But my argument is that part of behavioral realism's effect on the culture has been to imagine that human subjects can be extracted from time and history, and that this might even help to assess them in interesting new ways. I find it symptomatic, here, that McClanahan herself uses the term "interesting." The tendency to reduce individual psychology provokes new questions, and other anxieties. Behavioral realism does generate interest by trying to explain things it can't explain, or by trying to replace one explanation with another, such that attraction and anxiety create interest. The trial occurred in a period when anti-Muslim feeling was building throughout the United States, and the podcast narrates a situation where a courtroom full of people in traditional Muslim garb faced a prosecutor talking in stereotypes about "Islamic culture" and "besmirched honor" (Shah 2015). Koenig's performance of not having to address race generates relief, and keeps Serial provocative but merely interesting.

Serial is about what Koenig does and doesn't find interesting about the case, about the difficulty of explaining human being's inability to keep detailed accounts of their time, about memory—but not history, never about history. Value judgments seem to follow from factual ones but always revolve around Koenig's affect. Again in Ngai's terms, the seriality of Serial, its attention to the medium, and the act of checking the pleasures and displeasures of these aesthetic judgments against others' are marks of its aesthetic. And in fact, "citizen reporting" on the Syed case became a huge cottage industry, on Reddit. Interesting brought the *sensus communis* into existence. But this was explicitly a *sensus communis*, an aesthetic that seemed communal but that was not a community: the obsessed fans on Reddit had no strong ties with each other nor with the people whose lives they investigated and posted about publicly. They were not people who would see and bear witness to the victim's family, they were not jurors forced to consider each other and the consequences of their own actions, but they were an aesthetic community, bound together only by their interest and with a sense of their own agency partially suppressed by the show's aesthetic.

When Season Two of Serial came out, it promised another "deep dive" on a legal case, and the producers wrote in an email about the subjects: "What we can say is that they're very different from Season One, but no less interesting to us." And when Koenig announced that Bowe Berghdal would be the subject, she insisted that he was "such an interesting and unusual guy, not like anyone I've encountered before." The producers, Snyder and Koenig, used the word repeatedly in their interview with the *Wall Street Journal*. Snyder said that if listeners saw a headline that read "Pakistani, Afghan Leaders Discuss Resuming Afghan-Taliban Peace Talks," she wanted them to react differently after hearing the podcast: "I had sent it to these guys saying, 'I'd love it if, at the end of this story, listeners would see an article like that, want to read it, understand it, and actually have an emotional feeling about it.'" Notice how again, this sounds like System 2 being invited to the bar, where understanding could be linked to feeling. As with Planet Money, Serial is intended to change the listener's affect, as a means of driving and validating the explanation put forward in the show. Listeners will both understand more and be more interested in financial news or in peace talks. This describes, more than anything, a new relationship between System 2's reason and System 1's unreason, an explanation that also teaches the intuition not to find the financial news or peace talks boring. But of course, the financial news, the peace talks, or the truth of Adnan Syed's life might provoke not boredom but despair. The payoff comes in the relief offered when anxiety around the financial news, or the peace talks, or the justice system, is contained within merely interesting. But this relief is contingent and ultimately unsatisfying, because particularly in the historically specific moment in which behavioral realism arose, our issues and subjects cannot really be contained.

## Note

1 But for my purposes, the synechdocal relationship of individual to market-based whole predates the behavioral economists and comes straight from neoliberal architect Friedrich von Hayek and his understanding of tacit knowledge, neural networks, and the market as an information processor much like a human subject. The both impoverished and yet somehow more real version of a quantifiable human subject has many roots.

## References

Andrews, E. 2008. "Greenspan Concedes Error on Regulation," *The New York Times*, 23 October, p. B1.

Bennis, W. 2005. "How Business Schools Lost Their Way," *The Harvard Business Review*, May Issue, accessed online, https://hbr.org/2005/05/how-business-schools-lost-their-way.

Davidson, A. 2009. "Elizabeth Warren The Full Interview," *Planet Money*, 8 May, www.npr.org/sections/money/2009/05/the_full_warren_interview.html.

———. 2011. "It Stinks, But The Only Way To Fix The Economy Is To Squeeze The Middle Class," *The New York Times*, 9 November.

Glass, I. and A. Davidson. 2008. "The Giant Pool of Money," *This American Life*, 9 May, Audio transcript, www.thisamericanlife.org/radio-archives/episode/355/transcript.

Konings, M. 2015. "The Problem with Center-Left Critiques of Neoliberalism," *RoarMag.com*, 22 July.

La Berge, L.C., 2015. *Scandals and abstraction: financial fiction of the long 1980s*. Oxford University Press, USA.

Lewis, M. 2017. *The Undoing Project*, New York: W.W. Norton & Co., pp. 341–2.

Martin, R., 2002. *Financialization of daily life*. Temple University Press.

Mirowski, P. and E. Nik-Khah. 2013. "Private Intellectuals and Public Perplexity: The Economics Profession and the Economic Crisis," *History of Political Economy* 45(suppl 1): 279–311.

Seward, Z. 2008. "Adam Davidson Explains the Explainer," Nieman Narrative Conference at NiemanLab.org, 03 March, accessed online, www.niemanlab.org/2009/03/nprs-adam-davidson-explains-the-explainer-a-model-for-complex-news/.

Shah, M. 2015. "Improper race and religion references in Adnan Syed trial," *The Baltimore Sun*, 28 January, accessed online, http://www.baltimoresun.com/news/opinion/oped/bs-ed-syed-trial-20150128-story.html.

Zimmerman, D.A. 2006. *Panic!: Markets, Crises, and Crowds in American Fiction*, Chapel Hill: University of North Carolina Press.

# 38

# SERIALIZATION IN THE AGE OF FINANCE CAPITALISM

*David Buxton*

How might we critically approach the television series in a way that accounts for the nature of its form, a form which carries both ideological and economic ramifications? Few would deny that series fit awkwardly into an academic framework, by reason of their industrial volume, and because audience interest declines rapidly once they have disappeared from the screen. One could try to constitute a canon as in literary or film studies, but it is nevertheless difficult, if not impossible, to fully circumscribe a "work" sometimes extending to hundreds of episodes.[1] The choice made here is a synthesis, in very general terms, which encompasses the more commercial network series and the "quality" series produced by cable television, and which integrates on an equal basis the three terms evoked in the opening sentence: ideology, economy, and … form.

Any direct attempt to relate the ideological and economic dimensions of a particular series is more or less doomed to the reductionism of the base/superstructure model. We would do well to remember, however, that the very principle of seriality in its two historical forms, the serial and the series, was determined from the outset by commercial factors, beginning with the serialized publications, both in 1836, of Balzac's *La Vieille Fille* in France, and of Dickens' *The Pickwick Papers* in Britain. In effect, serialization was invented to increase and consolidate the circulation of the periodic press. For similarly commercial reasons, the recurring main character was a mainstay of popular genre literature, especially the detective novel.[2] For the sake of argument, in purely formal terms, *the television series can be seen as a derivative of what was originally a literary form.* Seriality in its different guises has never existed outside of considerations of economic rationality (unless one wants to stretch a point). The daytime serial and the weekly series were present at the beginning of the television medium as privileged forms that enabled the advance sale of advertising time on the basis of relatively predictable audience levels. I propose therefore to explore the link between the economic and the ideological through the mediation of form, especially through the internal variations within the series form. For my purposes, the internal form adopted by the series at a given historical moment *preempts* the analysis of the content of any particular series (and thus, *a fortiori*, of any particular episode).

Three theoretical suppositions anchor my argument. First, Adorno's claim that "form … is itself sedimented content" (Adorno, Adorno, and Tiedeman, 1997; see also the discussions in Jameson, 1990, 1992). The context here is a philosophical argument about the autonomy of "authentic" art, and Adorno would surely not have approved of its application to products of the culture industry. Yet in a little cited article on television fiction when it was still in its infancy, Adorno (1954) does seem implicitly to countenance such a reading. The principle of recurrence, inherent to the series form, is necessarily in tension with the criteria of realism that govern its perceived quality. The "pseudo-realism" denounced by Adorno is less a question of cheap sets and production values than of the sheer artificiality that stems from the recurrence of the same characters, leading to psychological stereotypes and predictable narratives.

Second, in an important book of neo-formalist criticism, Caroline Levine (2015) proposes a conceptual term borrowed from the world of design, *affordance*, to describe the potential uses or constraints latent in materials (glass, cotton) or in designs (fork, doorknob). From her reading of Foucault's *Discipline and Punish*, Levine argues that forms are always "portable" from one domain to another, like the monastic timetable that was subsequently transposed to schools, hospitals, and prisons. By the same token, the arrangement of elements within a social institution like, for example, the stock exchange could collide with other cultural forms in unforeseen and unlikely ways, due to its affordances.

Third, the distinction made by Marx in a "forgotten" chapter of *Capital* between formal and real subsumption to capital (Marx, 1990). Marx distinguished between formal subsumption in which the intervention of capitalist relations intervenes after the fact of artisanal production, and real subsumption wherein the intervention of capital occurs in the very organization of production. This comes in the context of a discussion of the transition between primitive and advanced capitalism, and between absolute surplus value based on the length of the working day and relative surplus value based on the integration of capitalist forms of organization of the workplace. Formal and real subsumption may seem at first sight somewhat removed from the subject at hand, but the distinction, extrapolated from the narrow context of Marx's original argument, is nevertheless essential to the notion of an asymmetrical periodization of capitalism, its uneven evolution, and the deepening of its internal logic. Real subsumption, which implies the intervention of capital in the design and conception stages of production, should be understood as a historical process whose absolute horizon is in all probability unattainable in anthropological terms (a society in which no human activity would exist outside of the extraction of surplus value). Nevertheless, Jason Read has argued convincingly that real subsumption extends to the production of a capitalist subjectivity, a form of continual existential adaptation. In other words, the (economic) concept of real subsumption involves an ideological dimension, wherein its translation into subjectivity is a contested historical process (Read, 2003).

## The "classic" series

During the 1950s, television seriality took the form of the anthology: a generic theme with different situations and characters each week. The best-known examples were *The Twilight Zone* (1959–62) and *Alfred Hitchcock Presents* (1955–65), in which seriality is most directly expressed through the continuity of the anchorman (Rod Serling and Alfred Hitchcock). The twenty-five-minute format, more common in the 1950s for filmed series, was conducive to adaptations of the short story form practiced by genre writers like Richard Matheson and Harlan Ellison.[3] The principle of weekly recurring characters came to dominate only in the latter half of the decade.

In the classic form of the series, a resolved, stand-alone drama is usually organized around one or several recurring characters against the same backdrop. Seriality is actually minimal, and these shows are closer to semi-anthologies than later series with multiple characters and storylines. Week after week, the main recurring character confronts a different problem posed by visitors ("tonight's guests"), as if the slate were forever wiped clean and time suspended. This relative minimalism accounts for the exceptional longevity of *Gunsmoke*, originally a half-hour radio series, which ran from 1955 to 1975 and *Bonanza*, which ran from 1959 to 1973. The western genre dominated television fiction in the 1950s, in part for reasons of convenience: the film western was mostly produced in the one-hour B-movie format, already calibrated for television programming, and the material infrastructures (ranches, trading posts, main streets, and saloons) were already in place and amortized. Furthermore, the production of "teleplays" was facilitated by the pillaging of a vast tradition of western novels and stories (Zane Grey, Max Brand).[4]

Ideologically, however, the simplified backdrop of the post-civil-war frontier town, its free citizens immune to problems of class or race, was the ideal setting for introducing action sequences into a moral theatre in which problems are posed by outside elements that disturb a generally harmonious micro-society (Rita Parks, 1982).[5] At work here is a social vision that owes much to Puritan instincts about the world: the breeding ground of disorder lies in the inability of certain individuals to control themselves, rather than in real conflicts of interest, and the threat to the town is always first and foremost a threat to the recurring characters. A variation on this formula saw recurring characters visit a series of locations in turn, confronting and resolving local problems before they continued on their way (*Wagon Train*, *Star Trek*, *The Fugitive*, *The Invaders*, *Time Tunnel*). The moral universe of the television western, with its attention to personal excess, was mostly at odds with the culture of mass consumption. The exploitation of its generic popularity to sell advertising space intervened after the fact of production.

The 1960s saw a formal evolution in the classic series: the organization of an episode into modular segments, which preceded the emergence of writing teams. In its demonstration of modern consumer skills (wining, dining, seducing, being at ease in a cosmopolitan setting), the "pop series" broke markedly with the relentless moralizing of the western (Buxton, 1990). Characters in this type of series, like *The Man from UNCLE* and *The Avengers*, were closely related to the pop culture of the time, and were already optimally designed as ideological machines without psychological depth. This opened the way for the conquest of an emerging international market: the exploration of an individual's psychological makeup is always rooted in a national culture, and as such is more difficult to export.[6] A memo for writers of the fourth and last season of *The Man from UNCLE* in 1967 expressed the need for humor, but stipulated that the protagonists should never joke when they are in danger (John Heitland, 1987). In other words, humor is reserved for sequences which are detachable from, and without influence on, the main storyline. The invention of modular segments allowed for a faster pace than the previous model based on theatrical drama, which was slowed down by the need to reveal and pass judgment on the moral value of each new character. Finally, this formal structure enables the rationalized distinction between a headquarters, where the recurring characters can establish themselves (through banter, running gags, etc.) in an ideologically controlled studio setting, and the outside world (themed studio settings, backlots for outdoor scenes), where they can apply their skills on a geopolitical stage. In consequence, this format requires that the recurring characters be the bearers of a *positive (social) project*, which legitimizes the use of violence or subterfuge in the accomplishment of their mission.[7]

## The "serialized" series

Modular segments assumed a new role in the 1980s. *Hill Street Blues* (1981–7), followed by *NYPD Blue* (1993–2005) marked the emergence of the mixed series (or serialized series), a hybrid of the serial and the (classic) series which could also integrate elements of soap opera and situation comedy: each episode follows several plotlines, some resolve, some do not (Stéphane Benassi, 2000). After the introduction of more finely-tuned audience measurements by Nielsen in 1969, advertisers were prepared to pay a premium for a "quality" (younger, more feminine, more urban) over a mass audience. This was a major step toward the real subsumption of the television series.[8] After this, the series becomes decentered, either through a duo of dissimilar partners (*Starsky and Hutch*, *Miami Vice*) or, more radically, through a team consisting of diverse ethnic backgrounds (*Hawaii 5-O*).[9] As it becomes incapable of a realist treatment of crime, which would involve a sociological explanation, and equally incapable of proposing a positive social project—not even the principled defense of the *status quo*—the police series takes refuge in interpersonal relations. Modular sequences reveal the personal problems of the recurring characters (alcoholism, sexual infidelity).

In its abandonment of the controlling male protagonist, the serialized series better "affords" (is less constrained in its material by) the absence of a positive project. In other words, it is the form best adapted to the *ideological passivity* of the series from the 1980s onward. In the episode "The Prodigal Son" (1986) of *Miami Vice*, a banker explains authoritatively that Wall Street is dependent on the capital flows of Colombian drug dealers. Drug consumption is shown to be widespread among ordinary citizens. The link between free enterprise and moral virtue, which provided an ideological bedrock for the classic series, falls apart here. So too does the pretension to realism, strained to the limit, which asks viewers to believe that regular narcs could operate as undercover dealers or hookers week after week, year after year, without being sniffed out.[10] Powerless in the war on vice and decadence, the police agent could at least look at himself in the mirror and savor his personal victories. From this point on, the series form was condemned to find different strategies to confront what was, in effect, a *structural* passivity resulting from the dominance of finance over productive capital, and the consequent near impossibility of interventionist social policies.

In the 1990s, with *The X-Files*, the classic formula of stand-alone episodes was punctuated by occasional serial episodes, which revisited the overarching mythology of the series, namely the replacement of humans by a genetically mixed species, through the secret collaboration of aliens and the powers-that-be. *The X-Files* was one of the first series to experiment with the season-long narrative arc, in which plotlines left dangling are taken up over differing intervals. But it was in the emblematic *24* (2001–10) that the logic of serialization was taken to its extreme. In *24*, each season covered a single daylong intrigue sliced into *24* episodes of real time. The classic series was an ideal vehicle for the masculine hero who, alone or with partners, demonstrated his mastery of a given situation. The introduction of serialized elements juxtaposed private lives and discrete criminal cases, invariably exposing weaknesses, difficulties, and moments of doubt. Tara McPherson has described *24* as a "techno-soap" whose technological innovations (split screen, ticking clock) served to "remasculinize" the serial form, after its historical grounding in domestic drama associated with female audiences (McPherson, 2007).[11]

The mixed or serialized series now dominates the series form, but with internal variations, ranging from the serialized season (*Dexter*, *Breaking Bad*) to the predominantly classic form with serialized elements (*CSI*, in which forensic scientists, "behind the scenes," replace an ideologically spent police force). Narrative arcs can occur in every episode (*24*) or sparingly (*Mentalist*). The more a series contains serialized elements, the more it is prone to reboots and changes of direction. One new development is the thematic series in which character recurrence is limited to a single season (*True Detective*, *Fargo*).

The most important consequence of serialization is character inflation. No longer can problems be dealt with by a single white male (the 1950s TV western), or two partners (the

1960s spy series). They now necessitate a strategically composed team of police officers (or lawyers, medical staff, etc.) in search of an elusive social equilibrium that might magically accommodate their various forms of diversity and personality traits: racial and ethnic categories, men and women, young and mature, gay and straight, liberal and conservative, and countless other possibilities. *Hill Street Blues* contained no fewer than 44 recurring characters (of which 20 were main characters). In general, some form of psychological development, synonymous with quality, required that these characters exist in and for themselves, their potential interactions harboring an exponential number of storylines.[12]

What then is the deeper meaning of the emergence and dominance of the decentered, serialized series? First, the recourse to multiple recurring characters, representing different approaches to the problems they confront, limits the damage of the structural passivity evoked earlier. Second, the very multiplicity of characters displaces the narrative center of gravity toward internal personal relations at the expense of sustained confrontation with social issues. Third, the serial form introduces elements of instability into a series, which is now forced to counter its own essentially entropic state through the creation of new characters and situations. The serialized series can only degrade, and thus corresponds to a society seen in this light.

In his discussion (1966) of Jules Verne's *Mysterious Island*, Pierre Macherey distinguishes between the *representation* of an ideological project (themes like scientific progress, the conquest of nature, etc.) and its *figuration* in concrete signs (characters, objects, habitats), which logically preexists any narrative movement. For Macherey, there is necessarily slippage, tension, and even contradiction between these two terms.[13] This form of analysis is particularly adapted to the classic series, in which the figuration of an ideological project is congealed into an immanent framework, producing incremental value on a weekly basis (simple growth). If a project's figuration is too rigid, the margin for narrative variation is duly limited (for example, *The Prisoner*, 1967–8). Conversely, a figuration that is too vague and open-ended contributes little or nothing to a series' brand identity in the face of competition. The classic series was forced to negotiate a position between these two extremes. The multiplication of recurring characters and the integration of private lives made it more difficult for the classic series to return to its point of departure, opening up the contradiction between the representation and the figuration of its ideological project. Serialization in its various guises becomes the only solution to this formal problem.

Both the commodity status and the economic value of the television series have changed enormously since the 1950s. Until the 1990s, the series was an indirect commodity, a means of organizing regular audiences whose attention was sold in advance to advertisers. For a long time, the use value of being able to watch televised images free of charge in the comfort of the family living room preempted questions relating to their quality, but rising expectations led to the increase in the average cost of series in real terms (constant dollars) by a factor of over 3 between 1965 and 2015.[14] The recent migration toward individual terminals and mobile devices, however, necessarily renews questions relating to form, commodity status, and the very future of televised fiction. The cost of early series was negligible, and most early television drama was seen as having no commercial value once broadcast.[15] Incredibly, every episode of the first season of the classic British series *The Avengers* (1961) was erased so that the videotape could be reused; several years later, it was exported to 70 countries. Since the economic model was established in the 1960s, the value of a series is realized, if at all, a long way downstream in the syndication and international markets. Since the 1990s, the series has also been proposed as a direct commodity to the individual consumer, first in the form of videocassettes, and then as box set DVDs containing entire seasons. Another economic model is the branded package sold to cable subscribers, where it is the channel (HBO, etc.) that is the commodity (Szalay, 2014). While broadcast and programmed television viewing is on the decline, especially among younger viewers, the latest emerging market is online video on demand. The series is now a mixed commodity, both indirect and direct, whose future sources of revenue are correspondingly uncertain. Not the least of these uncertainties is the long-term economic viability of paid streaming sites.

The tendency away from indirect to direct commodity status, which also entails fewer episodes in a season, cannot but have an effect on the series form. With the gradual decline of broadcast television, it makes increasingly less sense to generate hundreds of episodes from the same fixed framework over a long period; in any case, the serial turn makes this more difficult to sustain. On services like Netflix, a whole season is available in advance, calling into question the historical notion of seriality. Pitched in the same manner as a feature film, the series tends toward a variant of the latter: a ten-hour renewable epic, whose viewing rhythm is discretionary.

## The real subsumption of the series form

The argument for the real subsumption of the series form can now be made along several lines. First, the marketing department is now involved from the outset, before the production stage. As the sociologist John Caldwell has written,

> any screenplay or project developed in primetime television or feature film today generates considerable attention and involvement at the earliest story sessions and producers' meetings by personnel from the firm's financing, marketing, coproduction, distribution, merchandizing and new media departments or divisions. [...] [A]t the pitch and script stages, story ideas will be developed as diversified entertainment properties....
>
> *(Caldwell, 2008)*

In other words, the consumer is already conceptualized and targeted as an integral part of the production process.

In the case of *Lost* (2004–10), the producer, ABC, collaborated with amateur websites devoted to the series and participated in setting up a fan base to be mobilized as unofficial marketing auxiliaries. This has now become a common practice. At least one of the present functions of series is to help social media users "work" at constituting themselves as audience commodities, by providing cultural lubricant to define their profiles (for a discussion of the audience commodity debate, see Christian Fuchs, 2012). The series becomes a form of symbolic brand equity. Coming at this idea from another angle, Michael Szalay (2014) has suggestively argued, referring to several HBO series, that "dramas are futures markets [...] and should be understood as functionally equivalent to the class of financial instruments known as derivatives." Reproduction within and between seasons is conditioned by ongoing market research that determines the characters worth investing in, or liquidating.[16]

Second, real subsumption is also expressed in the way that the series form increasingly mirrors that of capitalist production itself. As a continual process of creating surplus value, capitalism depends on *compound growth* requiring exponential reinvestment, which exceeds the possibilities of productive capital (David Harvey, 2014). Marx calls this form of investment "fictitious capital" (credit, debt, speculation), whereby financial gain is dependent on the "fiction" that it will necessarily be convertible into productive capital (Marx, 1991). The inflation (accumulation) of characters in *Game of Thrones*, adapted from the books by George

R. R. Martin, at once the most advanced formal expression of the serialized series and the most regressive in terms of social relations, embodies an economy of this type. By season 3, this series had exceptionally amassed 250 or so named characters (Wikipedia). Each new season, dozens of characters, and potential storylines are speculatively produced, only a few of which can be developed.[17] Any purely psychological exploration is now contingent on budgetary considerations.[18] The point here is that the forward movement of the serialized series is dependent on a form of inflation which, as in its stock exchange counterpart, must periodically undergo a cull before it collapses definitively (generally after six or seven seasons in the case of success). Unlike the guest characters in the classic series, those created in the serialized series never entirely disappear unless killed off.

Third, the serialized series tends to imitate finance capitalism in its internal structure. Potential plotlines are created continuously, from episode one, to maintain a relentless rhythm of accumulation. The concatenation of these formally resembles the circuits of capital discussed in volume two of *Capital* in which the movements of money capital (M–M'), commodity capital (C–C'), and productive capital are imbricated (Marx, 1992). Credit (or finance capital, or the ongoing willingness of an audience to invest in new plotlines) is essential to prevent paralyzing breakdowns or delays in the metamorphosis of one form of capital to another; similarly, the series needs a stock of virtual characters to fluidify its multiple developments.

In terms of Levine's "affordances," the genre that best corresponds to these formal demands is the saga, in which character inflation is structured around the links "afforded" by membership of families, clans, hordes, networks, and more recently criminal or antiterrorist organizations. Without these, a series like *Game of Thrones* would fall apart under its own weight, as did *Lost*, now seen in this respect as a counterexample. The dramatization of narrative links between "free" individuals cannot be satisfactorily contained within the form of the serialized series. Vampires, aliens, zombies, psychopaths, gangsters, survivors, sociopaths, and lawyers flourish however as so many expressions of a near "degree zero" of social relations reduced to naked self-interest and power games in which "no-one is innocent."[19] Ideologically passive ("winter is coming"), fatalistic, the serialized series is increasingly at pains to "afford" normalized, serial relations within the framework of a functioning capitalist society, still less one that is evolving to the tune of a progressive master narrative.

## Notes

1 This difficulty could be circumvented in the case of the "classic" series of stand-alone episodes by treating a limited number of sample episodes as being representative of the whole. This option (used in Buxton, 1990) is no longer possible in the case of the "serialized" series, where one must wait until its termination before making definitive pronouncements, when a monographic treatment is less of a commercial proposition. A classroom exploitation of any one episode of, say, *Game of Thrones*, would be fairly meaningless.

2 One example will suffice: Earle Stanley Gardner wrote over 80 novels featuring the character Perry Mason between 1933 and 1973.

3 The passage to the fifty-two-minute format, generalized in the 1960s for drama series, required at least one subplot and an in-house "treatment," and was therefore less conducive to professional writers of stories for the "pulp" magazines (Buxton, 2011). The turn to "serialized" series led to the generalization of specific writing teams of up to a dozen persons, headed by a showrunner.

4 It is important to emphasize the dependence during the early years of serialized television production on a preexisting tradition of genre literature (westerns, detective novels, fantasy, and romance). In the first season of *Perry Mason* (1957–8), 38 of the 39 episodes were adapted from the original novels by Earle Stanley Gardner, written over the period 1933–57; by the second season, adaptations had fallen to 11 out of 30 (Buxton, 2010).

5 A memo for writers for Bonanza stipulated that "*the townspeople must not turn against the Cartwrights...[who] are too intelligent in their behavior, too respected and too prominent to have such a thing happen*" (Parks, 1982: 163).
6 The international market for series emerged rapidly at this time. Whereas *The Lone Ranger* was sold to 24 countries in 1961, *The Man from UNCLE* was broadcast in 60 countries several years later, followed by *Mission: Impossible* and *Hawaii Five-O*, which were exported to 87 and 80 countries (the socialist bloc being off limits). *CSI* was present in 150 countries in 2009 (Buxton, 2010).
7 In *Mission: Impossible* (1966–73), this involved a sexually and ethnically mixed, trans-class assemblage of actors, technicians, and managers (a "pop alliance") who clinically used their superior skills to intervene selectively against dictators and swindlers in foreign countries, always with a positive goal and outcome.
8 Since 2006, Nielsen IAG has measured, among other parameters, "viewer engagement" with series, an "active" mode of viewing expressed in the ability to remember minute narrative details. This explains why *Lost*, top ranked for viewer engagement in 2010, could charge significantly higher advertising rates than *NCIS*, despite the much larger audiences of the latter.
9 The choice of a disparate duo or socially diverse team of cops represents an ideological project in itself, an "upstream" resolution of social problems. For example, the pairing in *Starsky and Hutch* of the working-class (Jewish) Dave Starsky from New York and the college-educated Californian Ken Hutchinson in 1975 incarnates the "magical," national reconciliation of two social classes at odds over the Vietnam War. Add in a (grouchy) black boss and a (roguish) black informer for questions of race.
10 Even "quality" series like *Breaking Bad* and *Dexter* end up straining credibility to the limit for similar reasons.
11 Tellingly, one of the creators and leading writers on *24*, *Robert Cochran*, began his career on the daytime serial Falcon Crest.
12 In the daytime serial, character inflation could be diluted and contained over many years.
13 In *The Mysterious Island*, the figuration (an uninhabited island, an (all male!) society in microcosm, and science incarnated by an engineer) of its ideological project contains no internal conflict that might propel the narrative. As the story advances, the protagonists are no longer the conquerors of nature, but the (passive) objects of an external force, the secret experiments of the misanthropic Captain Nemo. Similarly, in the classic series, the figuration of an ideological project is sometimes completely at odds with the constraint of renewable episodes, most clearly in the case of *The Invaders* (1967–8), where the project of a surreptitious alien invasion takes a back seat to weekly encounters with small-town, personal problems, far more important (Buxton, 1990: 14–15; 46–60).
14 Figure calculated from diverse sources relating to the cost of individual series in Buxton (2010). The weekly budget for decors and accessories for the daily sci-fi/western series *Captain Video* in 1953 was a mere $25 ($207 in 2015 dollars). An episode of the western series *Cheyenne* came to $75,000 ($470,000) in 1960, and the spy series *The Man from UNCLE*, $155,000 ($906,000) in 1965. The average cost of an episode of a network or cable series in 2015 was between $3 and $3.5 million, and is typically "licenced" to channels at about 75% of its production cost. At the top end of the range, the average cost of an episode of the sixth season of *Game of Thrones* came to $6 million, and in the seventh season between $10 and $16 million, comparable to a feature film outside Hollywood, but in a different league from the cinema blockbuster at $150–200 million, plus marketing expenses.
15 As late as 1973, complete recordings of some 175 television series from the defunct network DuMont Television (1946–52) were unceremoniously dumped into New York harbor.
16 Sometimes in panic mode. Notoriously, *24* "misplaced" two presidents after assassination attempts, who disappeared from the series without further explanation. Initially, character inflation was seen as a form of insurance against excessive salary demands, each member of an expanded team being eminently replaceable.
17 For the two short final seasons, the producers made the conscious choice to close down the creation of new characters and plotlines, and instead to work on a projected derivative.
18 For example, during the first season of *Game of Thrones*, producer David Benioff spoke of writing supplementary, "intimate" exchanges between two actors, used to complete, at minimal cost, episodes whose allotted budget had run out (Cogman, 2012).

19 In the words of an Islamic terrorist in *24* (4:09). It is in these terms that I express the insights into the journalist Brett Martin (2013) concerning the end of the (patriarchal) American Dream in a number of "quality" series from the decade 2000–10 (*The Sopranos, Dexter, Mad Men, The Wire, Breaking Bad*).

## References


Adorno, T. (1954, ed. 1957). Television and the patterns of mass culture. In Rosenberg, B. and White, D. eds., *Mass Culture*. Glencoe, IL: Free Press.

Adorno, T., Adorno, G. and Tiedeman, R. (1997). *Aesthetic Theory*. New York: Athlone Press, p. 144.

Benassi, S. (2000). *Séries et Feuilletons TV. Pour une typologie des fictions télévisuelles*. Liège, Belgium: Editions du Céfal.

Buxton, D. (1990). *From "The Avengers" to "Miami Vice"*. Form and ideology in the television series. Manchester, UK: Manchester University Press.

Buxton, D. (2010). *Les Séries télévisées. Forme, idéologie et mode de production*. Paris: L'Harmattan.

Buxton, D. (2011). Richard Matheson et *The Twilight Zone*: la terre étrangère interne. In Chenille, V., Dollé, M., and Mellier, D., eds., *Richard Matheson. Il est une légende*. Paris: Encrages Université, pp. 141–9.

Buxton, D. (2014). The end of capitalism, the end of the world. *Out of focus*, 5, http://v2.outoffocus.biz/david-buxton/.

Caldwell, J. (2008). *Production Culture*. Durham, NC: Duke University Press, pp. 232–3.

Cogman, B. (2012). *Inside HBO's Game of Thrones*. San Francisco, CA: Chronicle Books, p. 75.

Fuchs, C. (2012). Dallas Smythe Today – The Audience Commodity, the Digital Labour Debate, Marxist Political Economy and Critical Theory. Prolegomena to a Digital Labour Theory of Value. *Triple C. Cognition, Communication, Cooperation*, 10(2), pp. 692–740, http://www.triple-c.at.

Harvey, D. (2014). *Seventeen Contradictions and the End of Capitalism*. London: Profile Books, pp. 222–45.

Heitland, J. (1987). *The Man from UNCLE Book*. New York: St Martin's Press, p. 188.

Jameson, F. (1990). *Late Marxism. Adorno or the Persistence of the Dialectic*. London: Verso, pp. 182–201.

Jameson, F. (1992). *Signatures of the Visible*. Abingdon, UK: Routledge, pp. 11–46.

Levine, C. (2015). *Forms. Whole, Rhythm, Hierarchy, Network*. Princeton, NJ: Princeton University Press, pp. 6–11.

Macherey, P. (2006). *A Theory of Literary Production*, 2nd ed. London: Routledge (original French edition, 1966).

Martin, B. (2013). *Difficult Men*. New York: Penguin Group.

Marx, K. (1992). Results of the immediate process of production. In *Capital: Volume I*. London: Penguin Books, pp. 1019–38. Trans. Ben Fowkes.

Marx, K. (1993. *Capital: Volume II*. London: Penguin Books, pp. 109–79. Trans. David Fernbach.

Marx, K. (1993). *Capital: Volume III*. London: Penguin Books, pp. 525–42. Trans. Ben Fowkes.

McPherson, T. (2007). Techno Soap. 24, Masculinity and Hybrid Form. In Peacock, S., ed., *Reading 24*. London: I. B. Tauris, p. 174.

Parks, R. (1982). *The Western Hero in Film and Television*. Ann Arbor: University of Michigan Research Press.

Porter, L. and Lavery, D. (2007). *Unlocking the Meaning of Lost: An Unauthorized Guide*. Naperville, IL: Sourcebooks.

Potte-Bonneville, M. (2015). *Game of Thrones. Série noire*. Paris: Les Prairies ordinaires.

Read, J. (2003). *The Micro-Politics of Capital*. Albany: State University of New York Press, pp. 103–51.

Szalay, M. (2014). HBO's Flexible Gold. *Representations*, 126(1), pp. 112–34.

# INDEX

Note: page references followed by 'n' refer to note section

For Product Safety Concerns and Information please contact our EU
representative GPSR@taylorandfrancis.com
Taylor & Francis Verlag GmbH, Kaufingerstraße 24, 80331 München, Germany

www.ingramcontent.com/pod-product-compliance
Ingram Content Group UK Ltd.
Pitfield, Milton Keynes, MK11 3LW, UK
UKHW050052200926
475702UK00019B/2790
* 9 7 8 1 0 3 2 1 7 8 5 6 1 *